The Civilization of the American Indian Series

Indian Dances of North America

Reginald Laubin (Tatanka Wanjila) and Gladys Laubin (Wi'yaka Wastewin) in Buffalo Dance costumes. Laubin Collection.

Reginald and Gladys Laubin

Indian Dances of North America

THEIR IMPORTANCE TO INDIAN LIFE

With Paintings, Drawings, and Photographs by the Authors

Foreword by Louis R. Bruce

University of Oklahoma Press : Norman and London

By Reginald and Gladys Laubin

The Indian Tipi: Its History, Construction, and Use, with "A History of the Tipi," by
   Stanley Vestal (Norman, 1957)
Indian Dances of North America (Norman, 1976)
American Indian Archery (Norman, 1980)

Permission for reproduction of any part of this book in any form must be obtained
from the authors, the artists, and the University of Oklahoma Press.

003082156

Library of Congress Cataloging-in-Publication Data

Laubin, Reginald.
   Indian Dances of North America.

   (The Civilization of the American Indian series)
   Includes bibliographical references.
   1. Indians of North America—Dances.   I. Laubin,
Gladys, joint author.   II. Title.   III. Series.
E98.D2L28   970'.004'97   76-40962
ISBN: 0-8061-2172-6

4   5   6   7   8   9   10   11   12   13

Dedicated to

our American Indians, in the interest of bringing about better understanding between the races and the preservation of the Indians' dances and rich heritage.

Observation and study of Indian dances in earlier days might have revealed the very soul of the people, for they were at one and the same time the focal point of all their material culture and the highest expression of their mystical yearnings.

Reginald and Gladys Laubin

Foreword

Reginald and Gladys Laubin's new book is an unusual one, depicting not only Indian dancing, but also Indian life, customs, rituals, and traditions from the time Jacques Cartier in 1534 first saw Indians dancing in a canoe, to the new revival of interest among Indians in their own heritage, now encouraged by the Government in the new acculturation program on the reservations today.

Aiding us with this new project, the Laubins have given concerts, demonstrative lectures, and have held seminars for Indian youth and leadership conferences in Wisconsin, Minnesota, and Montana and for Indian schools in Pierre, South Dakota, on the Fort Thompson, Lower Brulé, and Pine Ridge reservations, and for the new Navajo College at Many Farms, Arizona.

The Laubins were named Tatanka Wanjila and Wiyaka Wastewin when adopted by Chief One Bull, famous "fighting nephew" of the great Sitting Bull of history. Because of their adoption, Indians everywhere have accepted the Laubins as their own. I have known them and of their lifetime dedication to the preservation of Indian dance and culture for a long time, when they first presented their Ancient Indian Dances for the National Congress of American Indians, which now represents 105 tribes with a membership of 350,000. Without question, it was one of the finest programs I have ever witnessed and I have seen many Indian performances. We Indians are very skeptical of non-Indians interpreting our dances, but Reginald and Gladys are imbued with their true spirit and character, and are the first to present real Indian dancing on the concert stage, either here at home or abroad.

Chief One Bull and his brother, Chief White Bull, lived in the Laubins' tipi on several occasions on the Standing Rock Reservation. The two old men and their old cronies were so grateful for the Laubins' interest, when not even their own young people showed any, that they requested them to record and preserve the old ways. One Bull said, "You know exactly the real Indian ways. You are more Indian than our own Indian children." Kills Pretty Enemy added, "It is a good thing you are doing, keeping alive the old ways for coming generations, both Indian and white." No wonder our Indian people are warm in their praise of the Laubins.

This book, with its historical résumé and the Laubins' personal observations and experiences, is most timely and will be welcome, not only to the dancer, the anthropologist, the historian, and the educator, but to the layman and to the Indian people as well. Reginald and Gladys have spent most of their lives with and as Indians, and this book reflects their years of effort in our behalf. They have cut a clear path through the wilderness of misinterpretation, misunderstanding, and prejudice, making no concessions to preconceived notions, and present us as people with culture, intelligence, and aspirations worthy of any people anywhere. I know I speak for our Indian people when I say that we are proud to have the Laubins as our envoys. We appreciate this splendid book, which will create goodwill and understanding for our people. I know of no comparable book. These pages vividly reveal our thoughts and interpret our rituals and dances from the cradle to the grave. From the Iroquois in the Northeast, who furnished the pattern of the Constitution of the United States, to the Miwok of California, from the Eagle Dance of the Cherokee in the Southeast to the Spirit Dances of the Tlingits of Alaska, the Hunting and Harvest dances of the Chippewa and Menomini of the Great Lakes, the Warrior and Society dances of the Sioux and Crow of the Prairies, the Rain Dances of the Pueblo and the Sings of the Navajo of the Southwest, the Laubins present the fascinating lore of the First Americans.

Reginald and Gladys Laubin not only know, but they perceive, which is even more important than knowing.

Louis R. Bruce (Sioux-Mohawk)
Commissioner of Indian Affairs
1969–73

Preface

Indians are no longer the vanishing Americans. At the present rate of increase there will soon be as many Indians in the United States as there were when Columbus landed. It is the culture that is vanishing. This is why we feel it so important to come to an appreciation of Indian art and dance and to do what we can to preserve them. Indian arts and crafts are gradually being accepted for their true worth and not as mere tourist trinkets, but the Indian's dance may be the most important of all his artistic contributions, once we come to understand it, for it combined all of his other art expressions.

A leading anthropologist told us recently that scholars are just beginning to realize what an important part of Indian life the dance was. Those in the field in earlier days missed a great opportunity when they failed to study it, for dance was interwoven throughout an Indian's life.

We realize that, because of the cultural change, it will be impossible to preserve the dances in their entirety, or even perhaps in their purity, but certainly some knowledge of the original purpose and intent, as well as of the spirit and character, can and should be preserved.

It is no wonder that the average American knows so little about Indians. Much of the information he received in school was faulty and inaccurate. When we were in school we remember being required to read Francis Parkman's *The Oregon Trail.* Already being extremely interested in Indians, we were very much disappointed in the book. Parkman rather took the Indians off their pedestal, and we had a hard time trying to justify our Indian interest to our parents and friends.

Later we were introduced to George Catlin's writings, and our faith was restored. It was difficult then to understand how two men could have such completely different opinions of the same people. Catlin had very little criticism to make of Indian behavior and customs. In fact, he wrote so glowingly about them that even to this day people think he exaggerated his statements in the Indians' favor.

Parkman had very little good to say about them. Being a historian, he was saturated with historical accounts of savagery, treachery, and cruelty, written by people who made no effort to understand Indians but were rather interested in excusing the misdoings of their own countrymen. Parkman was looking for such characteristics, and when he did not find them, he imagined them.

He was ill during most of his trip. He could not but admire the Indian's health and strong physique, lacking these qualities himself. He considered the Indian merely a remarkable human animal.

Both men were in the West at approximately the same time, Parkman but five years later than Catlin. They visited the same camps, were entertained by chiefs of the same tribes. Parkman spent about six months in the country. Catlin was there nearly eight years. Catlin usually found Indians cleanly in their habits, was fond of their beautiful clothing, enjoyed most of their food—in other words, respected them from almost every point of view.

We are not sure that *The Oregon Trail* is still required reading in the schools, but in our lectures across the country we have found that it is still recommended for western history, and especially for a firsthand account of the Indians. The question that has always bothered us, and still does, is why is Parkman recommended above Catlin? Young people seldom hear about Catlin. Americans generally would have a much better understanding of Indians if they did. Perhaps Parkman is considered the better writer, but for human interest and understanding Catlin was as vivid with his pen as with his brush.

Many Indian nations had attained a high degree of culture and civilization long before Columbus set foot upon American shores. When the first Europeans came to this continent, they surpassed the Indians mainly in methods of destruction. They brought steel and gunpowder. They considered the Indians savages because they did not have such things. But these so-called savages surpassed the Europeans in many social and political achievements and had contributions to make in other fields.

The United States Department of Agriculture has estimated that four-sevenths of all the agricultural products grown in the entire world today originated in the New World.[1] What a dull diet we would have without some of the items the Indian has added to our table! "Irish" potatoes, sweet potatoes, corn, beans, squash, pumpkins, tomatoes, turkeys, cranberries. What kind of a holiday would we have without these foods? Or what sort of party would it be without popcorn, peanuts, chewing gum, and chocolate- and vanilla-flavored desserts? We should also mention maple syrup, pineapples, tapioca, and avocados, and—not in the food line—tobacco, quinine, and rubber. Even our frozen foods were inspired by natives of the American North, who have been preserving in this way for centuries.

What pleasing and colorful names Indians have given to features of our landscape—rivers, lakes, mountains—to cities and towns and the streets within them. Indian words have made their way into languages around the world.

In sports Indians originated lacrosse and contributed elements of baseball and football. Their love of the out-of-doors is reflected in sports such as hiking and canoeing, and they have provided widely used outdoor equipment—moccasins, canoes, pack baskets, tump lines, toboggans, snowshoes, hammocks, and sleeping bags, together with the dried foods now accepted as essential for any extended trip. These are *things* with which we are all acquainted and which we have been enjoying for many years, but we are only beginning to realize the importance of the Indian's attitude towards and appreciation of nature. He never tried to conquer nature but to live in harmony with her. The lessons he learned directly from Mother Earth may be among the most important he can pass on to his white brother, for they are essential to survival, that we may enjoy his other contributions.

One of the most important of the Indian's gifts lies in the realm of government. The philosophers of the eighteenth century were greatly influenced by the reports of early explorers on their contacts with various tribes of the Eastern seaboard. Here Europeans for the first time saw men who were truly free. Coming from nations ruled autocratically by kings, queens, and princes, they naturally dubbed Indian leaders with the same titles. In actuality, none of the Indian *kings*, with the possible exception of some in the southern United States and Mexico, had the absolute authority vested in the monarchs of the Old World.

Captain John Smith marveled that even children dared to talk to a "king," and Samuel de Champlain, speaking of Indians of New England, said, "They have chiefs, whom they obey in matters of war, but not otherwise, and who engage in labor, and who hold no higher rank than their companions."[2] John Long wrote that

The Iroquois laugh when you talk to them of obedience to kings; for they cannot reconcile the idea of submission with the dignity of man. Each individual is a sovereign in his own mind; and as he conceives he derives his freedom from the great Spirit alone, he cannot be induced to acknowledge any other power.[3]

Louis Hennepin, finding it difficult to convert the Indians, said, "Another hindrance lies in a custom of theirs, not to contradict any Man; they think everyone ought to be left to his own Opinion; without being thwarted . . . . they leave everybody at liberty in Belief."[4]

It is certain that John Locke was greatly influenced in his writings by his studies of American Indians and their lives of liberty. Thomas Jefferson was a great admirer of Locke and incorporated some of Locke's ideas when he drew up the Declaration of Independence. Jefferson made two remarks about Indians that are enlightening about his attitude toward them. He wrote in a letter to John Adams in 1812, "If science produces no better fruits than Tyranny, Murder, Rapine and destitution of national morality, I would rather wish our country to be ignorant, honest and esteemable as our neighboring savages are." On another occasion he was asked his opinion of the state of man and of the progress he had made. He replied, "The Ideal State of Man is that state in which we found the American Indian on our arrival in this country."

Few Americans have heard this, but it is now known that the Constitution of the United States was patterned after the League of the Iroquois Indians of New York State, who had one of the finest political organizations the world has known. Benjamin Franklin drew up his Plan of Union for the Thirteen Colonies at the time of the French and Indian War. It was rejected then, but later this plan influenced the drafting of the Constitution. Franklin wrote:

It would be a strange thing if six Nations of ignorant savages should be capable of forming a scheme for such a union, and be able to execute it in such a manner as that it has subsisted ages and appears indissoluble, and yet that a like union should be impracticable for ten or a dozen English colonies to whom it is more necessary and must be more advantageous, and who cannot be supposed to want an equal understanding of their interests.[5]

Possibly to stress his own statement, he called them "ignorant savages," but on another occasion he said, "We call them savages because their manners differ from ours, which we think the perfection of civility. They think the same of theirs."[6]

The late Frank Speck, an outstanding student of the Iroquois and head of the Department of Anthropology at the University of Pennsylvania, told us personally that the introduction to the Constitution is almost a literal translation of the preamble to the Covenant of the League, still recited by Iroquois leaders at ceremonies in the Longhouse.

It thus becomes evident that much of our present conception of personal freedom, liberty, even justice and democracy stems indirectly if not directly from contact with our First Americans. At least the Indians revived in Europeans a desire and a longing for these qualities that had long lain dormant or suppressed. It is something of a travesty that Americans, in their search and struggle for liberty, have not always seen fit to grant the Indians the same tolerance and freedom with which they themselves were greeted.

Even today Indians are still the victims of prejudice and misunderstanding. Our First Americans are the most neglected and poverty-stricken minority group in the United States. Although conditions have been gradually improving, they still have the highest tuberculosis rate, the highest mortality rate, and the lowest standard of living of any people within our borders.

There are a number of popular misconceptions regarding Indians, for example, that they are *not allowed* to leave their reservations. Reservations are no longer concentration camps, although at one time they were very nearly that. Indians are free to come and go as they please and have been for years. Reservations are tracts of land *reserved* for the Indian people. Poor as some of these tracts are, they are still home to many Indians, and most of them prefer to stay there.

Also, Indians are not wards of the government, although much of their land is still held in trust. They are citizens, albeit that some are second-class citizens because of ignorance, poverty, apathy, confusion on the reservations, and local prejudice. They were made citizens by an act of Congress in 1924 in token of appreciation of their great service in World War I (which ended in 1918). Indians have served with American forces in every war of American history. Most of the Indian wars would not have been won as readily without the help of friendly Indians in the service of the army.

Indians are not dying out. For a number of years the Indian population has been increasing very rapidly, almost twice as fast as the white population in the country. There are now about 900,000 persons of Indian blood in the United States and Alaska. This is still a very small minority of our over-all population, but a very important minority historically, economically, and from the standpoint of moral obligation, for we are still bound by treaties made with them during our early years when Indian tribes were important as individual nations.

The majority of the population in most of the Latin-American countries is Indian. Perhaps a better understanding of Indians would help us improve relations with some of these countries. The lesson can well begin at home. An understanding of Indian cultures should enable us to acquire a better understanding of other cultures around the world. A very great part of Indian culture was Indian dance, which we hope to make more understandable and meaningful in this book. You will find references to Indian manners and customs, physical appearance, disposition, and attitudes that are integral parts of dance and cannot honestly be separated from it.

Acknowledgments

While Savoie Lottinville was Director of the University of Oklahoma Press, he asked us to write this book, a comprehensive book on Indian dance and its relationship to Indian culture, generally to encompass the entire United States but specifically to treat of the Plains and Woodlands; to include our personal observations and experiences; and to appeal not only to the anthropologist and historian but to the layman as well. We are grateful to him for suggesting the book and for his assistance in obtaining a Guggenheim Fellowship, which enabled us to do the historical research.

Writing such a book has proved to be an involved task, particularly so because we have been interrupted by presenting concerts and lectures in Jackson Hole and in various parts of the country. So we are indeed grateful to Edward Shaw, present Director of the University of Oklahoma Press, for his patience and understanding in not "pushing" or hurrying us for the manuscript, and for his generous help, encouragement, and inspiring consultations.

Louis R. Bruce (Mohawk-Sioux), while Commissioner of Indian Affairs (1969–73), graciously offered to write the Foreword, for which we are also deeply grateful, as we are for his personal invitation to present our concert of Indian dances for the Indian leaders of the National Tribal Chairman's Association in Pierre, South Dakota, at the request of the Executive Director, Clarence Skye, of the United Sioux Tribes. We feel highly honored that the Commissioner and the Indian leaders held our work in such high esteem.

We are greatly in debt for the Guggenheim grant, which made it possible to supplement our active study on the reservations with research in important libraries and museums across the country, from the Smithsonian Institution in Washington, D.C., to the Huntington Library in California—the American Museum of Natural History and Public Library in New York; the Field Museum, Newberry Library, and Public Library in Chicago; Buffalo Museum of Science; Albany Historical Society; Denver Museum of Natural History; Sioux Indian Museum in Rapid City, South Dakota; museums and libraries in Santa Fe and Albuquerque, New Mexico, and Flagstaff, Arizona; Peabody museums and libraries at both Yale and Harvard universities; Wesleyan University and Trinity College in Connecticut; the University of Oklahoma in Norman and Gilcrease Foundation and Philbrook Art Center in Tulsa, Oklahoma. We appreciate the patience, courtesy, and assistance of many people associated with these institutions, and especially the help many years ago from Clark Wissler, who invited us to attend his classes and personally conducted us through the "poison room" in the American Museum of Natural History to observe and study many rare specimens not on public display. At a later time we received similar personal consideration from Harry Shapiro.

Frank Speck responded in the same helpful and generous way at the University of Pennsylvania, as did John Ewers at the National Museum in Washington, D.C., and Stephan de Borhegyi, while Director of the Stovall Museum in Norman, Oklahoma, and later of the Milwaukee Public Museum. Andrew Whiteford brought us to Beloit College several times for concerts, where we enjoyed good visits and personally conducted tours of the Logan Museum. Arthur Parker, a Seneca Indian related to General Ely S. Parker of Civil War fame, while Director of the Rochester Municipal Museum was most helpful and inspiring, as was also William Fenton, Director of the New York State Museum in Albany; Joseph Dunlap, Director of the Allen County Museum in Lima, Ohio, and Edward Fitzpatrick, Jr., Director of Dramatics at Ashland College in Oregon.

On several occasions Frances Densmore invited us to her home in Red Wing, Minnesota, where we enjoyed listening to her early experiences while recording songs among the Indians. Ella Deloria, noted Sioux ethnologist and writer, gave us much moral support and inspiration, as did Oscar Howe, Sioux "artist laureate" of the state of South Dakota, and his charming wife, Heide.

We are also in debt to James Rankin, who introduced us to John Pomfret, Director of the Huntington Library; to Arthur McAnally, late Director of Libraries, University of Oklahoma; to Arrell Gibson, in charge of the Phillips Collection there, and Alice Timmons, who succeeded him; to Margaret Blaker, Archivist of the National Anthropological Archives at the Smithsonian Institution, and to Ruth Butler, who introduced us to the Ayer Collection in the Newberry Library—all of whom were extremely helpful in aiding in our research.

In addition to the anthropologists already mentioned, we would like to express our sincere appreciation for the personal interest of Robert Bell and William Bittle, of the University of Oklahoma, and to Frederick J. Dockstader, Director of the American Indian Museum in New York. We also thank Peter J. Powell, who has been doing remarkable work with the relocated (dislocated) Indians in Chicago at Saint Augustine's Center, to Don and Sue Dietrich, of Olympia Fields, Illinois, and to G. D. Bartell and David Gradwohl, of Iowa State University.

We wish to express our appreciation also to Alfred Bailey, Director of the Denver Museum of Natural History; Jerry Bywaters, Director of the Dallas Museum of Fine Arts; Ruth Pershing Uhler, Curator of Education, Houston Museum of Fine Arts; Edith Quade, Curator of Education, Milwaukee Public Museum; Russell Fridley, Director of the Minnesota Historical Society; Clayton G. Rudd, President of the Minnesota Natural History Society; Samuel E. Beck and Mrs. H. E. Wheeler, while Directors of the Cherokee Indian Museum; Ross and Louise Caldwell, also of Cherokee, North Carolina; Arden DuBois, of the United States Department of State; Robert Treuer, Education Specialist, and Ada Deer (Menomini), former Community Services Coordinator for the Bureau of Indian Affairs, in Minneapolis; and Jack Williams and Arthur White of the National Park Service, all of whom have been especially interested in our work and helped us in many ways.

A warm friendship with Thomas Gilcrease over a period of many years, both in

Jackson Hole and in Tulsa, where he never tired of showing us his personal collections and "finds," will also be remembered, as will our friendship and association with Mari Sandoz, who was generous with her suggestions and references.

Marie and Onni Hakola, both fine artists, have been helpful and inspiring ever since we started our career, with constant encouragement, suggestions, and generous hospitality. To Anne Rudolph, a great dancer and teacher of body education, and to B. H. Bartfield, we wish to express sincere gratitude for deep friendship, inspiration, and the loan of rare books. To Yeffe Kimball, Oklahoma Osage, famous modern artist, we are grateful indeed for loving friendship, always making us welcome and sharing not only her rare books but her "tipi in the sky" in New York, enabling us to further our research in nearby libraries and museums.

To Gertrude Prokosch Kurath, of the Dance Research Center in Ann Arbor, Michigan, dancer, writer, sincere student, and researcher on ethnological dance, to R. W. Breckenridge, of Iowa State University, and to Albert W. Erkins, of Jackson Hole, Wyoming, we wish to express appreciation for information and the use of personal books and papers.

Ralph Hubbard, Curator and Librarian of the Indian Museum in Medora, North Dakota, an admired friend of many years, early inspired us and generously shared knowledge, experience, and his wonderful personal Indian collection.

Milford G. Chandler, adopted by Winnebagos, Potawatomis, Pawnees, and Mesquakies (Foxes), who was in charge of the Julius Rosenwald expedition for the Field Museum and who has collected priceless Indian specimens for many museums—Heye Foundation, Cranbrook Institute, Southwest Museum, Milwaukee Public Museum, Whitney Museum of Cody, Wyoming—not only has been a good friend for many years but has shared experiences and knowledge of many tribes and acquainted us with beautiful articles from his personal collection.

John Martin, former Dance Editor of the *New York Times*, and Walter Terry, formerly with the *New York Herald-Tribune* and now Dance Editor of *Saturday Review*, will never know how their generous praise and keen understanding have warmed our hearts and encouraged us throughout our career. Also, we shall always remember the inspiration and encouragement of Austin Wilder, former concert manager, and of his partner, James Gilvarry.

Our deepest gratitude includes the late Walter Campbell (Stanley Vestal), for his friendship and interest and for introducing us to Sitting Bull's people on the Standing Rock Reservation; and to Flying Cloud (Judge Frank Zahn), a friend of many years, interpreter for presidents and governmental dignitaries, yet serving us in the same capacity and adding much valuable information of his own to our quest for knowledge of his people.

And certainly this book would not have been possible without the help of Indian friends and "relatives" of many tribes and reservations, who patiently, willingly, and generously guided us on the long trail of discovery—especially my Indian "father," Chief One Bull, and his family, "mother" Scarlet Whirlwind and "sisters" Regina, Cecilia, and Margaret, and One Bull's famous brother, Chief White Bull; also the following Lakotas on the Standing Rock Reservation: Kills Pretty Enemy, Twin, Little Soldier, Makes Trouble, Crazy Bear, White Shield, Elk Nation, Rosebud, Two Face, Crow Necklace, Two Bulls, White Hand Bear, Young Eagle, Running Eagle, Magpie Eagle, Chase Alone, Loon, Eagle Man, Little Crow (son of Chief Little Crow, who led the Minnesota uprising in 1862), Kills Alive, Feather Earring, Long Chase, Iron Bull, Iron Boulder, Swims with Dog, White Buffalo, Lizzie Iron, Josephine Pleats, Mrs. Twin, Mrs. Iron Bull, Mrs. Two Bulls, Mrs. Has Tricks, Mrs. Stretches Himself, Mrs. Red Beans, Maude Young Eagle.

At Pine Ridge there were Sitting Bull's two sons, Little Soldier and John Sitting Bull (Deefy) (who escaped from Standing Rock when their father was killed), Jim Red Cloud, Long Wolf, Robert Horse, White Bird, Blunt Horn, Iron Hawk, Kills Enemy, High Eagle, Spotted Crow, Good Voice Iron, Returns from Scout, Holy Eagle, Crow Man, Henry Standing Bear, Fast Whirlwind, Walking Bull, Good Buffalo, all Oglalas, as well as High Hawk, White Eyes, and his son Daniel, Northern Cheyennes. And we shall always remember Black Elk, the Holy Man whom we visited many times, and his son Ben. When we sympathized with the old man because he was nearly blind, he remarked that it made little difference, as he could now see the real things of the spirit. He anticipated our visits and always "looked for" a special large, round Navajo pin Gladys wore, gently feeling it with his fingers. He gave me permission to use his invocation with the pipe and touched us deeply by stating he believed it would help to bring about a better understanding of his people.

Nor shall we forget John Calhoff, with his wealth of tribal lore and information, who with White Bear Claws, Thunder Bull, and Philip Romero often served as interpreter; nor the women who were kind and helpful—Mrs. Red Bear, Mrs. White Wolf, Mrs. Returns from Scout, and Eagle Nation.

We wish to express our sincere appreciation to many Crow friends, especially to the Deernose family, Yellowtail family, Old Coyote family, Joseph and Chester Medicine Crow, Max Big Man (Crow historian), Frank Hawk, Real Bird, Yellow Brow, Mountain Bull, Bull-over-the-Hill, Bird Horse, Pretty Shield (Mrs. Goes Ahead). We cannot speak highly enough about Donald and Agnes Deernose, Tom and Susie Yellowtail, Henry and Stella Old Coyote, Two Warriors, and Young Hawk, who were willing to leave families and loved ones for six months to accompany us overseas, where they helped us present concerts of true Indian dances in eleven countries from Finland to Israel, including a month's engagement at the famous Théâtre des Champs Élysées in Paris. It was the first time Indians were ever presented in concert instead of as Wild West or rodeo attractions. They were admired on both sides of the footlights in every country we visited.

We have fond memories of Chief and Julia Wades-in-the-Water, Rides-to-the-Door, and Theodore Last Star, Blackfeet of Montana. Julia and "Wades" liked to visit us in our tipi, for they said it reminded them of early days.

Many friends were helpful among the North Carolina Cherokees, especially Epps Welch, Will West Long, John Walking Stick, John Lossia, Molly Sequoia, the Owl family, and the Gloyn family.

Many individuals of various tribes have been much interested in our work and have assisted us in more ways than they realized. They include, first of all, Grey Wolf, a Cherokee, and Red Dog, a Sioux, who were the first Indians I met as a boy and who taught me dance steps which I learned later were among the most difficult to master. We were early acquainted with Buffalo Bear and Crazy Bull, two Sioux living in the East, and the Tantequidgeons, Mohegans of Connecticut, with whom we had many good times and who introduced us to Speck. Thunder Cloud, descendant of the great Ottawa, Pontiac, was always generous with the lore of his people and taught us steps and dances. His jovial good humor and warm friendship will always remain with us.

Tahan,* a Kiowa captive who later became a Kiowa war chief, was one of the most remarkable men we ever knew. He lived the wild, free life of the Kiowas before they were influenced by white men, later walked the white man's road, becoming a popular lecturer. He was a close friend for many years, calling us his "children," and shared with us his fascinating reminiscences of the early days until he took the Spirit Trail at the age of 105.

Our good friends the famous Pawnee-Creek artist Acee Blue Eagle and Swift Eagle, a Santo Domingo, spent many delightful hours with us and were most helpful with stories, songs, and dances. Other old friends, the McMullens (Chippewa and Potawatomi), who served with the Bureau of Indian Affairs for a long time, have both been helpful and encouraging. John Stands-in-Timber interpreted for old Cheyenne leaders—Ridge Walker, Little Chief, and Teeth—and visited us often in our tipi at Crow Fair. Lightning Star, Old Man, and their families, Arapahos, spent a summer with us and proved to be faithful and loyal friends. Joshua Wetsit and his wife, Assiniboins, Mark Big Road, Oglala medicine man, Evergreen Tree, Cochiti, long time performer at the Wisconsin Dells, Audrey Warrior, Sioux, Ramona Child, Sioux-Navajo, and Ferial Deer Skye, Menominis, all have been faithful, encouraging, and inspiring friends. Friends in the Southwest and among the Seminoles of Florida wish to remain anonymous, but we appreciate their kindness and help, nevertheless.

Words cannot express our deepest gratitude to Raymond C. Lillie and Vernon Johnson, first and present directors of the Jackson Lake Lodge. They made us very happy many years ago when they recognized the value of our work and invited us to appear at the lodge, where we have danced each summer ever since.

Eugene Petersen, director of the Motion Picture Unit at the University of Southern California, has shown great interest in our work, and to him we are indebted for many beautiful photographs of our dances.

Charles Nedwin Hockman, Director of the Motion Picture Unit at the University of Oklahoma, who directed our documentary color films on Indian dance and culture, was so interested and enthusiastic about retaining the lore of early days that he sponsored our pageant, *Arrows to Atoms*, in Oklahoma City. We cannot ade-

---

*This is the way he spelled it, but it is pronounced as if spelled Tehan (Tay-han'), according to our pronunciation key.

quately express our appreciation to him for his interest, or for his generous and tireless work and his excellent photography of our dances. We also wish to express our appreciation to Donald Clark, Dean of Fine Arts, who greatly helped with the direction of the pageant, and to all of the Indians who were so cooperative and performed so beautifully, and to Boyce Timmons (Cherokee), also of the university, who introduced us to leaders of various tribes and was influential in obtaining their assistance. Nor could we have done without the generous help of Joe and Amos Toahty, Linn Poahty, Mark Keahbone, David Apekaum, and George Watchetaker and that of Philip and Vinola Newkumet, who were so helpful with dances and stories about the Caddoes.

To all of these good people and to many others who have made our hearts sing by helping our dreams come true, we say, *Pilamaya* ("you make me grateful").

Reginald Laubin (Tatanka Wanjila)
Gladys Laubin (Wiyaka Waśtewin)

Moose, Wyoming
April 2, 1976 (The Awakening Moon)

Pronunciation Key

Vowels *a, e, i, o, u*— as in Latin

c— ch, as in *chair*

g— hard, as in *go*

h̄— guttural *h*

ġ— guttural *g*

j— a French, or soft *j*, like *z* in azure

n— in Lakota, nazalized at end of a syllable

ṗ— exploded p

ṡ— sh, as in *sure*

All other consonants are as in English.

In Lakota, the accent is on the second syllable unless otherwise marked.

Most Indian tribal names are both singular and plural, comparable to English *sheep* or *deer*. For example, Lakota may imply one individual or the entire tribe. There really is no such word as "Lakotas," but to harmonize with modern usage we have used plurals, such as Shoshonis, Pawnees, Arikaras, Chippewas, Ottawas, and so on, and designations like one Blackfoot, many Blackfeet.

Contents

Illustrations

COLOR PLATES

BLACK-AND-WHITE ILLUSTRATIONS

THE BEGINNING OF A NEW LIFE

Years ago it became apparent to me that Indian art could be the only indigenous art in America. Likewise, Indian dance can be the only indigenous American dance. My interest in Indian dance began when I was a small boy and met two Indians. I not only watched them dance, but they endeavored to teach me some dance steps. I found this experience so fascinating that I never outgrew my interest in the American Indian or his dances.

My parents were both concert musicians. My father had been first oboist in the newly founded Detroit Symphony Orchestra, and my mother was a fine soprano and pianist. With this early experience in the concert world, it was natural for me to think of someday giving concerts of Indian dances. Of course, no one had ever heard of such a thing, but nevertheless it was an idea that remained in my mind all through my school years.

As my interest in Indians broadened, I came to a greater realization of the abysmal ignorance of the average person concerning anything Indian. Gradually it dawned upon me that I could use my knowledge and skill at Indian dancing as a medium to bring about a better understanding of the Indians themselves.

I met Gladys Tortoiseshell at the Norwich Art School in Connecticut, and the idea began to take shape. She was of English and French-Canadian descent, with long dark hair, and was sometimes mistaken for one of the local Mohegan Indians. She was interested in making my dream come true, and we began to plan a career. I had an opportunity to study art in Paris, but instead we got married and went out West to live with the Indians. Because of the lack of appreciation of dance in general and of Indian dancing in particular, it has never been an easy road, but in many ways it has been a rewarding one. We fell in love with the country, as well as with the people, and the West has been home ever since.

Today our Indian friends tell us we are missionaries from the Indians to the white people. "Your skins may be white," they say, "but your hearts are Indian."

The fact that we had made a serious study of Indian material in museums and libraries, that we knew something of Indian dancing, and had made friends not only with local Mohegan and Pequot Indians but with every Indian who ever came to our area established a background for our first contact with Indians on reservations. Right from the start we were accepted, not as the usual curiosity-seeking tourists, but as Indians. We were adopted immediately into the Sitting Bull family.

We arrived during the big annual Indian Fair at Fort Yates, North Dakota, agency for the Standing Rock Sioux Reservation. Our first introduction was to Flying Cloud (Maĥpiya Kinyeyapi), who offered to be our interpreter. We learned that he was the best we could have, for he had a personal interest in the early days, which was important to us in learning from the old people. They had lived a life so different that they had terms expressing it that were not always understood by younger people or by many would-be interpreters. We were indeed fortunate that he not only became our interpreter but remained our good friend as long as he lived.

Flying Cloud took us over to the great camp on the prairie, telling us we should meet One Bull, who was their outstanding chief. He was known as one of the "fighting nephews" of Sitting Bull and had been instructed to take the place of his renowned uncle upon the latter's death. We found the old man and his wife in a little bit of a tent—a forester's tent—the kind the pack outfitters call a "tepee."

We had heard that a chief was often the poorest man in the village, because as "father" of his people he was expected to take care of them and sometimes gave everything he owned away. One Bull was certainly living according to tradition. His costume had been destroyed in a fire shortly before, and his everyday clothes were nothing but rags and patches, with moccasins of canvas made from an old tent.

Flying Cloud wanted us to get the old man's picture. We had heard of the usual Indian reluctance to pose for photographs, but we were assured that One Bull would do it gladly. We were delighted at the prospect. He had one of the strongest and most interesting faces we had ever seen.[*] A prominent Roman nose, lower lip protruding from loss of upper teeth, his brown, leathery skin and faded gray eyes gave rugged character to his features (see page 188). Age had shortened his frame and he stood only a little over five feet. In his prime he had been much taller, but always small for a Sioux Indian. It was one of the reasons he had received his name. Although small, he was courageous as a lone buffalo bull.

Still we hesitated to picture him in his rags. We thought we should show such a dignified, fine-looking old man in Indian dress, so we asked if he would mind wearing my costume.

Flying Cloud spoke to One Bull. The old man's face lighted up and he replied that he would be very happy to appear in my costume. This is when he first saw all of our Indian packing cases. We carried our costumes in old-time *parfleche* cases we had picked up at a trader's and in some we had made ourselves. When we got them out of the car it created quite a stir. One Bull said, "How is it these white people have all these Indian things? They tell us for fifty years they are no good. If they are no good, why do these white people have them?"

Flying Cloud explained that we were different from most white people they met. He said we liked the old Indian things and the old ways and had come to learn more about them.

---

[*]Later we arranged for Langdon Kihn to paint One Bull's portrait, which appeared in *National Geographic Magazine*, July, 1944, and in *Indians of the Americas*, published by National Geographic Society in 1955.

Left to right: Laubin, Chief White Bull, Gladys Laubin, and Chief One Bull. The chiefs are the famous "fighting nephews" of Sioux Chief Sitting Bull. In Indian relationship both chiefs are Reginald Laubin's "fathers." Laubin Collection.

I took the shirt and leggings out of their cases and the old man went into his little tent to put them on. A few minutes later he came out, elegantly attired in my buckskins. I took my war bonnet out of its cylindrical rawhide container and handed it to him. He was more amazed than ever to see that I carried it in the old Indian way.

Now, with the bonnet on, he looked the part—a real chief! What a contrast to a few moments before!

By this time I thought he would be interested in seeing the shield I had made (see page 189). Not being able to get real buffalo hide, I had made it by shrinking a heavy piece of rawhide from the shoulder of a steer. This had also been done in real Indian fashion—pegging the hide over a hole in the ground filled with red-hot stones, on which water was poured to create intense steam. (Later White Bull, One Bull's brother, showed me how he had made his shield.) Over the finished shield I had placed a painted canvas cover. In the old days a man removed the cover of his shield only when going into battle or for some very special ceremony.

The old chief said he felt highly honored that I would show him the "real shield" underneath. When I exposed it to his view, he gasped, becoming quite excited.

"This man has my name on his shield!" he called out in Lakota. Sure enough, I had painted a black buffalo on it, which could be as readily interpreted as One Bull. The old man immediately asked me to dance with him that night and invited Gladys to sit with his wife, Scarlet Whirlwind.

I loaned my chief's costume to One Bull for the remainder of the fair and for myself dressed in dance costume—breechclout, moccasins, porcupine-hair roach,

and feather bustle. We were stunned to find all the other male dancers attired in suits of dyed long underwear. Only in the last few years have some Indians begun to strip again, but they still wear bathing trunks under their breechclouts.

As an example of how the once sturdy Indian, who could endure all kinds of weather with almost no clothing, has changed, one of the dancers said to me, "You dance like old time. We ought to dress like that."

"Yes," I agreed. "Why don't you?"

"Too cold," he replied. "We catch cold."

At the dance Chief One Bull seated me on his left, the place of honor, among all the old dignitaries of the tribe. Here I got my introduction to the chiefs' "straight-up" dancing.

Gladys was seated on the left of Scarlet Whirlwind with the women, on the opposite side of the circle.

We must have acquitted ourselves well, for the next day One Bull sent word by Flying Cloud that he wanted to adopt us that night. His daughter Mini Capi, or Well, said to us, "Our friends, they come to us and say, 'Are they your relatives from up north who visit you?' They think you are *real* Indians!"

At the adoption One Bull first "counted coup," or told of his exploits in battle. Such "boasting," as some writers have called it, was formerly a requirement for participation in almost any dance or ceremony. We were fortunate to witness this, for One Bull was one of the last to retain the custom. He told of his fights with Crow Indians and of his part in the famous Custer Battle, where he was credited with leading the charge against Major Reno.

Following his counting of coups, the old man said:

I am the head chief here and you all know it. These two young people you see here I am going to adopt into our great Sioux Nation. They come all the way from the Land of the Eastern Ocean to be with us here. Although you see them dressed in the garb of our people,

The Laubins lived in their own tipi on the reservations. The blue-beaded dress was made by the daughter of Two Bears, the Yanktonai chief who greeted Lewis and Clark. Laubin Collection.

they are really white people who want to learn our ways and our dances so they can help bring about a better understanding between the red and white races.

This young man I am going to make my son and upon him I bestow my own name, Tatanka Wanjila, One Buffalo Bull,* the name of your chief. To the young woman I give the name Wiʹyaka Waśtewin, Good Feather, the name of my mother. My mother was Sitting Bull's sister, as you all know.

Now, my fellow tribesmen, recognize these two people by the names I have given them.

---

*The name Tatanka Wanjila refers to the Buffalo Spirit or Buffalo God, the controlling power of the buffalo, and could be better translated as the Only Buffalo Bull. It was pointed out to us that the bearer of the name represents a small part of the great power of the buffalo. Also, although small in stature, the chief was known as being as "brave as a lone buffalo bull." In English the name has been shortened to One Bull. Frances Densmore wrote it as One Buffalo because in Victorian times it was improper to use the word "bull." Brave Buffalo Bull was called "Brave Buffalo," Buffalo Bull Bear was "Buffalo Bear," and so on.

It was explained to us that to give one's own name to another was the highest honor that could be paid, and the old chief had so honored us. Later on, when we were alone with his family, his daughters interpreted for us, "When you go back to the white people to tell them about us, you will face opposition. But, when you meet that opposition, you put your head down, like an old buffalo bull, and push right on through."

Then looking at me, he continued, "That is why I give you my name, One Buffalo Bull. It is no longer mine but now belongs to you."

Turning to Gladys he said, "Look at me! I am an old man. That is because my mother took good care of me and raised me well. So, I give you my mother's name so you will look after my son and take good care of him."

Our adoption later proved to be an "open sesame" to Indians everywhere, for most of them had heard of Chief One Buffalo Bull of the Sioux and were glad to meet his new "son" and "daughter-in-law." Such a warm acceptance opened the way for us to live in our own tipi whenever we visited Indians on any reservation.

One Bull's words have always remained with us. There have been many times when we have had to put our heads down and push right on through, like buffalo bulls. It has not been easy to try to break down the old false, preconceived notions of Indians and their dancing.

We are sorry not to be able to include more illustrations in the historical sections of this book, but there were few artists on the scene during those times. The few who were present, such as John White, familiar to nearly everyone interested in Indians, did very little to portray the dances. Similarly, the advent of photography did little in this respect, for pictures had to be posed and could be taken only in bright daylight. Film fast enough to record action pictures came too late to be of any value in recording old-time dances. In more recent times it has not always been possible to get pictures for other reasons.

Often Indians would not permit pictures to be taken, and in our own case we felt it an honor to be invited to participate in the celebrations. It is difficult, if not impossible, to take part and take pictures at the same time. We doubt that we would have learned as much as we did, or have been accepted as "one of them" if we had gone around snapping pictures, like so many people—even Indians—do today.

Reginald Laubin

PART I. **History and General Discussion**

1. The First Explorers

Jacques Cartier stood on the deck of his ship, anxiously watching the return from the shore of his "onely boate," followed by seven canoes of "wilde men, . . . all of which approached neere unto our boate, dancing and making many signes of joy and mirth, as it were desiring our friendship. . . . Some of the women who came not over, we might see stand up to their knees in water, singing and dancing."[1]

Here we have the first mention of dance in the New World, in 1534. Cartier was greeted in this fashion near the mouth of the St. Lawrence River. It must have been something to see—warriors dancing in canoes!

From this time on we find reference to dancing in the accounts of most of the early explorers, but their reaction was usually curiosity rather than appreciation. There are no descriptions of the dances. Not all the early visitors had opportunity to see the dancing. They did not fraternize with the natives and so did not come into close enough contact to learn of their intimate lives.

On the other hand, early in American history there were many Europeans so fascinated by the Indian way of life that they deserted their own companions to go and live with the Indians. But almost none of these people ever wrote down their experiences, and we know about them only from other sources. For example, seven such desertions were recorded for the De Soto expedition of 1539.[2]

Columbus left some glowing accounts of Indian appearance and character and some mention of habits and customs. He stated that the Indians had beautiful physiques, mildness of nature all through the [Caribbean] islands and that they were "fairly white, and if they were clothed and protected from the sun and air they would be almost as fair as the people of Spain."[3] He reported further:

They are a loving people, without covetousness. . . . They love their neighbors as themselves and their speech is the sweetest and gentlest in the world, and always with a smile. . . . they have very good customs among themselves.

When the *Santa María* was wrecked, he said that the natives stole "not so much as a needle."[4]

But in all his journals the only mention Columbus made of dancing was when some of the Indians came to visit him in a canoe. He ordered a tambourine player and some of the boys of his crew to dance on the poop deck to entertain them. The Indians evidently thought it some kind of a war dance and responded by grasping their shields and bows and letting fly a cloud of arrows at the ship.[5]

Following Columbus was Giovanni Caboto (better known in history as John Cabot, for he sailed for the English king). He saw no one as he skirted the shores of this continent on his first voyage in 1497, but on his second voyage he captured three natives in the vicinity of either Prince Edward Island or Newfoundland and took them back to England. He was the first to see North American Indians, but it is doubtful that his exploit did much to assure future good relations between Europeans and American natives.[6]

Another Italian, Giovanni da Verrazzano, sailing for France, spent about fifteen days either in Buzzard's Bay or Boston Harbor in 1524 and was the next to write about the Indians. He was pleased with their appearance, saying they were "of as goodly stature and shape as is possible to declare," and that "the women are of like conformitie and beautie, verie handsome and well favored, they are as well mannered and continente as anye women of good education."[7]

But because the Indians did not have large, bulging muscles like European strong men, the French explorers considered them "not strong of body" and "of very little strength," and yet shortly after making these observations reported seeing one old woman, accompanied by a young maid of eighteen or twenty years of age, who hid themselves at the approach of the strangers. The old woman carried two infants on her shoulders, while hanging to her from behind was a child about eight years old, and the young woman "was laden likewise with as many." The explorers took the child away from the old woman to bring to "the most Christian king of France." There is no mention of Indian dancing.

Cartier was not as pleased with the Indians' appearance as Verrazzano had been ten years earlier. He said the men were "of an indifferent good stature and bigness but wild and unruly." He stated also that they painted themselves "with certain roan colours" and that they made their boats from the bark of the birch tree.[8]

On the day following Cartier's introduction to the Indians nine canoes arrived at the mouth of the creek near the anchored French ships. This time the French sent two men ashore to meet them, to "carry them knives with other Iron wares, and a red hat to give unto their Captains." During this presentation of gifts the Indians were continually dancing,

with many ceremonies, as with their hands to cast Sea water on their heads. They gave up whatsoever they had, not keeping anything, so they were constrained to go back againe naked, and made signes that the next day they would come againe, and bring more skinnes with them.[9]

Another time forty canoes containing about two hundred men, women, and children came to trade with them. "We gave them knives, combes, beads of glasse, and other trifles of small value, for which they made many signes of gladnesse, lifting their hands up to heaven, dancing and singing in their boates."[10] Again, "all their men, in two or three companies beganne to sing and dance, seeming to be very glad of our coming."

Cartier was able to get two of these Indians to accompany him so that he could train them as interpreters. He took them to France and apparently treated them well, for they gave him devoted service on his second voyage in 1535. On his return he was greeted by a chief, "the Lord of Canada, who made a long Oration, moving all his bodie and members after a strange fashion, which thing is a ceremonie and signe of gladnesse and securitie among them." The chief returned to his village, and another chief, with men, women, and children, called upon him, "who after the fashion of their country, in signe of mirth and joy, beganne to make a long Oration, the women still singing and dancing up to their knees in water."[11]

On these occasions, when gifts were exchanged, the Indians made "three great shreeks, or howles, in signe of joy and league of friendship . . . very loud with other ceremonies." At the conclusion of the trading the chief "commanded all his people to sing and dance."[12] It was apparently their custom to sing and dance whenever they were meeting or leaving strangers.

With all these references to dancing there is nothing to tell us how it was actually done or how it really looked, but it is interesting to see that it was important to the Indians. The same pattern of oration, singing, and dancing is still carried out at all Indian gatherings that we have attended.

Cartier believed that the Indians did not want him to go to the Iroquois village of Hochelaga up the river, but, after informing them that he was going anyway, "they altogether gave out three great shreeks and there upon beganne to sing and dance, as they were wont to doe."

The people he had been dealing with we believe to have been of Algonquian stock, but the Iroquois greeted him in the same way, "still dancing and greatly rejoicing at our coming." The French gave them "knives, beades and such small trifles," and the Iroquois filled the French boats with cornbread and fish "so thicke that you would have thought it to fall from heaven."[13]

More than seventy years after Cartier's visits, Champlain began to explore the same part of the country and continued his discoveries for nearly fifteen years. Early in 1605, near Cape Anne, north of present-day Boston, Indians approached in a canoe, then retreated, beached their canoe, and danced on the shore. Champlain gave them knives and biscuits, and the Indians drew him a map, with crayons and paper furnished them, conversing with the use of signs.[14]

Champlain reported these Indians as having

a very cheerful disposition, laughing often; yet at the same time they are somewhat phlegmatic. . . . All these people are well proportioned in body, without any deformity, and are also agile. The women are well-shaped, full and plump, and of swarthy complexion, on account of the large amount of a certain pigment with which they rub themselves and which gives them an olive color.[15]

Later, on meeting another group of Indians, he wrote, "They all began to dance and jump," and afterward seated themselves in a circle on the ground, "as is their custom, when they wish to celebrate a festivity or an harangue is to be made. Hatchets, paternosters, caps, knives, and other little knick-knacks" were distributed among them, when "all the rest of this day and the following night, until break of day, they did nothing but dance, sing and make merry."[16]

In another edition of Champlain's discoveries he wrote:

When I arrived at this village [Huron] it suited me to remain there while the warriors armed from the neighboring villages, . . . during which time there was continual feasting and dancing because of the delight they felt to see us determined to assist them in their war and of their assurance of victory.[17]

And so Champlain was greeted all along the way. At another time he said, "Many savages, men and women, visited us, and ran up on all sides dancing."[18] He gave good descriptions of some of the dances he saw and even tried to tell of the Indians' manner of dancing and how they executed the steps, which we shall take up later.

To go back to the earlier period, just a few years before the time that Cartier was exploring the northeast corner of the country, Pánfilo de Narváez in 1527, with another large expedition, was penetrating the interior of Florida, which in those days meant the entire region of the Gulf of Mexico. Narváez' arrogance and cruelty so antagonized the natives that his entire party was eventually forced to flee the country. When he finally made his way back to the predetermined place of embarkment, the ships supposedly awaiting him had already departed, their captain presuming him lost. He and his remaining men were forced to construct boats to effect their escape. The five leaky contraptions, each about thirty-three feet long, made their way along the Gulf of Mexico coast for nearly seven weeks, the men half starved and suffering from lack of fresh water, until finally all vessels were wrecked off an island near the present city of Galveston, Texas.

Indians rescued the survivors, and Álvar Núñez Cabeza de Vaca, who was to make one of the most remarkable journeys ever accomplished by man, wrote:

An hour after our arrival, they began to dance and hold a great rejoicing, which lasted all night, although for us there was no joy, festivity or sleep, awaiting the hour they should make us their victims. In the morning they again gave us fish and roots, showing us such hospitality that we were reassured, and lost somewhat the fear of sacrifice.[19]

We can hardly blame the Spaniards for their fear, since they had done nothing to encourage friendship with any natives. Less than two decades before, Narváez had massacred almost the entire population of Cuba, and word of Spanish misdeeds could have preceded him from tribe to tribe. Here again we have Indians dancing to honor their visitors.

During the winter the food supply ran out.[20] Eventually only fifteen Spaniards were left, and finally Cabeza de Vaca remained alone. Later on he met survivors from some of the other boats. Four of them, including the Negro slave, Estebanico, after eight years of travel, trial, and hardship made their way not only to the California coast but from there all the way down to Mexico City.

Cabeza de Vaca became a trader, using established Indian trade routes. He dealt in conch and cockle shells, deerskins (and perhaps buffalo hides), tassels of red-dyed deer tails, red ochre for face paint, hard cane for arrow shafts, flint for points, and glue to hold them together. The large conchs were used for knives, "especially for cutting a bean-like fruit used as medicine and in the ritual dances."[21] This may possibly be the first mention of the so-called mescal beans, which are still associated with the Peyote religion, or Native American Church, popular among many Indian tribes today, having largely taken over other native religions in the past one hundred years.

The Karankawa Indians, who lived near the gulf in what is now Texas and with whom Cabeza de Vaca often dealt, for musical accompaniment used gourd rattles, notched sticks (or *moraches*), and "a kind of rude flute, upon which no air was played, but which was softly blown in time to the chant." This latter sounds similar to the use of the Sun Dance whistles on the Plains. He said they had religious festivals at the full of the moon, or after successful hunting or fishing expeditions, and used the "black drink," found later all through the Southeast and South. He also said they settled disputes with their fists, which is certainly far different than among any other Indians with whom we are acquainted. Most Indians, seeing white men fight in this way, thought it ridiculous. If angry enough to fight, then you tried to kill your opponent. Otherwise you did nothing.

Cabeza de Vaca mentions a "shuffle dance," which we know as one of the dances found all across and up and down the country. He also mentioned a tribe of Marames, who were so poor they ate snakes, ants, lizards, and anything they could get. They were so swift they could run down deer on foot. He said:

They are a merry people; notwithstanding the hunger they suffer, they do not cease to observe their festivities and dances. To them the happiest time of the year is the season of eating prickly pears; they have hunger no longer, pass all the time in dancing, and eat day and night.

Another time he and a companion, Castillo, served as medicine men to the Coahuiltecans, on the Texas-Mexico border. They were apparently successful with their patients, for he wrote:

A great festivity was ordered; all that night and for three days after the Indians danced and sang and leaped with praise. And while the camp resounded with these discordant testimonies to divine power, the four Christians knelt on the sand and rendered thanks for God's compassion and his gifts.[22]

Castillo cured five Indians who had a kind of paralysis. He blew upon the affected parts, drew the sign of the cross upon their foreheads, spoke in Latin, and in other ways made a mystic impression upon the Indians, whose own medicine men did things in similar fashion. The sign of the cross could have been interpreted by them as either a star or the four directions, and the Latin as magical or sacred words.

When Castillo lost his nerve, Cabeza de Vaca took over and was also successful. In fact, this success enabled him and his companions to continue their journey in relative comfort and with great co-operation from the Indians, for their reputation as healers was carried by runners ahead of them as they traveled and they were welcomed with open arms and an abundance of presents wherever they went.

When among the Cuchendados, near the Río Grande, he found that these people, after preparing mesquite beans, had a great celebration:

7

A great dance followed the banquet; the Indians, men and women, leaped and caprioled, unretarded by their earthly ballast. With their faces painted with red ochre and minium, they circled about the fire, to the rhythmic scraping of grooved sticks. They kept their feet together, their elbows out, their shoulders hunched, and thus they hopped round and round, belly to rump, for the space of six hours, without ever ceasing their circular progress or their lamentable cries.

Any who fell out were scratched from shoulder to ankle with a rakelike tool armed with shark's teeth.[23] After all the time he spent with Indians, Cabeza de Vaca apparently never did learn to understand or appreciate their music.

Many people, in their limited knowledge of Indian dancing, have the idea that there is no leaping in it. But we have already seen references to jumping and leaping and we shall see more. We shall learn, too, that, although there were many tribal differences in dance styles across the country, there were at the same time many similarities. The dance just referred to by Cabeza de Vaca sounds like something we might see in many areas.

The stories of Cabeza de Vaca and of the Negro Estebanico led to Coronado's expedition in quest of the fabled Seven Cities of Cíbola.* With an army of 300 men, 70 footmen, and 1,000 friendly Indians he set out from Mexico in 1540 to explore what is now the American Southwest. He ventured as far as central Kansas. One of his first misdeeds was to capture a Yuma Indian and torture him for information about the "cities" to the north. And yet most of the Indians greeted him with friendship and honored him with presents of cotton cloth, dressed skins, corn meal, pine nuts, and turquoise. Some came as much as "seventy leagues" to see the white strangers. But the Spaniards' aggressiveness, lack of tact, and lack of morals or ethics prevented their seeing the real inside of Indian life. Whereas we now know that these people of the Southwestern pueblos had perhaps more ritual dances than any other Indians (and that today dancing remains more important to them than to any others in the United States), several of Coronado's chroniclers do not mention dancing at all.

They were often impressed by the appearance and conduct of the people in the various villages they visited or fought with. One Indian "captain" was called Bigotes—Whiskers—"because he wore a long mustache. He was a tall, well-built young fellow, with a fine figure." The mustache impresses us as most un-Indian, although we know that many Indians of Mexico, California, and the Northwest Coast wore them. To most Indians, however, the thought of hair on the face or body was repulsive. Plains Indians called white men "bear faces" or "old buffalo bulls" because of their heavy beards, and no Indian ever had a heavy beard.

---

*Some may wonder how the Spaniards came to use the name Cíbola. We know that it means "buffalo" in the Isleta dialect, but also the entire area once possessed by the Zuñi Indians was then known as Shi'wona and contained several multistoried "pueblos," or villages. The Spaniards may have mispronounced Shi'wona as Cı'bola. In Castilian Spanish a c is still pronounced "th," and so *thibola* would not be too far from *shi'wona*.

Vásquez, one of the writers, said that they also saw giants on the Colorado River, one so tall that the tallest Spaniard came only to his chest.[24] The nearest thing to a dance reported was that when they came to Cicuye (Pecos) the "people came out to welcome Hernando de Alvarado and their captain (who was being held a hostage by Alvarado) and brought them into the town with drums and pipes something like flutes, of which they have a great many."

There the Spaniards procured an Indian, a captive in the town, whom they called the Turk, because he had a shaved head and peculiar haircut, which they ascribed to the Turks. Bandelier thinks he was a Pawnee. We now find one of the first mentions of the well-known sign language of the Plains. Sign language was at least partly developed in other parts of the country, but nowhere was it used with such fluency as on the Plains.

The expedition met Querechos, whom we believe to be Apaches, then living in eastern New Mexico and Texas as full-fledged Plains Indians. The Turk carried on a conversation with them in signs, and the scribe reported, "That they are very intelligent is evident from the fact that although they conversed by means of signs they made themselves understood so well that there was no need of an interpreter."

They also found an Indian girl as white as a Castilian lady except that her chin was painted, or perhaps tattooed, like a Moorish woman. "In general they all paint themselves in this way here and they decorate their eyes."

Indians of both Plains and pueblos were reported wearing garments of the same pattern we know from more recent times. The Spaniards reported that the people of the Plains "have better figures, are better warriors, and are more feared" than those of the settlements, or pueblos. In our American history we learn that the Apaches were bloodthirsty and cruel, but the Spanish report said, "They are a kind people and not cruel. They are faithful friends."

Mendoza mentioned the hairdo of the women; his description sounds like the squash-blossom style of the Hopi maidens. He said:

The Indians have their dances and songs, with some flutes which have holes on which they put the fingers. They make much noise. They sing in unison with those who play, and those who sing clap their hands in our fashion. . . . They say five or six play together, and that some of the flutes are better than others.

Coronado, in his own report, wrote:

I am unable to give Your Lordship any certain information about the dress of the women, because the Indians keep them guarded so carefully that I have not seen any, except two old women. These had on two long skirts reaching down to their feet and open in front, and a girdle, and they are tied together with some cotton strings.

Casteñada wrote that the Pueblo girls went naked until they were married. How did he know? Did he see them when Coronado did not? With the soldiers' attitude toward women, it is little wonder the Pueblos kept theirs well guarded.

While Coronado was exploring the great Southwest, Hernando de Soto, with a retinue of six hundred men, more than two hundred of them mounted, wearing armor, carrying swords, lances, crossbows, and arquebuses and driving herds of cattle and swine, was pushing his way across Florida into Georgia, the Carolinas, Tennessee, and Alabama. In the entire account left to us by De Biedma, one of his scribes, we find only one reference to dancing, but worded in such a way that they must have seen quite a bit of it. The first reference says:

Apparently rejoicing, they began their customary songs and dances; and some fifteen or twenty women having performed before us a little while for dissimulation, the Cacique [chief] got up and withdrew into one of the houses.[25]

De Soto paid some of the penalty for Narváez' earlier indiscretion and brutality, but added enough of his own by constantly taking chiefs as hostages, burning Indians who refused to lead him to their towns, and enslaving others as he went along. Under such circumstances it is little wonder that he usually found the natives hostile. On the few occasions when they were friendly, he believed them to be treacherous, apparently judging them by his own inclinations. In the nearly four years of his explorations, De Soto captured and enslaved several hundred Indians, both men and women. He had to replace his slaves continually, as the Indians had no heart to live in such fashion and soon died.

On the occasion mentioned above, as soon as the cacique retired after the dancing of the women, the Spaniards attacked the town. De Biedma says the Indians fought "bravely on like lions. We killed them all, either with fire or the sword, or such of them as came out, with the lance, so that when it was nearly dark there remained only three alive." The Spaniards claimed there were five thousand people in the town, which was located near the present city of Mobile, Alabama.

Always the Spaniards reported that the Indians fought bravely, but they could not match horses and armor. Nevertheless, on one occasion the Spaniards admitted that twenty warriors held the entire army at bay, and in the fight above, although only twenty Spaniards were killed, the Indians inflicted seven hundred and sixty wounds with arrows, the armor notwithstanding. In three years the Spaniards lost 250 men and 150 horses.[26]

Not all the Spaniards were as cruel as were the leaders of the conquests. In fact, Ranjel, another of De Soto's chroniclers, seemed to be shocked by the actions of his superiors, for he said, "to Christians no such cruelty is allowable toward any ones and expecially toward an Indian who was ready to die to be loyal to his country and his lord. But later on the account was squared."[27] By this he referred to the final losses and destruction of the expedition.

Casteñada, writing twenty years after the Coronado expedition, was also critical of the high-handed methods used.

Both De Biedma and Ranjel mention several chiefs who were "giants." One of these led De Soto to his village, where, according to Ranjel, the Indians came out to dance, "and they danced very well in the fashion of rustics in Spain, so that it was pleasant to see them."[28]

Apparently referring to the incident near Mobile about which De Biedma wrote, Ranjel said, "Here the Indians immediately began an *areyto* [West Indian word] which is their fashion for a ball with dancing and song."[29]

It begins to look as if it were customary all across North America for Indians to greet strangers with dancing, and it also looks as if the women played more important parts in this role than the popular notions would lead us to believe.

Not too many years after these Spanish expeditions, in 1570 Sir Frances Drake was cruising along the California coast and put in for water in a little bay not far from the Golden Gate. Drake and his crew, during their several days stay in this region, built themselves a kind of rude fort on the mainland. While there, they had quite an experience with Indians.

First came a lone man in a "canow," who harangued the Englishmen. They in turn offered him presents, but he accepted only a hat.

Two days later Indians appeared again, and one man made a "tedious oration" from the top of a nearby hill, "delivered with strange and violent gestures, his voice being extended to the uttermost strength of nature," while all the people bowed their bodies "in a dreaming manner," crying, "Oh!" The men left their bows behind and came forward with presents. The women "used unaturall violence against themselves, crying and shreeking piteously, tearing their flesh with their nails from their cheekes, in a monstrous manner . . . they would with furie cast themselves upon the ground."*

Then three days later came the "king," preceded by "two Embassadors," one of whom called out the harangue while the other prompted him, evidently a ritualistic approach. The "king" and his guards had their faces painted, "some with white, some with blacke, and some with other colours," and each one brought presents. They were followed by women and children bringing baskets of meal, fishes, and other things. One of the "king's" companions carried his "scepter," which no doubt was a ceremonial wand such as used until recently by some of the California natives.

The scepter bearer, when at the foot of the hill near the fort,

with a composed countenance and stately carriage began a song, and answerable thereunto, observed a kind of measure in a dance; whom the king with his guard and every other sort of person following, did in like manner sing and daunce, saving only the women who danced but kept silence. As they daunced they still came on. . . .

They were permitted to enter the "bulwarke: Where after they had entred they yet continued their song and dance a reasonable time."

Following this dance, Drake was seated, while the "king" and others made ovations, and

the king himselfe with all the rest with one consent, and with great reverence, joyfully singing a song, set the crowne upon his head; enriched his necke with all their chaines [of shell beads]; and offering unto him many other things, honoured him by the name of *Hyoh*.

---

*The original printing used the Old English style (*v* for *u*, *u* for *v*), which we have changed to conform with modern usage.

Adding thereunto (as it might seeme) a song and dance of triumph; because they were not onely visited of the gods (for so they still judged us to be) but the great and chiefe god was now become their god, their king and patron, and themselves were become the onely happier and blessed people in all the world.

According to the anthropologists Alfred Kroeber and Robert Heizer, these Indians were probably the Coast Miwok, and they believed that Drake and his crew were returned spirits of the dead. Most Indians believed that it was very dangerous to touch or to be touched by spirits, which explains why the women scarified themselves, as in mourning, and the oration from the hilltop, with "strange and violent gestures," was a supplication for the Englishmen (ghosts) to go away, for none of the Indians wanted to be touched by the visitors. Following the ceremony, in which they honored Sir Francis, some of the Indians mingled with the Englishmen, but the women and the old men again began wailing and scarifying themselves. The sailors tried to stop them by holding their hands, which, of course, made matters worse, for they feared the personal contact with ghosts.

Despite the misunderstandings Drake's chronicler stated, "they are a people of a tractable, free, and loving nature, without guile or treachery." He found them "strong of body, swift in running, and of long continuance." They apparently ran most of the time, for, he said, "They seldom goe, but for the most part runne."[30]

No more English-speaking explorers saw these Indians until Captain Cook's visit to the region in 1776. Cook gave good descriptions of his dealings with the natives, of their appearance and behavior, but only one passage in his narration even suggests dance. He did mention that when the Indians approached his ships in their canoes they kept time to their songs with "the most regular motions of their hands; or beating in concert, with their paddles, on the sides of the canoes; and making other very expressive gestures."

Cook described the slat-and-leather armor of the region, also a

kind of leathern cloak, covered with rows of dried hoofs of deer, disposed horizontally, appended by leathern thongs, covered with quills [feathers?]; which, when they move, make a loud rattling noise, almost equal to that of many small bells. It seems doubtful, however, whether this part of their garb be intended to strike terror in war, or only is to be considered as belonging to their excentric ornamentation on ceremonial occasions. For we saw one of their musical entertainments, conducted by a man dressed in this sort of cloak, with his mask on, and shaking his rattle.[31]

This probably was a dance, but was not recognized as such because it was so different from the dancing to which the captain was accustomed.

2. The Colonial Period

One who did a great deal to publicize the new country and who wrote literally volumes to describe it was the famous Captain John Smith. He performed the roles not only of explorer, historian, pioneer, and diplomat but of trader as well. Early in his adventures along the East Coast he traded a pewter bowl to a "king" of the Florida Indians, who made a hole in it and wore it as a necklace. The captain was paid twenty "deere skinnes" for the bowl, and fifty for a copper kettle.[1]

These Florida Indians he described as having yellow skins and "blacke hayre," but he said the children had "very fayre Chestnut coloured hayre." Later writers often mentioned light hair and blue or gray eyes among Western Indians, particularly Mandans, which gave rise to many theories of their origin, such as being descended from the lost tribes of Israel, a lost Welsh colony, or remnants of early Norse invasions. Personally we have seen many Indian children, even from full-blood families, with brown or reddish hair, which turns black as they become older.

A bit later on Smith described Virginia Indians "of a colour browne when they are of any age, but they are borne white." They shaved half their heads, the other half being allowed to grow long. The women served as barbers, using two clam shells to shave off the hair "of any fashion they please."[2] The women also cut their own hair in various patterns, but always left some of it long. He reported that men had almost no beards. "It is a Miracle to see a Savage have any haire on their faces," except for one old man, whom Smith said was "eight score years olde." He had a white beard. "I never saw, read, nor heard, any have the like before," he wrote.[3]

And here we have the Welcome Dance again:

After they had feasted us, they shewed us, in welcome, their manner of dauncinge, which was in this fashion. One of the Savages, standing in the midst singing, beating one hand against another; all the rest dauncinge about him, shouting, howling, and stamping against the ground, with many Anticke tricks and faces, making noise like so many Wolves or Devils. One thing of them I observed; when they were in their dance, they kept stroke with their feet just one with another; but their hands, heads, faces and bodies, every one of them had a severall gesture; so they continued for the space of halfe an houre.[4]

This is the first mention we have of the individuality in Indian dancing found across the country in all areas but the Southwest. They kept time with their feet, but were allowed great freedom with bodily movements.

Captain Smith described another ceremony, which the Indians would probably have called a dance:

These people have a great reverance to the Sunne above all other things; at the rising and the setting of the same, they sit downe lifting up their hands and eyes to the Sunne, making a round Circle on the ground with dried Tobacco; then they began to pray, making many Devilish gestures, with a Hellish noise, foaming at the mouth, staring with their eyes, wagging their heads and hands in such fashion and deformitie as it was monstrous to behold.[5]

Most of the Europeans regarded the Indians as worshiping the devil, in hellish fashion, since the Indians were not "good Christians" like themselves.

It is possible that Smith did see a ceremony performed in honor of the sun, but what he saw may also have been a "medicine" ceremony of some kind, under the leadership of a medicine man.

Since any healing rite was also associated with mystery and magic, the Indian doctors had not only a knowledge of roots, herbs, and other natural medicines, but also used a great deal of singing and sometimes sleight of hand and hocus-pocus, which were just as much expected of him as we today expect none of it. But, since these magic performers were doctors, the French gave them their name for doctor— *medicin.* This came to be "medicine man" in English, and, when speaking of Indians, anything pertaining to magic or to the spiritual, holy, or supernatural has been termed "medicine." Indians themselves, when speaking English, use the same term.

The good captain made a number of other references to the dancing. Once he wrote:

... their dauncinge, which is like our darbysher Hornepipe, a man first and then a woman, and so through them all, hanging all in a round, there is one which stand in the midst with a pipe and a rattell, with which when he beginns to make a noyse all the rest Gigetts about wriing their neckes and stampinge on ye ground.[6]

We suppose that he referred to a hornpipe from Derbyshire; the hornpipe is a solo dance. This is an interesting observation, men and women dancing solos, for we have seen the same thing in recent years among Sioux in North Dakota, Sauks and Foxes of Oklahoma, and Winnebagos of Wisconsin. Among these tribes, the dance we saw was a contest dance, a remnant of the once prominent Calumet, or Pipe, Dance, which we shall take up later. Captain Smith may have seen a forerunner of this dance, but we do not believe the actual Calumet had reached the East that early.

When he spoke of "Gigetts," we would probably say "jigging," and by "wriing" he doubtless meant twisting their necks and shaking their heads, as is still done by proficient dancers of many tribes.

In another place he said that after a father named a new child the rest of the day was "spent in feastinge and dauncinge," also still an Indian way of celebrating such an occasion.

It seemed interesting to us, too, that he reported ceremonies where the Virginia Indians encircled the fire with meal, much as is still done in some of the ceremonies of the Southwest, where the culture is entirely different.[7]

One ceremony that apparently made quite an impression upon Smith, for he mentioned it twice, must have been a winter solstice ceremony, although it may also have been, as he said, a "conjuring" ceremony. At least, he was a central figure

One of the earliest dance paintings, a watercolor, by John White, about 1585, on the North Carolina coast among the Indians of the Roanoke region. The carved posts suggest those later found among the Delawares and other eastern tribes. Smithsonian Institution, Bureau of American Ethnology.

in it, and perhaps they were making some kind of magic to overcome any evil spell they believed he might have cast upon them! He was seated in the center of the circle and the performance was given around him. It could hardly have been a planting or harvest ritual, for it was given in midwinter.

Seven men, each with a rattle, began to sing around the fire, encircled it with meal, then about a foot or two beyond this circle laid concentric half-circles of "graines of wheate," by which he meant what we call corn. These half-circles were spaced about a handbreadth apart. The grains were added two or three at a time at the conclusion of each song, and little counting sticks were laid in between. Then a shaman, or medicine man, entered, "disguised with a great Skinne, his head hung round with little Skinnes of Weasels and other vermine, with a Crownet of feathers on his head, painted as ugly as the divell," and at the end of each song made "many signes and demonstrations, with strange and vehement actions." He cast deer meat, suet, and tobacco into the fire and "till six a clocke in the Evening

15

their howling would continue ere they would depart."[8] Smith was not much impressed with their singing, apparently. Few travelers were.

To this day Eastern Indians cast tobacco into the fire as an offering. The suet may have been to give more light, for it was not very bright in the bark houses, even in the daytime. Many other writers mentioned throwing fat on the fire to give more light. Plains Indians used buffalo tallow for the same purpose.

Apparently part of the ceremony was a seated dance, perhaps something like we hear of the ancient Hawaiian hulas, for he said, "In this manner they sat sixe, ten, or twelve houres without cease, with such strange stretching of their armes, and violent passions and gestures as might well seeme strange to him they so conjured." Smith thought they were making preparations to kill him, for he had already had the famous close call in which Pocahontas saved him. The ceremonies lasted "three or four daies," but each day ended with a great feast of which Smith partook, and "much mirth." They probably were honoring him rather than thinking of killing him.

One complaint that has sometimes been made about Indian dancing is that the women do so little, and when they do dance they are covered from head to toe with long heavy dresses. There is no "cheesecake." But let's hear what Captain John Smith saw:

Thirty young women came naked out of the woods (only covered behind and before with a few green leaves), their bodies all painted, some white, some red, some blacke, some partie colours; but every one different. Their leader had a faire paire of stagge hornes on her head, and an otter skinne at her girdle, another at her arme, a quiver of arrowes at her backe, and bow and arrowes in her hand. The next, in her hand a sword; another, a club; another a pot-stick: all horned alike. The rest, every one with their severall devices.

These feinds, with most hellish cries and shouts, rushing from amongst the trees, cast themselves in a ring about the fire, singing and dauncinge with excellent ill varietie, oft falling into their infernal passions, and then solemnly againe to sing and daunce. Having spent neare an houre, in this maskarado, as they entered, they in like manner departed."[9]

The captain does not tell us what this dance was for or what it was called, but it certainly had something to do with deer and hunting. In these early Colonial times, the Indian women of the East, except in very cold weather, did not wear much more than the men did—a wrap-around skirt, or kilt, instead of a breechclout; moccasins; and usually leggings. So there was considerably more cheesecake in those days, without any conscious effort to create it, than was found later on the westward march, where most of the Indian women did wear full dresses.*

---

*It did not take long for the missionaries to change the native innocence and instill in them the self-conscious "modesty" of the advancing white men. At the Gilcrease Museum in Tulsa, Oklahoma, is a life-size mural of Hiawatha and Minnehaha strolling through the forest. The artist, striving to produce an idyllic composition, portrays them both as nearly nude, which could be correct, too, of such early legendary times. An Indian woman, visiting the museum, was horrified, chagrined and offended when she saw this painting and complained directly to Mr. Gilcrease about it. Mr. Gilcrease, a Creek Indian himself, asked, "Do you think the Great Spirit made a mistake?"

Champlain was practically a contemporary of John Smith, so let's go north to find out what he has to say. In writing of a Victory, or Scalp, Dance held by *Etechemins* (Passamaquoddies), Algonquins, and Montagnais in northern Maine or southern Canada, Champlain said these united tribes killed "several hundred" Iroquois, and the event was celebrated with a great festival. (There were seldom several hundred killed in any Indian battle.) On the second day of the celebration the

Algonquins went by themselves to a public place. Here they arranged all their wives and daughters by the side of each other, and took position themselves behind them, all singing in the manner I have described before. Suddenly all the wives and daughters proceeded to throw off their robes and skins, presenting themselves stark naked. But they were adorned with *matachiats*, that is beads and braided strings, made of porcupine quills, which they dye in various colors. After finishing their songs, they all said together, *Ho, ho, ho*: at the same instant all the wives and daughters covered themselves with their robes, which were at their feet. Then, after stopping a short time, all suddenly beginning to sing and throw off their robes as before. They do not stir from their position while dancing, and make various gestures and movements of the body, lifting one foot and then the other, at the same time striking upon the ground.[10]

Let us see what some of the other writers of the period had to say about dancing. Roger Williams, ousted from the Massachusetts Bay Colony in 1635 because his views of religious freedom did not harmonize with those of the Puritan fathers, went south to found Rhode Island and preach to the Narragansetts. He saw many of their dances and ceremonies, but, like others of his time, his writings are very disappointing. We say he *saw* dances and ceremonies. We should say he could have seen them, but he saw only parts of them, for he wrote:

I confesse to have most of their customes by their owne Relation, for after once being in their Houses, and beholding what their Worship was, I durst never be an *eye* witnesse, Spectatour, or looker on, least I should have been partaker of Satans Inventions and Worships, contrary to Ephes. 5. 14.[11]

Then he mentioned that they did have feasts, or dances, of two sorts, public and private, and gave the briefest mention of them.

William Wood wrote at the same period—1634—and was much impressed by the Indians, their way of life, manners and customs, food, dress, and ornamentation. He was highly complimentary about Indian appearance and physique, virtues, courtesy, and dignity, but offered not one word about dance.[12]

John Josselyn, 1672, also was much impressed in the same way, writing about the Indians and wild life of New England, expressing interest in Indian and Colonial medicines and cures, admiring many Indian traits and customs, but making no mention of dancing.[13]

But finally we come to a prize observer, Daniel Gookin, writing at the same time and acquainted with the same Indians in the same part of the country. How is it he noticed the dancing when the others said nothing about it? He wrote:

They are addicted to gaming; and will, in that vein, play away all they have. And also they delight much in their dancings and revellings; at which time he that danceth (for they dance singly, the men, and not the women, the rest singing, which is their chief musick) will give away in this frolick, all that ever he hath, gradually, some to one, and some to another, according to his fancy and affection. And then, when he hath stripped himself of all that he hath, and is weary, another succeeds and doth the like; so successively, one after another, night after night, resting and sleeping in the days; and so continue sometimes a week together. And at such dancings, and feastings, and revellings, which are used mostly after the ingatherings of their harvests, all their neighbors, kindred, and friends, meet together; and much impiety is committed at such time. They use great vehemency in the motion of their bodies, in their dances; and sometimes the men dance in greater numbers in their war dances.[14]

Here we have gambling, dancing, and give-away all in one, a combination of activities still to be found among Western Indians even at this late date. There is no such thing as a "typical Indian," and yet, as we go along, we find many traits and customs that are more or less universal.

Moving on south, in a period almost a hundred years later, we have quite lengthy descriptions of dances among the Cherokees by Lieutenant Henry Timberlake, who visited them as an emissary of the British colonists, and in a few more years James Adair, a trader, wrote of a number of dances not only of the Cherokees but of other Southern tribes, as did also the botanist William Bartram.

Timberlake wrote:

I was almost every night at some dance, or diversion; the war dance, however, gave me the greatest satisfaction, as in that I had an opportunity of learning their methods of war, and a history of their warlike actions, many of which are both amusing and instructive.[15]

He wrote of Eagle, Green Corn, and Pantomimic dances, but the War Dance has been the fascinating one for white men from his time on, and if they did not find one they often made one up.

James Adair was one who tried to prove, all through his writings, that the Indians were descended from the Ten Lost Tribes of Israel, and he spoke of them as "red Hebrews." He considered most of the dances religious, but had the theory that the dancing was lengthened as the culture, and the rituals, degenerated. This is just the opposite of what happened to European dancing in religious festivals; as religion was emphasized, dancing was gradually eliminated.

Adair said they used two clay pots for drums, the tops covered with thin, wet deerskin. These must have been water drums, typical of the area, although the Cherokees seemed to prefer, at least in recent years, woodchuck skin (as did the Iroquois) and made little wooden kegs, or firkins, for drum shells. Adair wrote that while each of the noisy musicians beat the drums with sticks

the dancers pranced away, with wild and quick sliding steps and variegated postures of body, to keep time with the drum, and the rattling calabashes shaked by some of their religious heroes. . . . Such is the graceful dancing, as well as the vocal and instrumental music of the red Hebrews on religious and martial occasions.

Another time he said, "Each strikes the ground with the right and left feet alternately, very quick, but well timed."[16] The women wore terrapin shells, containing pebbles, tied to their legs, which is still the custom among present-day Stomp dancers. Adair mentioned the Scalp Dance, Friendship Dance, Eagle Dance, and an "annual feast of love," a religious ceremony to the great diety, for the various tribes of the Southeastern area.

Bartram seems to have been the first one to find the dances not only interesting or amusing, but intricate, for he says, speaking of a Ball-Play Dance of the Cherokees, "There was something singular and diverting in their step and motions, and I imagine not to be learned with exactness but with great attention and perseverance." He even makes an attempt to describe the execution of the steps and movements. He goes on to say:

The Cherokees, besides the ball-play dance, have a variety of others equally entertaining. The men especially exercise themselves with a variety of gesticulations and capers, some of which are ludicrous and diverting enough; and they have others which are of the martial order, and others of the chase; these seem to be somewhat of a tragical nature, where-in they exhibit astonishing feats of military prowess, masculine strength and activity. Indeed all their dances and musical entertainments seem to be theatrical exhibitions or plays, varied with comic and sometimes lascivious interludes.[17]

Speaking of the Creeks, he wrote:

These people, like all other natives, are fond of music and dancing: their music is both vocal and instrumental, but of the latter they have scarcely anything worth the name; the tambour, rattle-gourd, and a kind of flute made of a joint of reed or the tibia of the deer's leg on this instrument they perform badly, and at best it is a rather hideous melancholy discord, than harmony. It is only the young fellows who amuse themselves on this howling instrument; but the tambour and rattle, accompanied with their sweet low voices, produces a pathetic harmony, keeping exact time together, and the countenance of the musician, at proper times, seems to express the solemn elevated state of the mind: at that time there seems not only a harmony between him and his instrument, but it instantly touches the feelings of the attentive audience, as the influence of an active and powerful spirit; there is then an united universal sensation of delight and peaceful union of souls throughout the assembly.

Their music, vocal and instrumental, united, keeps exact time with the performers or dancers.

They have an endless variety of steps [italics ours], but the most common, and that which I term the most civilized, and indeed the most admired and practised among themselves, is a slow, shuffling alternate step; both feet move forward one after the other, first the right foot foremost, and next the left, moving one after the other, in opposite circles, i.e. first a circle of young men, and within, a circle of young women, moving together opposite ways, the men with the course of the sun, and the females contrary to it; the men strike their arm with the open hand, and the girls clap hands, and raise their shrill sweet voices, answering an elevated shout of the men at stated times of termination of the stanzas; and the girls perform an interlude of chorus separately.

To accompany their dances, they have songs of different classes, as martial, bacchanalian and amorous; . . .

Some of their most favorite songs and dances, they have from their enemies, the Chactaws; for it seems these people are very eminent for poetry and music; every town amongst them strives to excel each other in composing new songs for dances; and by a custom amongst them, they must have at least one new song for exhibition at every annual busk [Green Corn Dance].[18]

This requirement of new songs still holds among the Creeks of Oklahoma, and Speck reported it for the Yuchis at least as late as 1909. Many tribes are still fond of composing new songs and hold contests to feature them. And apparently all through history tribes have exchanged songs and dances with each other, whether enemies or not. The shuffling step Bartram describes sounds like the one still used in the stomp dances in Oklahoma. The girls performing a separate chorus reminds us of another custom still found among many tribes throughout the West. Especially is this true of the Shoshoni Sun Dance, where the women usually finish the dancing songs. It is also noticeable in certain phases of the present-day Grass, or Omaha, Dance.

During two hundred and fifty years of exploration, from 1600 to 1850, there was a steady flow of writings covering southern Canada, New England, the Great Lakes region, the Mississippi Valley, and even some areas of the Rocky Mountains and the Far West. The *Jesuit Relations*, recorded from 1610 to 1791, are full of French dealings with Indians, biased of course, by the prejudices of the Jesuit missionaries, who did not take kindly to any of the Indians' religious beliefs, customs, or amusements. In 1612 Father Biard wrote, "Their whole religion consists of certain incantations, dances and sorcery . . . they even have faith in dreams; if they happen to awake from a pleasant or auspicious dream, they rise even in the middle of the night and hail the omen with songs and dances."[19]

In the same year Biard wrote of an experience similar to what Champlain described. He called the Indians *Armouchiquois*, but we can find no such Indians formerly known by that name. They may have been Penobscots, for it was in their section of Maine. Six canoes, containing in all twenty-four warriors, approached the French ships.

They went through a thousand maneuvers and ceremonies before accosting us, and might have been compared to a flock of birds which wanted to go into a hemp-field but feared the scare-crow. . . . All night there was continual haranguing, singing and dancing, for such is the kind of life these people lead when they are together. Now as we supposed that probably their songs and dances were invocations to the devil, I had our people sing some sacred hymns, as the *Salve*, the *Ave Maria Stella*, and others.

The Frenchmen evidently ran out of hymns, for then they sang other songs

with which they were more familiar. When they came to the end of these, as the French are natural mimics, they began to mimic the singing and dancing of the Armouchiquois who were upon the bank, succeeding in it so well that the Armouchiquois stopped to listen to them; and then our people stopped and the others immediately began again. It was really very comical, for you would have said that they were choirs which had a thorough understanding with each other, and scarcely could you distinguish the real Armouchiquois from their imitators. [This is the first reference we have found of white men doing Indian singing and dancing.]

He said at another point, "When they had recognized us they showed their great joy during the evening by their usual demonstration; dancing, singing and making speeches."[20]

Father Le Jeune, in 1634, was quite complimentary about Indian characteristics:

If we begin with physical advantages, I will say that they possess these in abundance. They are tall, erect, strong, well proportioned, agile; and there is nothing effiminate in their appearance. Those little Fops that are seen elsewhere are only caricatures of men, compared with our Savages.

He also said they had minds of good quality and more intelligent than ordinary peasants.

Moreover, if it is a great blessing to be free from a great evil, our Savages are happy; for the two tyrants who provide hell and torture for many of our Europeans, do not reign in their forests,—I mean ambition and avarice. As they have neither political organization, nor offices, nor dignitaries, nor any authority, for they only obey their Chief through good will toward him, therefore they never kill each other to acquire these honors. Also, as they are contented with a mere living, not one of them gives himself to the Devil to acquire wealth.

They make a pretense of never getting angry, not because of the beauty of this virtue, for which they have not even a name, but for their own contentment and happiness, I mean, to avoid the bitterness caused by anger. . . . Whoever professes not to get angry, ought also to make a profession of patience; the Savages surpass us to such an extent, in this respect, that we ought to be ashamed. I saw them, in their hardships and in their labors, suffer with cheerfulness.[21]

Further on he says, "There are as many as twelve kinds of dances that are so many sovreign remedies for sickness. . . ." And then he says nothing whatever about them!

By 1665 the French were trading with and trying to convert the Indians around the Great Lakes and the Upper Mississippi Valley. Nicholas Perrot described a dance given by the Ottawas at the time a new "relative" was adopted in place of one deceased as lasting all day. This dance, as well as public dances, were held in honor of the dead. The person being adopted entered the cabin of the deceased dancing. He offered presents to the nearest relatives. His new parents stopped him in his dancing occasionally to add some article of adornment to his person and sometimes to repaint his face and body. At the close of his dance, at the end of the day, they gave him presents and he was then considered a son. This same ceremony was apparently conducted for adopting a daughter, for Perrot said the candidate might be "he" or "she."

He reported that already by this early date Indian customs and morals had retrograded from contact with the French. He said they were "as selfish and avaricious as formerly they were hospitable." They were even begging. Most people seem to think begging was a native vice. Perrot said that in the native state harmony prevailed and that there was almost no quarreling.[22]

Perrot said again that the Indian idea of a future world was a place where they would have finest eating, where they would mingle together, dancing and making merry forever.

Another Frenchman of the same period, La Potherie, described a great feast and dance, probably among the Ojibways, that sounds like the forerunner of the modern Grass Dance. He said:

It is difficult to make the reader understand the details of feasts of this sort, unless he has himself seen them. I was present at a like entertainment among the Iroquois at the Sault of Montreal, and it seemed as if I were in the midst of hell.[23]

Father Louis Hennepin, it has been learned, was not always accurate or even truthful in writing of his discoveries. He lifted material from both La Salle and Father Marquette, and from others as well, but there is, nevertheless, some interesting information to be found in his accounts. He gave quite a lengthy description of the Calumet Dance, but with little mention of the dance itself. The best attempt he made to describe dancing was among the Sioux, sometime between 1675 and 1681. They had just had a feast of bear's meat and were preparing to send out a war party.

Hennepin wrote:

After the Repast, these Savages having all of them certain Marks in the Face, and their Bodies painted with the Figure of some Beast, such as everyone fancy'd best, their Hair being also anointed with the Oil of Bears, and stuck all over with red and white Feathers, and their Heads cover'd with the Down of Birds, began to dance with their Hands all upon their Hip,* and Striking the Soles of their Feet with that violence against the Earth, that the very Marks appear'd. During the Dance, one of the Sons of the Master of Ceremonies, made 'em all Smoak in the Pipe of War, himself shedding abundance of Tears during the whole Action.[24]

After six years of association with Indians of many tribes, attending their ceremonies and celebrations, Hennepin was so biased, or obtuse, that he reported, "They have no outward Ceremony to signify that they worship any Deity: There's no Sacrifice, Priest, Temple, nor any other Token of Religion amongst them."[25] But he did say, "All these People naturally love Singing."[26]

Hennepin was one of the first to write about the Sioux, and he did get as far west as Lake Pepin and the Upper Mississippi. He and his party were captured by a band of Sioux and, it is certain from his story, he was adopted as a son by one of the chiefs. It was common Sioux practice, as it was among many tribes, to adopt captives in place of sons, brothers, or other relatives who had been lost. But Hennepin apparently did not know this and thought the entire adoption ceremony a special, long-drawn-out procedure for "sacrificing" him. He thought that his prayers for delivery were answered by a change of heart on the part of his captors and that

---

*First mention of hands on hips, typical Indian dance position today.

making him a son was merely the simple thing of declaring him one. But the ceremony he described, we know now, was definitely an elaborate one of adoption.

He said the warriors all cried and wept bitterly when some of the elders laid their hands upon his head. He interpreted this to mean that the elders wanted to spare his life, but that the others wept to entreat them to take it. Actually this ceremonial weeping was on behalf of the lost son of the chief who intended to adopt Hennepin in his place.

Hennepin, as did others, admired the Indian stamina and endurance. He said, "They'll row from morning to night without resting, or allowing themselves so much time as to eat their victuals . . . notwithstanding the fatigue of the Day, the youngest of the Warriors went at night and danc'd the Reed [Calumet] dance."[27]

Hennepin said he was given food and simple comforts when others were cold and hungry, and yet he complained all the time about the mistreatment he suffered as a captive. He never seemed to realize that, once adopted, he was no longer a captive.[28]

Hennepin claimed the honor of discovering the mouth of the Mississippi, attempting to take the credit away from La Salle, who arrived there in the winter of 1681–82. He evidently did get down to the lower Mississippi, for he reported on the Taenfas, a tribe living in Louisiana:

Men and women, who are half covered in that country, danced together before us. Their way of dancing is *much more difficult* [italics ours] than ours, but perhaps as pleasant, were it not for the Musick, which is very disagreeable. Women repeat every word the men have sung.[29]

He was also gracious enough to say that he thought the Indians, called "barbarous" by Europeans, had "more Humanity than many nations of Europe."[30]

In 1709 Antoine Denis Raudot wrote from Quebec that "there are several dances among the savages." He gave a description of the Calumet Dance, an Honor Dance, and a Discovery Dance, and also mentioned dances for curing the sick. Concerning the Honor Dance he said:

When several strangers arrive, a certain number of men, women, and girls step out right away and form a large circle in the middle of which four men place themselves. One of them beats a drum to the sound of which the other three accord their voices. All the circle, while dancing, turns around and each person takes different postures according to his caprice, striking the feet sharply on the ground and joining voices with those who are within the circle; he who received this honor signifies his gratitude for it by a gift such as he wishes to make.[31]

By 1720 the French were already established in Louisiana, and the Dutchman Le Page du Pratz, serving France, was living with the Natchez Indians. This tribe has long been extinct, but in the early French days in Louisiana was a power to be reckoned with. It had a high degree of civilization and was the only tribe in what is now the United States, except for some along the Northwest Coast, to have an absolute monarch. He was called the Sun and his person was considered so sacred that he was not allowed to set foot upon the ground, but was always carried in a litter. The tribe had a caste system, with two classes of aristocracy: Nobles and Honorables. The common people were Stinkers; captives were adopted into this group.

In a way, the Stinkers were the best off. They could marry as they pleased. The aristocrats, on the other hand, were not allowed to marry among themselves, so a man's children were one class lower than he was. Consequently, the children of an Honorable were only Stinkers.

Du Pratz says that the festival of the corn was greatest celebration of all. It was concluded with a dance by torch-light. Two hundred torches, made of dried canes, "each of the thickness of a child," lighted the central plaza, and men and women continued dancing until daylight.

The water drum seems to crop up again, for Du Pratz said the Natchez used a pot covered with deerskin for a drum. The drummer was seated in the center of the dancers, the women in a circle around him, "not joining hands, but at some distance from each other." The men formed another circle outside the women, each carrying a calabash rattle in each hand. The women danced left to right, the men right to left. The circles were sometimes narrowed, sometimes widened. New performers took the places of those who became weary.[32]

This was a typical dance formation all across the country. Another custom reported by Du Pratz common to other tribes, was that on entering a hut a guest was given a seat. He said nothing, nor was he spoken to for about ten minutes, "it being one of their prudent customs to suffer a guest to rest himself a little after his arrival, before they begin a conversation; and besides, they look upon the time spent in compliments as thrown away."[33] Du Pratz is the first we know of to give details of the War Dance, which we will describe later.

In 1731 the Sieur de La Vérendrye and his sons got as far west as the Red River country of North Dakota and by 1742 probably to the Big Horn Mountains of Montana and Wyoming. But they were interested primarily in finding the Northwest Passage, as had been so many Frenchmen before them, and incidentally in opening up new fur trade routes. In their journals there is plenty of reference to Indians—appearance, customs, visits, fights, trading, but not one to dancing. If they saw any at all, they were not interested enough to report it.[34]

The best accounts of dancing of the upper prairies were written a hundred years later, and we shall come to them by and by.

3. The Late 1700's and Early 1800's

By the late 1700's and early 1800's explorers were commonplace all over the West. There are so many reports that it is difficult to know which ones to choose. One of the best known was Jonathan Carver, who spent nearly three years in western travels from 1766 to 1768 and was one of the first white men to get as far as Minnesota. He spent quite a bit of time with the "Naudowessies," whom we call Sioux. Nadouessioux was the old French spelling of the Chippewa name for them, which meant adders, or enemies. Carver Anglicized the French word. Today we retain only the last syllable. The tribe itself prefers its own name, Dakota, Nakota, or Lakota, depending upon the dialect, and formerly did not like the term Sioux, naturally. They have become used to it in recent years and even use it in speaking of themselves when talking English.

Carver said, "No people are more hospitable, kind, and free than the Indians." He is speaking generally, for, although he spent more time with the Sioux, he also visited Chippewas and other Indians of the Middle West. He also said the Indians "usually dance either before or after every meal." He felt that they considered dancing a more acceptable sacrifice to the Great Spirit than a formal and unanimated thanksgiving.

He has a whole chapter on their dances. His observations are worth noting, for they help us to realize that, for all the cultural intrusions, the essentials of Indian dance remain the same today.

Dancing is a favourite exercise among the Indians; they never meet on any public occasion, but this makes a part of the entertainment. And when they are not engaged in war or hunting, the youth of both sexes amuse themselves in this manner every evening.

They always dance, as I have just observed, at their feast. In these as well as all their dances, every man rises in his turn, and moves about with great freedom and boldness; singing as he does so, the exploits of his ancestors. During this the company, who is seated on the ground in a circle, around the dancer, join with him in marking the cadence, by an odd tone, which they utter all together, and which sounds, "Heh, heh, heh." These notes, if they might be so termed, are articulated with a harsh accent, and strained out with the utmost force of the lungs; so that one would imagine their strength must soon be exhausted by it; instead of which, they repeat it with the same violence during the whole of the entertainment.

The women, particularly those of the western nations, dance very gracefully. They carry themselves erect, and with their arms hanging down close to their sides, move first a few yards to the right, and then back again to the left. This movement they perform without taking any steps as an European would do, but with their feet conjoined, moving by turns their toes and heels. In this manner they glide with great agility to a certain distance, and then return:* and let those who join in the dance be ever so numerous, they keep time so exactly with each other that no interruption ensues. During this, at stated periods they mingle their shrill voices with the hoarser ones of the men who sit around (for it is to be observed that the sexes never intermix in the same dance) which, with the music of the drums and chichicoues [rattles], make an agreeable harmony.

The Indians have several kinds of dances which they use on different occasions, as the Pipe or Calumet Dance, the War Dance, the Marriage Dance, and the Dance of the Sacrifice. The movements in every one of these are dissimilar; but it is almost impossible to convey any idea of the points in which they are unlike.

Different nations likewise vary in their manner of dancing. The Chipeways throw themselves into a greater variety of attitudes than any other people; sometimes they hold their heads erect, at others they bend them almost to the ground; then recline on one side, and immediately after on the other. The Naudowessies carry themselves more upright, step firmer, and move more gracefully. But they all accompany their dances with the disagreeable noise just mentioned.

The Pipe Dance is the principal, and the most pleasing to a spectator of any of them, being the least frantic, and the movement of it the most graceful. It is but on particular occasions that it is used; as when ambassadors from an enemy arrive to treat of peace, or when strangers of eminence pass through their territories.

The War Dance, which they use both before they set out on their war parties, and on their return from them, strikes terror into strangers. It is performed, as the others, amidst a circle of the warriors; a chief generally begins it, who moves from the right to the left, singing at the same time both his own exploits, and those of his ancestors. When he has concluded his account of any memorable action, he gives a violent blow with his war-club against a post that is fixed in the ground, near the center of the assembly for this purpose.

Every one dances in his turn, and recapitulates the wondrous deeds of his family, till they all at last join in the dance. Then it becomes truly alarming to any stranger that happens to be among them, as they throw themselves into every horrible and terrifying posture that can be imagined, rehearsing at the same time the parts they expect to act against their enemies in the field. . . . To heighten the scene, they set up the same hideous yells, cries and war-whoops they use in time of action; so that it is impossible to consider them in any other light than as an assembly of demons.

His description of the War Dance sounds more like that of the Woodland tribes. Certainly none of the oldest warriors we interviewed had any tradition of such a dance. The Sioux did use a pole in the Scalp, or Victory, dances. Perhaps in Carver's day they did also use it in a preliminary War Dance, as so many tribes did.

It is doubtful to our minds, too, that a man recited the deeds of his ancestors. At least we were led to believe that a man told only of his own exploits. He might, on occasion, have boasted of his lineage if he came from a distinguished family, but among most tribes it was a man's own ability that counted. He could not even inherit the office of chief unless accepted in that capacity by his people.

Carver mentioned a *Pawwaw* dance, or shaman's demonstration, which also seems to have crossed the country. We shall take it up later. *Pawwaw*, or *powwow*,

---

*This is the first mention of the Sioux glide, in which the feet make marks like figures of eight on the earth, to be mentioned in Chapter 22.

is an Eastern term for a medicine man, or juggler, and still carried that connotation in Carver's day. We have come to think of it as a gathering, or ceremony. The particular dance he described sounds like the *Midewin*, or Grand Medicine Ceremony, of other Lake Indians, and it is interesting to know that the Sioux, who at one time were on the western edge of the Great Lakes, had it too.[1]

He also described another medicine ceremony which sounds like the *Yuwipi* performance, still given by Sioux "doctors" today.

Carver also tells of a dance given for his benefit that he did not know how to classify. The Chippewas were allied with the French, who had just turned over Michilimackinac to the English. The Chippewas, who held an enmity for the English, resented this. While Carver and his party were encamped near Lake Pepin, on the Mississippi, he looked out of his tent to see "about twenty naked young Indians, the most perfect in their shape, and by far the handsomest of any I had ever seen, coming towards me, and dancing as they approached, to the music of their drums." He said they were all carrying torches on long poles and that they stopped every ten or twelve yards and "set up their cries and yells."[2]

He invited them in, which invitation they accepted without comment. They were painted red and black, as for war, and he thought that some of the movements of their dance were those of the War Dance. He believed they had been sent by the Chippewa chief, who had threatened all the English in his territory. He said they "continued their dance alternately," singing of their heroic exploits, and that after each period they struck the poles of his tent with their war clubs with such violence that he expected to have it tumble about them. Then, as the dancers passed him, each placed his right hand over his eyes and looked Carver steadily in the face, which he thought hardly a gesture of friendship. Toward the end of the dance he presented them with a "pipe of peace," but they would not accept it. He then made them presents of ribbons and other trinkets, whereupon they sat down, consulting together whether to accept them or not.

In a short time they did accept his pipe, lit it, and offered it to him to smoke, after which they smoked it themselves. Then they took up the presents, apparently greatly pleased with them, and left him "in a friendly manner."

It has been Indian custom, throughout many tribes, to "test the heart" of visitors, especially when from enemy tribes, even at a gathering to make peace. If the visitors could withstand the test, everyone was satisfied and the peace concluded. Such may have been the case with Carver. The dance he described also had some of the elements in it of the so-called Beggar's Dance, which we shall take up later. Carver himself stated that subsequently he was informed that the dance may have been such as was customarily given to honor visiting chiefs, and such would be our own interpretation. In the morning, when he was about to continue his journey, the womenfolk of the dancers brought him presents of sugar (undoubtedly maple sugar), and he found a few more ribbons for them, which made them happy.

Carver was one of the first to have an idea that the Indians originally came from

Asia. He based part of his reasoning on the fact that the Indians ate dog flesh in some of their ceremonials!

Carver made notation of the following dances: Pipe, or Calumet, Dance; War Dance; Marriage Dance; Dance of Sacrifice; the one above-mentioned that we might call Testing the Heart Dance; and Pawwaw, or Black, Dance. He does not give the tribe for the Marriage Dance, but it cannot be Sioux, for he later gives a different marriage ceremony for them. Whatever it was, he said the young couple took hold of a wand about four feet long, which symbolized that they were still separated, and, after an oration by an old man, one of the bridegroom's relatives danced and sang, still holding the wand between them. At the conclusion of the dance, they broke the rod in as many pieces as there were witnesses present, each witness taking a piece to preserve as a souvenir of the occasion. The Sacrifice Dance was given on the appearance of the new moon, following, as we might expect, a feast prepared for the occasion.

Only a few years later than Carver comes the story of William Biggs, who was a captive among the Kickapoos, another Great Lakes tribe. He resided among them until 1788. He described a Victory Dance in which the warriors danced around a peeled pole, and he danced the Beggar's Dance with them. They did this every spring, after coming in from a hunting party. They made trips to neighboring towns, dancing in front of the traders' posts, and the traders were expected to respond by giving the Indians presents.

From the accounts of earlier French writers, in the late 1600's—Allouez, Charlevoix, Cadillac—we know the Indians of the Lakes had Calumet, Discovery, Strike-the-Post, Scouting, and Honor dances.[3] Carver's and Biggs's notations go along nicely with this list.

That the Indians were fond of the dramatic is evident from the earliest accounts, and many of their dances incorporated a great deal of pageantry. When Perrot approached a Miami village with a Potowatomi escort, the Potowatomis charged the village, shooting off their guns, loaded with blank powder. The Miamis came running out, surrounded them, and discharged arrows over their heads. Then all mingled in a great sham battle, feinting with their clubs, yelling and shouting. It was ended by messengers bringing out the calumets, whereupon the "battle" was ended and the visitors were led into the village.[4]

By 1829, Thomas Forsythe listed for the Sauks and Foxes, another Lake group, "buffalow dance, otter dance, medicine dance, Mit-tee-wee," by which latter he evidently meant the *Midewin.*[5]

The difference in these lists does not imply that the Indians were changing their dances, but that each observer saw different dances. Few of them were with the Indians long enough to view their entire repertoire, and some who saw the same dances gave them different names.

Each of these observers judged the dances by his own personal standards. For instance, Count Francesco Arese, an Italian who came over here to see the Indians firsthand in 1837, liked the dog meat—he found it "perfect"—but cared little for the dancing or the music. Speaking of the Sioux, he described a dance that took place on the last evening with them:

The only music was a few singers who accompanied themselves by tapping with a piece of wood. At the start the dance was a sort of *adagio*, merely poses, grotesque and rather ugly. Then, so to speak, came the *allegro* which went in a *crescendo*. You would have said that the devil had entered into their bodies. Their feet, legs, hands and arms, their whole bodies moved in the most infernal and scarcely imaginable manner. Their singular music is very monotonous and made up of only two or three notes at most. Ordinarily it is in the minor, with no other modulations than that of emitting the sounds with more force or with less. At times it reminded me of priests in Italian villages who on very solemn feast-days put more than their usual rabidity into tearing God's ears and those of the faithful.[6]

According to such Italian musical terminology, the Sioux still have several dances which start with an *adagio*, gradually becoming *allegro* with *crescendo*, as do other tribes we have visited and which we shall talk about later.

About the same time that Carver was with the Sioux, John Long was living with the Chippewas, a little farther to the east. His *Voyages and Travels* make very interesting reading, for he served as interpreter and trader for a number of years and during his sojourn with the Indians came to understand them very well. Early in his report he said:

I also applied myself sedulously to obtain a complete knowledge of their manners and customs, and with that view partook of their amusements, and was soon noticed as a good dancer . . . by conforming to their ways, and taking pleasure in their diversions, I was soon endeared to them, and left them with regret.[7]

"The dances among the Indians," he continued, "are many and various, and to each of them is a particular hoop." (He probably meant whoop.) He listed eleven different dances,* including our old friends the Calumet, War, and Scalp dances, and wrote, "All these I was perfect master of, frequently leading the sett. [*sic*] If accidently a stranger came among us, (unless I chose to be noticed) no one could distinguish me from the Indians."

Often, following one of our concerts, we are asked, "Are the bells authentic? I didn't know Indians had bells." Here we are, back in 1768 to 1782, according to Long:

The Indians, in their war dances, sew hawk bells and small pieces of tin on [their moccasins] to make a jingling noise, and at a dance where I was present, there, with the addition of a large horse bell, which I gave the chief who led the dance, made a noise not much unlike a Dutch concert.[8]

Actually, bells have been "authentic" since Columbus, for he gave hawk bells to the Indians of the West Indies on his very first visit.

Long was adopted into the Chippewa tribe; the ceremonies included participation in the steam bath and being tattooed with needles dipped in vermilion. He was given

---

*The dances are listed in Chapter 4.

a new name, Amik, or Beaver. Following the adoption, he made presents to his new kinsmen, which included of course, Long being a trader, rum. In the following drunk, four Indians were killed by their own tribesmen. It seems a pity that a man of Long's appreciation and understanding had to deal in liquor.

When we heard of the narrative of John Tanner, who lived with the Indians for thirty years beginning in 1789, we thought surely that here would be an account full of dancing. But we found only a couple of references, although these were interesting and unusual. Tanner was captured by Shawnees in Ohio and almost immediately adopted by an old woman who had lost her son. He was taken to the boy's grave, which was surrounded by wooden pickets. The Indians brought many presents with them and danced around the grave, "dragging" Tanner with them. He said:

Their dance was lively and cheerful, after the manner of the scalp dance. From time to time, as they danced, they presented me something from the articles they had brought, but as I came around in the dancing to the party on the opposite side of the grave, whatever they had given to me was snatched from me: thus they continued the greater part of the day, until the presents were exhausted, when they returned home.[9]

Tanner never did explain, but after living with Indians so long certainly must have learned later that, because he was unable to give presents of his own, his captors gave presents to him, which he in turn was supposed to give away in honor of the dead. Since at the time he did not know that he was to give these things away, they were taken from him on the other side of the dance circle.

Having lived with Indians most of his life, Tanner probably had retained only a rudimentary knowledge of English, so his story was written for him in language which he perhaps could not even understand. In telling his adventures, Tanner mentioned one place that "the Indians now collected for the solemn ceremony of the meta, or medicine dance." Another place he said they were preparing for a *Wabano*, but he went hunting. He mentioned numerous war parties, but said nothing of dances, either before setting out or upon returning.

He must have known every dance in which the Ottawas (for he later went to live with them) and their allies participated, and the fact that he said so little about them shows either that he took them for granted or that his biographer was uninterested in them. To sell the book, it was more important to stress the exciting experiences, the warfare, hunting, and bloodshed.

The year that John Tanner was captured in Ohio, Alexander Mackenzie was traveling in the far Northwest. Between 1789 and 1793 he made trips as far as the Arctic Ocean and to the Pacific coast north of Vancouver. He was the first white man to cross the northern part of the continent. He had many dealings with the Crees, whom he called *Knisteneaux*, and also with the Chipewyans, Slaves, and Dog-Ribs, the latter three all Athabaskan groups. He found the Crees "mild and affable, as well as just in their dealings . . . also generous and hospitable, and good natured in the extreme." And yet these same Crees are the ones who pushed the Athabaskans farther into the Northwest, and whose term of contempt was accepted as the name for the Slaves, from which we derive the name Great Slave Lake, near which they lived.

He found the Chipewyans the most peaceable tribe in North America. He is another of the early explorers who lamented the great changes already taking place due to white contact. He said of the Chipewyans, "Their amusements or recreations are but few. Their music is so inharmonious, and their dancing so awkward, that they might be supposed to be ashamed of both, as they very seldom practice either."[10]

He met other groups which "enjoyed the amusements of dancing and jumping with those we had already seen; and indeed these exercises seem to be their favorite diversions." Again he wrote:

No sooner was the conference concluded, than they began to dance, which is their favourite, and, except jumping, their only amusement. In this pastime, old and young, male and female, continued their exertions, till their strength was exhausted. This exercise was accompanied by loud imitations of the various noises produced by the rein-deer, the bear and the wolf.[11]

Earlier we mentioned that we would probably have more references to leaping, or jumping. Here we have seen three more references to it, and in an entirely different part of the country. Indeed, it is difficult to tell whether Mackenzie's last reference to jumping is a separate sport or part of the dance, but there must have been some ceremonial implication connected with it, since the participants imitated the noises of various animals. It is beginning to look as if Indian dancing was not all shuffling.

We think of Lewis and Clark opening up the West, but there were a number of restless adventurers ahead of them. Pierre-Antoine Tabeau, a trader, was already with the *Ricaras* (Arikaras, Arikarees, or Rees) when the Lewis and Clark expedition arrived to spend the winter of 1804 with the Mandans in the same vicinity. No one, however, has too much to say about the dancing. These visitors, like so many others, were apparently concerned with more "important" things, such as finding the Northwest Passage, opening up new trade routes, and acquiring more territory for their governments.

Tabeau does give a report on a ceremony for procuring a sacred white buffalo cow, which he personally did not witness, and neither did Lewis and Clark, but their *engagés* did. In fact, the report carried to the two distinguished explorers must have sounded so bad that they did not even write it in the *Journals* in English, but in Latin![12]

In his narrative Tabeau also mentions a ceremony of sacrifice that was probably similar to the *Okipa* of the Mandans, the Sun Dance of the Plains tribes, or perhaps the *Hanbleciya*, or Day's Crying, of the Sioux. He said, "Some promise to dance four or five days without intermission, without rest, without smoking, without food, and especially without intercourse with women."[13]

Tabeau seemed to have little real understanding of the Indians, but at least did record much of what he saw. His observations uphold those made by many succeeding writers, especially regarding Indian attitudes toward war.

He also gives quite an account of a long ritual in honor of the dead, performed by the Bois Brulés (Sioux), but it differs in many respects from later accounts of a like ritual. Which just shows that, although some dances and rituals remain more or less static over the years, others change greatly, depending largely upon the overall life pattern and the changes affecting it.

Tabeau also mentioned a Pipe Dance for the "Ricaras," saying it was given at the time children's ears were pierced and for adoption.[14] He said the Ricaras and other Missouri tribes always held a ceremony of Blessing the Grain, which was celebrated for three days by dances and feasts of dog meat, but he does not describe these dances.

Captains Lewis and Clark, in their expedition to explore the new Louisiana Purchase and open up the territory for the government, made every possible effort to create friendly relations with the many tribes they met along the route. Although they were much more tolerant than most people of their day, yet they carried with them many of the prejudices common to the East.

In their packs were fourteen bales and a box of presents for the Indians, which included coats richly embroidered with lace, three kinds of medals—for great chiefs, in-between chiefs, and lesser chiefs—flags, knives, tomahawks, beads, mirrors, handkerchiefs, and paints. They also gave the chiefs whiskey at some of the councils, but found that the Ricaras not only refused it but even remarked that they "were surprised that their father should present them a liquor which would make them fools."[15]

As an example of the way in which they tried to establish good will and seek a common ground with their native hosts, the explorers not only presented vermilion paint to the Indians but performed the act of painting the Indians' faces with it. They realized that red was a favorite color and emblematic of peace. But they also "made" chiefs, which we doubt that the Indians understood, for they merely gave official recognition to leaders already acknowledged by the Indians. These chiefs received the medals, the officers' coats with lace and gilded epaulets—and the whisky.

The *Journals*, as well as the diaries of some of the men, have many references to Indian dancing, but very few intelligible details or even comments about it. Here is an example, written August 30, 1804, three and a half months after the start of the trip from St. Louis:

. . . in the evening, the whole party (Yankton Sioux) danced until a late hour, and in the course of their amusement we threw among them some knives, tobacco, tape and binding, with which they were much pleased. Their musical instruments were the drum, and a sort of little bag, made of buffalo hide, dressed white, with small shot or pebbles in it, and a bunch of hair tied to it. This produces a sort of rattling music, with which the party was annoyed by four musicians during the council this morning.[16]

The explorers gave a brief description of the Teton Scalp Dance, which was given to entertain them on their way up the Missouri in September. It followed a council and a feast of dog meat, buffalo, pemmican—which they called *pemitigon*—and ground potatoes, which were probably prairie turnips, or *pommes blanches.*

We sat and smoked for an hour, when it became dark; everything was then cleared away for the dance, a large fire being made in the center of the house, giving at once light and warmth to the ballroom. The orchestra was composed of about ten men, who played on a sort of tambourine formed of a skin stretched across a hoop, and made a jingling noise with a long stick to which hoofs of deer and goats were hung; the third instrument was a small skin bag with pebbles in it; these, with five or six young men for the vocal part, made up the band.

The "house" was really a large shade, or shelter, probably made of a number of lodge poles set in a three-quarter circle, thatched with tipi covers, for they said it was covered at top and sides with dressed buffalo skins. The "tambourine" should be plural, for each man played on such a drum.

People to this day think Indians are unemotional, but the *Journals* have entries that tell us differently. One place they state that a singer "put himself into a passion," broke one of the drums, and threw two others into the fire. A custom which still prevails among all the tribes we know is to give the singers (drummers) tobacco. This man evidently did not receive his proper share, which angered him. Such action was uncommon and when it did happen was usually ignored as unbecoming the dignity of the man or his audience. In this case the singer left the assembly, the two drums were rescued, and in place of the missing drum a buffalo robe was used. It was held in the left hands of several men, who beat upon it with their right hands, and the dance went on as before.

The *Journals* also contain a description of a "Medicine Dance" which sounds more like a puberty ceremony or a maiden's "coming out" party.[17]

The explorers celebrated the New Year of 1805 by entertaining the Mandan village with *their* dances and music, which delighted the Indians no end, particularly the antics of one of the French *voyageurs* accompanying them, "who danced on his head."[18] The white dancers were then presented with "several buffalo robes and quantities of corn." On several occasions the party entertained Indians along the route in this fashion.

Some months later, while with the Shoshonis, Captain Lewis was invited to the chief's lodge,

after which he was entertained with a dance by the Indians. . . . The music and dancing, which was in no respect different from those of the Missouri [River] Indians, continued all night; but Captain Lewis retired to rest about 12 o'clock, when the fatigue of the day enabled him to sleep, though he was awaked several times by the yells of the dancers.[19]

This chief turned out to be the brother of the young Indian woman, Sacajawea, who proved to be a better guide than her husband, Charbonneau, the Frenchman who had been hired in that capacity. The *Pahkees*, or Blackfeet, had recently attacked the Shoshonis and destroyed all of their tipis, except the one the chief now occupied. The rest of the people were living in conical willow-thatched huts. Under such dire circumstances it was common for the chief to have as poor a lodge as anyone else, but this last remaining tipi was probably reserved as a council lodge, and the chief, as host to the visitors, occupied it.

The fact that Sacajawea was the sister of the Shoshoni chief was perhaps the only reason the white men were welcomed, for at one time it looked as if trouble would ensue. The Shoshonis had had enough unhappy experience with strangers and were tempted to regard the white men, like all foreigners, as enemies.

Not long before this the Indian girl had pointed out the spot where she had been captured by the *Minnetarees* (Hidatsas)* a few years before. Lewis and Clark considered her completely unemotional, saying she displayed no sign of distress, or any joy, at the prospect of being reunited with her people. ". . . she seems to possess the folly or the philosophy of not suffering her feelings to extend beyond the anxiety of having plenty to eat and a few trinkets to wear."[20]

And yet, only a few pages farther on, with no retraction of this entry, we read:

We soon drew near the camp, and just as we approached it a woman made her way through the crowd towards Sacajawea, and recognizing each other, they embraced with the most tender affection. The meeting of these two young women had in it something peculiarly touching, not only in the ardent manner in which their feelings were expressed, but in the real interest of their situation. They had been companions in childhood: in the war with the Minnetarees they had both been taken prisoner in the same battle, they had shared and softened the rigors of their captivity, till one of them had escaped from the Minnetarees, with scarce a hope of ever seeing her friend relieved from the hands of her enemies.

Shortly after this meeting of Sacajawea† and her friend, a council was held by the captains and the chief. In order to better communicate with each other, they sent for Sacajawea. She

---

*The *Minnetarees* (Minitaris) have several different names. They are also known as Gros Ventres, or, more properly, as Gros Ventres of the Village, to distinguish them from an entirely different tribe of the same name farther west. Perhaps the best name for them is Hidatsas. Although they are associated with Mandans and Rees, they are not the same people, but are relatives of the Absarokas, or Crows. The Sioux call them "Psaloka," which name they also sometimes use for the Crows.

†Dr. Roberts, the early missionary to the Shoshonis, and others at Fort Washakie, Wyoming, pronounced the name with the accent on the third syllable, rather than on the fourth. In North and South Dakota she is still known by Indians and whites alike as Sakak'awea, which is approximately the word for Bird Woman in Hidatsa.

Lewis and Clark found much evidence of trade for European goods, even among tribes deep in the interior. They mentioned guns, beads, knives, axes, and other items similar to what they themselves were bringing as gifts and for trade. In the Peabody Museum at Harvard University are two dresses of elk skin, brought back by them, trimmed with little tin cone dangles and glass "pony" beads. Some of the Indians possessing these things had never seen white men. The goods traveled west through Indian channels.

came into the tent, sat down, and was beginning to interpret, when in the person of Cameah-wait she recognized her brother; she instantly jumped up and ran and embraced him, and throwing over him her blanket and weeping profusely; the chief was himself moved, though not in the same degree. After some conversation between them she resumed her seat, and attempted to interpret for us, but her new situation seemed to overpower her, and she was frequently interrupted by her tears.[21]

One of the most outstanding and dramatic incidents of the trip took place as the explorers neared the Pacific in October, 1805:

We had scarcely fixed the camp and got the fires prepared when a chief came from the In-dian camp about a quarter of a mile up the Columbia, at the head of nearly 200 men; they formed a regular procession, keeping time to the noise, rather the music of their drums, which they accompanied with their voices. As they advanced they formed a semi-circle around us, and continued singing for some time.[22]

This performance may have been similar to the Beggar's Dance, which is still per-formed by some of the Plains tribes. What a picture it must have been, to see that procession in the twilight, as the tired explorers prepared for their evening meal.*

On the way back east, when returning to the Nez Percés, the party got out the two violins and danced for the Indians, who returned the compliment

in a style of dancing such as we had not yet seen. The spectators formed a circle round the dancers, who with their robes drawn tightly round the shoulders, and divided into parties of five or six men, performed by crossing in a line from one side of the circle to the other. All the parties, performers as well as spectators, sang, and after proceeding in this way for some time the spectators join, and the whole concludes by a promiscuous dance and song.

Shortly after this the Lewis and Clark men danced for the the *Wollawollahs,* and a request was made of them to dance in return.

With this [request] they readily complied, and the whole assemblage, amounting, with the women and children of the village, to several hundred, stood up, and sang and danced at the same time. The exercise was not, indeed, very violent nor very graceful, for the greater part of them were formed into a solid column, round a kind of hollow square, stood on the same place, and merely jumped up at intervals to keep time to the music. Some, however, of the more active warriors entered the square, and danced round it sidewise, and some of our men joined in the dance, to the great satisfaction of the Indians. The dance con-tinued till 10 o'clock.[23]

To carry on a conversation with the Chopunnish (Nez Percés), one of the captains gave a message in French to Charbonneau, who relayed it in Hidatsa to Sacajawea, who in turn spoke in Shoshoni to a Shoshoni prisoner of the Nez Percé, who trans-lated it to the latter. It sounds like playing the old game of "gossip." We wonder just how the message did come out at the far end!

---

*The chief paid them the honor of personally bringing them a supply of driftwood, willows, and small bushes for firewood, which was scarce along the river.

Farther on in the Montana country the party found a deserted lodge, sixty feet in diameter, conical, thatched with brush, with eagle feathers on the tops of the poles, a stuffed buffalo skin hanging from the center, and opposite the door a cedar "bush" with a buffalo head on one side and opposite it several pieces of wood stuck in the ground. They were puzzled about the purpose of all this but did not conjecture what it was. As nearly as we can judge, it may have been the remains of a Crow Sun Dance, because as far as we know they were the only tribe to erect a Sun Dance lodge in this fashion. All other tribes used a center pole.[24]

Between 1809 and 1811, John Bradbury, a Scot, came over to America to study botany and visited the same Ricaras previously mentioned by Tabeau and Lewis and Clark.

Bradbury saw *"the dance of the scalp."* His account gives the pattern of the Scalp Dance common among many tribes, where the women did most of the dancing and often donned their menfolk's clothing and carried their weapons.[25]

Alexander Ross, another Scot who went west for John Jacob Astor in 1810, apparently took Indian dancing for granted, for in his entire journal he has only the following to say about it: "The Indians all the day kept dancing and smoking, and it was our interest to keep them so employed as much as possible." He is talking of Wallawallas, Shahaptians, and Cayuses of the Idaho-Oregon-Washington country. He goes on to say that, after smoking "the great calumet of peace," the women arrived, decked in their best attire, "when the dancing and singing commenced— the usual symbols of peace and friendship; and in this pleasing and harmonious mood they passed the whole day." Again, "The Indians smoked, danced and chanted all night, as usual, while we kept watch in turn." Another time he wrote, "Here a large concourse of Indians met us, and after several friendly harangues, commenced the usual ceremony of smoking the pipe of peace; after which they passed the night in dancing and singing." Ross and his party became so accustomed to this pattern of smoking and dancing, and considered it such a demonstration of peaceful attitude, that they no longer kept watch.[26]

Still another Scot, Robert Stuart, was in the far Northwest only a year or so after Ross and wrote of Indians at the mouth of the Columbia:

They pass a great portion of their lives in revelry and amusements, music, dancing, and play forms their customary diversions, as to the first it scarcely deserves the name, both from the deficiency of their instruments; and their manner of singing has something in it harsh and disagreeable to the ear, their song be, almost all extempore, on any trifling object that strikes the imagination; they have several kinds of dancing, some of which are lively, pleasant, and possess some variety, the women are rarely permitted to dance with the men, but form their companies apart, and dance to the sound of the same instrument and song.[27]

Although the first decade of the nineteenth century saw more and more travelers heading west, the West to most people was still the Ohio Valley and the prairies east of the Mississippi. Even western New York State was West to many people on the Eastern Seaboard. Estwick Evans made a pedestrian tour of this region in 1818 and visited the Seneca Indians of the Tonawanda district. He called them Tonan-wandeys. He found them possessing "much greatness, and many virtues," and felt that, considering the treatment they had received from most white people, they evinced "much forebearance, and even friendship towards us." He attended a ceremony in the long house, which he says was eighty feet long, with a large council fire at each end of it. Two parties were engaged in a War Dance.

This is a custom which these Indians will not relinquish. Some of them were naked, and many of them covered with ornaments. They wore strings of trinkets around their ankles, the object of which appeared to be to produce music in dancing. They also had much jewelry in their ears and noses. In their war dances, they imitate every part of an engagement: the onset, retreat of the enemy, pursuit, etc. Here the young warrior acquires a martial spirit, and the love of fame; and here too the aged veteran reminds his tribe of what he has done, and of what his spirit tells him he could do again.

One youth leaped over the dance circle and into the fire.

The dance commenced with the beat of an old kettle drum, and was ended by a rap with a club upon one of the benches. At the conclusion of each dance one of the chiefs addressed the company, and passed a piece of tobacco as a token, which they understood much better than myself.[28]

To this day the Senecas follow this same procedure in their dances.

Evans said these Indians would not allow any spirituous liquor brought into their village. He considered the women's voices soft and agreeable, contrary to most other writers, who seemed to think that they were harsh, guttural, or screechy.

In 1820 an Englishman, William Faux, saw western Indians while visiting Washington, D.C. They were Pawnees on a visit to the "Great White Father," and they danced in front of the President's house for a crowd of six thousand people. Faux did not say much about the dancing, but seemed to be quite impressed by their "war paint" and their nudity. He wrote:

They shewed their manner of sitting in council, their dances, their war whoop, with the noises, gesticulations, etc. of the centinels [sic] on the sight of an approaching enemy. They were in a state of perfect nudity, except for a piece of red flannel around the waist and passing between the legs. . . . They were painted horribly.[29]

In the same year, 1820, Major Stephen H. Long was leading an expedition to the Rocky Mountains. He had contact with Indians almost the entire way and sometimes gave a better account of their dances than of anything else he saw. His over-all report was so discouraging that much of the interest already manifest in the West was stifled, and no further governmental effort to explore it was made for a number of years.

Long briefly described a *Konza* Dog Dance he witnessed. Warrior societies, known variously as Dogs, Crazy Dogs, and Dog Soldiers, were found among most of the Plains tribes. The Kansas were among the village dwellers who used the large earth lodge. Into one of these the dancers came rushing and yelling. Then for some time they all sang to the accompaniment of a large hand drum, when the leader struck one of the posts near the center of the lodge with his lance "and they all began to dance, keeping very exact time with the music." Each dancer carried weapons and "rattles made of strings of deer's hoofs, some part of the intestines of an animal inflated, and enclosing a few small stones, which produced a sound like pebbles in a gourd shell." After dancing for some time, they departed, "raising the same wolfish howl." They repeated the performance in various houses around the village all night.[30]

Long wrote that "they also imitate the motions of different animals, playfully, sometimes grotesquely, in their dances."[31] Writing of the Omahas, he said, "They indulge much in the pleasure of dancing, and their dances are of various denominations, of which the following may be particularized. The calumet dance, *nin-ne-ba-wa-wong*, is a very favourite dance." Then he listed the Dance of Discovery (way out on the Missouri, so we have now seen it reported all across the country), Bear Dance, Beggar Dance, and Bison Dance.

"Among the Minnetarees is a ceremony called the corn dance; which, however, has but little claim to the title of a dance." Of these people he said later on, "In the same nation a singular night dance is, it is said, sometimes held."[32] Since he did not see it and so could not describe it, we wonder whether this was similar to the Night Dance given until recently among the Hidatsas, Rees, and their neighbors the Sioux.

Long also gave quite a good description of Calumet, Discovery, and Bison dances for the Omahas, some of the details of which we shall bring out when talking about specific dances. For the Bison or Buffalo Dance he said the dancers were painted black, wore buffalo-skin caps with a strip of hide, including the tail, down the back, and that they imitated bison, which would be a typical description of the Buffalo Dance all over the Plains.

Edwin James, who kept the records of the expedition, had this to say of Indian dancing, in writing of *Arrapahoes, Kaskaias* (Kiowa-Apaches), *Kiaways, Ietans,* and *Shiennes* he said:

Dancing is common amongst them, both as a devotional exercise and an amusement. Their gestures on both occasions are similar, except that on the former they are accompanied by solemnity, and on the latter by cheerfulness, and are characterized by extraordinary uncouthness, rather than by gracefulness. No ribaldry, however, or tricks of buffoonery are practiced on these occasions; on the contrary, their deportment is uniformly accordant with their ideas of decorum. This exercise is invariably accompanied by singing, or a kind of chanting, in which the women, who are usually excluded from a participation in the former, perform their part. Their music consists in a succession of tones of equal intervals, accompanied by occasional elevations and depressions in the voice. The modulations with which it is variegated are by no means melodious; the voices of all the chanters move in unison, and all appear to utter the same aspirations. The same series of sounds appears to be common to the chanting of all the tribes.

. . . Although in a region so extensive as that inhabited by them, and amongst so great a variety of tribes and nations, a considerable diversity of character is to be expected and admitted, yet it is believed that the traits above considered are common to the whole, as a race of barbarians. And although the shades of barbarism in which they are enveloped uniformly excludes the light of civilization, yet it is not to be presumed that they are equally dark and malignant in all cases.[33]

It may be interesting to know what these same "barbarians" thought of the "civilized" white explorers who were traveling through their country. When Dr. Roberts believed he had discovered the aged Sacajawea among the Shoshonis on the Wind River Reservation in Wyoming, he was convinced that he had found the right person because the Shoshonis sometimes referred to her as "the one who led the barbarians into our country." To this day, the Shoshoni word for white man is the same as their word for barbarian. And ethnologists have rated the Shoshonean peoples as lowest on the cultural scale in America!

Other tribes have similar uncomplimentary names for us. The Cree name for white people means "helpless ones." The Sioux word is the same as that applied to a monster. The Crows and Cheyennes call us "yellow eyes," the Blackfeet, "bear faces," because most Plains tribes abhorred hair on the face. Few if any tribes used a term comparable to "paleface." It is another white man's invention to cover up the less complimentary terms ordinarily used.

4. The Best Observers

Between 1830 and 1840 a genuine interest in Indians seemed to develop, and we have not only writers but artists of varying capabilities visiting them, often spending considerable time with some of the tribes. Of course, there were some artists with even the earliest expeditions, but most of them must have made field notes and finished their pictures after returning to Europe. Certainly most of their subjects are extremely un-Indian looking. Even weapons look European. Indian bows, arrows, shields, and clubs were quite unlike those shown in these early illustrations.

Even artists of the 1830–40 period sometimes took liberties, or were careless with details. Besides the famous artists such as George Catlin, Carl Bodmer, and Alfred Miller, there were others less well known, but whose drawings and sketches nevertheless are valuable and interesting. Paul Kane, Charles King, and Rudolph Kurz did beautiful work, which we occasionally see.

Many of these artists were from Europe. Perhaps the finest was Carl Bodmer, Swiss artist for the expedition led by Maximilian, Prince of Wied-Neuwied. Bodmer was an excellent draftsman and a keen observer. His water colors contributed much to the Prince's very valuable accounts of the journey, which occupied more than a year between 1832 and 1834. The expedition visited tribes up the Missouri River all the way from St. Louis to the last government outpost at Fort McKenzie.

Maximilian added further observations about the *Okipa* ceremony of the Mandans, reported in much detail by Catlin in his *North American Indians* and also in a separate book, *Okeepa*. Maximilian also reported a similar ceremony for the Minitaris. He said these people called it *Akupehri*. At any rate, the *Okipa*, or *Akupehri*, was similar in many ways to the Sun Dance of other Plains tribes, the Minitari version being even more like the general Sun Dance.

Maximilian also gives quite an account of a "Manitarie" Medicine Dance, which must have been an elaborate affair, and he says the entire ceremony was in charge of a woman. Six old men were chosen by young men to act as buffalo bulls and at one part of the ceremony these old men danced, "that is, they leaped as high as they could with both feet together," at the same time singing and shaking their rattles, which were long sticks with buffalo-calf hoofs dangling from them.

When they had danced for some time, they resumed their seats. . . . The whole was extremely interesting. The great number of red men, in a variety of costumes, the singing, dancing, beating the drum, etc., while the lofty trees of the forest, illumined by the fires, spreading their branches against the dark sky, formed a *tout ensemble* so striking and original, that I much regretted the impracticability of taking a sketch of it on the spot.[1]

The Medicine Dance was given in November, and, although it was in charge of

40

women, it was not *the* Woman's Medicine Dance, which the prince also wrote about. In it a medicine woman was the principal performer and she was assisted by four other women who "waddled like ducks," with short steps, their feet turned in, keeping time to quick beats on the drum. It was a sort of conjuring ceremony in which the leading performer went into convulsions and the music became "overpoweringly violent"; the whole performance sounds like others we have heard about among various tribes.[2]

Maximilian also mentioned a Dance of Old Buffalo Bulls, in which men danced with entire buffalo *skulls* and which continued four days and four nights, but he did not otherwise describe it.

George Catlin had more to say, and show, about Indian dances than any other writer before him, and more than most writers after him. He is the best known of the American artists who portrayed Indians. Some of his sketches are hardly more than cartoons, which he called them, but his finished paintings are usually very fine, with much detail, and his writings give us extremely valuable information.

Catlin's writings and paintings have been the most readily available sources of information, although some students have thought them unreliable. Catlin certainly wrote glowingly about the Indians at times, and he took liberties, as most artists do, in some of the details of his paintings. But he was really *there*, for the best part of eight years, and most of his observations still hold true in the light of what we know today. The late Clark Wissler told us that he considered Catlin the best source for information on Indians of his period. Catlin himself said that "the historian who would record justly and correctly the character and customs of a people, must go to live with them."[3]

(Indians were always pleased that we chose to live right with them in their homes instead of staying in a hotel or with "government people," as did most of the anthropologists, historians, and investigators who came to "study" them. Sometimes they even came to live with us in *our* tipi. They hadn't lived in tipis in more than fifty years and they told us many things we might not have learned otherwise.)

The Mandans were favorites of many explorers, from La Vérendrye to Maximilian and Catlin, but Catlin probably left us the best account of them. They were always friendly to visitors and were a strong and vigorous people until the smallpox epidemic of 1837, which almost exterminated them.

When Catlin first visited the Mandans in 1832 he said of them:

The Mandans, like all other tribes . . . devote a great deal of their time to sports and amusements, of which they have a great variety. Of these, *dancing is one of the principal* [italics ours], and may be seen in a variety of forms: such as the buffalo dance, the boasting dance, the begging dance, the scalp dance, and a dozen other kinds of dances, all of which have their peculiar characters and meanings or objects.

These exercises are exceedingly grotesque in their appearance, and to the eye of the traveler who knows not their meaning or importance, they are an uncouth and frightful display of starts, and jumps, and yelps, and jarring gutturals, which are sometimes truly terrifying. But when one gives them a little attention, and has been lucky enough to be initiated into their mysterious meaning, they become a subject of the most intense and exciting interest. Every dance has its peculiar step, and every step has its peculiar song, and that is so intricate and mysterious oftentimes, that not one in ten young men who are dancing and singing it, know the meaning of the song which they are chanting over. None but the medicine-men are allowed to understand them; . . . There is evidently a set song and sentiment for every dance, for the songs are perfectly measured, and sung in exact time with the beat of the drum; and always with an uniform and invariable set of sounds and expressions, which clearly indicate certain sentiments, which are expressed by the voice, though sometimes not given in any known language whatever.

They have other dances and songs which are not so mystified, but which are sung and understood by every person in the tribe, being sung in their own language, with much poetry in them, and perfectly metred, but without rhyme.[4]

Later on, Catlin says:

Dancing is one of the principal and most frequent amusements of all the tribes of Indians in America; and, in all of these, both vocal and instrumental music are introduced. These dances consist in about four different steps, which constitute all the different varieties: but the figures and forms of these scenes are very numerous, and produced by the most violent jumps and contortions, accompanied with the songs and beats of the drum, which are given in exact time with their motions.

If Catlin meant, by "four different steps," kinds of steps, or four different ways of executing steps, we would not argue with him too strenuously. But if he meant only four steps, we would not agree at all. There are dozens of variations of a few basic steps and from our observations over the years we are convinced that they were all indigenous. Nowadays there are still more steps, but a number of them have, without a doubt, come from contacts with the white man's dancing. We know one old Blackfoot dancer—and he is old, according to the usual concept of a dancer, about seventy years—who was a "show Indian" and had been all over the world with various Wild West shows. We questioned him about some of the steps he was using, which did not look traditionally Indian to us.

"I do all kinda dancin'," he said, "black bottom, jitterbug, big apple, ever'thin'." And that is just what it looked like, but we did have to admire his agility and remarkable sense of rhythm. Most of the younger Indians are incorporating the same sort of intrusions in their dancing, and with the great changeover in costume we sometimes wonder how much "real Indian" is left.

Dancing, Catlin said, was much more frequently practiced by Indians than by any civilized society,

inasmuch as it enters into their form of worship, and is often in their mode of appealing to the Great Spirit—of paying their usual devotions to their *medicine*—and of honouring and entertaining strangers of distinction in their country.

Instead of the "giddy maze" of the quadrille or the country dance, enlivened by the cheering smiles and graces of silkened beauty, the Indian performs his rounds with jumps, and starts and yells, much to the satisfaction of his own exclusive self, and infinite amusement of the gentler sex, who are always lookers-on, but seldom allowed so great a pleasure, or so signal an honour, as that of joining with their lords in this or any other entertainment.

He continued by saying that he was repeatedly honored with dances, sometimes paid to have them put on, and often watched them, so that he would be better able to talk about them.

I saw so many of their different varieties of dances amongst the Sioux that I should almost be disposed to denominate them the "*dancing Indians.*" It would actually seem as if they had dances for everything. And in so large a village, there was scarcely an hour in any day or night, but what the beat of the drum could somewhere be heard. These dances are almost as various and different in their character as they are numerous— some of them so exceedingly grotesque and laughable, as to keep the bystanders in an irresistible roar of laughter— others are calculated to excite his pity, and forcibly appeal to his sympathies, whilst others disgust, and yet others terrify and alarm him with their frightful threats and contortions.[5]

Other writers considered the Sioux to be superior dancers. As early as 1763 an English officer, Lieutenant Gorrell, said of them, "They are remarkable for their dancing; the other nations take the fashion from them."[6]

Besides the dances listed by previous writers, Catlin mentions several we have not heard of before. On the Fourth of July at Fort Snelling (now Minneapolis) the two old enemies, Sioux and Chippewas, gathered for a mutual peaceful celebration. He said they gave the "Beggar's Dance, Buffalo Dance, Bear Dance, Eagle Dance, and Dance of the Braves." We know that the Sioux had all of these, and perhaps the Chippewas had versions of the same ones. Catlin, in this case, made no distinction between them. The "*Dance of the Braves,*" as he described it, sounds like the Discovery Dance we have been following across the country, but he also listed that as a separate dance. He gave some odd ones ascribed to the Sioux—the "Woman Warrior" and "Dog Dance."

He did not give the tribe for the "Snowshoe Dance," which he seemed to like particularly well. He had illustrations of Sioux and Chippewa snowshoes, and in his painting of the "Snowshoe Dance" the dancers are wearing both Sioux and Chippewa snowshoes. He apparently was visiting Chippewas at the time, but they have a pair of Sioux snowshoes hung on a pole, so perhaps the dancers are Chippewas, and they have captured some Sioux snowshoes. Catlin said that this dance was given following the first snow as "thanksgiving to the Great Spirit for sending them a return of snow, when they can run on their snow shoes in their valued hunts, and easily take the game for their food."[7]

Returning home, Catlin visited the Sauks and Foxes on the Mississippi River and listed for them also the "Begging Dance" and the "Discovery Dance." But he gave them new ones too—a "Slave Dance," by a society of young men who volunteered to be slaves of the chief for two years, doing anything he required of them, no matter how menial; "Dance of the Berdache"; and "Dance of the Medicine of the Brave." The last was given by the companions of a man killed in battle for his widow, who hung his medicine bag on a green bush in front of her wigwam. His comrades danced in his honor about an hour a day for fifteen days.[8]

At about the time Catlin was engaged in his travels and painting, the McKenney

The *Snowshoe Dance*, painted by George Catlin at the time of a treaty between Sioux and Chippewas. Milwaukee Public Museum.

and Hall *Atlas* was published (1838), with excellent lithographs for that day of paintings by Charles King. Colonel McKenney was commissioner of Indian Affairs in 1826–27. His job was to "civilize" Indians, and so he had little good to say about their native customs. He wrote an interesting chapter on the dances for the *Atlas*, which we shall bring up later on.

Henry Schoolcraft was an agent of somewhat different caliber. He too was interested primarily in civilizing Indians, but he did show more sympathy and understanding for them as they were. He spent thirty years among them, mainly with the Chippewas, beginning in 1812 and continuing to 1842. He wrote a great deal about them, several volumes, in fact, and can be considered a reliable observer.

In his book *The Indian in His Wigwam*, published in 1848, he said:

Singing and dancing are applied to political and to religious purposes by the Indians. When they wish to raise a war party, they meet to sing and dance; when they wish to supplicate the divine mercy on a sick person, they assemble in a lodge to sing and dance. No grave act is performed without singing and dancing.[9]

A few pages later:

Dancing is both an amusement and a religious observance among the American Indians, and is known to constitute one of the most wide spread traits in their manners and customs.

44

It is accompanied, in all cases, with singing, and, omitting a few cases, with the beating of time on instruments. Tribes the most diverse in language, and situated at the greatest distance apart, concur in this. *It* is believed to be the ordinary mode of expressing intense passion, or feeling on any subject, and it is a custom which has been persevered in, with the least variation, through all the phases of their history, and probably exists among the remote tribes, precisely as it did in the era of Columbus. *It* is observed to be the last thing abandoned by bands and individuals in their progress to civilization and Christianity. So true is this, that it may be regarded as *one of the best practical proofs of their advance, to find the native instruments and music thrown by, and the custom abondoned.* [Italics ours.]

Everyone has heard of the war dance, the medicine dance, the wabeno dance, the dance of honour (generally called the begging dance,) and various others, each of which has its appropriate movements, its air, and its words. There is no feast, no religious ceremony among them, which is not attended with dancing and songs. Thanks are thus expressed for success in hunting, for triumphs in war, and for ordinary providential cares. Public opinion is called to pressing objects by a dance, at which addresses are made, and in fact, moral instructions and advice are given to the young, in the course of their being assembled at social feasts and dances. Dancing is indeed the common resource, whenever the mass of Indian mind is to be acted on and it thus stands viewed in its necessary connection with the songs and addresses, in the room of the press, the newspaper, and the periodical. The priests and prophets have, more than any other class, cultivated their native songs and dances, and may be regarded as the skalds and poets of the tribes. They are generally the composers of the songs, and the leaders in the dances and ceremonies, and it is found that their memories are the best stored, not only with the sacred songs and chants, but also with the traditions, and general lore of the tribes.

Dancing is thus interwoven throughout the whole texture of Indian society, so that there is scarcely an event important or trivial, private or public, which is not connected, more or less intimately, with this rite.[10]

No wonder the government and the missionaries, in their zeal to civilize and convert the Indians, struck at the dancing first of all!

Francis Parkman followed Catlin and Maximilian onto the Plains in 1846. He spent several weeks in Sioux camps in the vicinity of Fort Laramie, so he must have seen a great deal of Indian dancing. Just out of Harvard, he never could forget that all Indians were "savages," and all of his impressions of them were based on this premise. We must admit that his style of writing is much more vivid and colorful than that of most of his contemporaries and consequently is easy and interesting to read, but we have to judge the content by his prejudices. Also, he was very young and inexperienced, so that his judgment at that time may have been considerably different than it would have been had he made the same trip in later years.

In all of his book *The Oregon Trail* we find only two mentions of dance worth noting. The first is in a description of a visit to the Indian camp just outside the fort.

The Prairie Cock, a noted beau, came in at the gate with a bevy of young girls, with whom he began a dance in the area, leading them round and round in a circle, while he jerked up from his chest a succession of monotonous sounds, to which they kept time in a rueful chant.[11]

Here is his description of "the society of the 'Strong Hearts,'" which was holding a dance:

The "Strong Hearts" are a warlike association, comprising men of both the Dacotah and Shienne nations, and entirely composed, or supposed to be so, of young braves of the highest mettle. Its fundamental principle is the admirable one of never retreating from any enterprise once begun. All these Indian associations have a tutelary spirit. That of the Strong Hearts is embodied in the fox, an animal which white men would hardly have selected for a similar purpose, though his subtle character agrees well enough with an Indian's notions of what is honorable in warfare. The dancers were circling round and round the fire, each figure brightly illumined at one moment by the yellow light, and at the next drawn in blackest shadow as it passed between the flame and the spectator. They would imitate with the most ludicrous exactness the motions and voice of their sly patron the fox. Then a startling yell would be given. Many other warriors would leap into the ring, and with faces upturned towards the starless sky, they would all stamp and whoop, and brandish their weapons like so many frantic devils.[12]

Colorful as this description is, we do not think he saw the Strong Hearts at all, but got confused with another warrior society, the Foxes, for, from what we have been able to learn of the Sioux societies, the Strong Hearts certainly did not have the fox for patron. Few, if any, of the warrior societies danced around in a circle. Most of them jumped on both feet, in place. The most colorful thing about these societies was their regalia, each society having its own "uniform"—special headdresses, leggings, rattles, staffs or lances, face and body painting—and Parkman does not even mention these things.

Another writer who spent many years with the Indians and so is sometimes considered one of the best observers was Father Pierre-Jean de Smet, a Belgian by birth, who came to this country as a very young man and spent the rest of his life as a Jesuit missionary among Indians all through the Northwest, traveling back and forth over the prairies and mountains from the early 1830's until his death in 1873. Indians generally liked him, and he was welcome in some camps where no other white man would have dared to go. Apparently he always kept his word with them, but his word *about* them is something else. Certainly in the light of other writers and of present ethnological knowledge, De Smet reported many things that did not happen, or else happened to people other than himself and the Indians he was representing. He probably made some of his reports to impress his superiors with the seriousness of his work and the difficulties of his task in converting the "heathens."

For example, he fully describes the Morning Star Sacrifice of the Pawnees—the only example of human sacrifice among the Plains Indians—as if he personally saw it and knew all about it, whereas the last such sacrifice was made in 1818, a good many years before he even got to the West. Also, he said the Pawnees wore long hair, but we know that until very recently they were known for their shaved heads, like their neighbors the Poncas, Otos, Osages, Omahas, Kansas, and others of the Missouri and Platte rivers country. He said the Pawnees used a log drum, three feet long and a foot and a half wide. Such a drum has not been reported for any Plains tribe. The Pawnees used a large water drum, carved from a log to look something like an iron kettle, and the tambourine-type hand drum.

He said that the "Aricaras" and Gros Ventres horribly tortured their prisoners, while Maximilian made a special point of stating that the Mandans, "Manitaries" (Gros Ventres), Crows, and Blackfeet never tortured their prisoners, as did some of the tribes in the East. So it is doubtful that the Arikaras did either, since they were included in the three Village Tribes—Mandans, Arikaras, and Gros Ventres.

De Smet stated that following the announcement of the warriors lost in battle, the victory was announced and the celebrations begun, and that "by an inexplicable transition, they pass in an instant from frantic sorrow to the most extravagant joy." No tribe anywhere on the continent that we ever heard of ever celebrated a victory, if any of their own party was lost, until at least four days of mourning had been observed for the lost ones.

With so many discrepancies in his accounts, one wonders just how much of De Smet's writings he can believe. It is certain to anyone who has poured over some of the *Jesuit Relations* that he practically lifted accounts of earlier missionaries written in the seventeenth and eighteenth centuries about Indians of the Northeast and applied them to Western Indians. Hennepin did the same thing almost two hundred years earlier.

De Smet smoked the pipe with the Shoshonis at the Green River rendezvous and thought it "ludicrous." It would be interesting to know what the Indians thought of some of his ceremonies.

Early in his mission he reported a Calumet Dance for the Omahas.

Such a dance is really worth seeing, but it is not easy to give one an idea of it, because everything seems confusion. They yell, and strike their mouths, at the same time performing leaps of all descriptions, now on one foot, now on the other, always to the sound of the drum and in perfect time, pell-mell, without order, turning to the right and left, in every direction and in every shape, all at once.[13]

Such a dance sounds to us more like a Warriors' Dance or Grass Dance than Calumet, which has always been reported as being very dignified and ritualistic.

A few pages later he said, "I wish I could give . . . an idea of the architecture of an Indian village; it is as outlandish as their dancing."[14]

He interpreted the Indian oath of striking the ground with the hand and pointing to the sky to mean "that the earth produces nothing but evil, whilst all that is good comes from above." He should have known that the Earth was their Mother, the Sky the Father, and they were swearing by these holy "parents." In fact, most Indians believed that all good came from the earth.

De Smet said the Blackfoot women did the Scalp Dance, which tallies with other eyewitnesses, but his description of a Sioux Scalp Dance sounds as if he is borrowing from the East again, for he says the warriors flourished in their hands "the bloody scalps." We know that among the Sioux, although the men did take active part in the Scalp Dance, the scalps were carried by the women.

His account of an Assiniboin Sun Dance he admits came "from a credible eyewitness," and we shall take up his account of the Grass Dance when we treat with that subject. We know for certain that De Smet visited Sitting Bull's camps on several occasions. He was in the big camp at the mouth of the Powder River shortly after Sitting Bull has been elected head chief of all the warring Sioux in 1868. Concerning this occasion De Smet wrote:

The council was opened with songs and dances, noisy, joyful and very wild, in which the warriors alone took part. . . . Afterward there was a singing that roused the echoes of the hills and a dance that made the ground tremble. This was the end of the council; it closed tranquilly, in good order and harmony.[15]

De Smet did have this much to say in favor of Indian "amusements," which term he used to include singing and dancing. "These amusements among the Indians are perfectly innocent. I have never been able to detect the slightest gesture that could offend modesty."[16] And in a later letter he wrote:

Permit me to add the remark that the dances of the Indians (except the Scalp dance, which really makes one shudder) are generally modest and innocent. The sexes are never mingled. The men dance by themselves and the women form a ring around them. These savage dances certainly exceed in propriety many dances in civilized countries.[17]

Let us take a few more references from early contacts before going on with an analysis of some of the dances themselves. During this same general period we have been discussing, Dr. Josiah Gregg wrote of experiences along the Santa Fe Trail between 1831 and 1840, and in one statement, not mentioning any particular tribe, he said:

Among the amusements of the Indians generally, dancing is perhaps the most favorite. Besides a war accompaniment, it is practised as a recreation, and often connected with their worship. Their social frolics, in which the squaws are commonly permitted to join, are conducted with less ferocity of manner than their war dances; though even these are accompanied with the wildest and most comical gesticulations, and songs full at once of mirth and obscenity.

He also remarked that "in general, the Comanches are less fond of dancing than most other Indians."[18]

Around 1854, Edwin Thompson Denig wrote about the Assiniboins and included quite a bit about their dancing.

Dancing must be considered as a characteristic mode of expressing popular opinion on most, if not all, occasions and is generally done with the view of swaying the multitude, and conforming their actions to certain measures. It is also one of their principle means of publishing and handing down to posterity the rememberance of their gallant actions, of inspiring the young with a desire for distinction, and of awarding the praise due all brave warriors.[19]

Rudolph Friederich Kurz, the artist, was among these same people during Denig's time. It seems strange that an artist of Kurz's caliber had so little to say about the dances. He was fascinated by Indian life, the brilliant apparel, the excitement of the camps, but must have been very little impressed by the dancing. He wrote of one, which he did not even name:

Two young men leaped, one behind the other, around the open space between the fire and the circle of onlookers; each of them holding back his blanket with his left hand, carried in his right a slender whistle made of bone with which, inclining now to the ground, now towards the heavens, then toward the fire, then toward the guests, he blew a succession of harsh, tuneless sounds. The entire scene was in the highest degree animated and picturesque. . . .

Then, varying the movements, the two performers (they really cannot be called dancers) went slowly around the circle and addressed themselves to each of the older guests or to those who were actually taking part (as distinguished from the mere spectators). With the right hand they indicated the person to whom they would speak, said something flattering, whereupon the latter would reply "Hau" or "Hun." After they had spoken to everyone in the circle and had repeated the bounding and whistling act, the two young men and the drummers were relieved from further duty.[20]

And there you have the complete critique, except for a brief description of an Omaha Buffalo Dance, by an artist who spent many months among Indians.

We are now approaching the time of hostility, when most of the tribes of the Plains came to hate white men because of the great influx of emigrants into their country, the establishment of unwanted forts and towns, and the destruction of their food supply— particularly the buffalo, and other wild game as well. The white men who wrote of these times were usually more biased than earlier observers.

General O. O. Howard was more understanding and more fair than most army officers, but he nevertheless had the prevalent idea that the Indian's only salvation lay in accepting the white man's ways, at the sacrifice of his own. Here are some samples of Howard's observations. The very first comment he made on dancing concerned the *Stickeen* Indians—a village of Tlingits in Alaska, an area we have not touched on so far. He was sent there in 1875, only eight years after the purchase of that great territory from Russia. He wrote:

They have a characteristic dance of satisfaction, participated in only by the men and lasting for hours, in which they depicted, in rude pantomime, the departure of Fernandeste (their chief) on the steamer, his suicide, and the return of his body; they also portrayed our visit and the satisfactory settlement which I had just promised.[21]

The "rude pantomime" was apparently vivid enough that Howard understood the story they were portraying. Later, back in the Northwest among the Bannocks, he wrote:

Buffalo Horn (the war chief) asked permission to have a war dance, and I consented. The unearthly din of their wild wailing and singing, the weird shapes of the dancing Indians silhouetted against the blazing camp fires, and the sense of actual danger seemed to impress my whole command with a feeling akin to awe.

He saw Indians of many tribes up and down and across the West, but remarked that "the Brulés [Sioux] were the finest physical specimens of Indians that I had ever seen." As early as 1882 agency Indians had to get permission from their agent to dance.

Following is an amazing statement the general made:

Ceremonial dancing in various forms was a prominent feature in Indian life. Those tribes that were expert horsemen were generally shambling and awkward in walking or running on foot, the natural result of their being almost constantly on horseback from childhood to old age. Indian dances did not require much agility on the part of the performers. The body was kept stiff and the legs were moved forward and back, and up and down. It appeared to me as I watched the dances of the Indians that every dancer cultivated rigid action of the muscles, even when bending over or looking skyward.[22]

Howard's observation is contrary not only to what many other writers have said, but certainly different from ours. We watched old men, who were young warriors in General Howard's time, dance with an ease and grace that few old men in our civilization could match. Indian dancing may look angular to some who have observed only other kinds of dancing, but it is among the most relaxed forms. Otherwise the aged and the corpulent could not dance for hours, as we have seen them do. And to find more vigorous dancing than some done by the young people, one would have to go to the Caucasus or to some of the interior African tribes.

These same old men and women we knew, who had lived on horseback during the first half of their lives, seemed to glide along as they walked. Flying Cloud told the story at Fort Yates of Sitting Bull's race. Sitting Bull had been wounded in the foot in one of his early battles, a wound that slightly crippled him for the rest of his life. When he was about fifty years old, on a wager he ran a foot race against the fastest soldier on the post, and won, to the great chagrin of the army men, who had wagered most of their month's pay on their runner.

Before we take up one very special dance that gave its name to a unique religious movement, perhaps we should summarize the dances that have been reported so far.

SUMMARY OF RECORDED DANCES

Carver (1766–68), listing dances of both Sioux and Chippewas, with no distinction, and John Long (1768–82), for the Chippewas, give us the following dances for these two tribes:

Pipe, or Calumet Dance	Prisoner's Dance	Marriage Dance
Set-Out (for war party) Dance	Spear Dance	Death Dance
War Dance	Sacrifice Dance	
Return Dance	Testing the Heart Dance	
Scalp Dance	Pawwaw (Medicine Man) Dance	

In addition to Chippewa and Eastern Sioux, we have the French reports of the late 1600's, the reports of Forsythe, McKenney and Hall, Schoolcraft, and Catlin of the 1829–48 period for Sauk and Fox and other Great Lakes tribes:

Calumet	Peace	Medicine (Midewin)
Discovery	Begging	Wabana (Medicine Man)

Strike-the-Post	Green Corn	Slave
Scout	Green Bean	Mourning
War	Buffalo	
Honor	Otter	

Stephen H. Long listed for the Omahas:

Calumet	Bear	Begging
Discovery	Bison	

Maximilian listed dances as follows:

Mandans	Arikaras	Hidatsas
Six Warrior Societies	Six Warrior Societies	Medicine Dance
Hot Dance	Hot Dance	Women's Medicine
Okipa	Extended Robe	Old Buffalo Bulls
Corn	Scalp	Akupehri (like Sun Dance)
	Bird's Egg	
	Youngest Child	

In addition to Maximilian's list of Mandan dances, Catlin added Buffalo, Boasting, and Begging dances, and for Sioux and Chippewa:

Buffalo	Dog
Braves	Snowshoe
Begging	Berdache
Bear	Chief
Eagle	Pipe
Woman Warrior	

It is interesting that, although in those days the Sioux and Chippewas were usually at war and represented completely different linguistic stocks, several writers listed their dances together. Denig (1854) listed the following dances for the Assiniboins, to which Catlin added the Pipe Dance:

Seven Warrior Societies	Women's Dance
Scalp	Divining
Bull	

5. The Ghost Dance

The Ghost Dance of 1888 to 1890 marked the end of the Old Buffalo Days and the old Indian way of life. The buffalo were gone, and none of us today can fully appreciate the enormity of this catastrophe to these people whose entire existence depended upon them. In less than two generations millions of the great, shaggy animals, which had been the main support of all the tribes on the Plains, were ruthlessly slaughtered and all but disappeared. Cooped up on reservations, virtually prisoners of war, their treaties violated, their promised rations cut and long delayed in delivery, the tribesmen were suffering want and privation, misery and despondency such as they had never faced before. The proud Sioux, never really whipped in battle, defeated only because their commissary was destroyed, were ready for anything as a way out.

Word of a new religion being taught by a Paiute dreamer in Nevada, which promised the revival of the old Indian ways, the return of the buffalo, and the annihilation of the race responsible for all their troubles, naturally aroused their interest.

Actually, prophetic religions like the Ghost Dance were not new to Indian history. A Delaware prophet as early as 1764 had preached a revival of the old ways, demanded giving up everything obtained from the white men, even to firearms, and a return to the Indian way of life, if Indians were ever to be happy and to attain the destiny the Great Spirit had planned for them. The great leader Pontiac became a disciple of this new religion and attempted to organize all of the tribes of the East to throw out the white invaders and once more return the entire country to Indian domination.

After the failure of Pontiac's venture, the dream was revived by Tenskwatawa, brother of Tecumseh, the great Shawnee leader. The teachings of Tenskwatawa, the Prophet, helped Tecumseh in his effort to organize the tribes into an invincible confederacy, and Tecumseh came nearer to his goal than did Pontiac, carrying his doctrine as far south as the Creeks in Alabama and the Cherokees in Tennessee and North Carolina.

Kanakuk, the Kickapoo prophet, took up the teachings of Tenskwatawa and became a great influence among his own people in Illinois and among other Lake tribes in Wisconsin and Michigan. But he had no warlike motives whatever, preaching that if the Indians gave up liquor, violated none of the white man's laws, and lived peaceably among themselves they would eventually inherit a land of their own. He issued prayer sticks with religious symbols carved upon them, similar to prayer sticks used earlier by the Delawares. So as not to offend the white men, Kanakuk's disciples held their religious observances on Sundays.

All of these Eastern revivals, we might say, started with the Delaware prophet, passing from tribe to tribe and from generation to generation. After a lapse of thirty or forty years, and with no apparent connection, similar revivals began in the Far West. The revival spirit generally seemed to blossom again, and Kanakuk's doctrine was taken up once more, this time by a Potawatomi, whose influence spread among his own people and to Sauks and Foxes and Kickapoos in Indian Territory.

About 1870 a Paiute named Ta'vibo began to preach to the Indians near Walker Lake, Nevada. His words made such an impression that scattered bands of Paiutes came to hear him and his fame spread until he was well known to the Shoshonis and Bannocks of Idaho and to the Indians of Oregon. His doctrine preached racial equality, a return to the old way of life, return of the wild game, and resurrection of the dead. He taught a simple dance, which was done at night around a circle, but, contrary to the usual Indian custom, there was no fire in the center.

Ta'vibo's teachings spread to Indians in Utah, where they were considerably influenced by the Mormon missionaries. Ta'vibo was the father of Wo'voka, who spread the doctrine of the Ghost Dance a few years later.

Farther north, at about this same period of time, the news of another religious leader began to be heard. He was Smohalla, chief of a small tribe of Columbia River Indians in Washington, known as the Wa'napum; his followers were known as Dreamers. The Indian agent for this area claimed that Smohalla preached all the vices as virtues, but on reading his reports one finds that the vices largely consisted of resistance to his authority, the refusal to sell land to the whites, and opposition to removal to a reservation. Smohalla also preached a return to the old Indian ways, which included the belief that the Earth was the Mother, and consequently one would not plunge a knife into his mother's breast (plow the ground). He thus discouraged any attempts at agriculture, which the agent was trying to introduce.

Smohalla had gone to a Catholic school as a boy. He began to preach some of his doctrine as early as 1850. About 1860 he had a fight with a rival chief up the river and was left for dead. When he came to, he got into a canoe and drifted downstream. Later he was rescued by white men and eventually recovered from his wounds. He wandered on down into Mexico and, after hundreds of miles of travel and a long absence, finally arrived back home. He claimed that he had been dead and in the spirit world all that time. He preached that the Indians' miserable condition was due to abandoning the old ways, but he incorporated both Catholic and Mormon dogma and ritual into his new religion.

Smohalla's doctrine made converts among the Nez Percés and had some bearing on the outbreak of the Nez Percé war. After the Nez Percé defeat, even Smohalla finally agreed to go on a reservation in order to eliminate further trouble.

Shortly after Smohalla's doctrine began to make an appeal to Indians of the Northwest, another sect known as the Shakers came to light. This religion was taught by a Squaxin Indian named John Slocum and was also a mixture of Christian and Indian beliefs.

To the south about 1881 an Apache prophet, Nakai' Dokli'ni, proclaimed that the whites would soon be driven from the land. His converts formed the spokes of a wheel, all facing inward, while he stood in the center and sprinkled them with a sacred meal of pollen from the tule rush as they circled around him.

Nakai' Dokli'ni offered to bring two chiefs back to life, within a certain period, for a payment of horses. When the chiefs did not appear, he told the people that they did not want to come back as long as there were white men in the country. When the whites were gone the chiefs would come back, he said.

His preaching alarmed the agent, who called the soldiers. They were sent with orders to take Nakai' Dokli'ni dead or alive. Apache scouts led the troopers to him, and he surrendered without a protest. At night, however, the scouts joined their tribesmen in an attack on the soldiers, killing and wounding several, but the Indians were repulsed. The result was another long series of Apaches outbreaks.[1]

Most of these new Indian religions preached a return to the old way, abhorrence of liquor, living at peace with one's neighbors. All of them reinstated old dances or created new ones to coincide with the universal ancient Indian tradition of having a dance for anything important. All of these Indian doctrines preached the eventual destruction of the white men, but usually by supernatural means. White people already accepted by or living with Indians would survive as Indians.

Nevertheless, even the doctrines with peaceful intentions led to wars—the Pontiac War, the Creek War, participation by Indians on the side of the British in the War of 1812, the Modoc War, and finally to the last Sioux uprising, which ended the wars on the Plains.

Wo'voka, son of Ta'vibo, spent his early years as a ranch hand in Nevada and as a migratory worker in the hop fields of Oregon and Washington. He was sometimes known as Jack Wilson, because of his association with a Wilson family in his youth. In Washington and Oregon he had contact with Shakers and Dreamers. The new doctrines, coupled with the Christian teachings he had received from the Wilsons, fired him with dreams of glory and achievement. He returned home to add these new ideas to those inherited from Tavibo, and about 1886 began preaching to his Paiute neighbors. He introduced a dance that the Shoshonis later saw and said they had done fifty years earlier.

With a knowledge of sleight-of-hand, of hypnotism, and other shamanistic tricks, Wovoka was able to convince many of his hearers. In addition, he occasionally went into a deep trance, from which he did not recover for many hours. When finally recovered, he said that he had died and while dead had visited God, who had given him the message he was about to preach—that the dead would return to populate a new world, taking place of the old, which would be destroyed. To bring about this new world, the people must continue to dance the Ghost Dance that he had taught them.

When the new world failed to come and interest in the dancing lagged, Wovoka "died" again. Being able to read, he learned from an almanac that a total eclipse of the sun was due on January 1, 1889. His second "death," therefore, was chosen to take place at the same time, and had a profound effect upon the ignorant tribes-

Wovoka, prophet and dreamer. Unretouched photograph made by James Mooney in 1891. Smithsonian Institution.

men.* His return this time reestablished him not only as a great teacher but as the Indian Messiah, and he promised that if the dance was properly carried on it would be only a brief time before the old world would be destroyed. The new world would be ushered in with a great earthquake, followed by a flood, which would wash all of the old away and destroy all unbelievers. The new world would be covered with green grass and herds of deer, elk, antelope, and buffalo, and the Indians would live in a paradise, untroubled by disease, wars, or famine.

Wovoka's teachings spread like wildfire among the disheartened Indians of Nevada, Idaho, Oregon, and Utah, and before long the word was carried to Fort Hall, where it was accepted with enthusiasm by Shoshoni and Bannock Indians. One of the Bannocks went to visit a kinsman among the Shoshonis on the Wind River Reservation in Wyoming, and the Shoshonis decided to send a delegation to Walker Lake to see for themselves. Part of the Wind River Reservation is taken up by the Northern Arapahos. Although these two tribes had formerly been deadly enemies, this was no time for petty tribal differences, for the new religion preached the brotherhood of all men. An Arapaho named Sage joined the Shoshoni delegation to see Wovoka.

Sage was so enthralled by his visit to the Messiah that he immediately started a Ghost Dance upon his return home. Living with the Arapahos was an Oglala Sioux, Spoon Hunter, who had married an Arapaho woman. Spoon Hunter immediately became a convert to the new doctrine and called his son, a boy in the local mission school, to write a letter for him. The boy struggled through a letter in English (few Indians had yet learned to write in their own tongue), and the letter was sent to Spoon Hunter's nephew, Kicking Bear, a minor chief and mystic among the Minikon'ju (Minneconjou) on the Cheyenne River Reservation in South Dakota.

Kicking Bear was so intrigued by the message, which was read and interpreted to him at the local trading post, that he immediately saddled up his pony and started for the Wind River country, even though it was already winter. He did not bother to go to the agent for a pass, which was required in those days to leave the reservation, for he knew that it would not be granted anyway. He made his way to his uncle's lodge at Ethete, almost five hundred miles away, dodging white ranches and outposts of civilization all along his route. He became convinced that the new doctrine would save his people. On the way home he stopped at Pine Ridge to tell his friends and relatives there of his mission.

---

*When Tecumseh failed to arouse the Creeks in Alabama to support his cause, he told them that when he got back home in the North he would stamp his foot upon the ground, and they would feel it shake. Shortly after this pronouncement, in about the length of time it would have taken him to arrive in Ohio, an earthquake struck Alabama and actually shook down some of the Creek cabins. A number of Creeks thereupon went north to join Tecumseh. How was he able to predict an earthquake? Not even an almanac would have helped him.

Soon the word had spread to all the Sioux agencies. Bad off as most Indians were, none were in a worse plight than the Sioux. Commissioner Morgan, in his annual report, wrote:

Prior to the agreement of 1876 buffalo and deer were the main support of the Sioux. . . . Within eight years from the agreement of 1876 the buffalo had gone and the Sioux had left to them alkali land and government rations. It is hard to overestimate the magnitude of the calamity . . . to these people. . . . Suddenly, almost without warning, they were expected at once and without previous training to settle down to the pursuits of agriculture in a land largely unfitted for such use. The freedom of the chase was to be exchanged for the idleness of the camp. The boundless range was to be abandoned for the circumscribed reservation. Under these circumstances it is not in human nature not to be discontented and restless, even turbulent and violent.[2]

So the Sioux were more than eager to have a full report on the new religion and selected a delegation to go all the way to Nevada to visit the Messiah himself. Kicking Bear was the only delegate from the Minikonju. The names Short Bull and Kicking Bear have always been associated in history with the Sioux Ghost Dance uprising, or Messiah Craze. Short Bull was one of the two delegates from the Brulés, and there were four from the Oglalas at Pine Ridge. The seven slipped away from their reservations and made their way to the country of their former enemies, the Shoshonis. They had to traverse more than one thousand miles of country already occupied by ranches and towns. They cut their way through barbed-wire fences and carefully skirted the towns, so as to cause no alarm and raise no questions, following the old war trails that they had not been on for years. Eventually they arrived at the wickiup of Wovoka, on the Walker Lake Reservation in Nevada.

There the Sioux were joined by a member of their tribe who had been visiting the Northern Cheyennes and had come with a delegation of Cheyennes and Arapahos to see the Messiah. When Wovoka came out to greet them, all fell prostrate on their faces before him.

After the first meeting with Wovoka it seems that he made every effort to impress them with the actuality of his being the Messiah. He would appear to them out of clouds of smoke or from the top of a rock high above the river. On one occasion he called the various delegations together, and, although he talked in Paiute, the Sioux, Cheyennes, Arapahoes, and Shoshonis all claimed to understand him. He said that he was the Christ, the same whom the white men had persecuted, and showed them scars on his hands, feet, and breast to convince them. Since the white people had rejected him, he was coming back to save the Indian people from their oppressors.

These were the stories the Sioux delegation brought back the next spring, 1890, to their own people. Such words brought hope and encouragement even to the pagan Sioux, who knew little and believed nothing of Christian doctrines.

Indians home from school wrote letters for and read letters from Ghost Dancers back and forth across the country and helped to spread the doctrine. Only a month later, in May, rumors began to creep in to white settlements, and the alarm was spread that the Sioux were doing "some kind of war dance" and preparing for a big uprising. Most of the Sioux were unarmed, and they were outnumbered ten to one by white people all around the reservation, but knowledge and common sense were almost completely lacking among these settlers.

With no thought of war, but only of alleviating their present hopeless condition, the Sioux took up the doctrine in earnest. Even Chief Red Cloud, old and apathetic, gave his consent to the Ghost Dance. The Sioux delegates reported that Wovoka had told them they should live in peace, send their children to school, and follow the white man's road for the time being. If soldiers came to harm them, Wovoka would stretch out his arms and they would be powerless. The Indians' decimated ranks would be replinished by the returned spirits of the dead. As the spirits approached, they would be preceded by herds of buffalo and ponies. The Great Spirit was now on the side of the Indians and would help them. Bullets would be harmless. There would be a great earthquake and a flood that would drown all the white people. It would be followed by storms and whirlwinds.

The Ghost Dance beliefs were taken up mostly by the Teton Sioux, or Lakotas, although some of the Santees to the east were also affected by them. According to the Ghost Dance moral code, there must be no fighting; all good people must live together; troublemakers of both races were to be wiped out. "The entire Indian race, living and dead, was to be reunited upon a rejuvenated earth to live a life of aboriginal happiness, forever free from death, disease, and misery."[3] One must understand how depressed the Sioux were to accept a code like this. They had been some of the greatest fighters on the Plains. Their native culture was based on hunting and warfare.

The Sioux delegation told of Wovoka showing them his hat, and in it they saw the entire world, everything that was good and beautiful. They went into the Spirit World, where they saw dead friends and relatives. They saw herds of buffalo and horses. Only one member did not believe. All he saw was the inside of the hat.

Wovoka had told the delegations that they must dance four days, until the morning of the fifth day, when they should bathe in the river. They were to do this every six weeks. The Sioux seem to be the only tribe to incorporate the sweat lodge into the Ghost Dance, but it was an integral part of all their ceremonies. So, after a twenty-four hour fast, the leaders of the Ghost Dance ritual went into a sweat lodge, which in itself was the symbol of renewed life. At the rear of the sweat lodge was a pole on which cloth streamers and offerings of tobacco were hung.* When the steam bath was over, each participant plunged into the river. Even dancers who did not go into the sweat lodge were expected to bathe in the river before entering the dance.

---

*The streamers were not used in the usual sweat bath. They represented special prayers. Tobacco was offered in every ceremony. For more information on the ritual of the sweat bath, see *The Indian Tipi*, by Reginald and Gladys Laubin, University of Oklahoma Press, 1957.

Chief Little Owl (Young Bear), an Arapaho, wearing a buckskin Ghost Dance shirt, now in the Denver Museum. Western History Collections, University of Oklahoma.

Following the bathing, faces and bodies were rubbed with sweet grass. Then the dancers' faces were painted by the leaders of the dance. The sun, moon, stars, circles, and crosses were the emblems depicted. Many had faces painted red, with a black crescent on forehead or cheek. These preparations took all morning. The bodies were not painted, for they wore ghost shirts* and usually leggings.

---

*Wovoka himself disclaimed any knowledge of these shirts.

The early antagonism shown by the surrounding white people to the new dance and the fact that the government had now sent up troop reinforcements to alleviate the settlers' fears led to the adoption of the ghost shirt as the most peculiar property in the Sioux Ghost Dance. The ghost shirt was made of muslin, for buckskin was almost unobtainable, and was cut in the style of the old-time war shirt and sewed with sinew, as in early days. When possible leather fringe was applied; otherwise the fringe was also cut from cloth. The fringe and portions of the shirt were painted with a sacred paint obtained from the Messiah. Motifs included the emblems used on the face, as well as eagles, magpies, crows, and sage hens. The garments were also decorated with eagle feathers. Ghost Dance dresses were made in similar style. All participants—men, women, and children—wore such attire. Sometimes the leggings were also painted with red vertical or horizontal stripes.

The Sioux were the only Indians to make the garments of cotton and to proclaim them bulletproof. The Sioux medicine men started this belief in order to allay the fears due to the presence of soldiers.

Except for the muslin, nothing made by white men was to be worn or carried in the dance. A few participants wore beadwork, as a substitute for porcupine-quill embroidery, but all metal ornaments were banned. Later, when some Ghost Dance leaders were actually arrested and imprisoned, some of the dancers brought guns to the dance ground, not to display aggressiveness, but for self-protection. This, however, happened in only one of the Ghost Dance camps. It would have been impossible to carry guns in the actual dance, for each hand held the hand of a partner.

To allay fears on the part of the whites, the dancers tied an American flag to the top of the small pine tree erected in the center of their dance space. Cloth streamers, eagle feathers, stuffed birds, claws, and horns were fastened to the tree, too. The tree itself was referred to as the "sprouting tree," another symbol of renewed life. At the "four corners of the world," four points on the edge of the dance circle representing the cardinal points, were placed other ceremonial objects. On the west was a pipe, representing the Sioux nation. One translation of a letter written by Short Bull says it was a clay pipe, but it probably was of red claystone, or Catlinite.[4]

On the north was placed an arrow, symbol of the Cheyennes, whose most important tribal medicine is the Medicine Arrows and who formerly lived north of the Sioux. On the east was a symbol of hail, representing the Arapahoes, who formerly lived east of the Sioux and were known by them as the Blue Cloud people. To the south was another pipe, with a feather attached, representing the Crows, former enemies but now at peace.

The dancing started about noon. The leaders, or priests, sat near the sacred tree in the center of the dance circle. The dancers sat on the ground around the edge, intermixed men and women instead of men on one side and women on the other, as was the usual Indian custom. All the dancers wore eagle feathers tied in their hair, near the crowns of their heads, something else that had never been done before. A mournful chant was sung and a bowl of sacred food was passed around for everyone to partake of.

A company of men, as many as fifteen, then began another song and marched abreast, others falling in behind, parading all around the camp before returning to the dance circle and taking their seats.

A young woman next entered the circle and, taking her place near the tree, started the main ceremonies by shooting four arrows, one to each of the four directions, in Sioux order, west, north, east and south. The arrows had bone tips, which had been dipped in steer's blood. No doubt this young woman represented the Buffalo Ghost Maiden, legendary bringer of the pipe and of important ceremonies. The arrows were gathered up and hung, with the bow, on the center tree. Also hung upon the tree were a hoop and four sticks used in the old hoop game, which had sacred significance to many tribes.

On a signal from the leaders, everyone arose to his feet and a line was formed, all facing the sun, while the chief priest waved a ghost stick over their heads. He then turned and faced the sun himself, making a long prayer, while the young woman, or sometimes a different one, came forward carrying a pipe, which she held toward the west, from where the Messiah was to come.

The ghost stick was a special wand, peculiar to the Sioux Ghost Dance, to the upper end of which were fastened two buffalo horns, painted red, forming an up-right crescent. At upper and lower ends of the staff were sorrel horse tails, fastened in such a way as to look as if they were growing out of it. The staff itself was orna-mented with wrapped beadwork and trimmed with red cloth. It, too, was later hung from the tree (see page 191).

As the priest continued his prayer, the line of dancers closed in a circle around him. Most of them wore blankets and shawls, which they now wrapped around their waists, so that the fringe nearly touched the ground. The brilliant paintings on the ghost shirts and dresses now came to view. The dancers turned to the left, each one placing his hands upon the shoulders of the one in front, and all walked in a sun circle, singing, "Father, I come."

At the end of the song, all faced the center again, wailing and crying in a most fearful and heart-rending manner. Some clasped their hands above their heads, standing straight and still, asking the Great Spirit to allow them to see their loved ones who had gone on. Some grasped handfuls of dust and threw it over their heads. Then all sat down once more, to listen to another address by one of the leaders.

The next time they formed a circle, all took hands, intertwining the fingers. A leader began one of the Ghost Dance songs, all of which were plaintive and sad, with words such as this:

The Father says this, he commands all on earth to sing.
Mother, come back, little brother calls, seeking thee, weeping.
Father, all is gone, there is nothing here to satisfy me.

Referring to the Spirit World, another song was: "Joyous feast we now, Eating pemmican."

The Ghost Dance of the Ogallala Sioux at Pine Ridge Agency, Dakota, by Frederic Remington. Library of Congress.

Everyone joined in, all singing together, and the actual Ghost Dance began. The Shoshonis called this the "Dragging Dance." It was similar to the social Round, or Circle, Dance, the left foot leading, lifting higher than the right, but at the same time there was a plunge forward. The right foot then dragged to position, the left foot came to the rear, at the same time advancing again to the left, and again the right foot came to meet it. It was a grapevine step, but with much emphasis on the initial plunge left and forward. The left foot crossed the line of the circle forward and back. The right foot always remained on the line of the circle. This was the Ghost Dance step. No drum or rattle was used, and no bells, which had come from the white man.

Circles with as many as three and four hundred dancers were seen by some observers. They danced fast, "hands moving from side to side, their bodies swaying, their arms, with hands gripped tightly in their neighbors', swinging back and forth with all their might."[5] They often danced in dust two and three inches deep, so that sometimes they were almost hidden from view. They kept this up, going around and around, until first one, then another, broke from the ring, staggering and falling. Those who became tired first were supported by their partners on either side.

The leaders, priests, or medicine men watched for signs of exhaustion and approached the affected one with hypnotic gestures, waving a scarf or twirling a feather before his eyes, calling, "Hu! hu! hu!" like the rapid breathing of an exhausted runner. The hypnotist might change the twirling to an up and down motion as he slowly moved around the circle in front of his subject, until the latter was completely overcome, plunging from the circle, panting and groaning, arms waving wildly, eyes glazed and staring, and pitched forward on his face or fell flat on his back, to lie motionless, but with every muscle quivering and twitching. Sometimes a man or a woman would run from the ring "stepping high and pawing the air in a frightful manner."

Those who fell in these trances were allowed to lie where they fell with no effort to revive them, for they were on a visit to the Spirit World. Often a relative would stand guard over the person to prevent his being trampled upon. One spectator reported seeing a hundred people lying on the ground, unconscious, all at once.

Some dancers, exhausted but failing to go into a trance, merely sat at the side of the circle until they regained their breath and strength. On recovering from a trance, some awakened with violent tremors, arising to their feet and staggering away. Others moaned, sat up, and acted as if coming out of a deep sleep.

As the fallen dancers recovered, they were permitted to take places among the leaders in the center. They told their stories to the head priest, who shouted them to the people. Actually, only about one in ten had a vision, and even some of these did not really believe in it, but some claimed to have visited the Spirit World and to have seen long-dead relatives.

After the visions were related, which allowed all the performers a time to rest, the dance was repeated, sometimes as many as three times in one day. The Ghost Dance was usually started on a Sunday, the white man's medicine day, as another gesture of reconciliation. It ended with all participants shaking their shawls and blankets, replacing them on their shoulders, and going to their lodges.

When a person wanted special help from a medicine man or from one of the dancers who had had a vision, he first laid his hands upon the head of the one he was beseeching, then drew them down past the face, the chest, and along the arms. This gesture was often used in the Ghost Dance, but is also a typical Indian blessing used on many other occasions.

Certainly in the dance we have described there was nothing to cause alarm among any intelligent people. The few non-Indians who made an attempt to understand the ritual of the Ghost Dance said it was a better religion than the Indians had ever had before. It was based in part on the teachings of Christianity, but since it had not come from the missionaries, they preached against it.

Kicking Bear brought the good news proclaimed in the Ghost Dance to Sitting Bull's people on the Standing Rock Reservation in the fall of 1890. Many writers have claimed that Sitting Bull was the leader of the movement on his reservation, but people well acquainted with him say otherwise. Sitting Bull was interested, but skeptical. However, being the acknowledged chief of the people in his district, he told them that if they wanted to dance to go ahead and dance. He even joined them for a time, but when he did not go into a trance and received no personal help or inspiration from it he quit.

Agent McLaughlin tried to get Sitting Bull to order the dancing stopped, but Sitting Bull refused, as he felt his people had a right to dance if they wanted to. In order to learn if there was any truth in the Messiah story, he offered to go with McLaughlin to see Wovoka so that they both could judge for themselves as to the reliability of his teachings. McLaughlin, of course, made excuses and would not go. He tried to get the Indian police to arrest Kicking Bear, but this offended Sitting Bull's sense of hospitality and he refused to permit them to disturb his guest.

Given time for its prophecies to prove false, the Ghost Dance would have died a natural death or would have remained, as it did with some other tribes, as a promise of future bliss. McLaughlin himself knew this, but used the Ghost Dance to get rid of Chief Sitting Bull, who had more influence than had the agent himself. McLaughlin ordered Sitting Bull's arrest. The Indian police who belonged to Sitting Bull's immediate band turned in their badges, but some of the others were jealous of him. The agent's orders implied that they were to bring him in dead or alive. Old Indian friends of ours told us McLaughlin even issued whiskey to the police before they left to strengthen their hearts for taking their own chief.

Sitting Bull offered to go to see the agent of his own free will, but refused to be arrested by former warriors who had been under his leadership. In the scuffle that followed he was killed, both Lieutenant Bull Head and Sergeant Red Tomahawk shooting him fatally. But the police lost six of their number in the fight, and seven Sitting Bull followers, including Sitting Bull's young son, Crowfoot, were killed.

Thus ended the Ghost Dance at Standing Rock, on December 15, 1890. A number of the dancers fled the reservation, going over to the Cheyenne River Reservation to join the Ghost Dancers there under Big Foot.

In the meantime, the Ghost Dance was going at full force on the Pine Ridge, Cheyenne River, and Rosebud reservations, as it had been since June. At first there were small and frequent dances at each of the Sioux camps, but as the excitement at Pine Ridge grew, the smaller camps joined together into several larger ones, and dances were held every six weeks, according to the instructions from the Messiah.

In October a new agent was installed at Pine Ridge. He was immediately alarmed over the Ghost Dance and yelled loudly for military assistance in putting down the "outbreak." The Indians called him "Young-man-afraid-of-Indians." Soon there were about three thousand troops in the area, which alarmed the Indians. More than seven hundred lodges of "hostiles," including those from Rosebud, took refuge in the Bad Lands, about fifty miles from the agency, where the terrain would enable them to make some kind of defense. Kicking Bear was now back with them, as well as Short Bull.

The entire Sioux Nation in those days could possibly have mustered between six and seven thousand warriors, but most of them would have been armed only with bows and arrows, spears, and clubs. Actually, there were no more than seven hundred who could be considered warriors taking part in the Ghost Dance. So it is little wonder that the Indians were frightened, regardless of all the promises of the Ghost Dance leaders.

The news of Sitting Bull's death had such an alarming effect upon Big Foot and his followers that they made a desperate attempt to join the other Ghost Dancers in the Bad Lands. However, on the way they were intercepted by soldiers under Major Whitside. The Indians immediately surrendered to him, then moved under the supervision of the troops to a camp on Wounded Knee Creek, only eighteen or twenty miles northeast of Pine Ridge Agency. Four additional troops of Seventh Cavalry, under Colonel Forsyth, joined Whitside, so that there were now eight troops of cavalry, a company of scouts, and four Hotchkiss guns, making a total of 470 men against the 106 warriors in Big Foot's band.

The Indian tipis were pitched west of the creek, on the open plain, and were entirely surrounded by soldiers. The four Hotchkiss guns were set up on a hill to the north, commanding the entire area. Chief Big Foot himself was ill with pneumonia, but he ordered a white flag hoisted in the center of the camp.

Early on the morning of December 29 the Indian men were ordered to come out and to bring all of their guns. They were seated in front of the soldiers, but the first twenty men to come forward brought only two guns with them. So the soldiers sent a delegation of their own to search the tipis. They returned with about forty guns, mostly old and worthless, and in searching for them they nearly tore the tipis apart and molested the women and children remaining in them.

All this time Yellow Bird, a medicine man, was parading back and forth blowing an eagle-bone whistle and haranguing the people not to be afraid, to trust in their ghost shirts, for the soldiers could not harm them. He broke into the steps of the Ghost Dance, and moved around the open space where the parley with the soldiers was being held. He stooped to throw dust in the air, completed a circle, then sat down. In former times, throwing dust in the air would have been a signal to attack, but we have seen that this was also a common gesture in the Ghost Dance.* Regardless of Yellow Bird's intention, he had hardly sat down when an Indian gun went off, and immediately pandemonium broke loose.

The soldiers on the hill opened fire with the Hotchkiss guns, pointed directly at the tipis, where the women and children were trying to pack their belongings and break camp. A volley from the surrounding soldiers, who were almost near enough the warriors to touch them, killed most of them at once. These soldiers were of the Seventh Cavalry, Custer's old outfit, and they did not intend to let this chance to avenge the disaster of fourteen years previous go by. Their battle cry was heard above the din of the shooting, "Remember the Little Big Horn. Revenge for Custer."

Indians waved frantically at the white flag of truce. Later the army tried to explain the slaughter of women, children, and other noncombatants by saying that it was impossible to tell women from men in such a melee, and that the women were armed and fighting with their menfolk. This just does not bear out the facts. The

---

*Throwing dirt over oneself in the Ghost Dance was comparable to covering the head with ashes in biblical lore—a gesture of mourning and of humility.

warriors and noncombatants had already been separated. Already all but a very few guns had been turned in, so that most Indians were armed only with knives, clubs, and tomahawks. Furthermore, Indian women and children were found dead, shot in the back, as far as two miles from the actual scene of battle, showing that they had been pursued by the cavalrymen as they tried to escape. Altogether more than three hundred Indians—men, women, and children, mostly unarmed—were killed.

Thirty-one soldiers were killed in the fight, but there is good evidence to show that most of them were killed by their own cross fire. Yellow Bird is known to have killed a number of soldiers before he fell, riddled by the bullets he believed could not harm him. Big Foot was in an army tent, where he had been placed by the commanding officer and given medical care. When the fighting broke out he was one of the first Indians killed, for a cavalryman rode up to the tent and deliberately shot the old chief.

Fast Whirlwind was one of the Indian scouts with the cavalry. He told us that he did not believe in the Ghost Dance and felt that it would bring only harm to his people. He went with the soldiers to Wounded Knee with the understanding that they were only to escort Big Foot's band back to the reservation, where the Indians would be fed and their sick taken care of. He saw the whole ghastly affair. Fast Whirlwind said that the shooting started when a deaf and dumb boy, unable to hear the orders and consequently late in coming forward, was grappled by two soldiers. In the ensuing struggle his gun went off in the air.[*]

Indians reported that the soldiers were on a big drunk the night before and far into the morning. Even the officers apparently did little to stop the massacre, for massacre it was, if the Custer fight, where fully armed troopers were killed in warfare, can be called a massacre.

One old Indian we knew, Spotted Bear, who was still alive in 1964, was shot four times but each bullet went completely through, so he said he was shot eight times. His sister, Mrs. Knocks Them Down, was shot in the neck. Willy White Bird told us that he was a baby at the time, carried on his mother's back. She was killed while trying to run away, and he also was shot. We have had eyewitness accounts from many others.

So ended the Sioux attempt to bring back the glories of the good old days. (So also ended the Indian wars on the Plains, when the campaign was over on January 16, 1891.) News of the debacle at Wounded Knee speedily reached other tribes around the country, and upon hearing it, the Ghost Dance also ended for most of them.

---

[*]Since Wounded Knee has again been in the public eye, owing to the recent disturbances there, books and articles concerning the two "Wounded Knees" have been using army figures relating to the original incident. Army reports, endeavoring to whitewash the entire 1890 affair, indicated that the Indians were heavily armed with Winchester repeating rifles. If this was so, what became of them? The Indians did not turn them in, no Indians got away, and they were not found with the bodies after the "fight." Actually the Indians had been too poor for a long time even to think of buying expensive guns.

The movement had considerable influence in the Cheyenne and Arapaho tribes. Although of the same linguistic stock, the two peoples have always been very different from each other temperamentally. Arapahoes tend to be not quite so practical, to be more the dreamers, so the Ghost Dance made an immediate appeal to them and they carried it out with the keenest interest and the most detail of any of the tribes. Their Ghost Dance shirts and dresses were of finest buckskin and beautifully painted. Fine specimens can be seen in a few museums (see pages 59 and 190).

Tall Bull, a Cheyenne, and Black Coyote, an Arapaho, visited Wovoka at the same time. Wovoka held his big sombrero out in front of them and also held eagle feathers in his hand. Tall Bull saw him make a quick movement and take something black out of the hat. That is all he saw and he was not much impressed; he knew medicine men who could do as well or better. But Black Coyote saw Wovoka pass the feathers over the hat and when he looked in he saw the whole world, as the Sioux delegates also reported.

The Arapahoes said the four days of dancing represented the four days and nights during which the catastrophe would take place. A wall of fire would precede a landslide, driving the whites back across the Big Water. The sacred feathers the Indians wore and carried in the dance would enable them to rise above the fire and on the fifth day come down on a new earth. Old people would be rejuvenated. The dancing would revive the dead and all would return to this new world as they had been in their youth.

An Arapaho named Sitting Bull carried the dance to Oklahoma to Southern Arapaho relatives, to Southern Cheyennes, Caddoes, Wichitas, Kiowas, and others. Many writers have confused this Arapaho Sitting Bull with the famous Sioux chief; Sitting Bull the Arapaho did induce trances among the converts. The Southern Arapahoes sent one delegation after another to visit Wovoka and bring back instructions. They also bathed in a stream following the dancing and held the ceremonies every six weeks.

The Arapahoes opened the Ghost Dance with a ceremonial pipe, which was offered to the sun, the earth, the fire, and the four winds and then passed around to the participants. The head priest, or leader, then stood facing the country of the Messiah, eyes closed, arms outstretched, and made a prayer for the welfare of the tribe and for the early coming of the Messiah. After the prayer, songs were selected for rehearsal. However, the song used to close the dance could not be rehearsed, as it was to be sung only at that particular time. The Arapahoes composed many Ghost Dance songs, which spread from tribe to tribe and became the most important songs of the entire revival.

The Indians consecrated the dance ground by sprinkling it with a white powder and more prayers. Seven* men and women were made leaders. Crow, magpie, and

---

*Four is usually considered the sacred number among Indians, but in the Ghost Dance it was seven. The crow was the sacred bird of the Ghost Dance.

eagle feathers consecrated by a medicine man were given to these leaders, who made presents of ponies, blankets, and other things to the medicine men. Dancers also obtained special feathers, sometimes decorated, at a public ceremony from some of the leaders or from a person who had had a trance.

A dancer might paint his face according to the way he saw a departed relative painted in a trance. Those who had received no visions asked to be painted by one who had. The paint was supposed to aid in bringing about the promises of the vision and in bringing health. Designs of the sun, crescent moon, stars, crosses, and crows were painted in red, yellow, green, and blue, and the line of the hair part was painted in red or yellow.[6]

It took about two hours for this preparation, so the dance usually started after noon, and an hour or two were taken out for supper. The leaders went to the center of the circle, facing in, intertwined their fingers, and without moving sang a song in a low undertone. Then they raised their voices and the dance began. The Arapahoes did not, apparently, do the lunging step, as the Sioux did, but rather a side step, like the women's dance, although steady instead of in the three-quarter rhythm of the latter. Other dancers gradually joined in until a circle may have contained anywhere from fifty to five hundred dancers, men, women, and children. At intervals the dancers sat to rest and smoke, while leaders preached sermons or visions were related.

In the north the Arapahoes used a tree in the center, but the Southern Arapahoes did not. Like the Sioux, no drum, rattle, or other instrument was used, except that in relating a vision a person sometimes accompanied himself with a hand drum. The southern tribes did not ban the use of metal ornaments and belts. The hypnotism was carried out as among the Sioux, the medicine man using his hands, eagle feathers, or scarfs to induce a trance.

The Cheyennes who did accept the doctrine of the Ghost Dance performed in the same way as their Arapaho neighbors. The principal difference was that the Cheyennes built a bonfire at each point of the compass on the edge of the dance circle. They were the only ones to do so. The only people to use a fire within the circle were the Walpais in the Southwest.

Both the Cheyennes and Arapahoes incorporated with the Ghost Dance one they called the Crow Dance, which was done sometimes on an afternoon preceding an evening Ghost Dance. It was basically the same as the Grass Dance, the dancers being men stripped to breechclouts, with painted bodies and elaborate pendants of varicolored feathers hanging from the waist. Some even wore Grass Dance bustles. It was danced to a large drum and was different from the Grass Dance in that hypnotic trances were induced during its performance. The exciting songs and rhythm of this dance helped to promote the trances. When hypnotism was used it was most effective on young women, who were merely observers. Next, the older women, and lastly, the men were affected. But in the case of the Crow Dance some of the young men were greatly affected.

The Kiowas were interested in religious revivals some time before the Ghost Dance became known to them, so they, too, took it up avidly. A young Kiowa, Keeps-His-Name-Always, began preaching in 1881, at the time the southern buffalo herd was exterminated, that the buffalo would come back if the people followed him, but he himself died the next year. In 1887 another Kiowa, In-the-Middle, made the same claims, but went further in stating that the whites would be destroyed. He finally announced the time had come and that if all the Kiowas would leave their homes and come to his camp he would call down fire from heaven to destroy the agency, the entire white race, and all Indian unbelievers.

But nothing happened and the sorrowful people went back to their homes and to government rations of white man's beef. The prophet, of course, blamed the failure on someone who had violated his taboos and said everything would have to be postponed.

So, although the Kiowas lost faith in In-the-Middle, they were ready for the Ghost Dance when they first heard of it in June of 1890. They sent a delegation over to the Cheyenne and Arapaho agency to learn more about it. Soon after, the Kiowas gathered at Anadarko to receive lease payments and the Ghost Dance was formally inaugurated among them by Poor Buffalo, one of their delegates.

In September of 1890, A'piatan, or Wooden Lance, another Kiowa, went north to visit his mother's people the Sioux at Pine Ridge, primarily to learn more about the new religion. He then went to Fort Washakie to meet with the Arapahoes and Shoshonis, and from there went by railroad to Nevada to see Wovoka. But he was completely disappointed in his visit to the Messiah. He saw no scars, no dead relatives. Wovoka could not read his secret thoughts. So he did not stay, but went back to the Shoshonis at Fort Hall, Idaho, and from there sent a letter home, advising his people to have nothing to do with the Ghost Dance.

While Apiatan was gone, however, the Arapaho Sitting Bull went to see the Kiowas and assured them that the new earth would come in the spring of 1891. He consecrated seven men and seven women as leaders, giving them each a feather. Kiowa women, as other Indian women, had never worn feathers before. Sitting Bull taught them Arapaho songs and ritual. Later the Kiowas composed many of their own songs. They set up a cedar tree, instead of a pine, in the center of the Ghost Dance arena and were the only other ones besides the Sioux to hang things upon it.

When Apiatan returned, a big council was held in Anadarko. Everything had to be translated into English, Kiowa, Comanche, Caddo, and Wichita, so it took all day. Sitting Bull was also present. Both he and Apiatan gave their stories. There was no doubt of Sitting Bull's sincerity, but the Kiowas believed Apiatan and gave up the dance. However, it was revived again for a time in 1894 by two of the former priests.

In Oklahoma Arapahoes, Cheyennes, Caddoes, Wichitas, Pawnees, and Otos continued the Ghost Dance for some time, even after hearing the news of Wounded

Knee. But instead of the "feverish expectations" of the original teachings, they now regarded it in somewhat the same light as the Christian hope, a happier world to come at sometime in the unknown future.

The Pawnees took up the dance almost as avidly as did the Arapahoes. Otos and Missouris also became interested, but their agent arrested the leaders, which discouraged them so that they did not attempt to carry it on in full force. The Osages were already wealthy from oil discoveries and consequently could see no need for it. The Sauks and Foxes, Kickapoos, and Potowatamis, all remnants of eastern tribes and already under the influence of the Catholic Church, were only slightly interested and so practiced it only to a limited extent.

Arapahoes and Cheyennes taught the new religion to the Caddoes, Wichitas, Delawares, and Kiowas. The Caddoes showed the greatest interest and danced together with the Delawares. They and the Wichitas put heart and soul into the dance. They usually started in mid-afternoon and danced at least until midnight, sometimes until dawn. They danced all winter, even when it snowed. But such enthusiasm can last only so long. Eventually they, too, became discouraged, finally all giving up the dance except the Caddoes, who still carry on a version of it. Their Ghost Dance has become a sort of serious social dance, one in a series that they still perform occasionally. They do the Ghost Dance in the evening, men starting it and women then moving in between them. They hold hands and move in a circle to the left with the Ghost Dance step. The Caddoes have no bitter memories of this dance and its horrible aftermath such as still haunt the Sioux. To the older people it brings pictures of other days, to the younger people a hope for a brighter future and of better things to come.

As we might almost expect, the Paiutes, among whom the whole revival started, carried it out with more simplicity than did the tribes to the east, who were accustomed to longer and more elaborate rituals. The Paiutes, other than Wovoka himself, did not fall into trances. They did erect a large dance arbor and within it, to one side, a structure of branches where Wovoka sat. They had a fire on one side of the arbor. They danced four days, according to his instructions, on the fifth day ending by shaking out their robes and blankets to drive away sickness and evil. Wovoka, and certainly his tribesmen, had no idea of the far-reaching effects of the new doctrine upon Indians all across the country or of the terrible tragedy it would bring upon the poor, hungry Sioux.

The Shoshonis at Fort Hall were among the first to come under the influence of Wovoka's teaching, but they became skeptical and by 1891 had given it up. They said they had had the same dance fifty years earlier, and so they danced their Ghost Dance as they recalled it from that time. It was not just like that of other tribes. When men alone were dancing, they wore blankets, and instead of wrapping and tucking them at the waist, as the Plains tribes did, they held them with their hands. If, however, women entered the circle and one of them came between two men, they held her hands. The agent of the Western Shoshonis told them to play their

Indian games and have a good time, but not to do the Ghost Dance. At Christmas he gave them a big feast, which ended their interest in the movement.

The Ghost Dance spread as far as some of the California tribes on the west, to Oklahoma and some of the Southwestern tribes on the south, to Fort Peck and Fort Berthold on the north, and as far as the Missouri River on the east. It did not seem to affect the tribes of Washington or northern Idaho, although, as we have seen, they were greatly affected by earlier doctrines. The only pueblo affected seems to have been Taos, which has always been in close contact with Plains tribes, but even there it was taken up as a social dance rather than a religious revival. The Mohaves, Walapais, and Chemehuevis, all desert dwellers, took it up to some extent, but they were so far removed from other tribes and at the same time had so little contact with whites that not much is known of their reactions. It seems to have had no effect upon the Navajos.

Altogether thirty to thirty-five tribes were involved, with a total population of around sixty thousand. About half of some twenty-six thousand Sioux took part. It affected almost the entire tribes of Paiutes, Shoshonis, Arapahoes, Cheyennes, Caddoes, and Pawnees, but it made little impression upon the Comanches, who have been known throughout Indian history as skeptics.

More tribes came under the influence of the Ghost Dance than had been affected by any revival since that of Tenskwatawa, the Shawnee prophet, in 1805. Eventually it might have changed the attitudes and improved the outlook of Indians all over the United States. Without interference from the whites it might have continued to be a dream for peace, happiness, abundance—the good life.

6. Concepts of Indian Dancing

SHOW INDIANS

Today the average American places Indian dancing in one of three categories: he takes it for granted, as something still going on just as it always has been, and which he can see at almost any time he chooses to visit an Indian reservation; or he considers it a little-boy interest, now outgrown, and cannot visualize it as an American art form or as having adult entertainment value; or he thinks of it as wild West, or Hollywood hoopla dreamed up for motion-picture and television shows. He cannot believe that real, honest, authentic Indian dancing is of itself worthy of consideration as an art.

For some reason, to most people Indian dancing means a group of contorted, bent-over figures, feet moving awkwardly up and down, and a silly whooping punctuated by tapping the hand on the mouth, accompanied by weird and monotonous chanting undeserving of the title of "music."

In reality all Indian cultures have elements of great beauty, reflected in the dancing. Some of us are only beginning to catch something of the dignity, significance, and breadth of these cultures.

Indians have always been presented to the public as a type of side-show attraction. The effort has been to make them either savage or romantic figures, and the presentations have usually been cheap and gaudy. It started before the Revolutionary War and has been continued to the present day. When Lieutenant Henry Timberlake, an honest and true friend of the Cherokees, took some of them to England twice between 1756 and 1765, they were presented in this way against all his efforts to introduce them with dignity.

Through the years there has always been a class of person interested in the "news value" of a subject, and he often takes control. In the case of Timberlake, unknown to him an English earl sold admissions to see the Indians in their own living quarters at a hotel! The Indians did not object to being admired, at the proper time, but they were much displeased at the intrusions on their privacy and at being stared at like wild animals. They continually begged Timberlake to take them some other place or to furnish them with some diversion.[1]

George Catlin, nearly a hundred years later, had similar experiences in England and on the Continent, very embarrassing to him and to his Indian friends, but about which he could do little except protest. At one hotel he was asked to take his Indian guests and leave because the mobs on the outside, trying to get a look at the "savages," were literally tearing the building apart. The hotelkeeper admitted that the Indians were the "gentlemen" and that the "savages" were on the outside, trying to break in, but in the interest of his own financial welfare he was forced to demand their departure.[2]

The Indians have always been considered by those who knew them to be dignified, friendly, and courteous. Our personal contact with them in recent years bears this out. But they have seldom been so portrayed in popular works, whether written, pictured, or enacted. A stereotyped pseudo-Indian has been presented all through the years. The average person has had no personal contact with Indians and has accepted the false and the spectacular as his standard of Indian behavior and character.

William F. Cody, better known as Buffalo Bill, had enough experience with Indians to know something of their true character, but he, too, was a showman and so featured only the wild and warlike qualities of Indians wherever he went around the world. Since his day, the idea of the Wild West Show has been farther and farther removed from its source, so that later representations of Indians were even worse than those of earlier years. The idea of the Indian with a culture, art, and philosophy of his own has never been presented to or accepted by the public at large.

We have been told that the average person in Europe has a better understanding and more complete knowledge of American Indians than has the average person in this country. But this statement would have to be qualified, after our having been overseas several months with a troupe of Crow Indian dancers, the first time in history that Indians were ever presented in concert instead of as Wild West. The American impresario, even though accustomed to booking concerts, billed us without our knowledge as "American Indian Dance *Powwow*." He thought he was being clever, but everywhere we went the local impresario greeted us with, "What does *poh'woh'* mean?"

At the other extreme, the French think that anything connected with dance is ballet, and so they called us "Les Ballets Peaux Rouges" (the Red Skin Ballets). Thus we were announced on the posters and in huge letters over the marquee of the Théatre des Champs-Élysées in Paris, Belgium, and Algiers. In spite of the misleading titles, we did perform in many of the finest concert halls of Europe, North Africa, and Israel and pleased audiences wherever we went. In Belgium people waited for two hours in the cold and rain to thank us for dancing for them.

We received many excellent reviews in leading papers of each country we toured. But in Oran our American impresario greeted us gloomily the morning after our first performance. He said the review was terrible. "It says we have a show of poor art," he moaned, pointing to the large black letters across the front page of *L'echo d'Oran.* There we saw: "Les Ballets Peaux Rouges: un spectacle d'art pur." Of course it actually said, to our delight, "A spectacle of *pure* art," and went on to say:

The Indian Ballet has given us a show we were not expecting. Reginald and Gladys Laubin's troupe showed us the Indian spirit, with its songs and primitive dances of a strange beauty. We were expecting something picturesque. They gave us art, an art free of any spectacular artifice—a pure masterpiece of folk lore.

It is not an exhibition, but an extremely scrupulous reconstruction of Indian rites by the most infallible means of expression—song and dance.

The best of any Technicolor documentary pictures have never given us such colorful luxury.

The songs and dances have been selected in such a way that in every one of them is found an element of modern ballet. So the Indian Ballets constitutes a spectacle of art above all.

But for the initiated, what an enchantment!

We found that people overseas did have more sympathy for the Indians. They had never had to fight them, so had not erected a wall of propaganda against them and therefore were quick to recognize the Indians' real contributions to the field of art.

L'echo d'Alger caught the essence of our portrayal by reporting that "the word 'dance' is not sufficient to contain the symbolic representation of such manifestations where movement, song, color, poetry, legend, and drama are closely united."

But as far as really knowing Indian history, characteristics, tribal differences, and customs, nations abroad are misled as much by present-day Hollywood representations as the rest of us are. In staid, dignified, solemn Sweden they were disappointed because we did not burn a wagon train or scalp some white prisoners. They found our dances much too dignified and beautiful to be "real."

Then we learned that the local impresario in Stockholm had completely revised the notes we had given him, adding his own interpretation of Indian dances and his conception of their spectacular qualities. Fortunately a young anthropologist who was studying, of all things, Crow Indians came backstage to talk with us. Ours were the first real Indians he had ever seen, and they were Crows! He was perfectly delighted. But he questioned us about certain phases of the program. No wonder he was puzzled, from the way the dances were described in the Swedish text, which he translated back into English for us! Our dances did not coincide in the least with the impresario's concocted program notes.

When we presented the anthropologist with a copy of the notes we had sent on ahead, he was quite concerned. At our request he demanded of the management that a correction be announced over the public address system before each performance, and we are sure that from that time on our Swedish audiences had a much better understanding of what we were trying to do.

Photographers in every country tried to get the Indians to one side to pose with their "fiercest expression," with a knife in their teeth or a tomahawk in their hands. Newsmen overseas are the same as here, always trying to get something spectacular and "different." Our Indians knew that this was not their real character and thought the requests rather amusing. They were perfectly willing to oblige, being good fellows, until we pointed out that such pictures, misrepresenting them and their people, would do more harm than good—that they would overcome all our efforts to present Indians on the highest possible level. From then on they always consulted us before allowing pictures to be taken.

"Real Indian" showmen have sometimes been the worst offenders in giving a bad portrayal of their people. They have either done what they were told to do by some non-Indian producer or have played up to popular notions in an effort to please their audiences. Indians, like Orientals, are so polite that they often give answers they think are wanted rather than contradict their questioners. Even trained ethnologists have sometimes received wrong information in this way through asking leading questions. In addition, Indians have so often been unsympathetically reported on that they sometimes think, "What's the use?" So, rather than become involved in complicated subjects of customs, social behavior, and the like, they take the easy way out with simple answers. The show Indian applies the same technique to his audiences.

Show Indians of recent times have also often been handicapped by a personal lack of knowledge of the former life and customs of their people. The public expects every Indian to know all about his tribal history and in addition to be an artist, a singer, and a dancer. It is as ridiculous as expecting the rest of us to know all about *our* ancestral history or to all be artists, scientists, writers, and musicians. Nevertheless, many Indians not fitted for the entertainment world at all have been forced into it because they lacked the education to compete with non-Indians for other occupations away from their reservations.

Indian education has usually been much overrated. For instance, the famous Carlisle University was not a university at all, or even a high school. Strapping Indian youths, scarcely off the warpath, were sent there and they did produce excellent football teams. Yale, Harvard, Princeton, and other famous eastern universities did not like to admit being whipped by an Indian grammar school team, so the Carlisle Indian School became Carlisle "University." This naturally put the Indian to a great disadvantage, for thereafter he was expected to compete with real university graduates, which, of course, he could not do. So he was considered stupid and given menial jobs, or he "went back to the blanket," which simply meant that he went home to his people. But even there, after being away from home so long, he was apt to be a stranger, neither Indian nor white.

Today, with the great improvement in Indian education in recent years, there are still only a few Indian schools with college rating. Years ago, Indians leaving school with inadequate educations and having given their word never to go back to the Indian way of life often went into show business as the only available means of livelihood. They were not living as Indians; they were merely "playing Indian."

There has always been a tremendous interest in Indians, even though mostly in their spectacular aspects, but we feel it is high time that all of us came to know more of what they actually were and are like. If we do not learn soon, we shall never know anything except what we can glean from historical reports, written by non-Indians, often unsympathetic, for the lore is fast disappearing.

ATTITUDE ON DANCING

From 1665, when Nicholas Perrot complained that the Indians had retrograded through their contact with the French, to the present day there have been some

Makes Trouble (They Make Trouble for Him), a Hunkpapa warrior, a veteran of the Custer battle, and one of the last survivors of the buffalo days. Note the stance and figure of this man, photographed when he was in his eighties. Photo by Gladys Laubin.

people, closely associated with Indians and acquainted with their ways, who have lamented their decline at the expense of encroaching white civilization. It is remarkable that after more than four hundred years of contact with white men the Indians retain any vestiges of their own cultures.

In the late 1800's Indians were considered the vanishing Americans. By 1900 they were supposed to be well on the way to extinction. In 1903 an article in the *Overland Monthly* pertaining to the Klamaths of Oregon stated:

It is solely in the oldest Indians that traces of the aborigine remain; only with them live the customs, traditions and religion of their ancestors, and those weird, solemn chants, that in generations past always accompanied their games and dances.[3]

As recently as the 1950's, however, there were still old people living who had hunted buffalo and fought in the Indian wars, who were thorough Indians in every way. The greatest decline in the lore of the past has been within the past fifty years.

Realizing years ago that the old-timers would not be with us much longer, we went to the Standing Rock Sioux Reservation in North and South Dakota to learn what we could from them before it was too late. We had been told by Dr. Clark Wissler, at the American Museum of Natural History, and by Walter Campbell (Stanley Vestal), of the University of Oklahoma, that we would probably find the most conservative Indians* there. It was Sitting Bull's country.

Chief One Bull, who later adopted us, was nephew and adopted son of Sitting Bull. On the death of his famous uncle, One Bull inherited the rank of chief, and, even though government officials usually recognized only the "paper chiefs" whom they themselves "made" and supported, One Bull's influence was always strong among his people.

The people with whom we lived and studied were the last survivors of the Buffalo Days and of the Indian wars. All of them are gone now. Even old Indians today are a generation removed from those times and so can usually help very little with information on life in the Golden Age of the Prairie People.†

So, in a way, we are the connecting link between the early days and the Indians of today. Many of the young Indians nowadays are not much interested in the history

---

*The conservatives are the Indians who lived and retained the old culture. The traditionalists are products of modern schooling who have not actually lived the old Indian way but are now aware of their heritage and are endeavoring to preserve it. A large group of non-Indian students of Indian lore also call themselves traditionalists.

†One Bull, White Bull, Kills Pretty Enemy, Little Soldier, Makes Trouble, Twin, Antelope, Elk Nation, Crazy Bear, Red Bear, Roan Bear, Spotted Bear, His White Horse, White Shield, Eagle Shield, Wise Spirit, Male Bear, Two Bulls, Iron Boulder, Wades-in-the-Water, Rides-to-the-Door, Bull Over-the-Hill, Fast Whirlwind, Pretty Shield, Eagle Nation— these are just a few of our old friends who have gone over the Spirit Trail.

His White Horse and Rosebud, also veterans of the Custer battle, dancing at Bull Head, South Dakota. Photo by Gladys Laubin.

and lore of the past. There certainly was very little encouragement for them to retain any interest in their own heritage and culture. Today they realize more than ever that they must make their way on the "white man's road."

On the other hand, if the average Indian today had a deeper appreciation of his own heritage and of the contributions his people have made to our civilization, he would not be as mixed up and confused as he is. He would not feel such a stranger in his own land.

Americans, from the earliest colonial period to the present, have looked mainly to Europe for their ideas of art and culture. This was natural enough, since our earliest ties were with Europe. However, as our search for knowledge and culture has been carried to other parts of the globe, few have been aware that great cultures were in existence on this continent long before America was "discovered."

The interest in culture has extended to literature, art, music, philosophy, in fact the entire range of cultural activities with, for the most part, one exception—dance. Only in recent years has there been a sincere interest in this important phase of artistic expression.

The first white settlers in America, most of them seeking religious freedom, forgot that David "danced and sang before the Lord." The whites considered dancing a device of the devil. Later, both colonial aristocrats and ordinary people gave social dancing its place, but by and large they failed to see it as an art.

It is somewhat difficult to understand how the art of the dance lost its significance in European and American cultures when we consider the heritage from ancient Greece and the important place dancing held there. Greek generals danced their way into battle. They were known to demand praise for their dancing rather than for their courage in battle. Plato said, "Rhythm and harmony are made familiar to the souls of the youths, that they may grow more gentle and graceful and harmonious, and so be of service both in words and in deeds; for the whole life of man stands in need of grace and harmony." Later, in his *Laws*, he stated that "a good education consists in knowing how to sing and dance well."

We realize, of course, that the early Church did everything in its power to discourage dancing, believing it to be pagan and consequently immoral. But dancing persisted and played a part in religious dramas and festivals far into the Middle Ages. It seems that dance originally provided an important stimulus to religion, but gradually disappeared from religious observance. Some Indian tribes are in this transitional stage, with a few dances having religious significance and others now being entirely secular.

In modern society dance is secular only, but we still have two categories: social and as entertainment. Folk dances serve both purposes. In the entertainment division one purpose is merely to entertain. The other is to practice an art form. The difference seems to be in the thought, effort, and sincerity with which the dancing is conceived, executed, and projected. As art it stirs us; it is beautiful, dignified, polished. It gives us something to keep for ourselves, something to "take home." We feel that the best Indian dancing qualifies as art.

In recent years, with the interest in dance gradually mounting, Americans have brought to this country the greatest dancers of many nations. At the same time they have overlooked or completely ignored the dances of our native Indians, although our studies of earliest historical records, as well as of the best of their remaining dancing, leads us to believe that theirs was a dance art almost without equal in the rest of the world.

In Germany, where the modern dance received its greatest impetus, dance students were required to study the writings of George Catlin and of Maximilian for information on American Indian dance as the highest example of primitive art of any part of the world and essential to a thorough understanding of dance.

What other people have created as much interest as the Indians? What other people have been so emulated? Perhaps the reason the typical boyhood interest in Indians is not carried over into adulthood in America is that as we grow older and are faced with the crude historical portrayals of Indians we feel that our childhood interest was an illusion.

But civilization has progressed. We are, on the average, more tolerant of other peoples and other cultures than were our ancestors. The colonists and early settlers, as they moved across the continent, were completely satisfied with their own superiority over the "savages." Even the more tolerant among these early white Americans judged the Indians by their own standards, not the Indians'. Indian dancing was seldom understood or appreciated, but that here was a great American art worthy of understanding and of appreciation by all Americans there no longer can be any doubt.

To most Indian tribes, dancing, we are led to believe, was such an integral part of their lives that it is difficult for the average non-Indian American to understand its significance. Even in this day of increased interest in the dance, the public remains ill informed on this subject. However, in recent years, Indian art and arts and crafts have been gradually making their impressions upon us. Great Indian artists are winning recognition. Indian writers are coming to the fore; one recently won the Pulitzer prize for literature. Indian jewelry from the Southwest, as well as pottery, basketry, and hand weaving, are in great demand.

We believe that the dance was the greatest of all their arts, for it combined all other art forms. We hope that soon all Americans will be awakened to a greater interest in this truly American art, for, as Walter Terry wrote in the *New York Herald-Tribune* following one of our concerts in New York, "indigenous America needs bow to no one in matters of dance mastery. The American Indian's dance vocabulary is as rich as that of any other dance system in the world."

THE SUPPRESSION OF INDIAN CULTURE

It may be that some of the people in early contact with Indians did realize something of the importance of dance in Indian society. For this very reason they would have made every effort to discourage or suppress it. Until the last few years it was believed that the only hope for the Indian was to "civilize" him according to our meaning of the term.

Dancing was one of the first aspects of his culture to come under attack. For many years missionaries, educators, and even the government frowned upon Indian dancing. The great Sun Dance of the Sioux and other Plains tribes was forcibly suppressed, at the point of arms, in the early 1880's. All Indian dancing was feared as "war dancing." Even better-informed people who realized something of its real significance recommended its suppression because thus, at one blow, the entire social, political, and religious life of a tribe could be crushed. Dancing was the most Indian thing about Indians. The government wanted to destroy all tribal organization, everything Indian, and so struck at the dancing first of all.

Article No. 4 of the *Regulations of the Indian Office*, effective April 1, 1904, regarding Courts of Indian offenses, stated:

The "sun dance," and all other similar dances and so-called religious ceremonies, shall be considered "Indian offenses," and any Indian found guilty of being a participant in any one or more of these "offenses" shall . . . be punished by withholding from him his rations . . . or by incarceration in the agency prison. . . .

The regulations went on to list as other offenses Indian marriage customs, practice of "Indian medicine," even mourning customs. Actually, similar regulations had been in effect much earlier than 1904, but had never been printed. These regulations were not entirely repealed until 1934, when John Collier became commissioner of Indian Affairs.

We were adopted into Chief One Bull's family on the Standing Rock Sioux Reservation shortly after the bans on dancing had been removed. My Indian "sister," Hinto Agliwin (Brings Home a Blue Horse), told us just after the adoption ceremonies, "When they stopped our dancing we died. We stopped living. We felt there was nothing left to live for. Now we can dance again and it brings sunshine into our hearts. We feel j-u-s-t good!"

That is how important dancing was! To Indians it was not just recreation or relaxation. It was the way of life. During the bans more than a generation had been effectively removed from direct contact with the dance.

During this period, to be sure, Indians were occasionally granted permission to dance for fairs, rodeos, and Wild West shows; on white man's holidays, such as Fourth of July—Independence Day! Indians over forty years of age, that is, were given such permission. They were considered hopeless; it was already too late to civilize them. Young people were never granted permission to dance.

During these times, there were a few white people who sympathized with the Indians and did not sanction the intolerant attitude of the government. We knew an old trader who had formerly been an Indian agent for the Utes, but resigned because he could not agree with government policy. As agent he not only refused to stop all the dancing but encouraged it. Even the Sun Dance was held in some out-of-the-way place on the reservation, and he did nothing to interfere with it. He said they were better people for being permitted to retain their own customs.

Indian friends told us that when they went off to school they could not graduate before they had promised never to take part in Indian dances and ceremonies or to revert to any of the "savage practices" of their people. Naturally, few of them ever completely observed these promises. However, the most unhappy Indians on the reservations are those who attended the old Indian schools. They returned to their people neither Indian nor white. And so the old culture gradually died out and with it the majority of the dances.

We have a list, written in Lakota and given to us by Charley Brave years ago at Pine Ridge, South Dakota, of thirty-five dances once known to his people. He was an old man, but some of these dances had never been done in his day. Even before the government restrictions, Indian life was changing rapidly and with it the dances. But when we consider that at one time this one tribe, the Sioux, had such a number and variety of dances and that today they do only parts of three or four, and these on rare occasions, we can realize what a tremendous wealth of material has already disappeared. The same holds true for tribes all over the country, with the possible exception of a few in the Southwest.

Even in the Southwest an effort was made to prohibit the dancing during the 1920's. For the first time since the rebellions against the Spaniards in 1680 and 1696, the Pueblo Indians threatened to take up arms rather than give up their ancient ceremonies. Friends of the Indians finally prevailed upon Congress to have the Indian Office orders rescinded.

Since the lifting of the old restrictions, Indians have been allowed to dance when and as they please. But the change of heart on the part of the government has come almost too late. Most of the old religious and ceremonial dances and many of the artistic skills have now passed away. For a period of fifty years, on the few occasions when Plains and Woodland people danced at all, they did mostly social dances or "white man's dances." The Rabbit Dance and Indian Two Step are imitations of the white man's manner of dancing. The change-over from true Indian to this recent version is quite startling, to say the least.

The Cherokees of North Carolina no longer do any of their traditional dances. The last were given about 1946. To be sure, they still do an Eagle Dance in their big annual pageant, *Unto These Hills,* but it is largely a Broadway-type number that no old-time Cherokee would ever recognize. The Cherokees have become proficient in square dancing and once took first place in a national competition. Square dancing is quite similar to some of their old-time native social dancing. In Oklahoma today there are several Indian dances being done which are definitely versions of square dances.

Years ago, on our very first visit to the Pine Ridge Reservation, in South Dakota, we were introduced to a young missionary. When he learned that our purpose there was to learn what we could about Indian dancing, he remarked that he thought it was a worthwhile project, that something ought to be done to keep a record of the old ways and dances, but that the sooner the Indians gave them up the better off they would be.

"Why do you say that?" we asked.

"Because the dances keep them away from more important things. A dance never lasts just an evening, or even a day, but every time they have one it lasts for days. They travel miles to go to one of these affairs. They leave their livestock and crops unattended, and, besides, the dances are immoral," he replied.

"Where do you find these immoral dances?" we inquired. "We have been to a number of dances already and haven't seen anything out of the way."

He seemed quite shocked that we would expect him to go to an Indian dance. "I've never been to one," he said. "But I know they are immoral from the reports I get."

At the time of this incident there were no crops and no livestock on the Pine Ridge Reservation and not much in the entire states of North and South Dakota, for it was during the great drought. Most of the Indian cattle had died for lack of grass and water, and the crops had withered almost before they came up. It has been our experience that when Indians do have crops or livestock they leave someone in charge when the rest of the family goes off to a "doings." Of course, there are some irresponsible persons among Indians, as among any people.

As far as immorality at the dances is concerned, the nearest thing to it was at the "white man's dances," which the Indians were encouraged to attend. When the Indian speaks of white man's dances, he means just that. He does not consider Rabbit Dance or Indian Two Step as such, because he developed them himself. But on the same night that an *Indian* dance was being held, a "white man's dance" might have been going on nearby. There they did whatever was the popular dance of the day. That is where the liquor flowed and the young people got into trouble. We have seen almost no drinking at the real Indian dances, whether Sioux, Crow, Cheyenne, Arapaho, or in the Indian towns in Oklahoma.

Even today, Indians do not go to a traditional dance entirely for a good time. Although most of the dancing is social in nature and much of the old significance has been lost, a dance is still an opportunity for a social, political, and religious meeting all in one. The dance often opens with a prayer by some old man or woman, and during intermissions there are usually speeches on matters concerning tribal welfare.

Observation and study of the dances in earlier days might have revealed the very soul of the people, for they were at one and the same time the focal point of all their material culture and the highest expression of their mystical yearnings. The making or doing of any beautiful thing was a kind of prayer, a method of appealing to or communicating with the surrounding spiritual forces, of placing oneself in harmony with the great controlling power of the universe.

From this standpoint, all Indian artistic expression might be regarded as sacred. Every act of the day, every event of life, was strung on a sort of invisible chain of prayer. That prayer was expressed visibly through the painting on the Indian's face, the designs on his costumes and equipment and through his songs, his ceremonies, and his dances. The dance was the culmination of all other artistic endeavor and consequently the most important of all, for it combined all other art forms. Music, painting, sculpture, motion, rhythm, color, story, history, legend, poetry, drama—all were included in the dance. A dance of men on earth was a dramatization, a panto-mime, of the actions of the spirits above. Life was dancing, dancing was life.

Caleb Atwater, writing of his observations among the Indians of the Great Lakes region in 1829, compared Indian dancing to the Greek and Roman theaters.[4] Not many early observers were as understanding or as favorably impressed with Indian dancing, but, although Atwater was a commissioner sent by the government to make a survey of land, he happened to have a keen interest in the Indians as people and did not let his "civilized" prejudices stand in his way.

Considering the many years of continual suppression of Indian dance, it is little wonder that no great Indian dancers have appeared before the public in this type of presentation or that the average American has such queer ideas about this aspect of Indian art. Doubtless the Indians themselves never regarded dancing as art. Art and dance were customary parts of their lives, almost like breathing. We feel that the only way the dancing will be preserved will be through public interest, because so much of it has already lost its significance and importance to the Indians them-selves.

So far, they have been unable to project their dancing as art. In Oklahoma especially, but also in other areas, there is quite a revival of the so-called "war dancing," but it is entirely of a social nature and many of the dancers seem to strive to outdo each other in incorporating foreign movements and wearing overly ornate costumes. The beautiful dignified costumes of the past are seldom seen.

Nevertheless, interest in the dancing is continually growing, and in the past few years a regular "powwow" circuit has developed, which the best and most interested dancers of various tribes attend. Such powwows are held all summer long, and are actually a circuit, one following the other across many reservations. This in itself is encouraging and shows that Indian dancing is far from dead. But it is mainly "war dancing," and so far little effort has been made to revive other dances, which would be even more important from an artistic standpoint.

It is good to know that there is now some effort to encourage the young people to take an interest in the more important aspects of their own great heritage, towards an understanding and appreciation of the best of their own culture.

In the past few years a new attitude has developed in the Bureau of Indian Affairs, even to the extent of instituting courses in "acculturational psychology" in the Indian schools. It is heartening, but also rather pathetic and ironic, that now the old lore is nearly gone the government is encouraging the Indians to appreciate their own cultural values. We feel honored to have had some part in the new acculturation program by being invited to perform at a number of Indian schools and youth and tribal conferences and by our films on Indian dance and culture, produced by the University of Oklahoma, being used on various reservations to aid in the over-all project.

We hope the Indians themselves come to an understanding of dancing as an art and produce it and develop it as such. We hope, also, in succeeding chapters, to help other Americans appreciate this ancient American art form, for, as Walter Terry says, "if it does not belong to us by blood heritage it belongs to us through the heritage of the land itself."

SIOUX DANCES, RECORDED BY MA'ZA HO WASTE — CHARLEY BRAVE

1.	Peji wacipi	Grass Dance
2.	Skáyuha wacipi	White Horse Dance
3.	Iwakicipi	Scalp Dance
4.	Tokala wacipi	Fox Dance
5.	Suńka wacipi	Horse Dance
6.	Kangiyuha wacipi	Crow Owners' Dance
7.	Wi'ciska wacipi	White Marked Dance
8.	Cantetinza Wacipi	Brave Heart Dance
9.	Hańwacipi	Night Dance
10.	Hinhanjuwapa wacipi	Owl Feather Dance
11.	Winwanyank wacipi	Sun Dance
12.	Jiyowacipi	Prairie Chicken Dance
13.	Tatanwacipi	Buffalo Dance
14.	Wiwośte wacipi	Love Song Dance
15.	Katela wacipi	Warrior Dance
16.	Sotakayu wacipi	(No translation given)
17.	Ihoka wacipi	Badger Dance
18.	Owanka onasto wacipi	Preparation Dance
19.	Wakan wacipi	Medicine Dance
20.	Wanbliwacipi	Eagle Dance
21.	Aojanjan wacipi	Fire Dance
22.	Tekahapi wacipi	Wounded Dance
23.	Hinhankaha wacipi	Witch Dance
24.	Iyuptala wacipi	(A society, like Grass Dance)
25.	Hunka wacipi	Pipe Dance
26.	Heyoka wacipi	Clown Dance
27.	Nazunpeyuha wacipi	Tomahawk Dance
28.	Ptehinpte ptecila wacipi	Short Hair Dance
29.	Cehohomni wacipi	Feast Dance
30.	Śiyotankayuha wacipi	Whistle Carrier Dance
31.	Cunyuzeyuha wacipi	Forked Spit Dance
32.	Cinśkayuha wacipi	Spoon Carrier Dance
33.	Wanagi wacipi	Ghost Dance
34.	Maśtincala wacipi	Rabbit Dance
35.	Wakicicuwa wacipi	Charity Dance

PART II. **Music, Masks, and Paint**

7. Music and Instruments

Many of the historical observers quoted earlier mentioned the importance of music and of body and facial painting as adjuncts to the dancing. An understanding of these subjects will bring about a fuller appreciation of the dances which are to follow.

SINGING

No Indian would ever think of dancing without the proper song to accompany him. It would be impossible to separate song from dance, and it would be difficult to answer the old question which came first, music or dance. But it is certain that, even today, Indians are continually composing new songs for dances established long ago.

Many Indians now have tape recorders and enjoy recording songs of their own people and of other tribes at Indian "doings." One of our Kiowa friends obtained recordings of us singing Indian songs and tells us that he listens to them every day because they make him "feel good."[*]

But there was no such thing as a tape recorder during the period when we lived with the old-timers. The only available equipment was for disks—heavy, bulky, expensive, and dependent upon electricity. Most of the homes we stayed in were far from the agencies, and the Indians were lucky to have coal-oil lamps. We learned many of our songs the hard way, as the Indians do, by listening to them and singing along with the singers—only Indians are much faster at it than we are. They have remarkable memories and often can learn a song, even from a different tribe, by hearing it sung only a few times (see page 192).

Curtis reported that at Nambé Pueblo singers went to the river to bathe, and while there each singer placed a pebble under his tongue, which he kept there during the singing and dancing to help him remember the songs. If one lost his pebble, he had to report to the *cacique*, take another bath, and select another pebble.

Singing is one Indian art that is not dying out, although on the Plains some of the old manner of singing is gone, as are many of the old songs. Fortunately we learned some of these old songs, and our Indian friends tell us that we sing like the old people used to sing. "Too hard to sing that way," they say.

---

[*]Alice Fletcher made a profound study of Omaha and Pawnee music many years ago, and many other writers have contributed to the subject in recent years. Frances Densmore probably did the most to record, analyze, and interpret the music of many tribes. She has contributed reports from all the culture areas. She began with cylindrical wax records in 1909 and did her last recordings in the late 1950's with the most modern equipment.

The Smithsonian Institution can furnish a list of sources for Indian recordings.

Indians are constantly passing songs back and forth and composing new songs. Even in Bartram's time he said that the Cherokees had to have at least one new song for every annual presentation of the Busk (Green Corn Dance). In a contest among the Senecas, a man could make up a new song by the time the drum went around the circle and came back to him. Indians still have such contests today.

Speck, speaking of the Cayugas of Canada, said, "As for dance songs, it would be no exaggeration to say that almost five hundred, in a dozen chant series, have been heard in a single night of ceremonial festivity lasting about ten hours."[1]

Indians also take songs from other people and adapt them to their own use. Senecas still sing old popular songs, such as "Barney Google," "Red Wing," and "There'll be a Hot Time in the Old Town Tonight," in Seneca style so that they are hardly recognizable to non-Indians.

We have heard our Lakota friends on the Standing Rock Reservation sing "Indian Love Call" from *Rose Marie* and "Pale Moon" as Round Dance songs. One had to listen carefully to recognize them, but there they were!

Indians sing in unison, not in harmony. When women are called in to assist with the singing, which they do on many occasions, they sing an octave higher than the men.

The songs may sound strange to unaccustomed ears. Usually they are sung in a high, sometimes falsetto, voice, with a quaver, or tremolo, which white people think is bad. But the Indian likes this way of singing and strives to accomplish it. He says that the white man sings in his ordinary speaking voice, which to most tribes is just short of sacrilege. All songs, even humorous ones, are regarded in a certain religious light; the Indian sings in a high, quavering voice, the nearer to approach the strange world of the spirit, which is the true realm of song. Seneca singers refused to let a large recording company make records, even of funny or social songs, because of the sacred nature of all songs. They did not think it right to "make money on them."

Old-timers sang, to modern ears, "off key," which means that they used more notes, comparable in a way to the many-toned scales of the Orient, making it impossible to transcribe the songs accurately with the present system of musical notation. That they had their own standards of intonation and melody cannot be doubted, for, strange as the songs may sound to us, they were repeated the same way every time. Frances Densmore indicated these shadings of tones with notes on the five-line staff marked with plus or minus signs, showing that they sounded a trifle sharp or flat to European-American ears.

Miss Densmore recorded a Sioux journey song in 1911, when she was doing her work on the Standing Rock Reservation. At the World's Fair in Chicago in 1933 she found some of the same singers at the Indian Village and wanted to learn something about how the songs were retained or changed and asked them to sing the journey song again. The song sounded the same—even the key and tempo—but when partway through it, the leader made a couple of deep groaning sounds that certainly were not there before. Miss Densmore asked them to sing the song again, eliminating the extra sounds, for she wanted to get a good recording of it, comparable to the original of years before, and they willingly obliged her. Then, curious, she asked what the intrusive noises were.

They explained to her that recently they had gone to Europe with a wild west show, and when the ship was about to leave the harbor, the big whistle blew and frightened some of them almost to death. So they took the old journey song and added new words to it, which meant, as they explained it in English, "Don't let your heart go flutter when the boat holler," and the leader added the very realistic rendition of the boat whistle itself with a deep sounding, "Boeep, boeep!"

When we visited Miss Densmore one time, she played the record for us. We thought it most interesting and refreshing, and she said that she would give us a copy but that personally she did not like it at all. It was amusing and a good example of the way Indian songs are sometimes passed along, the original meaning lost, but the song still serving a definite purpose.

Many people think that Indian songs are in a minor key, but actually they have been analyzed as both major and minor, with the major predominating. They invariably start high and progress downward. Most of them have a short range, but occasionally the opposite is true. One Lakota song we know encompasses seventeen tones, according to our scale.

Of course, the Indians had no system of notation, if we except the mnemonics on birchbark among some of the Woodland tribes. These were not true musical notation, but symbols to recall songs to the minds of the singers. They were passed on, with their interpretations, from one generation to another. Nevertheless, students have found that Indian songs can be transcribed, not accurately, but very well, in accepted musical notation. The songs can also be analyzed as to key and mode, which of course the Indians did not understand either.

Often people are impressed with the wildness of Indian music. It is only natural that there should be an element of wildness in it, for they had the voices of nature, the animals and birds, the wind in the trees, the lapping of waves upon the shore, for their inspiration. Speck wrote that he had "never heard more beautiful melodies or sweeter sounding male voices in unison" than those he had listened to in the Long House.

The talents of no trained musicologist . . . can adequately transcribe the intangible qualities they possess or convey by a modern system of notation an adequate notion of the emotional effect of the melodies chanted through the winter night by a chorus of Iroquois singers.[2]

William Wood, writing 1629–34, said:

Their musick is lullabies to quiet their children who generally are as quiet as if they had neither spleene or lungs. To heare one of these Indians unseene, a good ear might easily mistake their untaught voyce for the warblings of a well tuned instrument. Such command have they of their voices.[3]

We are sure students of other Indian music, including ourselves, could say the same thing.

Most Indian songs have few or no words, merely syllables or vocables being used to carry the tune. For the tune is usually the important thing. Indians can tell by the tune, its melody and rhythm, just what kind of a song it is. However, when words are used they may be very important, and one word may be the symbol to represent a complete thought which would require an entire sentence in English for its translation.

An Indian was once asked, "What do you think of white men's songs?"

The Indian thought a moment, then replied, "White man's song? They talk too much."

Even modern songs such as those for the Forty-niner Dance, sung in English, are yet satisfied with a few words, just a short sentence to carry the main idea.

Many of the songs are complicated when analyzed. Rhythm may change several times in one short song, although the drum may be beating in one steady tempo. In many of the old songs, the rhythm of the drum was at odds with the rhythms of the song itself, all of which made them very difficult to learn and very confusing to non-Indians. Alice Fletcher explained it by stating that "the beat governs the bodily movements; the song voices the emotion of the appeal."

Indians did not sing to please an audience but, as with the dance, for the pleasure of participating. There were songs for every occasion of life, whether large or small, happy or sad, important or unimportant. Songs marked every step of the way from the cradle to the grave.

One of the most impressive remembrances we have was hearing old Two Shields sing to the dawn. Almost a mile away we heard his voice faintly coming across the dimly lighted prairie one cold and frosty morning. The words were simply, "The dawn appears. Behold it!" Another time Makes Trouble strolled back and forth through the camp, wrapped in an old army blanket, singing his morning song in a strong, penetrating voice. It was hard to believe that these old men, surrounded by poverty, had anything to sing about, but they were still grateful for the beauty of the morning and the promise of a new day. With the passing of the old people we never again heard the songs to the dawn.

It has been said that Indians do not have work songs, but it depends upon what we consider work. Certainly they did not have laborers' songs, like the Negroes, but they had occupational songs. We have heard women singing as they made moccasins, and One Bull used to sing while making a new eagle-bone whistle or pecking on a stone for a war-club head. Men had many songs for times of making or renewing ceremonial equipment, weapons, and other "man's things." In the corn-raising areas there are songs not only for planting and harvesting, but for cultivation and grinding the ripened grain. Adair wrote:

About an hour after sunrise, they enter the field agreed on by lot, and fall to work with great cheerfulness. Sometimes one of their orators cheers them with jests and humorous old tales, and sings several of their most agreeable wild tunes, beating also with a stick in his right hand, on the top of an earthen pot covered with a wet and well-stretched deer-skin thus they proceed from field to field, till their seed is sown.[4]

Often an individual might have the impulse to sing, so he picked up his drum and did so. Sometimes a small group gathered, just for the pleasure of singing together. Among the Crows and other Plains tribes, young people form a group and go around the camp at night serenading, boys and girls banding together. No drum is used, but the songs, designated by the Indians as serenade songs, are in the category of women's songs, in 3/4 time. When the serenaders stop in front of your tipi you are supposed to give them a present—food or tobacco—or they will sing for you most of the night. One time all that we could find to give them was a box of crackers. How they laughed! Crackers for throats already dry from long singing!

Although the serenaders are singing to other people, in no case can we imagine Indians singing, as in non-Indian concerts, exclusively to please an audience.

If you wish to learn a particular song, or record it, Indians insist that you go to someone whom they designate as a "good singer." We wanted to learn what is often called the Sioux National Anthem, or Flag Song. Everyone knew it and sang it at tribal gatherings, but when we wanted one of our close friends to teach it to us, she said, "You should get Red Legs to teach you that song."

We were about to drive out to find his cabin when we spied him coming over the hill, walking, carrying a sack over his shoulder. He reminded us of the story of Iktomi, the Spider Man, Sioux culture hero, carrying his bag of songs on his back. We waited until he got down to the road, then asked him, "Will you teach us the Flag Song?"

He replied, "By and by sometime. I been singin' all night for big dance and throat all sore."

"How far away do you live?" we asked.

"'Bout eight o' nine mile 'long this road," he answered.

So we offered to make a bargain. If he would just sing the song softly to us as we rode along, so he would not strain his voice, we would take him home.

"Okay," he replied eagerly, and got in the car.

So he sang the song and repeated it many times as we drove along. Later we made a final check with Jerome Standing Soldier, one of the best singers in the Fort Yates district, and that is how we learned the Sioux National Anthem.

Its words translate, "Grandfather, I love your country, and your war bonnet will wave above the earth forever."

The melody is sung first in vocables, then with the words. "Grandfather" is a term of respect, in this case representing not only the government, but our entire nation and all the people in it. The war bonnet, of course, is the American flag.

On one occasion we sang this song for the Indian Council Fire in Chicago, and Indians of many tribes in the audience all rose to their feet, just as any other audience would do if hearing "The Star Spangled Banner." Although this is a Sioux song, the *type* is familiar to many tribes, so even if they did not understand the words they recognized it as a patriotic song and stood up.

One time we were invited to a dance at Pine Ridge and as usual arrived early. Only the singers were present. We had seen them shortly before, walking along the road, their drumsticks tucked in their hip pockets. Now they were singing softly to themselves around a big bass drum and we were listening when one of them spoke up and said, "One Bull, you come and sing for us," handing me a drumstick.

So I sat with them at the drum and sang a song of Sitting Bull's that I had learned on the Standing Rock Reservation. Sitting Bull was admired as a composer among his people; being able to compose songs was one of the marks of a rounded-out man. This song was one Sitting Bull sang often toward the end of his life. "Once a famous warrior I was. It is all over and now a hard time I have."

They laughed and laughed, slapping me on the back and on the knee. "Hau! Hau!" they cried out. The song struck home, for they were also having a hard time. "That's a good song you sing," they said. "That's old time. Sitting Bull sing that kind. Where did you get it?"

Most Indian songs are quite short and are repeated as many times as necessary for the occasion. Ceremonial songs are usually sung through four times at each singing, and as a rule they must be sung absolutely correctly, but other less important songs are allowed considerable freedom of expression, especially by those considered good singers. By expression we do not mean shading, but phrasing, use of words, tempo, and the like. Indian songs are usually sung with full force. The singer is "intent on expressing the fervor of his emotion," as Alice Fletcher wrote.

For all the changes in Indian cultures, much of their singing remains as it was long ago. Jonathan Carver wrote:

During this [dance] the company who are seated on the ground in a circle, around the dancer, join with him in making the cadence, by an odd tone, which they utter all together, and which sounds, "Heh, heh, heh." These notes, if they might be so termed, are articulated with a harsh accent, and strained out with the utmost force of their lungs; so that one would imagine their strength must be soon exhausted by it; instead of which, they repeat it with the same violence during the whole of their entertainment.[5]

In the singing at dances sometimes the voices sound strained, but there is strength and power. Often a singer holds his left hand to the side of his mouth to "throw" his voice, while another may put a finger in his left ear to keep out the din of the singer beside him. With several men around the drum, all striking it together, all singing at the top of their lungs, the stirring, throbbing pulse of the music vibrates right through you. Anyone who has experienced such excitement will not soon forget it.

For anyone interested in learning to sing the songs as the Indians sing them, all the study in the world of written transcriptions will not enable him to do so. There are qualities that cannot be notated. There is a manner of singing—a pulsation of the voice and other peculiarities—that can be experienced only by hearing Indians sing.

Navajos sing in the highest falsetto of any Indians we have heard. However, other Indians occasionally learn their songs. A Santo Domingo friend of ours once sang us a Coyote Song of the Navajo Yeibichai and sang it just as high as they do. He jumped on both feet as he sang, shaking a rattle in one hand and a coyote skin in the other. The song sounds like coyotes howling. That he could sing so high and jump so hard at the same time is difficult to believe. This was one of the most thrilling songs we have ever heard.

In contrast, Pueblo Indians sing more in what we would consider normal voices. Next to the Navajos, the Sioux singing is highest and wildest. All through the Middle West the voices are also high, no particular difference being noted from the Plains. But when we get to the East Coast, the voices again tend to be more nearly "normal," although there are still Indian characteristics different from anything in European-style music.

There are tribal as well as regional differences and mannerisms in singing, so slight that non-Indians seldom recognize them at all, but Indian singers can tell instantly whether it is, for instance, a Crow, Sioux, Kiowa, or Blackfoot song.

All Navajo singing impresses us as being quite nasal. The Sioux use a nasal quality in love songs, but not otherwise.

There are many classes of Indian songs, but these, too, often defy the understanding of untrained listeners. The Chief's Song, for instance, may be a song about chiefs, sung by chiefs, or sung to honor chiefs. War songs may pertain to going to war, being on the warpath, or actually meeting the enemy in battle; may relate war experiences; may ridicule the enemy; or may be songs of longing by those left at home or prayers for the safe return of the warriors. Even songs of peace following a war may be termed war songs. Medicine songs might pertain to a certain ceremony; might be for healing, protection from harm, or working magic; and could be personal, tribal, or belong to a society. For all songs are regarded as property, and when transferred to other ownership must be bought and paid for, just as dances and ceremonies are. Songs which belong to a ceremony of course are transferred with the ceremony as part of it.

The following may illustrate the importance of a song to a particular "medicine."

One day One Bull said he wanted to show us something, and he brought out an old flour sack. We were sitting in the shade of the big cottonwood trees near his cabin at Little Eagle. Reaching into the sack he pulled out a large square of yellow-dyed cloth with an elk head painted on it. We thought we were alone, but when we looked up we found that we were surrounded by Indians. Where they had come from or how they knew what was going on is hard to say, but as soon as the old man opened up the square of muslin there they were. They all wanted to see Sitting Bull's medicine as much as we did.

However, because so many people had collected, One Bull would not sing the song that went with it. He merely told us something about it. This was a copy of the original medicine, for his brother, Chief White Bull, had given the original to Walter Campbell, his adopted son. But One Bull felt that some reminder of it should still be with his family at Little Eagle. In copying it, however, he did not make an exact copy, as this is never done. The original has an entire elk painted upon it, facing left, outlined in green and with red spots on it.

This is the medicine with which Sitting Bull one time made a storm to drive away a large party of Crow warriors who had surrounded a few Sioux in a little draw. One Bull was with his uncle when this happened. The Crows set fire to the grass surrounding the draw and the willows were so dry they were sure to flash into flame and exterminate the Sioux right there or force them out into the open. Sitting Bull got out his medicine, sang his medicine song, and went through a brief little ceremony, ending by slapping the cloth four times on the ground. Almost immediately a severe thunderstorm came up, putting out the fire and frightening the Crows away. Sitting Bull also had used this medicine before announcing the "little rain" for the Sun Dance.

This is the *wotawe*, or war medicine, that gave Sitting Bull his reputation as a medicine man among the whites, but among the Sioux any man was allowed to own such a medicine, if fortunate enough to come into its possession.

Walter Campbell told us he once showed the medicine to some people on the French Riviera. They were complaining about a drought, and Walter rather jokingly remarked that he had an Indian medicine that would make it rain. He never learned the song that went with the painted cloth, but he waved it briskly in the air and suddenly the sky became dark and a terrible storm sent everyone scurrying for shelter. The Frenchmen thereafter crossed themselves every time they saw him and gave him a wide berth.

But possibly because he did not know the song, Walter had such bad luck while Sitting Bull's medicine was in his possession that he eventually gave it back to the family. Years after seeing the copy One Bull had made, Mini Ca'piwin and Magli, two of One Bull's daughters, showed us the original medicine. We were alone in the little log cabin this time and Mini Ca'piwin sang Sitting Bull's medicine song for us.[*] In this case she sang it merely to bring us all good luck. She made no maneuvers with the cloth. The words translate something like this: "*Wakan Tanka*, to him I am related. The sacred people are my friends. From a sacred place an elk is my friend. A sacred person is my friend."

We asked if we could make a sketch of the elk, and Magli said, "Yes, if you think your medicine is strong enough, you can." But we felt, because this was *wakan*, she was concerned for us and really did not want us to copy it, so we did not.

Sitting Bull's medicine was kept in a little painted cylindrical case, and the family recently gave it to the Sioux Indian Museum in Rapid City, South Dakota, where we last saw it.

Strangers have difficulty in understanding how a dancer knows when a song is really going to stop. The song may be repeated any number of times, so counting does no good; when it ends depends upon the singers. Perhaps we should say it

---

[*]The song was sung by One Bull for Frances Densmore and may be found in her "Teton Sioux Music." Sitting Bull's medicine is described in *New Sources of Indian History* by Stanley Vestal (Walter Campbell), published by the University of Oklahoma Press in 1934.

depends upon the song leader, or drum chief, for he is the one who gives the cues. As we listen carefully, when a song is started the leader sings a phrase first alone, then the other singers chime in, repeating the phrase and singing the entire song through to the end. But, before it is actually finished, the leader begins his introduction again, overlapping the other singers as they draw to the end of the song. As long as the leader does this toward the end, the dancers know there is to be another repeat. Otherwise they know it is the last time through and are ready to put their flourishes at the end and come to a sudden halt on the last beat of the drum.

Also, there is usually another cue, quite decided at least among the Sioux. On the last time through, the singers strike the drum more softly, in unaccented beats, then build up to a loud climax for the last beat. This signal may be five, seven, or nine beats so it sounds something like this: ONE, two, ONE, two, one, two, three, four, five, six, seven, eight, *One*, two *three, four, FIVE*.

Most Sioux Grass Dance and Round Dance songs do have a few words. These come in only one small part of the song, and often the song is sung through once in vocables only, then the words appear in the second rendition. All vocables, then vocables and words are alternated in this fashion during the repetitions of the song. And, as we mentioned for Rabbit Dance, sometimes a Rabbit Song is sung through first in vocables only, the second time in Lakota words, the third time in vocables again, and the fourth time in English.

The Stomp Dance songs of the East and Southeast are antiphonal and give one the impression of having an African relationship. A leader sings a short phrase, which is echoed by the chorus of dancers, and this is kept up through the dance. Perhaps these songs were influenced by runaway slaves, many of whom took refuge in Indian camps; some of the Indians themselves were slave owners in Colonial times. These songs have a "swing" to them that we do not find in other Indian music.

The Winnebagos have songs comparable to our ballads, sung about tribal or legendary heroes, with verse after verse. To most tribes a verse would be merely exchanging one or two new words in the worded part of the song.

Indians have often been portrayed as having harsh speaking voices, but we have found their voices to be most pleasant. When among themselves, at home or at a gathering, both men and women usually speak so softly that we have to listen carefully to hear them.

If any loud talking needs to be done, a crier or master of ceremonies is engaged to do the announcing. In the old days, a warrior recounting his coups could also throw his voice with such power and force that he could be heard distinctly by a large gathering, but that was a matter of training his voice, much as great singers do, rather than of straining and screaming. We used to enjoy listening to old Bull-over-the-Hill when he woke up the whole Crow camp before sunrise with his harangues on proper living.

To be sure, there are gutturals and nasal tones in many Indian languages (as there are in many non-Indian languages), but this does not make them unpleasant to listen to. Indians have always been extremely "fussy" in their use of speech, and one of the biggest complaints of the older people today is that the young people are not using their languages properly.

Caleb Atwater, the United States commissioner sent to treat with Indians of the Upper Mississippi in 1829, wrote of the women's voices:

While scolding, their voices are disagreeable, as harsh and as grating on the ear, as can be imagined; whereas, when good nature prevails, as it generally does, no earthly sounds can be more harmonious, more soft, more soothing, more melodious. As there is more elasticity in the mind of the female, than in the mind of the male, so there is in their voices, which can either grate harsh thunder, or produce sounds as agreeable as the music of the spheres.

He found the tunes of most of the Indian songs dull and monotonous, "Yet, even such tunes sung by some clear, soft and melodious voices, both of males and especially of females, the music in them is quite agreeable and even enchanting."[6]

Atwater was evidently a cultured, well-educated man, who was so interested in Indian music that he intended to transcribe some of the songs. So he prevailed upon the chief of one of the villages to procure for him a table, chair, pen, ink, and paper, which must have been quite a project in a community where few yet had these white man's things. But the chief obtained them from someplace and seemed to be delighted that Atwater was so interested. Atwater became even more interested in the general festivities and the dancing, however, and never wrote down a single word or a note. He even joined the Indians in some of the dancing, which pleased them so much that they completely overlooked his not using the table and materials they had brought him.

Making a record of the music became a much easier matter by the end of the century, with the development of the phonograph. Poor as it was compared to the wonderful machines we have today, it was much faster and easier than transcribing songs by hand, and so much more accurate.

Atwater is the one who compared Indian dances to the Greek and Roman theaters, believing the Indians to be better actors, speakers, dancers, and singers than were those ancients. Comparing Greek music to Indian, he said, "The music, read it as you will, either backward or forward is not one whit better than the Winnebagoes possess now." Again he wrote, "What nature had done for man in giving him musical powers, the Winnebagoes showed us at Prairie Du Chien, in July and August of 1829."[7]

But the Italian, Count Arese, was not quite as well impressed. He wrote:

A quarter of an hour after our departure the savage began a song of departure . . . and if I hadn't had a sample of Sioux music the night before, I should have thought my guide was going mad or was taken with cholera. The savages have several songs that they call by bizarre names: for instance, the song of the bull, of the eagle, the bear, of death, war, departure, arrival. It is not that a given song sings the praises of the bull or the bear, or that there is any imitation of the noises they make, but simply that one melody (since they call such howling melody) is dedicated to the merits of a certain animal or event. Generally their songs have no words: and those that have are made up of only four or five repeated over and over, as for instance: "I arrive, open the door for me, open, open, open, open the door for me, open the door for I arrive." and so on until the voice gives out.[8]

Catlin tells of his Indians in Europe attending a concert by a famous soprano in Paris. Afterward, one of the Indians said to her, through an interpreter, "You have a beautiful voice. It sounds just like a coyote." This, to him, was the highest compliment he could pay her.

INSTRUMENTS

Indians of North America had many musical instruments, most of them percussion, some wind, but no strings, except the Apache fiddle, which is believed to have been developed after the coming of the Spaniards, and the musical bow of California, which can hardly be regarded as a musical instrument. It was an ordinary hunter's bow, which in California was extremely short, some just over three feet in length. It was held straight out, string up, one end in the player's mouth. The string was tapped with the nail of the index finger and the melody made by changing the size of the oral cavity.[9] The effect was something like a Jew's harp. The player sometimes played lying down, as this type of music was mainly diversion.

Most songs were accompanied by some sort of rhythm-producing instrument, but north of Mexico there seems to have been no combination of instruments which could be considered an orchestra. Among most tribes a group of singers served in its place.

Because of the spiritual nature attributed to music, drums and rattles too were believed to have great power. The drum represented all of life's forces and its rhythm was symbolical of the rhythm of the entire universe, the heart throb of all creation.

Drum rhythms among Plains and Woodland tribes are usually simple and yet must be executed precisely by the singers or there is complaint on the part of everyone listening and especially from the dancers. An outsider would never detect the slight differences that Indians recognize.

In the Southwest rhythms are often extremely complicated. But if the singers or dancers make a mistake they are whipped with yucca switches.

For men's dances, such as Grass or "War" dances, the rhythm is usually steady or slightly accented 2/4 time. Sometimes the drum is struck steadily in half time, that is, every other beat. We have given some mention to the rhythm used in women's dances. Never have we heard, on any reservation in our many travels among Indians, the usual conception of an "Indian" rhythm, the loudly accented beat followed by three softer ones: *One*, two, three, four. This seems to be another contribution of non-Indian musicians with more imagination than fact at their disposal.

DRUMS

Drums consisted of anything from a board beat with a stick to beautifully made ceremonial drums with painted rawhide heads and beaded skirts, hung from elabo-

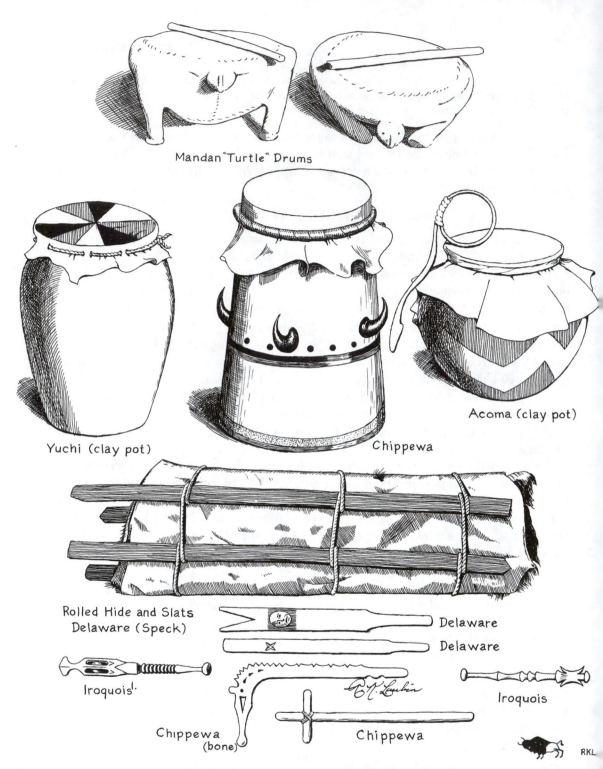

Mandan "Turtle" Drums

Yuchi (clay pot)

Chippewa

Acoma (clay pot)

Rolled Hide and Slats
Delaware (Speck)

Delaware

Delaware

Iroquois!

Chippewa
(bone)

Chippewa

Iroquois

RKL

Drums and beaters. Top row: Mandan "turtle" drums (from a photograph by Edward S. Curtis). Second row: left, Yuchi clay-pot drum (after Frank G. Speck); center, Chippewa *midé* water drum, decorated with black-bear claws, in the Field Museum of Natural History, Chicago; right, Acoma clay-pot drum and beater (after Frances Densmore). Third row: Delaware drum of rolled deer hide and slats (after Speck). Fourth row: drum beaters, Iroquois (one after Speck, one in the Rochester, New York, Museum of Arts and Sciences); two Delaware (after Speck); a Chippewa *midé* beater of bone, in the National Museum of History and Technology, Smithsonian Institution, Washington, D.C.; and a simple Chippewa beater.

rately decorated stakes. In some of the oldest ceremonies the drum was merely a rolled hide, sometimes with wooden slats roped to it, which was struck in time with the singing. Utes made a drum for some of their ceremonies by sewing together two large buffalo hides, then stretching them taut and drying them. Slits were cut at intervals around the edge and thongs to serve as handholds inserted. Both men and women stood around this "drum," each holding a thong in the left hand and beating on the hide with a stick.

Hand games in the Northwest were usually accompanied by beating on boards raised off the ground an inch or so. Supporting sticks were first laid on the ground and the boards were placed upon them.

A favorite stunt of the Boy Scout Indian dancers is to dance on a large drum, five or six feet across. No Indian tribe we ever heard of did this. It started a number of years ago when Jaques Cartier, a famous concert dancer, performed a Haitian voodoo dance on such a drum. Later he was engaged to do an "Indian" dance in the motion picture *Rose Marie,* and so he wore Indian costume and transferred an Indian-type dance to the big drum for spectacular effect. Some Scout leader saw the picture, and it has been popular ever since. Nowadays the Scouts usually do an Eagle Dance on the big drum.

The only references we have found to foot drums are from California. There at least two tribes did dance on drums. According to Densmore, the Maidus used half of a hollow sycamore log five or six feet long placed over a trench. A dancer played this drum by dancing on it in time to the song. Sometimes two or three men also beat upon it with heavy sticks or clubs at the same time.[10]

Split- or hollow-log drums were also known in Mexico and South America, as well as in the South Pacific. The Aztecs had a similar drum made of stone.

The Maidus also used the board drum described above and sometimes held a short board in the left hand, resting it on the lower arm in a horizontal position while striking it with a stick held in the right hand.

The Makahs of California also used a board drum, but they arranged the boards to form three sides of a square. According to our friend George Stoddard, who spent some time with the Miwoks of California some years ago, they came nearest to dancing on a real drum. An oblong hole was dug in the ground, eighteen to twenty-four inches deep, and over this a green hide was pegged on opposite sides, leaving openings of eight or ten inches on either end. When the hide dried it made a very resonant drum, and he said the dancer danced on it in an odd sort of three-beat rhythm. As further accompaniment several men also shook split rattles, or clappers, in time with the song. These were made of elderberry shoots about a foot long, split almost their entire length and the pith scraped out, bound with rawhide or bark for about two inches at the lower end to keep them from splitting all the way. A clapper was held in each hand and shaken in a jerky manner so that the two sides slapped together.

It is difficult to learn just what drums were like in the East. Early explorers usually passed them over as "rude." John Smith said they made a drum of a "wooden platter," over which they stretched a hide:

They cover the mouth thereof with a skin, at each corner they tie a walnut, which meeting on the backside neere the bottome, with a small rope they twitch them togither till it be so taught and stiffe that they may beat upon it as upon a drumme.[11]

Occasionally in recent times we have seen drums made of wooden chopping bowls. Maybe Captain Smith's drum was something similar, or perhaps it was even a water drum, for to this day the heads of Peyote drums, which use an iron kettle for a shell, are fastened by tying to marbles attached to the skin in the same way. The Peyote religion was introduced on the Southern Plains from Mexico, and so water drums must have been used there too. Some Plains tribes used water drums of various kinds, and we know that the water drum was used all over the East and the Middle West.

As far as we know, it is the really native drum, indigenous to America. Old ones were made of hollow logs, with a plug or disk in the bottom to hold water. For many years the Iroquois have been making water drums of tiny kegs, or firkins, and fastening the heads in place with iron hoops made by their own blacksmiths. The drums are small enough to be held in the hand, as are some of the Cherokee water drums. Some Cherokees learned the cooper's trade and made their own kegs. The last old man to do so was John Walking Stick, and we bought several of his drums before it was too late. The Cherokees preferred the skin of a woodchuck for the drumhead, for it is thin but very tough.

Chippewa water drums were much larger than the Eastern type, a foot or more in height with heads eight or ten inches across. A few Cherokee drums were of such a size. Such drums were too large to be held in the hand and so were rested upon the ground—not set flat, but tilted, so that only a corner touched the ground. Otherwise they would suffer a loss of resonance. Chippewas and other Lake Indians used tanned buckskin for the head. The single head on all these log or keg drums is held in place by a hoop of some kind, the drum shell being larger at the bottom than at the mouth, the slight taper making it possible to tighten the hoop securely.

Some accounts say the drum should be half full of water. No one who ever saw Indians prepare a water drum would say this. The Seminoles use only two *mouthfuls* for their little drums. A cup would be plenty for an average Cherokee drum. The wooden water drum has a small bunghole through which water can be added or drained, the tone being partially adjusted in this way. The water serves mainly to keep the head wet. A small amount serves as a resonator, but too much has the opposite effect and kills the tone. Indians spend a good deal of time tuning a water drum. When it is finally right, the end of each beat clanks like a little bell. Such a drum, although seeming not to make much noise, has such penetrating vibrations that it can be heard for two or three miles through woodland and as much as ten miles across open water.

Playing the water drum. Note that the drum is tipped, not flat on the ground.

Perhaps the main reason the water drum was popular in the East is that the wetter the head the better the tone. In a damp climate this is something to consider, for the rawhide heads on other drums go "flat" and lifeless when damp. A rawhide drum is as good a weather prophet as some of the most modern instruments and will surely predict a coming storm.

The water drum was often played near a fire, so that as the head dried out the tone rose higher and higher. Then it was tipped to splash the water on the head again and the tone dropped instantly back to its original level.

The water drum is just about the opposite of the ordinary drum in several respects. It has a soft leather head and must be wet to sound well. Also, it requires a hard stick. The rawhide drums must be very dry, the head is hard, so we use a soft beater—a stick padded on the end. Indians sometimes spend a great deal of time making carved and fancy drumsticks for their water drums. In some tribes the stick is more important than the drum, for the Indian says the drum is no good without the stick.

We know of no case in North America where any kind of drum was played with the hands, as in some other parts of the world.

The Peyote religion apparently came to the Kiowas and Comanches in the late 1870's, and their drum has been a little iron kettle with three legs, so it can be set on the ground without loss of vibration. The Indians buy these kettles and file off the ears for the bail. Since the kettles are now made entirely for Indian trade, it seems that the foundry would cast them without the ears! White buckskin is used for the head, which is laced on ceremonially before each meeting and removed again at the close of the meeting. Seven marbles are used for lacing the head to the kettle, and it must be done in such a way that a seven-pointed star is formed across the bottom. Yet it must be laced without overturning the drum, which would spill out the water, and there is no way of putting water in, once the head is in place. At the end of the ceremony the drum is turned upside down, showing the star.

Care is taken not to leave it turned over long enough to lose the water, for the head is then removed and the kettle passed around so that everyone may have a sip, the water having become holy because of its use in the ceremony. Now one can see that four little pieces of charcoal had been placed in the water before making up the drum. None of the written accounts of the Peyote rites that have come to our attention mention the charcoal, but people who have been present tell us this is so. They represent the four directions and symbolize peace, as they are the residue of former sacred fires—life, light, knowledge, and wisdom.

The technique of lacing the drum to marbles is the same as that used for fastening peg loops to the bottom of a tipi cover. It is an old Indian invention or discovery and probably the same as Captain John Smith saw in 1609. We have seen tipi peg loops fastened to pebbles, walnuts, pieces of corncob, chips of wood. Some reports mention that in the early days four pebbles were used for securing the water drum instead of the seven marbles, but seven is also a sacred number and enables one to apply more tension to the head. In tuning the kettle drum, a prong from a deer antler is used as a lever to tighten the cords. Once the head is in place and stretched as tightly as possible, a little hole is pricked in it to one side, near the rim, to release the air pressure. This has the same effect that the larger holes have in the shell of a rawhide drum.

Of course the Peyote drums are not dance drums, although it is believed that long ago dancing played a part in the original Peyote worship. Peyote in its present form came to the tribes near the end of the Buffalo Days when dancing was not only dying out on its own but was being discouraged by official circles. But the other water drums we have been talking about were used for many dances, being important ceremonial adjuncts to them.

In the Southeast and also the Southwest, both pottery-making areas, a water drum was often made of a clay pot, jar, or vase with a piece of buckskin tied tightly around the rim or lip. As a rule, in most tribes women were not supposed to play or handle drums, but in Acoma pueblo a girl played a pot drum in the Flower Dance, using a beater with a loop on the end, striking the edge of the loop.[12] Such a beater is common in the Southwest and is also used in the Apache Mountain Spirit Dance.

The Yaquis of southern Arizona and northern Mexico have about the most unusual drum of all. In their Deer Dance they use half of a large gourd inverted and floated in a pan of water. The drummer steadies the gourd with his left hand, lightly touching it with his fingers or holding it by an attached cord. With his right hand he strikes it with a supple stick wrapped with corn husks. The water is considered holy and is splashed on the spectators as part of the ceremony.

Mention will be made of the turtle drums formerly used in the Mandan Okipa. Someone told us that he had seen a drum in the South Pacific made from a real turtle or tortoise shell. The Seris, of western Mexico, beat on a sea turtle shell placed over a hole in the sand, but nowhere else have we heard of any drum connected with turtles. Rattles, yes, but not drums.

All drums, among Indians, were regarded as having sacred or mysterious power. So not just anyone could own, or even play, a ceremonial drum. The big dance drum—the "hung drum" mentioned earlier—was regarded as a personality and was in the keeping of a special officer, the Drum Keeper. In some tribes the drum was actually treated like a person, kept in the back of the lodge in the place of honor, and offered food and drink to support its spirit. Among the warrior tribes of the Plains only a man who had counted coup was allowed to strike the drum, so the "orchestra" was made up of outstanding individuals.

Generally speaking, Middle Western Woodlands and Plains Indians preferred dance or ceremonial drums about the size of bass drums, with two heads, laced together with rawhide thongs. Nowadays most of them do use bass drums, and they are not supported from four stakes, but usually placed right on the ground, with the singers sitting around them. At most modern gatherings the singers sit on chairs or benches; sometimes a few of them hold the drum off the ground to bring it within

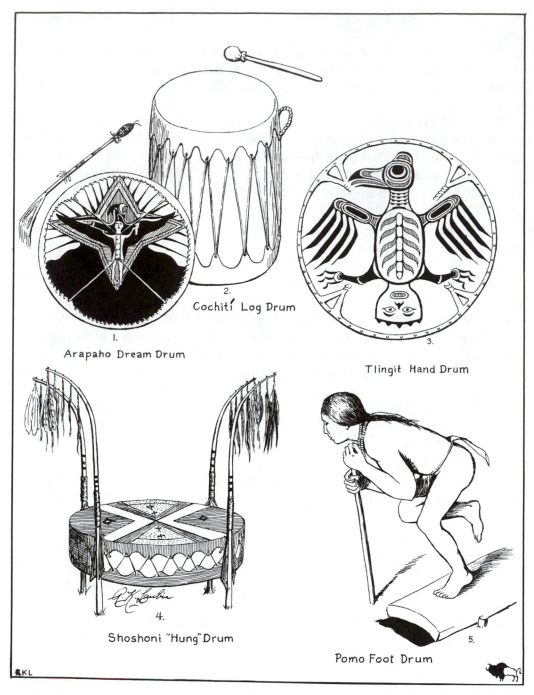

2. Cochití Log Drum

1. Arapaho Dream Drum

3. Tlingit Hand Drum

4. Shoshoni "Hung" Drum

5. Pomo Foot Drum

1. An Arapaho dream drum, painted on the inside to represent a vision. The outside is painted in a different design. The diameter is eighteen inches. 2. A Cochití drum made from a hollow cottonwood log. The diameter is sixteen inches, the height twenty-three inches. 3. A Tlingit (Northwest Coast) hand drum, also painted on the inside, in the National Museum. The diameter is twenty-four inches. 4. A Shoshoni "hung" drum, in the Field Museum. 5. A Pomo (California) foot drum of wood.

106

easier striking distance. In Oklahoma we have seen two bass drums used at one dance with fifteen or sixteen singers around each drum.

The old Indian drums are now seldom seen except in museums. They were usually made of large hoops of cedar or willow, occasionally of a section of a great cottonwood log. Or sometimes, even years ago, a bass-drum shell was used, on which heavier rawhide heads were laced in Indian fashion. Lake Indians, in recent times, made their drums for the Dream Dance from wooden wash tubs. Of course this meant that the lower head was smaller than the upper, but these drums were decorated with fancy beaded and elaborately decorated skirts so that only the top head was seen. It hung from four curved stakes, which were also decorated with beads, feathers, and tufts of hair hanging from their tips.

In the Southwest the ceremonial drums are of approximately opposite proportions. They are made of hollow logs, usually cottonwood, occasionally oak, with two heads laced on, but the log frame, or shell, is about twice as long as the diameter of the heads. Here, too, the drums are regarded as sacred, having individual personalities, even being given personal names, and are under the care of especially appointed guardians.

At Santo Domingo two ceremonial objects are placed within the drum before the heads are completely laced on. One is a little wooden ball of oak about three quarters of an inch in diameter, painted yellow with two dots of red, representing the earth, the other a little oaken cylinder about three quarters of an inch long and three eighths of an inch wide, painted yellow with red on each end, representing the universe.[13]

The Santo Domingos seldom made the entire drum, usually obtaining the shell from the Cochitis, who are famous for their drum making. The Santo Domingos boast of never having sold a drum, so none of theirs are to be seen in museums, but the Cochitis sell many to those willing to pay their price, which is high—as much as two hundred dollars even in the early 1900's.

We have seen drums from a number of tribes which had a small hole somewhere in the shell to release the air pressure and avoid splitting the heads, like one finds on bass or snare drums. But the long drums of the Southwest do not have them, except for Santo Domingo, where in each drum there are two small holes, a very small one near the top head for the "eye," and a slightly larger one directly below it for the "mouth." The Santo Domingos use bullhide for the heads. The other Pueblos also use bullhide or steerhide and apparently find them heavy enough not to require any holes for releasing the pressure.

Pueblo drums are sometimes painted simply, but symbolically, with the scallops cut from the heads representing rain clouds.

The most common drum is the hand drum, song drum, or tambourine drum. No Indian drum should be called a tom-tom. Most Indians object to this term and in speaking English call them drums. To them the drum is full of meaning, and they feel that "tom-tom" is a slighting reference to it. The hand drum is a one-headed drum on an open hoop, usually with crossed strings or even wires over the open back for a hand hold. These drums are laced together in many ways, depending upon tribe or maker's tastes. The heads on many recent ones are even tacked on with brads or brass tacks. Anything that will make a hoop is used for one—iron, wood, an old snare-drum shell, an old banjo shell.

Although these drums are often used ceremonially, they are not under as strict regulations as the larger drums, and almost anyone could own one. Some individuals had personal visions or taboos which forbade the ownership or handling of any kind of a drum, but such restrictions were rare. Hand drums vary in size from about twelve inches to as much as two feet in diameter, those on the Northwest Coast being particularly large. Sometimes we find square ones, made on a frame like a shallow wooden box. Among Plains Indians these often belonged to medicine men, but we find them also on the Northwest Coast. Lakes Indian medicine men often used a small tambourine-type drum with two heads, usually with snares on one side. Snares are occasionally found on single-headed drums, too.

Medicine men also used a sort of drum rattle. The frame that supported the heads was made of a long slat, looped at one end for the drum shell. It looked like an oversized drum beater as described for the Apache and Acoma—a very small, double-headed drum on a handle, with a few pebbles, seeds, or shot inside.

RATTLES

There were even more kinds of rattles than there were drums, and in some rituals they were as important or more so. They were not children's toys but instruments of power. Among the Lakotas and some other tribes as well, rattles were supposed to be especially effective against evil forces. Some society rattles would sell for as much as a horse.

In the East rattles were usually made of gourds, with seeds, later shot, to produce the sound. Pebbles were sometimes used too, but they wore out the gourd and also gave too harsh a sound. In the West no gourds were available, yet the tradition remained, so rattles were made of rawhide to look like gourds. Iroquois still make rattles of snapping-turtle shells, hickory bark, and cow horns, as well as gourds, each type being reserved for particular ceremonies. We have a snapping-turtle rattle made in recent years exactly as were the old ones, except that the handle is wrapped with friction tape instead of buckskin!

Small terrapin shells were used for the leg rattles worn by the women rattlers in Stomp dances, before the advent of tin cans, which now take their place. Tin cans have been used for hand rattles for many years, too, and some of these are elaborately decorated with quillwork to hide the can. Before sleigh bells were available, dancers all across the country wore rattles around their knees of small turtle or terrapin shells, on which were hung pieces of deer, elk, or buffalo hoof which jangled against the shells with the movements of the dancer. Leg rattles were also made of pieces of horn or hoof hanging in clusters so that they sounded with the dancer's movements. Hand rattles were made by hanging such pieces of horn or hoof to a stick. Beautifully carved wooden rattles were used on the Northwest Coast.

Speck, speaking of the Cayugas again, but in terms that could apply to almost any tribe, said:

> The drum and rattles of different types are held in semisacred esteem.
> Every material used in their construction is symbolical of some phylum or class of animal and plant life that contributes its substance to the life support of the people. It is not easy for modern folk to sense the feeling of communion of spirit that underlies the use of a turtle's shell, splints of hickory, threads of animal sinew, animal skin wrappings, and kernels of maize, combined in the making of a large snapping turtle shell rattle and blended into the purpose of a man who uses such a combination of spirit forces as a rhythm marker to accompany the voice. . . . These are only a few examples of the kind of nature appreciation so deeply set in the Indian mind and so feebly felt by most persons reared in European cultural environments.[14]

The notched stick is sometimes referred to as a rattle, for it does sound like one. It was sometimes called a *morache*, which seems to be a Spanish word, but in Spanish it is usually called a *raspador*. Usually the notched stick, or rasp, was made of wood, but it was often scraped with a scapula, or shoulder blade, of a small animal. For resonators the lower end of the *raspador* was placed against an overturned basket, a gourd, a piece of sheet metal, or a metal washtub. Such instruments are still used to accompany the Ute Bear Dance every spring.

WIND INSTRUMENTS

In the wind instrument class there were whistles of great variety—bird-leg and wing bones, reeds, deer tibia, carved wood. Some importance of eagle-wing-bone whistles is given in the account of the Sun Dance. Eagle-bone whistles were also used by warriors to give signals in battle. Whistles of many types were used in many ceremonies. The most interesting is the *ši'yotanka*, used for the Grass Dance, which blows in harmonics and sounds like a bull elk bugling.

Pan pipes were used in Mexico and the principle was known to many North American tribes. Sometimes they were merely a pair of bone whistles of different tone blown together—the nearest Indians came to true harmony—but in Mexico there were some with as many as five tubes, made of bone, wood, or clay. Also in Mexico and parts of the United States a multiple flute was known, consisting of two, three, or even four tubes blown through a single mouthpiece. In some cases the tubes were all the same, sounding the same note. In other cases some of the tubes had finger holes, so that a tune could be played while the other tubes set up a drone—the same idea used in bagpipes and hurdy-gurdies. The ocarina, or "sweet potato," is also native to Mexico, but we have not heard of its being used among our own Indians.

Indians everywhere apparently had flutes, and these were true flutes, not whistles. Although they were all *flûtes à bec*, no transverse flute being known to native America, they nevertheless contained a baffle plate in the mouthpiece which deflected the air on the same principle as the transverse flute. Miss Densmore did report seeing one transverse flute at one of the pueblos, but it was a modern instrument.

The flute was mainly a courting instrument, although it was used in some ceremonies among the Pueblos. A flute was usually made of cedar, but some were of sumac. The wood was split, hollowed out, and glued together again. Each maker made his flute according to the size of his own hands, and the holes varied from five to seven, again a matter of personal choice. So it would be difficult to find two flutes that sounded alike or played in the same key, although I have played on many that came very near to reproducing our scale and were very well in tune. There is some evidence that the nose flute, blown with the nose instead of with the mouth, an instrument found in Polynesia, was also known in California.

The Santo Domingos made a flute of bamboo (earlier of native cane) and attached to the lower end of it a bell made of half a gourd, so that the instrument resembled a shepherd's pipe, or we might say a clarinet. Bamboo is not native to America and not even cane is native to New Mexico, so they must have imported their material from some other region or used something else originally.

Most Indians preferred a flute that produced a strong tremolo, or warble, and the maker strove to incorporate this quality into his instrument, just as singers strive to accomplish the same effect in their singing. Atwater said the Indian flute "produces the most melancholy music in the world," and we might almost say it still does.

But, so far as we know, flutes were not played together, as an ensemble or an orchestra, north of Mexico, unless possibly by some Pueblo group. A young man used a flute to serenade the young lady of his choice. Often he made up a song, which he sometimes sang and then played upon his flute as well.

Occasionally a flute was used to give signals in time of war. If scouts reported an enemy lurking near the village, the alert might be given on a lover's flute, the enemy thinking it was only a serenade and not aware of a trap being laid for him.

The conch-shell trumpet was known to many tribes, not only in Mexico but along the Gulf and Southeastern seaboard—even as far north as the Iroquois, where at one time it was used to call the people to council.

BULL-ROARERS

Perhaps the simplest of all instruments is the "bull roarer," which is merely a thin slat of wood from six inches to two feet long and one half to two inches wide, attached to a cord and whirled rapidly about the head. It makes a noise like a bull roaring or like distant thunder. So it is usually associated with Thunder, with lightning, winds, clouds, and rain. This instrument is found in many parts of America and is also known in other parts of the world, including Australia. It was known to the Eskimo, Kwakiutl, Arapaho and other Plains tribes, as well as tribes of the Plateau and of the Southwest.

In some tribes it is now considered merely a children's toy, but in others it still has sacred significance. A similar instrument, the "hummer," also apparently only a toy, was used by Plains children. It was made of a bone from a buffalo hoof attached to strings or thongs, the bone making the center, the strings extending from both sides of it. These strings were tied on their outside ends to little sticks which were held in the hands, the strings whirled to twist them, then pulled and released, untwisting and twisting them in the same way as the discs white children sometimes play with and call "whizzers," or "buzzers."

The Hopis regard the bull-roarer as the prayer stick of Thunder, and the noise it makes is the wind accompanying the thunderstorm. They make it of a piece of light-ning-riven wood and measure the string from the heart to the tips of the fingers of the outstretched right hand. Navajos also use lightning-riven wood and consider the noise to be the voice of the Thunderbird. Apaches make the blade from wood of a tree struck by lightning on a mountaintop.

So the bull-roarer is usually decorated with designs representing lightning or the Thunderbird, and sometimes its edges are scalloped to add to the lightning symbol. In regions of little rainfall it is employed in ceremonies to bring rain. In areas of much rainfall, however, it is used to implore the wind to bring fair weather. The Kwakiutl associate it with ghosts.[15]

8.   Masks and Paint

MASKS

Among the many questions asked us about Indians is: "Did Indians use masks?"

Many tribes did to a limited extent, but only a few used elaborate masks comparable to those of other parts of the world. And yet, perhaps the most elaborate of any in the entire world are those of our own Northwest Coast. Certainly they are the finest in this hemisphere. Grotesquely but beautifully carved and painted, some are so large it is difficult to imagine a person being able to wear them. They offer more variety in size and shape than masks of any other part of the globe. Some are double or even triple masks, the mouth of the outer mask being opened by a hidden string, revealing an inner mask, which within itself may contain yet another mask.

The subject of masks could fill a volume in itself, and our better museums have excellent collections where one could spend hours in their study.

Wearing a mask usually was thought to impart to the wearer the identity of the being represented by the mask. It was not worn as a disguise in the way we usually think of disguises. While wearing a mask he was that being, whether god, demon, mythical character, ancient hero, or some animal spirit. To most Indian minds, people as well as animals with power could change their appearance at will. An animal could take on human form, or powerful medicine men might change themselves into animals, large or small. Such transformations were portrayed in the masks of the Northwest Coast, the wearer being able to demonstrate them by showing the inner mask or masks.

The masks were kept concealed until the time of a performance, so that the ordinary person never had a chance to become familiar with them. The performances, given at night in a great lodge, were awe-inspiring even to those familiar with them. As one observer reported:

The scene in one of these lodges, dimly lighted by the fires which show the faces of the assembled spectators and illumines the performers, presents a most weird and savage spectacle when the masked dancers issue forth from behind a screen of mats, and go through their barbarous pantomimes. The Indians themselves, even accustomed as they are to masks, feel very much afraid of them, and a white man, viewing the scene for the first time, can only liken it to a carnival of demons.[1]

The carvers of these masks were not only masters with their tools but artists with a profound knowledge of construction and anatomy, and their creations were cleverly executed.

We might say the same thing for the masks of the Iroquois. The False Face Society is still active, alive, and strong among our Senecas, Cayugas, and Onondagas of New

Kwakiutl masked dancers, Northwest Coast. Photo by Edward S. Curtis, 1914.

York State and Canada. This is a society of "doctors," and its function is that of healing. Whereas the masks of the Northwest Coast represent mythical beings, birds, animals, and monsters, the Iroquois masks represent disembodied spirits which have the power to drive away disease. Although there are many ways of carving the various characters represented by the masks, there is yet a certain limitation, so that the character is always recognizable. There are two classes of these wooden masks, and several varieties, and different students of the Iroquois have enumerated from one dozen to more than two dozen types. A few represent animals, but most are wind or disease gods—spirits, all heads, no bodies. Grotesque, sometimes hideous and horrible, these masks nevertheless show real knowledge of facial construction and are beautifully made (see page 193).

Formerly these wooden masks were always carved on a living basswood tree, after appropriate ceremonies and offerings of tobacco to the spirit of the tree. They

113

say that when the tree was properly propitiated the scar healed and the tree continued to live.

A mask on which carving was begun in the morning was painted red; in the afternoon, black. Some masks, half red and half black, were called "divided" or "whirlwind." Eastern warriors also painted their faces like this when preparing for battle.

Iroquois masks were sometimes consecrated with little bags of tobacco and were anointed with sunflower oil.

Long horsehair (formerly basswood or nettle fiber) was fastened to the masks, with a part to resemble human hair. It often hung to the dancer's knees. Eyes were made of tin, copper, and brass; before the introduction of metal, clamshell was used. These masks are worn when the society performs, the dancers making weird, angular movements, shaking turtle-shell rattles, and uttering a sort of hissing sound through the mouths of the masks. During the ceremony they blow ashes over the patient being cured. Dr. Speck told us he had seen a number of cures wrought by the False Faces in Canada on patients who had been given up by the best non-Indian doctors. Speck was a thorough scientist, with a reputation as the foremost ethnologist on Indians of the Eastern Woodlands of his day. But he said he had no scientific explanation for these cures.

Some of the masks in the museums in Buffalo and Rochester, New York, are still used by the Indians of nearby reservations at the times of their festivities, especially at those of the winter solstice. The Indians come for them, use them in the ceremonies, then return them to the museums.

The Senecas also have another society of masked healers known as the Husk Faces, whose masks are made of corn husks, braided or twisted and sewn together. They, too, perform at the time of the annual ceremonies. The Husk Faces play a part in the agricultural beliefs of the Senecas. At the midwinter festivities the dancers wearing them carry digging sticks and hoes to represent the coming planting season. Since the feminine power was the one representing fertility, in most tribes women did the planting, cultivating, and harvesting of crops. But these masks were also associated with hunting, so men were the dancers, but women made the corn-husk masks. The wooden masks were made by men.

Iroquois and Cherokees apparently made the greatest use of masks among Indians of the East, but used them for entirely different purposes. So far as we know Cherokee masks did not belong to a medicine society, but were used in the Booger Dance, as we shall see. The wooden ones were usually carved of buckeye and are not nearly as beautifully done or as artistically conceived as those of the Iroquois. Some of the most interesting were made of gourds, the gourd stem serving as the nose.

Algonquian and southeastern Siouan tribes also used masks to some degree. The controlling Spirit of Game was represented by a masked dancer in the Delaware Big House Ceremony. The Spirit of Game was often called the "Living Mask"; he had been made guardian of all the wild creatures of the forest by the Creator. He

A Seneca False Face dancer with a snapping-turtle rattle. New York State Museum and Science Service.

was sometimes seen riding on a buck, herding the deer, but he lived in the western mountains, high above the earth. His face was large and round, the right half painted red, the left half black, and his body was covered with long dark hair, like that of a bear.[2]

The dancer portraying this being wore a similar mask, with a flap of bearskin fastened to it behind, concealing his own hair. He also wore a pair of bearskin leggings and a bearskin coat and carried a rattle made from a turtle shell. The mask was left in charge of a certain family during the year, and tobacco was burned for it periodically.

Other deities were represented also by masks carved on the posts of the Long, or Big, House. Christian missionaries jumped to conclusions and proclaimed all of these mask-using Indians as idolators or pagans. The masks were not worshiped, however, and neither were the faces carved on the posts. They represented the spirit force, or power; they were symbols of the beings, and endowed the wearers with power and the temporary ability to behave like the beings. The masks, whether worn or stationary, were "something to focus attention upon" and aided the participants in a ceremony to concentrate on the power represented.

Sometimes the False Face Dancers engaged in droll and humorous demonstrations. It was not only proper but expected that the audience laugh on such an occasion, but *with* the performer, not *at* him. No one dared laugh at the performer or the mask, no matter how funny or how hideous it appeared, for the over-all purpose of the mask and of the performance was utterly serious. The few who made the mistake of laughing *at* them always suffered some dire consequence, often going mad.

Dr. Speck told us of an occasion when a young fellow made fun of a False Face. Within a few days he went stark, raving mad. The best physicians in Canada were unable to help him. His parents, who did not believe in the False Faces and belonged to the Anglican church, finally had to condescend to ask the False Face Society to heal their son. The False Faces never turn down a request for a healing. They put on a ceremony for the young man, and within a few days he came back to his senses. Speck said that neither the doctors nor anyone else had a scientific reason to offer. The patient was kept under observation for awhile and sent back home.

The price for such a cure is that the person cured and the persons making the request for healing all become members of the False Face Society.

Masks, striking and spectacular in appearance, are also used in the Southwest, where they represent gods or spirits controlling the universe and life forces. Many of the Pueblo Indians have Kachina dances, the kachinas being these spirits, represented by masked dancers. Weird and impressive as the masks are, they do not exhibit the beautiful carving shown in Northwest Coast and Iroquois examples. Navajos also have a number of masked dances, but few white men have seen them. Their masks are similar to but usually simpler than those of their Pueblo neighbors. They also represent deities and are used during the Mountain Chant.

PAINT

On the plains, where there were no carved masks, realistic masks were used in bear and buffalo dances and simple ones of rawhide in the Elk Dance. Clowns, like Heyoka, made masks of buckskin (later of muslin), covering the entire head, usually having a long nose attached and eye and nose holes cut in the fabric.

In areas where masks were scarce or nonexistent, painting the face and body was the alternative, although, of course, this was also done in the mask areas. Sometimes face paint served the same purpose as a mask, hiding the real identity of the wearer or endowing him with the power of the creature or spirit he represented.

Face painting at one time was an important part of costume for almost any dance, as well as in every ritual and for all tribal games. The ritual of painting face and body, for example, was very important in the ball game of the East and the Southeast. Nowadays few dancers bother to paint, but here and there we find some who still take the face painting seriously and consequently produce some interesting, some-times weird and striking, and often beautiful facial decorations. Crow dancers are some of the best in this respect. Formerly an Indian did not think himself properly dressed without some paint on his face and a pretty pair of moccasins (see pages 194 and 197).

The use of face and body paint was universal among Indians of America, as it was among many peoples around the world. It could mean many things. Some face paintings had secret meanings for their wearers. Some showed membership in certain warrior societies. Some were purchased from dreamers or medicine men because they were believed to have protective power or power to aid the wearer in accomplishing feats of bravery in war or skill in hunting. Hence they are often spoken of as "war paint," but even during family life at home it was customary for both men and women, and even children, to have some painting on their faces. Red and yellow were favorite colors, for both are sun's colors, red usually representing the morning sun, the source of life, light, energy, and power; yellow, the setting sun, symbolic of beauty, sincerity, and peace.

In the days before the Indians wore so much clothing, the entire body was painted, the paint mixed with tallow or grease and serving as protection from the weather. Indeed, the Indians acquired the name "redskins" from the custom, in the East, of painting the entire body with red ocher. Since this custom has long since disappeared and the Indians themselves do not even know about it, they sometimes ask, "Why do you call us redskins? Our skins aren't red; they are brown." Then, pointing to someone with a fresh sunburn they will say, "You people are the redskins."

Oftentimes, especially for some social function, Indians did paint just for decoration, to make themselves attractive, using designs according to individual taste and fancy. But other designs were limited to certain uses and could be worn only by certain individuals. Still other patterns were handed down from father to son. Except for members of certain societies, or for individuals who were inactive about camp, one would seldom if ever see two people painted alike, for even the least important "dress-up" paint was an individual and personal matter.

Women especially, but sometimes men also, painted the hair part or hairline either red or yellow, and sometimes a half-circle beneath the hair part on the forehead.

Women often painted on each cheek a red or yellow spot, representing the rising and setting sun, the half circle on the forehead being the noonday sun. One old woman we knew, Mrs. Red Bear, always painted her entire face yellow. We never asked her why, for such things are personal.

For many years powdered paints obtained from white traders were mixed with grease or water and used for face and body painting. Before the traders came, native earths and clays were used in the same way, along with some colors obtained from plants—barks, roots, leaves, and berries. Some of the dancers today—the few who use paint at all—are using theatrical makeup.

On the Pine Ridge Reservation in South Dakota is a hill known as Red Hill, where Indians still obtain a bright-red earth. Rosebud Reservation also has sources of many colors. The Bad Lands are full of colored earths that were once used for coloring materials. The Sioux once owned a place in Minnesota, now the White Earth Chippewa Reservation, which yielded a white earth highly prized for paint. The Sioux also got a brown pigment from a place still known as Brown Earth. Two towns in Minnesota are named Blue Earth and Mankato. Mankato is a corruption of the Sioux Makato, which also means Blue Earth. Blue was a precious color and prized, as was bright red. Sioux obtained a green also from Minnesota; their name for green earth is *makatozi*, or "blue-yellow earth." They also got a clear blue from a place near Lusk, Wyoming.

One of the yellow ochers found by the Sioux, if burned in an ash-wood fire, turned to a beautiful rose color. Other clays and ochers were also found to give different shades by heating or burning.

Tunnels as deep as twenty-five feet have been found in various parts of the country where Indians had mined different ores for use as pigments. Usually these were iron ores, giving red, yellow, and gray, but they also used copper ore for green and blue.

Of course the pigments used depended upon tribal location. Sioux made a yellow from cottonwood buds, as probably did other tribes where the cottonwood is prevalent. Still farther west many tribes used rabbit brush for a bright yellow. Curtis said the Hopis made a beautiful turquoise paint from a soft grade of turquoise, which they pulverized and added to a mixture made from piñon gum. This paint was further mixed with masticated squash seeds when applied to the face or body. Whoever wore this beautiful turquoise blue had to be careful not to approach the fire too closely, as the heat turned it black.

He also said they made a red by pouring the liquid from boiling red corn over crushed ripe berries of skunk bush, giving it substance by adding a certain variety of white clay. The dried berries were kept on hand and the paint made up as needed for decorating the bodies of Kachina dancers.[3]

When Chief One Bull adopted us, he painted both our faces during the afternoon preceding the ceremony. My face was painted with a series of yellow dots across the nose and both cheeks. He began with a small dot on the bridge of the nose, then continued with more dots out across the cheeks, each one perfectly round, becoming a little larger, until the last ones, near the ears, were nearly the size of a dime. Old as he was, we wondered how his hand could be so steady. These dots, he said, represented the tracks of the mountain lion, and this was the paint he wore into battle, especially on horse-stealing raids against the Crows. The mountain lion stealthily approaches his enemies and yet is courageous if forced to fight.

He painted Gladys' face with a design that showed that he had rescued a wounded comrade under fire. Certain conventional designs did have specific meanings which could be interpreted by all members of the tribe. This "rescue" design was a small solid triangle of red containing within it a yellow cross and was painted on each cheek.

The family also suggested tattooing Gladys' chin with the three blue perpendicular stripes formerly used to distinguish girls who had gone through the *Hunkayapi* adoption ceremony, so the old woman who stands at the fork of the Milky Way would let her pass. This old woman examines everyone on the way to the Spirit World. Any woman showing these tattoo marks was immediately allowed to proceed, as were men who could show Sun Dance scars. Others were detained until they could show proper identification. Those who could not be identified had to take the short fork and drop back to earth. This tattooing has not been done in a long time, but we knew several old ladies who still showed these blue marks.

In early historic times many tribes did tattoo as well as paint, with the same purpose in mind, the tattooing being permanent. Both on the Northwest Coast and in the East it was customary to tattoo totemic designs on face and chest, thus identifying oneself with his family clan. William Wood wrote between 1629 and 1634 about

many of the better sort [Indians of New England] bearing upon their cheekes certaine portraitures of beasts as Beares, Deares, Mooses, Wolves, some of fowls as Eagles, Hawkes, etc. which be not superficial painting, but a certaine incision, or else a raising of their skin by a small sharpe instrument, under which they conveigh a certaine kind of blacke unchangeable inke, which makes the desired forme apparent and permanent.[4]

Thomas Auburey, a British officer in the American Revolution, wrote of some of his experiences with the Indians. In telling a friend about their dress he commented:

Joined to these strange dresses, and added to the grotesque appearance, they paint their faces of various colors, with a view to inspire an additional horror. It is almost incredible to think what a prodigious degree of conceit and foppery reigns amongst the savages in decorating their persons, perhaps not inferior to that by which some of our pretty fellows of the present are so conspicuously distinguishing themselves. The following striking instance of it, several other officers, as well as myself, were eye-witnesses to, and it afforded us no small entertainment. In our way to their encampment, we observed a young Indian who was preparing for the war-dance, seated under a wigwam, with a small looking-glass placed before him, and surrounded with several papers filled with different paints. At our stopping to observe him, he was at first a little disconcerted, and appeared displeased, but soon after proceeded to adorn himself. He first smeared his face with a little bear's grease then rubbed in some vermillion, then a little black, blue, and green paints, and having viewed himself for some time in the glass, in a rage wiped it all off, and began again, but with no better success, still appearing dissatisfied. We went to the council, which lasted near two hours, and on our return found the Indian in the same position, and at the same employment, having nearly consumed all of his stock of colors! What a pity it is that the ladies in England, adept in this art, have not such a variety of tints to exercise their genius with; in my mind, if they must paint, the more ridiculous they appear the better. Bear's grease, indeed, would not be a very delicate perfume, but no matter—if nature must be patched up, it little signifies with what—I could laugh at the streaks of an Indian, but am struck with contempt at the airs put on by young flirts, from a penny-worth of carmine, and touched with pity when sixty would assume the glow of fifteen, through a false shame, or a childish want of admiration![5]

Generally black symbolized death, so it was used in war and mourning ceremonies. Red and black both were regarded as war colors, but an excess of colors or many colors used at one time could signify excitement, hence war. But warriors did not necessarily use a horrid face paint to frighten the enemy. The paint disguised him and protected *him* not only from the enemy but from evil forces as well. So, regardless of how horrible the painting looked, the real purpose was to protect and strengthen the wearer.

Painting was so important in some ceremonies that the Yuchis, for instance, at their annual ceremony peeled a large piece of bark off a tree at one edge of the ceremonial square and smeared it heavily with a lot of red paint mixed with clay and grease, to supply the dancers with face paint.

Among Lakotas, the first coup striker on a war party painted his face all black and let his hair hang loose. Other coup strikers painted the lower half of the face black. Sometimes the first coup striker painted his entire body black as well.

Painting was an important feature of the Indian's life as long as he lived. As a little child his face was painted to dress him up for social functions and ceremonials. He painted his face for every important occasion from then on and even when idling about camp. When death finally overtook him his face was painted for the final journey over the Spirit Trail, and in some tribes, after the body had disintegrated on the burial scaffold, the bones were gathered up, ceremonially painted, and buried.

James Buchanan in 1821 reported a visit with one of his Indian friends, who had spent a great deal of time in plucking his scanty beard and painting his face.

Having finished his head-dress, about an hour before sunset he came up, as he said, to *see* me, but I and my companions judged that he came *to be seen.* To my utter astonishment, I saw three different paintings or figures on one and the same face.

From the front view the nose looked very long and narrow, with a round knob at the end. On one cheek was a red spot the size of an apple, on the other a black spot. The eyelids, upper and lower, were in reversed coloring. The nose in profile on one side looked like the beak of an eagle, with the mouth open. The other side resembled the snout of a pike, with open mouth and teeth.[6]

Much face painting was symbolical rather than naturalistic, and yet within a tribe such symbolism was often intelligible to tribal members. Among the Haidas of the Northwest Coast a red circle indicated an eagle's nest, a black semicircle was the

120

moon, arching lines above the eyes represented a grizzly bear's ears, and a square was a fish-drying rack. Many tribes represented the moon by a black crescent, because black was the color of night, when the moon is seen.

Whether we want to speak of face painting as "war paint" or not, it is certain that no warrior would think of going into battle without first applying the proper paint. Even when caught by surprise a man might take a few moments, if at all possible, to daub some paint on his face before meeting the enemy. Count Arese told of an incident when he and his party hired an Indian as guide. He and a Canadian, with the Indian, went off to locate some buffalo when they came unexpectedly near an Indian camp which they were afraid might be hostile.

We at once halted, looked to the saddle-girths, changed our primings, got our guns ready—in short prepared to defend ourselves or flee. . . . The Canadian and I were soon ready, but not the Indian. He had stuck an arrow into the ground, hung his mirror on it, and was busy painting his face red and black and putting feathers on his head; that is, he was completing a toilet for presenting him-self worthily to the enemy—a thing an Indian never fails to do.[7]

The count further described his guide, named Eagle, as having "two little stars tattooed, one on his forehead, the other on his chin, and four lines on his cheeks." He said he was a fine-looking man, "tall, spare, with well-developed muscles, a good frank expression, although a little (or even a great deal) hard and ferocious, especially when he painted himself red around the eyes."

A mirror and little pouches of grease and paints were almost as important to a warrior as his weapons and were always carried with him. Mirrors were one of the first articles of trade and Adair, himself a trader, wrote in 1770:

It is their usual custom to carry nothing along with them in the journie but a looking-glass, and red paint, hung to their back—their gun and shot pouch or bow and quiver full of barbed arrows; and frequently, both gun and bow; for they are generally in a state of war against each other.[8]

There were times when it was just as important for women to paint as it was for men. For instance, during the puberty rites for a girl among the Luiseños of California, her face was painted and a similar painting was made upon a rock. At the end of a month her face was painted with a different design, and this new painting also was placed on the rock. "This was repeated every month for a year, each month a different painting being placed on the girl's face and a similar one added to the original one on the rock."[9] At the end of the year she was lectured on proper behavior and on her place in the tribe and, among other injunctions, was told not to neglect her painting.

In the records of the English settlement at Jamestown there are many references to painted Indians, women as well as men. There are two accounts of meetings with the "king," Powhatan, the first one dealing with the sentence to execute Captain John Smith and the second at a later date, when Smith and his company were in Powhatan's good graces. The first says:

Before a fire upon a seat like a bedsted, he sat covered with a great robe, made of Rarowcun [raccoon] skinnes, and all the tayles hanging by. On either hand did sit a young wench of 16 or 18 years, and along one side the house, two rowes of men and behind them as many women, with all their heads and shoulders painted red: many of their heads bedecked with the white downe of Birds; but everyone with something: and a great chayne of white beads around their neckes.

The second account says:

Powhatan strained himselfe to the utmost of his greatnesse to entertain them [Smith's company], with great shouts of joy, Orations of protestations, and with the most plenty of victuals he could provide to feast them.

Sitting upon his bed of mats, his pillow of leather embrodered (after their rude manner with perele and white Beads) his attyre a faire robe of skinnes as large as an Irish mantell: At his head and (at his) feete a handsome young woman: on each side his house sat 20 of his Concubines, their heads and shoulders painted red, with a great chaine of white beads about each of their neckes. . . .[10]

The first account could mean that both the men and women had heads and shoulders painted red, but the second definitely states "Concubines." Whether they were really concubines or not, at any rate a number of women were painted all alike for specific occasions—times of festivity and importance.

More than sixty years later, Daniel Gookin said of the Indians of New England:

They used to oil their skins and hair with bear's grease heretofore, but now with swine's fat, and then paint their faces with vermillion or other red, and powder their heads. Also they use black and white paints; and make one part of their face of one colour; and another of another, very deformedly. The women especially do this; and some men also, especially when they are marching unto their wars; and hereby, as they think, are more terrible to their enemies. The women in time of their mourning, after the death of their husbands or kindred, do paint their faces all over black, like a negro, and so continue in this posture many days.[11]

Because of lack of understanding and appreciation, most European and early American observers classed all types of face painting as horrible or frightening, but in reality many were attractive, some even beautiful, and the objective of painting for social occasions was to glorify and beautify one's person.

The matter of judging whether an Indian's face was painted beautifully or horribly was brought home to us once while on tour on the East Coast. On one occasion, a lady chairman came to our dressing room to see if we were ready. I stepped to the door to greet her and she pulled back in alarm when she saw me in full costume, face painted and all.

"How terrible!" she exclaimed.

The very next day, in a town not twenty miles away, and when I was wearing the identical costume and paint, the chairman who came to the dressing room gave an equal gasp, but this time of delight.

"Oh, how beautiful!" she cried. "Did Indians really paint their faces so attractively?"

PART III. **The Dances**

9. Dances of the Life Cycle

In an earlier chapter (Best Observers) we listed dances we might consider associated with the life cycle of Indians in former times. We will take up some of them in more detail, for the entire trail of life, from cradle to the grave, was marked by dancing.

BIRTH AND CHILDHOOD

In many tribes, families of importance celebrated the birth of a child with a big feast, give-away, and dance. Although there was no effort to commemorate actual birthdays, it was customary to have another celebration at approximately the first anniversary. Most tribes had elaborate puberty ceremonies for both boys and girls, which also included the customary orations, feasts, give-aways, and dancing. The same might be said for weddings. In fact, the only marriage ceremony many tribes recognized was such a celebration, when parents of the girl, the young man, or both made the announcement of the new couple with a big public display.

While with the Crows we were asked to attend a wedding dance. When we arrived we discovered that the actual wedding had taken place almost two years earlier and the couple was celebrating the first birthday of a pair of twins. But it was called a "wedding dance," nevertheless. The guests, who must have included nearly a hundred Indians, were seated at a long table built under an arbor of poles and branches. The twins, a girl and a boy, had been given "white man's names," Victoria and Victor, because they were born on VE Day at the end of World War II. In those days most of the Crow women were still wearing their attractive cotton-print dresses, with wide leather belts and high, boot-type moccasins, their hair in two braids, and gay Spanish or Pendleton shawls. The men dressed cowboy style, with high-heeled boots and high-crowned hats, although many still wore long hair, in three braids. Beaded hatbands and fancy silk scarves were added decorations.

It was a colorful assembly by present-day standards, but not as rich as in earlier times, when everyone would have worn fringed and beaded buckskins and beautiful moccasins and had their faces properly painted for the occasion.

Following a feast of beef, boiled potatoes, fry bread, and chokecherry pudding, the dancers gathered to add the finishing touches to the celebration. Brilliant in their costumes of dyed long underwear, displaying most of the colors of the rainbow, with tail feathers and perky porcupine roach headdresses, they added sparkle and gaiety to the occasion. The dance was the usual Crow "War Dance," or Hot Dance.

It is probable that a similar kind of dancing took place even in ancient times, for it was mainly a social occasion, and a long, involved ritual was not considered necessary.

Children were taught to dance even before they could walk, and so naturally there were many dances for children, and children took part in many tribal dances. They were never left at home. Everyone attended a dance. Babies slept through the booming of the drum, and the rhythm came to be as natural as breathing.

Flying Cloud would clap his hands and sing for his little boy, not yet old enough to walk. The child would climb up, grasp the side of his crib, pull himself to a standing position, and, while holding on to the railing, bounce in time to his father's song. A Kickapoo father used to carry his tiny child on his back when he danced to accustom the little one to the feel of the motion and rhythm.

Today we usually think of the Rabbit Dance as an adult social dance, but the Kiowas had a Rabbit Dance that was entirely for youngsters. They held contests to see who could act the most like a rabbit and jump up and down the highest, fastest, and longest.

THE DOLL DANCE

We think of dolls as children's playthings, and Indian children have dolls, just as children do everywhere. But dolls were also used in many ceremonies and had feature roles in many dances across the country. Lewis and Clark mentioned a doll as having an important role in a Mandan Buffalo Dance. Dolls were also used in the Crow and Kiowa Sun Dances. The Leni Lenapes, or Delawares, had, until very recent years, a Doll Dance that was supposed to bring good fortune and good health to the family who owned the doll and to those taking part in the ceremony. According to the legend, this particular doll was a child's toy that was discovered to have life, and it demanded that its owners give it a feast and new clothes and hold a dance for it every spring. The Delawares accepted this doll as a minor deity and held the celebration in its honor each spring, as directed.

Instead of a drum the singers used a sewed-up dry hide stuffed with grass, upon which they beat with sticks. They sat in the center of the dance ground. The doll was fastened to a pole and was addressed as "grandmother." The dance leader took the pole to which the doll was tied and commenced to dance around the circle, following the song of the Doll Dance. The people fell into line behind the leader, then formed two circles, this time the men inside and the women outside.

At the completion of each set the doll was passed to the next man in line, until six men had danced with it. Then it was passed to the women, until they also had danced with it six times in all. Twelve was the Delaware sacred number, and thus the doll danced twelve times.

There were other dolls among the Delawares that also had powers of preserving health and of healing the sick. Some of them had an element of witchcraft about them. A medicine man might demand that such a doll be made for a healing rite. The doll represented the patient in perfect health, and proper ceremonies were arranged to bring about the patient's transition from the state of illness to that enjoyed by the doll.[1]

Dolls play an important role in the Kachina rituals of the Southwest and were used in hunting and fertility rites of the Plains.

PUBERTY RITES

Since the future of the people depended upon the women of the tribe, puberty rites for girls were usually more important than those for boys. The Apaches probably had the most elaborate puberty ceremonies of all. The famous Mountain Spirit Dance, also called Crown Dance, Devil Dance, and Ghost Dance by whites, is an essential part of the girls' puberty rites. It is one of the finest of all Indian dances and shows real choreography, with many interesting patterns and movements. Although one of the most entertaining dances, it still has much religious significance and is performed only for important occasions. It can be used to cure sickness and to avert catastrophe as well as to bring a young girl into womanhood.

In the latter ceremonies, the girl becomes White Painted Woman, or Mother Earth, and the dancers represent the Mountain Spirits, who are intermediaries between man and the Life Giver. There is some amount of danger in becoming a masked Mountain Spirit dancer, for, if certain taboos are broken or if the dance is not executed properly, some dire consequence may result. The dancer may have trouble with his ears or eyes, or have a swollen face, or even become paralyzed. If he does not put on the mask-headdress properly, he may go mad. Such are the beliefs, so it is not always easy to find persons willing to be dancers.

But once a man has danced in the Mountain Spirit Dance and has become familiar with its ways and traditions, he usually becomes enthusiastic about it and stays with it into old age. Such dancers take pride in mastering all the intricacies and details associated with the ritual and vie with each other for best dancing, striving to become leaders.

The ceremonies take place in a large, tipi-shaped arbor especially erected for the occasion. The dancers are "made," or prepared in another brush shelter some distance away. "Making" them is the most dangerous part of the ceremony, so it is not done within the camp. All must be done under the guidance of competent medicine men, or shamans, and their orders followed explicitly. The dancers have no power of their own but, because they represent powerful supernatural beings, power emanates from them. They are painted with designs representing the cosmos—morning star, planets, lightning, raindrops, rainbow, sun, and moon. For healing rites, the most important dancer of all is the Clown, who represents a comet, but in the puberty rites he merely adds comedy. He does anything he is told to do by the onlookers and serves as a messenger for the other dancers, who are not permitted to talk to anyone else during the performance.

A group of Apaches from Fort Sill did the Mountain Spirit Dance for us in our *Arrows to Atoms* pageant. They considered it an important enough occasion that they not only consented to do it for us, but did it in the afternoon, whereas usually the Mountain Spirits dance only after sunset. Before each performance they had a little private ceremony, offering tobacco to the spirit powers. The Clown was painted in huge letters on the front of his bare body "U.S. Indian Service." Across his back was "Post No Bills."

There are usually at least four masked dancers, in addition to the Clown, and for most occasions two girls also take part. After the dancers are "made," they line up, facing East, and hold their mask-headdresses out in their hands while the shaman sings a set of four songs. The dancers then spin clockwise, spit into their headdresses four times, and put them on, feinting three times, actually placing them over their heads on the fourth time. This is much like many Plains ceremonies where each ceremonial act is accompanied by three feints before the actual movement. The Mountain Spirits are protectors of game animals, most of which have horns, so they call their headdresses "horns."

The puberty rites last four nights. The first fire in the ceremonial lodge is made with rubbing sticks. During the day there are a feast, social dances, and games. Each evening, just after sunset, the Mountain Spirits come from the east, enter the lodge, and circle the fire four times. They approach it from the east again, coming within seven or eight yards of it, and make a strange little call, which sounds much like an owl. They go around the fire once, then stop on the south side, approach the fire, sway, and make the call. This is repeated to the west and north, and ended back at the east, where it began. Thus they complete the circle, which represents time, or eternity. After "worshiping" the fire, they circle around the lodge, blessing each pole with yellow ochre and pollen from a nut tree, and then trot off to the east and vanish in the darkness. If there is any sickness in camp, they may first dance around the camp circle. Or if there is sickness or trouble within any certain dwelling, they dance back and forth before it.

For this first part of the ceremony, a water drum is used. It was the usual drum of the South, a pottery jar with a buckskin head. For our pageant they used a drum of a small tin bucket over which was stretched rubber from an inner tube. A friend of ours tells us that he saw San Carlos Apaches use a large tin can with a piece of wet muslin for a head.

By and by the dancers return. This time several water drums are used along with a piece of heavy rawhide, placed northeast of the entrance, which another singer strikes in place of a drum. The dancers come bounding into the firelight, rapidly circling the fire. Special songs are now sung. Some of these are individually owned and are sung only by their owners, but everyone joins in on a sort of refrain, which all know. When sacred things are mentioned in the songs, the dancers make their cry, and also when they want to "say something" they make it, for they are not allowed to talk or make other sounds. These songs are of three classes, and according to Morris E. Opler are referred to as "free step," "short step," and "high step," so the dancers dance accordingly.

The "short step" is the one we see most, with short, choppy movements, rigid body, angular contortions of the arms with their "swords." In a "free step" song, the dancers can do about as they please.

An Oklahoma Apache Mountain Spirit dancer performs for puberty rites. Photo by A. C. Hector, Anadarko, Oklahoma.

The dancers circle the fire sidewise, with their backs to it, facing outward, in the "high step." Although they do not get down quite as low as in the Russian *trepak*, they use much the same movement, "high" referring to the motion of the legs rather than to the position of the body or the elevation of the jumps.

Captain John Bourke, speaking of all the dancers as "medicine men," which of course they really are not, wrote: ". . . the medicine men . . . resumed their saltation, swinging, bending and spinning with such violence that they resembled, in a faint way perhaps, the Dervishes of the East." He said they danced as long as the fuel in a large pile was unconsumed.[2]

On the fourth night the girl for whom the ceremony is given is brought in to the dance. She does a shuffle step, moving sidewise, left and right, alternately pivoting on her heels and toes, with her arms upraised, upper arms horizontal to each side, lower arms at right angles, elevated upward and with palms forward. In between these movements she dances in place, swaying her body, with her hands on her hips.

About midnight the Mountain Spirits go around and chase all the people into the center of the camp for a big social dance. From now on the Mountain Spirits are allowed to talk, but they still do not touch anyone. They may even be invited into the social dance, but do not touch their partners.

The social dances sometimes take place during the day as well as each of the four nights. The first social dance is like the ordinary Round Dance of the Plains tribes, except that the water drums are used. The second social dance is a couple dance, where the women choose the men, another custom found everywhere. The partners face each other and move about four steps toward the fire and four back again, sometimes holding arms. The same partners dance each night and on the fourth night the man is supposed to pay the woman. Sometimes a woman takes *two* partners, and both are expected to pay her. Even a Mountain Spirit dancer must pay his partner when he is invited to dance. The social dances last till dawn and the puberty celebrations end on the morning of the fifth day.[3]

John Collier says that the puberty ceremonial is "the Apaches' most momentous ritual."[4] Preparations are made a year in advance. The garments to be worn by the girl are of the finest doe or buckskin, designed with symbols such as those used by the Mountain Spirit dancers themselves, representing the forces to be supplicated on the girl's behalf. The dress is dyed yellow, the color of pollen, which in itself represents fertility. Fringes attached to the centers of decorative circles represent sunbeams. An old woman "sings over" the dress sometimes for a period of two months. A singer and his wife, who serves as his assistant, act as ceremonial parents.

The ritual brings joy, blessing, and good fortune not only to the girl and her family but the entire tribe and is filled with mysticism and beauty. The girl remakes herself into the image of Mother Earth and establishes herself in proper relationship with the entire universe.

THE MAIDEN'S DANCE

Among many tribes there were times when the virgins held a public ceremony, with a feast and dance. Each girl proclaimed her purity. If any man could contest her claims, she was publicly disgraced and forever looked down upon by the people. But if such a man's claims were proven false, woe unto him! He was lucky to escape with his life, for all of the accused girl's family and relatives sought revenge.

Married women also staged similar public ceremonies, proclaiming their faithfulness to one man. The Sioux had a society of such women known as the Owns Alone, which often appeared in public with rituals and dances, just as men's fraternities, or societies, did.

THE DANCE TO THE CARDINAL POINTS

While he was still a small boy, Flying Cloud saw a dance he called the Dance to the Cardinal Points, given by the Yanktonais on the Standing Rock Reservation. This was just before the Indian police began to clamp down on the old ceremonials, and it was the last time it was given. It was a prayer for long life, for the participants and for the entire Sioux Nation. So it may well be included in this series of dances pertaining to the life cycle.

A circle of stones about thirty feet in diameter was laid out, with two lines of stones crossing the center and forming four spokes of a great wheel. In the center where the two lines crossed was placed a larger stone painted red. Little turtles, fifty or sixty of them, were placed between some of the stones in each spoke. The turtle is the emblem of long life and of fertility.

Four couples took part, the men lining up four abreast on the right of the center line of stones, on the south side of the circle, the women on the left, making a line eight abreast altogether. In this case the women were being honored, for their usual place was to the right of the men.

The men wore only clouts and moccasins. Their bodies were painted with gray mud, their hair combed out loose and mud rubbed on it too. Their clouts were dyed blue. Each man carried a bunch of sage in his left hand and four eagle feathers in his right.

The women wore white dresses, their faces were painted yellow with red crosses on the foreheads, their hair was braided, and they also carried sage and feathers like the men.

Four singers with hand drums, also stripped to clouts and moccasins, took places in a line abreast north of the circle.

The eight dancers advanced with a trot step to the center rock and retreated, circled to the left, approached the center and moved back again, facing east, continued on around, the next time following the line of stones to the south, and finally approaching the center from the east facing west. This seems to be the opposite of other Sioux ritualistic procedure, and Flying Cloud did not remember any reason for it. But he did say it was a very hot day in August and the sweet grass "smelled real good."

VISION DANCES

The enacting of visionary experiences was important in many sections of the country. Later we shall take this up with some of the societies of the Plains. It was also important among a number of Eastern tribes, and particularly so with the tribes of the Northwest. There the Spirit dances, which were mainly the portrayal of personal dreams or visions, made up the most important cycle of dances, lasting all winter long. But we shall talk about the Northwest later. Here, since we have been dealing largely with Plains and Woodlands, let us just mention a Vision Dance of the Leni Lenapes, or Delawares, as an example of what we might have found among other people of the East. The Delawares were giving their Vision dances until about 1930.

Visions were usually associated with the male members of a tribe, but not always. Often important visions were revealed to boys not yet in their teens and were held sacred by them for the rest of their lives. Delaware boys went on a vigil fast at the time their voices were changing, hoping that when they returned they would have the voices of mature men. But they hoped even more to receive a vision, showing them spiritual helpers who would guide them throughout life. Boys of most tribes went on similar vigils.

Ordinarily a person seldom if ever spoke of his vision, but in many tribes it could be expressed through song and dance. The participants in the annual Big House ceremony of the Delawares were those who had had visions, most of them having been received during late childhood or early youth. Nevertheless, a person was not regarded as mature enough in religious experience to take active part until he was at least thirty-five years of age.

The Big House ceremony lasted twelve nights. On the twelfth night, after all the serious ritual had been completed, young men and women were given an opportunity of telling their visionary experiences. It was a sort of initiation into the form and style of delivery considered proper for actual participation in later years.

The leader of the annual ceremony started the first night's ritual with a recitation of his vision, but not in a natural or normal voice. He and the other participants were regarded as having direct communication with the Spirit World. The leader arose from his seat north of the center pole in the long house, or Big House, rapidly shaking his rattle of box-tortoise shell. He recited his vision in a high monotone, pausing after every phrase to allow an assistant, or "follower," to repeat it and shake *his* rattle.

Two singers used a rolled dried deerskin, to which four slats were bound lengthwise, for a drum. When the speaker had finished, they struck a rapid series of beats on the hide and called out, "Ho-o-o!" several times.

Each visionary had a song concerning his vision. The leader now sang the words to a verse of his song and the singers used the song as a dance tune, striking the rolled hide in time. There were two fires in the Big House, one at each side of the center post. The leader danced counterclockwise in an oval around the two fires. He could stop the singers whenever he wanted by whooping. He might recite another verse, which the singers would sing after him as he danced again.

Other people could join in the dance if they cared to, men forming a file behind him, women following after the men. The leader might stop several times on his way around the oval. The other dancers would do likewise. Each verse was an installment toward the complete recitation of the vision. There were usually six or seven stops around the oval.

When the leader came to the singers on the south side, he stopped again, shaking hands with each one and calling them by terms of kinship. All the dancers did the same. They danced past the singers facing them, as a gesture of respect, then turned into file once more.

On returning to his starting place, the leader began to move toward the center post, the file following. He stopped once more before reaching it, then circled it, making his final recitation and song before the post itself. On it was carved a face representing the Great Spirit. The Delawares say they did not worship it; it was merely "something to focus attention on." At the end of the leader's final recitation, all made the prayer call, "Ho-o-o!" and raised their hands, to "lift the prayer."

When the leader finished dancing, he handed the rattle to another man. If that one did not care to dance, he handed it to another, until someone wished to dance. In these intermissions, the men sat and smoked their pipes. People were allowed to enter or to leave the Big House only between dances.

The next dancer repeated the same procedure, first reciting his vision in a monotone, then the words of his song, the singers learning them and singing the melody in dance time. These dances were Stomp Dance type, just a shuffle or trotting step to the right. They are another example of how the same dance could be used for both religious and social functions.

The meeting continued until everyone had had a chance to recite his vision and dance and the rattle came back to the leader. The length of such a meeting depended upon the number of visions recited, but usually lasted until nearly dawn. It was closed with all present being served bowls of corn meal mush, which they ate using mussel shells as spoons. The meeting was ended with the call "Ho-o-o!" being repeated twelve times.

The Vision Dance occupied the first two nights of the Big House annual ceremony, which altogether ran twelve nights. As we have mentioned, on the twelfth night young men and women were permitted to recite their visions. On this night the dancers formed a column, or double file, the men following the visionary doing the recitation, the women following his assistant. They approached the center and circled the center post from the opposite side of the oval, entering in front of the singers this time.

The visions played an important part in giving the people a feeling of union with the supernatural forces controlling the universe.[5]

MOURNING DANCES

When we spoke about John Tanner and his thirty years among the Indians, you may recall that one of the few dances he mentioned was one held when he was adopted by the Shawnees, being given at the grave of the boy whose place he was taking. Perhaps we should call such ceremonies memorial services rather than mourning rites. They were held in honor of the deceased, and at such times relatives usually went through a period of wailing and singing. The accompanying ceremonies, however, were often quite festive, and merrymaking prevailed. There were occasions, too, when dancing was performed at or near the time of actual mourning, as when a man's warrior society danced in his honor following his death. Usually four days of intense mourning were set aside following it, and then the society members danced their customary routine in full regalia.

Some tribes even had Skeleton Dances as part of their mourning rites. Several writers mentioned one for the Wolf Clan of the Delawares. It seems to have been introduced by the Nanticokes, a Virginia tribe at one time neighboring the Delawares. We think similar rites were known to other tribes in the East and also on the Plains. Among many of the latter the bodies of the dead were allowed to disintegrate naturally, then the bones were gathered up and honored in special ceremonies.

But among the Delawares, the flesh was stripped from the bones immediately after death, as a means of hastening the spirit on its journey, and the flesh buried at once. The bones were dried for twelve days, then wrapped in white buckskin and carried to the dance ground. A couple of men held up the bones, shaking them in time to the dance songs so that they rattled, while the rest of the assemblage danced around them. Following the dance, the bones were buried.

We have attended a number of memorial services—for Crows, Sioux, Cheyennes, Kiowas, and Blackfeet. Sometimes such services were repeated year after year; sometimes they were given only once, or only occasionally. They were costly, for the sponsor was expected to furnish a feast and give-away in honor of the departed one.

Some writers have expressed the opinion that the elaborate mourning rites were mostly for show and that the grief was not genuine. But in our experience there are no more emotional people anywhere. On our very first visit to Standing Rock we came upon an old woman sitting at her daughter's grave, keening and wailing. Then she smoked her little pipe, sitting quietly, and afterward was heard talking, as if carrying on a conversation. Then she cried and wailed again. We supposed that the loss of her daughter was recent, but learned that it had occurred eleven years before! The old lady visited the grave each year on the anniversary of her daughter's death. Although too poor to sponsor a public memorial, her grief must have been real enough.

We went to the Blackfoot country as special guests of Julia Wades-in-the-Water when she held a celebration in honor of her husband. This was two years after his passing. It had taken the old lady all that time to save enough to put on the festival and buy the necessary goods. But since her husband was a chief she wanted the occasion to be worthy of a chief. She invited many people from many tribes, for Chief Wades-in-the-Water was well known and well-liked. A chief is supposed to be generous, so Julia gave away almost everything she had. Stacks of quilts and blankets, canned goods, flour, sugar, and coffee were presented to the visitors.

A framed colored photograph of the chief, draped with an American flag, was set up in the center of the circle near the goods. Julia came forward, wailing in the high, keening voice all Indian women use when mourning the dead. She broke into a song of honor for "Wades," in which all the other women joined. She wore the pretty red flannel dress, decorated with appliquéd ribbon and jingling little metal thimbles, that he had liked so well, and his gray felt sombrero.

Following the give-away it was the visitors' turn to sing a song in Wades' honor. But all of the visiting Indians seemed to have "lost the song," and no one volunteered. So Julia came to us and asked us to sing a Sioux song for him. We began an old chief's honoring song, and, surprisingly, an Assiniboin friend joined in with us. The dance which wound up the day's activities was the customary Grass Dance, now used for social gatherings among Indians everywhere.

But the memorial services were not yet over for Julia. She cooked for and fed all the visitors—about thirty of them—for three more days. But, rather than being worn out and discouraged with all the work and expense, she beamed afresh every time a new family arrived. By the end of each day she had used up all the food on hand, so she would go into town to buy more provisions and while there ate in the restaurant! We never saw her take a bite all the time she was serving the rest of us.

We have attended Memorial Day services on the Standing Rock Reservation. While Indians formerly had no such special day as this, they have put our Memorial Day to good Indian use and made it the occasion for many families to honor their dead at once, all in Indian fashion. They have taken over the white man's way of decorating graves with flowers, which was only occasionally done in olden times. But few flowers grow wild at this season, so they decorate the graves with paper ones they make for weeks in advance. On the graves they also place fruit—mainly oranges—but father One Bull asked us to bring apples for *ina*, mother Scarlet Whirlwind, who had been very fond of them. The fruit is for everyone. Candy and popcorn are there for the children, tobacco for the men, sometimes articles of clothing. Formerly real Indian articles were used—war bonnets, moccasins, beadwork. All these things are given away in honor of the dead. Some families bring along food for a feast to serve relatives and close friends. Speeches, prayers, and songs—both old Indian ones and hymns translated into Lakota—are part of the proceedings.

A big gathering takes place at night in the community hall at the agency. There considerable time is devoted to Mourning and Honor Dances, which are very similar, one for the dead, one for the living. The drum is "muffled" by striking only the edge of it and is beaten softly and steadily to nearly the end of the second repetition of the song, when it is struck three times loudly by the song leader and then continued in fast 3/4 rhythm, like a woman's dance. During the soft drumming the dancers— relatives of the person honored—use a shuffling step as they circle around to the left. On the loud beats they continue around, single file, using the limp step of the women's dance, but faster. Men and women alternate in the line. Sometimes the dance is repeated for friends to join in.

A Mourning Dance was given for Matthew American Horse, killed in action overseas. Six women relatives performed this, one carrying a large American flag. The woman following held the flag to keep it from waving, as another gesture of mourning. Mrs. Many Horses turned a horse loose in the dead soldier's honor; anyone catching the horse could keep him.

An Honor Dance was given for a returned soldier who had lost a leg. He was presented with a beautiful eagle-feather war bonnet. A give-away occupied a good portion of the evening.

Sometimes in the honor parade three, four, or five relatives marched abreast, while the other dancers followed in single file. These dances are not costume dances, although if costumed dancers are present they join in. The men remove their hats, sometimes waving them in parts of the song.

At another Honor Dance, Mrs. Long Chase carried a staff with ten eagle feathers fluttering from it, representing ten members of her family, all in Service. The Mourning and Honor dances were followed by the customary present-day dances—Grass Dance, Round Dance, Rabbit Dance, and *Kahomni*. *Kahomni* is much like Rabbit, except that there is no back step. The feet move forward all the time and when the leader shouts, *"Kahomni!"* everyone—each couple—turns completely around.

Most tribes have taboos against mentioning the names of the dead. The names may only be sung in a song. After being given to a living person, they may be freely spoken again.

Formerly a Mourning Dance was important in the Osage cycle of dances. When a warrior died, his closest friend was selected to be principal mourner. He went into the hills to fast and pray for an entire moon. He took no weapons with him and subsisted on food he could take with his bare hands. When he came back, gaunt and emaciated, he was met by two medicine men, who conducted him to a special lodge set aside for him.

A ceremonial arbor covered with cottonwood boughs was built. Each clan furnished four or more dancers, who gathered at the mourner's lodge and painted themselves from head to foot. Their bodies were painted with red ocher, on which certain designs were marked in yellow. On their faces a yellow stripe was drawn across the eyes, and red and black designs were painted on the cheeks.

Two sets of singers were named and the dancers were divided into two groups so that the dancing could be carried on continuously. At sunrise the dancers circled the arbor, then danced out from it and back again, members of different clans going opposite ways. They met and passed each other many times during the day. By alternating the dancers the ritual went on all day until sunset, except for a brief recess at noon, when they ate lightly.

The wife of the dead man sat near the entrance of the arbor, dressed in old clothing, her hair and face covered with wet mud and ashes, which she replenished as it dried and fell off.

At the next sunrise, the drums began again and the songs, dancing, and prayers continued through the second day. The procedure was repeated on the third day. At sunset a party of six dancers broke pell-mell from the arbor, yelling and shouting, and made a wild rush for their horses. Leaping upon them, they tore from the village, sworn to kill the first stranger they met. It seems that, according to Osage belief, the dead warrior could not enter the Spirit Land unless the hair of an enemy accompanied him.

In more recent years, closely watched by government agents and troops, medicine men decided that enemy hair was all that was necessary. It did not have to be a scalp. So they paid someone from an alien tribe for his hair, which was cut off with a knife, to simulate scalping. It was tied to a stick, as was formerly done with real scalps, and the six warriors returned to their village. Approaching it at a mad gallop, as they had left it—perhaps several days before—they shouted their victory. The lost soul could then begin its journey. The wife washed her face and hair and put on the best clothing she had worn while her husband was alive. The dancers also washed off their paint, and the whole village rejoiced.[6]

The Cherokees had a Burial Dance at the home of the deceased to alleviate the grief of the bereaved and to enable them once more to turn their thoughts to normal living. They danced for seven nights. Some writers have referred to the burial rites as the most poetic of all Cherokee ceremonies, and Morgan gives the same impression for the Condolence Ceremonies of the Iroquois, a similar dance.[7]

The Iroquois also had a Dance for the Dead, in which only women took part. It was usually held about a year after the passing of an individual, but was sometimes given for the dead in general, in the spring and fall, when the spirits of the departed were supposed to visit the earth and dance with the people.[8]

Tabeau mentioned a long ritual, reminding one somewhat of the Calumet Dance, for the Brulé Sioux, which also had similarities to the Sioux Spirit Keeping—a long ceremony of mourning—but in neither of these was there any dancing. Whether other tribes had a Mourning Dance comparable to that of the Osages we cannot say, but the important thing was that they did dance on occasions of mourning, and at memorials, thus completing the cycle of dances along the trail of life.

10. The War Dance

From the eighteenth century on, and certainly during the early period of our national history, white Americans feared and dreaded the Indian War Dance. At the same time they were fascinated by it. The government tried to prohibit all Indian dancing largely on the notion that it was all war dancing. But when permission was granted for Indians to hold a dance it was the War Dance that everyone wanted to see!

We find no specific mention of a war dance in the early writings until we come to Timberlake. He remarked that the War Dance gave him the greatest satisfaction. To be sure, there were many references to Scalp and Victory dances and other dances pertaining to war, but nothing that could specifically be called the War Dance until Timberlake wrote about it. Nevertheless, all through the East and the Middle West, in the Woodlands, a real War Dance performed preparatory to going into battle seems to have been standard procedure. This was not the so-called War Dance that Indians are doing across the country today. The present-day War Dance is really Grass, or Omaha, Dance, which we shall take up later.

GENERAL DESCRIPTION

The custom everywhere apparently was to set up a post in the center of the village. Sometimes this post was merely peeled of bark. At other times it was painted, either red or black, depending upon the tribe. It may have been symbolic of various things, but mainly it seems to have represented the enemy. According to most accounts, the chief who wanted to raise a war party began the ceremony by striking the post with his war club or tomahawk and reciting his brave deeds against the enemy. Then the drummers began a War Dance song, the chief dancing in time to it. Other warriors came forward, one at a time, striking the post and telling their deeds and then joining in the dance, thus signifying their eagerness to join the party.

In the McKenney and Hall *Atlas* is a detailed account of the War Dance:

Dancing is among the most prominent of the aboriginal ceremonies. There is no tribe in which it is not practised. The Indians have their war dance and their peace dance, their dance of mourning for the dead, their begging dance, their pipe dance, their green corn dance, and their wabana. . . . In the war dance the actors are distinguished by a more free use of red and black paint, except in mimic representations in time of peace, when the colours are not so closely adhered to. . . . It rarely happens that two of a group are painted alike.

The music consists of a monotonous thump with sticks upon a rude drum, accompanied by the voices of the dancers, and mingled with the rattling of gourds containing pebbles, and the jingling of small bells and pieces of tin, worn as ornaments. . . .

The war dances are pantomimic representations of the incidents of border warfare, and, although by no means attractive in themselves, become highly picturesque when contem-

War Dance of the Sauks and Foxes, from a lithograph in McKenney and Hall, *Indian Tribes of North America, 1836–44*, after a painting by Peter Rindisbacher, about 1825–35. Smithsonian Institution, Bureau of American Ethnology.

plated in connection with their significant meaning. The persons engaged are warriors, the leaders of the tribe, and the great men of the day; and the allusions are to the heroic deeds or subtle stratagems of themselves, or of their ancestors, or to some danger that threatens, or some act of violence about to be perpetrated.

The dances of the Indians are not designed to be graceful amusements, nor healthy exercises, and bear no resemblance to the elegant and joyous scenes of the ball room. . . . the war dance, in which the warriors only engage . . . is a ceremony, not a recreation, and is conducted with the seriousness belonging to an important public duty. The music is . . . without melody or tune; the movements exhibit neither grace nor agility, and the dancers pass around in a circle with their bodies uncouthly bent forward, as they appear in the print, uttering low, dismal, syllabic sounds, which they repeat with but little perceptible variation throughout the exhibition. The songs are, in fact, short, disjointed sentences, which allude to some victory, or appeal to the passion of revenge, the object of which is to keep alive the recollection of injury, and incite hatred of the tribe against their enemies. From the monotony of most of these dances there are, of course, exceptions. Sometimes the excitement of a recent event gives unwonted life and spirit to the ceremony, and occasionally an individual, throwing talent and originality into the representation, dramatizes a scene with wonderful force and truth.

The writer then proceeded to say that Keokuk, the Sauk chief, was considered a great orator, bringing his oratorical talents to bear on such occasions, while an Oto chief brought a "rich fund of humour" into the celebrations, along with practical jokes, to the delight of the spectators:

Sometimes the dance is suspended, as it were, for a few moments, and a prominent actor in it addresses his companions in a short speech, when the dance is renewed with increased activity. But it seems to be chiefly by their expressive countenances, the significant gestures, that they convey ideas on these occasions, and produce an interest in the savage assemblage of spectators, who, like most other human beings, are ready to applaud whatever is done by their chiefs and leading men.[1]

As we have noted before, the early writers could see neither grace nor agility in the dances because the movements were so different from anything they were accustomed to. McKenney implied as much by his own statement, when he wrote that dancers had "their bodies uncouthly bent forward, as they appear in the print"—and in the print they are all erect! It is interesting to see that he did recognize "talent and originality" among some of the solo performers, and he must have been one of the first white men to realize that Indians have a sense of humor.

THE NATCHEZ

Du Pratz gave a good account of the War Dance of the Natchez, who, for all the differences in social and political structure, seem to have had many "typical" traits. Du Pratz wrote that the pole was seven or eight feet high, with a "war pipe" hung at the top and a roast dog at its foot. An old man first told of his exploits—or "counted coup," as it is spoken of in later literature.[*] All those assembled then ate the dog but kept walking around while eating, signifying that they were always on guard. One young man went into the brush and made the "death cry," whereupon all seized their arms and rushed to the place where they heard the noise. The young man then appeared, making the cry again. All answered and returned to the feast. These same alarms and searches were made two or three times. A war drink made of boiled cassina leaves was passed around, and all assembled at the post, each striking it in turn and recounting a coup. Following these recitations, all participated in the dance, weapons in hand.

This War Dance celebration, with the feasting, took place on three successive days, after which the party set out on the warpath. In the meantime the women had prepared food to be taken on the trip, and an old man had prepared a hieroglyphic identification of the tribe to be left at the scene of the attack, so that the enemy would later have no doubt about who had dealt the blow.[2]

There is good reason to believe that the dog too symbolized an enemy, and eating the dog represented the devouring, or conquering, of the enemy. Ceremonial can-

---

[*] *Coup,* French for "blow," has been used to designate striking the enemy, and *count coup* for the subsequent telling of the deed.

nibalism existed among a number of tribes in North America. It is probable that, although only parts of an enemy, such as heart, liver, arm, or shoulder, were eaten, thereby imparting some of the qualities of the brave enemy to the victor, formerly the entire body was consumed. The Tonkawas were abhorred and despised by other tribes in recent years because they were cannibals. The dog, being the Indians' only domesticated animal and consequently nearest to man, would be the obvious substitute in a changeover from actually eating human flesh to devouring the enemy symbolically.

THE CHEROKEES

Timberlake said that the War Dance of the Cherokees gave him the greatest satisfaction because it also gave him the opportunity of learning the Cherokees' methods of war and the history of their warlike actions, and he found it "both amusing and instructive."[3] In connection with the War Dance, Timberlake was much impressed with the giveaway associated with it. He wrote:

The Indians have a particular method of relieving the poor, which I shall rank among the most laudable of their religious ceremonies. . . . When any of their people are hungry, as they term it, or in distress, orders are issued out by the head men for a war-dance, at which all the fighting men and warriors assemble; . . . one only dances at a time, who, after hopping and capering . . . relates the manner of taking his first scalp and concludes his narrative, by throwing on a large skin spread for that purpose, a string of wampum, . . . or anything he can most conveniently spare; after which . . . another takes his place, and the ceremony lasts till all the warriors and fighting men have related their exploits. The stock thus raised, after paying the musicians, is divided among the poor. The same ceremony is made use of to recompense any extraordinary merit. This is touching vanity in a tender part, and is an admirable method of making even imperfections conduce to the good of society.[4]

In Speck's day the Cherokees of North Carolina were still doing many of their dances. They had two that might be designated as War Dances. The one generally called War Dance is also known as Snake Mask Dance. The leader wore a wooden mask with a coiled rattlesnake carved on the forehead. The Cherokee dance dramatized the warriors' defiance of enemies, witches, and ghosts, and the mask showed that they had no fear of anything. Speck believed this to have been originally an enlistment dance, a challenge to join the war party.

The second dance was similar to the Striking-the-Stick Dance of the Iroquois and was called the Warrior, or Brave, Dance. Ceremonial clubs* were painted red, for blood, or black, for anger and fearlessness. The dancers formed only one line but danced forward and backward and on a signal gave a prolonged war cry. Then the dance quickened in pace, and the dancers made motions of striking the enemy, finally milling about and concluding with four war whoops.

---

*The original Cherokee war clubs were made of oak or hickory, but in recent years for ceremonial purposes buckeye, a much lighter wood, was used.

THE IROQUOIS

Lewis Morgan, a noted authority on the Iroquois, writing about 1850, gave perhaps the best account of the War Dance. He wrote:

The Feather dance and the War dance were the two great performances of the Iroquois. One had a religious, and the other a patriotic character. Both were costume dances. They were performed by a select band, ranging from fifteen to twenty-five, who were distinguished for their powers of endurance, activity and spirit. . . . The two dances mentioned . . . were the highest in the popular favor. All things considered, however, . . . the War dance, *Wä-sä-seh*, was the favorite. It was the mode of enlistment for a perilous expedition, the dance which preceded the departure of the band, and with which they celebrated their return. It was the dance at the ceremony of raising up sachems, at the adoption of a captive, at the entertainment of a guest, the first dance taught to the young. . . . The characteristic feature of this dance is to be found in the speeches which were made by those surrounding the band of dancers between each tune, or at each break in the dance. From this source the people derived as much entertainment as they did excitement from the performance itself. It was the only dance in which speeches and replies were appropriate, or ever introduced; and in this particular it was a novelty, leading often times to the highest amusement.

The War dance was usually performed in the evening. It was only brought out on prominent occasions, or at domestic councils of unusual interest. . . . In an adjacent lodge, the band assembled to array themselves in their costumes, and to paint and decorate their persons for the occasion. The war-whoop ever and anon broke in upon the stillness of the evening, indicating to the listening and expectant throng within the council house that their preparations were progressing to a completion. A keeper of the faith, in the meantime, occupied the attention of the people with a brief speech upon the nature and object of the dance. Presently a nearer war-whoop ringing through the air, announced that the band were approaching. Preceded by their leader, and marching in file to the beat of the drum, they drew near to the council house. As they came up, the crowd gave way, the leader crossed the threshold, followed quickly by his feathered band, and immediately opened the dance. In an instant they grouped themselves within a circular area, standing thick together, the singers commenced the war song, the drums beat time, and the dancers made the floor resound with their stirring feet. After a moment the song ceased, and with it the dance; the band walking around a common center to the beat of the drum at half time. Another song soon commenced, the drums quickened their time, and the dance was resumed. In the middle of the song there was a change in the music, accompanied with a slight cessation of the dance, after which it became more animated than before, until the song ended, and the band again walked to the beat of the drum. Each tune or war song lasted about two minutes, and the interval between them was about as long. These songs were usually recited by four singers, using two drums [water drums] . . . to mark the time, and as an accompaniment. The drums beat time about twice in a second, the voices of the singers keeping pace, thus making a rapid and strongly accented species of music.

It would be difficult, if not impossible, to describe the step, except generally. With the whites, the dancing is entirely upon the toe of the foot, with rapid changes of position, and but slight changes of attitude. But with the Iroquois, it is chiefly upon the heel, with slow changes of position, and rapid changes of attitude. The heel is raised and brought down with great quickness and force, by muscular strength, to keep time with the beat of the drum, to make a resounding noise by the concussion, and at the same time to shake the knee-rattles, which contribute materially to the "pomp and circumstance" of the dance. In the war dance, the attitudes were those of the violent passions, and consequently were not graceful. At the same instant of time, in a group of dancers, one might be seen in the attitude of attack, another of defence; one in the act of drawing the bow, another of striking with the war-club; some in the act of throwing the tomahawk, some of listening, or of watching an opportunity, and others of striking the foe. These violent motions of the body, while they, perhaps, increased the spirit and animation of the dance, led to disagreeable distortions of the contenance, as well as to uncouth attitudes. But, at the same time, the striking costumes of the dancers, their *erect forms* [italics ours] at certain stages of the figure, their suppleness and activity, the wild music, the rattle of the dance, together with the excitable and excited throng around them, made up a scene of no common interest.

In this dance, the war-whoop and the response always preceded each song. It was given by the leader and answered by the band. A description of this terrific outbreak of human voices is scarcely possible. It was a prolonged sound upon a high note, with a decadence near the end, followed by an abrupt and explosive conclusion, in which the voice was raised again to the original pitch. The whole band responded in a united scream upon the same key with which the leader concluded, and at the same instant.

In this celebrated dance, therefore, which had doubtless been used for centuries, and been performed throughout the whole area of the American republic, we find this simple succession of acts: the war-whoop and responses, the simultaneous commencement of the war-song and the dance, the slight cessation at the middle of the tune, with a change in the music, the renewal of the dance with redoubled animation, and the final conclusion of the war-song in perhaps less than two minutes from its commencement; and lastly, the walk at the beat of the drum around a central point for about two minutes, until the war-whoop again sounded, and another war-song was introduced. This round was continued until the spirit of the dancers began to flag, and the desires of the people had been reasonably gratified. Without any speeches between the tunes to relieve the band, it usually lasted about an hour; but with speeches, it often continued for three hours with unabated animation.

Any one present was at liberty to make a speech at any stage of the dance. His desire was manifested by a rap.[*] At the sound the dance ceased, or, if finished, and the band were walking, they were required to stop, and all present, as well as the music, to be silent. The only condition affixed to the right of making a speech was that of bestowing a present upon the dancers, or upon the one to whom it was addressed. After the speech was concluded, and the present delivered, the war-whoop and response were again sounded, the drums beat, the song and the dance commenced, and were ended as before. Then followed another speech, and still others, alternating with the songs, or suspending the dance at the moment of its highest animation, at the pleasure of the speaker. In this manner the War dance was continued until the spirit of enjoyment began to subside, when the final war-whoop put an end to the dance, and the band retired.

These speeches were often pleasantries between individuals, or strictures upon each other's foibles, or earnest exhortations, or perchance patriotic ebullitions of feeling, according to the fancy of the person and of the moment. Some of them were received with rounds of applause, some with jeers, and others with seriousness and deference. They usually lasted but two or three minutes. The Indian has a keen appreciation of wit, and is fond of both jest and repartee, as well as of ridicule. . . .

Among the dancers were men of all sizes, figures and heights. There was one warrior, especially, of such herculean proportions that he might be called a giant. He furnished a theme for the next speech, which was made by *Hä-sa-no-an'-da*, the dance having ceased, as follows: "Friends and Relatives—I admire the ease and grace with which *Hä-ho'-yäs* manages his wonderful proportions. He has every reason to be proud of his size and dignity. I propose to give him a present of two plugs of tobacco, supposing that it will be sufficient for *one*

---

[*]A cane or staff was struck against the floor.

quid." Gives tobacco. *Hä-ho'yäs* received the tobacco with seeming pleasure, and the people the jest with considerable merriment. At the conclusion of the next song, he thus replied: "Friends and Relatives—I return my thanks to *Hä-sa-no-an'-da* for his present. I assure him that my intellectual capacities correspond very justly with my physical dimensions. I hope my brother will publish my fame from the rising to the setting sun." Again the war-whoop sounded, the music opened, and the dance was renewed.

In the many addresses and witticisms that the War Dance called forth, the Iroquois took the highest delight. They served the double purpose of relieving the dancers themselves, who would soon have been exhausted by continuous exertion, and of entertaining the people in the interval. This was the secret of its great popularity as a dance, and of its universal adoption. To this day, a well-conducted War dance is the highest entertainment known among the Iroquois.[5]

We make this long quotation not only because it is the best description of a War Dance we have seen, but for the following reasons. Morgan, although he evidently believed this War Dance to be ancient, said it was acknowledged to be foreign by the Iroquois, generally ascribed by them to the Sioux. Their name for it is *Wä-sä'-seh,* or Sioux dance. It is interesting to us that the Sioux themselves have a similar word for the Osages, *Waja'-je.* But then, the Osages are a Siouan people, and whether the Iroquois got the dance from one or the other, it nevertheless shows that there was interchange between tribes that we now consider Western with those of the East. The Sioux, in our early history, were on the western edge of the Great Lakes, and the Iroquois in their travels often went that far and controlled all the country in between.

The dance as described by Morgan certainly has Sioux characteristics, if we may judge by what we personally know of Sioux dancing.

But it is also interesting that the Sioux do not claim a War Dance as such. They say there was no honor in going to war and that it was unnecessary to "stir up courage" with a dance. It was expected of every young man. The honor came with the success-ful return from a war expedition. That was the time for celebrations!

This same attitude was shown by other tribes as well, and some of them in the East. Morgan says the War Dance was also used on the return of a war party. Dances described by early writers as War dances often took place on a war party's return, so might better be labeled Scalp, or Victory, dances.

The "rapping" and the interspersed speeches are probably a transition from earlier days when the Iroquois also "struck the post" and "counted coup." Even in Morgan's day, the Iroquois had not been on a real warpath in many years. With no actual coups to recite, the type of speechmaking gradually changed to its present form. The Iroquois still rap and speak, as Morgan reported over a hundred years ago.

Although Morgan did not mention it, the dog feast was formerly also a part of the Iroquois War Dance. In fact, according to Dr. Fenton, the Iroquois have *two* War dances. The other is called *Striking-the-stick Dance,* and is said to have come from the Shawnees, an Eastern tribe that was first encountered in the Southeast, moved up into New Jersey, then Pennsylvania, Ohio, Kansas, and finally Oklahoma, but that still retains traces of its early Southeastern sojourn. In this dance, two lines of dancers face each other, advance, and as they meet strike their war clubs together, turn, and return to their original lines. They demonstrate fighting and scalping. Formerly a war pole, striped diagonally with red paint, was set up at one end of the lines, and a speaker struck it at the end of each song.[6]

Although the Sioux have a give-away connected with nearly everything that they do, we cannot consider this phase of the Iroquois dance as typically Sioux, because it was also typical of tribes all across the country.

In early historical times, the Hurons, Mohawks, and Oneidas all used an enemy's head in the kettle at the War Dance. Later they substituted dog, and finally hog. Dog's heads, in soup, were passed around to great warriors to excite their courage. A timid person was likely to have ashes put on his head. Today a hog's head is the ceremonial head.

Another great change is in the purpose of the War Dance. Since this dance no longer has any function as an actual war dance, it has become a rain dance.[7] In most tribes Thunder had a great deal to do with war, so the transition is logical.

Frank Speck, in his study of the Yuchis in 1909, said that this tribe formerly gave its entire repertoire of ceremonial dances before setting out for war. Many of these dances were animal dances and were done to secure the favor of the various clan totems for protection on the journey and in battle. White men referred to all of these dances as "war dances."[8]

THE OSAGES

Victor Tixier, who was on the prairies in 1839 and 1840, mentioned "striking the post" for the Osages, living at that time in Missouri. The post was painted red. The warriors struck it one after the other with their tomahawks, then "extending their hands toward it, they listed their acts of courage and the reasons for their hatred of the Pawnee."

The war chief made the rounds of the lodges, exciting younger men to anger and courage. Ceremonial "war fires" were built and at one of them a great heap of powdered charcoal was mixed with fat to use as war paint. After striking the post, the warriors all rode around the camp on horseback, stopping in front of the lodge of the man they wanted for leader. If he accepted their invitation, he painted himself black from head to foot with the charcoal.

The Osages had two ceremonial war lodges. A group came out from each lodge, turned in opposite directions, and danced around the camp. Whenever they met they stopped to face each other.

The warriors made maniacal contortions, jumping and capering like madmen. These people, so serious and so composed the day before, looked as if they were possessed of the devil. They were making such faces that they seemed to be on the point of dislocating their jaws, rolling their eyes wildly and twisting their limbs about, mumbling indistinct words, and uttering the war cry in a low voice, beating drums or blowing *tsu-tsehs* [reed flutes]; some took up a warlike song, which they accompanied by striking their fans on some pieces of wood. After this intermission, they completed the turn of the camp and came back to their lodges. The dancers, out of breath and covered with perspiration, began to eat. Such was the first part of the *dance du charbon*.

He even described the costumes as being "picturesque":

Some wore deer tails placed on their heads like the crests of ancient helmets; others had their foreheads crowned with a band made of crow's beaks painted in green. They held now a spear, now a calumet, now a stick, sometimes a tomahawk, a fan, or the old-fashioned war hatchet. Tufts of swan's down, eagle feathers, buffalo tails, small calabashes filled with pebbles, skins of white wolf and of panther were also parts of their attire, with the wings of the calumet bird (the bald eagle) which they used as a fan.[9]

Whoever inserted "bald eagle" in parentheses as the "calumet bird" was unfamiliar with his subject, because the golden eagle is the one the Indians admire as the war eagle and whose feathers were commonly attached to the calumet and whose wings were used as fans.

Tixier's mention of the deer-tail crests refers to the type of headdress still popular with Indian dancers. It is usually made of porcupine hair (not quills) and hair from the tail of the white-tailed deer, but many of the old crests, or roaches, were made of turkey beards and deer-tail hair. The hair roach was found throughout the Woodland area and was mentioned in the earliest reports. It simulated the roach of hair left as a scalp lock on the shaved heads of warriors. A man who had earned war honors was permitted to decorate his scalp lock with the hair roach; with further honors he could add feathers to it. It had much the same significance to the Woodland Indian that the eagle-feather war bonnet had to the Plains Indian. The feathers, being set in bone sockets on swivels, were flexible and consequently suitable for forest wear. The Winnebago call the roach a *casin' djera*, meaning a deer-tail headdress. The Chippewa call it a *gi' cida*, meaning a "full warrior," or a "full man" (see page 195).

M. G. Chandler says the "crow's beaks" were really beaks of ivory-billed or pileated woodpeckers. The bird's scalp—crest of fiery red feathers—was taken, the upper mandible pulled back and the inside painted blue or green. Scalps of the same birds were used on the calumet (see pages 194, 195).*

The Stephen Long expedition noted the custom of striking the post for the Otos, who are related to the Osages, and said that having struck the post a warrior was bound to tell only the truth, and many jealous watchers made sure that he did.[10]

---

*Grinnell said that only sons of chiefs among the Pawnees were entitled to wear the beaks on a headband or headdress. At any rate, they were rare and disappeared from the scene long ago. Paul Warner, while associated with the Field Museum, saw one among the Pawnees in recent years. The only one known to be in existence today is in the Osage Tribal Museum in Oklahoma. For illustrations see the paintings of Charles B. King in the McKenney and Hall *Atlas* and Oliver LaFarge, *An Illustrated History of the American Indian* (New York, Crown Publishers, 1956), 100.

Porcupine and Deer-Hair Roaches

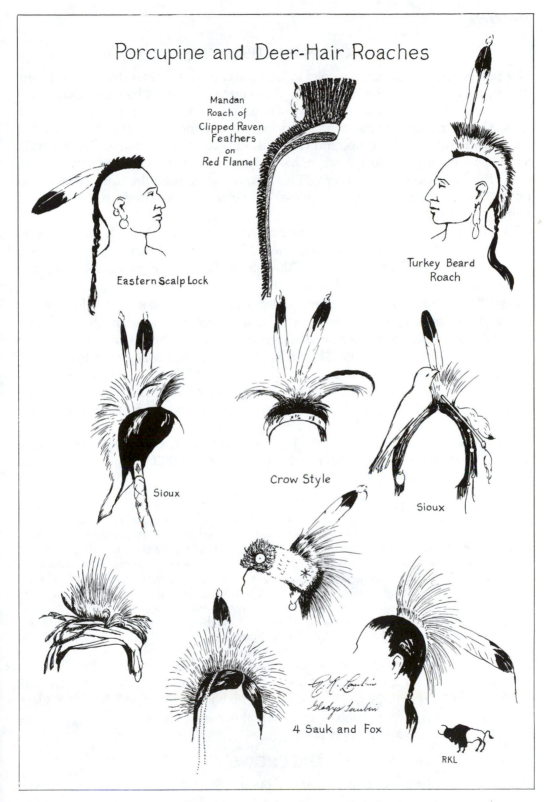

Mandan
Roach of
Clipped Raven
Feathers
on
Red Flannel

Eastern Scalp Lock

Turkey Beard
Roach

Sioux

Crow Style

Sioux

4 Sauk and Fox

RKL

Porcupine- and deer-hair roaches.

COMMON CUSTOMS

The procedure of choosing the chief to lead the war party seems different from the usual custom. In most tribes a chief raised the war party, and if he were known as a man of experience and a good leader he usually had no trouble gathering his warriors. The preparation of the charcoal paint was common to many Western tribes and particularly to the Poncas, and Omahas, relatives of the Osages. But generally a man painted his entire face black, or his body, only when he had been first to count coup, that is, first to strike the enemy. This meant that he used the black paint on his return rather than on setting out, unless, of course, he had previously earned the right to paint black.

Tixier was the second to mention a war cry in a "low voice." Usually it is described as high-pitched. Indian cries we have heard have always been so high that the average white person cannot approach them in pitch. It took a great deal of practice on our parts to be able to duplicate them.

As with most tribes, there were long and strenuous purification rites before setting out on a war path, and often similar rites again following the return home.[11] The strict rules of behavior and the taboos associated with the war path among most, and perhaps all tribes, make it unrealistic to believe the stories concerning the rape of women captives which are so prevalent in accounts of the Indian wars. Any such intimacy with a woman would destroy a warrior's power and make him liable to defeat, injury, or death. The perpetrators of these stories, and believers in them, show a complete ignorance of Indian customs, habits and beliefs.

The following is an example of the kind of nonsense that has been published in regard to Indian dancing. An article written by an artist in 1903, pertaining to a Crow celebration he witnessed, reads:

Owing to the hostile attitude those in authority hold towards Indian celebrations, I was glad of the opportunity of witnessing this dance, which might not be given again in a long time. . . . The air was heavily laden with the perfume of sweet-scented grasses, and seated upon robes and mats were the spectators and the participants. [He said they started with a Calumet Dance, then followed with a War Dance] . . . faces, full of grimaces, expressed the ferociousness and cunning of the savage; eyes rolled and glared; teeth snapped with fiendish leers; breath came through inflated nostrils; the very hiss of death and battle was in the air. With unabated zeal the dancers continued their movements until by force of sheer exhaustion they reeled from the ring, while others standing near took their vacant places, and performed the same ceremony until they, too, fell from exhaustion.[12]

This writer sounds as though he had been reading from someone like Tixier, or perhaps he read Catlin's account of the Sioux Scalp Dance. No doubt Indians did use facial grimaces and danced with some frenzy back in the days when they were dancing in earnest and portraying their actual experiences, but no one ever sees them in dances performed nowadays.

THE CROWS

The Crows, like the Sioux, had no real War Dance. Since 1875 they have been doing

War Dance of the Mandan Indians, by Carl Bodmer, 1833. From the attire of the dancers this may instead be a warrior-society dance. From Prince Maximilian Wied zu Wied, *Travels in the Interior of North America, 1832–34*. Smithsonian Institution, Bureau of American Ethnology.

the Hot Dance, which is a version of the Grass Dance, or Omaha Dance, of other tribes. In speaking English they call it War Dance because that is what the whites call it. It formerly was a warrior's dance, but it always has been largely a men's social dance.

The only dances in which Indians fell from exhaustion, so far as we know, were the Sun Dance and the Ghost Dance. The Crows have not given their own Sun Dance since 1874 and never did the Ghost Dance. Although the writer lamented the fact that Indian dances were frowned upon by the authorities and were "passing," such reports did much to discourage their preservation and encouraged a continuance of the official attitude of censure.

When the *wolves*, or scouts, of a Crow war party returned with news that they had discovered the enemy, a pile of buffalo chips was made and the warriors sat down in a semicircle near it. The leader kicked over the pile of chips before making his report. The Sioux had a similar custom but knocked over a stick stuck in the ground.

If a Crow leader wished to harangue the tribe for war, a big pile of stones was built up in the center of the camp, the warrior societies paraded around the village, halting at the pile, and the herald made speeches honoring brave men as examples for others to follow. Sometimes a pile of buffalo chips as high as a man was used instead of the stones. The war leader approached it with four ceremonial stops and then sang his song four times. On the last song the warriors gave the victory call, the women trilled, and the leader attempted to mount the pile, waving eagle wings in each hand to imitate the flight of that bird of war. He wore a buffalo calfskin robe, his entire body was painted black, and he carried his shield on his back. If he was successful in reaching the top of the pile, it indicated that they would go to war. Once at the top he laid down his "wings" and rolled the shield down the heap of chips. If the shield landed face up, the success of the expedition was assured. If it fell face down, disaster would ensue, which meant that he would have few if any followers.[13]

This ceremony certainly cannot be considered a dance, but was the Crow substitute for the War Dance. The piles of chips or stones may have been substituted for the pole or post used in other tribes, although, except for the leader of the scouts kicking it, it was not struck, as when an actual pole was used.

THE APACHES

One of the most vivid accounts of a War Dance was by Captain Bourke, who fought in the Apache campaigns but came to be fond of the Apaches and learned to know them well. He wrote of a dance given by Apache army scouts and his story would seem to agree with our previous statements that most Indian "war dances" were in reality "warrior dances" and were more often given for social occasions than as any preparation for war.

All night long the Chiricahuas and the Apache scouts danced together in sign of peace and good will. . . . Not much time need be wasted upon a description of their dresses; they didn't wear any, except breech clouts and moccasins. To the noise of an improvised drum and the accompaniment of marrow-freezing yells and shrieks they pirouetted and charged in all directions, swaying their bodies violently, dropping on one knee, then suddenly springing high in air, discharging their pieces.[14]

OVERSEAS PERFORMANCES

George Catlin wrote of the startling effect the War Dance had on spectators in London when he was traveling through England with a troup of nine Ojibwa Indians in 1845:

. . . the large room of the Egyptian Hall was filled at an early hour, and the Indians received with a roar of applause as they entered and advanced upon the platform. . . . Indian looks and Indian costumes, etc., were supposed to have been pretty well understood before this, by most of the audience, who had studied them at their leisure in my rooms on former occasions; but Indian dances and Indian yells, and the war-whoop, had been from necessity postponed and unappreciated until the whole party (as they sprang upon their feet) announced the war-dance as having commenced. The drum was beating, the rattles shaking, war clubs and tomahawks and spears were brandishing over their heads and all their voices were shouting (in time with the beat of the drum and the stamp of their feet) the frightful war-song!

With the exception of some two or three women (whose nerves were not quite firm enough for these excitements, and who screamed quite as loud as the Indians did, as they were making a rush for the door) the audience stood amazed and delighted with the wildness and newness of the scene that was passing before them; and, at the close of the dance, united in a round of applause, which seemed to please the Indians as much as seeing the queen.[15]

But they were pleased with seeing the queen. They were so excited that they celebrated the occasion the next day by having a dog feast, such as was associated with the real War Dance. They observed all the forms accompanying it in their home country. Catlin procured the dog for them; he does not tell us how.

There are many Indians who believe that their special dances and ceremonies helped win World War II. The landing on Okinawa followed a big ceremonial put on by the Indians in the First Marine Division. One of the last stories the well-liked war correspondent Ernie Pyle wrote was about these Indian marines. Apparently most of them were Navajos, but Sioux, Comanche, Apache, Pima, Kiowa, Crow, and Pueblo tribes were also represented.

The Red Cross furnished colored cloth and paint to use on their faces. The rest of the costumes were made from anything available—chicken feathers, sea shells, cocoanuts, empty ration cans, and empty rifle cartridges. Several thousand marines, realizing that their Indian buddies were entirely serious in the performance, gravely watched as the Indians danced and sang to give strength to the American forces and to put the finger of weakness on the Japanese.

Some of our Crow friends ascribed their success in the war to the effectiveness of the Sun Dance, which we shall take up later, but Sun Dance or War Dance, Eagle Dance or Mountain Chant, the Indians were there with their ancient ceremonies to help win a modern war.

11. Victory and Scalp Dances

If there was any such thing as a universal dance among Indians of North America it was the Victory, or Scalp, Dance. It seems that all tribes had such a celebration, even those noted for their peaceful pursuits rather than for any interest in war. In many cases Victory dances have been confused with War dances, but Victory Dance is a better designation than Scalp Dance.

THE PRACTICE OF SCALPING

There is good reason to believe that the practice of scalping was originally limited to a few tribes in the Northeast. To most tribes, any trophy was sufficient, so long as it was evidence of vanquishing the enemy. Most were satisfied with heads, but a hand, arm, or ear would do.

It is thought that the Mohicans, of the Hudson River Valley, were the ones who originated the practice of scalping, at least in that area. An offshoot of the Mohicans migrated into Connecticut and became known as the Pequots. During the Pequot War the colonists offered bounties on the heads of slain Pequots, but soon discovered that it was much more convenient to adopt their enemies' custom of merely bringing in the skin and hair of the crown of the head. Full heads were heavy and bulky; a soldier or scout could handle only a couple at once. By following the Pequot custom the same man could bring in a whole beltful of scalps.

The only drawback lay in the fact that there was no identification of the former owner of the scalp. In later wars, when sizable bounties were offered for enemy scalps, scalp hunters were not always too particular and sometimes brought in scalps of friendly or neutral Indians; they were much easier to get and paid just as well.

In 1755 the Massachusetts Colony declared war on the Penobscots, offering forty pounds for each Penobscot warrior's scalp and twenty pounds for the scalp of a woman or child. Because of ensuing arguments as to which was a man or a woman's scalp, and because the Penobscots were not too easily taken unaware, the next year the bounty was raised to three hundred pounds "for every Indian enemy." This was at the time of the French and Indian War and most Indians in the direction of Canada were considered enemies.[1]

At the same time bounties were offered by the French for English scalps and by the English for French scalps, so a thriving business in scalp hunting developed. The scalps with the longest, blondest, silkiest hair brought the most money, which meant, of course, scalps of white women and children. The same practice was carried out in the Revolutionary War, the English offering high bounties for American scalps, and vice versa.

This brisk trade in scalps encouraged the practice among neighboring Indian tribes, as well as among the colonists, and as "civilization" spread west the emigrants found the custom had preceded them. But it seems that the Europeans were the ones actually responsible for the spreading of it. A number of tribes, especially of the desert regions and notably the Apaches, considered so fierce and bloodthirsty, never did adopt it.

COUNTING COUP

Most tribes had certain military codes, similar, in a way, to the chivalry of the Middle Ages. Among the tribes of the Plains the actual taking of a scalp was not an honor. The only honor really worth mention was the *coup*, the touching of an enemy with the hand, a stick, or a hand weapon. In other words, the coup implied personal combat with the enemy. Nothing else rated. A coup could be counted on either a living or a dead enemy, and while it naturally rated higher on a living enemy, it nevertheless took great courage to count coup on a dead enemy, because the Indians did not abandon their dead on the field, except in extreme cases. A fallen warrior was immediately surrounded by his companions, and the coup striker was in a hornet's nest.

Four men could count coup on the same enemy in the same fight. All four rated high honor, but the first to touch was the acknowledged hero of the day. Scalping could be left to the laggards or the timid. In the case of a lone warrior, or a few companions out on a mission of revenge or horse stealing, scalps would be proof of hand-to-hand contact with the enemy, but such an enemy might have been killed from ambush or in stealth. Although the warrior counted his coup, his deed was never given the importance attached to one which had numerous witnesses who could declare that there had been a real fight.

The emblem for counting a coup was a tail feather from the golden eagle, and by the position in which it was worn an observer could tell at a glance just what kind of a coup had been earned. Among the Lakotas, the feather straight up at the back of the head signified a first coup, the highest honor. The second man to touch the enemy slanted the feather to the right, the third wore his horizontally, and the fourth wore his feather hanging down from his scalp lock.

M. G. Chandler, who was adopted by Winnebagos, told us that they had one ornament even more important than the eagle feather. It was simply an oak twig, shaved down, with the shavings still attached and dyed red. The Winnebago warrior wore it in his hair along with feathers he had earned, or sometimes placed it in his war bonnet; it showed that he had won all the honors it was possible for him to attain. Bodmer pictures a similar ornament as part of the headdress in one of his Mandan portraits.

Thus we see that Plains Indian warfare was not so much a matter of bloodshed and manslaughter as we have supposed. It was in a way a mounted game of tag in which a man fought mainly to distinguish himself in the eyes of his fellows. It was a reckless, daring, exciting game. Its rewards were honor, glory, prestige. The forfeit for failure was death at the hands of the enemy. A man who had counted no coups was a nobody. He had no place in the council, could not take an important part in any ceremony or dance, could not even name his own child.

Even reliable writers have sometimes confused the issues in scalping and counting coup. Clark Wissler said that the taking of a scalp rated very highly among the Sioux, but his observation is certainly contrary to the information we have received from all our friends and "relatives" who fought in the Indian wars. Both he and Miss Densmore state that the killing of an enemy was the highest honor, but again this has been denied by all of our acquaintances. We think the confusion comes from the interpretation of the terms used. The Sioux warrior used the terms "killed," "vanquished," or "overcome" to express the counting of a coup. He might say, "I killed that man," when he really meant, "I struck," or "I counted coup on that man." It was ceremonial usage and implied that he *could have killed* him. But to leave the enemy unhurt after striking him was the greatest honor of all, for it was the most dangerous way of earning the honor.

Nowadays, at all Indian gatherings, we see women wearing beaded headbands, even beaded crowns, and one or two erect eagle feathers. Where it all started is anyone's guess. In the old days the only woman who could wear an eagle feather was one who had gone to war and counted coup, just as the men did. Not even a chief's wife or daughter could wear one otherwise. In all our time among the Sioux the only woman we ever saw wearing an eagle feather was Mary Crawler, Tasina Maniwin, who went into the Reno fight on the Little Big Horn to avenge the death of her little brother, Wicoȟanla, or Deeds, who was the first one the soldiers killed. When we knew her as an old, old woman, she still wore an eagle feather erect at the back of a big gray Stetson, and she danced with the men!

We have never seen Crow women wear eagle feathers at home, on the reservation, but we have seen Crow entries for the Miss Indian America contest in Sheridan, Wyoming, wear them.

THE SIOUX VICTORY DANCE

Some writers have implied that Indians did a War Dance before going to war to stir up courage. The courage and enthusiasm were already there. It was part of the upbringing of every Plains Indian boy. Boys often went to war the first time at twelve or fourteen years of age. But no matter how many enemies were killed or how many horses and other booty were taken, if a war party suffered the loss of even one man the expedition was not considered a success and there could be no celebration until at least four days had been set aside for mourning the lost one. After that, with permission from the dead man's relatives, a Victory Dance might have been held.

Old Sioux veterans we knew were horrified when they learned that some accounts of the Custer Battle had stated that the Indians had held a big victory celebration the night after it took place. Reno survivors declared that they heard a big Scalp Dance going on in the village below them. The Sioux said there were too many warriors lost even to think of a Scalp Dance. According to our standards, Indian losses were insignificant compared to the victory achieved, but not to the Indian mind.

The "noise" the Reno men heard was probably wailing for the dead. The village was already removed to a safer place, but relatives of slain warriors returned to the scene of their passing to mourn their loss.

In the case of a victorious homecoming, the successful warriors usually hid out in the hills near the village and took time to dress up to look their finest, paint their faces, and decorate their ponies. Sometimes during this interval they even sent an advance runner to give the impression that the venture had been a failure, that the few survivors were delayed because of carrying their wounded. The entire camp was thrown into a confusion of wailing and mourning, but before it became too serious and relatives began to cut off their hair, gash themselves, or cut off fingers in their grief the war party came thundering into the village circle, yelling and shooting their guns in the air. Feathers flying, war bonnets streaming in the wind, they tore around the camp like an enemy war party, driving their captured loose horses before them.

After about so much of this "horse play," they settled down into a dignified parade, singing their war songs and shouting their latest exploits. Now all could get a close look at the new heroes and their booty. Many of the newly acquired horses were immediately given away, often to women relatives. The onlookers had the right to take personal items from their heroes. Leggings and moccasins were sometimes stripped right off them as they rode by. A hero often wore second-best articles on such an occasion, for he stood a good chance of losing them.

Scalps and other trophies were handed to the women, who prepared them for the big celebration that night. The scalps were usually stretched on small willow hoops and the flesh sides painted red or black—sometimes half red, half black. The hoops containing the scalps were then tied to long willow wands to be carried in the dance.

In the evening, when the Victory Dance took place, a young warrior who had just counted his first coup might be especially honored. A pole was set up in the center of the dance ground and painted all black or with black rings. It represented the conquered enemy, but was used only on the occasion of honoring a special warrior. The new coup striker was painted black from neck down, and, if his honor was a first coup, he also had his entire face painted black. At this time he might have his name publicly changed. His father, if he had counted coup, or some great warrior gave him a new name and announced it for everyone to hear. The warrior himself might choose the name, if there was a special one he wanted, but it was customary for the one giving the name to choose it. The one receiving the new name gave away horses, and so might the one doing the naming, and also the young man's family.

Men counting second, third, or fourth coups could paint the lower halves of their faces black. Others taking part in the Victory Dance had their faces painted by a specially chosen young woman, who dipped her hand in black charcoal paint and drew four fingers across the lower portions. All wore their hair loose.

Victory Dance— counting coup.

A huge fire was built up near the black pole, a little east of it, and the singers took their places nearby. Women who had already been presented with scalp poles or trophies gathered to form a compact circle, and the returned warriors made another ring on the outside, facing the center, the women facing them.

First the man who had counted the most coups stepped forward and told of his exploits. He then presented a scalp pole or other trophy to some woman on the side-lines, and she joined the others in the center of the arena, giving the woman's tremolo, or trill, waving the trophy aloft. The singers pounded a tattoo on the drum, and a chorus of "*Hau,*" and "*Wašte,*" greeted the telling of each honor.

The songs for the Victory Dance were many and varied. Sometimes the drum was steady, unaccented 2/4 rhythm, but the singers might suddenly change into a rapid 3/4, or rather 2/4 in triplets, an accented beat preceded by an unaccented one, no third beat—like woman's dance but much faster. Thus the character of the dance could change instantly with the drumming. Tempos also changed at the decision of the singers.

On a rather slow, steady beat the dancers moved to the side, as in the Round Dance, while the man who had just recounted his coups danced within the arena, between the warriors and the group of women in the center. A few more dancers might join him within the circle, pantomiming attack and retreat or portraying their own exploits. On a faster song the solo dancers could become even more dramatic, while the circle of dancers continued around, now stepping in half time. On one of the fast 3/4 rhythm songs they danced in a low squat, both feet far apart and coming down hard at once on the accented beat, sometimes moving them slightly nearer together on the unaccented beat, apart and stamping hard again on the accent, the circle of dancers at the same time progressing slightly to the left.

On yet another song all the men massed, still moving to the left, and on a sharp drum beat all paused in their tracks to listen while the women and children bowed low, crying, "Ku'tiyaye!" ("they [the enemy] fell over!").

If the party had been a large one, the dance might be carried on for several nights. Catlin said that the Scalp Dance was usually given for fifteen successive nights. During the days feasting around the camp in the various heroes' lodges was the rule.

During the portion of the Victory Dance devoted to the pantomiming of personal exploits, Two Shields used to do a dance like the old Discovery Dance mentioned by many early writers. He first looked for the enemy trail, followed it, enacted the attack and victorious homecoming, all the time the other warriors were doing the side step.

No Heart and Gray Whirlwind once pantomimed a battle. No Heart pretended to be killed. Then two men came out from the circle, portrayed lifting No Heart onto a horse and leading him off, then the two actually carried him out of the arena.

This "Wounded" Dance was often given along with the Victory Dance, and has been even in recent years. Two war bonnets were hung on a post in the center. Men and women formed two opposite lines, facing each other. The women turned to the left, forming an inner circle, moving with the sun. The men turned to the right, forming an outer circle going the opposite way. A scout danced outside the circle, with stealthy motions.

On a signal from the singers all reversed and went the opposite direction. As they passed the pole the leading woman put on one of the war bonnets, the leading man the other. Another scout entered, riding a cane with a horse's head, like an old-time hobby horse. The two scouts met, the one on horseback overcoming the one on foot, "riding" around his "enemy" in triumph, after which the fallen warrior was carried off.

This Wounded Dance was a bit different from one sometimes called that, to be described under the women's society known as the Shield Bearers, which was also given at times of the Victory Dance.

Following the Custer Battle, the Sioux sang a song at the Victory dances which translated, "Long Hair [General Custer] is your friend. Here is his hair." Of course, they did not have his hair, as Custer had short hair at the time and was not scalped. The song was a sort of satire. It was used even in recent years, the Indians taking a sort of sly delight in singing it before white people who did not understand the words.

In Warrior and Victory dances a man who carried a wooden knife painted red, with horsehair tied to its hilt, showed he had taken a scalp. If his face were painted with white spots he had probably distinguished himself in a snowstorm, or he might have thunder medicine. Carrying a lance with a blade painted red showed it had been used to kill or wound an enemy. A man painted his old wounds red, spots for bullets, lines for arrows. One who had been wounded might also wear a feather dyed red or one with a red tip, as Young Eagle did. If he wore a split feather it showed that he had been wounded many times. A man who painted a red hand on his chest had been struck by an enemy. Although the coup had been counted on him, it nevertheless rated as a war honor, but *he* could not claim it as a coup.

Horse tracks painted on a horse showed captured horses, a track for each horse. Stripes on the horse's legs indicated the number of times enemies had been struck from that side. An imitation scalp fastened to a horse's bridle showed that that particular horse had been used to ride down an enemy.

While the above account pertains to Sioux customs, other tribes had similar celebrations and ways of marking their exploits. An Arikara warrior who had struck an enemy in the enemy's camp wore fox tails on his heels as he danced. An oak twig with curled shavings, dyed red, has already been mentioned for the Winnebagos. A Hidatsa who wore a similar decoration depicted that he had been wounded many times.

The Victory Dance was a peculiar combination of rejoicing and exulting over vanquishing the enemy and of mourning for the loss of him as a brave man. Part of this, no doubt, was out of fear of reprisal on the part of the dead enemy's spirit, but at the same time Indians, for all their taunting of an enemy as a coward, preferred to fight a brave one. It is possible that they did lament the loss of such a man. It was more of an accomplishment and consequently more to be proud of to fight a brave enemy.

The Sioux preferred to fight Crows, Shoshonis, and Flatheads to white soldiers, whom they considered much inferior as warriors. The enemy Indians fought them on their own terms, as individuals. The soldiers took orders from a man who sometimes did not know any more than they did and was no better a fighter, something Indians could not understand. Besides, they said the white men took all the fun out of fighting. They fought when it was cold, when they were wet and hungry. There was no sense to that!

Following the Victory Dance the scalps, on their poles, were set up on a distant hillside. Food and water were placed before them and they were left there to the elements, their spirits returning to the souls of the dead warriors. The offerings and the scalps were never molested.

SCALP DANCES

If there is any distinction between Victory and Scalp dances, then perhaps we may think of the Scalp Dance mainly as a woman's dance. Everywhere women played an important part in it. Among the Sioux the Shield Bearers dance was very much like the Scalp Dance of other tribes, where the women danced wearing men's headdresses and sometimes other articles of men's apparel. Lewis and Clark gave an account of a Teton (Lakota) Scalp Dance. Ten men, some with hand drums, others with rawhide and deer-hoof rattles, formed the "orchestra."

The women then came forward, highly decorated, some with poles in their hands on which were hung the scalps of their enemies; others with guns, spears, or different trophies, taken in war by their husbands, brothers, or connexions. Having arranged themselves in two colums [sic], one on each side of the fire, as soon as the music began they danced towards each other till they met in the center, when the rattles were shaken, and they all shouted and returned back to their places. They have no step, but shuffle along the ground; nor does the music appear to be anything more than a confusion of noises, distinguished only by hard or gentle blows upon the buffalo skin; the song is perfectly extemporaneous. In the pauses of the dance any man of the company comes forward and recites, in a sort of low guttural tone, some little story or incident, which is either martial or ludicrous, or, as was the case this evening, voluptuous and indecent; this is taken up by the orchestra and the dancers, who repeat it in a higher strain and dance to it. Sometimes they alternate, the orchestra first performing, and when it ceases the women raise their voices and make a music more agreeable, that is, less intolerable, than that of the musicians. The dances of the men, which are always separate from those of the women, are conducted very nearly in the same way, except that the men jump up and down instead of shuffling, and in the war dance the recitations are all of a military cast.[2]

The dance Lewis and Clark saw on this occasion may not have been a real Scalp Dance but only a semblance of one given to entertain the white visitors. It seems the Indians were not very serious about it. The captains certainly had little idea of the actual content of Indian music. The songs may have sounded "perfectly extemporaneous" to their ears, but the same songs would have been sung identically each time they were repeated.

They also were unimpressed with the recitations they heard in the dance. Any warrior who tried to get away with "some little story or incident" in a real Scalp

Dance would have found himself the laughingstock of his people. He had to be able to prove any statement he made.

Except for the Shield Bearers' Dance, which we shall take up later, no other report we have read and none of the old-timers of our acquaintance ever mentioned the two lines of women dancers for the Sioux, but apparently the dance had better choreography in earlier days and would have been even more interesting than in its more recent form.

The Utes also had a Shield Dance done by the women, who carried shields and spears as well as scalps, but the real Victory Dance was given by the men.

Only recently we saw Crow women do the Scalp Dance. Most of them wore their husbands' bonnets and some carried weapons. Using the customary woman's step, they circled the dance ground in single file, and to the right, which is unusual in Plains dances (see page 199).

THE CROW VICTORY CELEBRATION

The Crows had several other customs concerning the victory celebration peculiar to them. Their highest coup was taking a gun away from an enemy. This was also the Blackfeet's highest honor. The man who took the gun and/or the first coup striker painted his robe or his shirt black all over. The second and third painted their robes or shirts half black, and the fourth painted the sleeves of his shirt black. The paint used was charcoal mixed with buffalo blood that had been carried home in the paunch.

When near home, the warriors fired off their guns, so that people knew a success-ful party was returning, and those who had counted coups went into camp to pro-cure hand drums for each warrior. The women, carrying scalp sticks, gathered ahead of the war party and danced into camp while the warriors followed, singing their victory songs.

A night or two after their return, the warriors painted their faces and paraded through camp, the war leader in the rear, followed by a herald. The herald cried out for the women to come to the leader's or pipe carrier's lodge for a feast. After the parade the men took their seats around the inside of the lodge and the women en-tered, each sitting behind her warrior. When the scalp and scout songs were sung, each woman took the robe and tomahawk of her man, went to a conspicuous place by the door, and danced.

After a feast of cherry pudding, the women took what was left home. While they were gone, boys cut willow rods, or poles, and leaned them against the outside of the leader's tipi, then lined up to await the women's return. The singers in the party took their hand drums, but everyone else, men and women, each took a willow. As the singers beat the wild rhythm for the lusty victory songs, all rushed on the tipi and struck it with their sticks. Some of the men fired their guns into the air. After this striking, the couples moved to the center of the village, where they danced, the men with their blankets wrapped around their partners. The dance was like the Owl, or

Round, Dance and moved both left and right, but the songs were victory songs. After dancing awhile, they rushed to strike the tipis of former war leaders, dancing between each striking. Such a celebration might last several days. At times the women did the dance already described above.[3]

THE STEAL-THE-DRUM DANCE

Still another form of Victory Dance, or it might even be called an honor dance, which could be given at almost any public celebration is one the Crows call Steal-the-Drum. It proved to be a very popular dance in our repertoire overseas with the Crow dancers, who remembered seeing old warriors do it years ago. A number of distinguished warriors, each with a hand drum, took their places standing in the center of the dance arena and began to sing Owl Dance songs. The women started an ordinary Owl Dance, forming a crescent and moving in a circle shoulder to shoulder around the singers. Gradually men from the surrounding onlookers broke in on the crescent, each man forcing his way between two women. It looked as if the dance could go on forever, but suddenly a man who had honors outranking any of the singers stepped forward out of the crescent and into the ring. Dancing sidewise in front of the crescent, and with longer steps, he made his own circle around the ring, overtaking the others as they continued to dance side by side.

When he came to another warrior with an outstanding record, he tapped him on the shoulder. The second likewise stepped out into the ring, following the first with the long steps, and he in turn tapped another prominent warrior. This kept up until there were as many of these important warriors dancing within the circle as there were singers with drums, when they began to circle the singers. Each made a feint at taking a drum from a singer, and just as the song drew to a close each snatched a drum, holding it aloft and yelling. The dancers then dispersed. Such a dance might continue as long as there were challengers to the records of those holding the drums.

Maximilian reported an Extended Robe Dance for the Arikaras, given by the bravest warriors. Someone started it by giving a present to a brave warrior, who accepted by pointing his gun at the donor. Another brave man could then take the present away from him by recounting a deed of still greater bravery. This was kept up until the bravest of all finally came into possession of the gift.[4]

The Hidatsas are also reported to have had something like Steal-the-Drum. At one of their celebrations, a warrior might take a drum from a singer, striking it for each deed he recited. Someone with a greater honor could then take the drum from him and return it to the singer.[5]

At the time of the Omaha Wawan, or Calumet ceremony, a man could end the ceremony by taking a drum from a singer and telling a deed which no one could surpass.[6]

THE BLACKFOOT VICTORY DANCE

Father De Smet gave an interesting account of the Blackfoot Victory Dance.

On returning from the late field of battle, the warriors, at the head of whom was a young chief, chanted songs of triumph, accompanied with the beating of drums; at each beat they sent forth a wild and piercing shout, then followed the song, and so on alternately; wild as the music was, it was not without harmony. It continued thus during almost the whole of our route. We marched up the right bank of the Yellowstone river, having on our left a chain of mountains resembling those old fortresses told of in the histories of ancient chivalry. We had scarcely arrived at the encampment, when the Blackfeet commenced, under the shade of a beautiful cluster of pines, their arranging for a dance, insisting, at the same time, upon showing the Blackrobes how highly they valued their presence among them, and how gratified they would be to have them witness this display. There was, indeed, nothing in it that could give occasion to offended modesty to turn aside and blush. I need not tell you it was not the polka, the waltz, or anything resembling the dances of modern civilized life. The women alone figure in it, old and young; from the youngest child capable of walking, to the oldest matron present. Among them I have seen several old women upward of eighty years, whose feeble limbs required the aid of a staff in their movements thus to dance. Almost all appeared in the best costume of the warriors, which, however, was worn over their own dress, a sort of tunic they always wear, and which contributed also not a little to the modesty of their appearance. Some carried the arms that had done most execution in battle, but the greater part held a green bough in the hand. In proportion as the dresses increase in singularity, the colors in variety, and the jingling of the bells in sound, in the same degree is the effect upon the rude spectator heightened. The whole figure is surmounted by a casket of plumes, which by the regular movements of the individual is made to harmonize with the song, and seems to add much gracefulness to the whole scene. To lose nothing of so grand a spectacle the Indians mount their horses, or climb the neighboring trees. The dance itself consists of a little jump, more or less lively, according to the beat of the drum. This is beaten only by the men, and all unite in the song. The women take the treble and the men the bass. To break the monotony, or lend new interest to the scene, a sudden, piercing scream is added. If the dance languishes, harangues and those skillful in grimaces come to its aid. As in jumping the dancers tend toward a common center, it often happens that the ranks become too close, then they fall back in good order to form a large circle, and commence anew in better style.[7]

De Smet's account of a Sioux Scalp Dance is not as good and sounds like hearsay. He says the pole was painted red, which does not agree with other accounts or with what we have heard personally. He also said "the warriors surround it, flourishing in their hands the bloody scalps which they have brought back from the field of battle," and states that they struck the post with their weapons. Perhaps the Sioux struck the post in the Victory Dance in those days, but a number of our old friends were alive in de Smet's time and never mentioned it. We know the warriors did not dance with the scalps.

THE ARIKARA VICTORY DANCE

Around 1810 John Bradbury told of "the dance of the scalp" by the Arikara women. "The ceremony consisted in carrying the scalps elevated on sticks through the village, followed by the warriors who had composed the war party, dressed in all their ornaments, and painted as for war." Further on he gave more details, saying that the women put on their husbands' clothes, carried their tomahawks and moved in a circle, brandishing the weapons at intervals as they faced the center. One by one they stepped into the center, each boasting of her husband's war deeds. He neglected to say in which direction they danced, but said they ended with a dog feast.[8]

Tabeau, the trader with the Arikaras in Lewis and Clark's day, stated that small war parties were successful more often than big ones. He wrote, "A victory, however complete it may be, must not be bought at the price of a single one of his [war leader's] warriors." If they lost a man, the party returned, its members covered with dirt and dust, "looking ashamed and vanquished."

When, on the other hand, the party returned victorious and without loss, those who are on racers announce from afar, by particular cries, the meaning of which is known, the number of scalps, of prisoners, and of captured horses. The whole village with cries of joy answers this announcement, which is repeated many times as the war party approaches. At length the warriors appear, chanting their victory, and come on at a slow pace. At once the women pounce upon them, seize their arms, and disrobe them completely. The cries of joy, the feasts, and appropriate dances succeed one another for many days; the scalps are produced with ceremony, and change owners several times a day. They are carried in triumph journey after journey and often to a friendly nation. All those who have had the honor of striking an enemy dead or alive, that is to say, for the first, second, third and fourth stroke only, count this deed for themselves and then generally take a new name. They wear also the feather of the calumet bird or other honorable marks according to the number and nature of their great deeds and the rank they had while fighting.

A man who brought back horses could wear hair on his leggings.[9]

This description of the victory celebration tallies closely with accounts for other tribes and periods. It is almost identical to what we have been told by old Sioux friends, with the exception of keeping the scalps. Occasionally scalps were cut up to serve as trimming and decoration on certain war paraphernalia—leggings, shirts, and the like—but they were not retained otherwise.

Maximilian said that the Mandans, "Manitaries" (Hidatsas), and Crows saved the scalps and used them for ornamenting their clothing. The prince stated that they painted in various ways for the Scalp Dance but that warriors who had performed certain exploits painted their faces, even their entire bodies, black. They formed a circle, advancing and retreating to the rhythm of drum and rattle, their wives carrying the scalps on long rods. He also said that to the leader of the expedition belonged all the scalps and the horses taken on that warpath. We doubt this very much and think he was misinformed.

Old men and old women went out to greet the incoming victorious party, singing scalp songs. The leader made them presents, giving away all the horses and other booty, leaving himself poor but respected. This latter sounds typical enough, and in other tribes would apply to all the members of the party, as well as to the leader.[10]

THE ASSINIBOIN VICTORY DANCE

About twenty years after Maximilian, Denig, writing of the Assiniboins, said that the scalps were given to people who were in mourning for relatives lost at the enemy's hand. They were told to cease mourning, blacken their faces, and take part in the victory celebrations.

Scalp Dance of the Minatarres, by Bodmer, painted at Fort Clark in 1834. From an engraving in Prince Maximilian's *Travels*. Smithsonian Institution, Bureau of American Ethnology.

An old man went around camp, beating a hand drum and singing, inviting everyone to join the dance. Both men and women painted their faced black, except for the tips of their noses. All dressed in their best attire, but the men carried no weapons. The women had the weapons and the scalps and shook them up and down in time to the music.

Old men with hand drums lined up first, then the male dancers, then the women, holding the scalps and trophies out in front of them, formed a circle, standing so close together that they pressed against each other.

"After swinging to and fro a moment, they all move around in a circle by short side steps, lifting their feet together and keeping exact time with the drums." After two or three circlings, the dance ended with a shout by the men, the scalps were shaken again, and the warriors one at a time stepped forward to recount their coups. Shouts of approbation greeted these recitations, the drums struck up again, and the dance was resumed, perhaps for hours. Sometimes an old woman took a scalp in her teeth, shaking it as a dog would, then throwing it to the ground.

In a large camp small groups of young people danced around fires scattered all through the village. If they also had scalps, so much the better, but if they had none, they danced anyway. Sometimes there were twenty or thirty of these smaller dances going on at once, and the celebrations might be carried on for weeks. The paint might wear off, but it was improper to wash it off. According to Denig,

This dance is not attended with any violent gesticulation or eccentric motions, as has been represented, but is an orderly affair, and seriously performed. Unless a scalp has been brought no singing or dancing can take place. Even if many enemies were seen to fall, yet the enemy must be struck, which is the coup, and the hair procured, which is the proof.[11]

THE CHIPPEWA VICTORY DANCE

Henry Schoolcraft, who spent thirty years among the Indians, mainly with the Chippewas, from 1812 to 1842, wrote of a War Dance, but with the exception of the post it seems to us more like the Victory dances we have been discussing.

This ceremony, together with what is called *striking the post*, was performed during our stay. The warriors, arrayed for war, danced in a circle to the music of their drum and rattles. After making a fixed number of revolutions, they stopped simultaneously and uttered a sharp war yell. A man then stepped out, and raising his club and striking a pole in the center, related a personal exploit in war. The dance was then resumed, and terminated in like manner by yells, when another warrior related his exploits. This was repeated as long as there were exploits to tell. One of the warriors had seven feathers in his head, denoting that he had marched seven times against the enemy. Another had two. One of the young men asked for Lieutenant Clary's sword, and danced with it in the circle.

An old woman, sitting in a ring of women on the left, when the dancing and drumming had reached its height, could not restrain her feelings. She rose up, and, seizing a war-club which one of the young men gallantly offered, joined the dance. As soon as they paused, and gave the war whoop, she stepped forward and shook her club towards the Sioux lines, and related that a war party of Chippewa had gone to the Warwater River, and killed a Sioux, and when they returned they threw the scalp at her feet. A very old, deaf, and gray-headed man, tottering with age, also stepped out to tell of the exploits of his youth, on the war path.[12]

THE CHEYENNE SCALP DANCE

The Cheyennes had a form of Scalp Dance wherein the women were all tied together in a line. This not only prevented any one of them from slipping off to her lodge if she became bored or tired, but added to the fun.

On one occasion, however, it brought disaster. The Cheyennes, under Dull Knife, were making their famous retreat to the north after escaping from their confinement in Indian Territory. The Elk Soldiers were supposedly in charge of the camp. Knowing that Mackenzie's army was pressing close, they ordered the camp to move to a safer place. But the chief of the Fox Soldiers insisted that since the Scalp Dance had been started it would have to be continued. Rather than cause open friction between the two warrior societies, the Elk Soldiers gave in and the dance was continued. When American forces attacked the camp, the women, tied together, could not escape. They fell and tumbled in heaps and most of them were killed or captured.[13]

THE ALGONKIN VICTORY DANCE

To go back East for awhile, one of the earliest references to a Victory Dance was made by Samuel de Champlain, writing of the Indians on the coast of Maine in 1615. A great feast of elk, bear, seal, and beaver was prepared in a number of "boilers." Before the meat was cooked, one man arose, took a dog and hopped around these boilers from one end of the cabin to the other. Arriving in front of the great Sagamore he threw his dog violently to the ground, when all with one voice exclaimed, *Ho, ho, ho,* after which he went back to his place. Instantly another arose and did the same, which performance was continued until the meat was cooked. Now after they had finished their *tabagie* [feast], they began to dance, taking the heads of their enemies, which were slung on their backs, as a sign of joy. One or two of them singing, keeping time with their hands, which they strike on their knees: sometimes they stop, exclaiming *Ho, ho, ho,* when they begin dancing again, puffing like a man out of breath.

Sagamore is a word coming from a Hebrew term for "great prince" and was used early in American literature. Champlain at other times used the term *tchi-okimau,* Algonkin for "great chief." Here we have the dog again, apparently representing an enemy, and we see that heads, rather than scalps, were preferred by these people, who were a mixed gathering of *Etechemins* [Malacites or Passamoquoddies], Algonkins and Montagnais. They were celebrating a great victory over the Iroquois. Champlain said they killed "several hundred."

This was the same celebration we spoke of previously where Champlain reported that in a certain part of the ceremonies all the wives and daughters threw off their clothes, except for ornaments of beads and porcupine quills. They put their robes back on again, then threw them off alternately during the ceremony. Champlain gave no explanation or interpretation of these actions, merely reporting what he saw, and not having seen any other report on it we are at a loss to interpret it.

The Algonkin sagamore was seated before these women. In front of him stood two sticks on which hung enemies' heads. Sometimes he arose and harangued the gathering, saying, "Look! how we rejoice in the victory we have obtained over our enemies; you must do the same, so that we may be satisfied." These words were always answered by "Ho, ho, ho," much as Western Indians would say, "Hau." The sagamore and his companions then removed their robes, appearing only in clouts, and distributed presents to the other Algonkins, who took them home. It seems strange that the Etechemins and Montagnais were left out. At Plains gatherings the visitors were the ones who always received the most presents.[14]

OTHER TRIBES

Speck reported that the Yuchis, originally from the Southeast and affiliated with the Creeks, had a Scalp Dance, given by the women, who carried the scalps on poles and danced with them at night, as on the Plains.[15]

The Cherokees had a Scalp, or Victory, Dance in connection with their Eagle Dance, which in itself was given as part of the victory celebration. In this dance the warrior who recited his honors took the head of the line, carrying his Eagle Dance wand and a scalp. He spoke and re-enacted his exploits, while the others walked slowly behind him. Each warrior in turn had an opportunity to recite. The water drum was thumped to give approval to the recitations, and there was much shouting and yelling. As each warrior finished, he handed his wand and scalp to the dance leader; when all were collected, the Scalp Dance was ended.[16]

We understand that even the peaceful Pueblos formerly had Scalp dances and that even now the Custodian of the Flint Society at Santo Domingo, one of the most conservative pueblos, has charge of a set of scalps procured years ago that he must care for ceremonially each day.

The Navajos formerly had a Victory Dance in which the warrior who had killed an enemy painted himself black so that the enemy spirit could not recognize him. This is one of the reasons that the black paint has been used by all tribes, in addition to its symbolizing the charcoal and ashes remaining after the fires of war have been extinguished. Because of this fear of reprisals on the part of enemy spirits, Plains tribes often hacked the body of a brave enemy to pieces so that he might not return to do them harm.

We have a report for the Columbia River region that "Scalp dances are performed by women, hideously painted, who execute their diabolical antics in the center of a circle formed by the rest of the tribe who furnish music for the dancers."[17]

VICTORY DANCES TODAY

At some Indian gatherings today, snatches of the old Victory and Scalp dances are given, but they are greatly watered down from what they once were. At many we have attended throughout the West the women wave white handkerchiefs in place of scalps. An American flag is usually carried by one of the dancers. We were at Cannon Ball, on the Standing Rock Reservation in North Dakota, when news of VE Day came, ending World War II in Europe. The Indians immediately called a big dance. The usual Grass Dance was interspersed with old Victory songs, to many of which they added new words referring to the Sioux boys in the armed forces and to the "Bad Talkers"—the Germans. The boys, still being overseas, were represented by their parents, who told of their experiences in the war.

This was the first time we had ever heard the war cry made by slapping one hand over the mouth. Most people think this is the common "war whoop" of all Indians, but we had come to the conclusion that it was just another popular misconception. Now we learned that it was used only in battle, when victory was imminent, or in the Victory dances. Nevertheless, the way the old-timers made the call was quite different from the usual school-boy notion. It is the same as the whoop that we hear interspersed in some of the more vigorous dancing—a yell in high falsetto, coming to full volume, then dropping sharply at the end. The victory whoop is the same yell, but the mouth is tapped rapidly with the fingers, which are held tightly together and cupped over the mouth at each tap, completely stifling the sound, so that, when done rapidly, the result is an ear-splitting tremolo.

The women's tremolo sounds much the same, but is not as violent, and they do not use the hand at all. They make the sound with the tongue against the roof of the mouth.

Catlin wrote:

The frightful war whoop is sounded at the instant when Indians are rushing into battle, as the signal of attack. It is a shrill sounded note, on a high key, given out with a graded swell, and shaken by a rapid vibration of the four fingers of the right hand over the mouth. This note is not allowed to be given in the Indian countries unless in battle, or in war or other dances, when they are privileged to give it.[18]

Following World War I some of the Sioux veterans wanted to know if they could wear eagle feathers. The old men held a council and these soldier boys were asked to tell of their experiences. They told of the horrors of modern war, of fighting in trenches, the gas, the strafing by planes, but they made no impression whatever upon the old-timers, who were used to hardships, privation, and starvation. They just laughed and said, "You didn't fight the enemy. All you did was shoot a gun at him!" Unless the soldiers had "gone over the top" and actually fought the Germans hand to hand, they got no eagle feathers.

By the time of World War II, most of the old-timers had gone, and so had the interest in coups and eagle feathers, but the parents of the present soldiers were proud of them just the same. One old lady paraded with a Japanese sword her boy had sent home; he had taken it from a Japanese officer he had captured, a real war honor. An old man danced with a captured Nazi flag sent home by his grandson.

During a lull in the festivities, we strolled through the town and came to the house of Mrs. Has Tricks. She was cutting wood with a large, long-handled ax. All at once, from across the flat, open field, we heard the drum and another victory song. The old woman could not resist the challenge of that music. She stopped her chopping and began to dance, all alone, where she was, swaying and waving her ax in the air.

We were with the Crows when they put on their celebration for VJ Day. Families of the boys overseas carried their pictures in a victory parade, American flags flying, the big bass drum booming, the old victory songs ringing in the dusty summer air. During intermissions, people gave away in honor of their soldier boys. Some threw handfuls of small coins on the ground and the youngsters scrambled to pick them up. Later some of the women donned the war bonnets and did the Scalp Dance previously mentioned.

Recently we visited Kiowas in Oklahoma. A boy in service had just come home for the funeral of his mother, and a dance was given in his honor. Donations were made by most of the people present to pay his expenses to and from his base in the Pacific; they even had a raffle for a blanket to add to the funds. A society of War Mothers gave a Victory Dance. The older women who had had sons in the Services had dark blue blankets; the younger women with husbands and brothers in uniform had blankets of lighter blue. All these blankets were embroidered in gold with the emblems of the various branches of the Armed Forces. Even mottoes and slogans were emblazoned in gold embroidery and beadwork in large letters stretching across the shoulders when the blankets were worn. These blankets were used only in the Victory Dance, not in the social dances that followed.

At this same ceremony we saw a revival of the old Gourd Society Dance, which had not been given in more than fifty years.* We were told that we had helped in

---

*Indians, in English, refer to societies as "clans" and so usually say Gourd Clan Dance.

A Crow give-away— horses, blankets, buffalo robes, war bonnets. Note the high hat and spotted skunk skin worn by Chester Medicine Crow (left). Photo by Gladys Laubin.

this revival by putting on the *Arrows to Atoms* pageant, stressing traditional costumes and dances. The Gourd Dance was like other warrior society dances we shall describe later. On this occasion the Gourd Dance songs were sung especially for the young soldier and the dancing was done in his honor.

In resumé, we might say that the Victory Dance, generally speaking, consisted of these divisions:

PARADE—A parade exhibiting the trophies and booty taken on the raid.
GIVE-AWAY—The successful warriors gave away most of their booty and had their clothing and ornaments taken from them.
WARRIORS' DANCE—Each warrior had an opportunity to recount his coups and portray his part in the battle.
WOMEN'S DANCE— The scalps and other trophies were actually "danced."
GENERAL DANCE—Everyone could take part, like a Round, or Circle, Dance, in celebration of the victory.
FEAST—Feasting about the village, the feasts furnished by the warriors' families in honor of their safe return.

169

Perhaps the Scalp and Victory dances were largely women's dances because, when it is all summed up, the women made the greatest sacrifices in war. They not only lost loved ones but also lost their providers when the young men failed to return from the warpath. Also, since women ordinarily did not take part in the fighting, this chance to wear their husbands' finery, carry their weapons, and boast of their deeds built up their own egos and helped make up for the lack of finery and glamour in their everyday lives.

12. The Green Corn Dance

Throughout the entire corn-growing area, from southern Canada into Mexico and from the East Coast to the Rocky Mountains, we might expect to find ceremonies governing the planting and harvesting of this great crop. The development of maize, or Indian corn, is one of the most remarkable achievements in agricultural history. It was first cultivated by prehistoric Indians in the Neolithic era and was the basic food of the earliest high cultures on the American continents. Even in prehistoric times Indians had many varieties of corn for many uses and many climatic conditions. There were kinds that would grow from sea level to elevations of fifteen thousand feet, in deserts and in heavily watered areas from Canada to the tip of South America.

Although the corn ceremonies of the many regions varied with the differences of seasons affecting the planting and harvesting, many of the rituals were remarkably similar.

Often the harvesting rites were more important than those of planting. When blessed with a bountiful harvest, the Indians expressed their gratitude through elaborate rituals of thanksgiving, purification, and sacrifice. Many of these rituals were actually new-year celebrations. Old clothing, utensils, and pottery were destroyed and houses completely renovated. All the old fires were extinguished, and new ones symbolizing renewed life, health, vigor, and spiritual power were started from a new sacred fire kindled by a holy man.

THE CREEKS

We have already given Du Pratz's account of the corn festival of the Natchez as he reported it in 1720. One of the most written-about ceremonies from the Southeast was that of the Creeks, but Cherokees and Choctaws also figure in the early descriptions. This ceremonial was known as the Busk, but one might read a dozen accounts of the Busk and never find out what it really means. We finally learned that it is a corruption of the Creek *púskita*, meaning "fast." Creeks and Cherokees each had a series of six great ceremonies concerned with the varying seasons during the year, but the Busk seems to have been the most important of all. Other ceremonies usually took place at the new moon, but for the Busk the most important ceremonies took place on the full moon.

Cherokee, Creek, and other southeastern Indians observed alternately a year of twelve moons and a year of thirteen moons. There were celebrations for each new moon, with especially elaborate ones for the moons of the vernal and autumnal equinoxes.

Indian towns of the Southeast were permanent villages. The dwellings were of heavy poles, or small logs, set up endwise, interwoven with withes and plastered with clay. The roofs were thatched, usually with grass but sometimes with bark. These cabins were built around a town square, which was used for celebrations and ceremonies. The square itself was surrounded by an embankment of earth two or three feet high; during ceremonies only the select few were permitted to go within its borders. (Lewis and Clark mentioned a similar mound of earth completely surrounding Omaha villages. Similar low mounds were also reported as encircling some of the early Mandan and Arikara villages.)

A preliminary to most of the ceremonies of the Southeast was the ritual of the "black drink." It was a decoction made by boiling certain herbs, mainly *Ilex cassine*, in water. It was a strong emetic and was believed to purify not only the body but the spirit, to leave one in a state of innocence, and to promote keen thinking and a vigorous mind and body. It was used in pledging friendship and also was supposed to endow great prowess and daring in war. At one time a special dance accompanied the making and taking of the black drink.

Bartram wrote that

The busk, or feast of first fruits, is perhaps their principal festival; this seems to end the last and begin the new year.

It commences in August, when their new crops of corn are arrived to perfect maturity: and every town celebrates the busk separately, when their own harvest is ready.

If they have any religious rite or ceremony, this festival is its most solemn celebration.

Each family provided itself with new belongings, the whole town was swept and cleaned, and the old things were thrown on a pile and burned. Everyone drank of the black drink and then fasted three days. On the fourth morning the priests made a new fire with a fire drill in the center of the square and each dwelling procured a new flame from it. Everyone put on fine new attire and the men assembled within the square to be served a feast of the new corn. At night the entire population gathered within the square

where they dance, sing and rejoice during the whole night, observing a proper and exemplary decorum: this continues three days, and the four following days they receive visits, and rejoice with their friends from neighboring towns, who have purified and prepared themselves.[1]

The ritualistic procedure no doubt gradually changed over the years. An account of the Creeks from about 1798, just a few years after Bartram, says the sacred fire was made on the very first day, after the village was cleaned and white sand had been sprinkled over the square. Four logs were laid in the form of a star, pointing to the four directions, and the fire built where they met in the center. After the new fire was made, the women did a Turkey Dance during the preparation of the black drink. Drinking of this sacred potion occupied the day from about noon until the middle of the afternoon. The Tadpole Dance followed next, done by four men and four women. (Does it symbolize new life?) The men took part in another dance called

Hintha by the Creeks, which lasted from evening until dawn of the following morning.

On the morning of the second day, the men fired off their guns while the women did the Gun Dance, and at noon the men went to the sacred new fire, rubbing themselves with ashes, then ran to the river and plunged in. While they were washing in the river, women prepared new corn for a feast. When the men returned they rubbed themselves with some of the meal before eating.

It seems that the third day was devoted mainly to resting, the men sitting in the square. On the fourth day the women kindled fires on their own hearths, where small logs were laid in the same pattern as those of the sacred fire, bringing coals from it to their dwellings. They followed this ritual with ash rubbing and bathing as the men had previously done, and then did the Long Dance.

In the larger Creek towns the Busk was continued another four days. On the fifth day, the four logs of the sacred fire having been consumed, four new ones were similarly placed, a new fire kindled, and the men drank the black drink once more. They sat in the square two more days, and on the eighth day the final ceremonies were held, many of them outside of the square. They involved more drinking of medicinal herbs and rubbing the body with various "medicines." Tobacco played an important role. Two men carried flowers of "old men's tobacco" to the chief's house, and everyone present received a portion of them. The chief and the counselors paraded around the new fire four times. Each time they came to the east they threw tobacco in the fire as an offering, then halted their march on the west side. It was followed by a parade of all the warriors of the town, who repeated the performance.

A cane with two white heron feathers was placed outside the chief's cabin. At the moment of sunset, a man from the Fish clan took this wand, followed by the rest of the villagers, to the river. Halfway to the water's edge, this leader stopped and gave the "death whoop," doing this four times before he reached the bank. As the crowd collected, each person placed a bit of tobacco on his head and in each ear and on a given signal, repeated four times, each threw some in the water. When the signal was repeated again, the men dived into the river and each brought up four stones from the bottom. They crossed themselves with the stones four times, each time throwing a stone back into the river and yelling the death whoop. They washed, the leader picked up the wand, and they headed back for the village. There the wand was stuck up in the square and everyone visited and made merry until nightfall, when the Mad Dance ended the Busk.[2]

The Busk, or Green Corn Dance, was a time of amnesty. Hatred was forgotten, crimes and injuries forgiven. It was a season of change of mind, of openheartedness and friendliness. Marriages were contracted. Tribal problems were considered and attempts made to solve them.

The Creek Indians near Arbeka, Oklahoma, still hold vestiges of the old Green Corn ceremonies. It seems remarkable that this much of their traditional culture is left. The Creek male performers wear ordinary farmer clothes, and when it is hot, as it usually is at the season of the green corn, many of them strip off their shirts, ap-

The town square for the Green Corn Dance of the Creeks at Arbeka, Oklahoma, 1957. The square is surrounded by a two-foot earth embankment, as in early days, and has thatched arbors. This and the following three photographs are reproduced from a sixteen-millimeter film photographed by Ned Hockman, University of Oklahoma.

pearing in undershirts or bare from the waist up. Many of the Creek women have pretty dresses of early 1800's style.

The Creeks still have the town sqaure surrounded by an earthen embankment, or levee, about two feet high. They have three arbors on this square, the difference being that the north side is the open side, instead of the east, as formerly with the Yuchi and most other tribes. They have a sacred pole, but it is on the north, and near it is a buffalo skull—an addition doubtless made since arrival in Oklahoma and association with Plains tribes.

They have four Heralds, who might be called Marshals, carrying staffs, who make announcements and enforce discipline.

The *first* day is devoted to the making of the black drink. Women wash themselves in it as an act of purification. All fast, and many prayers are made. Boys go through the scratching ceremony (described in the following section), which serves as a sort of initiation, to make them brave and worthy members of the tribe. Apparently the one scratching is now considered enough to carry them through life. Each of four men brings in a log for the sacred fire.

On the second day the women hold the Ribbon Dance, which bears some likeness to the Scalp Dance of many tribes. The heralds have ribbons fluttering from the tips

The Ribbon Dance of the Creek women, performed at the time of the Green Corn Dance.

of their staffs and go around making announcements about every hour during the morning. The women wear their Indian dresses, with long varicolored ribbons hanging from headbands or fancy combs and streaming down their backs. With the children they first walk around the square four times, stopping the first time in front of the lodge of the Chief of the West. A singer with a gourd rattle accompanies them. The Chief prays that the Great Spirit will keep them in the ways of their fathers and offers thanks for the good things they have had since last they met. As they make four more circles they stop again each time at the west to receive the commendation of their menfolk. As they march, the "shakers" accent their foot beats to shake their knee rattles. The women carry knives, which they say shows that they are willing to prepare food for the men. Following the slow march, they dance around four times with a fast step, quite different from the usual Stomp Dance step. One foot advances, then both feet come down at once, alternating left and right.

Men and boys drink the black drink on this second day.

On the third day the men have a Feather Dance. All the men carry wands, or poles, of cane with two white heron feathers and one gray feather tied to the tip of each. All gather in a group and shout at the four quarters, east, north, west, and south, then walk around the square four times. They trot around the sacred fire and around

The Feather Dance, of the Creeks, performed on the third day of the Green Corn Dance. The dancers are carrying wands with heron feathers attached.

the sacred pole once, then stand the wands up against the arbor and go to the river to bathe. Afterward the wands are broken and the pieces, with the feathers, are burned.

The dance is accompanied by singers with rattles and by a *rubber*-covered drum. Formerly a clay-pot water drum was used. The only face paint used nowadays is by the Assistant Chief, who paints his face all white. They say the Feather Dance is a dance for peace and white, the color of peace.

On the fourth day the Indian-ball, or stick-ball, game is played, followed by a feast, and the Busk is over for another year.

THE YUCHIS

None of the early accounts of the Green Corn Dance actually tell us much about the dancing, but in 1909 Frank Speck made a report on the Yuchis which is more enlightening. The Yuchis came from the Southeast, where they were neighbors of Shawnees, Cherokees, Creeks, and Catawbas—all different stocks, and the Yuchis entirely different from any of the others. During Colonial times they were almost completely crushed by the Muskogian Confederacy, which they later joined. Now the remnants of this once powerful tribe live in Oklahoma, once more neighbors of the Creeks and Shawnees. During the early 1900's they were still doing their old dances and ceremonies with very little change. They were almost identical to those of the Creeks, whom they say took the ceremonies from them, although the Creeks claim they were revealed supernaturally.

The Stick-Ball Game played at the end of the Creek Green Corn Dance.

There were still seventeen clans among the Yuchis, each represented by an animal totem and each having its own dance in honor of the animal. The dances were all of the Stomp Dance type, which is merely a running shuffle, or trot, on the part of all but the principal women, who wore knee rattles made of several small terrapin shells and little pebbles. (Nowadays the rattles are made of small tin cans, but the women wearing them are still called "shell shakers.") These "shakers" emphasized each step with a decided stamp of the heel in order to make the rattles resound with as much noise as possible. The step is executed by scraping and jarring each heel, the toes not touching the ground.

The dancers circled the fire counterclockwise, imitating with arms and bodies the motions of the clan animals. Everyone was free to join in any clan dance, but the clan of the particular animal being represented was in charge. Other animals, as well as clan totems, were represented in dances. A man carrying a coconut-shell (formerly a gourd) rattle in his right hand led each dance, and singers with a water drum added to the accompaniment of most of them.

The Yuchis believed they were descended from the Sun. The town square, including the cabins around it and the fire in the center, was called the "rainbow." It was also known as the "big house" and was spoken of as "thoroughly beautiful" and "good all over." The actual square of earth, sprinkled with sand, represented the earth. Each side was about 75 feet long.

The Yuchis elected a tribal chief for life. Each town had a Town Chief, who came from the Bear Clan and served as the civil and religious head. Worthy clansmen were chosen to assist him; one would succeed him. A Master of Ceremonies was chosen from the Panther Clan. He was the highest official of the Warrior Society and acted as a sort of policeman, being in charge of the dances and of the fire. He had three other Warriors on his committee. There were also four young men who served as Marshals, who kept women and dogs out of the square at designated times and prevented the men participants from sleeping, or even leaning against anything for support, during actual ceremonies. One of the Warrior committee served as Scratcher. He had an instrument made of a turkey quill, bent to form a square, through which were inserted six metal pins, used to scratch the arms of the male dancers. All the officers carried staffs about seven feet long, with a couple of heron feathers attached at their tips.

The Town Chief decided when the annual ceremony was to be held. It was supposed to come on the full moon of the first ripening of the corn. Formerly this celebration was the real Green Corn Dance, and the big celebration, which we might call the New Year, came a bit later, after the corn had matured. But by 1900 the entire sequence of celebrations for the year were united in the one ceremony, held when the green corn was ready to eat.

The head of each family was given a little bundle of sticks by the Chief. They represented the number of days until the ceremony was to be held. Each morning a stick was discarded until the actual time was at hand. During this period dances were sometimes held as practice for the coming ceremony. During the period of the festival no one could eat salt and there were no sexual relations.

After cleaning and sweeping the ceremonial square and the houses, most of the refuse was piled behind the house on the north side of the square, but a pile about three and a half feet high was also made on the east side of the square. The fast began on the morning of the first ceremonial day, continued for twelve hours before taking the black drink, and followed the drinking of it into the second day. The four Marshals went after the four green logs, symbol of vegetation, for the sacred fire. On their return they whooped to announce their coming. They marched around the fireplace three times in a sun circle, then placed the logs, as described before, in the form of a star, one pointing to each direction.

Arbors had been erected on the north, west, and south sides of the square to take the place of the ceremonial cabins of earlier days. The Chief did not dance but sat under the arbor on the west side. He whooped occasionally to encourage the dancers. Two of the Warriors sat under the north arbor and two under the south. A post was erected at the southeast corner of the square. Formerly prisoners were burned there as a sacrifice to the Sun.

The posts supporting the west arbor, which represented peace, were peeled of bark to make them "white." The supporting posts of the north and south arbors were painted red, representing war. Ashes from the new fire were scattered to the three arbors, or lodges, to make sacred trails. A "horned serpent" made of deerskin and stuffed, painted blue, and with two yellow horns on its head, was placed in front of the benches under the north arbor and the two Warriors seated there placed their feet upon it. It was venerated in the first night dance, the Big Turtle Dance. The horned serpent, known all the way down into Central America, perhaps shows some past connection between Indians of Mesoamerica and our own South.

On the evening of the first day, dancing of a semisocial nature took place until about midnight. Then followed the Big Turtle Dance. The dancers massed near the post in the southeast corner of the square, the leader in the center, carrying his rattle. He began to shake it and to move in a counterclockwise circle, calling, "Ho! ho!" The dancers formed close ranks behind him, echoing his shouts. As he moved toward the fire, all joined hands, spreading out in single file. One woman, sometimes two women, wearing the shell knee rattles now joined the line, coming from the northwest corner of the square and taking a place directly behind the leader. He led the line around the fire, "with the sun" this time. When the men whooped, two more "shell shakers" came in, the dance continued for a time, and then was led the other way around, the customary direction. After going in a sun circle it was necessary to "unwind," just as we have learned for the Plains, only here, in the Southeast Woodlands, the entire conception was reversed.

When the men whooped the second time, the women left, and the men continued alone, making several more circles within the square. Then the leader stopped, stamped, and whooped, and everyone dispersed, going to the various houses nearby.

After a short interval the leader returned, circled the fire alone, started another song, and the other dancers gradually joined in again. The leader led the line to each of the four corners, circled around the square, and moved back to the fire. This was the time when all the women, children, and visitors were invited to participate.

The same kind of dancing, with a leader calling and dancers responding, was common to Eastern tribes all the way up to Maine.

The men sometimes danced with left hands extended toward the fire and their heads lowered slightly so as not to be blinded by the light. The women did not dance in this way, but except for imitative dances kept their arms to their sides and did not raise their feet high off the ground. Occasionally men dancers included fancy steps and flourishes.

By 1909 the men wore good clothing—not Indian—but in their hats they wore a heron feather, its quill shaved part way, to make it limber and a bit top-heavy. It was fastened to a small coiled spring, which was attached to the hat, so the feathers moved and "danced" with the men. Some men wore little bunches of red, black, blue, and white feathers in their hatbands. Such feathers, and a few designs painted on their faces, seem to be all that remained of former Indian apparel.

In most tribes the women have been more conservative in their dress than the men. The Yuchi women, like others of the Southeast, often wore a silver comb at the back of the head, from which hung ribbon streamers of many colors. Such a head-dress traces back to Colonial times.

The Big Turtle Dance lasted about two hours. No drum was used, just the leader's rattle and the knee rattles. The leader carried the songs, the others joining in or responding in a chorus to the leader's phrases. The songs and manner of singing in the Southeast makes one think that perhaps they have been influenced by the Africans. At one time many runaway slaves were given refuge, some being adopted into these southern tribes. But the over-all picture is still Indian and the same kind of singing was used in "Stomp Dances" all over the East. All things considered, the ceremony was very little changed since the earliest reports of it.

One change seems to be in the time of making the sacred fire. We have seen it reported for the first, fourth, and fifth days. According to Speck, the Yuchis made it on the morning of the second day. Fire-making materials hung in a bag over the Town Chief's head in the west arbor. He made the new fire with flint and steel, using dried pith and decayed wood for tinder. One of the marshals then carried the lighted tinder in a bark tray to the sacred fireplace and kindled the new fire. The four marshals then marched around the fireplace four times.

Another change was the use of flint and steel instead of the traditional fire drill, but it was still unthinkable to use matches for the new sacred fire.

On the second day, the black drink was again prepared and during its preparation the men and boys were ceremonially scratched. The scratching tool was dipped in a solution of the same plants that went into the black drink and used to scratch the arms from elbow to wrist enough to make the blood run. This ritual was always associated with the ball game in former times and was not mentioned in connection with the annual ceremonies. But lately the ball game has been a part of the combined ritual, so we find the scratching too.

The Rainbow was believed to be the "town square" of the supernatural beings above. The Sun brought the rituals to earth, teaching them to his people, the Yuchis, to protect them from evil influence and so that they could honor the spirit beings, who were emulated in the ceremonies. The Sun himself was the offspring of a supernatural woman and the Chief of the Sky World. He was taken to the Rainbow and scratched, and from his blood, which dripped to the earth, the Yuchis were created. So the ceremonial scratching of the Yuchi males was done in the square, that their blood might drip on the "rainbow," thus insuring the future of the tribe. The scratching was supposed to make them strong, in inure them to pain and hardship. It symbolized hardihood and endurance. It was not used to punish children, as has sometimes been stated, but to initiate them into the responsibilities of manhood. The Yuchis believed that, if the ritual of the annual ceremony were not carried out correctly, the Sun would rise high in the sky, see no performance, and retreat to set back in the East, nevermore to shine on earth.

Following the scratching, the Feather Dance was performed. In it there were four leaders, two abreast, the first two holding a feathered wand in each hand. The wands were about four feet long, with six heron feathers attached perpendicularly to the shaft, much like the Eagle Dance wands of the Iroquois. The following two leaders each carried rattles. The dancers strung along behind the four leaders, they also being two abreast. They ran in a sunwise circle toward the pile of sweepings on the east side of the Square. Facing the Sun, they leaped over this three-and-a-half-foot pile as they came to it. There was no explanation of this act, but it may have symbolized the Sun's "jump" during the night from setting in the West to rising in the East. Any who failed to make the leap were taken by the four Warriors and ducked in the river. Anyone who fell or dropped something as he danced received the same treatment.

The Feather Dance symbolized the Sun's journey over the dance square. It was also called *the* Green Corn Dance, whereas actually the entire annual ceremony was often called that. Whites sometimes called the ceremony "War Dance," because formerly, in preparing for war, the entire list of dances—the same ones given for the annual ceremony—were performed. The Feather Dance was probably the original dance for the ceremony, before the later consolidation.

During the scratching, a barbecue of beef was being prepared behind the Chief's arbor, and during the Feather Dance the women brought food to the edge of the square. The hungry men, who had not eaten since the previous morning, were expected to carry this food to the scene of the barbecue without tasting any of it. It was a further test of their stamina and self-control. When they returned to the square the two pots containing the black drink were set to the east of the sacred fire. The Chief and leading men drank of it first, followed by those of lesser rank, and finally by the townsmen. Two men dipped from each pot at a time, four taking the emetic at once. They always approached the pots from the north side. The drinking was repeated several times. Finally the four marshals took their share, which was a signal that the ordeal was nearly over. After the potion had taken full effect, the second, or assistant, chief finally led them to the river, where they washed their hands and washed the paint from their faces.

While they were gone, the Town Chief hung four ears of green corn on the fore log of the west arbor, and on their return everyone rubbed his hands over these ears and then over his face, and then went to his proper seat under an arbor on the square. Cobs of last year's corn were burned on the sacred fire, symbolizing the passing of the old crop. Tobacco was passed around and all smoked while the Chief made a short speech, enjoining the people to forgive all past offenses and reminding them of the purpose and importance of the ceremonies.

Formerly the Feather Dance was then performed once more, but on more recent occasions the feast of the new corn, barbecued beef, and other victuals began right after the Chief's talk. The women prepared all the barbecue; the butchering had been done by two men called "white men," giving us some idea of the opinion held of white people.

The feast was followed by a ball game, the two sides having been chosen by the Warriors. Formerly the ball game itself was an important rite, at least among the Creeks and Cherokees, being accompanied by all the forms of their worship—

fasting, scratching, the black drink, prayers, washing in the river.

All during the second day's activities, no performer was allowed to sleep or rest. Even during intermissions and periods of sitting, the men were not allowed to sit against a tree or post. If one was caught dozing, a Marshal struck him a sharp blow with his staff.

On the second night, any of the dances could be given, but the activities usually ended with the Crazy, or Drunken, Dance. This was probably similar to the Mad Dance of the Creeks, with this exception: The Yuchis used whiskey in this dance, originally believing it to be of divine origin, but its abuse by the younger men led the chiefs to decide to discontinue the entire annual ceremony, and the one Speck witnessed in 1909 was apparently the last one the Yuchis gave. Speck said the character of the Drunken Dance was extremely obscene, and self-respecting women refused to join in the dance. The men whinnied like stallions or mules and the dance ended with an uproarious song, followed by general debauchery. In older times, among various tribes, similar unrestraint was permitted at a certain period in annual ceremonies of this nature, the entire affair being symbolical of the passing away of evil followed by the entrance of self-control, purity, goodness, and common sense.

The first two days of the Green Corn ceremonies were the most important. The third day was usually given over to resting, with a few minor observances, as was also the fourth, but on the fifth day the townspeople assembled at the square again for more dances, and on the sixth day they had another feast, mostly meat this time. It was followed by dancing and revelry, as on the second night, and on the seventh day all participants finally dispersed to their homes.

The following dances were given, not only at the time of the green corn, but at almost any time of year on an informal basis:

CLAN DANCES

Bear	Panther	Fish	Skunk	Turkey
Wolf	Wildcat	Beaver	Opossum	
Deer	Fox	Otter	Rabbit	
Tortoise	Wind	Raccoon	Squirrel	

Formerly there were supposedly Eagle, Buzzard, and Snake clans as well.

OTHER DANCES, DIFFERENT FROM CLAN DANCES

Horse*	Quail	Lizzard	Leaf
Cow	Turkey	Opossum	Feather, or Corn
Buffalo*	Owl	Raccoon*	Crazy, or Drunken
Big Turtle	Buzzard*	Skunk	Shawnee*
Pike*	Chicken*	Gun	
Catfish*	Duck*	Negro	

This list might be considered typical for tribes of the Southeast.

---

*Accompanied by the water drum.

At one time the Yuchi drum was made of a hollow log about three feet high, with a head stretched over the upper end. More recently a large earthen pot was used. A piece of wet hide was stretched over the top and bound in place with a heavy cord. The pot stood about eighteen inches high and contained a little water. The head was often painted with a wheellike design representing the cardinal points. The drum occupied a place near the Chief's lodge in the west.

Rattles were used for all the dances except the Shawnee. This latter was borrowed from the neighboring Shawnees, and Speck said it was a very picturesque and animated dance, a general favorite. A Shawnee visitor, a girl, usually led the dance, heading a line of women who filed out from one corner of the square, holding hands. Men from different places around the square then came in, breaking in between the women, so that the line soon became one of alternate men and women. It wound about the square, imitating the movements of a serpent. One of the men gave a whoop and the entire line reversed, going the other way, until another whoop turned it back again.

We saw the Shawnees give this dance only recently. The women were beautifully dressed, mostly in a dark silken material, profusely decorated with small silver medallions, in traditional Woodland fashion. The line wound up into a compact mass in the center, then unwound again, going faster and faster, and as it stretched out again, the front part came to a sudden stop, "cracking the whip" on the end members, who went flying in all directions, amidst great hilarity.

The Leaf Dance was given in gratitude to the welcome shade of trees in hot summer weather. It was exceptional in that several women carried hand rattles. As the dancers trotted or shuffled around, they waved their hands gracefully, in imitation of leaves being rustled by the wind.[3]

THE SHAWNEES

We saw the Shawnee Bread Dance in the middle of May, 1960. The Shawnees live near the Creeks and Yuchis in Oklahoma, but are a very conservative group and never advertise their "doings." While doing research in the Library of the University of Oklahoma, we ran across a book on the Shawnees giving some description of their Bread Dance.[4] From this account it seemed as if this was the important annual ceremony of the Shawnees, although held in the spring, before planting, thus setting it apart from the Green Corn dances we had been studying.

The Bread Dance was supposed to be held just after the first full moon of spring, when the leaves were in bud and after the geese had migrated northward. It was exactly this time of year when we came upon the account in the library. We had heard about the conservative Shawnees, only a few miles from the university grounds, and wondered if it were possible that anything of the kind were still to be seen.

Several of our inquiries were greeted with statements such as: "I never heard of the Bread Dance, but the Shawnees have a Squirrel Dance sometime in the spring." This was encouraging, for the title "Bread Dance" is only a rough translation of the

Shawnee term *Takuhaw-naguway.* It seems more to refer to *food* and to both meat and corn cakes. Later we met an old-timer in the area and he did call it "Bread Dance." So the problem now was to learn if it were still being held, when, and if we would be permitted to attend.

Most Indian affairs in Oklahoma are now advertised over the radio each week, but never a word from the Shawnees. Most of the people we questioned knew nothing of any Shawnee ceremonies. One person said he had heard of the Squirrel Dance and had been trying to see it for years, but never learned of it in time. Eventually we did hear that the Shawnees at Little Ax were getting ready for something the coming week end, and with more inquiry we finally received an invitation to attend direct from the old chief's family. It would be the "Bread Dance"! Only one other white person was invited to attend this Bread Dance and he had an Indian wife. We were told that we had been invited because of our interest in bringing about a better understanding of Indians.

For this occasion the Shawnees have permission to hunt squirrels out of season to furnish the ceremonial food. Formerly all kinds of meat were procured—especially venison, but also wild turkey, grouse, and squirrel. Squirrels are the only game available today. Many Shawnees now work away from the community, so the Bread Dance was held over the week end. On the previous Wednesday evening the men selected as hunters began their fast, eating nothing from then on until late Saturday afternoon. During the intervening days they collected approximately two hundred squirrels, which were roasted over open fires to be served following the dance on Saturday.

Another modern note is heard in the method of taking the squirrels, which live in hollow trees. The hunter lights a firecracker and tosses it into the hole at the base of the tree. The squirrel pops out of the top and is easily shot.

The ceremonial ground, an opening in a blackjack oak thicket, was in the shape of a square, with an arbor on the west side where the old chief sat with the singers and officers. There was no mound or embankment. One officer is the Guard, another the Woman Pusher, who sees that the women get into the dance and helps direct them in their parts. The women play a very important part in the Bread Dance. They wear the pretty dark dresses we mentioned before.

The drum used was a water drum, made of an ordinary galvinized pail with a leather head bound on with a piece of heavy cord. Two men with rattles assisted the drummer. Another elderly man acted as assistant to the chief and served as a priest. Six wall tents were pitched around the square, but the east side was left open. Just north of this opening sat the men dancers. On the south side of the arbor the women performers sat on a bench. We sat with our little group of Delaware, Caddo, and Cherokee Indian friends on a log just outside the square, north of the arbor.

The Guard, who served as leader of the men dancers as well as Master of Ceremonies, was a Caddo Indian who had married into the Shawnees and became interested in their old religion. One of his duties was to see that no one except the dancers entered the ceremonial arena.

The active ceremonies of the Bread Dance began about noon. The roasted squirrels were already piled on a tarpaulin near the fire in the center of the square. On another tarp were baskets full of various kinds of corn bread. Squirrels and bread were covered over by another canvas. The women were supposed to have raised the corn to make the meal, but only a few had done so.

With no preliminary introduction or announcement, the singers began a song and the women rose from their benches and began to circle the dance ground to the right. In early days the hunters danced on their return in the morning, after being gone three days, but this seems no longer to be done. A dozen women, some hardly more than girls, took part. In fact, the leaders of the women were the youngest ones. Each had a large bright-red spot painted on each cheek.

The Shawnees, as other Indians, respect age, so older people were in charge of the ceremonies. The frail old Chief was said to be nearly one hundred years old and was the only one who knew the full ritual and all the songs. He made an impressive appearance with his long white hair falling over his shoulders.

The Shawnees do not approach the Great Spirit, whom they call Grandmother, with fear or in an attitude of gravity and sadness, but with joy. They believe that in seeking a blessing they should be merry and cheerful, and the appeal should be made in the spring, when the birds are singing and Nature is waking from her long winter sleep. After this period of festivity, which is also one of thanksgiving and supplication, the crops are planted. No one would venture to plant otherwise.

The women danced twice before the men joined them. Their dance was not disciplined like a chorus line, but showed evidence of a good deal of practice. The formations seemed more important than any uniform step. These afternoon dances were slow and dignified. Most of the women used a double-beat step, similar to the "toe-heel." But some did a trot or shuffle instead. The tempo was about two beats each second.

The third dance was begun by the men, twelve of whom formed an inner circle, while the women danced in an outer circle. The men wore beautiful soft-soled moccasins of Woodland type and had silk kerchiefs tied around their heads. A few had on bright shirts, but otherwise did not wear Indian clothes.

Instead of following each other in strict single file, the men danced obliquely in their circle. After some time they made a double file and continued around the inner circle. Occasionally they called out, "U-u-u-u! E'-e-e!" At first the rhythm was steady, then in accented 2/4 time.

At the conclusion of this dance, which lasted several minutes, the women all went under the arbor to be blessed, after which the cycle of two women's and one men and women's dance was repeated.

After the second blessing of the women, they danced with a twisting movement of their feet, as Sioux women do. They danced in place, then to the left, then to the right, all side by side, facing the audience in "company front."

Next they formed two lines, single file, and one moved to the right, one to the left. As the two lines approached each other on the opposite side of the circle, the men joined in again. The two lines of women joined in a double rank and the men, also in twos, followed them around, calling out occasionally, "Haw haw!"

On the third set of dances, the women again used the twisting step near the center of the circle. When the song stopped, they walked around about halfway and then went completely around in the original two-beat step. The drum was steady. The new song seemed to be made up of short phrases, with pauses between phrases. On the second time around the women doubled ranks after completing about three quarters of the circle. When the drum stopped, the two women on the end dropped off, one going one way, one the other; pairs continued to "peel off" in this way until the entire line had disbanded.

Between dances sometimes there was repartee accompanied by songs between the men and women, in which they made fun of each other. The women claimed to have conquered, and so did the men. Everyone seemed to enjoy this.

The next time out, the men went first, followed by the women. All walked around for a time, then the leader called, "Hiu', hiu', he-he-he-i'!" Still walking around, one dancer called, "Yo-ho-o-o'," and the whole line answered in response, "Yo-ho-o-o', hi-i-i-e'!" This was much like the typical Stomp dances of the South. The line doubled again, and all began dancing. The leader called, "Hi-o-o-ho-o-o'!" and the line responded, "Yo-o-o-o'!" From then on the dance continued with calls and responses marking it all the way. The leader shouted, "Yo-ho-o'!" and the response was, "He-he'!" repeated fifteen times in all. As they danced they sang, "Hia ho' hi ye'!" As the "ye" was being enunciated, others called, "He-he'!" so that the entire effect was like an exuberant "round," with the added interest of the calls and responses. The drum was steady all the way and four thumps on it followed a final loud shout that ended the dance.

Altogether the women danced eight times and the men four. After this final dance the old Assistant Chief made a long prayer. The entire assemblage had previously been cautioned by the Guard to remain completely quiet. Many of the younger people no longer speak Shawnee, showing that even this conservative tribe is now rapidly changing. The Guard said, in English:

Some of you here may not understand the Shawnee language. I do not understand it well myself. But this is no excuse not to be quiet and respectful while we have this prayer for all the blessings of the earth, and all of us should be quiet and attentive from now on until it is finished.

The old man spoke in Shawnee for forty-five minutes and not a soul moved, not even the youngsters. Dressed in old-style blue-cloth leggings, tied at the knees with bright cerise scarfs, and a bright orange shirt, the old priest was one of the most colorful figures on the grounds. His graceful hands with their long, beautiful fingers were extended above his head as he spoke, and he held them there throughout the entire long prayer. His voice was soft and rich, a pleasure to hear, even without understanding a single word.

Wildcat Alford, a Shawnee, great-grandson of Tecumseh and keeper of the tribal

COLOR PLATES

Color Plate 1:   Chief One Bull, a nephew of the famous Chief Sitting Bull, the Indian
                   "father" of the Laubins, at age ninety-two. He lived to see ninety-four
                   winters. Photo by Gladys Laubin.

Color Plate 2:   Reginald Laubin with the shield he made that led to the Laubins' adoption
                  by Chief One Bull. The stone-headed club was used by One Bull in the
                  Battle of the Little Big Horn. The porcupine-quilled shirt and leggings
                  were a gift from Flying Cloud. Photo by Gladys Laubin.

Color Plate 3:   A rare and beautiful Arapaho buckskin Ghost Dance dress in the Logan Museum, Beloit, Wisconsin. The headdress is from an Arapaho women's society and has no connection with the Ghost Dance. Photos by Gladys Laubin.

Color Plate 4:
A Ghost Dance
wand (after
James Mooney).

Color Plate 5:   Black Elk (left) and Kills Enemy (center) teaching Laubin old-time songs, keeping time with a cane, clapping hands, and pounding with the fist. Photo by Gladys Laubin.

Color Plate 6:   Iroquois and Cherokee masks, a Sun Dance buffalo skull and a "Ghost stick" in the Laubin home. Photo by Gladys Laubin.

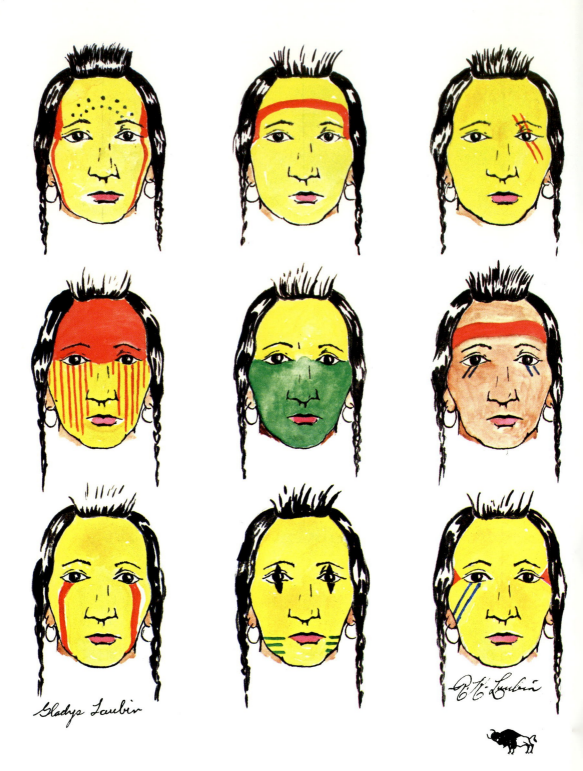

Gladys Laubin

C. H. Laubin

Color Plate 7:   Crow facial designs, sketched at Sun dances. The center design on the
right-hand page is Oto (after McKenney and Hall), showing dyed pileated
woodpecker beaks, set on a strip of red cloth, and worn with a turban and

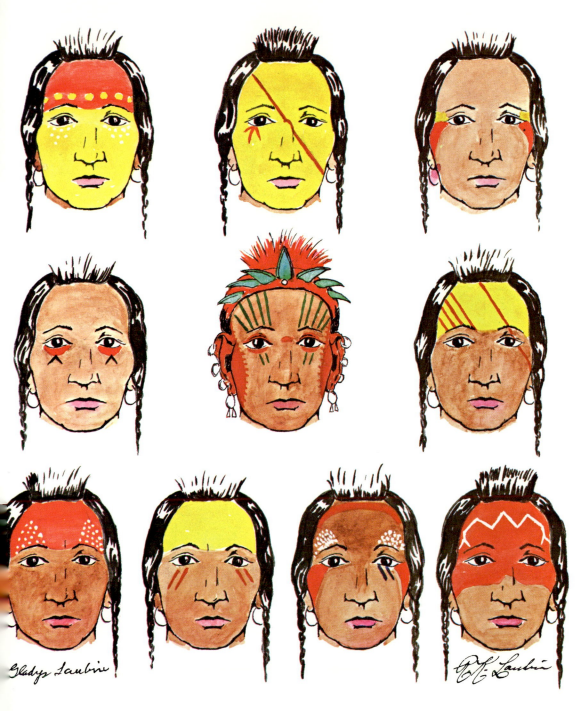

Gladys Laubin

RKL

roach. The center "beak" was often a grizzly-bear claw, which Catlin mistook for a "boar's tusk."

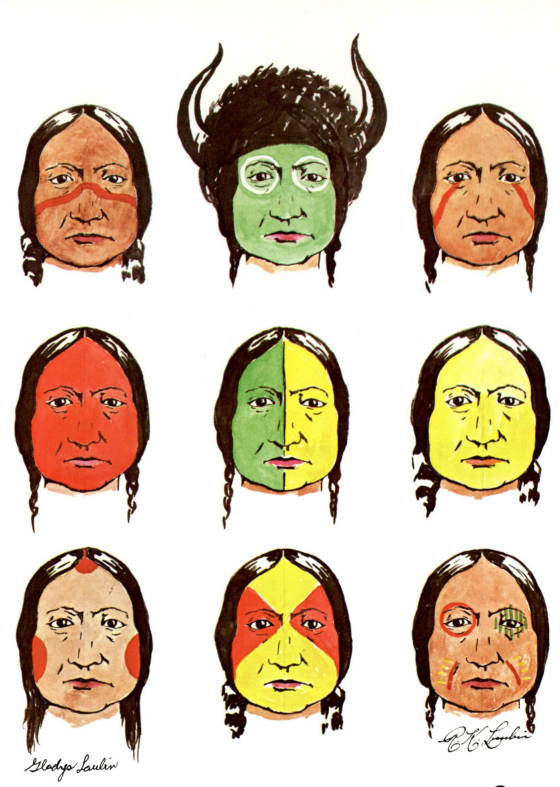

Color Plate 8:   Lakota facial designs sketched at dances. The center sketch on the top
row on the left-hand page shows Makes Trouble's buffalo paint. At the
lower left corner is a typical women's design. The right-hand page shows

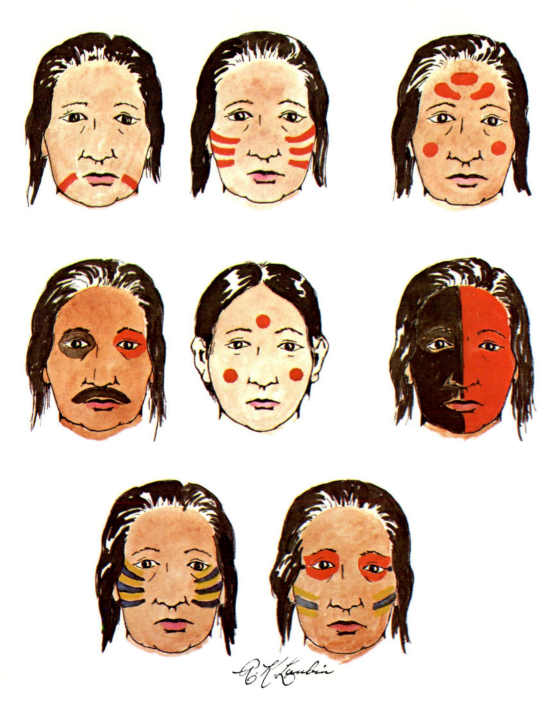

Yuchi facial designs (after Frank G. Speck). Similar designs were commonly used among the Woodland Indians.

Color Plate 9:   Sioux porcupine hair roaches. Left to right: Iron Moccasin, One Bull (Laubin), and Kills Enemy. Old-time Sioux dancers usually wore some ornament over the forehead to prevent anyone from looking directly into their eyes. Photo by Gladys Laubin.

Color Plate 10:   Crow women performing the Scalp Dance at a Crow fair. They are wearing their husbands' war bonnets. One is carrying an imitation scalp. Laubin Collection.

Color Plate 11:   The Lakota Sun Dance.

Color Plate 12: The Crow Sun Dance—raising the Sacred Pole. Photo by Gladys Laubin.

Color Plate 13: The Crow Sun Dance—looking up at the eagle on the stringers and the buffalo head on the Sacred Pole. Photo by Gladys Laubin.

The Crow Sun Dance as it was performed during World War II. The service flag represents Crow men in the armed forces. One dancer touches the Sacred Pole with the fluffy on his whistle. Photo by Gladys Laubin.

Truhero, the Sun Dance Priest, blessing a Sun dancer at the Sacred Pole. Photo by Gladys Laubin.

The Crow Sun Dance — the Sunrise Ceremony. Photo by Gladys Laubin.

Yellow Brow in his late eighties, blowing his eagle-wing whistle in the Crow Sun Dance. Photo by Gladys Laubin.

Chief One Bull, Laubin's Indian "father," wearing a war bonnet made by the son of Little Crow, the chief who led the Minnesota "Massacre" in 1862. One Bull's war shirt, made by his daughter, Margaret, symbolizes his part in the Battle of the Little Big Horn. The three bars on the sleeve, of blue and yellow, represent the three troops of Major Marcus A. Reno's cavalry. The red and blue triangles are the opposing Indian and white forces, and the red zigzags show that the Indians struck like lightning. Photo by Gladys Laubin.

Laubin wearing a Wi'ciska headdress of split buffalo horns and crest of eagle feathers, carrying a fur-wrapped crooked lance like those used by several warrior societies. Photo by Gladys Laubin.

A Cree Wolf Society cape, reproduced by Reginald
Laubin from the original in the Peabody Museum, Harvard University, Cambridge. Photo by Gladys Laubin.

A Sioux Heyoka dancer at Standing Rock Reservation, South Dakota. He is carrying Laubin's bow. Photo by Gladys Laubin.

Laubin performing the Prairie Chicken Dance at the Théatre des Champs-Élysées in Paris. Laubin Collection.

Laubin and Flying Cloud dancing the Grass Dance on the Standing Rock Reservation. Flying Cloud is wearing Crow leggings backward to symbolize that his grandfather, Flying Cloud, was killed in a battle with Crow Indians. Photo by Gladys Laubin.

A hungry horse eats a Grass dancer's belt. Photo by Gladys Laubin.

The Laubins live close to Indian reservations, with the beauty of nature to inspire them. Laubin Collection.

records, wrote that the prayer was usually given by one known as an orator, and so it seemed to us. Alford said that first the Great Spirit was petitioned for fruitfulness in the coming season, that the Shawnees might be given an abundant crop of corn, beans, and pumpkins; the prayer continued for the general welfare of the people, for success in their undertakings, for an increase of game. Then thanks were given for the success of the hunters and finally for all the good things that had come to them during their whole lives.[5]

The Guard told us that the old man also admonished the people to hold to the old traditions, to be honest and faithful, to leave whiskey alone. In short, he reminded them of all the virtues necessary to a happy and good life with each other.

The prayers finally over, all the little boys present were called to the north side of the square, where women served them corn bread. They were honored as the coming generation, whose duty it would be to carry on the traditions and watch over the welfare of the tribe. The bread was of different kinds, made from several varieties of corn meal. Some was in small patties, hard and dry, some was as large as a pie plate.

The only difference in the account of Alford, speaking of many years ago, and the ceremony as we watched it was in the sequence. He mentioned the dance of the returning hunters, which was not given, and he said the prayer was made before the dancing began.

After the boys were served, the men dancers, who according to Alford formed a committee (as did the women dancers), served the squirrels to the women—first to the women dancers, then to all the women present. When the squirrels had been eaten, the women dancers served the men, dancers first, the corn cakes. Even we visitors came in on this part of the feast. This was the first food the men dancers, who had also been the hunters, had eaten in nearly three days. They had had almost no sleep as well, and yet had been dancing most of the afternoon.

Following the feast, all dispersed to their homes or tents, and no more activity took place until evening, when the general Stomp, or Frolic, Dance was held. We have already spoken of this dance, which lasted far into the night, lighted only by the big fire in the center of the square. At times the dancers left the square completely, weaving in and out among the trees, their ghostly shadows adding weirdness to the scene.

The usual stick-ball game was supposed to be played on the following day, Sunday, which would end the festivities, but, the weather becoming rainy and unpleasant, it was called off until the following week, and we were unable to attend. This was another difference in sequence from that reported by Wildcat Alford. He said that the ball game was the opening of the Bread Dance ceremonies. But all in all, the Bread Dance we attended was remarkably close to the one he described.

The Shawnees some time ago lost the follow-up ceremony to the Bread Dance. Another great festival was formerly held in the fall about the time of the vernal equinox. According to Alford, it was much like the spring festival, except that it was entirely one of thanksgiving. After enduring all these many years, is the Bread Dance now doomed to follow the trail into extinction that so many Indian ceremonies have taken? The old chief, being the only one who knew the full ritual and songs, was constantly prompting the singers, and we could not help but feel that we had seen the last of the Bread Dance. If the ceremony is continued, it will probably be much simplified from that of earlier days.

THE SEMINOLES

Many people do not realize there are several groups of Seminoles. One group in Oklahoma and two groups in Florida are known by this name. Some of the Florida Seminoles still have their old ceremonies.

Actually, there is no such thing as a Seminole tribe. It has been said that *siminoli* in Creek, or Muskogee, means "wild," but this is not a complete or an accurate connotation. Rather, it refers to those who moved away from the main towns. By 1700 most of the Indians native to Florida had died out. Early in the century Indians from Georgia, Alabama, and South Carolina began to move into Florida to escape white pressure from the north. The remnants of the former Florida tribes joined these newcomers, who were mainly Hitchiti-speaking tribes, Hitchiti being one of the Muskogean languages. After the middle of the century other Muskogean peoples joined these first emigrants. A band of Yuchis also joined them, and before long a number of runaway African slaves took refuge among them. This conglomerate "tribe" of people are the ones we mean when we use the term Seminole. Most of them spoke Muskogean tongues, which though related were mutually unintelligible. At the time of the Seminole War (1835–42), the Muskogee-speaking peoples were most numerous, but most of the leaders were Hitchiti. The ones subdued and conquered by the army and sent to Oklahoma were Creeks, or Muskogees; the Hitchitis fled into the swamps of the Everglades. Today the Hitchiti-speaking Seminoles in Florida are known as Mikasuki.

Both groups of Florida Seminoles, except one band of Mikasuki, hold Green Corn dances, which are apparently much like those of the Creeks and Yuchis. The Florida Seminoles have no reason to trust or be friendly with white people and so are reticent about their customs and dances. However, they are known to have at least thirty different dances that they still perform at one time or another each year.

Most important of all is the Green Corn Dance. One group of Mikasukis holds its Green Corn Dance in May or June, another group holds the dance in June or early July, and the Cow Creek Seminoles hold theirs sometime between late June and middle July.

The Seminoles apparently have the usual sacred square of the southeastern Indians for their ceremonial ground. From people well acquainted with them we learned that this square is bounded at its corners by four posts, northeast, northwest, southwest, and southeast, and a special ceremonial post is set farther out beyond the southeast post. There is no longer a mound of earth surrounding the square. The ceremonial arbor is on the west and the opening of the dance ground on the east.

One phase quite different from other Green Corn or Busk ceremonies is that of owning medicine bundles. The Cow Creek band and Big Cypress group each still has one such bundle. Those who live along the Tamiami Trail have six bundles. The keepers of these bundles are the priests in charge of the ceremonies.

On the first day the leading priest, or medicine man, purifies himself and then directs the preparation for the ceremonies. Men and boys gather wood for the fire. A ball game is held in which young men and boys play against young women and girls. This certainly must be a ceremonial game, for ordinarily this is one of the roughest games that can be played and only the most rugged individuals can endure it. At night some of the tribal dances are given, including some different from other tribes.

Buffalo*	Quail*
Catfish*	Screech Owl*
Sandhill Crane	Chicken*
Switchgrass	Crawfish
Feather*	Snake, or Hunting
Alligator	Crazy*
Woodpecker	Steal Partner

On the second day there is feasting, barbecued meats of various kinds being served. One Seminole family told us that alligator is best of all. The men feast in a ceremonial arbor called the "big house," reminding us of the Creeks. The women and children eat separately nearby. After the feast a man goes out to kill a white heron, whose feathers are to be used in the ceremonies (Feather Dance is the name given to this dance by the few white people who have seen it. The Seminoles have a different name for it, which has no translation, so that it must be a very old ritual). At night the men begin to fast, and on the third day the priest and assistants bring out the medicine bundle (or bundles). The black drink is prepared and drunk by the men. The Feather Dance is held in the morning and afternoon. Long wands with heron feathers at the tips, like those of the Creeks, are carried. Only the men take part. In the other dances men, women, and children participate.

Between the two performances of the Feather Dance, a tribal court is held, where cases involving the breaking of tribal rules are tried. No white people have ever been permitted to attend these courts, so it has been presumed that penalties are severe, but if the customs are anything like those of the Yuchis and Creeks, all past offenses except for extreme crimes are forgiven.

Another ball game follows the Feather Dance and more dancing takes place at night. One dance given every night is the Snake, or Hunting, Dance. The Seminoles prefer, in English, the term "Hunting Dance," although their own term translates "snake."

---

*Familiar from other Green Corn ceremonies.

At dusk on this third day the priest makes a ceremonial fire, using flint and steel from a bundle, the contents of which are now displayed. Four ears of corn are placed around the fire, seemingly in place of the four logs in the sacred fires of other Green Corn dances. Over the new sacred fire another black drink, containing several ingredients, is brewed, boiling until midnight, the dancing going on in the meantime.

Before the brew is drunk, the four ears of corn from the fireplace are added to it. After the men take the drink and purge themselves, the dancing is resumed. It is done in two lines, men and women alternately in each line, but in other respects it is much like the dancing in the Shawnee Bread Dance. The dancers wind in and out among the four poles and around the square, finally winding around the ceremonial post, which is also a goal for the ball game.

At dawn of the fourth day the priest hides the sacred bundles and the men and boys are scratched. The Seminoles believe the scratching will insure a healthy life. The men then retire to a sweat lodge, where steam is made by pouring the last of the black drink on the red-hot stones. Coming out of the sweat lodge, all plunge into the water, and the long fast is broken. A feast of new corn follows.

We have not heard of the sweat lodge for the other tribes doing a Green Corn Dance, but undoubtedly they used it at one time, too.

The Seminoles also have a Hunting Dance, or Ceremony, in the fall—or at least they did have. The accounts we heard sounded much like the Bread Dance of the Shawnees, except for the time of performance. The men go out after meat four days before the celebration, procuring any kind they can find, but preferring deer and alligator. Turtles are also used. The women make corn cakes of several kinds of meal. This Hunting Dance, or Ceremony, lasts four days, so is a different thing from the Hunting, or Snake, Dance we mentioned above. At this ceremony the other dances listed are also given.

All the dances are accompanied by rattles, except the Buffalo Dance, which uses a small water drum. It is made of a tin can, or small pot, covered with a thin, wet rawhide head. The drum contains *two mouthfuls* of water, and is beaten with a straight stick. The medicine man, or priest, does the Buffalo Dance, pawing the ground, snorting, tossing his head, like an angry buffalo bull. Just how old this dance is is hard to tell. Certainly the Seminoles have not seen a buffalo in many generations. It is therefore either a very old dance, having come with them in their migrations, or learned more recently from visiting Oklahoma relatives.

On the fourth night of the Hunting Dance a feast follows the last performance. Men and women sit in the same positions in which they danced—two lines facing each other. Each line alternates men and women, and the opposite line is so placed that a man is opposite a woman. At a call from the leader, a woman feeds corn cakes to the man opposite her and he feeds her meat. This exchange of food goes on until everyone is "full." Everyone looks straight ahead, never turning his head while the food is passed along the lines or during the ceremonial feeding.

The ball game plays an important part in the Seminole rituals, as it did all through the Southeast. The Seminoles use two rackets, as do the Choctaws, Creeks, and

Cherokees. Formerly they used two goal posts, but now the one ceremonial post is the only goal.

THE CHEROKEES

The Cherokees were perhaps the most important tribe in the Southeast, but because their Green Corn ceremonies, according to early writers, were very similar to neighboring tribes, we need to go into little detail. Timberlake, writing with more understanding than most men of his day, said:

They have a few religious ceremonies, or stated times of general worship: the green corn dance seems to be the principal, which is, as I have been told, performed in a very solemn manner, in a large square before the town-house door: the motion here is very slow, and the song in which they offer thanks to God for the corn he has sent them, far from unpleasing.[6]

Speck said that the Cherokee year was punctuated by six festivals:

First—Festival of first new moon of spring about the time the grass began to grow.
Second—New green corn feast, when the corn was first fit to taste.
Third—Mature or ripe green corn, forty to fifty days after the second festival. The corn was hard and perfect.
Fourth—First new moon of autumn—New Moon Feast.
Fifth—Propitiation festival, about ten days after the fourth feast.
Sixth—Festival of exultation, somewhat later.

Of these festivals, Speck said that the third, for mature or ripe green corn, was the most important and comparable to the Creek Busk.

THE IROQUOIS

To see if there is much difference in the Green Corn rituals across the country, let us now say something about the Iroquois, the Cherokee's northern relatives. In the first place, the Iroquois name for the celebration is "a feast" instead of "a fast." Morgan said it was a four-day affair and that a feast was held at the end of each day. The Iroquois believed they best showed their gratitude to the Great Spirit by being joyful and happy, as did also the Shawnees.

We find that they also had a series of six festivals annually. Whether one was more important than the others is difficult to say, but since they celebrated their new year in mid-winter—about the first of February—and it was the one which carried their prayers directly to the Great Spirit, perhaps it may be considered the most important. It was an indication of their faith in the Great Spirit; they knew spring, with its promise of happiness and plenty, was coming.

Following the New Year festival, which lasted seven days, the Iroquois held a Maple Dance at the time of making maple syrup and sugar. Such a festival was held by all Northern Indians in the sugar-maple belt.[*]

---

[*]Maple sugar was an Indian contribution to the world's table; they learned to make it long before the coming of the white man. The sap was boiled down in bark utensils. The present

Next on the list of annual festivals was Planting. Then followed the Strawberry Festival, when the wild strawberries were gathered. The fourth was the Green Corn Dance, and it was a very important occasion. The Iroquois believed that corn sprang from the bosom of the Mother of the Great Spirit, after her burial, so it was a sacred plant indeed. Although the Iroquois and other agricultural tribes cultivated other crops, particularly beans, squashes, and tobacco, corn was the most important. The Iroquois referred to their crops as "Our Life" or "Our Supporters," according to Morgan. People who think that Woodland Indians were chiefly hunters and merely supplemented their diet with agricultural products are unacquainted with the facts.

On the first day of the Green Corn Dance (or festival), following introductory speeches the Great Feather Dance is given. We have seen that Feather dances were an important part of the Southeastern ceremonies, but they were quite different from the Great Feather Dance of the Iroquois. Morgan said:

This dance was the most splendid, graceful and remarkable in the whole collection, requiring greater powers of endurance, suppleness and flexibility of person, and gracefulness of deportment than either (any) of the others. The *saltandi ars*, or dancing art, found in the Feather dance its highest achievement, at least in the Indian family; and it may be questioned whether a corresponding figure can be found among those which are used in refined communities, which will compare with it in those particulars which make up a spirited and graceful dance.[7]

Two singers, who sit facing each other astride a wooden bench, keep the rhythm by striking the bench with rattles made of snapping-turtle shells. The songs for this dance are all religious in nature. The Great Feather Dance is one of *four* sacred ceremonies which the Great Spirit, or Master of Life, gave the Iroquois in the beginning, and all of them are performed at all the sacred festivals. The other ceremonies are Drum Dance, Individual Chant, and Bowl Game.

The Great Feather Dance takes its name from the single eagle feather which stands erect, in a swivel socket, on the warrior's cap, or headdress, the *gustoweh*, of the Iroquois. After the introduction of silver in Colonial times, a highly ornamented silver band surrounded the cap, which was made of fine trade cloth and ribbons, and further decorated with a bunch of white feathers near the eagle feather. Those having the right to wear the Woodland style war bonnet, in which the feathers stood erect instead of spreading in a circle like the war bonnet of the Plains, wore it in the Great Feather Dance. In recent years the Plains-style bonnet has also been used. The male dancers are usually stripped to the waist and wear the Iroquois-style front-seam leggings, with kilt, silver arm bands, and various necklaces. The eagle feather, coming from the bird which soars closest to the realm of the Great Spirit, symbolizes prayer ascending—another reason for the title of the dance.

The steps used in the Great Feather Dance are much like those of the War Dance, but the feet are raised very high and the dancers always remain erect, even though

---

method of making maple sugar differs from the Indian only in the use of more modern equipment. Maples of similar variety grow in northern Europe, but Europeans knew nothing of the use of the sap for sugar before their discovery of America.

there are many body movements and many gestures with the arms. The heel is brought down with great force, sometimes stamped three or four times before alternating to the other foot.

Although the eagle-feather cap is a warrior's ornament, the Great Feather Dance is a dance of peace, and the movements are graceful, dignified, and imposing, portraying mild and gentle feelings. A dancer who wins popular acclaim for his graceful and spirited dancing is expected to lead the next dance. In this way there may be several changes in leaders before the ceremony is over.

The Great Feather Dance opens with a call and response much like the Stomp dances of the South. The dancers arrange themselves in single file, moving in an elipse to the right around the council house. First they walk around, then the tempo quickens and the dance begins. The women form a line at the foot of the men's column. But they dance sideways, alternately raising their heels and dropping them on the accent of the turtle rattles. Sometimes a particularly animated woman will step high and leap like the men. Everyone is invited to join in, even little children. Old people, unable to dance, stand at the end of the singers' bench and try to follow the rhythm with their bodies. To end the dance, one of the singers strikes his rattle twice on the bench.

Following the Great Feather Dance, tobacco is burned as incense and thanksgiving speeches are made. A man known as Keeper of the Faith makes these speeches, thanking the Master of Life who has caused the Supporters to yield so abundantly. The speeches follow an age-old pattern in both content and manner of presentation.

After the speeches may come several social dances, which in turn are followed by the Corn Dance. It, too, is like the Stomp Dance, being antiphonal between the leader and his assistant, who carry rattles made of horn, striking them on their palms. Dr. Fenton says that the Onondagas form two lines, men in front, as usual, women bringing up the rear. But the Senecas usually form only one line, the men beginning the dance, the women falling in at any time. Any or all of these dances are given at all the Iroquois festivals, the season giving the name to the particular occasion. The Corn Dance is sometimes led in zig-zags and figures around the room, in and out around the fire and benches, much like the Shawnee Stomp Dance.

Theoretically, the religious part of an Iroquois festival is supposed to end about noon, but in actuality is often carried on until nearly twilight. But all songs and dances are believed to have sacred significance, so we cannot draw distinct lines. Following the social dances, games are played, and then comes the feast.

On the second day of the festival, another speech of thanksgiving is made and the Thanksgiving Dance is performed. This is like the Great Feather Dance, with minor exceptions. It is not necessarily given in costume and it is frequently interrupted between songs with more speeches of thanksgiving. During the speeches the dancers walk around the room. Even at the time of the Green Corn, there are speeches thanking the Maple, Bushes, and Trees for providing fruit. Thanks are given also to Mother Earth; to Rivers and Streams for furnishing water to sustain life; to herbs for providing medicines to cure diseases; to the Corn and her sisters, Beans and Squashes; to the Wind for moving the air; to the Moon and Stars for furnishing light when the Sun is absent; to the Sun for his light and aid to the crops; and of course the Great Spirit, who embodies them all and directs all things for the good of his children.

After the Thanksgiving Dance, there are other dances and again a feast. Any selected dances may be held at night.

The third day is much the same, with many speeches and many songs, both individual and sung by all. Gratitude is expressed for acts of kindness, for personal and political achievements, for anything that affected the happiness and welfare of the people. Dances and a feast again follow.

Formerly there were four days set aside for the Green Corn Dance, the fourth day winding up with the Bowl Game, a game of chance, but important ceremonially. In recent years the activities of the third and fourth days have been combined into one. Succotash is the principal food at the feasts, the real Indian succotash including not only fresh corn and green beans, but squash as well, formerly cooked with venison, but recently with beef or pork. Some succotash was even made with fish—a very special kind of fish chowder.

THE PLAINS INDIANS

The Green Corn dances so far described are more or less typical of the entire Woodland area. Back in 1674 Daniel Gookin mentioned that great festivals, with games, feasts, and dances, took place after gathering the harvests in New England. Traveling westward to the Plains we find similar ceremonies, worked out according to their own ceremonial patterns. All the earth-lodge people were as dependent upon their crops of corn, beans, and squash as were those of the Woodlands or those on the Southern Plains, such as the Caddoes and Wichitas.

Tabeau, one of the earliest writers on the Arikaras, northern relatives of the two last-named tribes, gave an account of the Blessing of the Grain, which was one of their most important ceremonies. At least it was important enough for him to write about it, whereas he said nothing about a green corn ceremony. The Arikaras believed they would have no harvest without this Blessing of the Grain. It involved the construction of quite an elaborate altar, typical of Plains religious concepts, and dancing and feasting occupied most of a three-day period, while much gaiety prevailed.

The ceremonies were held in the lodge of the principal chief, with the altar at the far side, opposite the door. The altar must have been colorful, according to Tabeau's description, but he gives no interpretation of its symbolism. Six red-painted gourd rattles lay upon it. In front were three strung bows and four arrows, with white feathers lashed on at only one end, so that they hung like "leaves of corn." Between the bows and the arrows was a pipe, crowned with leaves and on which lay a green branch and a piece of dried meat. On the second day of the ceremony, six nude young men stood with their backs to the altar while the oldest man in the village made a long prayer. When it ended, the young men hastily seized the pipe, the branch, and the meat, walked the entire length of the assembly, and went outside to make offerings to the powers of the universe, the winds, and the Missouri River. When they re-entered, the pipe was lit and carried to each man within the lodge, not passed from person to person. When the pipe was exhausted, it was replaced before the altar and the young men took places in the assemblage.

A naked "sacristan" placed six buffalo-shoulder-blade hoes (which Tabeau called pickaxes) and six little baskets made of osier withes in front of the bows and then added six crowns, or wreaths, of straw. These crowns, Tabeau said, were offerings to snakes, worms, locusts, and other pests not to prey upon the crops. The hoes were a prayer for more buffalo as well as for crops. The empty baskets were a prayer that they might be filled and also an acknowledgment of the expected abundance.

A couple of hours later four women, in full attire, took places at the foot of each of the four center posts of the lodge. Each held an artificial bird, and four warriors advanced to seize these birds, uttering cries such as each bird would make. Other birds were also brought in and their cries also imitated. This apparently wound up the ceremony. It was followed by a dog feast.[8]

Omahas and Pawnees had great festivals of thanksgiving at the time of harvesting the green corn. The Omaha festival is described with sympathy and understanding by Alice Fletcher in her report on that tribe.[9]

THE PUEBLO INDIANS

Perhaps the best-known Green Corn Dance today is held at the Santo Domingo Pueblo in New Mexico. Many summer tourists make a special effort to see it and it is one of the few Santo Domingo ceremonials which outsiders are permitted to attend.

All the Pueblos have similar dances, but that of Santo Domingo is the largest and most elaborate. The various Pueblos hold their dances on the days of their patron saints. Saint Dominic's Day is August 4. Sometimes as many as two hundred dancers turn out. For all the importance of this dance to the Santo Domingos, they say the name Green Corn Dance is a misnomer. It is just another ceremony to pray for rain and final growth of the crop. All the Pueblo ceremonies are, in the long run, prayers for rain, which is easily understood in a desert country. A similar ceremony is held late in the fall. Jemez has one on November 12.

For one hundred and fifty years the Spanish Inquisition was a power to be reckoned with in the Southwest. The Indians were forced to manifest an acceptance of Christianity and any infraction was punished by flogging and even execution. Coronado smoked the men of one village out of their kivas, where they were holding a religious ceremony. He had evidently tried to convert them at one swoop, for they understood the significance the cross had for the Spaniards and made the sign as an entreaty for peace. Whereupon Coronado burned two hundred of them at the stake, as an example of what happened to pagans. The few that escaped were lanced from horseback. So the Indians accepted the white man's God as a means of preserving their own lives, never in the least relinquishing their loyalty to their own gods, whom they understood better. One writer says, "They are devout Catholics and unregenerated pagans at the same time, with no thought of inconsistency."[10] The only exceptions are the Zuñi and Hopi Indians, who were so isolated that the Spaniards never conquered them. They massacred every missionary who attempted to force the new God upon them.

The Green Corn Dance of Santo Domingo begins with a consecration in the local church. The bell rings and muskets are fired. The dancers tour the village, finally arriving at the saint's shrine near the kiva. It is built of leafy boughs and lined with fine cloths and skins, and candles are lit to receive the saint. Indians with muskets stand guard all day, but there is not the remotest connection between the rites for the saint and the ancient ceremonies. As Erna Ferguson says, "They sit side by side, that is all; they do not touch."[11]

The ceremony itself is started by the Koshares, or Delight Makers, pouring out of the kiva. They represent departed spirits and pantomime past history. They send runners out as scouts to watch for enemy tribes—Navajos, Comanches, Apaches— who in the past raided the Santo Domingo corn fields and destroyed what they could not carry away.

When the principal dancers begin dancing, the Koshare act as valets to them, but the dancers never let on that they see them, for they cannot see spirits. The leader carries a pole with yellow feathers, the sun's color, at its tip. The dancers lift their feet high and bring them down with a hard stamp, pounding power from the earth and sending this power into action. The women dance barefooted, in order to have closer contact with the earth and partake of its fertility. They carry pine boughs representing growing things and eternal life. The *tablitas* the dancers wear on their heads represent the mesas and clouds and are painted blue for the sky. Tiny tufts of eagle down hang from the headdresses and are worn in the hair, also symbolizing clouds, hence, rain.

There are two kivas in the village and each furnishes a group of dancers, who dance alternately all day long, suggesting that their prayers are continuous and constant and insisting that they be heard.

We were told by a friend who formerly lived near Santo Somingo that the pueblo was offered one hundred thousand dollars a few years ago by a motion picture company for permission to photograph the Green Corn Dance. Realizing that the Indians never allowed the taking of pictures of their ceremonies the company explained that this was only to assure that a record would be made, promising that the film would be stored until such time as the tribe decided it could be shown. Nevertheless, the offer was refused.

We have seen that the Green Corn Dance differed in the various areas of the country. In most areas planting and harvesting were both celebrated with elaborate ceremonies, usually accompanied by much dancing. Sometimes there were ceremonies in between to assure the full development of the crop. The festivals combined prayers for fruitfulness with those of joy and thanksgiving. We think that most tribes felt about dancing as the Iroquois do, that it was taught to mankind to enable him to communicate with the Great Spirit, to express thoughts and feelings he could transmit in no other way. No other form of communication with the spirit world is as adequate and complete.

13. Calumet and Eagle Dances: In the East

It is certain that the Calumet, or Pipe, and Eagle dances were related. In some of the early records we hear only of Calumet Dance, but a similar dance among Iroquois and Cherokees was spoken of as Eagle Dance. The Iowas and the Choctaws, widely separated and with entirely different cultures, had both Calumet and Eagle dances. There is some tradition that the Sioux also had an Eagle Dance, as well as Calumet Dance and Medicine Pipe ceremonies. Charley Brave listed Eagle Dance as one of the thirty-five dances formerly known to the Sioux.

Both Calumet and Eagle dances, wherever found, were used to greet strangers, to create ceremonial friendships, and often to bring success in hunting or war, to bring good luck or oppose bad luck, to cure sickness, as well as to make peace between warring tribes.

The earliest reference we have found to the Calumet Dance is in the writings of Nicolas Perrot, who in 1665, speaking about the *Outaoüas* (Ottawas) and other "savages," said they "sang the *calumet*. . . . The Calumet also compels the suspension of hostilities and secures the reception of deputies from hostile tribes. . . . It is, in one word, the calumet which has authority to confirm everything, and which renders solemn oaths binding."[1]

He made one of the first references to the Sioux, who were first mentioned in the *Jesuit Relations* of 1640, saying that they "sang the calumet" for an *Outaoüa* chief. He also wrote that the sun gave the calumet to the *Panys* (Pawnees) and that it had been communicated from village to village as far as the *Outaoüas*.

The tradition that the Calumet ceremonies originated among the Pawnees has been accepted by scholars. Until recent years they had the most elaborate ritual of all, indicating that they have had the concept the longest, but we also have the evidence of tradition among many tribes. By 1665 or shortly thereafter the Calumet was reported for other tribes as far east and south as the Cherokees, Catawbas, and Choctaws.

Calumet is a term the French gave to the ceremonial pipes they found in use among the Indians, from *calumus*, Latin for "reed." The stems of the early pipes may have been hollow reeds, but in more recent times have usually been made of ash, the center pith being removed to make the hole. The smoking of such pipes was known to most Indians across the country long before Columbus. They were always sacred and handled in ritualistic ways, often with elaborate ceremony. Indian pipes usually had bowls of stone, the most prized being Catlinite,* which comes from only

---

*Named for George Catlin, who first described the quarries.

two places—the well-known quarry at Pipestone, Minnesota, and a smaller, little-known quarry in Wisconsin, Catlinite was a popular trade item, even in pre-Columbian days, and articles made from it have been found in very early sites, in many sections of the country. It is not surprising, therefore, to find the region where Catlinite was found to be the center of greatest development of the "peace pipe" concept.

Indian pipes were always used in peace-making ceremonies. But a pipe could also be a war pipe, for in many tribes war parties were gathered by means of the leader presenting a pipe to those who wished to follow him, and the leader carried the pipe on the expedition. It bound the members of the party in conradeship and expressed their mutual loyalty to each other and to their leader.

Because the pipe itself was sacred, the elaborate ceremonies with many songs and the Calumet Dance evolved, probably in the early 1600's. Most of the early accounts state that the calumets had stone bowls and fanlike decorations made of golden eagle tails. The bowl was an altar, in which the sacred incense burned, wafted to the spirits above. The feather fan decoration symbolized the brushing away of evil.

The eagle was revered by tribes everywhere. He was the greatest and most powerful of the birds, ruler of the air and the creatures of the air. He was powerful, fierce, and fearless. Such power could be used to end wars as well as to make them. The eagle often symbolized purity as well, for he flew high into the pure atmosphere. He came closest to the realm of the Great Mystery, or Great Spirit, and was his special emissary. It is not difficult to understand how, when the calumet was decorated with eagle feathers and there was ritual dancing in association with it, the dance naturally involved movements symbolical of the eagle and of his power.

The Pawnees were a good way west of the early explorations, but the Calumet ritual had already reached the Mississippi River tribes by the time the French came into that region. French explorers, traders, and missionaries helped to spread the ceremonies.

Although reports for the Mississippi region mention the stone bowls, the stem alone was used in the ceremonies of most of the eastern tribes; later, tribes in the West were using only the stems also. These decorated pipe stems were the true calumets. In the West and Middle West they were usually drilled, even though not smoked. The hole was said to represent the spirit trail and also the direct light of the sun. By the time the ceremony reached the Iroquois and Cherokees, the calumet and the dance were separate items. The wands used in the dance were no longer calumets, but merely decorated batons.

One trail of diffusion was apparently from the Pawnees to the Iowas, then to the Foxes, the Illinois, and the Miamis, tribes successively adjoining each other to the east. The Miamis already had a fully developed cult of the calumet, as we might call it, when the French first met them. Perrot was met by a Miami chief at the head of three thousand warriors. Each village chief in the company, naked except for embroidered moccasins, carried a calumet. They came forward, singing and dancing, "bending their knees in turn almost to the ground" as they approached Perrot in their greeting.[2]

Northern Plains tribes already had greatly developed "medicine pipe" rituals, so the Calumet Dance, to them, was a different thing. However, there are similarities in the two. Plains Ojibwas (western relatives of the Chippewas), Assiniboins, Crees and Blackfeet all had Pipe, or Calumet dances. Arikaras and Omahas had rituals similar to that of the Pawnees. Other tribes, such as the Kiowas, Arapahos, and Cheyennes, do not seem to have had a Calumet ritual. The Omahas claim that they learned it from the Arikaras and that the Arikaras also taught it to the Poncas, Iowas, and Otos. The Crows got it from the Hidatsas, their relatives, who were neighbors of the Arikaras.

The ceremony went down the Mississippi River all the way to the Gulf. Both the Caddoes and the Natchez had it, as did the Chitimachas at the mouth of the river. From that region it spread to Creeks and Cherokees, even the Catawbas and Shawnees learning versions of it.[3] Wherever the calumet lost its significance, the Eagle Dance served as a substitute of equal importance.

In earliest times the Calumet Dance seems to have been primarily a solo dance, as it has been in recent times in the Middle West. In the West it has been recorded as a duet dance. In other regions it was sometimes performed by a company.

Fenton points out that for the seventeenth century the best records come to us from the Illinois, Miamis, Potawatomis, and Iowas. We have further reports on the Miamis for the eighteenth century, as well as for Natchez, Cherokees, and Catawbas. Shawnee, Iowa, Omaha, Pawnee, and Osage Calumet dances lasted into the late nineteenth century; Cherokee, Fox, and Sioux, into the early twentieth, as did a weakened version among the Menominis. The Iroquois Eagle Dance is still in existence.[4] The Foxes still retain enough of the tradition to do a demonstration each summer at a celebration in Illinois (Rock Island). We might say that we have seen a diluted performance among the Crows in the 1940's and that there are still several Crows who know the ritual, although it has not been given lately.

THE CALUMET DANCE

As we look back at the early records, we find that the Calumet Dance followed a pattern similar to that previously given as typical of other Indian dances. First, there was a parade, carrying the calumets and other paraphernalia, greeting the recipients of the ritual. Then we have the Pipe, or Calumet, Dance proper. At first it was given by solo performers, one after another. Later this changed, depending upon the location, to two, four, and up to a dozen or more performers taking part all at once. Then we have the Discovery Dance, Striking-the-Post, with a recitation of war honors, a Giveaway, followed by actual smoking of the pipe and a feast. This is the usual order. It varied, depending upon the tribe, but these elements were all part of the Calumet, Pipe, and Eagle dances. The combination served as a drama, or play, in several acts, a drama personalized by all those present being not only spectators but participants in it.

Each dancer originally carried a calumet, or stone-bowled pipe, decorated with a fan of golden eagle-tail feathers. As the number of dancers increased, the "pipes" became mere wands with the feather decorations. Everywhere the dancers ritualistically imitated the movements of eagles, but made no attempt, other than painting their bodies white, to look like eagles, as the present-day Eagle Dancers in the Southwest or in Oklahoma do. The stems, or wands, with their fan attachments, symbolized eagles.

The wand was usually held in the left hand and later accounts tell of the gourd rattle in the right, which was shaken in time with the music, while the wand was waved and swayed in graceful arcs. Also, a whistle of eagle wing bone was added, with which the dancer imitated the cries and screams of an eagle. There was much knee action, the dancers at times bending "almost to the ground," as Perrot said. Some of the steps were executed in a deep-seated squat, still to be seen among the Senecas and Onondagas.

THE DISCOVERY DANCE

The Discovery Dance was also, usually, a solo dance, in which a warrior enacted his experiences on the war trail. Long said it was sometimes given to honor strangers, which would certainly be true when associated with the Calumet Dance. Writing of the Omahas, he said the chiefs sat in an inner circle, others in an outer ring. The dancer wore a crowbelt and carried a club. At first the dance was slow, then the music quickened, became very fast, and stopped. The warrior advanced to the center post, struck it with his club, and told of a war deed. The song began again, the performance was repeated, until in this fashion he had recounted all his war deeds. He then gave the crowbelt and club to another dancer, who likewise told of his experiences. When each man had finished, he made presents, usually horses, to the chiefs.[5]

A hundred years earlier Raudot told about the Discovery Dance of Lake Indians, saying they danced to drum and rattle. "They are nude, and only one man dances at a time. He is girded with a crow, which is his totem. After he has finished and has recounted all his exploits, he is replaced by another and in this fashion the dance continues until all the warriors have performed." He said each man struck the post before telling his deeds. The dancers were called to the dance lodge by the singers beating on the drum. The report of each deed was greeted by "a great cry" from the audience, but if a warrior tried to deceive them by claims he could not uphold, he was promptly contradicted and had his head rubbed with ashes![6]

Long and Raudot both mentioned the "crow" for this dance. We might get the impression from Long that this ornament was a sort of communally owned affair, and we do know that among the early Omahas only an extremely brave man was allowed to wear one. But Raudot must have been mistaken when he said the crow was the dancer's "totem." Raudot, personally, had seen little, if anything, of the Indians about whom he wrote. He based his writing on memoirs of others who had been witnesses.

Catlin briefly mentioned a Sauk and Fox Discovery Dance. By his time this tribe, at least, was doing the dance in a group. He said:

It was exceedingly droll and picturesque, and acted out with a great deal of pantomimic effect—without music, or any other noise than the patting of their feet, which all came simultaneously on the ground, in perfect time, whilst they were dancing forward two or four at a time, in a skulking posture, overlooking the country, and professing to announce the approach of animals or enemies which they have discovered, by giving the signals back to the leader of the dance.[7]

Generally speaking, in the Discovery Dance a warrior pantomimed the finding and following of a trail, watching and listening for the enemy, the discovery of an enemy camp, the stealthy approach, the attack, and the victorious homecoming. Plains Indians even included the capture and running off of enemy horses, which they acted out with a vigorous double-beat step, knees lifted high, to a fast tempo. At the same time the eagle was represented by spins and turns, with swooping movements of outstretched arms.

SIGNIFICANCE

When we ordinarily think of the calumet as a "peace pipe," and the Calumet Dance as a dance for peace, it may be difficult to understand how all these warlike concepts played a part in it. But we must remember that all the tribes with which it was associated had cultures in which warfare played an important role. Peace would follow a victory over neighboring enemies. So it was logical to incorporate within the ceremonies for peace the concept of the victory which brought it about. With this concept of victory went also the matter of personal war honors, which made up the honors of the tribe and symbolized the bravery of the people as a whole.

A peace solemnized with the calumet was seldom broken. The only known violations were by Ottawas and Iroquois, both Eastern tribes that apparently did not ascribe to the calumet ritual the same importance given it by other tribes. Their indigenous peace rituals were based on the symbolism and mysticism of the wampum belts. To tribes of the West, the calumet was as sacred as wampum was in the East.

THE MIAMIS

Allouez, in the *Jesuit Relations* for 1667, wrote concerning the *Iloumec*, who were probably Miami:

They acknowledge many spirits to whom they offer sacrifice. They practice a kind of dance, quite peculiar to themselves, which they call "the dance of the tobacco-pipe." It is executed thus: they prepare a great pipe, which they deck with plumes, and put in the middle of the room, with a sort of veneration. One of the company rises, begins to dance, and then yields his place to another, and this one to a third, and thus they dance in succession, one after another, and not together. One would take this dance for a pantomime ballet and it is executed to the beating of a drum. The performer makes war in rhythmic time, preparing his arms, slaying the enemy, removing his scalp, and returning home with a song of victory,—and all with astonishing exactness, promptitude and agility. After they have danced, one after the other, around the pipe, it is taken and offered to the chief man in the whole assembly, for him to smoke; then to another, and so in succession to all. This ceremony resembles in its significance the French custom of drinking, several out of the same glass; but in addition, the pipe is left in the keeping of the most honored man, as a sacred trust, and a sure pledge of the peace and union that will ever subsist among them as long as it shall remain in that person's hands.[8]

There was a definite relationship between the Calumet, Discovery, and Strike-the-Post dances. In some tribes all three were part of the same ceremony. Marquette called the Discovery Dance the "second part of the calumet dance." Striking-the-Post usually followed the Discovery.[9]

Allouez's account of the "dance of the tobacco-pipe" sounds as if the first part was Discovery Dance. The ceremony also included the actual smoking of the pipe, which was later given up as the Calumet Dance changed and developed. Antoine Denis Raudot wrote from Quebec in 1709 that

the dance of the calumet, which is a savage pipe with a stone head, where the tobacco is put, and a wooden stem, is an honor that one nation goes to render to another in order to renew an alliance. The one who is delegated to offer the pipe and to dance addresses a war chief and presents it lighted to him, dancing to the songs of several men and women, who have accompanied him. They name in these songs the person to whom they offer the calumet, tell the reason for which they give it to him, and accompany the dance with a present. The savage and the nation to whom it has been presented also give a present to reply to the honor that has been done them and send back this ambassador of sorts and all his following after having regaled them for several days. This calumet is of red stone and has the shape of some animal or of an ax to adorn it; the stem is very long and adorned with several feathers painted different colors; some of the feathers are fastened to it and others wave freely in the wind.[10]

In another account, Miami ambassadors carried a pole with the white under-feathers of an eagle decorating it and a "grand calumet ornamented with bones and feathers" hanging from it. These ambassadors had a blue streak painted on their foreheads and a blue heart painted on their chests. Later, after learning of flags from the Whites, they carried a calumet in one hand, a white flag in the other, and a belt of white wampum.

Four calumets were laid at the place where the actual ceremonies were to be held. The pole was planted in the ground nearby. The chief marched to the pipes, picked up one of them, struck the pole with its stem, and counted coup. He then turned around and selected a young man, to whom he presented the pipe. This young man then danced to the rhythm of drum and gourd rattle.

After a short dance, another chief repeated the same action and presented another pipe to another dancer. Four dancers each did a solo dance with a calumet.[11]

THE FOXES

Nearly a hundred years after Allouez, another Jesuit, Jacques Le Sueur, wrote of the Calumet Dance of the *Renards* (Foxes), neighbors of the Miamis.

The first part of the dance is performed by one person, who throws himself into various attitudes, and exhibits gesticulations with the calumet in his hand. In the second part he invites some warrior to join him in the dance; the latter approaches with his bow and arrow, and hatchet or club, and commences a duel against the other, who has no instrument of defense but the calumet. The one attacks, the other defends, the one aims a blow, the other parries it, the one flies, the other pursues; then he who flies wheels about, and in his turn puts his adversary to flight. All these movements are performed with set steps, and in cadence, accompanied by the sound of voices and drums, and in civilized countries might pass for the commencement of a ballet. . . . For the calumet, for the chiefs, for war, for marriage, and for public sacrifices, distinct dances are appropriated. That of the calumet is the most striking, and appears to be the most serious. It is danced only on particular occurences, when strangers pass through the country, or when the enemy sends ambassadors to offer conditions of peace. . . . This dance was a true religious cult not only among the Renards, but also among almost all the upper nations; that it was called the Dance of the Spirit, that one was said to be dancing not at all with the calumet, but to be dancing in honor of the calumet; in a word the calumet was the god of this nation.

It is interesting to hear these early writers compare Calumet Dance to ballet. Le Sueur also said that the power of the calumet could kill enemies. It was used to conciliate foreign nations and enemies, to bring good weather or rain, according to need. It could cause favorable winds and keep away evil. But all this being pagan, to Le Sueur's mind, he tried to prohibit the calumet ceremonies. He said there could be no choice between Christianity and the calumet—they had to choose one or the other. So the Indians chose the calumet. From then on this missionary could see no good in an Indian, and he listed all their bad qualities.* He said, "It is possible to say without calumny that the savages are scarcely men in outline, etc."[12]

The Foxes carried the Calumet Dance all the way to the Abenakis, near Montreal, early in the 1700's. They used two redstone pipes with eagle feather fans attached. A *pole*, painted red and decorated with feathers, was set up by the door of the lodge where the ceremony was to be given. They used four dancers, symbolizing the world quarters. The dancing was concluded with a feast of dog meat, sacred food, the head being especially important in the ritual. In recent times they have used a hog's head.

The pole, or post, figured in the Calumet and Eagle dances of a number of tribes. Besides the Miamis, it was used by Menominis, Winnebagos, Omahas, Iowas; Quapaws, Osages, Iroquois, and Cherokees. It seems that the Foxes did not strike it in this ceremony, but they had a pole, nevertheless.

THE ILLINOIS

Back again in Allouez's time, Hennepin wrote:

I must speak here of the *Calumet*, the most mysterious thing in the World. The Scepters of our Kings are not so much respected; for the Savages have such a Deference for this Pipe, that one may call it, *The God of Peace and War*, and *the Arbiter of Life and Death*. One, with this *Calumet*, may venture amongst his enemies, and in the hottest Engagement lay down their Arms *before this Sacred Pipe*. The *Illinois* presented me with one of them which

---

*Times change. Within the past few years the pipe has been accepted as one of the sacred objects on the altars of both Catholic and Episcopalian churches in Indian services.

was very useful to us in our Voyage. Their *Calumet of Peace* is different from the *Calumet of War*; They make use of the former to seal their Alliances and Treaties, to travel with safety, and receive Strangers; and the other to proclaim War.

It is made of a Red Stone like our Marble; the Head is like our common Tobacco-Pipes, but larger; and it is fixt to a hollow Reed, to hold it for Smoking. They adorn it with fine Feathers of several Colours; and they call it, *The Calumet of the Sun*, to whom they present it; especially when they want fair Weather or Rain, think that that Planet can have no less respect for it than Men have, and therefore that they shall obtain their Desires. They dare not wash themselves in Rivers in the beginning of the Summer, or taste the new Fruit of Trees, before they have danc'd the *Calumet*, which they do in the following manner:

This Dance of the *Calumet* is a solemn Ceremony amongst the Savages, which they perform upon important Occasions, as to confirm an Alliance, or make Peace with their Neighbors. They use it also to entertain any Nation that comes to visit them; and in this Case we may consider it as their Ball. They perform it in Winter-time in their Cabins, and in the open Field in the Summer. They chuse for that purpose a set Place among Trees, to shelter themselves against the Heat of the Sun, and lay in the middle a large Matt, as a Carpet, to lay upon (it) the God of the Chief of the Company, who gave the Ball, for every-one has his peculiar God, whom they call *Manitoa*. It is sometimes a Stone, a Bird, a Serpent, or any thing else that they dream of in their Sleep; for they think this *Manitoa* will supply their Wants, by Fishing, Hunting, and other Enterprises. To the Right of this *Manitoa* they place the *Calumet*, their Great Deity, making round about it a kind of Trophy with their Arms, *viz.* their Clubs, Axes, Quivers, and Arrows.

Things being thus disposed, and the Hour of Dancing coming on, those who are to sing, take the most Honourable Seats under the Shadow of the Trees, or the Green Arbours they make in case the Trees be not thick enough to shadow them. They chuse for this Service the best wits amongst them, either Men or Women. Every Body sits down afterwards, round about, as they come, having first of all saluted the *Manitoa*, which they do in blowing Smoak of their Tobacco upon it, which is as much as offering it Frankincense. Every Body, one after another, takes the *Calumet*, and holding it with his two Hands, dances with it, following the Cadence of the Songs. This *Preludium* being over, he who is to begin the Dance, appears in the middle of the Assembly, and having taken the *Calumet*, presents it to the Sun, as if he would invite him to smoke. Then he moves it into an infinite number of Postures, some-times laying it near the Ground, then stretching its Wings, as if he would make it fly, and then presents it to the Spectators, who smoke with it one after another, dancing all the while. This is the first Scene of this famous Ball.

The Second is a Fight, with Vocal and Instrumental Musick; for they have a kind of Drum, which agrees pretty well with their Voices. The Person who dances with the *Calumet*, gives a Signal to one of their Warriors, who takes a Bow and Arrows, with an Ax, from the Trophy already mentioned, and fights the other, who defends himself with the *Calumet* alone, both of them dancing all the while. The Fight being over, he who holds the *Calumet*, makes a Speech, wherein he gives an Account of the Battles he has fought, and the Prisoners he has taken, and then receives a Gown, or any other Present, from the Chief of the Ball. He gives then the *Calumet* to another, who having acted his Part, gives it to another, and so to all others, till the *Calumet* returns to the Captain, who presents it to the Nation invited to the Feast, as a Mark of their Friendship, and a Confirmation of their Alliance. I can't pretend to be so much Master of their Language as to judge of their songs, but methinks they are very witty.[13]

Hennepin said earlier that the calumet of war was distinguished from that of peace by its feathers.

THE QUAPAWS

The "Akansas" (Arkansas), now known as Quapaws, in their Calumet ceremonies set up the war post, as in War and Scalp dances, in the center of the dance ground. Poles were also erected on which gifts were displayed. Guests and chiefs were seated near the center. The singers used water drums and gourd rattles. Warriors struck the post with their weapons and counted coups. The gifts were presented to those for whom the ceremony was given.

THE WINNEBAGOS

Charlevoix, in 1721, said that the Winnebagos gave the best performance of the Calumet Dance, but they danced with feather fans. The Iroquois and Cherokees also used fans, as did the Yuchis, Creeks, Chickasaws, Catawbas, and Coasàtis— all southern tribes except the Iroquois. But the Tuscasoras, the sixth nation to be added to the original Five Nations of the Iroquois League, came up from the South between 1712 and 1800 and took their place in the League in 1722. The Cherokees are also an Iroquoian people. So it is not strange that the Iroquois showed Southern influence, but it is difficult to explain why the Winnebagos used fans instead of calumets.

THE CHEROKEES

The Cherokees were one of the largest and most important tribes of the East. They were moved west to Indian Territory in the 1830's, but some went into hiding and there are still several thousand living in North Carolina, which was part of their early domain. Formerly they occupied much of Tennessee, South Carolina, and Georgia as well.

DeSoto must have seen Cherokees in 1540, but little was written about them until British contact began in the early 1700's. In 1759 hostilities arose between the two and except for limited truces there was little peace until after the Revolutionary War. During one of these peaceful interludes, the Indians demanded that, if the colonists were sincere in their desire for peace, they send an emissary to live with them to show that they could get along well together. Army officials hesitated to order anyone on such an assignment, but Lieutenant Henry Timberlake volunteered to go. He was received well and apparently enjoyed his stay with the Cherokees. He later took groups of them to England twice, to see "their father, the king."

On his first visit, in 1756, he was received by a body of three to four hundred Indians, ten or twelve of them entirely naked except for clouts about their middles,

painted all over in a hideous manner, six of them with eagle tails in their hands, which they shook and flourished as they advanced, danced in a very uncommon figure, singing in concert with some drums of their own make, and those of the late unfortunate Captain Damere; with several other instruments, uncouth beyond description. Cheulah, the headman of the town, led the procession, painted blood-red, except his face, which was half black, holding an old rusty broad-sword in his right hand, and an eagle's tail in his left. As they approached, Cheulah, singling himself out from the rest, cut two or three capers, as a signal to the other eagle tails, who instantly followed his example. This violent exercise, accompanied by the band of musick, and a loud yell from the mob, lasted about one minute, when the headman waving his sword over my head, stuck it into the ground, about two inches from my left foot; then directing himself to me, made a short discourse (which my interpreter told me was only to bid me a hearty welcome) and presented me with a string of beads.

Then they took him inside the townhouse, or council lodge, a man holding him by each arm, and seated him in one of the first seats, which were benches. Cheulah addressed him the second time, professing his friendship.

He had scarcely finished when four of those who had exhibited at the procession made their second appearance, painted milk-white, their eagle tails in one hand, and small gourds with beads in them in the other, which they rattled in time to the musick. During this dance the peace-pipe was prepared; the bowl of it was of red stone, curiously cut with a knife, it being very soft, though extremely pretty when polished. Some of these are of black stone, and some of the same earth they make their pots with, but beautifully diversified. The stem is about three feet long,* finely adorned with porcupine quills, dyed feathers, deers hair and such like gaudy trifles. . . .

This pipe was offered to Timberlake, who smoked it, and it was then smoked "by 170 or 180 others." Then "The Indians entertained me with another dance, at which I was detained till about seven o'clock next morning, when I was conducted to the house of Chucatah, then second in command, to take some refreshment."[14]

Other writers have given some mention to the "Eagle Tail Dance" of the Cherokees, so we can conclude that the Cherokee form of the Calumet Dance from the beginning used an entire eagle tail as a fan rather than a wand or an actual pipe stem.

James Adair was with the Cherokees about 1735. He said that an Indian delegation came to greet him, and in advance of them all was a man painted in streaks of white and bearing a *swan's* wing. In making peace they first smoked "out of the friend-pipe" and ate together, drank the *Cusseena,* or black drink, and then proceeded

to wave their large fans of eagle-tails— concluding with a dance. The persons invited appoint half a dozen of their most active and expert young warriors to perform this religious duty, who have had their own temples adorned with the swan-feather cap. They paint their bodies with white clay, and cover their heads with swan-down; then approaching the chief representative of the strangers, who by way of honour, and strong assurance of friendship, is seated on the central white or holy seat . . . they wave the eagles tails backward and forward over his head. Immediately they begin the solemn song with an awful air; and presently they dance in a bowing posture; then they raise themselves so erect, that their faces look partly upwards, waving the eagles tails with their right hand toward heaven, sometimes with a slow, at others with a quick motion; at the same time they touch their breast with their small callabash and pebbles fastened to a stick of about a foot long, which they hold in their left hand, keeping time with the motion of the eagles tails: during the dance they repeat the usual divine notes, YO, &c. and wave the eagles tails now and then over the stranger's head, not moving above

---

*There are some pipe stems in existence as much as five feet long.

two yards backward or forward before him. They are so surprisingly expert in their supposed religious office, and observe time so exactly, with their particular gestures and notes, that there is not the least discernible discord. If the Hebrews danced this way, (as there is strong presumptive proof) they had very sweating work, for every joint, artery, nerve, is stretched to the highest pitch of exertion. . . . The Indians cannot shew greater honour to the greatest potentate on earth, than to place him in the white seat . . . and dance before him with the eagles tails.[15]

The Eagle apparently was always important to Cherokee religious beliefs. Bartram, the naturalist, stated that they revered only the golden eagle. Cherokees, Iroquois, and other tribes, especially those of the South, believed that, because of his magic power, the eagle could cause either sickness or health, sickness coming from improper observance of the customary forms of respect due him. So the procuring of eagle feathers was often a special profession. Timberlake said that on one occasion a party came home from a hunt,

bringing with them an eagle's tail, which was celebrated at night by a grand war-dance, and the person who killed it had the second war-title of Colona conferred upon him, besides the bounty gathered at the war-dance, in wampum, skins, etc., to the amount of 30 pounds, the tail of an eagle being held in the greatest esteem, as they sometimes are given with the wampum in their treaties, and none of their warlike ceremonies can be performed without them.

Another time he said that about six hundred persons of both sexes assembled for a "grand eagle's tail dance," but that about midnight, "in the heat of their diversion," news was brought of the death of one of their principal men, which put a stop instantly to the celebration.[16]

So we find the Cherokee Eagle Dance used for greeting strangers, for making both peace and war, and as we learn later for curing sickness, especially the "eagle sickness" caused by improper contact with the birds. The dance was given on the occasion of killing an eagle, to welcome the eagle spirit to the town. It was used to celebrate a victory, which in more recent years meant the winning of the Cherokee ball game, similar to lacrosse, except that these Southeastern tribes use two rackets for each player.

Dr. Frank Speck first told us about the Cherokee Eagle Dance, but his account of it was not published until after his death. The last Eagle Dance, as well as the last Cherokee dance of any kind, was given around 1946.* Although we personally have never seen a complete Cherokee Eagle Dance, we were fortunate in having some of the old men demonstrate it for us. Even then there was some argument as to what

---

*With the usual pressure against Indian dancing applied to the Cherokees, they gradually gave up their dances in favor of square dancing. A few years ago a Cherokee square-dance team won contests all over the country. It is quite amusing to watch a capable square-dance group going through all the maneuvers using Indian Stomp and War Dance steps. But then, square dancing is about the best substitute they could have found for their old Indian dances, for some of them were very similar to the square dancing we know today.

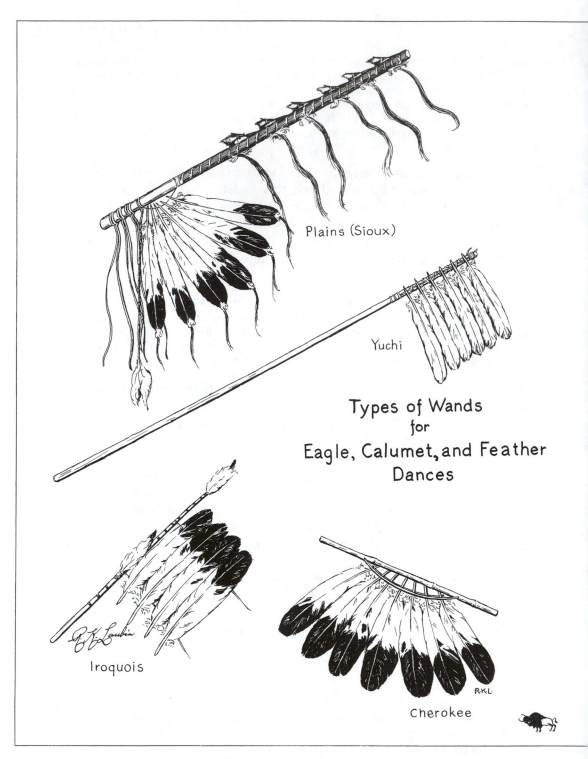

Plains (Sioux)

Yuchi

Types of Wands
for
Eagle, Calumet, and Feather
Dances

Iroquois

Cherokee

Types of wands for Eagle, Calumet, and Feather dances. Some Sioux calumets had only four feathers and four pileated woodpecker scalps. Densmore, in *Teton Sioux Music*, shows a wand with woodcock heads and a fan of hawk feathers— no doubt a recent wand and mislabeled "pileated woodpecker and eagle tail feathers."

was right and what was not. Will West Long insisted that only one wand was used. Epps Welch said they used two and that the wands were made of cane, which is hollow, and shot was placed in the tube to make it rattle. Perhaps both men were right, the double wands being used in a solo version we shall discuss later.

Such a dance, using two wands that also served as rattles, might be very interesting. This version evidently got to the people in charge of the drama, *Unto These Hills*, which has been presented at Cherokee, North Carolina, every summer in recent years. It features an Eagle Dance wherein each dancer uses two wands. None of the written records or anything we have heard from anyone, Dr. Speck included, bears out the use of two wands for the main Eagle Dance. *Unto These Hills* is advertised as being authentic, but the dancing performed there bears little resemblance to old Cherokee dancing. They do not even use a drum for the dancing; it is accompanied by thumping on an electric organ. However, they do have a beautiful outdoor theater.

Old accounts always mention dancers carrying an eagle tail in one hand and a rattle in the other. The most unusual thing about the Cherokee dance is that the tail is carried in the right hand and the rattle in the left, which makes it extremely difficult for a right-handed person to perform the dance. Speck said the fan frames were of *sourwood* (tupelo, or sourgum), which was sacred to the Cherokees. Its use prevented contamination that might result from handling eagles or their feathers. But recent frames have been made of cane, with the arch for spreading the feathers made sometimes of sourwood, sometimes of ash or oak. Just when the fan was introduced is hard to tell. The early reports give the impression that an eagle tail alone was used. A full eagle tail has twelve feathers, but the fans have only five, seven, or nine. It is possible that as eagles became more scarce the fans took the place of full tails.[*]

Eagles and rattlesnakes were deadly enemies, so the Eagle Dance of the Cherokees was formerly given only in winter or in times of frost when the snakes were asleep and would not hear the eagle songs. If antagonized, they became doubly dangerous. The eagles themselves were not supposed to be killed at any other time, either. The Cherokees had other special winter dances, too. Among these were Booger and Bear dances. To give them at any other season might attract cold and death and prevent crops from maturing. However, when given at the proper time, the dances could overcome the evil potential of animals, plants, human beings, and ghosts.

The Cherokee Eagle Dance was unique in several respects, among them the fact that women played an important part in it. Although in 1714 John Lawson mentioned the part women played in Cherokee dances, it is doubtful that women took

---

[*] Old Cherokees insisted that seven was the proper number, as there are seven Cherokee clans.

an active part in the Eagle Dance in very early times; but in the last hundred years, at least, equal numbers of men and women have participated.

The Cherokee Eagle Dance seems to break down into four parts. There was a dance with wands and rattles, comparable to the Calumet Dance of other tribes; a dance to honor the peace pipe, or calumet; an interlude to honor the Eagle Killer; and a Scalp Dance, wherein warriors recited their brave deeds, quite as with other tribes. This apparently was the usual order of performance, but it was not compulsory. The various parts of the Eagle Dance could be performed separately or in a different sequence. In its final years, the Eagle Dance was usually a part of the Booger Dance ceremonies.

The first part of the Eagle Dance symbolized victory and was further divided into two sections, with different formations and movements. The women carried only wands, no rattles, but the lead woman wore rattles of terrapin shells enclosing small pebbles around each knee. Since Cherokee women have been wearing long, full skirts, these rattles are not visible, but they are certainly audible. The same kinds of rattles are used in the Stomp dances by other Southeastern tribes as well.

The men all carried gourd rattles in their left hands. At first men and women formed opposite lines, stretching east and west, facing each other in pairs. Originally a pole was in the center of the dance ground. It had a sort of umbrellalike top, made of green boughs, to shelter the singers, who sat under it. In later times, when the dances were in an indoor hall, the pole was dispensed with. At a cue in the song, the leader of the men made a right turn, the two lines doing likewise, and he led in a circle to the right, the women following behind the men. The wands were held vertically and shaken in quick, short motions up and down, the rattles shaken in unison. The step was the same as the Stomp Dance, a sort of running shuffle.

Following this movement, the women formed an inner circle, moving to the right, the men in the outer circle going to the left. The position was now a crouch. Rattles and wands were held close together, but waved up and down instead of in the previous jerky manner. The men dancers stooped, bending one knee almost to the ground, the feet in a double-beat step much like Western Indian dancing. There was a good deal of freedom in individual movement. The action was varied by jumping on both feet, marking time, and much waving of the wands and rattles, while the women continued circling in their ring. At the conclusion of this set of songs, the dancers retired for a time.

When they returned they began the second series of dances, which honored the peace pipe, although apparently no pipe was yet in evidence. This time they used wands only, holding them horizontally in both hands. They formed lines as before, in opposite pairs, and about ten feet apart. They stepped a pace forward, and back again; then to vary the movement partners alternately waved the wands over each other's heads, swinging them sidewise and with a fanning motion at the same time. When the song changed they reversed positions, continuing the fanlike motions, then changed back to the original position again, alternating in this way throughout this period of the dance.

In a second group of songs the same advance and retreat of the two lines was carried on, but the wands were waved with more side swing and greater motion as the partners met in the center. Then, as they retreated to their lines, the leader of the men led his line in a half circle to the left, and the woman at the opposite end of her line led the women in a half circle to the right, so that when they straightened their lines out again, this time extending north and south, the partners had changed. The dancers now turned around, so that the lines were back to back. The wands were waved toward the sky in time to the music of drum and song, then the lines moved together and apart, back to back, to the end. The dancers again dispersed.

When they returned this time, the men had their rattles again, and each woman carried an empty basket. Forming two east-and-west lines, as at the beginning, they marked time a few moments, wands again held vertically, then all did a right-face, the leader of the men leading off with a sort of stiff-legged march to form a circle, men ahead, women following, moving counterclockwise. The wands and rattles were used more like wings now, each dancer following the postures of the leader, who sometimes extended his arms to the sides, as if flying. The baskets symbolized the feast which was to follow the dance and, allegorically, represented feeding the eagles to compensate them for their feathers and so preventing them from working evil.

Following the march with the wands and baskets, the wands were all collected by the leader, and the first part of the Eagle Dance was over.

There seems to have been an eagle cult among the Cherokees. A person who dreamed of eagles or eagle feathers had to go on a lone vigil and fast, then arrange for an Eagle Dance at the first opportunity, lest someone in his family should die. But to go through with the ceremonies assured him of eagle power. There were occasions when the Eagle Dance was done for the double purpose of preventing a calamity for the dreamer and of curing someone who was already ill.

To stumble while doing the Eagle Dance was regarded as an omen of impending death. Such a belief was not unique with the Cherokees, but was common to many tribes in reference to various important or sacred dances. Also, the wands were never allowed to touch the ground, for that would defile them and bring calamity.

Between the Eagle Dance and the Scalp Dance was an interlude in which the Eagle Killer was honored. It was also customary, at this time, to offer smoke to the singers, who sang a song demanding tobacco. They were presented with a stone-bowled pipe by the driver, who held it to each singer's lips. In early times, as we have seen, the pipe was also offered to strangers and guests or to delegations wishing to make peace. It was interesting to us to learn that the Cherokees had a driver for their dances, just as we had found among Western Indians for the Grass Dance. He preserved order, urged participation in the dances, and acted as Master of Ceremonies.

Long ago an eagle was killed for each performance of the Eagle Dance, thus acquiring fresh eagle power, and new wands were made up for the dancers. In more recent times no eagle was killed, but some person was honored with the title of Eagle Killer for the ceremonies. The driver placed a deerskin in front of the Eagle Killer and on it donations were spread as "ceremonial compensation to the dramatic star of the evening."[17] Formerly these donations consisted of deerskins, tobacco, a knife, powder and lead, buttons and pins, symbolizing tribal concern for his general welfare—skins for moccasins; tobacco for ceremonial or spiritual well-being; knife, powder, and lead for his livelihood, and buttons and pins for his womenfolk. Later the donations were coins—about five cents from each donor.

Now came the time for the special Scalp Dance in the Eagle Dance schedule. A line of warriors appeared painted for war, each bearing a wand in his right hand and a scalp or a weapon in his left. This time a singer was a member of the dancing line, carrying his little water drum and singing as he danced. The dancers circled to the right with the running trot, or shuffle step, giving occasional whoops and yells as they progressed. These were all victory songs now. When a song stopped, the leader recited and enacted his war experiences as the others marched slowly behind him. Much yelling introduced and ended each song and recitation. When the leader had finished, he retired to the end of the line and the next man repeated the performance, dramatizing his own experiences. This kept up until each dancer had had a chance to tell his story. When the Scalp Dance ended, the leader gathered up the wands and scalps and put them away, then everyone gathered for a feast, the usual way of ending an Indian ceremony.

THE BOOGER DANCE

In recent times the Eagle Dance became part of the Booger Dance in the winter ceremonies. The Booger Dance was a masked dance representing "people from far away or across the water."[18] The chief of the masked dancers used to bring with him a live sparrow hawk as emblem of his chieftainship. The masks were often made of large gourds, or sometimes were carved from buckeye wood. The Iroquois and Cherokees did more with masks than any other Indians except those of the Northwest Coast and the Southwest deserts. Even so, Cherokee and Iroquois uses of masks were quite different. The Cherokee Booger Dance took its name from the English "bogey," so refers to ghosts, frightful animals, or the spirits of strangers who came into Cherokee country.

The Booger dancers dressed as grotesquely as possible. They took particular delight in burlesquing the white man. They pretended to speak strange languages. Europeans were represented by exaggerated features—bushy eyebrows, mustaches, chin whiskers. (Most Indians detested hair on the face and body.) They gave themselves big noses, ghastly white skin, red cheeks, bald heads. They stuffed abdomens, buttocks, and shins to look even more ridiculous.

Some dancers represented hunters, carrying bows and arrows, guns, clubs, and sometimes a dead chicken or dead lamb to represent the game they had taken. We would think of the Booger Dance as a clowns' dance, which it was, but it also had the serious purpose of pointing out the terrible things that had happened to the Cherokees since the coming of the strangers and reminding them to retain their old ways.

Sometimes a dancer wore a hat made from a hornet's nest, representing all "mean creatures." The dancers were boisterous, discourteous, and vulgar, depicting every attribute the Indians abhorred. They acted as if they were anxious to start fights, pushed each other around, and when asked what they wanted the reply was always, "Girls!"

The Boogers danced clumsily, one leg raised horizontally and then the other, in imitation of the ridiculous dancing some white people do in trying to imitate Indians. They danced to the music of a singer with a water drum, assisted by a number of other singers with rattles. Each Booger had a chance to dance solo. His name, or rather the ridiculous name he used while being a Booger, was sung in the song, and the song was sung four times for his dance. Every time his name came out in the song the audience cheered and yelled, like white people do.

Actually, the Booger Dance had its origin before the coming of the white man, which was foretold in a prophecy which prepared them for the coming of strangers. John Lawson wrote about a masked-clown performance of neighboring Catawbas in 1714. He said their faces were covered with "vizards made of gourds" and that they wore bells of various sorts on their ankles and knees.

They danced an hour, showing many strange gestures, and brandishing their wooden weapons as if they were going to fight each other; oftentimes walking very nimbly round the room, without making the least noise with their bells, a thing I much admired at; again turning their bodies, arms and legs into such frightful postures that you would have guessed they had been quite raving mad; at last they cut two or three high capers and left the room.[19]

The Booger Dance itself shows some relationship to the Calumet Dance. In the old days strangers could ask for the Calumet ritual, which established their friendship and desire to cooperate with their hosts. The Boogers, representing strangers, could ask for the Eagle Dance, which of course traces back to the Calumet. Or they could ask for the Bear Dance, which also has a relationship to the Calumet. The pipe which the Driver offered to the singers sometimes had a bear effigy carved on the bowl.

After the Boogers had finished their cavorting and asked for the Eagle Dance, a number of women equal to the number of Boogers joined them. The woman leader wore the leg rattles and danced opposite the Booger leader. The women were nicely dressed in Cherokee style, adopted from the long, full skirts and tight bodices of the early nineteenth century. Their entry into the dance symbolized the submission of the Cherokees to the invaders. The dance was like the real Eagle Dance, but at its conclusion the Boogers left the room, making a great deal of noise and trying to drag some of the women with them.

The Driver then came forward with the pipe and danced in a circle with it, ending with a cry of "Stop," whereon the dance ended and the rattles and drum were gathered up and put away. From then on the night was spent in performing the old Cherokee social and animal dances. The Booger Dance was supposed to weaken the harmful powers of alien tribes and races, represented either by living individuals or by spirits, who caused disease and misfortune.

In the National Museum in Washington is a figure representing a Cherokee Eagle dancer wearing a mask. None of the early writings mention masks for Eagle Dance, and the performers of this century did not wear them, except in this Booger version, which may explain the figure in the museum. Just how far back the Booger and Eagle dances were combined is difficult to tell, but it probably did not take place until late in the nineteenth century.

THE SOLO EAGLE DANCE

The old Cherokee men we mentioned earlier demonstrated a duet form of Eagle Dance and also a solo version. Just when these were performed is not clear, but the story is similar to the one we heard in other parts of the country. After dancing together for awhile, the two eagles fight and one goes off limping, with wings drooping. A similar story for a solo dance has the eagle wounded by a hunter. He pantomimes a struggle to keep flying but flutters to earth and ends the dance falling to the ground. Thunder Cloud, an Ottawa Indian we knew years ago, told us this latter story. He even said there was a second duet version, in which the hunter carried the eagle off at the end of the dance.

To get back to our Cherokees, the two dancers started side by side, with a *wand in each hand*, giving a partially naturalistic portrayal of eagles. They began in a crouch, quivering both wands with a movement of the fingers. They advanced in a running step, kneeling at the end of the run and shaking the wands hard. They retreated and repeated the same motion, with the kneeling, three or four times.

The next movement was a stiff-legged march in a circle to the right, one dancer following the other, swinging upper bodies side by side, waving the wands like wings, slowly. Then they came side by side again, running forward together, swooping. Next they paused, shaking all over, with short, choppy little steps, as are used in Prairie Chicken dances of the Northwest. Then they separated, faced each other, and circled again, this time advancing toward each other and pantomiming eagles fighting, advancing, swooping, striking, retreating. One eagle was wounded; the dancer depicted it by dropping one arm loosely to the side and limping as he went off. The other continued circling around, "flying" higher and more vigorously, triumphant after the battle.

We were told that this same dance pattern was sometimes done by a solo dancer. Either the solo or the duet version must have been done at times of tribal gatherings and largely for entertainment. It is possible, also, that the solo dance was used as a contest. In several tribes today the last vestiges of the Eagle or Calumet dance are now used as contests between solo dancers.

THE CHOCTAWS

The Choctaws, living west and south of the Cherokees, are known to have had both Calumet and Eagle dances. Some students are of the opinion that the Choctaw Eagle Dance belonged to an Eagle Cult. Be that as it may, they had an Eagle Dance. Although Catlin did not write much about it, he was much impressed with it, particularly because the step was so difficult, done in a low squat. He wrote:

This picturesque dance was given by twelve or sixteen men, whose bodies were chiefly naked and painted white, with white clay, and each one holding in his hand the tail of the eagle, while his head was also decorated with an eagle's quill. Spears were stuck in the ground, around which the dance was performed by four men at a time, who had simultaneously, at the beat of the drum, jumped up from the ground where they had all sat in rows of four, one row immediately behind the other, and ready to take the place of the first four when they left the ground fatigued, which they did by hopping or jumping around behind the rest, and taking their seats, ready to come up again in their turn, after each of the other sets had been through the same forms.

In this dance, the steps or rather jumps, were different from anything I had ever witnessed before, as the dancers were squat down, with their bodies almost to the ground, in a severe and most difficult posture. . . .[20]

THE IROQUOIS

For many years we have been interested in the Seneca and Onondaga dances that are still performed in New York State. The best of the Iroquois dances are given during the winter solstice; the Eagle Dance is still the most important. For all the many years of contact with European civilization, the Iroquois retain much of their traditional manner of living. Our friend Dr. Speck used to tell us of his visits to the Senecas and Onondagas. We feel as if we had seen the dances ourselves because of his vivid descriptions. In their Eagle dances these tribes use wands somewhat similar to those of the Cherokees and gourd rattles.

Usually four, but sometimes five or six, eagle feathers are suspended parallel to the wand, which is about eighteen inches long and made of ash, hickory, or maple. Four is the ceremonial number to the Iroquois, as to most tribes.

The Eagle Dance of present-day Senecas belongs to the Eagle Society, which is a medicine society. Some of its members have dreamed of eagles, or other birds, or have been cured of "eagle sickness." Some have power for curing wounds or for preventing accidents. Each member has a bundle containing two wands, two rattles, a single feather, a whistle, and a package of sacred tobacco. Although these bundles remind us of some of the medicine bundles of more western tribes, there are no ceremonies or dances connected with the bundles as such. Sometimes the bundle is merely wrapped in newspaper or kept in a flour sack. A bundle is suspended from a pole outside the house where a meeting is to be held. The Eagle Dance is usually given at the request of someone suffering from some complaint which he believes the ceremonies can cure.

The eagles associated with the Iroquois dance are not ordinary eagles; they are often spoken of as "Dew Eagles." They are supernatural creatures that fly above the clouds, and if they come to earth at all it is only to alight on a mountaintop. So the only way they are ever seen is in dreams. Some say there are three colors, but all agree that some are red and some are pure white. The red Dew Eagles are the most powerful. They can take away bad luck, but also can bring it to people who do not live virtuously. They can restore wilted things. The Dew Eagles are partially responsible for watering the earth, sharing the responsibility with the Thunderers. They can be appealed to through sacred tobacco.

In the Iroquois beliefs about the origin of their league, a bald eagle sits on the top of the Tree of Peace. The bald eagle is much less fierce and warlike than the golden. He watches for any evil thing that might destroy the peace and screams alarm and defiance at the appearance of any danger. The Iroquois knew that "eternal vigilance is the price of liberty" and that there could be no real liberty without peace.[*]

Golden eagle feathers decorate the Eagle Dance wands, which are supposed to represent the Dew Eagles. The Iroquois did not kill the eagles to obtain their feathers. They dug a trench large enough for a man to lie down in and covered him over with brush so that he could not be seen from above. When an eagle came down for the bait which was placed on the brush, the eagle catcher tried to hold him and pluck some of his feathers. Sometimes he was able to get only one or two. An eagle with a five-to-seven-foot wing spread would be quite a handful, and extremely dangerous in the bargain. In the West eagles were trapped in similar fashion, but usually from a pit in which a man could stand.

Originally the Eagle Dance was associated with war in the minds of the Iroquois, as with other tribes. To the Iroquois the wands did not symbolize calumets, although they doubtless originated from the decorations on that instrument, and a number of phases of the Iroquois Eagle Dance bear resemblance to the Calumet ceremonies of the Middle West. Although the Iroquois have a tradition that they received the ceremonies from the Cherokees, we know there are many elements related to other tribes farther west, rather than south.

The present Iroquois Eagle Dance evolved from ceremonies pertaining to both peace and war. There are still portions of it reminiscent of the Scalp and War dances of old. In order to keep a dance alive, it must have a function. The original function being gone, the Eagle Dance now serves a different purpose. Instead of creating new friendships, it celebrates existing ones. It is used to cure disease, to bring rain, to hearten the unhappy and depressed, and as a thanksgiving. At times it has also been used to bring luck in hunting.

Formerly a special pole was erected for the Eagle Dance. It was of sycamore, about the height of a man, with a small fork at the top, reminding one of a miniature Sun Dance pole. It was peeled and painted with a red stripe which started at the bottom and spiraled counterclockwise to the top. With the pole also went a "striking stick," with a loop on it so it could be hung from the fork. The striking stick was striped in the same way. So were the wands. The use of the pole has long since been discontinued, and an ordinary cane is now used instead of the striking stick.

The Iroquois did not have a driver, but did have a conductor, who served in the same capacity. He was also the leading singer and had charge of the ceremonial

---

[*]Students of the Iroquois believe the bald eagle, as our national emblem, stems from this source.

The Seneca Eagle Dance, by Ernest Smith, of the Tonawanda Reservation, New York, about 1900. Smithsonian Institution, Bureau of American Ethnology.

regalia, in addition to conducting the ritual. The conductor appointed a whooper, who had about the same position as a cheerleader.

Recent performances of the Seneca Eagle Dance have employed two dancers, but we have drawings and written accounts from around 1900 which show four dancers. Each dancer wears Iroquois-style costume—leggings of cloth with seams down the front, kilt or wide breechclout, arm bands, and a close-fitting cap with a single eagle feather erect in the center. Any warrior could wear a cap and one feather; a war chief was entitled to wear two feathers. The feather twirled in a bone socket—"looking around."

Formerly Eagle dancers painted their entire heads red, or half red and half black. This was in the days when Iroquois wore shaven heads and scalp locks. Nowadays members of the Eagle Society paint a red spot on each cheek.

The Conductor brings out the little water drum and places it upside down on the floor, so that the head will become wet. Beside it he places a beater and a rattle of cow horn. Formerly the rattle was of bark. These instruments are for the "orchestra." Then he appoints the Whooper, and people to serve in other capacities, as Speakers, a Gift Custodian, and those to present the wands to the dancers.

He then opens the meeting with a prayer of thanks to the Great Spirit and Spirit Powers and for the sacred tobacco. There is also a Priest of the Society who, with the Conductor, takes the wands and gourd rattles to the kitchen stove, where they are purified over incense from tobacco sprinkled on the fire. A rattle is tied to each wand. Of course, in the old long-house days, this was done over an open fire. The Conductor brings the tobacco back into the main room, where each member fills his pipe. The wands and rattles are brought in, the Priest keeping one set, the other set being handed to a Speaker.

The Whooper then calls out, answered as by an echo from the entire assemblage. The Conductor strikes the drum twice and begins the first song, joined by another singer with the horn rattle. There are fourteen songs for the Seneca Eagle Dance. Each one is started by the Whooper, but is ended by someone striking against the floor with the striking stick (cane). This recalls times of old when a warrior would interrupt the song by striking the pole with the striking stick in order to recount his deeds.

The story has come down from the past that long ago a warrior pledged his word, or took an oath, by striking the skin of a dead enemy. This was known as "striking a skin." It later changed to "striking a drum." The Eagle Dance is also known among the Senecas as "Striking-a-Pole," the names apparently being used interchangeably. (The Senecas also have a Shawnee War Dance called "Striking-the Stick," which lead to some confusion among observers.)

When the pole or the floor was struck, the drum was also struck, and the speaker's deeds were applauded by thumps on the drum, so we can see a relationship among these various "strikings." Whenever the Dew Eagles or the Creator are mentioned the drum is also struck.

Now, instead of counting coup, the speakers in the Eagle Dance tell of personal experiences connected with the dance; also of testimonials of cures, beliefs, prayers for cures in behalf of stricken members, prayers of thanksgiving, encouragement to others to carry on the traditions. Sometimes a Speaker talks in jest, or makes fun of someone in the group, but in order not to hurt anyone's feeling he always makes a present to the person he ridicules. Presents are given out to various members following each song, and crackers and apples distributed by the Custodian to those designated by the Speakers.

In this way the first three songs are sung, with no dancing at all. After the first song the Priest hands a wand and a rattle to one of the dancers, who remaining in his seat unties the rattle from the wand. After the second song the Speaker with the other wand and rattle hands them to the other dancer. These two dancers are seated on chairs at one end of the room. In the old days they would have been on benches. After untying the wands and rattles, they hold a wand in the left hand, a rattle in the right.

A bit of meat, corn, or even a penny is placed on the floor in two spots near the center of the room, one for each dancer. On the fourth song, the dancers sway in their seats, waving the wands horizontally and shaking the rattles in time with the music. They represent birds on their perches. During this first part of the song there is no accent, just a tremolo beat. When the song changes to an accented beat, the dancers hop off their chairs and begin a crouch dance, advancing with short hops, like birds, turning from side to side and shaking wands and rattles in time. The rattles represent birds scratching on the ground.

The drum changes again to vibrato, and the dancers charge the food, weaving their shoulders and shaking the wands and rattles far out to the side in the position of wings, vibrating rapidly like wings. They lunge for the food, and good dancers will pick up the meat, corn, or penny with their lips without touching their hands or knees to the floor.

Once the "meat" is in his mouth a dancer retreats to his seat, twisting his body and looking around, as a feeding bird does. These dances are ordinarily quite short, but the song and dance must be repeated until someone strikes with the cane, which brings it to a stop. Usually a striker waits until near the close of the song, but he can stop it any time he wishes.

The dance is repeated for each of the ten remaining songs, the only variation being in the individuality of each dancer and his interpretation of an eagle in action.

The Iroquois songs remind one to some degree of the songs of the Southwest. The changes of rhythm, with three short beats occasionally interspersed, sounding to the uninitiated as if coming at random, make the songs complicated and difficult to learn, even though they are very short. Analysis shows them to have a definite pattern, and the dancer must learn all the songs perfectly in order to follow them with exactness.*

It takes great agility to pick up the food from the floor. Old men in the group are sometimes singled out and honored for their great agility as Eagle dancers in their youth. We are reminded of the "Feather" dances of Oklahoma tribes, especially Cheyennes, which are occasionally performed at Indian "doings." "Feather" dance is a confusing term, for there are many feather dances across the country, bearing no resemblance to each other. The one we refer to is usually done only by boys and is a contest dance, testing their agility. The usual thing is to pick up a tiny fluffy feather, stuck into the ground, with the teeth in much the same manner as the Iroquois Eagle Dance. Sometimes the boys pick up a handkerchief, or dollar bills, in the same way.

The Seneca dancers used to pick up the "food" twice during each song, but now do it only once. The dance ends on three quick beats. The dancers simultaneously rap sharply with the heels and the rattles, then go to their seats.

---

*Some recordings of Cherokee and Iroquois Eagle Dance songs are available through the Music Division of the Library of Congress.

After the last, or fourteenth, song, the dancers lay the wands and rattles on the floor in front of them. The conductor picks them up, ties them together again, and wraps them in the bundle. He then thanks the dancers, singers, and all who took part, then thanks the Creator and the Spirit Powers and asks that all present may return safely to their homes.

Now we have the feast. Meat and corn soup are passed around, counterclockwise, to everyone present. In early days this was a dog feast, and the heads of the dogs were presented to the bravest warriors. Later a hog's head was substituted for dog, presented to some honored person, and now it comes down to any kind of meat, usually chicken, and corn soup.

The over-all ceremony of the Seneca Eagle Dance follows the usual Iroquois pattern, but the crouch dance and bundle are not known to any other Iroquois ritual. We can see that a number of other tribes have influenced it. The songs are more like the songs of the Mesquakies, or Foxes, than any other. We have mentioned that the Eagle bundle was hung to a pole outside the house where the meeting was to be held. The bundle was also displayed in times of drought in order to appeal for rain. A similar practice has been noted for the Menominis near the Great Lakes, who hung a drum, gourd rattle, and eagle-feather fan on a pole as a prayer for rain.

On the other hand, the Iroquois may have done some influencing themselves. At one time their warriors ranged as far as Lake Superior on the west and as far south as the Carolinas and Tennessee. There is no doubt that they had great influence all over the Middle West.

NIGHTHAWK DANCE

A division of the Delaware tribe, long ago adopted by the Iroquois and still living on the Six Nation Reserve in Canada, has a Nighthawk Dance which is very similar to the Cayuga version of the Iroquois Eagle Dance. Two to four dancers take part, like the Iroquois wands in the left hand, rattles in the right, a water drum and cowhorn rattle for accompaniment, with similar squatting and crouching positions, jumps, and other birdlike movements. They also paint a red spot on each cheek.

THE SHAWNEES

The Shawnee Eagle Dance, which in some ways is more like the Choctaw dance, at the same time has the feature that the dancers pick up objects from the floor with the mouth. The Shawnee dance was associated with an eagle bundle, which would indicate western contact, but has other features that are typically southern. In the bundle, as well as eagle feathers and tobacco, is a raven's wing, which in the Southeast, from where the Shawnees came originally, was a doctor's emblem. And yet the Shawnee dance was not used for curing or for making friendships. Neither did it incorporate the striking post, or counting coup. Apparently it was given only to honor the bundle and the power, or spirit, of the eagle. The bundle also included a raw (untanned) hide, used in place of a drum, with a stick for a beater, and a gourd rattle.

The ceremony employed twelve dancers, again showing the group, or company, aspect of the Cherokee and Choctaw rituals.*

Other tribes of the Southeast—Creek, Yuchi, Chickasaw—also used either a buzzard's or a raven's feather as a doctoring emblem. The Cherokee war leader wore a raven skin when he went ahead to scout the country and gave a raven's cry as alarm. In many tribes ravens, buzzards, and eagles, all birds of prey, were associated with war activities. Consequently, it is not surprising sometimes to find these other birds also associated with Eagle dances. Although the Iroquois do not use them in their Eagle Dance, they do have a mythological giant crow that figures in some of their ceremonies.

We have already mentioned "eagle sickness" among Cherokee and Iroquois. The same belief was held by the Creeks, Yuchis, and Chickasaws.

Some people wonder why it was always the eagle's tail, or tail feathers, that were used in Eagle and Calumet dances instead of wings. There may be two reasons. The first is that the "war eagle" is the one admired. He was the young but mature bird, usually not over a year old, with black-tipped white feathers on the tail. They are completely different in appearance from those of the older bird. Each year thereafter, the feathers become more speckled and darker. The wings, however, do not show such marked change. In addition to distinctly representing the war eagle, these yearling tail feathers are also the most beautiful. In capturing live eagles, without destroying them, the way the Iroquois did, it was probably easier, too, to get tail feathers. Apparently the only tribe not to ascribe importance to eagle feathers in the Calumet ceremonies was the Chitimachas on the Gulf, who used flamingo feathers.

---

*The Catawbas sent a delegation all the way from South Carolina to Albany, New York, to perform the Calumet Dance on a peace-making mission in 1751.[21]

14. Calumet and Eagle Dances: In the West

Now let us see what happened to the Eagle Dance in the West. We have mentioned that the Pawnee ceremony was perhaps the most elaborate of all the Calumet rituals. It was recorded in its entirety by Alice Fletcher in the *Twenty-Second Annual Report* of the Bureau of American Ethnology, so we shall not say too much about it here.

We know that although there is a thread of resemblance running through Calumet, Eagle, and Pipe dances everywhere, there were also many differences in the middle western and western versions of the ceremony. We still find the counting of coups, the distribution of presents, and the feast, but most of them incorporated adoption rites not found in the eastern ceremonies. The adoption was often, if not usually, of adults, who became ceremonial children, rather than of actual children. The "child" was "captured," with coup being counted upon him. It also seems strange that even tribes which raised no corn at all used ears of corn in their symbolism, whereas tribes in the East, almost as dependent upon corn as upon the chase, did not include it in theirs. A buffalo skull also played an important part in the Western rituals, and a wild-cat skin was given a prominent place by many Western tribes. We do not know the symbolism, but certainly it is one of the softest and most beautiful of furs.

To most tribes, regardless of location, piercing children's ears was an important occasion. It had about the same significance for them as a christening or baptism has for Christians. Tabeau (1803–05) mentioned that among the "Ricara" (Arikaras) the Pipe Dance was given at the time of this ear piercing. He saw it performed by naked dancers at nineteen degrees below zero! At the same time the children were bathed in ice water. Strangers visiting at the ceremonies were given presents and, because of the nature of the Pipe Dance beliefs, were not expected to make any return.[1]

The actual Calumet dancing in the Western areas, although it represented eagles, was not done in a squat, or low crouch, as was the case in the Eastern dances. We have mentioned before that there has been too much emphasis, in the popular mind, on the crouch dancing of the Indians. What there was of it, however, was more typical of the Plains than of the Woodlands, and yet, in these Calumet and Eagle dances, we find the crouch in the East, with little if any of it in the West. Where dancers were actually depicting eagles, a crouch would aid in simulating the appearance and action of the bird.

In the West the ceremonies were more elaborate and involved, with the use of more paraphernalia. The calumets were highly decorated, with much symbolism attached to them. In some tribes each calumet of a pair was different. Usually one represented male and one female, although the Iowas, who had one of the earliest forms of the ritual, have one story that both of their calumets, or wands, were male. However, another Iowa story says they were male and female.

The number of feathers in the fan varied from six to twelve, depending upon the tribe. In museums we have seen wands with two fans each. Osages used seven feathers in each fan. A Hidatsa buffalo robe in the American Museum of Natural History is painted with the Sacred Pipe design and shows seven feathers on each pipe. Old Sioux drawings show four feathers on each wand. Black Elk said the famous Buffalo Calf Pipe of the Sioux had twelve feathers—a full eagle tail—but when Sidney Thomas examined the actual pipe in 1941 it had six eagle feathers, which had been stained red. Even though Black Elk was a keeper of ceremonies and one of the last of the real holy men, he may never have seen the actual Buffalo Calf Pipe, for it was kept by a family on a different reservation.[2] Wissler's account of the Oglalas says there were six golden-eagle feathers on each wand.[3]

In some tribes the calumets were tribal property. In others they were personally owned. The female wand represents, among the Pawnees at least, the night, the moon, the north, kindness, and gentleness. It cares for the people, is the mother. Although the male wand represents male attributes—the fatherhood of nature, as well as prowess in war, protection of the family, and the like—it can bring injury, so must follow in the ceremony, rather than lead, which is the opposite of the usual male role in Indian society.

THE IOWAS

Both Iowa wands were perforated. The Iowas, being an Eastern Plains tribe, were already mounted by the time of their first contact with French and Americans. So, when they sent a delegation to perform the Calumet Dance, the two dancers rode horseback. They halted four times on their approach, dismounting to dance each time. They carried the wands, or calumet stems, in their left hands, rattles in the right.

With the Iowa Pipe, or Calumet, bundles went also a deer-bladder skin, painted blue, filled with tobacco; a forked stick to support the calumets when not in use; and a wildcat skin on which to rest the lower, or bowl, ends. We first found blue paint mentioned for the Miamis. It seems to have been an important color for the Calumet rituals.

The Iowa ceremony had the usual Western concept of adoption. Tobacco was sent to the one to be adopted. If he accepted it he accepted the invitation to go through with the ceremony, and was considered the son of the donor from then on. The wand bearers danced as the people came out to meet them, waving the feathered calumets gracefully through the air in front of them, shaking their rattles, and singing, "We bring health, power, and prosperity to our new son. He shall live to be white-headed and to carry a cane."

After the fourth dance, all went to the special lodge prepared for the ceremonies, where the forked stick was set up and two servants detailed to watch the wands as they rested against it. A song accompanied the setting up of the stick and placement of the wands.

The donors furnished a feast, but the recipient and his family and friends reciprocated with valuable gifts. The ceremonies lasted several days. If the recipient had a child, it was also adopted. The donors charged the lodge, "captured" the child, took him to their camp, dressed him in fine clothes, painted his face, and placed eagle down upon his head. They then brought him back, dancing again with the wands. Whenever they met the child in the future they were expected to give him presents.

Catlin said this Calumet, or Pipe of Peace, Dance was also given at the conclusion of a peace treaty, after smoking the sacred stems. The dance was also given in honor of a very brave warrior to compliment him for his bravery. He, of course, to show that he was not overrated, made valuable presents to the donors.

The Iowa Calumet Dance was started by a distinguished warrior, who handed the wands and rattles to the dancers and counted coup.

The Iowas were among those tribes who had both Calumet and Eagle dances. Catlin said the Eagle Dance was a war dance. The dancers represented soaring eagles, heading against the wind, looking down, preparing to swoop. The wind was strong, so they would fall back, advance again, fall back and advance, blowing eagle-bone whistles to represent cries of the eagles. Each dancer carried an eagle *tail* in his left hand, but a weapon in his right. After each dance some warrior counted coup, and after each recitation the dance was resumed with renewed vigor. In the midst of the noise and excitement a medicine man jumped forward, flourishing shield and spear, counted coup, and portrayed war experiences in a dance.

Skinner, who made a study of the Iowas, did not believe that the Eagle Dance was a war dance but that it belonged to an Eagle Cult, or Eagle Bundle. It is probably what we have run into before, a *warriors'* dance rather than a *war* dance.[4]

THE KANSAS

The Iowas belong to a group of Siouan tribes known as Chiwere, which includes Otos and Missouris, so it might be expected that calumet ceremonies of this group were all similar. Another group of Siouan people, the Dhegiha, includes Omahas, Poncas, Quapaws, Osages, and Kansas. We should expect them, too, to have similar ceremonies, but they also had some differences. The Kansa calumets were drilled, or perforated, and to them the hole represented the sun. On the end of the wand where a pipe bowl ordinarily would be attached was a mallard duck's head. In addition to the usual fan of eagle feathers was a bunch of owl feathers, and a series of pileated woodpeckers' bills and attached crests was lashed to the stem. Tassels of red-dyed horsehair were also fastened to it. The duck's head represented good weather, for ducks fly quacking when the weather is fine. The owl feathers symbolized rain, for it rains after the owls hoot. The woodpecker bills also represent good weather, and the horsehair was a prayer for more horses. This horsehair decoration was common to all of the Western calumets. The Sioux even call the calumet wands "horse tails."

With the Kansa bundle was also a forked stick, painted red, on which to rest the calumet, duck head down. The forked sticks represented crotched trees, where eagles build their nests. Four grains of corn and a wildcat skin were also in the bundle.

With the Kansas it was apparently always a child who received the adoption, although his father was the one who received the invitation and who furnished the feast and presents for the donor. The child's face was painted green (for the earth?), with an outer circle of red. He was led from the lodge, placed before a drum, and two men with wands danced before him. At this time the donors were given presents of blankets, horses, and other valuables. One wand had a fan of dark feathers from the old golden eagle, which was the female wand. The other fan was of the young eagle, white with black tips—the male wand.

A single grain of corn was quartered and dropped in a bowl of water. A horse tail was dipped in the bowl and drawn in a circle around the child's face, symbolizing washing off the paint, and he was then ceremonially dried by motions with the wildcat skin. Bundles of grass were placed in each of the four directions and the child's feet were placed on each in turn, showing that he would live to see four generations of his own.

The Omahas, relatives of the Kansas, used similar wands, but the Osages, also relatives, did not perforate their wands. Even the Crees, Algonkins living far to the north, had similar wands. They kept the upper mandibles of the woodpeckers' heads tied back over the crests in time of peace, but in war time cut the sinew binding so that the crests would stand erect in anger and defiance. Perhaps other tribes had similar symbolism. The woodpecker, probably because of his red crest and because he darted so swiftly that he looked like a shaft of red light flickering through the trees, was closely associated with the sun.

THE CREES

The Crees had a bowl with the calumet; some writings would lead us to believe that only one calumet was used in a ceremony. The bowl was filled and placed on a pile of offerings while an invocation was made to the sky, the four quarters, and the earth, the performer pointing the feathered stem and circling with it as the invocation progressed. The entire assembly then sang while he danced with the stem, swinging it before him and over his head and shoulders in graceful arcs. After the dance, the bowl was placed on the stem and the pipe was lit and passed around, each one smoking it, or rather pretending to smoke it, and stroking the stem with his hands. The pipe was passed to the left, in a sun circle. In making peace, the pipe was smoked first by the former enemy, then by the Crees, each person taking four puffs. Then, after a series of songs, the Pipe Dance was performed, following which the pipe was smoked again.

Paul Kane, the Canadian artist, spoke as if each Cree band had a Medicine Pipe Stem, or Calumet. He saw eleven of them all at one time. A Pipe Stem Carrier was elected for a single term of four years. The honor cost the holder as much as fifteen or twenty horses. With the office of Carrier went a "highly ornamented skin tent," a bear's skin upon which the pipe stem was to be exposed to view, a "medicine rattle," and a wooden bowl. The latter was always carried with him, as he was supposed to eat from it whenever food was served.

A pipe stem was wrapped in "manifold coverings" and was usually enclosed in a large bag of "parti-colored woolen cloth" which hung on the outside of the lodge. It was never taken inside except when it was uncovered and used in a proper ceremony. In moving camp, the Carrier's wife carried the bundle. It was considered a very bad omen for it to fall to the ground.

At the time of Kane's visit to the Crees, the head chief was going from camp to camp in an effort to raise a large war party for an attack on the Blackfeet in the spring. He had with him, in addition to his own pipe stem, ten others, as commitments from their owners that they would join him. He was in mourning for the loss of four relatives at the hands of the Blackfeet, so he wore old, dirty clothing, and as he harangued the villages in which he appeared the tears streamed down his face.

Kane prevailed upon the chief to open the bundles containing the eleven pipe stems, whereupon he first made a fragrant incense, burning "dried leaves of a plant collected on the Rocky Mountains." While it was burning he filled the bowls with "tobacco and some other weed," then took off his clothes, with the exception of his breechclout. It was between thirty and forty degrees below zero, but the cold did not disturb him in the least. He threw over his shoulders a highly ornamented wolfskin, then removed the wrappings from one of the stems. He inserted it in one of the bowls and sang a song which Kane could not understand. Following the song, he lighted the pipe, inhaled a puff, and turned his face upward, offering the stem in the same direction while making a prayer to the Great Spirit for success on the coming expedition. Another puff of smoke was blown to the earth, pointing the stem toward it, with a prayer for plenty of buffalo and the good things of the earth. At this point a woman lifted the door flap and the ceremony ended right then. No woman was supposed to see these Cree pipe stems, which seems to place them in a different category from the usual calumets.

Later on, with more ceremony, the other stems were unwrapped, each stem being inserted in a bowl and smoked by the men present. After Kane had sketched them, they were carefully rewrapped and removed from the lodge.

Kane said the chief traveled six or seven hundred miles on snowshoes to accomplish his mission. Prior to starting for the enemy's country, the warriors gathered, in the spring, at a designated place, where they feasted and danced for three days before leaving. The pipe stems and "medicine dresses" were all exhibited, and everyone decorated himself with all the finery he could command. This may explain Kane's painting, which shows what looks like a typical Calumet Dance except that the two dancers are in full regalia, instead of being stripped. Kane painted the picture sometime between 1848 and 1855 and in his note gives the impression that it was typical of Blackfoot, Blood, "Surcee" (Sarsi), Gros Ventre, and "Paygan" (Piegan) Indians. So apparently a type of Calumet Dance was known to these tribes, as well as to the Crees. What puzzled us was the dancers appearing in fringed and quilled shirts and leggings, the costumes of chiefs and headmen. All reports up to

"*Medicine Pipe Stem Dance*, Blackfoot Indians, Blood Indians, Sur-cees, Gros-Ventres and Paygans," by Paul Kane. Royal Ontario Museum, Toronto, Canada.

this date mention the nakedness of the dancers, and even as late as 1891 we shall see that the Omaha were mostly nude for this ceremony. Perhaps his story of the Cree chief raising the war party and his mention of the "medicine dresses" explains it, but Kane said that he made the sketch for the painting while visiting a Blood encampment. He said nothing about the dance itself, what it looked like, or how it was done.[5]

THE OMAHAS

The Omaha ceremonies seemed to be most like the original ritual of the Pawnees. As might be expected, the Omahas being farmers, as were the Pawnees, a sacred ear of corn was an important ceremonial object on their altar. S. H. Long, about 1820, wrote that among the Omahas the Wawan was "a very favourite dance."

The Omahas had the same idea of adopting the son of the recipient of the ceremony that the Kansas did. The child in the ceremonies represented the coming generations. But Long said that presents were given to the adopted son and to his son, who represented him, by the *donor* of the ritual. All other reports say just the reverse. It is the recipient who gives presents to the donor, to pay him for the honor. He also mentioned only one calumet, belonging to the "father," which was placed on a forked-stick support in back of the lodge, but later said there were two dancers with calumet stems. The Omahas, at that time, were living in large earth lodges.

The ceremonies lasted two or three days. Each night the calumet was wrapped in cloth and "put to bed," with a lullaby sung to the accompaniment of a rattle. In the morning it was awakened by another song and placed back on the rack.

A striking post was set up near the entrance of the lodge and a dancing arena was marked off by screens of hanging skins. The principal men sat around the post, another difference from the usual custom in which the seat of honor is at the rear of the lodge, opposite the door.

The adopted son led his youthful representative (his own son) and two dancers decorated with paint and wearing only breechclouts to the ceremonial lodge. The dancers each carried a decorated calumet stem and a rattle "of dried skin or a gourd."

They dance in the ordinary manner of the Indians, and pass backwards and forwards between the entrance and back part of the arena, endeavoring to exhibit as much agility as possible in their movements, throwing themselves into a great variety of attitudes imitative of the actions of the war eagle, preserving at the same time a constant waving motion with the calumet in the left hand, and agitating the gourd in the right, more or less vehemently, agreeably to the music.

Long evidently implied a difference between donors of the ritual and other donors of gifts. He said presents were given by warriors. One donor tied horses to the post. An old crier announced his name, then this donor struck the post, told of his deeds, and gave the horses away. Following the actual Calumet Dance, the donor of the ritual struck the post and recounted his war deeds.

In Osage ceremonies, which were similar, the coup strikers struck either a pole or a shield suspended from the pole.

Sometimes a gift giver lightly struck the person of one of the dancers instead of striking the post before relating his deeds and making his presents. Still another way was to pick up a hand drum (a gong, Long called it) and strike it once for each deed related. No one could then touch the drum unless he could relate a greater honor, which sounds like the Crow Steal-the-Drum Dance that we described earlier. Apparently the Discovery Dance was also a part of the Calumet ceremonies of the Omahas in Long's day, but later was dropped.[6]

Later accounts of the Omahas say the two stems were placed on a rack of red forked sticks with their lower ends resting on a wildcat skin. When they were first picked up they were waved to the rhythm of rattles only, but later in the ceremony the rhythm was augmented by a drum. Omahas and Pawnees used large water drums for this ceremony. The wands were grasped by the ducks' necks in the left hand, the rattles in the right. The female wand was blue, with ten dark eagle feathers; the male, green, with seven dark-tipped white feathers. The bundle also contained a bladder of tobacco; an eagle-bone whistle; three downy eagle feathers, or "fluffies"; sweet grass, for incense; and a wildcat skin.

The Omahas had special songs for laying down the wands. The dancers tied the rattles to the wands and simulated eagles settling on a nest, which reminds us of the Iroquois, far to the east. A design was painted on the child's face similar to the one on the gourds. It represented birds' eggs and also showed the horizon and the path of the four winds. The red markings in the design symbolized the light of the sun, as did the woodpecker feathers on the wands. Green represented the earth, blue the sky, red the sun and life.

One of the most sympathetic accounts of the Omaha *Wawan*, or Calumet ceremony, was written by John Comfort Filmore, who witnessed it in 1891. He said that the dancers were mostly nude, with magnificent figures. "I never saw finer physiques," he wrote. He said the ceremony was performed at night, and

a very impressive scene it was. . . . The only light was that of a blazing campfire, which shone on the barbaric figures and costumes of the Indians with telling effect, and made the whole camp a weird and fascinating spectacle. The sacred pipes were brought out and their coverings removed, the officiating Indians treating them with a reverence comparable only to that with which a priest of the Roman Church treats a crucifix. These pipes were not to be smoked; indeed they had no bowls, and their use was symbolic only. . . . When they were waved in the act of laying them to rest ceremonially, they described the most graceful arcs imaginable.

The significance of these eagle feathers is to symbolize Power turned into the service of Peace. The eagle here plays precisely the same part as is played by the lion in the scripture text: "The lion and the lamb shall lie down together and a little child shall lead them." In both, the thought is of an animal of prey, the strongest, fiercest and most successful, using all his powers in the interest of peace and good-will.

Christian Indians noted this parallel and pointed it out to Alice Fletcher when she was making her notes on the Wawan ceremonies. To complete the parallel, the child was brought in and gifts made over his head, in his name, quite similar to our own Christmas. Filmore continued:

He is the symbol of innocence and peace. The Indian mind is highly poetic and imaginative, and all their religious songs and ceremonies are brim-full of poetic imagery.

Not only the dances, but all the movements employed in the Wa Wan ceremony are dramatic. For example, when the Pipes are ceremonially raised, the image in the Indian mind is of the eagle rising from his nest to take his flight. He is pictured as repeatedly fluttering his wings preparatory to flight, and the songs and the movements of the Pipes are meant to suggest this. The drum and rattles accompany each phrase of the song with a tremulous motion until the point is reached when the eagle is imagined as about to take wing; then the regular beat of the drum begins and is kept up until the end of the song. In the song when the Pipes are ceremonially laid to rest the process is reversed; the drum-beat continues until the eagle is imagined to have reached the branch where his nest is. Then the tremolo of the drums and rattles accompanies the fancied fluttering of his wings as he prepares to settle down into his nest. There are corresponding movements of the Pipes, with their long hanging plumes of eagle feathers; movements which are exceedingly beautiful and dramatically effective.

Filmore evidently saw this ceremony in the open, as he mentions camp and campfire, and it took place in July. Few people could see any good in an Indian ceremonial in his time, when some of the most severe pressure was being exerted to root them all out. But he went on further to say, "I should be sorry to see these Indians allow the memories of the deeds and customs of their ancestors to die out. The remembrance of them is not likely, I think, to interfere in any degree, with their advance in civilization."[7] Filmore was ahead of his time in his attitude.

The final rites of blessing the child were secret with the Omahas, only the immediate participants being present. But the Poncas, whose ceremonies otherwise were quite close to the Omahas, although less elaborate, conducted all the rituals in public.

THE OSAGES

The Osages, too, had a sense of power being applied in the efforts of peace, of the timid and the ferocious living together in harmony. Their ritual for peace was addressed to the spirits of the birds—golden eagle, pileated woodpecker, mallard duck, owl, cardinal, and bluejay. When the storm clouds of war cleared away, these birds inhabit the bright blue sky of peace. Although they represent different species, they are all "chief birds." The eagle is chief of the sky, the woodpecker chief of the trees, the duck chief of the water, the owl chief of the night. The cardinal represents the sun, as also does the woodpecker, and the bluejay warns of enemies approaching.

THE PAWNEES

The Pawnee wands were much like those of the Omaha, but with still more symbolism. They even grooved the stems, as most Western Indians grooved their arrow shafts. An arrow had three grooves, whereas the calumet wand had only one, and that one straight and painted red, symbolizing the pathway of a shaft of sunlight. The stem was perforated and also feathered, like an arrow, with split eagle-wing feathers. The eagle flies near the abode of the Great Diety above. On the stems were mallard-duck necks and heads, as with other tribes, but so placed that a pipe bowl could be attached below the bills.

Pawnees, Omahas, and Osages "fletched" the stems like arrows, and like Iroquois arrows at that, for the Iroquois used two vanes on their arrows, not three as most tribes did.

THE CROWS

Lowie said that as late as 1910 there were probably twenty-six owners of Sacred Pipe bundles among the Crows. In 1931 he witnessed an "indifferent" performance of the ritual, which was held in a circular shade instead of in a large tipi. We might say that when we saw the Sacred Pipe, or Calumet, Dance, still more recently it was at the time of the Crow Fair and also held in an open shade.

A prospective "father" would take food to the one he wished to adopt. If it were accepted, the chances were that the proposed "son" would accept also the invitation for adoption. The Crows had a number of "medicines," all of them implying adoption, but according to Lowie it was the very essence of the Sacred Pipe ritual. He agrees that the ceremony came rather recently to the Crows from the Hidatsas, probably in the early 1800's. The Hidatsas, being neighbors of the Arikaras, must have been among the earliest recipients of the Calumet ritual, so it is somewhat puzzling as to why they passed it on to their Crow relatives so late.

In many ways the Crow ritual was similar to those we have been discussing. In recent times a Crow "father" could perform adoptions four times, but he seldom did so more than three times, thus always having one more to go. Whereas in recent years the "father" usually initiated the proceedings, it was customary, formerly, for a "child" to seek adoption. The adoption included the "child's" wife.

A Crow Calumet bundle contained the usual two pipe stems, with eagle-feather fans attached; ears of corn; braids of sweet grass; and a red stone bowl. The corn and stems were painted blue, and in this case, as we found for the Iowas, we have the stems representing the male element and the ears of corn, the female. The bundle was wrapped in flannel or in a buffalo-calf hide.

The candidate, or "child," and his wife were instructed for four nights. The bundle was laid out each night. Four hand drums were smoked over sweet-grass incense and used to accompany four songs, each of which was sung four times. The adopter, and his wife, the "parents," sat by their prospective "children" and gently swayed their bodies in time to the singing. On the fourth night, the bowl was placed on one of the stems, and all in the gathering smoked from it.

When the actual adoption took place, the candidate and his wife, dressed in ragged clothing, were supposed to hide in some tipi. The bundle owner came out of the ceremonial tipi to look for them. A man dancing and carrying one of the wands led the procession, the rest following him, all abreast. The one on the extreme right carried a buffalo skull slung from his back by a rope of sweet grass. The party pretended to search for the missing couple by lifting the door flap of each tipi they approached. Singers with hand drums sang for the dancer.

Finally they "discovered" the tipi where the candidate and his wife were "hiding," and four men with coups to their credit entered to "capture" them. The first tapped the candidate lightly on the shoulder, gently raised him off of his couch, and recited a coup. The second man seized an arm and counted coup. The third seized the other arm, also counting coup. The fourth man also counted coup, then all four made speeches expressing wishes for the prosperity of the captured couple. The fourth warrior took the candidate by the hand and led him out, two of the others each supporting an arm. This ceremonial capture, or seizure, reminds us of the way in which Timberlake was taken to the council house of the Cherokees.

The adoption lodge was made of two large tipis, pitched close together with their covers overlapped, really making a large shade. The candidate and his wife were led to this lodge. The man carrying the buffalo skull took his place in the center and the skull was taken off his shoulders and laid on blankets. Presents were piled all around it and were claimed by the skull bearer, who was usually a close relative of the bundle owner.

The dance followed. Two young men, chosen for their dancing ability, were selected. When we saw them, they were dressed in the usual present-day dyed underwear, with porcupine hair roaches and bustles. Formerly a kind of altar on which the wands rested was arranged in the back of the lodge. The "father," or adopter took the wands and handed them to the dancers. When we saw the ceremony, there was no altar, and as we have said it was held in an arbor, or open shade. The dancers entered from the outside. They began with the wands in their left hands, the rattles in their right, but occasionally they switched them to opposite hands. Four songs were sung, the dancers performing for each one, then the wands were laid down. The dancers bent quite forward at times, gently waving the wands, and occasionally knelt down, waving the wands and shaking the rattles. When they finished they were given a choice of any four articles from the gifts which had been made to the bundle owner.

The performance Lowie wrote about was much the same, as far as dance goes, but the one we saw was given mainly as an entertainment, no real adoption taking place at that time. Lowie believed the crossing of wands and rattles was a recent innovation, peculiar to the Crows. In the old days, after the dancers had laid down their wands, an ordinary pipe was smoked by everyone present.

Following the smoking, the candidate's face, and the faces of his wife and family were all painted with a pipe design on both sides, and a corn stalk was passed over their faces as if they were being rubbed with it. Then one of the four warriors who had led the candidate in arose and touched the candidate's ear with an awl, symbolizing piercing a child's ears, and another made motions with a knife to represent cutting the navel cord. Then the new "babe" was cleansed by the "father" pouring water on his head and wiping it off with a new cloth. This rite was quite like that of the Kansas, who used a wildcat skin instead of the new cloth.

The candidate and his wife received fine new clothing and food from the new "parents"—the donor and his wife—and finally the bundle was wrapped, presented to the "child," then placed on his wife's back, and she carried it to their own tipi. Afterward, when moving camp, she so carried it. During fair weather the bundle was hung over the tipi door, but in rainy weather it was taken inside and hung from the rear tipi poles. Meanwhile, the donor made a new bundle for himself.[8]

The Crows believed that good luck went with the possession of a Sacred Pipe, but the pipes really belonged to the Sun, so some people were afraid of them. As with other tribes, they could be used for making peace. They also had healing power and were used to patch up or prevent quarrels within the tribe. Also, the dancing was not *with* the wands but *in honor of* them, and the feast that accompanied the ceremony was to "feed the pipes" rather than the assembly.

THE SIOUX

The Lakotas, who raised no crops at all, nevertheless attached a great deal of symbolism to corn in their Calumet ritual. They have a tradition of having received the ceremony from the "Rees" (Arikaras). In one story they even speak of the wands as "cornstalks," which were waved as the corn waves in the breeze. It is probable that the entire ritual originated with the Rees, as we know they carried it north from their relatives, the Pawnees, but the Lakotas ascribe it to a long-ago holy man. They call it the Hunka ceremony, and the ones who have partaken in it, Hunkayapi. It is also known as Alowanpi, or "Singing for Someone." Hunka is a term of respect, used in many ways, but implying brotherly or ancestral relationship; it could be applied to any beloved or respected person or personage. The Sun might be called Hunka, for example.

We can readily see that the Hunka of the Sioux is merely their version of the Calumet, Sacred Pipe, or Eagle Dance, although they may also have had a separate Eagle Dance. Their sacred paraphernalia included ears of corn; two calumet stems, or wands; pipe rack; rattles; red and blue paint; buffalo skull; dried buffalo bladder; tobacco; sweet grass, eagle fluffies, and dried meat. The stems were perforated and were decorated with pileated woodpecker heads and feathers, strands of red horsehair, and fans of eagle-tail feathers. The Lakotas explain the presence of the woodpecker scalps on the wands by saying that "it is a simple, humble bird, which stays near its nest and is seldom seen."

It is certain that the Sioux have had the ceremony for a long time, for Hennepin spoke of it several times. According to him, it must have been used to enlist members for a war party. After strenuously paddling their canoes all day, when Hennepin and his companions were so exhausted they could hardly move, Indians in the party danced far into the night. They were Eastern Sioux, who in those days were using birchbark canoes. Hennepin wrote that:

Notwithstanding the fatigue of the Day, the youngest of the Warriours went at night and danc'd the Reed dance before four or five of their Captains, till Midnight. This sort of Ceremony is always concluded by the two Youngest of those who have any Relatives kill'd in the Wars.[9]

Whatever the significance of the Calumet Dance in Hennepin's time, by the early 1800's adoption was the important thing to the Sioux, as it was to other Western tribes. We are sure this latest form of the ceremony did not develop until about 1800 because it appears for the first time on the Hunkpapa calendar for 1801. And yet, the Lakotas (Western Sioux) tie the ceremony in with the instructions received from the White Buffalo Calf Maiden, who brought them their great tribal medicine, the Buffalo Calf Pipe, and all their important ceremonies. Her appearance would seem to be in the late 1600's.

Old Sioux informants said the calumet wand represented the original Buffalo Calf Pipe, which could not be available for the average Hunka ceremony.

Again a child played the important role, both actually and symbolically, for a child was the greatest gift from Wakan Tanka, the Great Mystery. Children who went through the Alowanpi were more carefully watched and protected than other children. The father of a child whom he wished to become Hunka would send an invitation to the Holy Man who had the right to perform the ceremony. The invitation, instead of being made with a pipe, as in most ceremonies, was made with a dried buffalo bladder containing little packets of sacred tobacco. If the Holy Man opened the bladder pouch, he accepted the invitation.

A ceremonial lodge made by uniting two ordinary tipis, as with the Crows, was erected, but it faced West, instead of East, for the Buffalo Calf Maiden came from the West. The entrance to the Hunka lodge was shielded, or screened, on both sides with hides, making a kind of hallway, several yards long, just as with the Omahas and Crows, so that the public could not press too close.

Within the lodge, just back of the central fire, an altar was prepared by removing the sod from a square of earth. Behind the altar was placed a buffalo skull, painted with red lines, resting on a bed of sage. Sage was also stuffed into the openings of the skull and strips of red flannel were tied to the tips of the horns. Behind the skull was a rack formed of two forked sticks set in the ground and another stick laying across the forks, all painted blue; against this rack the two wands were leaned, each with a red rawhide rattle beside it. Also leaning against the rack was a perfect ear of corn, painted and impaled on a blue stick. From the upper end of the ear of corn was attached a white eagle plume, or fluffy, representing not only the tassel on the live corn but the spirit force of the corn. Similar fluffies were also attached to the heads of the rattles, which were shaped like gourds.

There have been a number of accounts of the Hunka rites, and no two of them agree, which leads to two conclusions: the Holy Man in charge was allowed certain liberties, according to his own visions and understanding; and sometimes Indian informants deliberately misled outsiders, whom they felt would not understand. Thus, some accounts say the stick which held the ear of corn was red, or that the eagle fluffy was yellow, or that the corn was painted in four stripes of various colors. Generally, we have seen that blue and red are the colors associated with the calumets. To the Lakotas red represented the power of the Sun, life, light, fruitfulness; blue, the Sky, the creatures of the air, peace, harmony, beauty.

Although a child always figured prominently in the Lakota ceremony, adults[*] were also adopted, just as in other tribes. The "children" wore old clothes, hid, and were captured, just as with the Crows, with the same counting of coups at the time of "capture." Really small children were carried to the ceremonial tipi on the backs of adult participants. Sometimes a man to be adopted was carried on a buffalo robe,

---

[*]Sometimes the adopted "child" was older than the adopting "parents"!

supported by men holding it on each side, just as was done in "raising a chief." The parade to the sacred lodge stopped four times, the men in the party giving a wolf call each time to signal their approach.

In Hennepin's time it seems that both the "Calumets of War" and the "Calumets of Peace" were actually smoked, but in the Hunka the smoking was done with other pipes. There was a great deal of smoking, at first with a common, "everyday pipe," later with a ceremonial pipe, but the wands themselves were not smoked.

The Hunka ceremony, strange to say, was held more often for girls than for boys. They might be considered the "debutantes" of Lakota society, for they were always from important families. Only the "wealthy," the families of prominent warriors, with plenty of horses, could afford the ceremony.

Gifts were heaped up in the entrance "hall." Horses to be given away were tied just outside. A crowd collected to see as much of the ceremony as possible. The Holy Man leading the ritual sat to the rear of the altar, usually with assistants on either side of him. The candidate was brought in and seated between the fire and the altar, facing the Holy Man. Singers sat around a big drum to the left of the entrance. The Holy Man might wear a headdress with buffalo horns, hawk quills, and weasel skins adorning it. His face was painted with red perpendicular stripes, and his hands were painted red. Sometimes his body was also painted red, with red zigzag stripes on his arms. He lit an ordinary pipe with a buffalo chip that had previously been kindled in the fire and placed on the altar. The pipe was passed to the "father," then to the "son" (but not to a female candidate), and then around to the men at the gathering, who sat on the right, or south, side of the lodge.

The pipe was emptied with proper ceremony, the ashes placed on the altar, then an incense of sweet grass was made, and the ceremonial pipe purified over it and lit. The Holy Man offered it to the Powers Above, the Earth, Four Winds, and stooped low to offer it to the Sun, as if looking up at it from inside the tipi door. This ceremonial pipe was not passed around. The Holy Man smoked a few puffs himself, then laid it aside.

The wands were then purified in the sweet-grass smoke and handed, with the rattles, to the two dancers previously chosen. An old drawing shows these dancers painted all over, one with red ocher, the other yellow. The drum began a moderate, steady beat, then as the singers started the song the drum changed to a staccato beat, same tempo, but with a rest between each beat, and the dancers moved toward the entryway, gracefully swinging the wands in their left hands and shaking the rattles in their right, in time, dancing in the "hall," towards the West. Knees were bent and they leaned forward, but not in the crouch of the true Eagle dances. The songs would transcribe in 2/4, 3/4, 4/4, 6/8, and 12/8 time, but the drum was either steady or in accented 2/8.

The song was repeated four times, and during the singing the dancers moved back toward the altar, where they paused. On the second song, whose words indicated the movements, they waved the wands four times in each direction, circling to the

North, East, and South, then waving four times to the Sky, the Earth, and over the buffalo skull.

On the following song the dancers separated, going to each side of the lodge, dancing first to the rear, then forward again to the entrance. This song also was sung four times. Another song was sung for laying down the wands; at the end of it the dancers placed them back on the rack.*

Now came another interlude with the ceremonial pipe, the Holy Man offering it to the West, North, East, South, and West again, thus completing the circle of time, then stooping to offer it to the Sun once more. When he laid the pipe aside this time, the "child" was ceremonially dressed in new clothing, his (or her) hair combed and oiled, face painted, and then a fluffy eagle plume, with a lock of red horsehair and a tiny tuft of green mallard feathers, was attached to the hair. We were told that a woman wore such a tuft on the right side of the head, a man on the left.

The face was painted with a blue line from the hair part to the tip of the nose, with another across the upper forehead and down each cheek, ending opposite the one on the nose. Then red perpendicular stripes were added, of the same length, in between the blue ones. It cost an extra horse to be permitted to wear two or three extra red stripes. This face paint could later be worn when dressing up for any important occasion.

The *child* was then handed the ceremonial ear of corn, symbol of growing things, fertility, and prosperity, and given a lecture as to proper behavior, while another song was sung. A girl was told to practice the virtues of chastity, hospitality, industry, honesty, generosity, and gentleness; to show kindness to the old, the sick, and the poor; to have compassion for those in distress and tenderness toward children.

A boy was similarly exhorted in the practice of the manly arts and virtues—which latter included all those to be possessed by the women—and in addition to show respect for the ceremonies, to share the women's sorrows, and to be strong so as to protect the women and children in their weakness.

When this lecture was concluded, the Holy Man picked up the two wands, leading a song in which everyone present joined, waving a wand in each hand over the head of the *child*, then over the heads of everyone, while the drum kept the rhythm.

He next picked up the rattles, one on each hand, telling that their color was the color of the Sun and of the Earth and that the feather plumes gave them potency. He sang another song, shaking the rattles in time, while the drum accompanied him, then shook the rattles over the *child* and danced around the lodge, shaking them over everyone's heads.

Again the pipe was lit, this time being offered to the buffalo skull, the smoke blown over it and into the nostril cavity. The pipe was handed to the *father* and to the *child* if an adult male, who smoked it and handed it back. The Holy Man blew smoke over

*Transcriptions of Sioux Alowanpi (Hunkayapi) songs may be found in Frances Densmore's *Teton Sioux Music* and in E. S. Curtis' *The North American Indian*, Vol. III.

a red-painted rock beside the altar and over the altar, representing Mother and Grandmother Earth. The rock was symbol of strength and durability; its power could make one strong and prevent fatigue.

The *father* then ceremonially fed the *child* from a wooden bowl containing dried meat with a horn spoon. There is also an account that a miniature meat rack was set up to one side of the altar on which both lean and fat meat were hung, and the ceremonial food taken from it.

Father and *child* were then tied together by a cord around their wrists and given another talk on the duties of Hunkayapi to one another. Some stories have come down that there were times when two men went through the Hunka ceremony to be united as brothers, instead of father and son, and tied in the same way. They were known among the Sioux as "brother-friends." In literature they are sometimes spoken of as "blood brothers."

The wands and corn were wrapped up in a bundle and presented to the new *child*, now known as Hunka. The Holy Man turned the buffalo skull over, upside down, forcing its horns into the ground, extinguished the fire, and the ceremony was over. He and the assemblage then paraded the *father* and *child* back to the father's home, stopping again four times en route to give the wolf calls. The *child* and his real parents had made valuable presents to the adoptive father and the Holy Man. Others had piled up gifts for them and also for the child and his family. It was customary now for the recipients of these gifts to give most of them away to the assembled crowd. The ceremonial lodge was taken down, and the Alowanpi was over.[10]

According to Wissler, there was a simple form of adoption in which one person merely waved a horsetail over another and pronounced him Hunka. The full wands were also known as horsetails (as well as cornstalks), and the entire Alowanpi was sometimes spoken of as "waving horsetails over each other."[11]

The Calumet, Pipe, or Eagle Dance is a good example of the way a dance can play a very important role in a long elaborate ceremony. Without an understanding of that ceremony the dance itself becomes meaningless. We find in F. W. Hodge's *Handbook of American Indians North of Mexico* the following:

Nature is prodigal of life and energy. The dance is universal and instinctive. Primarily the dance expresses the joy of biotic exaltation, the exuberance of life and energy; it is the ready physical means of manifesting the emotions of joy and of expressing the exultation of conscious strength and the ecstasy of well-directed energy.

. . . The dance is only an element, not the basis, of the several festivals, rites, and ceremonies performed in accordance with well-defined rules and usages, of which it has become a part. The dance was a powerful impulse of their performance, not the motive of their observance.[12]

And, we might add, important nevertheless. As the dancing was dropped out of the Alowanpi and other Calumet rites, the rites themselves disintegrated until today all we have left, generally speaking, are suggestions and fragments.

THE BRAVE HEART DANCE

One of the dances we do is called the Brave Heart Dance, and we received the information about it from White Eyes, an old Northern Cheyenne living with the Oglalas on the Pine Ridge Reservation in South Dakota. We feel sure it traces back to the Calumet rites, even though there is no evidence that the Cheyennes ever observed them as such.

The Brave Heart Dance was a dance of greeting, given by one of the bravest warriors. The dancer used *two* globular rattles, which was not usual for the Calumet Dance, but we have seen that there were occasions when the Lakota Holy Man used the two rattles, and the two wands, separately. As described to us, there were many movements in a deep crouch, or squatting position, although the dancer was allowed almost unlimited freedom in steps and figures because of his special rating as a great warrior.

THE PIPE DANCE

Even before we met White Eyes, we had learned another related dance from a Winnebago; he called it the Pipe Dance. It was strictly a contest dance and the only thing that suggested a pipe was an eagle-tail fan held in the left hand. A rattle was carried in the right. The Winnebagos still had songs called Pipe Dance songs. There were a few customary movements expected of the performer, but otherwise as long as he followed the song and ended properly he was free to dance as he pleased. One dancer performed, then handed fan and rattle to another dancer, who tried to outdo him. This went on until every dancer who cared to try had done so, and the judges then decided on the winner. Some kind of prize was always offered; in recent years it has usually been a small sum of money.

We saw this Pipe Dance performed years ago at the Wisconsin Dells Stand Rock "Ceremonial." Several dancers took part, and even a couple of women were given a chance at it. The dancer begins with a circular motion of his arms, shaking fan and rattle in time with the music. Then he balances on one foot, continuing to circle the fan and rattle, and breaks into a double-beat step, stamping both feet together but moving first one ahead and then the other by twisting his body. A good dancer manages to get in the circling with fan and rattle again at the end of the song, finishing by shaking the rattle near the ground and extending his right leg to the rear as far as possible, tapping the toe on the last beat of the drum.

The day after the program we went to the camp where the Indians were staying and met one of the dancers. We complimented him on his Pipe Dance of the night before. "I didn't do Pipe Dance," he said. "I do Tomahawk Dance." It certainly looked like Pipe Dance to us, and we said so. He explained that the song was different; they sang a Tomahawk song, so he did a Tomahawk Dance!

On a visit to the Sauks and Foxes in Oklahoma one time, we had the Pipe Dance demonstrated for us by two women. Of course, they do not go through the violent steps and attitudes of the men. We told them we knew the Winnebago dance, and the singers sang their Pipe Song for us. They said they also used it now as a contest, passing fan and rattle from one to another.

A Chippewa Indian once demonstrated his Pipe Dance for us. It was also a contest. He said that one dancer challenged another by "sticking his pipe in the ground" (a straight pipe, with no fan) in front of the other's wigwam. Actually, the pipe was leaned against a forked stick which was thrust into the ground. When the pipe was picked up and taken into the wigwam, the challenge was accepted and they "danced it out" at the next dance.

In the contest the pipe was placed on one side of the fire and the solo dancer danced on the opposite side. The singers at the drum really controlled the dance. They beat fast or slow, changed rhythm, or stopped completely. During slow movements the dancer was required to step only on the drum beat and was not allowed to sound his bells in between. This takes a great deal of ability and muscular control. Likewise when the drum stopped he had to hold the position he was caught in, without sounding his bells, until the rhythm picked up again. During the slow parts of the dance he was supposed to "look like a pipe," that is, to be in a nearly squat position, with upper legs and body at right angles to each other, so that he represented a stone pipe bowl. This was supposed to be a ridiculous-looking posture, and the people all laughed, whether it was done right or wrong. Being able to stand this ridicule took a strong heart. At the end of the song, the dancer was expected to leap over the fire and snatch the pipe, raising it up on the last beat.

We recall that Frances Densmore mentions such a dance for the Chippewas in one of her books on Chippewa music, but she does not mention leaping over the fire to grab the pipe. Perhaps this was a later addition. At any rate, the dancer who gave the best performance won. If he were the one challenged, he kept the pipe; otherwise, the challenger was given the pipe. This dance looks to us as if it had probably developed as the Calumet and Eagle dances faded away.

The Cheyenne Feather Dance, already mentioned, also has some element of Eagle Dance, as we have seen, at least in comparison with the Iroquois version.

Catlin wrote about a Pipe Dance for the Assiniboins, which he thought peculiar to this tribe. He said that in the center of the dance ground, near a little fire, sat a dignitary with a long pipe, which he smoked incessantly, "grunting forth, at the same time, in half-strangled gutturals, a sort of song." The dancers sat on buffalo robes surrounding the fire. One fellow began beating on a hand drum and singing, and another

sprang instantly on his feet, and commenced singing in time with the taps of the drum, and leaping about on one foot and the other in the most violent manner imaginable. In this way he went several times around the circle, bowing and brandishing his fists in the faces of each one who was seated, until at length he grasped one of them by the hands, and jerked him forcibly up upon his feet; who joined in the dance for a moment, leaving the one who had pulled him up, to continue his steps and his song in the centre of the ring; whilst he danced around in a similar manner, jerking up another, and then joining his companion in the centre; leaving the third and the fourth, and so on to drag into the ring, each one his man, until all were upon their feet; and at last joined in the most frightful gesticulations and yells that seemed almost to make the earth quake under our feet. This strange manoeuvre, which I did but partially understand, lasted for half or three-quarters of an hour; to the great amusement of the gaping multitude who were assembled around, and broke up up with the most piercing yells and barks like those of so many affrighted dogs.[13]

We include this only because Catlin said it was a Pipe Dance, but it is different from anything else we have come upon. Another time Catlin mentioned both Eagle and Discovery dances for the Sioux, but did not describe them. He merely said they were far more graceful and agreeable than the Dog Dance, which he witnessed at the time. At a combined gathering of Sioux and Chippewas at Fort Snelling he saw a number of dances, including Eagle and Brave dances, as noted earlier. The Brave Dance sounds like the Discovery Dance, but he also listed Discovery Dance, as such, for both Sioux and Chippewas.[14]

THE PUEBLOS

One of the most popular dances for tourists in the Southwest today is the Eagle Dance, performed in many of the pueblos. It is one of the few dances that might be classed as solo, although it is really a duet dance.

In recent years a very similar dance has been performed in Oklahoma. However, Oklahoma Indians sing their own songs for it, although even some of these have some resemblance to Eagle Dance songs of the Pueblos, which are very complicated and "tricky" rhythmically. Although today we find the Pueblo-type Eagle Dance migrating to the Plains, there is good evidence that originally the Pueblos learned it from the Plains tribes.

Here is a strange thing: most of the Pueblo dances are highly conventionalized, but their Eagle Dance is very naturalistic. Most of the bird and animal dances of the Plains and Woodlands were naturalistic, but the Eagle Dance, as we trace it through those areas, was extremely conventionalized. The mere fact that Indian dances were not static, but could change with conditions, increases our interest in them. Most of the Pueblo Eagle dancers actually simulate eagles, the dancers wearing complete wings of eagle feathers, painting their bodies to represent eagles, and usually wearing down feathers and a large beak attached to their caps.

Taos, however, has always shown more Plains influence than the other pueblos and now is doing the Eagle Dance in Plains costume, using a porcupine roach and beaded "suspenders," like so many Oklahoma dancers, but retaining the Pueblo-style wings. But Oklahoma dancers are using identical costumes, and so to one who has not tried to follow the Eagle Dance back and forth and across the country, it would be hard to say whether the Taos dance came from Oklahoma or the Oklahoma dance came from Taos. The music is the distinguishing feature. Taos Eagle songs are more like those of other pueblos, with complicated rhythms and changes of drum beat. Oklahoma Eagle songs are scarcely different from ordinary War Dance songs, being steady without the complicated changes.

The Pueblo Indians have much of the same symbolism associated with their Eagle dances that we have found in other places. The eagle, most majestic of the birds, is venerated. He lives near the gods and is associated with the Thunderbird. His feathers carry prayers to Those Above. In the Southwest rain is the all-important thing, so most of the ceremonials are prayers for rain. The Eagle Dance is one of these prayers. There is a story that Pueblo Eagle dances trace back to the overcoming of a great plague. The Thunderbird started the wind to blowing, rain clouds formed, and the rain washed away the plague. The Eagle, as an impersonation of the Thunderbird, was then honored through the Eagle Dance.

One report says that at Tesuque Pueblo in New Mexico the Eagle Dance may be done at any time of year, but is usually given when the wild yellow roses are in bloom. It is a dance for curing; they say the "eagles are always strong, so can cure anything." The ceremony begins with a four-day fast. On the third night the sick person is treated in a ceremonial chamber, where an altar has been erected. The dance is held on the fourth day and is open to visitors.

The dancers are given strength by a treatment of "medicine water." Erna Ferguson writes, "It requires unusual skill and an amazing control of leg muscles in its stooping, swooping, varied movements."

The two dancers wear caps of raw cotton, with long yellow beaks fastened to them. Their faces are painted yellow, with red under each eye. Body, legs, and arms are yellow, with eagle down stuck on in various places. Long strips of cloth, with eagle wing feathers, are carried to represent wings. They dance "hopping, swooping, performing maneuvers of the greatest intricacy with quick steps and inconceivable grace. The dance is highly conventionalized and at the same time very naturalistic."[15]

For all the importance of the eagle in Southwestern mythology, the Eagle Dance there might almost be regarded in the light of a secular dance. Certainly it is not as involved in ceremony, and consequently is not as important, as their other rituals. The Hopis, however, do have a ritualistic Eagle Dance, as well as the more popular version. It is a "masked dance," in the same category as their other masked dances, whereas the Eagle Dance usually seen by white visitors to the Hopi mesas uses no masks and is very similar to the others we have been talking about.

The pipe and smoking have never been as important in the Southwest as in the Plains and Woodlands, so we could hardly have expected the Pueblo Indians to accept the full Calumet rites, but the Eagle Dance fits into their understanding of the powers of the universe. While the Eagle Dance may have been an indigenous development, ethnologists are convinced that much Pueblo lore is related to the Plains.

Since the Eagle Dance is still being performed by the Pueblos and is a favorite of all who see it, we hope they continue to keep it for a long time to come.

TRIBES OF THE NORTHWEST COAST

Tribes along the Northwest Coast had dances pertaining to animals and birds, but these were associated with their concept of "spirit dancing." During the long winter months these dances were sometimes held nightly. The dancers portrayed visionary experiences, either their own or legendary ones.

Curtis, in Volume X of his *North American Indians*, shows a photograph of an extremely dramatic Kwakiutl Thunderbird dancer, in complete costume of feathers to look like a huge eagle, including a superb carved mask of the type used in many ceremonies of the Northwest Coast Indians.

Those who had received power from some spirit helper portrayed their visions through pantomime and dance. The portrayals of various spirit helpers were not necessarily naturalistic, and no spoken reference was ever made to the vision, but through costume and movement the dancer made it evident to his audience what his helper was and the nature of his vision. His "orchestra" was trained to sing songs he had received, or composed songs using themes he suggested, with symbolic words which hinted at the identity of the helper and of the visionary action without revealing their true nature.

So in a way we might even include the Northwest Coast in our distribution of the Eagle Dance, for they did have Eagle dances and they were associated with healing, magic, and spiritual power.

CONCLUSION

To this day, most Indians smoke more in the nature of a rite than a habit. Among old-timers, at any rate, if one accepts your tobacco he does so as a gesture of friendship. There are still, among the Plains tribes, old men who remember the pipe rituals, even though they are almost never performed any longer, and they hold the memory sacred. The kind of pipe used by the Lakotas in recent times, in the Sun Dance and other rituals as well as in council, had much the same significance as that of the calumets of old. Although it lacked the eagle-feather fan, it was usually decorated with porcupine-quill embroidery, feathers from the neck of the mallard duck, horsehair, and sometimes a bit of buffalo wool. The mallard is a peaceful bird who minds his own business; his feathers show that man should shed trouble and discord as ducks do water. The bowl of the pipe was the altar where the sacred fire burned. It represented the earth and the rock. The materials and colors used symbolized the four elements of nature—earth, fire, air, and water, and the creatures of earth, sky, and water. The whole represented the union of all forces and consequently represented harmony and perfect life.

No symbol in Christendom was ever more sacred than was the pipe to old-time Indians. Even young Indians, who may know little of the traditions and symbolism, still regard the pipe with a spirit of veneration.

15. The Sun Dance: The Teton Sioux

The Sun Dance is perhaps the best known of all Indian religious festivals. At the same time, it is the least understood. Frowned upon by missionaries of various Christian faiths and government officials alike because of its "bloody" features, it was nevertheless brought to the attention of the public because of its spectacular aspects, such as the bloodiness.

It was the severity of the self-torture, of course, which horrified and shocked the white observers. They did not understand the Indians' attitude or know that according to ancient belief it was a poor sacrifice indeed to offer material possessions as a token of gratitude for delivery from great stress or as an appeal for supernatural help. Possessions all came from the Great Mystery in the first place; to offer them to him was only to give him back his own. So the only sincere sacrifice a man could make was of his own body and blood. As Frances Densmore wrote:

Strange as it may seem, the element of pain, which ennobled the ceremony in the mind of the Indian, was a cause of its misunderstanding by the white man. The voluntary suffering impressed the beholder, while its deep significance was not evident. It is probable that no Indian ceremony has been misinterpreted so widely and so persistently as the Sun Dance.[1]

The Sun Dance, in one form or another, was given by most of the Plains tribes. The Comanches seem to be the only ones with no ceremony of this type. Strangely enough, the Sioux proper and the Poncas were apparently the only tribes that had a term for it comparable to "Sun Dance." The sun was the highest manifestation of the Great Mystery, the visible symbol of his power, the bringer of light and life.

The Utes, Shoshonis, Plains Crees, and Plains Ojibwas call it Thirsting Dance. Cheyennes and Arapahos call it Sacrifice, Offering, Medicine Lodge, or Medicine Dance. The Cheyennes also refer to it as New Life Lodge, or Lodge of the Generator (Creator). The Assiniboin term was Making a Home, signifying the Thunderbird's nest in the fork of the sacred tree.

Ethnologists believe that the ceremony had its origin with the Village Tribes, and with the Cheyennes, and Arapahos, who at one time were all in the same vicinity. The latter two tribes certainly have the most elaborate and highly developed ritual, which would indicate that they have done the Sun Dance for the longest time. Tribes within the entire sphere of Plains influence gradually adopted it, the rituals became progressively simpler toward the edge of the sphere.

The last celebration of the original Sun Dance of the Standing Rock Sioux was given in 1882 and was broken up by United States troopers. Every effort by Indians to continue any form of native worship was persecuted vigorously from then until the late 1920's, when restrictions were somewhat relaxed. They were finally dropped altogether in 1934 with the passage of the Wheeler-Howard Bill in Congress, and since then a number of tribes have revived the Sun Dance.

In 1935 Chief One Bull partially revived it at Little Eagle, on the Standing Rock Reservation. It was attempted the next summer in the Cannon Ball district, but was given up for reasons to be mentioned later. One Bull also pledged the Sun Dance in 1942, and in recent years it has been given on the Pine Ridge Sioux Reservation.

A few tribes, among them the Shoshonis and Arapahos, never gave up the Sun Dance. Even during the period of persecution they persisted, as also did the Southern Cheyennes, the Blackfeet, Crees, the Assiniboins, and the Poncas.

As well as being the only organized ritual of many of the Plains tribes, the Sun Dance served a number of other important functions. It was held at the only time of the year when the widely scattered hunting bands reunited and so served as a social and political rally, as well as a religious one.

Different tribes had varying ways of determining the time of the Sun Dance, but it was always held during the summer. The Lakotas held it in the full moon of June or July, when all the world was green and nature and men were rejoicing. The ceremonies might be considered a dramatization of the entire spiritual and emotional life of the people. It was a presentation of the old, old story of good overcoming evil. It combined prayers of supplication for future help and strength with those of thanksgiving for past blessings.

Depending upon the tribe, the Sun Dance festivities lasted eight to fifteen days. Everyone knew where they were to be held, and for many days in advance the people of the various bands of the tribe gradually made their appearance at the large campground. Each band camped in its accustomed place; every individual knew the relative location of his own lodge and where to find his relatives and friends. With the exception of the Crees, Ojibwas and Hidatsas, the great tribal circles opened to the east. The center of the campground was reserved for the sacred tipi and for the Sun Dance lodge. As with all ceremonies, the Sun Dance was involved in symbolism from start to finish. The great camp itself symbolized the horizon, as well as the constellation of the Northern Crown, the council ring of the spirits.

During the days of preparation, all sorts of social activities took place. The pulsating voices of tribal singers and the throb of many drums filled the air. Young people engaged in social dances, and warrior societies paraded about the great camp, performing their special dances.[*]

PREPARATION

The preliminary preparation for the Sun Dance began months in advance. With the Lakotas the leading priest, sometimes spoken of as the Intercessor, was selected

---

[*]Each year the Sun Dance was held in a different place, on "new ground," and even nowadays a new site is selected each time. It may be only a few feet from a former location, but it is never actually the same.

each year, but the office always went to a holy man well qualified to hold it, and only a few men were known to possess these qualifications; thus often the same priest led year after year. The active participants, whom we might call "candidates," of course varied from year to year, and the leader of these dancers was usually the first man to vow to give the Sun Dance that year.

The candidates offered themselves in the Sun Dance as the result of vows made in times of danger or stress. In the old days such vows were often made on the war-path as a promise of sacrifice for delivery from a particularly dangerous situation. A vow might also be made to avert calamity or disease or to aid a sick or injured relative or friend. A man might also seek supernatural aid for a friend, or for himself, or seek *power* for himself, which was akin to becoming a holy man.

At the time of making his vow, a man made an offering of some choice possession or of a game animal just killed—one of the few occasions when an animal was killed and not used. But to the Indian's mind it served an even greater purpose. To fulfill his vow, the candidate was expected to make a still more outstanding sacrifice at the Sun Dance itself. The least he could do was go without food and water for the duration of the ceremony. But it usually implied much more than that. In the days when the warriors were real men, they usually sacrificed a "red blanket" to the Great Mystery. This meant a sacrifice of their own blood.

To give a red blanket a candidate offered pieces of his own flesh—tiny pieces of skin, from ten to a hundred pieces, cut from his arms and shoulders by an assistant, usually his best friend, who thus aided him in his offering. Sitting Bull sacrificed such a red blanket of one hundred pieces of flesh in the Sun Dance he gave shortly before the Custer fight, at which time he had his famous vision showing the destruction of the soldiers. One Bull also sacrificed a red blanket, the little scars being visible on his arms all through his long life.

Even more severe forms of torture were common. For his first Sun Dance vow a candidate usually offered himself to be fastened to the sacred pole by skewers thrust through the loose skin of his breast, to which were tied long thongs attached to the top of the center pole. He might go even further than this and have similar skewers thrust through the skin of his back; to these were tied heavy buffalo skulls. Sometimes he was hoisted completely off the ground, there to dangle until the weight of the skulls pulled them free and the weight of his own body tore the skewers from his breast and dropped him to the ground.

About a month before the Sun Dance was to take place, medicine men gathered to make ceremonies assuring fair weather for the occasion. An altar of bare earth was prepared, sweet-grass incense burned, and pipes were offered to the four directions, the sky, and the earth.

In the old days, the great camp gathered a week or more before the Sun Dance was to take place. Among the Lakotas, the Sun Dance itself was divided into two periods of four days each. The first four days involved more or less secret instruction and initiation of the candidates, while the rest of the village celebrated with feasting and dancing. The Begging Dance, described in another chapter, took place several times during the first period. A stick was placed upright in the ground before some-one's tipi and was not taken down until the owner presented the serenaders, both men and women, with food.

On the first day a council tipi, where chiefs and Sun Dance leaders met, was erected in front of the main circle of tipis and opposite the eastern entrance to the camp. Behind it, at sunset, was pitched another lodge, the tipi of preparation, where the candidates met for rehearsals and instruction. Sometimes this was a new tipi; always it had at least new lacing pins, new smoke poles, and new pegs, all of which were purified in sweet-grass smoke. Sweat lodges were built by the various bands, and those who were to take an active part in the Sun Dance purified themselves with the vapor baths.

THE FIRST PERIOD

Buffalo skulls served an important part in the Sun Dance. One was placed on a bed of sage behind the council tipi during these first four days.

The camp crier and marshals (from *akicita* societies) were appointed on the *first day*.

On the *second day*, while the candidates rehearsed in the sacred tipi, names of persons to serve in other capacities were announced, as were the names of children whose ears were to be pierced—their initiation into tribal life and their introduction into society.

On the *third day* the actual appointments to the various offices were made—the scouts to look for the sacred tree, their escorts, and the musicians. They appeared dressed in their finest attire, and as soon as the appointments were confirmed by the tribal leaders all mounted their horses and rode hard to the top of the nearest hill and back, feathers and fringes streaming in the wind, yelling and shouting like an enemy war party. On the evening of this third day there was a big feast of buffalo tongues. (Buffalo tongues seem to have been an important feature of Sun Dances of many tribes.)

On the *fourth day* announcement was made of the four virgins who were to cut the sacred tree and of the women who would take an active part in the Sun Dance. The virgins selected had to make public proclamation of their virtue, challenging anyone to dispute them.

Women played important roles in the Sun Dances of many tribes. Among the Blackfeet a woman was the real leader who pledged the dance. A woman might pledge it also among Cheyennes and Arapahoes. Among the Sarsis a woman pledged the dance and her husband assisted. A woman could also pledge the dance among the Canadian Dakotas.[2] Often women went through the fasting and thirsting sacrifice. Sometimes these took their places in the line of dancers, and oc-casionally a woman had pieces of flesh cut from her arms, but women never, so far as we know, took part in the other self-torture rites.

We have seen how a post or tree was important to many Indian rituals. It was per-haps most important of all in the Sun Dance, where it was involved in many symbolisms. On the fourth day the four scouts went looking for the sacred tree. It had to be a cottonwood, as nearly perfect as possible, and about eight to ten inches in diameter at its base. Cottonwood was a sacred tree because it will grow where no other large tree will grow. It can always find the life-giving water. Its rustling in the slightest breeze represents continuing prayer to the Great Spirit, and its fluffy white down looks like the sacred eagle down so important in many ceremonies.

The young men who had been selected as scouts dressed as for war—stripped to breechclouts, painted and wearing their warlike insignia, carrying their shields and weapons. The entire tribe gathered to see them start on their quest, singing war songs as they rode away. At this time the tree was looked upon as an enemy which must be overcome. When the scouts discovered the tree of their choice, they returned to make their report to the Sun Dance Priest. Once their decision had been made it could not be changed and no other tree could be used. On the way back they were greeted by friends on horseback riding in wide circles around them as they moved along. When they arrived at the village they found people dancing around the big drum and singing praise songs as for victorious warriors. The scouts were required to recite their discovery in the ceremonial manner prescribed for all scouts, then a feast was given for the young men. Everyone except those under Sun Dance vows partook of this feast, and little tidbits were sent to the candidates.

According to some reports, a ceremony by people who belonged to the Buffalo Cult followed the return of the scouts. They had their own parade, to honor the Buffalo Spirit, companion of the Sun, and bring his power to the Sun Dance. At the conclusion of the procession one of their medicine men performed a solo Buffalo Dance to complete the rites. The buffalo, being so important in the lives of the Plains Indians, played a great part in the symbolism and ritual of the Sun Dance.

That night (of the fourth day) the candidates sat around the inside of the secret lodge, the leader in the place of honor in the rear, with the Priest who served as instructor. All wore buffalo robes, with the hair outside, while smoking their individual pipes. They rehearsed their songs and got up to dance, blowing whistles of eagle wing bones. All had a *wa'cinhi*, or fluffy eagle plume from the tail of the golden eagle, bound to the lower end and some were beautifully decorated with quill or bead embroidery done by women relatives. The whistles were a very important part of the Sun Dances of all tribes. They represented the voices of Thunderbirds and also the call of the spotted eagle, who flew higher and closer to the realm of the Great Mystery than any other creature.

As the dancers blew upon their whistles the downy feather at the end danced in time with their movements, so the whistling also represented the breath, or life, of man. The constant blowing of the whistles symbolized the intensity of their prayers and showed that man's thoughts should rise high, as the eagles do.

The Sun Dance Priest, or Leader, had also prepared a sacred pipe, which would be an important instrument all through the long ceremony. It, too, was decorated with braided porcupine-quill wrapping. The woman selected to do this work felt herself highly honored.

At the end of the rehearsals on the fourth night, the sacred pipe was passed to the candidates by the priest, who had first purified himself with sweet-grass smoke. He held the pipe to the candidates' lips, as they were not permitted to touch it with their hands.

THE SECOND PERIOD

On the morning of the *fifth day*, the first day of the second, or sacred, period and one of the most momentous days of the entire Sun Dance, the selection of the site for the Sun Dance lodge was finally made and a "war party" was sent after the tree. Before it left, the Priest made a ceremony to insure clear weather for the day and dancers performed what might be called a "war dance" to drive away all evil and sanctify the dance ground. A procession followed, marching around the sacred spot where the holy tree was to be erected. Buffalo chips were placed on the spot and lighted, and on them sweet-grass incense was burned. Following the burning of the incense, the place where the tree was to stand was marked by a stake, after which the warriors departed.

About this time the candidates ate their last meal. They would not eat again until the ordeal of the Sun Dance was over, three days later.

THE TREE

On the arrival of the war party at the selected tree, the Priest pointed his pipe at its tip and made a speech honoring the cottonwood for its gifts to mankind and its protection of the winged creatures which sought refuge in its boughs.

You, sacred tree, have been chosen to represent the center of the hoop of our nation. There you will represent the people, and you will be the sacred pipe, reaching from earth to the sky above. The weak will lean against you and you will support the people. You will stand at the crossing of the four sacred paths [four directions] and will be the center of all the Power of the universe.

During the address, the Priest pointed his pipe at the tip of the tree, lowered it in four movements to the bottom of the tree, then circled the tree touching the pipe stem on the west, north, east, and south sides of it.

Now came the chiefs, in full regalia, who danced a Victory Dance around the tree. Then the four virgins came forward. For this episode the tree represented an enemy and the virgins were to be given the honor of counting coup upon it. Since they actually had never done such a thing, male relatives with war honors recounted their coups for their benefit.

The first young woman stepped near the tree, her relative counted coup, and she struck the tree on the west side, using a brand new ax. After the introduction of steel tools by the whites, a new ax was always used in the Sun Dance. Formerly the tree had been burned down and the char periodically chipped away with a new stone ax. The second young woman came forward, her relative counted his coup, and she struck the tree on the north. The action was repeated by the third and fourth young women, who struck the tree on the east and south sides, then the ax was returned to the first woman, who chopped the tree down so that it would fall to the south, "the direction we are always facing." From the time it fell the candidates were allowed no more food or water.

As the tree fell, the crowd of onlookers shouted victory cries, and during the yelling and commotion many people gave away presents in honor of the Sun dancers. Some of these gifts were made to poor or old people; others were in the nature of offerings and decorations for the Sun Dance lodge.

An incense of sweet grass was now made to purify the tree, and all the branches were trimmed off close to its trunk except for the large fork at the top, twenty to thirty feet up. Sometimes a little tuft of leaves was left at the tip of the tree also. The priest rubbed red paint in the wounds of the tree and from then on the tree was regarded as sacred. No one dared touch it or step over it.

At least twenty men were designated to carry the tree back to camp, and, since they were not allowed to touch it, stout sticks about two feet long were thrust under it, two men handling each stick, and the tree was carried on this litter, top foremost, back to the site of the Sun Dance lodge. Again a great parade formed, making a haphazard procession back to the camp, young people riding back and forth and around the marchers as they advanced. On the way more gifts were made and the whole affair was another simulation of celebrations honoring the return of victorious warriors.

The procession halted four times en route and each time the warriors howled like wolves, the call of victory. During these rests, the tree was supported on crotched sticks cut especially for the purpose, for it must not touch the ground while on the march. The fourth halt was near the site of the Sun Dance lodge. This time, the warriors all charged an image, made of sticks, which had been placed near the proposed entrance. Each one endeavored to be the first one to strike it, so it was quite a rough-and-tumble affair. The man who struck the image first also ran ahead and cut down the stake that marked the site where the sacred tree, or pole, was to stand. Sometimes a bush or small tree growing in a position where an image would be placed was the "enemy," substituting for an image.

The person designated earlier to dig the hole for the tree now did so, using a new spade, and the tree was brought in, its tip turned to point to the west, and its base close to the hole. There it was supported on the forked sticks while it was prepared for its final position. The priest removed the bark, and people scrambled forward to pick up pieces of it for good luck. He then painted the pole with four vertical stripes running from the fork to the base. Usually all four were red, but some priests used red on the west, blue on the north, green on the east, and yellow on the south.

A crossbar the "length of a man," saved from one of the branches, was fastened at the base of the fork, and to it a bundle of cherry branches was tied. Some say this bundle represented the Thunderbirds' nest, but the important symbolism was that it was a prayer for plenty, choke cherries growing in clusters being an obvious analogy.

Within the bundle of branches was a large rawhide bag painted with beautiful designs. Inside of it was a buckskin bag, and in that was a piece of buffalo hump (the choicest of all meats), pierced by a sharp cottonwood stick painted red. It represented the arrow that had killed the buffalo, and also a picket pin used to tether a horse taken from an emeny.

From the crosspiece thus made, two images of rawhide were suspended, much as the dancers themselves would be suspended later on in the ceremony. One image was cut to represent a buffalo, the other a man. Both were usually painted black, although sometimes the man was painted red. The buffalo represented the herds upon which the people depended. The man represented the people themselves. To the fork were also fastened the long cords from which the dancers would hang. Each cord was made from a buffalo hide, cut round and round in a spiral. It was fastened to the fork at its center, thus leaving two thongs hanging. To the top of the tree was fastened, formerly, the skin of a buffalo calf—in recent years a large strip of red trade cloth. (The Sissetons placed a stuffed buffalo calf in the fork.)

Buffalo fat was placed in the hole, with red paint, the sun's color, and the signal was given to raise the tree. This was a most solemn occasion, for the tree *was no longer an enemy but* now implied all its sacred meanings, and the people stood in silence and in awe as it was lifted into position. It was raised by the aid of rope slings and was done in four movements. It must not fall back or slip, or the entire ceremony would be useless and only disaster would result. On the fourth pull it was dropped into place in the hole, the rope slings removed, and the earth tamped tightly around its base. It was hoisted in such a way that the crossbar pointed north and south. Now it looked like a huge cross, and many Indians will tell you that it represented the Christian cross. Originally it was a practical way of displaying the offerings and was said by some to represent the morning star, the symbol of wisdom and the patron of warriors, but One Bull said it represented the Four Winds.

As the tree slipped into place the crowd cheered and songs of praise and cries of victory were raised. Dancers circled the pole in an honor dance. The tree was now the center of the universe, the connection between man and the spirit world, the symbol of life itself.

THE ARBOR

Now it was time to erect the Sun Dance lodge. This was a circular enclosure, from fifty to more than one hundred feet in diameter, depending upon the number of dancers and spectators present. A circle of forked posts was set up, leaving an opening to the east. Black Elk said there were twenty-eight posts, representing the days of one moon. Within this outer circle of posts was set another inner circle of a corresponding number. Light poles, including extra tipi poles, were laid across the forks; these were thatched with buffalo hides, tipi covers, and brush to form a shade for the spectators. Brush was also stacked all around the outer "wall," with the exception of the doorway to the east. The finished lodge was a circular shade, or arbor, surrounding the sacred pole. Offerings of various kinds, including cloth, beadwork, and articles of clothing were hung on the support posts. *There were no stringers, or connecting poles, between the outer arbor and the sacred pole in the Sioux Sun Dance lodge.* The Sioux and Poncas were the only ones to make this type. All other tribes had poles leading into the center pole.

When the Sun Dance arbor was completed, the warriors gathered once more for a big dance, similar to the present-day Grass Dance, to "smooth the ground." Special dancers who had been selected gathered on the west side of the pole. They danced toward the west and back, then to the north and back, to the east and back, to the south and back. In this manner they danced in the form of a cross, the four directions. Then all the dancers massed, dancing again around the pole, discharging their guns and shooting arrows at the rawhide figures hanging from the crosspiece, this action representing the overcoming of enemies and the success of many buffalo hunts. The dance also symbolized the overcoming of evil.

A Victory Dance naturally followed the dance of driving away evil powers, and the new lodge was purified with cedar incense, which could appease, or perhaps we should say counteract, Thunder's influence.

It was time now for the purification rites in the sweat lodge. A virtuous woman was honored by being selected as custodian of the sacred pipe. The Priest carried the Sun Dance pipe into the *initipi*, or sweat lodge, and took his place in the rear, or west. Candidates entered from either side, so as not to pass in front of the priest, and last the Holy Woman came in, taking her place by the door. The lodge was covered with the candidates' buffalo robes, which were thus purified along with the participants. The sacred pipe had already been filled and sealed with the fat from a buffalo's heart and another pipe was used for the actual smoking in the ritual. The Sun Dance pipe was placed in front of the Priest during the smoking of the other pipe, then wrapped in sage and handed to the Holy Woman, who represented the White Buffalo Maiden of Sioux mythology. She carried it, "walking the sacred road," to a little mound of earth a few feet in front of the doorway, on which a buffalo skull had been placed, facing into the lodge. She placed the pipe on the skull, its stem pointing east, then turned back to the lodge to tend the door while the men within took the steam bath.

During the steam bath the people of the great encampment, dressed in their best clothes, paraded around the camp circle. After the ceremony in the sweat lodge, the candidates returned to the sacred tipi of preparation to be painted for the coming ceremonies.

At sunset the young people rode around the village, the men singing and the women responding, and the candidates danced again within the sacred tipi.

THE FIRST DAY OF DANCING (THE SIXTH DAY)

Each morning the Priest repeated his ceremony for clear weather and warriors danced to drive away evil. Before sunrise on the *sixth* morning, the candidates marched around the sacred tipi four times, then proceeded to the Sun Dance lodge. The procession was led by the Holy Woman carrying the Sun Dance pipe. Behind her came the Priest, carrying his pipe, the only one to be smoked during the ceremonies. Beside him was the Sun Dance leader, carrying the sacred buffalo skull, which had been painted the night before with a red stripe across its brow and two perpendicular red stripes down the sides of the face to the nostrils. The candidates marched on either side of these two leaders, forming a single line as they approached the Sun Dance lodge. Warrior societies flanked them as they moved along, but did not enter the lodge. The candidates circled around it slowly four times in a sun circle and entered to the left, circling to the west side of the lodge, where they sat, singing holy songs.

The dance leader laid the painted buffalo skull on a little bed of sage to the west of the sacred pole. Balls of sage were stuffed in the eyeholes and the nostril opening, for sage is a sacred plant. A rack of two forked sticks with another stick across them was made in front of the skull, and the Holy Woman handed the sacred pipe to the Priest, who placed it upon the rack, its bowl resting upon the mandibles of the skull. The little rack was painted blue and symbolized a drying rack full of meat.

Just as the sun came up over the horizon, the candidates, whom we may as well now call the dancers, rose to their feet and lined up on each side of the sacred pole, raising their hands in greeting to this most important manifestation of *Wakan Tanka,* the Great Mystery, blowing upon their eagle-bone whistles. At the same moment the Priest called out, "*Wakan Tanka,* be merciful to us. We want to live. We sacrifice ourselves that our people may live."

The singers took up a song having words of similar meaning and the entire assemblage wailed and lamented. Recent interpreters have said the Priest called out, "Repent, repent!" applying Christian concepts to the old rite, but the old-time Indians had no conception of sin, as the missionaries told of it. Certainly they had a deep understanding of right and wrong, but wrong could only be righted by restitution, a concept not applied to association with the Spirit World. Our old Kiowa friend, Tahan, told us, "We knew nothing of the devil or of hell. The white man told us about the devil and has been giving us hell ever since."

The singers were seated on the south side of the arbor, one group around a large drum, another group around a dried buffalo hide. In this case, the drum may have been a late innovation, for it was of the same type used in the Grass Dance—about the size of a bass drum, highly ornamented with a decorated "skirt," and hung from four beaded, or quilled, and painted stakes. Utes and Shoshonis use a drum, and we know the Arapahos now use one, but in early days most Sun Dances were given to the accompaniment of beating on the dry hide only. Just what the significance of the dry hide is we have never learned, but it seems to have been a part of the original Sun Dance. Whatever the type of drum, its rhythm represents the rhythm of the universe, the pulse beat of the people. It has the power to command life and shape creation.

The Dance Step

After the first greeting to the Sun the dancers withdrew to the area in the west of the lodge, behind the buffalo skull and pipe, and danced in place, always facing the Sun, so that they gradually shifted position as the Sun advanced in the heavens. The step used, and still used in Sun Dances today, is simply a slight raising on the toes and bouncing of the entire body in time with the music. As the dancer moves, he blows his whistle in time with the song. The whistles, all being closely registered but no two exactly of the same note, have an eerie, pulsating quality, reminding one of the bell-like chorus of the peep frogs we hear in early spring. Perhaps this is one of the things they do represent, for certainly the Sun Dance is a ceremony for the renewal of life and a drama of the continuous cycle of nature.

Costume

The dancers all appeared barefoot and with hair hanging loose, the traditional manner of wearing the hair both after conquering an enemy and when seeking supernatural assistance. Hands and feet were usually painted red, and each dancer wore a kilt of buckskin about his waist and hanging below his knees. Some reports say that these kilts were dyed red, but old-timers at Standing Rock insisted that they were always white. However, it was customary to wear a long breechclout, which hung over the kilt before and behind, and these could be red. The dance leader was sometimes distinguished from the other dancers by having his kilt elaborately embroidered in porcupine quills and having his body painted differently from the others.

Each dancer engaged a person to do the painting, and each painter was free to use whatever colors and designs he deemed suitable, for he was a person who had himself taken part in a previous Sun Dance. A dancer was usually painted in a solid color above the waist with contrasting designs on this background. Symbols might also be cut from rawhide and hung about the neck. The motif was often the sunflower, for it turns its face to the sun all day. Buffalo, eagles, hawks, swallows, sun, moon, and morning star, were other designs used. The emblems were painted in green, yellow, blue, and black. The colors used in this case had symbolism relating to the heavens. Red, as well as being the tribal color, also symbolized the red of clouds at sunset; light blue represented a cloudless sky; green, earth and the power of growing things; yellow, the forked lightning; white, the light; and black the night. Even the moon was painted black (or dark blue) when used as a design on the dancer's body.

In his hair each wore a little scratching stick, about eight inches long, nicely quilled and with a little dangling feather. He might have four of these. He was not allowed to touch his body during the Sun Dance and so used these sticks, taking one from his hair for the purpose.

In former times it would have been possible to tell just what sort of torture a dancer intended to undergo by the way he was painted. Other participants were also painted with distinguishing marks. For instance, the scout for the sacred tree had a red circle painted around his right eye, the one who dug the hole for the tree had a red stripe on his right cheek and his hands painted red, the musicians painted a red circle around their mouths, and their assistants, both men and women singers, had red stripes on their foreheads.[3]

An Indian drawing made many years ago shows one dancer with a red body and a yellow face, another with a blue body and a yellow face, a third all yellow, and a fourth all red.[4] Black Elk said that the dancers in the very first Sun Dance were all painted red, for it is the sacred paint, and each had a black circle painted around his face, for there is much power in a circle. Each also had a black stripe from the forehead down to a point between the eyes, a line down each cheek, and one on the chin, representing the four directions. There were black rings around ankles, wrists, elbows, and upper arms; black is the absence of light, hence the color of ignorance, and black so represents the bonds that tie us to the earth. In recent times dancers have been permitted other ways of painting, according to their visions or the visions of the ones doing the painting.[5]

Each dancer was permitted to wear a headdress or other ornaments to which he was entitled, but most wore an eagle fluffy at the back of the head, erect, and some wore capes of otter skin, armlets of shed buffalo hair, and anklets of rabbit skin. The shed buffalo hair reminded one of the buffalo and of his importance to the people and was endowed with magical influence. The rabbit fur showed that one was meek in the presence of the Great Mystery. All dancers carried small willow hoops in one hand and a sprig of sage in the other.

One Bull told us that he was entitled to wear the full war bonnet of chieftainship, but that he preferred to appear before *Wakan Tanka* as he came into the world, poor and helpless.

The Priest wore buffalo horns upon his head, and his hair was braided, instead of loose, and often wrapped with otter fur. He might wear bands of buffalo skin with loosening hair on both ankles and wrists, and his buffalo robe was taken from a buffalo which was shedding. Shed buffalo hair was also tied in his own hair, and he wore a strip of buffalo skin down his back. Priests were allowed some freedom in their costume, and some wore otter fur wristlets and anklets instead of buffalo hair.[6]

Since the Priest had probably danced the Sun Dance several times before, he was not required to dance now, but sat in the west, behind the altar. During intermissions he sometimes took the sacred pipe from its rack and held it aloft as he made a prayer. At other times he lit his own pipe, offering it in the customary manner to the six directions—west, north, east, south, sky, and earth—and then passing it to the dance leader and the other dancers.

A Chief, or Holy Man (sometimes he was both), sanctified a pipe in the smoke of sweet grass, sweet sage, or cedar, then offered it to *Wakan Tanka*, pointing its stem to the heavens, then in turn to the four quarters, offering it to *Wiyohpeata*, the Winged Power in the west; to *Waziyata*, the Great White Cleansing Wind in the north; to *Wiyohinyanpata*, whence comes the morning star, the dawn, and the light of wisdom; to *Wóhpe*, the Beautiful One and the south, the power of growing things,

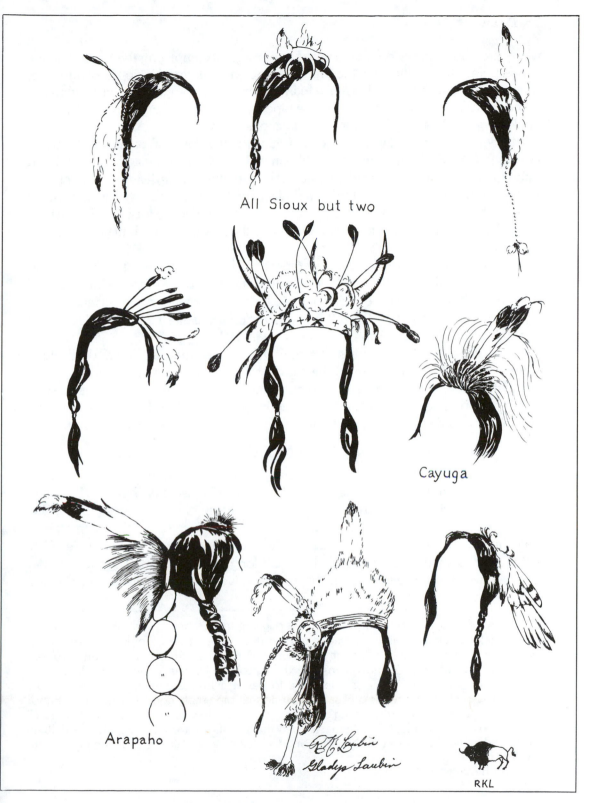

All Sioux but two

Cayuga

Arapaho

Miscellaneous headdresses.

where life begins and ends; then pointed it west again, completing the circle. Thence it was pointed to *Mahpiyata,* the Heavens and the Spotted Eagle dwelling there, closest to *Wakan Tanka;* and to *Maka Ina,* Mother Earth, from whence all good things come. Following such an invocation, the pipe was lit, and the same routine followed in blowing smoke to each of the "six directions."*

At noon of this sixth day, or first day of dancing, the dancers' paint was renewed. Otherwise, the dancing continued until some dancer fell exhausted, when a short intermission might be declared. During such rests, the dance leader threw himself prone on the ground, west of the sacred place, pressing his head against the sacred buffalo skull. The other dancers retired to the western section of the arbor, where beds of sage were spread for them. On these they placed their buffalo robes and rested.

Although it is not mentioned in any report on the Sun Dance with which we are familiar, One Bull stated that the Holy Woman lifted the pipe from the altar and held it, stem pointing to the Sun, dancing in place just in front of the other dancers. During lulls in the dancing she replaced it upon its rack. One Bull's daughter, Magli, held this office furing the last Sun Dance he gave in 1942.

Except for a few brief respites, the Sun Dance continued all day and all night, stopping just before dawn. During the night a fire was kindled near the entrance, on the east, symbol of the coming light. Dancing throughout the night, the dancers symbolized the darkness of men's minds, living in ignorance. The fire represented the coming of knowledge and understanding.

THE SECOND DAY OF DANCING (THE SEVENTH DAY)

At dawn of this seventh day, or second day of dancing, men and women paraded once more around the camp, the women in advance, praising Wohpe, the Beautiful One, the Feminine Power, and Maka Ina, Mother Earth, the men singing of the Sky and Wind.

At the same time, the Priest prepared the sacred altar at the west of the pole. With a knife he outlined a square about three feet long, carefully removing the sod and finely pulverizing the earth within the square. Two intersecting lines were traced

---

*When we presented our *Arrows to Atoms* pageant in Oklahoma, with about a hundred Indians taking part, we wanted someone to open the program with a pipe ceremony, as in early days almost any public gathering was opened. But with fifteen tribes represented, which head man should we ask? The Indians solved the problem by paying me one of the highest compliments I ever received and asking me to perform the ceremony. Afterward an old Kiowa-Apache came up to me and said, "You do that pipe putty good, but not quite right." When I asked him what I did wrong, he said, "You point to west first and should be east."

I replied, "Our people, the Lakota, received the pipe from a sacred person, the Buffalo Calf Maiden, who came out of the West, and to honor her we always offer the pipe first to the West."

"Oh!" he said. "O.K!"

inside the square, forming a cross whose lines were parallel with the sides of the square. Tobacco was offered to the sky, earth, and four quarters and placed in the incisions forming the cross. Over the tobacco he spread powdered red paint and over the paint mica dust. Downy eagle feathers were placed at the intersection of the lines and at their ends.

The turf and excess earth removed from the square were placed to the west of it, and over the little mound thus formed was spread a bed of sage, on which the buffalo skull was again placed. The Priest carried a coal from the fire to the altar and made an incense of sweet grass, over which he purified the knife to be used in the sacrifices. The exposed and mellowed earth represented the earth's power, available to man. The square was the four winds and the four directions. One report says the altar was round, but round altars were usually reserved for ceremonies other than the Sun Dance. Again we have the powers of the universe, even the forces of creation and of destruction, all united in one symbol, the sacred altar. The pipe itself has the same symbolism.

Promptly at sunrise the Holy Woman picked up the Sun Dance pipe, bringing it to the entrance and offering it to the Sun. The dancers followed her, extending their hands in greeting to the rising sun, and this time the song was one of rejoicing at the coming of the light and the dawn of wisdom. The Sun dancers then began to dance, turning first to face the south, then the west, the north, and finally the east. Again turning, they looked at the top of the sacred pole, bathed in the brightening light of the new morning Sun.

After this dance they retired to their places of rest in the rear and assistants rubbed off their paint with sage and repainted them. On this second day of dancing they were sometimes painted differently than on the first day, and except for those wearing special headdresses all now wore wreaths of sage upon their heads. The wreaths represented the circle of the sky, and stars, and heavenly bodies. Some dancers added two eagle primary feathers inserted straight up in the wreaths, one on each side of the head, looking much like long horns, symbolizing plenty of buffaloes and buffalo power.

The Buffalo Dance

While the dancers were being painted, it was customary in former times to present a special Buffalo Dance. For its duration the Holy Woman continued to hold the pipe, because the buffalo skull, upon which it was supposed to rest, was a necessary accessory to the dance. A medicine man feigned to lift the skull three times. On the fourth time he actually picked it up and carried it to a place near the center of the circle, in front of the sacred pole. The Buffalo dancers continually gazed at the skull as they danced. The rhythm was similar to that of the women's dances, in 3/4 time. They scraped their feet on the second, or unaccented, beat, bringing the heel down hard, imitating the defiant actions of an angry buffalo bull.

At the close of the Buffalo Dance the skull was replaced behind the altar and the pipe was again rested on its rack. The most important part of the Sun Dance was about to begin.

After the dancers were painted they all stood up at the west of the tree, raising their right hands and gazing at its top, blowing upon their whistles, while the Priest prayed that those about to undergo torture might successfully pass the ordeal. The dancers then moved in a sun circle around to the east, still looking at the top of the tree. Here they again raised their hands, blowing the whistles, while the singers intoned, "Grandfather has given us a sacred path." They continued around to the south, looking north, still blowing their whistles; around to the west, facing east; then north, facing south—always facing the Tree—then retreated to the west, again facing east.

Here they all wailed while the dance leader, starting at the north, went completely around the circle, stopping at each supporting post as he went, and returning to the north. Each one who intended to make a blood sacrifice then did likewise, going around the entire Sun Dance lodge, stopping at each post to pray.

A man who was to give a "red blanket" might sit with his back against the center pole while an assistant, one who had performed similar actions before, lifted the skin of his arms with the point of the purified knife, which was really more of an awl, being ground down to a very sharp point. With another knife he sliced off the little piece of raised skin and deposited it at the foot of the sacred tree. This was done as many times as the man had offered. There is a story of one man who offered two hundred pieces of flesh as well as being suspended from the sacred tree, but his two sisters were so concerned that they each offered to give fifty pieces in his stead, leaving him to sacrifice only one hundred! After offering his "red blanket," a dancer resumed his dancing with the rest, keeping it up until he fell exhausted or until all the dancing ceased.

Drama

We might consider the torture phase of the Sun Dance as a drama in four acts, representing capture, torture, captivity, and escape. A dancer who was to be tied to the tree came forward, leaned against the tree, and grasped it with both hands, when he was seized by the assistants who pretended to throw him roughly to the ground. If he was to be pierced on the chest he was turned face upward and the awl was thrust through on each side, above the breasts. The assistant raised the loose skin with his thumb and forefinger, then pushed the awl through and thrust a little plum-wood skewer through the incision. The skewers were painted blue, one being inserted over each breast. To these skewers were attached two of the thongs hanging from the tree. The dancer was lifted to his feet before the thongs were fastened; they were usually adjusted so that only his toes touched the ground, but a particularly brave dancer might request to be raised entirely off the ground (see page 201).

The suffering the dancer underwent was symbolical of the fate—calamity or even death—which threatened to overtake him or some loved one before he made his vow to take part in the Sun Dance. Thus he proved his courage and demonstrated complete mastery over his body, his unconcern for physical pain and suffering, his dominion, we might say, of mind over matter. Indians believed they were better able to understand the oneness of all things through participating in this suffering, themselves becoming the sacrifice to *Wakan Tanka.* When the bonds of captivity to evil and darkness were finally broken, the spirit was freed from the flesh, representing ignorance. The old body was destroyed and a new one created.

During the capture, the singing and drumming became more intense, but the other dancers maintained the same simple step as before, merely rising on the toes a little faster. This represented the first act of the drama. The actual piercing of the flesh was the second act. As the newly captured dancers began to dance, suffering the excruciating pain of the skewers in their flesh, the rhythm was again slower, the songs softer, while they acquired equilibrium and became adjusted to their new role. Their assistants came near them, handing them buffalo tails to be used as fly brushes and as fans.

In this third act, which was divided into four periods, twenty-four songs were required, six for each period. In the second period the actions became more violent, the singing and drumming corresponding, the women in the audience making their high-pitched trill of applause and victory. The "captives" now began their struggle to escape, pulling back on their thongs, trying to tear loose from the skewers holding them. The assistants might take hold of them, also pulling back, using their added weight to try and free them.

Each period became more intense. During the fourth period they danced with still greater fury, jumping, pulling back, straining, finally jerking free from their bonds and falling to the ground, exhausted. Sometimes a dancer fainted, only to be revived and raised to his feet to try again. If he could not free himself by the end of the fourth period, a medicine man was called to cut the flesh from the skewers, for it was forbidden to pull the skewers out. The assistants who attempted to help with the release and the medicine men were rewarded by rich presents from the dancer's relatives. Many people made gifts, too, at this time, in honor of relatives suffering in the Sun Dance.

Once free, the dancer was carried to his place at the rear of the Sun Dance lodge, there to recline and rest until the entire ceremony was over. A medicine man rubbed a healing herb into his wounds, and no case of infection or permanent injury was ever reported. The recovery was further proof of the goodness and power of Wakan Tanka, who had intervened to save the dancer or his loved ones at the time of his making the vow.

Those who underwent other forms of torture were, of course, also dancing during the periods of the captivity. Sometimes a man said he would carry four of his relatives on his back, meaning that he would drag four buffalo skulls. On his chest he had painted a buffalo, and along with the wreath of sage he wore in his hair two horns made of sage.[7] Men who elected to drag buffalo skulls might have from two to eight. If only two were used, they were fastened high up on his back, so that he literally carried them. All were fastened to skewers through the flesh, beginning at the shoulder blades near the spine, others set a bit lower and farther apart. Sometimes one was secured to each upper arm. Each skull weighed about twenty-five pounds, so the dancer could not stand erect and support all this extra weight. The skulls were fastened by the thongs running through the nostril opening so that they hung horns downward. As the man moved they constantly bumped against him, the sharp bony structure and horns digging into him.

Sometimes a man chose to be fastened to four stout poles, set in the ground at the corners of a square, within which he stood, thongs attached to skewers in his back and breast. This was the most severe torture of all, so also rated as the highest type of sacrifice. The sufferer was fastened so tightly to the four posts that he could barely move, but he, too, attempted to dance to the music, pulling and jerking until all four bonds were broken. The posts represented the four directions, so he regarded himself as being in the center of the world, with the entire weight of it upon him. When he finally became free, he was also freed of his great responsibility, for he had now served his people well, having offered himself that they might live. One such candidate was "captured" in the morning and it took him until evening of the next day to break free—more than thirty hours!

Individuals sometimes went through the above sacrifice at times of the year other than the Sun Dance, when seeking a vision or special help. It was then known as Hanbleciya, or Day's Crying.

It is told that at a Sun Dance one man rode up to the sacred pole on horseback, where he had the skewers thrust through his back and the thongs from the pole tightly fastened to them. The horse was then driven off, a free gift to whoever might catch him, and the candidate was left swinging in the air. There he struggled until the flesh was torn loose and he dropped to the ground.

It is said that the torture phase of the Sun Dance seldom lasted more than an hour, although occasionally it took much longer, as we have seen, unless the dancer agreed to have the skewers cut loose. Of course it took more endurance, consequently brought more approbation from the people and rated as a greater sacrifice, to break the bonds naturally. While a man was undergoing torture he constantly prayed for his people, and the Lakotas believed that Wakan Tanka granted requests to those who thus fulfilled their vows rather than to those who were careless of their obligations. This did not imply that Wakan Tanka was a cruel god, for Wakan Tanka was the power in everything, largely impersonal, and yet concerned with the welfare, proper balance, proper relationship, of all his creation. Wakan Tanka, the Great Mystery, or Great Spirit, is the innermost self, the hidden reality of all things. He is infinitely above mankind, and yet within mankind. Through sacrifice, the Indian believed he could come closer to this reality.[8]

During the "captivity," children were introduced to their role in tribal life by being brought forward to have their ears pierced. A medicine man punctured the lobes with an awl (formerly of bone), then inserted a little piece of copper or brass wire or sometimes just a piece of grass, which remained until they were healed. The healing was said to be more rapid when wire was used. Often the children's ears were pierced as a result of a vow. If a child were ill, the parents might offer to have its ears pierced if it recovered for the next Sun Dance. Only children of "wealthy" parents could afford to have their ears pierced, for it was a public ceremony, consequently requiring many presents. These were left within the Sun Dance lodge, to be appropriated by the "poor" at the close of the ceremonies.

As was mentioned earlier, candidates often took part in the Sun Dance to seek supernatural aid in the form of a vision. At the great Sun Dance on the Rosebud River prior to the Custer Battle, Sitting Bull saw soldiers falling from the sky, their hats tumbling before them, and there were no ears on their heads. They had no ears! They would not listen to advice or reason.

The physical exhaustion, hunger, suffering, and high emotional tension easily induced visions in many of the dancers. One Bull told us that after two days and a night he heard a horse nicker in the west, and from the south came a herd of buffalo heading north. He saw white people killing buffalo until they were all gone. So he knew what was coming, but the things foretold in a vision could not be prevented. Later, however, during the great drought of the 1930's, with its disastrous dust storms, he said the buffalo had returned to "hook up the ground!"

Soon after his Sun Dance, One Bull's younger brother captured a horse on the warpath—the same horse seen in the vision. In his vision a figure of a man appeared in the sun—the spirit power of the sun—which became One Bull's guardian spirit, of "medicine." It was not too unusual for a warrior to have power from the Sun. It was truly "great medicine."

There are some accounts of the Sun Dance which say that it ended on the evening of the seventh day, but it was more usual for the dancing to continue all through the night again and come to a conclusion on the morning of the eighth day. During the tortures, the men not participating in them continued to dance. But they, too, were suffering from hunger and thirst. It was their third day without food or water. To make their suffering worse, an officer known as the tantalizer brought out plates of food, eating in front of them, pouring water on the ground, to test their hearts and make them strong. Such temptation was almost more than a man could bear. It was not uncommon by now for dancers, one after another, to fall from exhaustion. At such times brief intermissions were called and during them sometimes other dances were presented for the benefit of the audience.

The Scalp Staff Dance

Usually the first dance given was the Scalp Staff Dance, to be followed by the Women's Dance. In the former, dancers, both men and women, formed a crescent-shaped line, the women on the left, men on the right as one faced them. They danced in place, much as the Sun dancers did. The leader, usually an elderly man, carried a scalp stick, to which was fastened an imitation scalp. He danced in front of each man, around behind the line and back to his place again. Others might also carry scalp sticks, and each of those who did repeated the dance in the same way.

As they danced there were times when the men cried out, "U-hu-hu-hu!" and the women responded with "U-wu-wu-wu!" The unusual thing about this Scalp Staff Dance was that men, not the women, carried the scalp sticks.

The Women's Dance was the usual side step, or shuffle dance.

THE FINAL DAY OF THE CEREMONY

Just before dawn of the eighth day the dancing stopped, the dancers retiring to their resting places in the rear of the Sun Dance lodge. A few minutes before the sun rose they came forward to greet it for the last time during the ceremonies, arms extended and whistles blowing as before. The Priest sang his song to the new day. Then the dancers retired again to the rear of the lodge, now sitting in a row behind the altar. The Priest gave the usual invocation with his own pipe, lit it and passed it to each dancer for a few puffs, and the public part of the Sun Dance was over for another year.

When the pipe was smoked out, the ashes were carefully placed on the altar; several men gathered the ashes from the fire (over near the entrance), which were also placed on the altar. Wreaths, willow hoops, the rawhide symbols, feather dangles, fur wristlets and anklets, all were placed on the altar and on top of the entire heap of ceremonial objects the buffalo skull was placed.

The dancers, led by the Holy Woman with the sacred pipe, filed out, marched sunwise around the exterior of the lodge four times, proceeded to the sacred tipi, went around it also four times, then entered. Inside, the Priest broke the seal on the sacred pipe and placed the seal of buffalo fat on the altar within the tipi. He lit the pipe, after the invocation to the six directions and powers of the universe, and offered it to each man, who smoked a few puffs and handed it back. Sometimes the dance leader, who had provided the sacred pipe, gave it to the Priest, but he might also keep it himself as a memento of the important occasion. From then on, only people who were entirely worthy ever smoked it. No one with the slightest blemish on his character would dare to touch it.

After smoking the sacred pipe, the dancers all went to the sweat lodge and the Holy Woman guarded the door while they had a vapor bath. All the sage which had been spread in the rear of the Sun Dance lodge was burned in the fire heating the rocks for the steam bath. As was customary, the door was opened four times. The first time the cover was raised, a bowl of water was passed around, with a braid of sweet grass, which was dipped into the water and merely touched to the lips of each dancer. Then the pipe was smoked again. The lips were again touched with the moistened sweet grass during the second opening.

The third time the door was opened each man took a mouthful of water. The fourth time he could drink as much water as he wanted. The pipe was smoked after each raising of the door cover. When the men came out of the sweat lodge, they rubbed themselves with sage and returned to the Sacred Tipi. There a feast of soup, dog meat, buffalo ribs, and choke-cherry pudding was brought to the famished dancers, and their ordeal was over.

The tipi poles, covers, and buffalo hides used in thatching the Sun Dance lodge were now recovered by their owners, the gifts hanging to the posts were collected by needy people, and by sunset the entire camp was disbanded. Only the sacred pole with its offerings, the surrounding posts, and the things piled on the altar remained, there to stay until completely disintegrated over a period of many years. They were never molested by Indians.

Because all Indian dances were so involved with the entire life of the people, we felt it necessary to give as complete a picture of the Lakota Sun Dance as possible. Some recent reports would lead one to believe that it consisted only of dancing in a line, in place, facing the sun. In recent revivals this is about all that has been done, but we know from earlier reports and from the stories of One Bull and other old-timers that there was considerable pattern, ritual, and action to the former Sun Dance, as we have tried to show.

THE REVIVAL OF THE SUN DANCE

One Bull was completely in earnest in giving both of his recent Sun Dances in 1935 and 1942. He and his family had to serve as sponsors, which involved great expense, and they were extremely poor. They were also the principal participants, for most of the people were uninterested. Consequently, the dances were on a small scale, with few dancers. The most important ones were very old men, so they could not be expected to produce a ceremony with the vigor and spectacle of former times, but in the main they followed the old pattern very well.

There was some change in the very purpose of the dance. One Bull promised to give the 1935 dance as a result of recovery from a serious injury. The bans on Indian dancing had just been removed. During his illnes he saw a rider of early days, war bonnet flowing in the wind, riding a white horse across the sky. He decided then to give the Sun Dance if he recovered. This prayer was in keeping with the teachings of old, but in addition One Bull determined to make his Sun Dance a prayer for rain, to break the terrible drought that had plagued the Dakotas and other prairie states for several years.

Although there is no record of an earlier Sun Dance having been given as a prayer for rain by the Lakotas, a number of old-timers we knew told us this story. During one particularly dry Sun Dance, when it was very dusty and even the spectators were suffering from the heat, Sitting Bull came out during an intermission and announced that he thought there should be a little rain to settle the dust. He had hardly spoken when a small cloud gathered above them and a shower descended. It lasted only a short time, but was enough to settle the dust and revive everyone's spirit. When it was over, they saw that the ground where the chief had been standing was still entirely dry! Such stories as this, of course, contributed to the yarn that Sitting Bull was a medicine man. He was not regarded as such by his people, but owned a very powerful "medicine."[9]

Shortly after One Bull'a Sun Dance the drought was broken and South Dakota has had no extended period of drought since. One Bull believed so strongly in the

One Bull, age eighty-two (center) and two of his granddaughters dancing the Sun Dance at Little Eagle, South Dakota, in 1935. The man on the left is Bear Comes Out, the Ikoncan (Master of Ceremonies). Laubin Collection.

power of his dancing that he warned all the people to hang their belongings high in their cabins, for the water was sure to rise high in the river. He and his family packed up and went to the Black Hills, to work in a pageant for the tourists during the summer. They had no more than gone when the rain came. And how it rained! One storm brought five inches of rain in one night, washing out roads and bridges and flooding houses. Then the people said One Bull's medicine was too strong and some of them wished him and his family bad luck.

We followed them later to the Hills, and when we found them we told the old man what the people back home said. He just laughed and laughed. We could not see anything very funny in having people wish him bad luck, and we said so. "Why is he laughing? What is so funny?" we asked Magli.

"Oh!" she said, "Father says the people, they never know what they want."

One Bull's second revival Sun Dance was given as a prayer for victory for our armed forces in World War II and for a just and lasting peace. During the ceremonies, soldier boys home on furlough were especially honored.

The minor differences in these recent Sun Dances and earlier ones were these: Only two women tapped the tree with the ax; the final cutting was done by a man. These two women also helped carry the tree back to the site of the lodge. Also, the tree was carried on a wagon, which brought it to the edge of the camp ground, *but* the four halts were observed before it was placed in the wagon, four halts were made while it was in the wagon, and again there were four halts after taking it from the wagon while carrying it to its final location.

The ceremony lasted only two days and two nights, but even that was a long time for men in their nineties, as were One Bull, his brother White Bull, and their old friend Kills Pretty Enemy, who served as the Holy Man, or Priest.

The women participants smoked the sacred pipe at the close of the ceremony and also took part in the sweat-lodge ritual, which was given only following the dance. Two buffalo skulls were used on the altar, which was known on some occasions in the past. When we read reports on the Sun Dance, we never find two exactly alike, and yet all may be correct. Each Priest had a right to use his own paintings and regalia, even a certain amount of his own ritual. The underlying reasons and principal motives, however, were the same.

The fasting and thirsting must have been torture enough for old men. There was no laceration of the flesh in either of One Bull's Sun Dances. All the old men taking part had undergone various phases of torture many years ago, so they were well acquainted with it. There have been reports that Sioux dancers at Pine Ridge have undergone the torture dance several times in recent years, for an annual Sun Dance has been revived there, but many features of the old-time Sun Dance are no longer to be seen.

In the later years of the Sun Dance the offerings placed on the altar at the conclusion of the ceremonies were sometimes burned in order to prevent curious white people from gathering them up and carrying them off. But we went over the Sun Dance grounds at Little Eagle after One Bull's ceremony of 1935 and found one sage wreath still lying on the ground. It was now late summer and our old friend Flying Cloud was with us. We picked up the old sage wreath, and Flying Cloud assured us it was all right for us to keep it, for he knew it would not be a mere souvenir to us, but instead a keepsake, full of memories. Later, One Bull also assured us he was happy for us to have it. It still occupies an honored place on our log wall, placed above a great old skull of one of the original priarie bison.

Because of the success of One Bull's dance in 1935, the people of the Cannon Ball district of the reservation decided to put on a Sun Dance the following summer. But things went wrong from the very start. There were arguments as to leadership, bickering as to proper procedure, and finally a good deal of trouble stirred up by non-Indian commercial interests trying to capitalize on the affair.

A big camp was set up, including a couple of real tipis, and the ceremonies finally got under way. But hardly had the dancing started than a cloud burst descended upon the camp, with frightful lightning and thunder and heavy hail. Many of the tents were blown down. The Sun Dance ended right there.

Just before the storm a well-known photographer got some beautiful pictures, which appeared in the *Saturday Evening Post* with an article giving the impression that the entire ceremony was concluded and that they got the rain they were asking for. But such was not the case, and to this day the Cannon Ball district has not tried to give another Sun Dance. Such a storm showed the presence of evil, and Thunder came in his ancient role of cleanser. Some people said the storm was caused by white men coming uninvited into the sacred lodge and stepping across the altar.

16. The Sun Dance: Other Tribes

THE MANDAN *OKIPA*

Since it is believed that the Sun Dance may have originated among the Mandans, let us see how it was performed by them. The Mandans as a tribe almost ceased to exist after the terrible smallpox epidemic of 1837. The best account of them comes from Catlin, who spent more time among them than among any other Indians he visited. They called their great annual ceremony Okipa (Okeepa), which Catlin not only covered in his Letter No. 22 in his *North American Indians*,[1] but about which he also wrote an entire book entitled *Okeepa.* Catlin found a great deal to admire in the Mandans and praised them many times and in many ways. But he was horrified by the cruelties of the Okipa. With the remarkable tolerance he showed, yet not being able to accept Mandan self-torture, it is little wonder that other observers were willing to go to almost any lengths to destroy similar "heathen rites."

Catlin claimed that the Mandans in their beliefs recognized both a Good Spirit and an Evil Spirit. Also, in common with most tribes in North America, they had a tradition of a great flood. It seems strange that many Indian religions have stories parallel to some in the Bible, including many legends of virgin birth. Some of the Sun Dance origin stories ascribe it to the teachings of a legendary hero, son of a virgin, or to an earthly mother with Sun or Morning Star as father.

The Okipa was largely a celebration of deliverance from the catastrophe of the flood and an assurance that it would never happen again. (So they were wiped out by smallpox instead!) In addition, it served as a prayer for an adequate supply of buffalo and as an introduction into manhood for the youth of the tribe.

The Mandans were one of the Village tribes who lived in large earth lodges along the upper Missouri River, in what is now North Dakota.* Although they were largely dependent upon their crops, their most important meat supply came from the buffalo herds which frequented their area. But, because they also used other wild game, many other animals were also represented in the ceremony.

In the center of the Mandan village was an open plaza about one hundred and fifty feet across, reserved for ceremonies and public gatherings. In the very center of the

---

*High on the bluffs overlooking the Missouri River, on an original site near the present city of Mandan, North Dakota, are several reconstructed earth lodges. These dwellings are most impressive to anyone interested in former Indian life. They might suggest very large Navajo hogans, but average about thirty feet in diameter, with a council lodge some sixty feet across. The site of the Mandan village visited by Lewis and Clark and by Catlin is farther upriver.

plaza was a greatly venerated object that Catlin translates as the "big canoe." It was apparently a ceremonial representation of the legendary vessel responsible for their rescue from the flood, corresponding to the ark of the Bible tale. So far as is known, the Mandans had had no contact with Christian teachings, and the *Okipa* was ages old. One theory has been advanced in recent years, however, that Christian Vikings got as far west as the Mandan country in the 1300's, so could easily have influenced native beliefs.[*2]

Catlin describes and pictures the "canoe" as looking much like a great barrel, being constructed in this form from posts set up in a circle and bound with withes.

The *Okipa* was held when the willow leaves had reached full size. The ceremonies began amidst a great din, in the morning, people gathering on the rooftops of their lodges, women and children wailing and crying, as if asking deliverance from a great calamity. In the distance a strange figure approached and the men made preparations as if for war, stringing their bows, drawing arrows from their quivers, and readying lances, knives, and war clubs.

As the figure drew closer it could be seen to be a man, painted entirely white, wearing a cloak of four wolf skins over his shoulders, a headdress made of the skins of two ravens, and carrying a long pipe in his left hand. He called out that no one should take alarm, as he was the First, or Only, Man and had come to save them. He proceeded immediately to the great medicine lodge, which had been built solely to house these annual ceremonies and was closed the rest of the year. Only Man, portrayed by one of the tribal leaders, was the legendary hero who came from the sacred mountain far to the west.

Four men were chosen to clean the medicine lodge, which they then lined with fresh willows, sage, and sweet-smelling herbs. Four offerings, which we might think of as flags of blue and black trade cloth, but tied in such a way as to represent human figures, were hoisted above the lodge. Inside an altar consisting of a scaffold of light poles erected in a square, like a drying rack, about five feet high, with two buffalo skulls and two human skulls on each side, occupied a prominent place just west of the central fire. A small "medicine," which Catlin could not see well enough to de-

---

*There is much evidence that a Viking expedition penetrated North America as far as present-day western Minnesota in 1362. At that time the Mandans lived farther east than they did when Verendrye, Lewis and Clark, and Catlin found them. Those who believe in this Viking journey cite as further proof, in addition to the famous Kensington runestone, a number of authenticated sagas, and many Viking artifacts that have been picked up along the route, the fact that the Mandans had religious beliefs quite different from those of other tribes, which they think came about through the teaching of the Vikings who were Christians. All early reports on the Mandans state that many of them had light skins, hazel or blue eyes, and light hair. Belif in an Evil Spirit, tradition of a white man who came to them as a teacher, and reverence for the "canoe" are also cited as evidence.

scribe but which impressed him as representing a small turtle (although no one would tell him about it), was hung to the center of the scaffold. Beneath it was a knife and a bundle of skewers. On each side of the fire were two drums, four in all, which Catlin described as "sacks" made of heavy buffalo rawhide, cut and sewn to represent huge tortoises and partially filled with water.

Two of these drums were in existence at the time Edward Curtis made his remarkable photographs of Indian life in the early 1900's. They are flat on top, as a drum would be expected to be, which led Catlin to think they represented tortoises turned over on their backs. According to Indian belief, however, if these drums were ever turned upside down, the world would come to an end, for they represented the great legendary turtle of creation, which thrust its back up through the waters to form the earth. One of them was made for each direction, each containing water from the direction it represented— another example of the way Indians expressed the separate parts of a whole, yet all united as one entity.

Two rawhide globular rattles were also placed near the drums, one near each pair.

Only Man went around the village, stopping at every house, telling the inmates that he was the last survivor of the flood. As he circulated around the village he was presented with sharp-edged tools, which he carried to the medicine lodge in the evening.

No one knew where he stayed that first night, but he appeared again at sunrise the next morning, and as he entered the medicine lodge he was followed by about fifty young men, who were to take part in the ceremonies and sacrifice themselves during the rituals. Some were painted yellow, some white, and some red. Each carried his medicine bag, quiver, and shield on his left arm and a bow and arrows in his right hand. Marching to their places around the inside wall of the lodge, they hung their weapons above their heads and sat or reclined beneath them.

Only Man lit his long pipe and smoked it for some time, addressing the young men and telling them to trust in the Great Spirit, who would enable them to withstand the ordeal they were about to undertake. He then called another old man, whose body and hair were painted entirely yellow, whom he appointed as master of ceremonies, presenting him with the sacred pipe as his badge of office. Only Man shook hands with him, passed out of the lodge, went around the village once more taking leave of the chiefs and dignitaries, and departed for "his home in the mountains in the west." From then on, the master of ceremonies was in charge, and it was one of his duties to see to it that no one left the lodge for four days and nights, during which time they could not eat, drink, or sleep.

Outside, in the plaza, other ceremonies were taking place. The most important was the Bull Dance. Eight dancers took part, wearing costumes of buffalo skin, with great masks made of buffalo heads, a strip of hide down the back, ending with the tail hanging behind. They wore buffalo hair around their ankles, had a bundle of green willows on their backs, and carried slender staffs about six feet long in their left hands and rawhide rattles in their right hands. These rattles were ring-shaped, like a doughnut, with dew claws hanging around their circumferences.

The Bull dancers were elaborately painted, even their faces, although hidden beneath the tremendous buffalo masks. In his book *Okeepa*, Catlin describes and pictures them. The faces were painted with red and white stripes across the forehead, nose, and chin, with red at the top of the forehead and bottom of the chin. All joints were painted black, with white rings. Their backs were black, faded over the shoulders, becoming reddish on their bellies. The backs of arms and legs were also painted black, with perpendicular bright red and white stripes on the fronts. Hands and feet were black.

Two pairs of "bulls" represented each of the four quarters, and between each pair another character danced. Two of these latter represented day and the two others, night, the two "days" dancing opposite each other, the two "nights" also opposite, all facing outward from the "big canoe." Night was represented by bodies painted black, with white spots for stars, and day had red and white perpendicular stripes—red for the morning rays from the sun, white for the ghosts which the bright rays chased away. They wore kilts of eagle feathers and ermine skins, and headdresses of the same materials, those of the "days" natural in color, of the "nights" dyed red. They also carried staffs and rattles.

The Bull Dance was conducted by the master of ceremonies, carrying his medicine pipe. He came out of the ceremonial lodge and went to the "big canoe," where he wailed and cried. Four other old men painted red, who up to now had been guarding the sacred lodge, went inside and came out carrying the sacred turtle drums, which they placed near the "canoe." Another man, also painted red, brought the two rattles which had been lying near the drums.

The master of ceremonies smoked his pipe to the four directions, and the Bull Dance began. It was given four times the first day, once for each direction, each performance lasting about fifteen minutes. During the intermissions, the master of ceremonies danced back to the sacred lodge, the singers carried their drums to it, and the dancers retired to their special lodge. The entire performance was given eight times the second day, twelve times the third day, and sixteen times the fourth day. The Bull dancers, dancing in pairs, acted the parts of buffalo bulls, snorting, pawing, and bellowing. But, while they did the most active dancing and played the most important role in the drama, there were many other fascinating characters who joined them to add interest and excitement to the scene.

There were two "grizzly bears," dressed in the skins of these animals, who took positions near the "big canoe," growling and giving a realistic portrayal of real bears. They threatened to break up the Bull Dance, but women brought them food to appease them.

Two "bald eagles," bodies and limbs painted black, head, feet, and hands white, occasionally swooped in to snatch food away from the bears.

As many as a hundred or more naked boys, their bodies painted yellow, their hands white, and wearing tails made from white deer hair, were "antelopes," who chased the eagles away and took the food from them, driving them out onto the prairie. Catlin believed this symbolized that "bountiful gifts at last fall into the hands of the innocent."

There were two "swans," with white noses and feet painted black. There were two "rattlesnakes," painted yellow on the backs and on the back of arms and legs, with black spots and rings on the yellow and white clay down their fronts. They carried gourd-shaped rattles of rawhide in their right hands and sprigs of sage in the left.

Two "beavers" were entirely covered, except for their heads, with buffalo skin, hair out, and they wore rawhide tails cut to look like beaver tails. Two "vultures," naked, were painted brown, with blue heads and shoulders and red noses. Two "wolves," also naked, wore wolf skins down their backs.

The wolves chased the antelope, and when they caught one, the grizzlies came up and took it away, pretending to eat it. All these various animals and birds had different songs to which they danced, or rather enacted their parts, including all the various cries and calls. So the Mandans depicted the relation of one form of life to another and the constant struggle for existence.

Maximilian, who saw the Okipa not long after Catlin did, even reported that two men represented *dried meat.* They wore caps of white hare skin, their bodies were painted with zig-zag stripes, and they wore girdles of green boughs. He did not give nearly as complete a description of the ceremonies as did Catlin, but the two compare very well. He saw the antelope painted differently; they were red on the back, with bodies and limbs white, and black on the nose and mouth. He added two coyotes, with the tops of their heads white and yellow-brown on their faces. He said the eagles, beavers, and coyotes were "modern," showing that in his day, as throughout history, Indian dances were never static.

About noon of the fourth day an Evil Spirit appeared on the prairie about a mile west of the village, in nearly the same place where Only Man was first seen. He approached in zig-zag fashion, which to all Western tribes was a signal of warning or of calling attention. He was naked, painted black from head to foot, with white rings over the black and canine teeth painted at his mouth. Maximilian said the same character wore a black cockscomb and a mask with white wooden rings around the eyes and cotton yarn hanging from the mouth for teeth. He had a sun painted on his abdomen and a crescent on his back, with white circles around each joint, and he wore a buffalo tail.[3]

Catlin said he carried a staff, eight or nine feet long, with a red ball on the forward end, which he pushed ahead of him as he went. Maximilian described it as a small stick in his hand, with a ball of skin at the end, to which a scalp was attached, painted red on the under side. Either way, it represented the misuse of sex.

This creature advanced, screaming and yelling, and began to chase the women, whereupon the master of ceremonies approached him with his sacred pipe, completely cowing him. This act was repeated a number of times. Each time the pipe was withdrawn, the Evil Spirit regained some power and chased the women again. Of course this was a dramatization of the familiar story of good overcoming evil, as well as the overcoming of darkness by the approaching light of day.

The Utes had a legend of a party of warriors a long way from home at the time of the annual Sun Dance, who consequently held the ceremony on their own. Not being on sanctified ground, they were attacked by an Evil Spirit, who was about to destroy them when the Sun sent a white spirit to drive the evil one away and saved them from a horrible fate.[4] The Utes were on the far outer fringe of the Sun Dance area and yet had somehow learned the story, so closely related to that of the Okipa, many miles to the east.

Eventually the Evil Spirit of the Mandans was entirely overcome by the power of the pipe and began a retreat from the village. The women then began to chase him, beating him with sticks, showering him with dirt, which stuck to the greasy paint and made him look worse than ever. One woman took his lance away from him and broke it. Other women took the two pieces and broke them into smaller pieces. As he ran, warriors also pursued him, firing guns loaded with blank powder at him. Whatever honor there was in being elected to this role was pretty well offset by the misery he was forced to endure through this realistic portrayal. As he finally disappeared over the horizon, all raised shouts of victory and returned to the medicine lodge.

The Evil Spirit was sometimes known also as the Owl, the owl being associated with night and the forces of evil. The woman who snatched and broke the lance was especially honored, being escorted back to the sacred lodge by two other women, who lifted her up over the doorway (which projected from an earth lodge like a tunnel, similar to that of an igloo), where she harangued the multitude. She now claimed power over the earth, the buffalo, and all creation, taking upon herself a new role as Earth Mother. She ordered the turtle drums carried back into the medicine lodge, and the Bull Dance was over. All of its participants returned to their lodge of preparation, and the Earth Mother invited the chiefs into the sacred lodge. She ordered the master of ceremonies to smoke his pipe again, and the torture ceremonies to begin. Afterward she could demand the most beautiful dress in the village, for she led the dance held at the Buffalo Feast that night.

But there was no feast for the candidates undergoing the torture. The little scaffold in the center of the lodge was removed and the skulls were taken up and hung from the two rear center posts. The candidates were pierced in the same manner as described for the Lakotas and hung from the rafters, some by their chests, others by their backs. Two men had been selected to make the incisions and implant the skewers. The candidates came forward one at a time until as many as eight were hanging from the ceiling at once. The cords by which they were suspended hung down from the roof of the lodge, and each man was raised four or five feet off the ground. In addition to being hung up on skewers, they were also pierced by skewers on their arms, thighs, and below the knees. Shields and quivers were hung on the arm skewers and buffalo skulls from those in the thighs and legs. Each man held his medicine bag in his left hand, holding it tightly until he fainted and dropped it.

As each candidate hung in space, an assistant turned him around with a long pole. These assistants were painted red, with black hands and feet. Eventually each candidate did faint, whereupon he was lowered to the ground and the skewers which held him to the thongs were pulled out. All the other skewers, however, had to be torn out. When he revived, he crawled to a large buffalo skull near the center of the arena, placing the little finger of his left hand upon it, where it was chopped off as a further offering by a man who had been chosen to make these amputations. No treatment was given and the candidate neither groaned nor flinched; the fasting and thirsting evidently reduced the flow of blood. The chiefs and head men sat around the wall of the lodge, watching carefully to select the bravest candidates.

As each group fainted and was lowered to the ground, the master of ceremonies went out of the lodge and over to the big canoe to wail. He was followed by six or eight victims at a time, who crawled and staggered after him.

Around the "canoe" a circle of about twenty young men, all wearing eagle-feather headdresses like an arc at the backs of their heads, but otherwise naked, was formed. Each was painted half blue and half red, blue on the right side and red on the left. The circle was linked like a chain, but instead of holding hands they held willow boughs between them. All danced wildly about the "canoe" while the victims struggled to get as near the outside of this circle as possible. The young dancers then divided into pairs, each pair wrapping a stout thong about the wrists of a victim and dragging him in what Catlin said the Mandans called "the last race." And well it might have been, for it seems impossible that a human being who had already suffered so much could withstand this final trial.

Each victim tried to remain on his own feet and actually to run with the other two, endeavoring to remain "alive" as long as possible. To the Indians, fainting was a form of death, the only difference being that the spirit returned to its body instead of leaving it forever. Of course, none of them were able to keep their feet very long, so they were literally dragged, until the force of bouncing and bumping over the ground, the buffalo skulls banging along behind them, eventually tore them loose and freed them from their bonds. Most of them did faint, but upon recovering made their way to their homes.

At sundown the master of ceremonies carried all the tools which Only Man had gathered to the river and threw them in as a last sacrifice, thus symbolizing that the first big canoe, which had saved mankind from the flood, was made with such tools.

That night the village criers, usually old men who yet retained powerful voices, circulated around the village, shaking rattles, and announcing that the Earth Mother was now in charge of all mankind. She in turn invited certain people, who gathered around the "big canoe" for a feast. The eight Bull Dancers, now washed free of their paint, the master of ceremonies, the four drummers, the man who shook the rattles, the old chiefs, and eight or ten young married women were those invited. Everyone else was required to remain at home, indoors. Meat was first handed to the Bull Dancers in wooden bowls, while the women danced before them. Each woman then chose one of the men, and the couples went off together. A man could buy his way out of this arrangement with a present, but this was the finale of the Okipa ceremonies.

So we see that, for all its dramatization of the forces of life, of sacrifice, of gratitude for delivery from catastrophe, and prayer for deliverance, the Okipa was also important as a fertility ceremony to insure a continued supply of buffalo, most important of all creatures to the Indian way of life.

Both Catlin and Maximilian reported a ceremony similar to the Okipa for the Hidatsas, but it was done in an outdoor arbor, like other real Sun Dances, with a forked center pole. Although they also underwent torture, Catlin said that it was a feeble imitation of that of the Mandans. For rhythm they beat upon a dried hide, typical of most Sun Dances. The entire story of the Hidatsa ritual was different, however, being more like that of their relatives the Crows.

THE CHEYENNES

On the Northern Cheyenne reservation in Montana, Last Bull was a reservation policeman, certainly a very necessary officer in these times, but one looked down upon by most Indians because he represents the white man's way and white man's justice, which has not always been just with them. Some of the young fellows made fun of Last Bull for being a "white man." They said he was not really brave, but had authority because he was backed by white men.

Knowing that all bans had been removed from Indian dance and religion, Last Bull said that he would show them whether he was an Indian and whether he was brave or not, and dared anyone to undergo the old Sun Dance sacrifice with him. There were no takers, so Last Bull offered his sacrifice all alone. He was actually suspended from the tree by slits cut in his chest. He came through the ordeal with flying colors, and in fact did it again another year, as a prayer for his people, that they might take a new lease on life and become the dignified, prosperous, and happy people they once had been. There has been no question about Last Bull's courage or sincerity since.

In many ways the Cheyennes' Sun Dance is similar to that of the Sioux. Although their lodge is the more typical type, with twenty-eight rafters, or stringers, running to the center pole, they use rawhide images, as do the Sioux. They have an even more elaborate altar. The dance itself is much the same, even to the wearing of the sage wreaths. The Cheyenne story of the origin of the Sun Dance, however, is entirely different. It came from the Suhtai division of the tribe (formerly a distinct tribe), which was located near the Mandans in earlier times. This helps to bear out the contention that the entire Sun Dance concept originated in that area. An old Cheyenne, Little Chief, told us that the Medicine Lodge Ceremony came to the Suhtaio from a legendary hero, Erect Horns, or Standing-on-the-Ground, who saved the people from a cannibal monster that could change its shape and character at will. Erect Horns also brought back, from inside the Sacred Mountain, the Sacred Hat, a buffalo-horned bonnet still preserved as one of the sacred relics of the tribe.

The Cheyennes, during the time of government restriction on the Sun Dance, gave up the torture feature because they knew the entire ceremony would be prohibited if it were carried on. Actually, although torture was often undergone at the Sun Dance to fulfill vows, it was not the important feature of the Cheyenne ceremony, according to Grinnell.[5] Such vows could be honored at any time. The Sun Dance was a good time because of its great importance to the people. Although they never did call it "Sun Dance" except in English, they did not even refer to the ceremony by their name, calling it instead "Willow Dance" in order to get around the government "snoopers."[6]

Formerly there were other dances included at the time of the Sun Dance, as we have seen for the Sioux. The Cheyennes had a Crazy Society, similar to the Sioux Heyoka, which performed the morning after the Sun Dance started. Both men and women belonged to the Crazy Society. They served a feast of dog meat and took it from the boiling kettle with their bare hands. Men and women were painted black, with white spots, the women wearing skirts tucked up between their legs instead of breechclouts.

The Sun Dance, or more properly Medicine, or New Life, Lodge, of the Cheyennes, began at dark of the first day, as was the case also with the Arapahos and the Shoshonis. The dance itself lasted until sunset of the fourth day, meaning that the participants danced three nights and three days. It was given largely as a prayer for renewed life. Consequently, the wife of the man who pledged the Sun Dance surrendered herself to the leading priest, who was the ceremonial "grandfather," as part of the fertility rites—another phase that drew the ire of the missionaries and government officials. The Arapahos had the same rite—but they were known among early explorers as rather loose morally, whereas the Cheyennes have always been credited with being extremely "straight-laced." However, morality in any culture depends upon the standards of that culture, not upon the standards of outsiders.

It is probable that in early times the Cheyennes hung a captive to the center pole, and there are stories that the Crows also sacrificed a captive at the time of their Sun Dance. But the Pawnees were the last Plains tribe to offer human sacrifices and their last Morning Star Sacrifice was about 1818.

THE ANIMAL DANCE (MASSAUM CEREMONY)

Since all tribes were hunters to some extent, and all recognized the relationship of man to other creatures, it is to be expected that animal dances played an important part in their repertoires. Edward Curtis saw the Animal Dance of the Cheyennes as recently as 1926. It was given in the summer, often at the time of the Medicine Lodge, or Sun Dance, and points again to the relationship of these dances one to another and to the origin of the Sun Dance in the Mandan country.

The Cheyennes separated into two divisions in prehistoric times. They wandered around, not too far from each other, and eventually, meeting again and recognizing a mutual language, joined together once more. This happened as they were moving west and after they had crossed the Missouri River, probably in the early part of the eighteenth century. These two divisions, known as Suhtaio and Tsistsistsas, or Cheyennes proper, had separate culture heroes and many different traditions. The Sun Dance supposedly came from the Suhtai hero Standing-on-the-Ground, while the Animal Dance was brought to the Cheyennes by Sweet Medicine. At one time each division had its own separate annual ritual. In later years the united tribe accepted both rituals, and it is difficult to say which was the more important.

The Animal Dance is also known as the Massaum Ceremony, Buffalo Dance, and Crazy Dance. Parts of it are typical of the Sun Dance; it is given to fulfill a vow; a green cottonwood is cut, in ritualistic manner, for a center pole; and a special lodge is erected. Since both divisions of the tribe were living at least part of the time during their long separation in the region of the Mandans, it is possible that each took to itself a portion of the Mandan Okipa. Animals are the important feature of the Massaum, and the renewal of man's physical and spiritual life, with attendant self-torture, was important to the Medicine Lodge.

The Animal Dance might come under medicine, or healing, ceremonies, for healing was also an important part of it. The Massaum, like the Medicine Lodge, was given to assure the reanimation of all living things, but it was evidently also a hunting ceremony, to assure an adequate food supply.

The full Massaum ceremony was pledged, as was the Sun Dance, or Medicine Lodge, by a man and his wife. It was a long and complicated ritual, lasting four days and nights. The first three days were given over to a semisecret performance. The public ceremonies began on the afternoon of the fourth day. The participants were members of various animal societies who were chosen to assist.

Much ritual, smoking, painting, symbolical movements, and singing were involved in the preparation of a special wolf skin to be worn by the pledger on the final day. A buffalo skull played an important part, as did also an altar and whistles similar to those of the Sun Dance. The morning star was a featured symbol, and a dog feast had its place in the Animal Dance, as in so many ceremonies.

The tribal circle, as usual, opened to the east, but the ceremonial tipi in the center, often referred to as the Grasshopper Lodge (no one knows why), faced west. On the morning of the fourth, or final, day, separate lodges were erected for each animal society and for the "Contraries," who acted like clowns. There were two Buffalo societies, each with a separate tipi.

The Pledger served as a Leader. The wolf skin he wore was painted yellow, the wolf head formed a headdress, and he was painted yellow all over his body. He used two yellow canes, with scarfs and little balls of sage hanging from their tops to represent forelegs, reminiscent of animal characters we find in the ceremonies of the Southwest. Two other most important characters were another wolf, a gray one, and a fox. The Gray Wolf wore a natural wolf skin with a scalp hanging from its nose. Behind the ears was attached a strip of buffalo hide which dragged on the ground, and fastened to each side of it, between the wolf ears and the wearer's shoulders, were polished buffalo horns. He was painted white, the paint then streaked with the finger nails.

The fox skin was painted blue down the back, with a blue disk to represent the sun on the right side and a crescent on the left side, over the heart. Dots of yellow marked the rest of the fur, with blue lines up each leg from the foot to meet the blue line of the back. The Fox Dancer was painted yellow all over, with blue spots, and black lines under his eyes and nose.

These performers blew upon whistles and carried on a sort of parade and pantomime around the camp circle, the Yellow Wolf circling outside the camp, then inside, later followed by the Gray Wolf. Then the Fox and another man, with hair loose, painted yellow, and carrying a staff with green leaves tied to its tip, entered the scene, running, circling, doubling back, the Wolves joining in.

Grinnell gives a very complete description of the ritual.[7] Curtis described the ceremony for the Southern Cheyennes.[8] He states that the men in the Buffalo Societies wore buffalo headdresses and had their arms and legs painted black. But Grinnell, speaking of the Massaum Animal Dance he witnessed, said there were thirteen women, two little girls, and two men acting as buffalo in the first Buffalo Society. The women and girls made long headdresses of slough grass and carried in their right hands sage wreaths with strings across them. The men were painted gray above the waist, with yellow legs, a red sun on the chest, and a red moon over the left shoulder blade; they carried bunches of buffalo hair in their right hands. This may be another example of different priests, or medicine men, carrying on ceremonies that differed in detail.

A Coyote, painted yellow with striped face, a coyote skin down his back, and a whistle in his mouth, took a position on the west of the camp, constantly pacing back and forth, always trotting.

Then came the Buffalo, led by a "cow," a fat woman especially chosen for the office. (A fat woman would have been hard to find in early days and still is rare among the poor Northern Cheyennes.) The two Bulls brought up the rear. People who were sick and ailing were brought into the camp circle and the Buffalo danced and circled around each one, the Cow performing healing incantations. As the Buffalo began to file away, the Bulls finished the shamanistic ministration before proceeding to the next patient.

A society of Otters performed in much the same way, followed by the Deer. These two societies carried willow wands. Women, children, even babies took part in the Otter Dance. The two male leaders wore feathered headdresses. The other Otter men wore otter skins down their backs and had red crosses on their right shoulder blades. The bodies of the Deer were painted yellow, and the Does wore an eagle feather on each side of the head to represent deer ears, wearing their hair in a single braid down the back.

Sometimes four Elk Dancers entered in. They painted their lower legs, arms, and shoulders black, the rest of the body yellow, and wore sage wreaths on their heads, with bare twigs to represent antlers. They also carried willow wands.

Grinnell also mentioned a group of eleven men—the first five painted yellow, the next three red, then two white, and the final dancer red—who enacted the dream of a famous Cheyenne named White Bull. They represented white-tailed deer.

A group of seven Young Wolves together with the wives of the two other Wolves came into the wings of the Massaum Lodge bearing the sacred straight pipe of the Cheyennes, while the Yellow Wolf and the Fox zig-zagged, stopping and turning, back and forth from the sacred tree to the entrance.

The Contraries, painted white even to their hair, which was done up in knots over their foreheads with single eagle feathers, wore scant loin cloths and carried minia-ture bows and arrows, painted red. They danced and cavorted around all during the other performances, doing things backward, moving in opposite directions to the other dancers, like Sioux Heyokas, darting in and out like lightning in a thunder-storm. They served as Hunters and Clowns all at once. They pretended to shoot the Buffalo and were charged by the Bulls. They doctored the sick by jumping over them.

After circling the camp, the first Buffalo Society filed to the center lodge and danced before the circle of singers. The Coyote joined in, whistling his way in and out among the Buffalo. The Buffalo then entered the lodge. The Otters came next. They too, after circling the camp, danced before the lodge, when the Buffalo came out and joined them. Then the Deer joined in. After that, all went to their respective tipis while the second Buffalo Society circled the camp. These Buffalo were painted black, with white discs on their shoulders, elbows, wrists, hips, knees, and ankles. They also wore anklets, shoulder belts, and wristlets of hop vines. Some of them wore wreaths instead of horned headdresses, and all carried wreaths of willow or cottonwood in their right hands.

When the second Buffalo Society had completed the circle, all the other dancers joined them in the center again, and each group then danced four times.

These parades and dances went on all day, interspersed with proper rituals. Finally dried meat was hung on the tip of a lodge pole, which was then leaned against the sacred Massaum lodge. The Yellow Wolf got down on all fours and the Coyote attempted to go under him. Three times he tried, and on the fourth attempt was successful. During this bit of pantomime, the Fox was trying to grab the dried meat, but as he leaped for it a man raised the pole out of reach. This, too, was done three times, and on the fourth time the Fox got his meat. But no sooner had he grabbed it than the Contraries took it away from him.

All the animals then gathered again in the wings of the sacred lodge, while all the old men and the women walked toward them. The animals formed in groups again and all marched to the river, the Coyote in the lead, followed by the Deer, the two Buffalo herds in the center, the Wolves on the north side of the procession. Almost everyone in the village followed the parade, which stopped four times en route to the water to sing sacred songs. At the fourth stop the Coyote sprang from the group and ran for the water, the others all following in a mad rush. The first one to reach the stream would count coup on the enemy in the next battle. All splashed water on their heads and faces, then reformed in ceremonial order for the march back to the encampment. Again they stopped four times to sing. The Clowns shot various ani-mals, who pretended to be wounded, and their fellow society members doctored them, supporting the "injured" ones and rubbing the feigned wounds. On reaching the center of the village again, the sacred pipe was lit and when it was smoked out the ceremony ended, everyone dispersing to his own tipi.

In olden times even more animals were represented, further evidence that it all started with the Okipa of the Mandans. Horses, cranes, antelope, bears, mountain lions, bands of wolves and coyotes, foxes, even blackbirds were represented. Grinnell says there were seven Clowns, but formerly there were four, two painted white, with bows and four arrows each—one blunt, one chewed soft on the end, one sharp, and one with a rawhide point. The other two Clowns were painted with black stripes on the arms and legs to represent lightning.

THE KIOWAS

We have seen how the representation of animals was an important feature of the Okipa, had a relationship to the Cheyenne Medicine Lodge, and had a part in the Sioux Sun Dance. But as the Sun Dance spread farther and farther from its apparent source, animal representation became less important or nonexistent. Also, torture was a minor aspect or was lacking entirely. The Kiowas, who once lived in the presumed region of origin and who moved south in comparatively recent times, nevertheless got the Sun Dance secondhand. Theirs incorporated features common to several other tribes, including a special buffalo hunt such as held by the Shoshonis, Crows, Blackfeet, Gros Ventres, and Arikaras.[9] Most of these tribes required the killing of a buffalo with one shot. Tahan, our old Kiowa friend, said it had to be shot with one arrow in such a way that no blood showed on the hair. It had to fall on the arrow so that it did not bleed freely and what little blood did come dripped into the ground. The head and a strip of the hide down the back, including the tail, were used in the ceremony. But the Kiowas did not include torture rites. Not only was there no torture, but no blood was to be seen at all. Even the use of the color of blood, red, was prohibited.

The Kiowas were among those who made a ceremony for rain to introduce the Sun Dance. On one occasion a young medicine man, an apprentice we might call him, made the ceremony. It was followed by a violent thunderstorm, instead of the desired light rain, and a visiting Cheyenne was killed by lightning. The friends and relatives of the dead man immediately protested to the Kiowa council that the Kiowas were responsible for his death because they had made the storm. The Kiowas replied that there was no doubt the young medicine man had made too strong a ceremony and brought too much of a storm, but they disclaimed all responsibility for the Cheyenne's death, saying:

Look, your man was wearing a red blanket! You know our customs. You know we do not permit the wearing of red during the time of our Sun Dance. That is why your young man was killed. We are very sorry for this, but neither we nor our new medicine man caused his death. He was wearing a red robe and Thunder was offended.

That settled that. Some of the Kiowas gave presents to the Cheyennes to ease their hurt and make their hearts sing again. The Cheyennes agreed that the Kiowas were right, and good feelings were restored.

THE UTES

As with the Kiowas, neither the Shoshonis nor the Utes practiced torture in their Sun dances. The Utes apparently accepted the dance very late, learning it from their relatives, the Shoshonis, changing it and adapting it to fit their own tribal concepts. The Utes sometimes called the Sun Dance lodge the "tipi of the people," also the "Indian church." Their Sun Dance actually welded together a number of former concepts into a unified whole.

Just before dawn on the first day of the Ute Sun Dance, a large party of men and women went to attack the tree. It represented an enemy chief, and the leader of the party shot his "heart"—the tree fork—with a bullet or arrow. Others of the party then charged the tree, and two men chopped it down, while the rest circled around, shouting victory. Women stripped the bark from the limbs, as they would strip the body of a fallen enemy, and on returning to camp there was a sham battle with those who did not go after the tree. The "chief" (tree) and all the arbor poles were regarded as captives and were brought to the dance ground in wagons.

Most of the bark was stripped from the tree trunk, from the base upward, which the Shoshonis do not do. While the "chief" was lying on the ground it was painted at what would be eye level when raised with a broad black band, flanked on either side with red. Above these bands, on the side of the tree which the dancers would face, was painted a heavy red arrow pointing to the fork, to remind them to always look at the fork (not the sun) while they danced. There were fourteen arbor poles, whereas the Shoshonis use twelve. But the Utes say, as do the Shoshonis, that twelve posts (excluding the two door posts) are the Twelve Apostles. There is no altar. The dance was, and still is, given to obtain power for the individual participants and for the good of the people.[10]

THE SHOSHONIS

The Shoshonis are among those who never gave up the Sun Dance, even during the period of its prohibition. Never having performed the torture rites, there was less effort on the part of government officials to carry out the orders for its suppression. If pressure did become too strong, the Shoshonis merely went up some hidden draw or canyon and held it anyway.

The Shoshoni form of the dance is one of the simplest, indicating recent development, which may be another reason it survived. In the form in which it was brought to the Crows, it is still "given," or sponsored, by one or two individuals who make the extra sacrifice of sustaining its cost. To this day generosity is recognized as the crowning virtue among many Indian tribes. To make such a gift as the Sun Dance to the entire community brings great honor, as well as sacrifice, to the sponsors.

Early on the morning of the day on which the Sun Dance is to begin, old men gather to select the place for the sacred lodge. They dress almost entirely in present-day store clothing, but when we saw them they were colorful figures just the same, with their tall "reservation" hats, usually adorned with a bright-colored silk scarf and sometimes with a fluffy eagle plume, another brilliant scarf about their necks, long pigtails, and beaded moccasins. These old men sit in a circle, passing around and smoking a ceremonial pipe. Near them are the ceremonial objects that later will be hung from the sacred pole in the center of the ceremonial dance lodge—the buffalo head, stuffed eagle, and colored pennants.

At the conclusion of their meditation, a hole is dug for the Sun Dance pole at the spot the old men indicate. The cottonwood tree has previously been selected, with appropriate ceremony similar to that of other tribes, and is now brought to the camp. (We saw it brought first on a wagon, later on a truck!)

Formerly the Hidatsas, Arikaras, and later the Shoshonis prepared the head of a buffalo killed in the special hunt so that it looked alive. Nowadays the Shoshonis, and consequently the Crows, use a mounted buffalo head, which they keep from year to year for the Sun Dance. It is cared for during the year by the last sponsor, until a new one is named; he then takes it to his home.

THE CROWS

The original Crow Sun Dance was different, in most respects, from that of any other tribe. It was given primarily as a vow for revenge and was not necessarily given each year. The lodge itself was also quite different. The structure was based on four poles, as is the Crow tipi, one of these poles serving as the main, or Sun Dance, pole. The last real Crow Sun Dance was given about 1875.

In 1941 the Crows imported the Sun Dance from the Wind River Shoshonis, in a desire to go back to something truly Indian. Since that time they have incorporated minor changes, but it is primarily the same dance. During World War II, their Sun dances were given largely to protect Crow boys in the armed forces and to bring an end to the war. Several were given each summer, in different districts of the reservation. In the agency district, a Sun Dance was given in June of 1942 and each succeeding summer through 1945 as a prayer for victory. The ceremony of August, 1945, completed the cycle of the sacred number four. Before another moon had grown full the last of our enemies had surrendered, so of course the Crows felt that their prayers had been answered and that their Sun dances had contributed towards ending the war. In 1946 the dance was given again as a thanksgiving for the victory and as a prayer for a lasting peace. During these dances a Shoshoni medicine man came over to take charge of the ceremonies. The Crows now have their own medicine men who have learned the rituals.

Crow boys in the armed forces used Sun Dance paint on their faces and sang the Sun Dance songs before going into battle. They were always successful, and so unperturbed in the face of danger that some of the white boys became interested and joined them in their rituals. A couple of these boys later visited the Crow reservation and took part in the Sun Dance.

The Crows, like all Plains Indians, were "rugged individualists." Each man lived his own life in so far as he did nothing to harm his tribesmen while pursuing personal goals. And yet, the goal of the individual was also to do something for the benefit of his people. The welfare of the tribe was always considered above a man's own personal interests. Great power for the common good could be invoked through united action, and this took its highest form in the Sun Dance.

The Crow Tobacco Dance was similar to the original Crow Sun Dance, being held in a lodge of like construction. The main difference was that it was held by a society, representing only a small percentage of the population, but they danced to insure public good. On the other hand, the Crow Sun Dance, participated in by the entire tribe, was largely for individual ends.[11]

At the first Crow Sun Dance we witnessed, an old man counted coup on the tree. At those held later, returned soldier boys had this honor, telling of some deeds they had performed overseas. The coup striker charged the tree on horseback, striking it with a long willow stick, but one could not help noticing the difference in the attitude of the old Indians and that of the soldiers. The old men told their deeds with vehemence and expression, as if the honors they were reporting took place yesterday. The younger fellows were self-conscious and we could hardly hear them speak.

After the counting of the coups, three black rings are painted around the tree about the height of a man above its base. The rings represent the three nights of suffering the dancers are to undergo; they will be fasting from this morning until the end of the dance. A coup is recited for each ring.

The bark is left on the tree. In the fork a bundle of willow shoots is tied, giving the appearance of a cross. Indians today insist it represents the Christian cross, but originally it must have symbolized the Morning Star, Thunderbird's Nest, or Four Directions. Willows grow by the water, the sustainer of all life. Just below the fork, so that it will appear on the west side of the pole when erected, is tied the mounted buffalo head. White rings are painted around its eyes and sage is stuffed in its mouth and nostrils. Representing the great herds upon which the tribes once depended, it is still a symbol of plenty. To the tips of the fork are tied streamers of cloth, blue for the night on one, white for the day on the other. These colors also represent truth and purity.

Now the tree is ready and is raised in a ceremonial manner. Tipi poles, tied together in pairs, and at varying distances, are used as props, and the tree is raised in four symbolic movements (see page 202).

At one of the Crow Sun Dances we attended, just as the tree was raised into position and its butt slipped into the hole, the buffalo head came loose from its upper ties and turned completely around, so that it hung upside down. In the old days this would have been regarded as a very bad omen and might have ended the dance then and there. But the Crows, completely unabashed, sent a man up the tree with pole-climbers attached to his shoes, and he turned the head back right side up, refastened it, and came down again. A few of the Indians thought this amusing, making jokes about the incident and the climber, who responded good-naturedly to their jests as he worked high up above them.

The center pole, or tree, once erected represents, as with other tribes, the center of the world, the power of fruitfulness, the tree of life, the trail from the earth to the sky, even the Great Spirit Himself. The dancing lodge is erected in a circle around it, with an entrance facing the east and the rising sun. Twelve posts about eight feet high, with small forks at their tips, are set in the ground to form the circle, connecting poles are laid in the forks, and long stringers are run from each support post to the fork of the tree in the center—the usual form of Sun Dance lodge with all tribes except the Sioux and the Poncas, and of course the old-time Crows (see page 202). They will tell you these twelve stringers represent the Twelve Apostles, but they will also tell you that the lodge is constructed just as it was hundreds of years ago. It is doubtful that the Sun Dance existed hundreds of years ago, but at least it is older than any Christian contact.

Indians nowadays give a number of Christian interpretations to their Sun dances in an effort to break down prejudice on the part of the whites. Many Christian Indians do attend the Sun Dance, some merely as spectators, but others join with the singers at the drum. The Crow-Shoshoni dance does use a drum and not the dried hide formerly used in many Sun dances. Most Indians have always had a very tolerant attitude toward religion, and it is hard for them to understand how any one group can claim to have the only direct path to the Great Mystery.

During these first performances of the Shoshoni-type Sun Dance by the Crows, a stuffed golden eagle, chief of all the creatures of the air, powerful in battle, was fastened to the rafter over the entrance as a prayer for victory. The eagle is still used, for he is the guardian protecting the people from evil.

All kinds of fresh, green brush are gathered and leaned around the lodge, except for the entrance, and thatched over the outer perimeter of the rafters to form a shade. As with other tribes, the floor of the lodge represents the world; the arbor, the dome of the sky.

Early in the evening, after the completion of the lodge, the dancers arrive. Barefooted; wearing colorful kilts usually made of Pendleton shawls or blankets; upper bodies bare except for ceremonial red, yellow, or white paint; sacred, mystical designs upon their faces; long hair; and medicine whistles, they present a thrilling sight. They parade around the outside of the lodge, sunwise, then enter, line up around the inner "wall" facing the sacred pole in the center, raise their arms, and make the opening prayer of the Sun Dance, blowing their eagle-bone whistles in a long, sustained tremolo.

Once the dance begins, the whistles are blown in time with the song, the fluffy eagle plumes attached to them dancing in time. There are literally hundreds of Sun Dance songs, the choice being up to the leader of the singers. The men singers sit around a large bass drum, placed to the south of the entrance. They are assisted by a number of women, who sing an octave higher and keep time by shaking willow wands up and down. The drum, the songs, everything and every action used in the Sun Dance have symbolical meanings and are the visible forms of specific prayers. The spirited dancing songs, the trembling willows, the blowing feathers all unite to

The Crow Sun Dance. The dancers' stalls have not yet been erected. The rope in the foreground prevents spectators from entering. Photo by Gladys Laubin.

give an impression that everyone, everything, is moving in harmony with the great rhythm of the universe.

The dancers charge in to the center pole, whirling eagle fluffies in each hand, then slowly retreat, facing the pole, constantly blowing their whistles. The drum beats louder and the song becomes stronger as they approach the pole; the rhythm remains steady throughout, but the drum softens as they retreat. While dancing in place their step is like that of other tribes, but in the charge to the pole various steps are used. Some run ahead, others use a limping step, some advance jumping ahead on both feet. The Sun Dance is a pageant of movement and color (page 203).

The Crows have had turnouts of from seventy-five to one hundred and fifteen dancers, which means that it is practically impossible for them to keep changing posi-

Yellow Brow in his late eighties, blowing his eagle-wing whistle in the Crow Sun Dance. Photo by Gladys Laubin.

tion during the day so as to continually face the sun, as is the case with other tribes. Whether this was so with Shoshonis, too, in earlier times, we do not know. But we do know that they consider the pole the important thing, and so always face it. The Crows have doubtless had the greatest numbers of Sun Dancers ever to take part in the ceremony.

Women go through the ordeal of fasting, just as the men do, neither eating nor drinking for the duration of the ceremonies. Sometimes they even stand in the line of dancers at the rear of the lodge, but they do not advance to the pole and retreat. One Crow woman we know has taken part in several Sun dances and tells us she always feels better as a result.

The men dancers have ranged in age from fifteen to eighty-seven years—the age of Holds-the-Enemy when he went through the entire ritual of fasting and dancing in 1943. In 1945 the oldest dancers were Yellow Brow and Buffalo, both past eighty. Each of these men fasted two days before beginning the Sun Dance, then continued to fast and dance three more days and nights. During the ceremonies of 1944, young fellows home on leave from the Armed Forces had had difficulty with the Sun Dance ordeal. Yellow Brow had harangued them, "Did you come here to rest or to dance?" They replied, "All right, grandfather! If you think it is so easy, why don't you do it?" So Yellow Brow did the dance the following year. Not only that, but he danced with more spirit and vigor and fasted longer than any of the young fellows. Afterward we asked how he and the other old man, Buffalo, made such a superior showing over the young men. He answered, "It is the way we think."

According to what the dancers tell us, thirsting is the greatest hardship. One dancer told us that after the first day he was no longer hungry but that every mud puddle and water hole he had ever seen in his life came before his eyes. Another said he felt as if he "could spit cotton." When dancers are so nearly overcome with thirst that they can endure it no longer, the medicine man doctors them and gives them permission to dance to the pole and touch it with the plume at the end of their whistles. They claim that they thus draw water from the pole, that all trace of thirst vanishes, and they are renewed in strength.

When Buffalo was so nearly exhausted he could hardly stay on his feet, he took hold of the pole with his hands and asked the medicine man to bless him (see page 204). Bad Boy, a medicine man's apprentice, borrowed the whistle from the Shoshoni medicine men, placed it against the pole, sucked on it, and sprayed "something cold, like water," all over Buffalo's shoulders and back. Bad Boy himself said it tasted like sap from the tree. Certain it is that he himself, after dancing almost continuously for two days and nights without water, had no saliva left to make such a spray. Truhero, the Shoshoni medicine man, performed this feat several times for exhausted dancers and seemed to be able to transfer his "medicine" to others.

Healing is considered one feature of the present-day Sun Dance, and the Crows claim that various ailments, diseases and vices, have been cured by participation in it. They believe they have replaced their old bodies with new ones, discarded evil thoughts, and taken on a new attitude. We saw one Indian spectator crippled with arthritis go in to the sacred pole on crutches and, after being blessed by the medicine man, throw them away and walk back to his seat without assistance.

All through the night a fire is kept burning just inside the entrance. It has the practical purpose of lighting the lodge for continued dancing and the symbolical one of signaling the approach of the sun at dawn. Among some tribes the fire was originally fed by sticks which brave warriors, counting a coup for each one, placed on it.

One of the most impressive ceremonies takes place at dawn each morning (see page 205). As the first rays of light appear, the dancing becomes more vigorous, for the approaching day will bring a new world to all mankind. Just as Grandfather Sun appears over the horizon, the dancers form a line facing him with outstretched arms and open palms, blowing steadily upon their whistles, as they did at the start of the

Big Day, Crow Sun Dance Leader, offering a prayer. Under his leadership the Sacred Pole was peeled, rather than painted. The partitions to the dancers' stalls have been erected. Photo by Gladys Laubin.

319

dance the previous evening. When the sun has cleared the horizon they gather their robes and seat themselves on the ground, to the west of the fire, pulling their robes over their heads, while their leader makes an earnest prayer for the benefit of people everywhere. The dancers respond with a morning chant, or hymn, repeated four times. Following this prayer period the dancers are allowed a couple of hours' rest while the singers and drummers leave the lodge. Except for this early-morning rest, someone must be dancing all the time.

On the second morning, during this rest period, peeled willow rods about an inch and a half in diameter are used to erect a little stall for each dancer along the inner wall of the lodge, at the rear. These rods, or thin poles, are painted yellow and white. A tired dancer can hold on to the two forming his stall for support as he dances. When the dancing is resumed friends and relatives bring armloads of fresh rushes and mint, which are spread upon the ground in the stalls. It seems as if a cool breeze from the north has suddenly come up, so fragrant and refreshing are the rushes. In later periods of rest the dancers lie on them.

During lulls in the dancing, some of the spectators are brought forward to touch the sacred pole and to be blessed by one of the medicine men. To tread the bosom of Mother Earth within the sacred lodge, one must show proper respect by removing his footwear. The Sun Dance Priest places his hands on the shoulders of his patients and makes prayers for them, then symbolically drives away all evil by fanning them with the eagle feathers he carries in his hand.

Each morning the ceremonial paint on the bodies of the dancers is renewed, usually in completely different colors and designs from those of the previous day. Each dancer engages some older man to do this for him, a man who has power. The colors and designs and the manner in which they are applied all express the potency of the dancer's prayer. As the paint changes the appearance of the individual, so the prayer can change his character and his old self.

About noon of the fourth day the consummation of the prayer of the Sun Dance is achieved, the dancers' vows have been fulfilled. Once more they all face the center pole, stretch out their arms, and blow steadily upon their eagle-bone whistles, bringing the rituals to a close. The Priest blesses a special drink they are to take to break their long fast. It is contained in a large bowl which he passes from dancer to dancer. The dancers claim that this bowl was empty when placed at the foot of the tree but full when the Priest picked it up. After drinking this sacred potion, the dancers are allowed to drink as they choose. Yellow Brow and Buffalo asked us for water and for orange juice, but the younger fellows wanted pop or beer!

The participants then retire to sweat lodges, where the ancient rites of the vapor bath are performed. With this final act they believe themselves to be purified both spiritually and physically and to have received inspiration and courage to face whatever trials may present themselves in the coming year. A feast is prepared for the dancers by friends and relatives, and the Sun Dance is officially over.

But whenever you see a full moon you will know that members of the Sun Dance Society are gathering to hold a Sun Dance "sing." There they unwrap their "medi-

A Shoshoni Sun Dance Priest blessing patients with eagle feathers near the Sacred Pole. (The present-day Crow Sun Dance is the same as the Shoshoni). Photo by Gladys Laubin.

cine feathers," given them by the medicine man—a recent innovation from the Shoshonis—sing Sun Dance songs, and have a prayer meeting.

On one such occasion, when the Sun Dance proper was over and the great camp had been dismantled, we had the only tipi remaining on the ground. The Sun Dancers gathered for their meeting under a brush arbor and as the evening wore on, it began to look like rain. The Sun Dance sponsor asked me if he could leave the sacred buffalo head in our tipi. The painted white rings around the eyes and the sage stuffed in the mouth and nostrils, in addition to its being a very large head, gave it an extremely grotesque appearance.

Gladys had already gone to bed, but I helped carry it into the tipi and placed it beside the door without disturbing her. Then I went back to the meeting. By and by the sky cleared and the full moon came out in all its beauty. About that time Gladys awoke. Looking across the tipi, she saw that tremendous buffalo head silhouetted against the doorway in the moonlight. She nearly went straight up through the smoke hole!

SUMMARY

Some of the recent innovations in the Sun Dance suggest that the underlying motives are gradually changing or dying out. For instance, during the most recent Sun dances many of the dancers have been wearing sunglasses! Also, some of the younger dancers are wearing silk scarfs around their chests, instead of appearing bare-chested like the old-timers. When we first went to the Sun Dance, even men with short hair attached braids to their headbands. After that, the ones with short hair made no effort to change its appearance.

Shoshonis and Arapahos on the Wind River Reservation in Wyoming often hold their Sun dances at the same time, but on their own sections of the reservation. The Arapahos use sixteen stringers, or rafters, to the center pole, each decorated with pennants and offerings. They have a very elaborate altar. Otherwise, their Sun Dance is much like that of the Cheyennes. They dance in place, changing position gradually so as always to face the sun, but they do not charge in to the pole and back. So to the tourist, the Shoshoni dance presents more of a spectacle.

From all the study that has been made, it seems that the Sun Dance, as we know it today and as it has been known for the past hundred years, is a recent phenomenon. But it had its origin in other, much older ceremonies. Even tribes which had no real Sun Dance had older rituals which seem to be related to it. The Omahas had an annual summer ceremony, following the tribal buffalo hunt, in which a green cottonwood tree was cut, ceremonially painted, and erected as the center of the ceremonies. It had the usual Sun Dance significance, representing a man, an enemy, tribal unity, and the like. We had the privilege of attending a dozen Sun dances over the years.

One more note of interest: in the original Crow Sun Dance, a special character known as the Bird Man was supposed to "raise" the four main poles by flapping his arms like wings, while several men did the actual raising. To show how some of these seemingly inconsequential details spread from tribe to tribe, among both Blackfeet and Arikaras a man stood on the center pole before it was raised, flapping his arms in birdlike movements.

The Crows formerly had a very important fetish in the shape of a doll which was placed on the altar. Long ago Kiowas and Crows were neighbors, and later, when separated by long distances, they remained friends and visited back and forth. So the Kiowas also used a doll in their Sun Dance. The sacred headdress worn by the Black-foot Sun Dance Woman also has a doll attached to it. All these dolls seem to be stuffed with tobacco seeds, the most sacred plant of most Indian tribes.

To those who may be primarily interested in dance, the important thing in studying a ritual as involved as the Sun Dance is that dance, no matter how simple, played such an important part. To learn something of the significance of the dance, we must understand the relationship of dance to ritual. The dancing was not done to be spectacular, or to entertain, but to participate to the fullest, to play an important role in the drama of the ritual. In no other way but dance can one put so much of his being into the occasion. Even when the dancing was limited to a slight movement of the body or of the hands in time with the songs, it nevertheless was important enough that the Indians called the entire ritual a *dance*.

The Crows still hold a Sun Dance each summer, as do many of the tribes we have mentioned. But some of our friends have ranches up in the hills and have been unable to attend. So, they travel all the way to Fort Hall, Idaho, to take part in the Sho-shoni-Bannock Sun Dance, which comes later in the season, after their important ranch work is done. They usually call us up on the telephone from Yellowstone Park on their way, asking us to have a sweat lodge ready for them when they arrive at our home en route.

17. Society Dances: The Warrior Societies

The warrior societies make up a complicated and involved subject. Their significance and importance have not been generally understood, and many writers have given confusing accounts of them. Few have pointed out the importance of dance to them, for these societies were not only greatly involved in tribal life and welfare but were also dancing societies.

The following is but a brief synopsis of societies we consider outstanding and contains new material from my Indian father, Chief One Bull.

Each warrior society, of whatever tribe, had its own songs, dances, and regalia. Robert Lowie says that among the Crows "each club welcomed volunteers attracted by its dance or regalia."[1] The same statement might be made for many tribes. Costume was very important; some of it was extremely colorful, even spectacular. A man could hardly help being proud to appear in such fancy garb. Much of the glory of belonging to one of these societies came in taking part in the many parades through the camp.

Maximilian seemed particularly interested in these "bands," or "unions," as he called them. Other writers speak of them as "clubs," "lodges," or "fraternities." In some ways they were comparable to our civic and fraternal organizations. With Plains Indians, however, these societies usually did have important military significance, although they rarely went to war as a unit. In some tribes, notably the Village tribes (Mandans, Hidatsas, and Arikaras) in the North and the Kiowas in the South, they were graded according to age. The child and teen-age groups might be considered as training units for future warriors.

Some writers call these clubs "soldier societies." Among the Sioux one class, the largest, was known as *aki'cita oko'la-kiciye*. *Aki'cita* would best translate as "soldier." Translated into English, most of the Cheyenne societies were known as soldier societies, too. Because certain of these Cheyenne and Sioux societies played an important role in the late Indian wars, it has been supposed by some that the Dog Soldiers, for example, were known to every Plains tribe. We shall see that there was a good deal of similarity among the various societies, but there were also many differences.

Maximilian listed six societies each for the Mandans and the Arikaras. For the former he named Foolish Dogs; Crows, or Ravens; Soldiers; Dogs; Buffaloes; and Black-tailed Deer. For the "Arikkaras" he gave Bears; Mad Wolves; Foxes; Mad Dogs; Mad Bulls; and Soldiers. He said, "Besides these bands, the Arikkaras have, at least, seven different dances." These were Hot Dance, Bird's Egg, Dance of the Youngest Child, Prairie Fox, White Earth, Dance of the Spirits, and Dance of the Extended

Hidatsa Dog Dancer, the familiar painting by Bodmer, from Prince Maximilian's *Travels*. Seldom, if ever, has it been mentioned that similar headdresses were worn by leaders of Dogs or related warrior societies of many tribes. Smithsonian Institution, Bureau of American Ethnology.

WARRIOR AND OTHER SOCIETIES*

Mandan	Arikara	Hidatsa
1. Foolish Dogs	4. Mad Dogs	Crazy Dogs
2. Crows, or Ravens	Crows	Ravens
3. Soldiers (Black Mouths)	6. Soldiers	*Black (Muddy) Mouths
4. Dogs	2. Mad Wolves	Dogs
5. Buffaloes	5. Mad Bulls	Bulls
6. Black-tailed Deer		
———————————	——————————	——————————
———————————	1. Bears	
	3. Foxes	Kit Foxes
Little Dogs	Young Dogs	Small Dogs
——————		*Strong Hearts
	——————	——————
Half-shaved Heads	——————	Half-shaved Heads
——————	——————	——————
——————		Stone Hammer

Hot Dance

Women's Societies

Band of the Gun
River
Hay
White Cow

---

*Numbers for Mandans, Arikaras, Crows, and Blackfeet are Maximilian's.

326

Crow

Crazy Dogs, Long Crazy Dogs
3. Ravens
_____
8. Big Dogs
1. Bulls
_____
_____
2. Prairie Foxes
7. Little Dogs (Muddy Mouths)
_____
*5. Lumpwoods (4. Half-shaved Heads)
   Muddy Hands (Foxes)
*6. Stone Hammers
_____
_____
_____
_____
_____
_____

Hot Dance
_____
_____
_____
_____
_____
_____
_____
_____

Crazy Dogs Wishing to Die
_____
_____

Blackfoot

Crazy Dogs
4. Carry the Raven
6. Soldiers
2. Dogs
7. Buffalo Bulls
_____
Kit Foxes
3. Prairie Dogs
*5. Buffalo with Thin Horns
_____
_____
_____
_____
_____
_____
_____
_____
_____

Grass Dance
_____
_____
_____
_____
_____
_____
_____

1. Mosquitoes (Atsina—Flies)
_____
_____
_____

---

*Most important of their class or type.

Sioux

Assiniboin*	Oglala	Hunkpapa
6. Crows	Raven, or Crow, Owners	Kangiyuha
3. Soldiers		
Big Dogs	Dogs, or Wolves	Sunktokeca
8. Bulls	Chiefs	Tatanka Wapaha
1. Kit Foxes	*Kit Fox	*Tokala
Small Dogs		
	*Strong Heart	*Cante Tinza
2. Braves (Nappaishene)	Napeyasni (No Flight)	
	Badgers	Iȟoka (Hin'p̓op̓opa)
	Sotka Yuha (Bare Lance Owners)	Sotka Yuha
	White Marked	Wi'ciska
	Miwatani	Miwatani
	Sotka Tanka	
	*Sacred Bow	
Grass Dance	Omaha	Ohitika, Pejiwacipi, Omaha
		O'iglapta (Help Themselves)
		Ozuye (Warpath)
		Ska akan'yanka
4. Ducks		(White Riders)
5. White Cranes		
7. Mice Comrades		
Gakoges (Scrapes)		
Gakemeze (Stripes)		
	*Heyoka	Heyoka
		*Naca
		Wabilénicá (Orphans)
	Women's Societies	
	Shield Owners	
	Winyan Tapika	
	Wild Carrot	
	Owns Alone	
	Prairie Chicken	
	Wi'cilo (Favorite Son)	
	Tanners	
	Porcupine Quill Workers	

*Denig's numbers.

Santee

———————————
Raven Owners
———————————
———————————
———————————
———————————
———————————

Kit Fox
———————————

———————————
No Flight
———————————

———————————
Badgers
———————————

Owl Feather
———————————

———————————
Omaha
———————————
———————————
———————————
———————————
———————————
———————————
———————————
———————————
———————————

Heyoka
Thunder
———————————

Cheyenne

Northern Crazy Dogs
———————————

Dog Men and Wolves
*Shield Soldiers (also known as Bulls)
———————————

Fox
———————————
———————————
———————————
———————————
———————————
———————————
———————————
———————————

Bowstring Soldiers
    Omaha?
———————————
———————————
———————————
———————————
———————————
———————————
———————————
———————————

Elk Soldiers
Inverted Soldiers (Contraries)
———————————
———————————

Robe. In the latter the dancer held a buffalo robe over one arm, like a shield, and imitated battle maneuvers. It was participated in only by the bravest warriors.

Maximilian said that the Mandan Foolish Dogs were boys ten to fifteen years of age. But already, in his day, things had begun to change, for he wrote that formerly older people had also belonged and that when in battle they dared not retreat. The Crows, or Ravens, were young men twenty to twenty-five years old; the Soldiers consisted of the most eminent and esteemed warriors; the Black-tailed Deer were men about fifty years old.

The Ravens' ritual sometimes lasted forty nights! The Soldiers had two members who carried staffs decorated with owl feathers. Once a staff was stuck in the ground, its owner dared not retreat. The only way he could be saved in case of an overwhelming enemy charge was by some brave companion pulling up the staff, thereby "setting him free" and allowing him to escape with the others. This same custom was carried out by certain members of most warrior societies.

The Mandan Dogs had elaborate feather headdresses and costumes like the one shown in Bodmer's famous painting of the Hidatsa Dog Dancer; the Mandans and Hidatsas were neighbors. The Dogs danced with rattles made of deer hoofs, or dewclaws, fastened to a stick.

The Buffaloes had two members who wore masks; they could not retreat.

Using Maximilian's list of Mandan societies as a basis, we have made a chart showing societies of Northern Plains tribes with which we are most familiar. We can easily see how several tribes had organizations of the same or similar names, and we know that warrior societies were much the same among them all. The numbers used for Mandan, Arikara, Crow, and Blackfoot societies are Maximilian's, so that you may see the order in which he listed them. The numbers for the Assiniboins are Denig's. One might make a similar chart for tribes of the Southern Plains, or a large enough one to take in both North and South.

Among all the tribes there were certain of the societies which served as camp police. The ones the Sioux designate as *akicita* were the ones that could be called upon for police duty. Usually only one society served as police at a time, taking turns with the others. The police were especially in charge of the tribal buffalo hunts. In war, and in everyday life, the individual was free to do just about as he pleased, as long as he did not disturb or endanger his neighbors. Even the chief of a war party had little actual authority. A plan of attack or of ambush might be made, but if some young fellow decided he would rather distinguish himself in a rash personal attack on the enemy he tried to do so. The police might try to hold him back, but if he succeeded in eluding them no punishment was meted out, even if the entire plan of attack had to be discarded or changed as a result. Instead of being punished, such a hothead if he succeeded in counting a coup would be the hero of the day.

Not so with the tribal buffalo hunt, however. At that time no man was allowed to hunt alone, and no one could start the hunt until the signal was given by the police in command. To risk their disfavor on such an occasion would mean that, if caught, the culprit would be whipped unmercifully, his best buffalo horse would be killed, and his lodge would be cut to shreds.

The police were also responsible for seeing that orders of the tribal council were carried out in other matters, but seldom were they as severe as on the tribal hunt.

Among people such as the Mandans, whose societies were graded according to age, when a member of a lower society became old enough he could purchase membership into the next-higher society with presents to a member of that society. This member either stepped out altogether or tried for the next-higher society to which his age and accomplishments entitled him. Society membership was thus more or less stable. The drums, rattles, and regalia likewise had to be purchased from outgoing members. For example, a Raven bought a Half-shorn Dance and costume from a Soldier before being eligible for entrance into the Soldiers.

Dances and songs were also regarded as property, either personal or belonging to a group, and were purchased with material goods—horses, blankets, beadwork, and so on—or they could be exchanged as property. No one could perform a dance or sing a song unless he had the right to do so.

There were three classes of Dogs: Little Dogs, Dogs, Old Dogs. The Little Dogs had a Hot Dance in which they danced barefoot on hot coals and dipped meat from a boiling kettle with their bare hands, eating it hot. They painted their lower arms, feet, and ankles red. Late-comers had to go the deepest into the boiling water. The Old Dogs bought their dance and regalia from the "Buffaloes" before being admitted into membership into that society.

We find no Black-tailed Deer among the other tribes we have listed, but since its members were older men, it may have been the equivalent of the Chief's Society of the Sioux.

Among both the Hidatsas and Mandans the Soldiers painted their mouths black, so they were also known as Black, or Muddy, Mouths. They were the only ones among the Village tribes to serve in the capacity of police.

Boler mentioned Stronghearts for the *Minnetarres* (Hidatsas). It is possible that he was confused with some other society, for otherwise this seems to be a society of the Teton Sioux, or Lakotas.

Speaking of the Mandans again, Maximilian said the women also had "bands" and that they also had their "peculiar dances." "These bands, or unions," he wrote, "give occasion to many festivities, with singing, music and dancing." After dances of the "unions" he gives Scalp Dance as most important.

He said the Hidatsas had eleven bands among the men, three among the women, plus two distinct dances—the Dance of the Old Men and the Scalp Dance, danced by the women.

THE CROWS

The Absarokas, or Crows, close relatives of the Hidatsas, nevertheless had a somewhat different conception of the warrior societies. Age played a minor part in the membership, and one did not have to "buy" his way into a club. He came in through invitation, which sometimes was made because of very strong hints on his part that he would like to join. In Maximilian's time the Bulls were the most important society among the Crows, but in later years the Lumpwoods and Foxes took over, being rivals for the number one position. As a rule a man joined one society and remained in it the rest of his life, so all ages were represented in each society. There was no initiation fee. Apparently, to the Crows, the hazards a club member faced in battle were fee enough.

Some time after 1870 the Crows received the Hot Dance and the Crazy Dog Dance from the Hidatsas, so to distinguish their original Crazy Dog Dance from this late-comer they called the newer one the Long Crazy Dog Dance. Although the Crows purchased membership in religious societies, such as the Tobacco Lodge and the Sacred Pipe Lodge, they did not apply this system to warrior societies until borrowing these two new ones from their relatives. Then they "sold" certain offices within the club, but still did not demand an initiation fee. In fact, they practically bribed some influential persons to join. With the coming of these new societies, some men belonged to an older one and a new one at the same time. Previously it had been customary to belong to only one club.

THE LONG CRAZY DOGS

The leader of the Long Crazy Dogs wore a cap with two polished deer antlers, and the members all carried ring rattles, which were characteristic of the Cheyenne Dog Soldiers and the Sioux Strong Hearts. The Hot Dance and Long Crazy Dog societies were rivals. Actually, their dancing was much the same and today we have only the Hot Dance left, which will be included under the discussion of the Grass Dance.

THE MUDDY MOUTHS

Many years ago the Hidatsa Muddy (Black) Mouths visited the Crows and taught the members of the Little Dogs their dance. So the Crow Little Dogs then changed their name to Muddy Mouths. In more recent time, when the membership of the Muddy Mouths dwindled, they joined the new Long Crazy Dogs. When the Muddy Mouths held a dance, all the people tied up their dogs because if a dog went after a Muddy Mouth dancer he was supposed to turn on it and kill it.

The Muddy Mouths' two head men carried rattles. The members formed two lines, facing each other, a rattler in front of each line. They began to sing and shake their rattles, dancing toward each other. As they crossed each other's paths all the others shouted and began to dance. When the dance ended, the Whipper, wearing a bear-skin belt, touched each man with his quirt before he could be seated. He also approached them when they were to dance again. In the case of the Muddy Mouths, the dancing was quite different from that of most societies, because it was reported to be like the Hot, or Grass, Dance, which can be very vigorous and active, with many fancy steps and flourishes. So we have this society and the Long Crazy Dogs dancing in the style of the Hot Dance.

But the older society, the Crazy Dogs, jumped in place, hard, on both feet, shaking and jarring their bodies as they shook gourd-shaped rawhide rattles in time to the songs. Crows also had a society of Big Dogs, which danced in no particular order, but jumped and leaped forward individually, leaning their bodies forward as they progressed. Each song got faster, and on the last song they danced more vigorously than ever.

THE LUMPWOODS AND HALF-SHAVED HEADS

Maximilian named the Lumpwoods and Half-shaved Heads as separated societies, but according to Lowie the original society was the Half-shaved Heads. They plucked, or shaved, the front of their heads almost to the crown. After one of the members counted a coup with a knobby, or lumpy, club, the society changed its name to Lumpwoods. There were often divisions within a club or society, especially among the Crows and the other tribes that did not observe age grouping. The Lumpwood younger members were known as Lumpwoods without Sweethearts, the older members were called Old Lumpwoods, and those in between were the Tall Lumpwoods.[2] The Lumpwoods danced in place, swinging their right arms as far back as possible and forward to normal again.

THE MUDDY HANDS AND FOXES

The early writers did not mention the Muddy Hands for the Crows, but this was once an important society. Apparently its members were older men, and when membership dropped to about fifty, between 1865 and 1870, they accepted an invitation to join the Foxes. As one mark of peculiarity, the Muddy Hands seldom extinguished a fire, because the fire represented the enemy. After the group had moved off and left a fire burning, a very brave member might go back and put it out, but by so doing he pledged himself never to retreat from an enemy.

The Foxes roached their hair after the manner of some of the Woodland tribes. This seems to be a distinctive mark for the Fox Society among many tribes. This is probably the society Maximilian called the Prairie Foxes.

When the Foxes danced, they formed an arc of a circle, moving to the left, jumping on both feet. But the Muddy Hands, before joining the Foxes, had a different procedure. Two of their members, dressed for war, weapons in their hands, rode up and struck a pole to which a buffalo hide, which represented the enemy, was tied. These two men then acted out their war experiences.

THE HAMMER SOCIETY

Maximilian listed a Stone Hammer Society for the Crows, but the stone hammer emblem was used by the Hidatsas. The Crow hammer emblem, although similar in pattern, was made of wood, and they called their society merely the Hammers, or Hammer Owners.

THE BEARS AND BULLS

Among most tribes, a Bull Society was made up of older men—men who had been great warriors but whose fighting days were over. But among the Arikaras, Maximilian names the Bears as the number one society, and it was composed of distinguished older men.

In the former Crow Bull Society there were two men who wore masks and portrayed blind buffalo bulls, the most dangerous of animals. In the National Museum in Washington, D.C., there is a Mandan bull mask, made from the skin of a buffalo's head, which looks like the entire head of a buffalo bull. The eyes are covered with red flannel and tin and, of course, are much farther apart than are a man's eyes. We wondered how the dancer could see, for upon examining the mask we found no eye holes in it whatever. Members of the anthropological staff could offer no solution. When we heard about the bull masks of the Crow society, our puzzle was apparently solved. For, if the dancers were imitating blind buffalo, what could be more realistic than a mask which made them, in effect, blind?

THE BLACKFEET

Maximilian said the Blackfeet had seven warrior societies and a Scalp Dance, performed by the women dressed as men, carrying arms. Also they had a "dance of the braves, or warriors, who form a circle, within which several dance, imitating all the movements of battle, and firing their guns, on which occasion their faces are painted so as to give them a fierce expression."[3]

We think that on this occasion the prince fell for the usual story of "war paint." Face painting for war was usually protective to the wearer rather than an effort to frighten the enemy. But some warriors may have believed their particular paint was powerful enough to frighten him!

THE MOSQUITOES

We find some new names among these Blackfoot societies, such as Mosquitoes for the youngest. The Atsinas (often called Gros Ventres or Gros Ventres of the Prairie), neighbors and allies of the Blackfeet, had a society of youngsters known as Flies. The nearest thing to these names among other tribes with which we are familiar was the Mice Comrades of the Assiniboins, who used to raid the drying racks for meat and otherwise get into mischief.

THE PRAIRIE DOGS AND HORNS

The Blackfeet had a society known as Prairie Dogs who served as police. According to Maximilian, their Soldiers were also the most distinguished warriors, but the Buffalo Bulls ranked highest because they were retired warriors with great reputations.

In recent years one of the most famous of the Blackfeet societies was the Horn Society. We wonder if this might have been the Buffalo With Thin Horns listed by Maximilian, for some of its members did wear bonnets with split, or thin, buffalo horns, just as some similar societies of other tribes did.

THE ASSINIBOINS

THE KIT FOXES

Edwin Thompson Denig, reporting on the Assiniboins in 1854, gave a different pattern to the Fox, or Kit Fox, Society dance of that tribe, from the others we have mentioned. They started at "a swift pace," representing the movements of a coiling snake, much like the snake dance at a football rally. After the line was "wound up," the dancers began to jump up and down, striking one foot immediately after the other, keeping exact time and all singing along with the main singers. This dance lasted about a minute, when there was a flourish on the drums, a shout from the dancers, and all formed a line again. One man stepped out, counted coup, and the drummers thumped their approval. The dance was repeated after each counting of coup, and each man was given an opportunity of telling his exploits.

These Foxes were all young men in their twenties. Instead of fox jawbones, Denig says they wore fox teeth, bored and strung across their foreheads from ear to ear. Instead of shaving the head and roaching the hair, they gathered the front hair in a bunch, tied like a horn, the rest hanging loose behind. Four eagle feathers were attached near the center of the head. But they did wear the fox skins on their shoulders, like the Lakotas.

THE BRAVES

Denig also listed a Braves Dance, Nappaishene, which must be like the Napeyaśni of the Oglalas. He said their dance was similar to that of the Foxes, except that the song stopped while the drum continued. This sounds like a contest dance still done today by several Plains tribes. At each step the dancers grunted. First they danced in place in a circle, then, bending low, they pressed to the center, turning and looking in every direction, without order. When they were huddled close, the song stopped, but the dancing continued for a time, when they all yelled, broke from the huddle, and formed the circle again.

Their outstanding costume was no costume at all. They danced completely naked, with painted bodies. A favorite way of painting was with red and yellow stripes from head to foot. Another was a red face and yellow body, or red face and white-striped body. Some faces were painted with white, yellow, or red spots. Skunk or fox tails were worn on the heels of the moccasins, and all members carried their weapons. Everyone was given a chance to count his coups, the drummers responding with thumps on the drum, the number depending upon the value of the exploit. In this way the dance might last for hours. It was given two or three times a year.[4]

THE CHEYENNES

Much has been written about the Cheyenne warrior societies, and sometimes several names have been used for one society, resulting in some confusion. Originally there

Cheyenne Soldier Societies Dancing, by Dick West, Cheyenne artist. Photo by Bob McCormack.

were five societies among the Cheyennes—Fox Soldiers, Elk Soldiers, Shield Soldiers, Dog Soldiers, and Wolf Soldiers. After the tribe had split into Northern and Southern divisions, the Wolves of the Northern half became the Northern Foolish Dogs and those of the Southern half became the Bowstring Soldiers.

Other names have also been associated with some of these groups. The Foxes were also known as Kit Fox, Swift Fox, and Coyote. The Elks were known as Elk Horn Scrapers, Hoof Rattle, Crooked Lance, Headed Lance, Medicine Lance. The Shields were often called Red Shield, Buffalo Bull, Buffalo, or Bull. The Bowstring

Soldiers were sometimes called Owl Man's Bowstring or also Wolf Soldiers. The Dog Soldiers were called Dog Men or just plain Dogs.[5]

THE DOG SOLDIERS

The Dog Soldiers were in the unusual position of being all of one band, or tribal division. When the society was first organized long ago, all the male members of the Flexed Leg Band joined the Dogs, and the society retained this unique association. Consequently it camped as one unit in the tribal circle, whereas other society memberships were divided among several bands and thus scattered throughout the camp circle. So the Dog Soldiers exerted a great influence on the political life of the Cheyennes. They also fought as a unit, which other societies seldom did. For these reasons they were well known outside the tribe and were written about more than any of the others.

THE LAKOTAS

We find that among the Lakotas the warrior societies were most numerous. Clark Wissler made an extensive study of the societies among the Oglalas, as did Robert Lowie for the Eastern, or Santee, Sioux. We are drawing on our own experience with the *Huńkpapa* for an account of the societies within that division. In a tribe as large and with as many subdivisions as the Sioux, we could hardly expect to find all divisions having the same societies. As we can see from the chart, the Oglala and Hunkpapa did have some of the same societies, but each also had a number of different ones.

It was customary among the Lakotas for a true *akicita*—soldier, or police—society to select new members at a secret meeting, and one was not notified until he was "captured." A delegation was sent to take him. As soon as he heard that he was to be made a member he struggled to escape, making as much of a show of it as possible. It was, of course, a great honor to be selected for membership in one of the warrior societies, but as part of the game the candidate was expected to try to run away from the responsibilities and dangers entailed in joining such a band of daredevils. After he was "captured" he was dragged, or carried, to the ceremonial tipi for the initiation rites.

Most of our information came from my Indian "father," Chief One Bull. By birth, One Bull was a Minikon'ju, the son of one of the leading chiefs, Makes Room (They Make Room for Him). But as a lad One Bull was adopted by his uncle Sitting Bull, who was Hunkpapa, and so from then on in tribal matters he always considered himself of that division.

THE NACA

Flying Cloud, our interpreter, spoke of the warrior societies as "lodges." One Bull said that if a young man belonged to no society he was known as a No Lodge. All the Hunkpapa societies, except Omaha, and Naca, served as *aki'cita*—soldiers or police. The Hunkpapas rated Naca highest of their lodges, for Naca members were

Chief One Bull as a young man, a member of the Naca, Strong Heart, and Fox societies. Laubin Collection.

in training for chieftainship. One was usually invited to join Naca after thirty years of age, but because he came from a chief family One Bull was asked to join as an honorary member while in his twenties. His real father was a chief, he was "son" of Chief Sitting Bull, at that time the elected chief of all the Lakotas, and he was also related to Four Horns, another prominent Hunkpapa chief. He was given the office of Pipe Keeper. This particular pipe was all catlinite, bowl and stem. The Naca interceded in quarrels, and it was One Bull's duty to offer the pipe to the angry participants and thus stop the fight. "To make peace between two tribesmen is your job," the Naca men told him.

The Naca members wore headdresses made of an entire golden eagle skin. The beak was over the forehead, the wings hung over the sides of the head and down over the shoulders, the tail hung behind.

Among the Lakotas, a person joining a society as a full-fledged member paid an entrance fee, which consisted of furnishing a feast for the other members or of giving them presents. But when One Bull was invited in as an honorary member of Naca they gave *him* presents.

After his second warpath, against the Crows, One Bull joined the Tokalas, or Foxes, direct from No Lodge. This was no usual occurrence, for the Foxes were among the oldest and most important of the warrior societies. One Bull was highly honored in this way out of respect for the record he had already made as a warrior.

Although the Sioux did not have the graded-age societies of some other tribes, age, family standing, and certainly war experience had a great deal to do with receiving an invitation to join a certain society. The boys did have societies imitating those of the adults but they were not true age societies.

THE FOXES

One Bull rated Foxes, Strong Hearts, Silent Eaters, and Naca as the foremost societies, Naca being highest. (Strong Hearts and Silent Eaters were divisions of the same society.) All other societies were of equal rank among themselves. Wissler lists Tokala as Kit Fox, but Flying Cloud referred to it merely as Foxes. The Foxes regarded themselves as foxes and called their enemies "marrow bones." They were supposed to find enemies, like foxes do bones. Initiates into the Fox Society had their heads shaved in a roach, Eastern style. After the hair grew out again, if no more initiates were being taken in, two to four members volunteered to have the "Fox haircut." A couple of these shaved-heads always sat with the drummers, assisting with the globular rattles the society used.

The drum was an important piece of society property and was kept in a special cover when not in use. The Drum Keeper took this cover with him when he went into battle. The large dance drum was made of a hollow cottonwood log, with the skins of black-tailed deer for heads. The sides were decorated with bells, scalps, and eagle feathers. The drum was supported on four forked stakes, with porcupine-quill wrappings on the forks and eagle feathers hanging from them. Four special drumsticks were used.

The Foxes had two Whippers, who acted as marshals at the meetings. They brought in new candidates, and, if any member was discharged for cowardice or breaking of society rules, the Whippers ejected him. The whips were "medicine" and gave power in war.

The Lakota Foxes had a dance similar to that of the Fox Society of the Crows. In addition to the Fox haircut, members wore fox skins, slit so as to go over the head, the fox head hanging down over the chest, the tail behind. These skins were decorated with quill work, little bells, and feathers. Fox jawbones, painted red or blue, were fastened to strips of otter skin and worn as headbands, with crow feathers sidewise at the back of the head and two eagle feathers straight up. The officers painted their faces and bodies yellow, with red over the mouth.

When a dancing song was sung, the Foxes, who had been sitting in a circle, rose and danced toward the center. The two Whippers stayed to the outside, pretending to whip the dancers into a bunch. This dance is sometimes spoken of as a begging dance, for the members marched around the camp, stopping at homes of leading men. After a dance, the owner of the tipi was expected to come out with a pipe, of-

Laubin in the Crow Beggar's Dance,
performed by some warrior societies for the benefit of the poor.
Photo by Gladys Laubin.

fering it to the drummers and "giving away" to someone in honor of a child or relative. The performance was staged as a benefit for the "poor." The Foxes themselves received nothing.

The Foxes had, among other regalia, four lances, which was usual to most societies, but two of these were bow lances, as described later for Sotka Tanka and the Sacred Bow Society, except that these had bone points.

When One Bull was in full chief's costume—buckskin war shirt, leggings, and war bonnet—which he wore on important occasions, he at the same time always wore an otter-skin collar with a conch-shell "moon" at the throat, and loops of otter skin attached to his leggings, like garters, just below the knees. These special ornaments, he told us, were emblems of the Fox Society. Even though he had gone on into Strong Hearts and Naca, he always considered his membership in the Fox Society important.

The Foxes had a different ceremony following a feast. Then the lay members were painted red, and all marched around the camp, occasionally stopping to dance. The society had one flat quilled pipe but two Pipe Keepers, who took turns in carrying the pipe. The Pipe Keepers were the leaders of the society and headed the parade, the Pipe Carrier in advance. Next came the two Bow-lance Carriers, then two beaded straight lances, the Whippers, and two Food Bearers, and finally the lay members. When the Pipe Carrier stopped and turned around, all the others gathered around the two leaders and halted. The drum was carried by four singers, who now began to beat and sing. The men owning the special regalia held it up and danced, after which everyone except the singers danced.

After each dance, all lined up again, the Pipe Carrier first, followed by the other officers in order, each falling in as the line marched on, the lay members moving up on a run. Following the last dance, all lined up in the same order, but this time taking their places with the line halted. The Pipe Carrier passed down the line, past the officers, past the main body, around each end of the line and back to his position at the head of the line, like an army officer reviewing his troops. Again taking the lead, the others followed him back to the ceremonial tipi of the Fox Society.

During our participation in the Crow Fairs of the early 1940's, a "begging dance" similar to that of the Foxes was still being given each year. Four men wearing capes of eagle wings led the "Indian file" parade, followed by the dancers, wearing their dyed underwear, porcupine roaches, and "tail feathers"—and, of course, bells. Four men carrying the big bass drum marched near the end of the line. These singers were the only ones not in single file, for two of them had to be at the sides of the drum. They drummed in a steady, marching rhythm, no song, until the leaders stopped in front of an important man's tipi. Then they began a lively song, and the dancers capered in usual Hot Dance style about them. At the close of the song, the tipi owner came out and made a donation to the Fair. Another dance was given in his honor and the parade resumed, marching on until it arrived at another head man's tipi.

THE STRONG HEARTS

One Bull next joined the Strong Hearts, which was perhaps the best known of all the Sioux societies. There seems to be no record of a Strong Heart ever being accused of cowardice or of breaking rules, and its members remained members, whether attending meetings or not. Nevertheless, members were threatened with dismissal if they ever showed cowardice and, if a man did not show up at a meeting, the Strong Heart Whippers (they also had two) might cut up his robe. He could escape this punishment by promising a feast for the whole society.

Within the Strong Hearts was a select group known as the Hanhe'pi Cante' Tin'za, usually translated as the Midnight Strong Hearts, perhaps because they usually held their meetings at night. They might have been called the campaign managers who were responsible for getting Sitting Bull elected to the Chieftainship. Following his election another group of about twenty prominent members of the Strong Hearts formed an elite club known as A'inila Wo'ta—the famous Silent Eaters. This group served as an advisory council, and because of its serious nature ate in silence. They permitted no storytelling, no jokes, and they had no dance.

One Bull, although a very young man, was selected to belong to the Silent Eaters after a year with the Foxes and almost immediately after joining the Strong Hearts. According to his statements, a man was a life member of any society he joined. Becoming a member of another society did not terminate membership in ones previously joined. One Bull also joined the O'iglapta, Help Themselves. Instead of rivalry between societies, as we found among the Crows, the Lakota lodges often cooperated. In a battle, members of various lodges might help a new warrior count his first coup. When a man won an honor, he also brought honor to his society, so by belonging to several he could bring honor to them all. The Help Themselves and the Silent Eaters combined to assist One Bull in becoming a head man of the Foxes. They presented him with a war bonnet and a pipe. One Bull's brother, Chief White Bull, was previously head of the Minikonju Foxes, but he said the head man there was the Drum Keeper.

When it was necessary to punish someone for violating the regulation against solo hunting at the time of the great tribal hunt, the Four Councilors (Civil Chiefs) usually designated either Foxes or Strong Hearts to carry out their sentence. All societies collaborated in electing a chief. When the choice was made, the Four Councilors substantiated it.

No murderer could belong to any of the warrior societies. A murderer was anyone who killed a tribesman.

Tribal moves, whether in hunting, warfare, or just moving camp, were governed by four "Advisors" who were selected by the Four Councilors. The Advisors could be appointed from any warrior society. They in turn were assisted by two other *akicita* and all were directed by Naca.

The Strong Heart bonnets had two split buffalo horns. These bonnets had beadwork on the brow band and a wide piece of yellow porcupine quilled work, like we see on pipe bags, hanging down in back. Two men were selected to wear these bonnets and long sashes, which were also staked down with picket pins. In addition there were two straight and two crooked lance carriers, who also were bound not to retreat. When dancing, all the dancers carried ring-shaped rattles and wore eagle-wing-bone whistles around their necks. The rattles were swung sidewise and not up and down.

In "Teton Sioux Music" is a photograph of a rattle which Densmore said was from the Strong Hearts. It is globular, but it nevertheless has a ring, or band, of fur around it. It is incised with lines representing a turtle, symbolic of good protection against attackers. All of our own informants, and Wissler's accounts, mentioned *ring-shaped* rattles. We wonder if Miss Densmore's is not really a Raven, or Crow, Owner rattle, which was globular.

When they held a dance, the Strong Hearts circled the camp, two abreast, their two Whippers riding horses on the flanks of the marchers. They stopped to dance at the tipis of head men, just as the Foxes did. Their entire ceremony was much like that of the Foxes.

On days when the Strong Hearts were to have a meeting, four young members went out in the morning in search of meat. Two in advance carried rattles, as a warning of their approach. The two following had bows and arrows, and woe unto any dogs they encountered, for they would serve as food for the society meeting, following the singing and dancing. It was supposed to make a "strong heart" to have your dog killed and not show anger.

Within the Strong Hearts, besides the Midnight Strong Hearts and the Silent Eaters, there was another group known as the Icu Sapa, or Black Chins. They painted their chins black, whereas the rank and file members of the Strong Hearts painted their faces red and wore eagle feathers in their hair. Among the Icu Sapa were another four who wore bonnets and sashes, the bonnets being of bunched owl feathers with a crest of six eagle feathers in the center.

THE NAPEYASNI

The Oglala Napeyasni, or No Flight Society, was a branch, or offshoot, of the Strong Hearts. They had four bonnet wearers who wore caps, or bonnets, with a pair of split buffalo horns and a long sash trailing over the left shoulder with the right arm through the opening. They also carried picket pins with which they staked themselves in position in battle, not to retreat until the pin was pulled up by a comrade. They did not carry lances, the picket pins serving in their stead. After returning from a warpath they danced around the camp, and the sash wearers had their sisters, or other young women, hold up the sashes as they paraded from tipi to tipi.

THE BADGERS

The Oglalas said they got the Ihoka, or Badger Society, from the Crows, but the Crows have no tradition of it. Also the Sotka Yuha, or Bare Lance Owners, is supposed to have come from the Crows. The Iȟoka was another society severe on members who did not come to meetings. Their robes were cut up, and if the owners protested they were whipped by the Whippers. The Badgers had no special costume and they painted any way as long as they did so in pairs. They paraded also in pairs, first a Whipper, then two Pipe Men in advance, followed by two crooked lances, two straight lances, two short buckskin-wrapped lances, then the lay members, with the singers, drummers, and the other Whipper bringing up the rear. They started off at a trot. When they slowed down the singers began a song and the men faced backward and danced. When they came to a head man's tipi they formed a circle about the drum, but facing outward, dancing away from the center instead of towards it, as was customary in most dances. Their herald then addressed the "host," telling him how honored he was to have the Badgers dance for him, inviting him to come out and speak.

The host then appeared, usually bringing out a favorite son or daughter, and "giving away" in their honor. The presents were given to some poor person in the village, rarely to members of the society. The Badgers proceeded around the camp circle in this way until returning to their own society tipi.

The Badgers seem to have had an inner, or associate, society known as the Hîn'popopa, or Crackling Robes, but we were able to learn nothing else about it.

Another society mentioned, but for which we obtained no additional information was the Wabile'nica', or Orphans. One Bull named them at the top of his list, but then he said that with the exception of Naca, Strong Hearts, and Foxes all societies were of equal rank or importance. But orphans, among Indians, are almost outcasts, for everyone of any respectability has relatives. A child who had lost his parents was almost always immediately adopted by some family, and even friends called themselves by terms of relationship, such as "brother" or "cousin." So these members of the Orphan Society may have been a desperate bunch, with no ties to hold them back!

THE MIWATANI

The Miwatani was also known as the Mandan, or Owl, Society. It was much like the Mandan Dogs. Leaders wore owl-feather headdresses much like those Bodmer painted for the Hidatsas, except that the latter was largely raven and magpie feathers, with a crest of wild-turkey feathers. They carried the same kind of stick rattle of dewclaws, as did also the Crow Big Dogs. The Miwatani also had a fire trick. After first putting "medicine" on their hands, members carried burning brands by their flaming ends from an outside campfire to the fireplace inside the lodge.

Two leaders wore headdresses with split owl feathers over the cap, a crest of eagle feathers, crow feathers hanging from each side, and crow and spotted-eagle feathers hanging behind. Lay members had similar headdresses but without the eagle-feather crests. In the early days of the society the caps were covered with crow feathers and the crests were of turkey-buzzard tails, according to tradition. The reason for the change was not noted, and in more recent times the bonnets were changed again, when the caps were made of buffalo hide with the hair on. The Miwatani also had eagle medicine. The two (some say four) bonnet wearers wore sashes, made of either buffalo or elk leather, on the right side. These had transverse stripes of quill-work, with white plumes at the ends, four rows of rabbit ears and weasel tails, and little bags of medicine and white plumes hanging to them. They also tied a little bag of medicine and a white plume in the hair at each temple, and around the neck wore an eagle bone whistle, which was blown when they were attacked.

Most of the societies among the Lakotas each owned a large double-headed drum, which hung from four stakes decorated with eagle feathers. The Drum Keeper of the Miwatani was the most important man in the society. He was usually an old man, so did not go to war. But he removed a feather from each stake, tied it to a wand, and gave the four wands to members to carry into battle. If the bearer of one of these wands counted a coup, he could then wear the feather. The drumsticks, drum stand (four stakes), and drum were all treated with great ceremony and respect.

The only way the society could have new officers was for all the officers to resign at once. Lay members who had distinguished themselves in some way were invited to fill these open offices, and outsiders with high reputations might be solicited also.

We have the expressions "drumming up trade" and "drumming up candidates." The Indians were literal about it. When the officers in the Miwatani wished to resign, the drum was painted red, but no one beat it, although the members sang. The old Drum Keeper then came forth, beat the drum, and threw a stick to the audience, signifying that he was throwing a horse away. Whoever picked up the stick got the horse. Other officers could then follow suit. Occasionally a man even threw his wife away, saying "Whoever gets this stick can send my wife for water." This display of generosity was associated with the officers' bravery and established prestige in the eyes of the public, proving they were worthy of membership in such a famous organization.

Although regalia was not renewed each spring, as it was in some societies, each new officer furnished material for his "uniform," and the retiring officer helped him make it up, for which he was paid in horses. During this manufacture the newly appointed officers acted as servants. When it was time to eat, they went to some-one's drying rack containing meat, blew their whistles, ran and seized the meat they wanted, and scurried back to the ceremonial tipi with it.

Each morning while the new regalia was being made up, it had to be purified. The new officers, taking turns, carried live coals in their bare hands, slowly, without showing any pain, and placed them on the altar in the tipi. The bonnet maker then made sweet-grass incense, rubbed the smoke over his hands, and held the materials over it. When the bonnets were finished, the new Bonnet Men brought hot coals into the lodge for making more incense while a large crowd watched. Then other society members pretended to look for the new Bonnet Wearers, and when they were found an experienced warrior recounted coup and presented the regalia to them, placing the sashes over their shoulders and the bonnets on their heads.

Each member had a buffalo robe with a quilled rectangle in the center, the rest of it painted red, and for every wife discarded he hung an owl's leg and foot on it. New members were usually taken into the Miwatani in pairs.

Members painted their bodies, leggings, and moccasins red and for formal occasions wore buckskin* shirts with long fringes. Shirts and leggings were embroidered alike, in the same wide beadwork designs, which were in black and white. Since this was an old society, the embroidery was probably in "pony" beads originally, which came in dark blue, which the Indians called "black," and white.

The Miwatani dance was similar to the other society dances we have been discussing, but when it was finished each dancer stood in the circle with bowed head until a Whipper tapped him, when he could take his seat.

The Miwatani was definitely borrowed from the Dogs of the Mandans. In turn the Mandan Dog Society was much like that of the neighboring Hidatsa, who had the fantastic and beautiful headdress shown in the Bodmer painting. Dog Society headdresses of other tribes may have used crests of feathers from different birds and perhaps had different feathers on the crown, but the over-all type was like the Hidatsa headdress. Perhaps the entire Dog Society idea originated there. There were similarities of pattern, behavior, and costumes wherever the Dog Society was found. Even in the Southwest, a Dog Dance among a number of the Pueblos features a headdress with a crest and sometimes a tail of feathers.

So the Lakota had not only their own Dog Society, but the Miwatani as well—in effect, two Dog societies.

THE DOGS, OR WOLVES

The Dogs, sometimes called Wolves, had four officers who wore coyote skins, decorated with crow feathers, similar to the capes of fox skin the Foxes wore. There is a similar cape, or stole, of the Cree Wolf Society in the Peabody Museum at Harvard University (see page 212). The coyote skin has a slit to go over the head. It is mounted on red flannel, has little hawk bells on the nose and tail, and is decorated with feathers of seven different birds of prey, including those of both bald and golden eagles. The Dogs all carried bone whistles. There were two lances wrapped with otter skin and two feather banners. Members painted their faces with a red band across the mouth and a vertical stripe over each eye. This paint was supposed to represent coyotes feeding. The Dog dancers danced in place, as in the Sun Dance, but without even raising the heels, merely flexing the knees and lifting their bodies. They blew their whistles and ended the dance in a wolf howl. On some occasions the Dogs served as clowns, but they were not Heyoka, which we will discuss in the next chapter.

THE SOTKA TANKA

The Sotka Tanka of the Oglala was similar to the Miwatani and was not a true *akicita* society. But it had a special lance, like a double-curved bow, with a lance point of iron at one end. It had a buckskin string decorated with white weasel strips. The bow was not painted but from its curves hung clusters of eagle feathers.

---

*Buckskin is any soft, tanned skin, sometimes antelope or mountain sheep.

THE SACRED, OR MEDICINE, BOW SOCIETY

The real Sacred, or Medicine, Bow Society was never large and went out of existence long ago. But as recently as 1934 there were old men living who remembered it. The Sacred Bow was associated with thunder and the spider. The society was more ceremonial and had more spiritual significance than other societies but in other ways was much the same. Its members fought to the death, even if deserted. The Sacred Bow Leader also had rattlesnake medicine, something generally not known to the Sioux. Besides representing a great power on the warpath this medicine was supposed to be a cure for snake bit. The Sacred Bow men had an elaborate ritual and a dance, but it was performed only when some officer wished to resign and a new member was taken in his place. Because a member was supposed to "fight to the death," if he returned from a harrowing military experience he was free to resign as an active member. Only men of unquestionable courage, generosity, and integrity were invited to become officers.

No Sacred Bow man could use any metal. There were four of the sacred bows, which were double-curved, each attached to a shaft with a flint tip at one end. They were not used as weapons, only as emblems. Each bow was painted red and also with designs representing dragonflies, flying insects, and lightning. Elaborate pendants of magpie, hawk, eagle, and other swift flying birds hung from the curves of the bow. Ordinarily these bow-lances were carried with the points down, but if pointed at the enemy the carriers had to make a stand and never retreat. The sacred bows were never allowed to touch the ground and when not in use were kept in long buffalo hide cases, painted red.

There were also four men who carried hangers made of forked cherry, ash, or elm saplings, painted red, with a single eagle feather hanging from the longer end of the fork and sometimes a piece of buffalo hide wrapped around the shank. These hangers were thrust into the ground and the bow-lances hung from their forks. The Hanger Carriers painted themselves yellow, with red faces.

The four men who carried the sacred bows painted their faces and sometimes their entire bodies red or brown-red, representing a buffalo wallow. In addition to the red background, a blue line was drawn from the corners of the mouth around the forehead, with a little fork at each end. Wavy lines of blue or black, with forked ends, were painted down arms and legs. Blue bands were painted around the ankles, arms, wrists, and shoulders, and sometimes rabbit fur was worn on wrists and ankles, over the painted bands. Others wore shed buffalo hair from the hump. All of this painting and decoration referred to lightning.

A second way of painting was to draw a blue crescent representing the moon on the forehead and a blue line from ear to ear across the nose. The same blue or black wavy lines were added to arms and one leg, but the line on the other leg was made straight, so the wearer "could think straight."

Altogether there were ten officers, including two Club Carriers, but no mention was made of a special paint for them. Officers wore little three-inch hoops on thongs over the left shoulder, hanging on the right side, and eagle-bone whistles to which were attached rawhide emblems of a conventionalized spider. The hoop was crossed with two rawhide thongs painted blue and was wrapped with a buckskin thong. From the center hung a little pouch of the special medicine and the tail of a white-tailed deer. Members wore headbands of rawhide, cut in the shape of a snake, embroidered with porcupine quills. They wore their hair loose with an eagle feather thrust through the headband horizontally across the forehead.

Robes were of buffalo hide, taken when the hair was still short after shedding. A snake, running left to right, was painted toward each edge of the robe, top and bottom, and below the top snake was a red-breasted swallow. A dragonfly adorned the center. At the center of the top edge hung two streamers of buffalo hide, painted red. Moccasins had a quilled deer-track design embroidered on the instep and deer tails hanging at the heels. Shields were painted with the spider design.

Their mounts were painted also, dark horses with white lightning, white or light horses with red lightning, running from withers to hoofs and from withers to flanks. All painting and decorations pertained to Thunder, storm, and death-dealing agents.

In front of a sacred tipi that faced west was a large sweat lodge where all were required to purify themselves before a ceremony. What that was finished, four men carrying hand drums came out of the tipi, and when they began to sing, the Leader of the Bow Carriers came out and pointed his bow-lance to the west, blowing his eagle bone whistle. He was followed by the two Club Carriers, with wooden clubs, then by the Hanger Carriers, and finally by the Sacred Bow men, all blowing their whistles and raising their right hands to the west. Then they raised their weapons in their left hands and pointed them to the west, as the Leader had done. All took a step forward, pointed north, another step and pointed east, another and pointed south.

A pole had been set up at each cardinal point on the circumference of a large circle, and the dancers now charged in company-front formation toward the pole marking the west, all in time with the singing and the hand drums. As they neared the pole, all turned to the right and circled it single file, every man striking it with his weapon. All turned company front again and ran back to the pole on the east, circling it, as they had the pole on the west, then charged on to the north. They circled and struck the pole at the north in the same way, pivoted, and ran south, circling the pole there in the same manner. All then hung up their regalia in proper arrangement near the sacred tipi and retired to the sweat lodge again. The hangers were stuck into the ground and from them the bow-lances and clubs were hungs.

For some special occasions the performance was given as a race, each man for himself, no formation being attempted. In this case, the poles were erected on the circumference of the camp circle and, instead of going from west to east and from north to south, the men raced first to the pole on the west, back around the tipi, then to the north, east, and south, returning to circle the sacred tipi after circling each pole. Apparently the decision as to which form to take was up to the Leader of the society.

We do not usually think of deer in connection with death-dealing power, but in Indian belief all forked-horn animals had magic power. The spider is always associated with creation, for it spins its web out of its own body, so it is associated with higher powers, especially Thunder—powers of creation and of destruction. Rattlesnake medicine brought bad luck to the enemy.

The Sacred Bow Society was known to the Minikonjus as well as to the Oglalas, but we did not hear of it for the Hunkpapas. It definitely came from the Southern Cheyenne Bowstring Soldiers. During the Indian Wars the Cheyennes were more closely associated with these far western Sioux divisions than with others of the Tetons.[6]

THE SOTKA YUHA

Sotka refers to a tall, thin tree standing out among smaller ones, but the name of the society known as Sotka Yuha is usually translated as Bare Lance Owners. It was much like the Iḣoka, or Badgers, with two Leaders, four Lance Carriers, two Pipe Carriers, two Whippers, a Herald, a Food Passer, and eight Singers, four of whom sat at the drum, and any number of lay members. Everyone was assigned a seat, and he sat in that place at all meetings. They say the society was in existence for about ten years, from 1866 to 1876, but toward the end there was only one man at the drum.

THE WI'CISKA

The Wi'ciska, or White-Marked Society, of the Lakotas—also known as They-Dance-With-Toes-Pointed-Forward—seemed to be something of a mixture from other societies. Most of their songs were the same as those of the Sotka Yuha; they also used some Badger songs. Each spring, in common with several other societies, new paraphernalia were made up. While the members went on a search around the camp for the various materials necessary, four old men stayed in the ceremonial tipi, smoking, until the others returned. Two men were designated to do the work, which included rewrapping the ceremonial lances and whips and repairing bonnets.

There were two Bonnet Wearers who had headdresses with split buffalo horns, rabbit fur and eagle down on the cap, and a crest of eagle feathers over the crown running into a long tail down the back. The bases of the feathers were wrapped with red flannel. The two Whippers wore bunches of split owl feathers, with two eagle-tail feathers, on their heads; their whips were decorated with fox or otter skin and eagle feathers.

The Whippers were mounted, while the other Wiciska performed their dance, closing inward toward the center and firing their guns repeatedly.

THE RAVEN, OR CROW, OWNERS

The Kangi Yuha, Raven Owners, sometimes called Crow Owners, in contrast to other societies used four hand drums, painted black, instead of a large dance drum. They had two Sash Wearers, who carried short lances with which to pin themselves down; they were not allowed to retreat unless the lances were removed by a friend. There were four other Lance Carriers, using longer lances decorated with otter skin and crow, or raven, feathers. Their faces were painted black, or with black stripes. These men were expected to take the front in a battle, but were not bound to stand.

The Raven Owners wore skunk fur on their elbows and ankles, a crow skin around the neck, one eagle feather over the forehead, and three or four more at the back of the head. They painted their bodies and limbs black and carried their quivers, with bows and arrows or guns when they danced. After every performance the otter skin and feathers were removed from the lances. A man who failed to come to a meeting was taken a large quantity of food. If he could not eat it all he had to give away a horse.

The dance was led by two men with globular rawhide rattles. A Pipe Carrier took the central position, with the Lance Carriers on either side. Those carrying guns fired them off during the dancing.

When going into battle, the Raven Owners wore their finest regalia,

so that, if they were killed, they would die in a manner worthy of their position. The sleeves of the war shirts were not sewed, but were tied together under the length of the arm. Before a fight the warrior untied these fastenings and threw back the sleeves to permit free use of his arms.[7]

All the old-time war shirts were made in this way, so that they could actually be worn into battle without hampering the movements of their wearers. Even men who had no right to special, fancy regalis sometimes borrowed it to go into battle. They usually did this to acquire power from these ceremonial things, but on one occasion White Bull, before he had acquired his later reputation as one of the greatest warriors the Sioux ever produced, borrowed an elaborate horned bonnet just so if he were killed the enemy would not think they had killed a "poor man."

LANCE EMBLEMS

Most of the warrior societies, of whatever tribe, had a number of lances, some straight, some "crooked" (shaped like a shepherd's crook), which were important items. The Comanches have a story that the crooked lance was originally used to unhorse an enemy.* Most society lances had a blade, or point of metal, but at the *lower* end, and they were not used as weapons except for striking an enemy for a coup, with the upper end, in a charge.

The two straight lances of the Strong Hearts were like the well-known "Indian battle flag"—a tall staff with a full string of eagle feathers, like a war bonnet trailer. Each lance had the usual long blade at its lower end. There were also two similar staffs in the Dog Society and two in the Chiefs' Society, but the latter had no blades.

---

*All the members of the Crooked Lance Society of the Southern Cheyennes carried crooked lances.

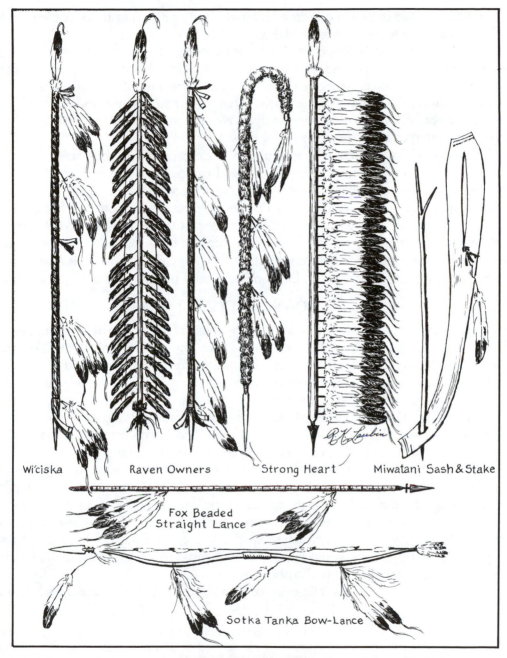

Wi'ciska   Raven Owners   Strong Heart   Miwatani Sash & Stake

Fox Beaded
Straight Lance

Sotka Tanka Bow-Lance

Warrior Society lances.

An old man in full buckskin costume and two-tailed war bonnet used to carry such a "battle flag" in the parades at Crow Fair.

The man who carried a lance into battle was expected to thrust it into the ground, thereby marking his place, and was not supposed to leave that position until rescued by a friend, who pulled it up and released him. The society members given the lances were, therefore, the bravest of the brave. They regarded themselves as "made to die." If they did die, they could depend upon a grand funeral, with all their fraternity brothers putting on a big dance in their honor.

Among the Crows, a man who accepted a lance carried it in the society dances, but he turned his back on his companions and danced backwards, thus signifying that he was willing to hold off the enemy alone, if necessary.

In many societies the Whippers, or Drivers, were important officers. They were sometimes the only ones who could release a Lance Owner or a Sash Wearer from his station in front of the enemy. They pulled up the lance or picket pin and ceremonially whipped their owners into retreat. Among the Crows, most society whippers wore belts of grizzly-bear skin, and Maximilian noted this also for the Village tribes.

DANCE STYLE

Many of the warrior societies had died out by the 1870's. A few held on into early 1900's, but very few old people living today have any memory of them. We have seen a few demonstrations of this type of dancing. We once saw an old Cheyenne trying to teach a Dog Soldier Dance to some young fellows. It was really quite pathetic, for they did not catch the spirit of it at all. As far as dancing goes, most of the warrior society dancing was extremely simple. It consisted largely of jumping in place on both feet. But the old-timers put so much of themselves into it that it was delightful to watch them. Without this spirit and power it is nothing.

Maximilian wrote "the dances of the several classes are in the main very similar, but there is a particular song belonging to each, and sometimes a different step."[8] We might point out also that the difference in the various society dances was most likely to show up in the routines and formations. Simple as the dances were, a prime requisite for joining any of the societies was being a good dancer. So we might say that, although the dances would appear to be simple to us, the Indians had standards of performance which had to be met.

Henry Boler, writing of the Hidatsas, or Gros Ventres, between 1858 and 1866, said:

Some of the dances were very wild and picturesque, that of the Lance Band in particular, being composed of warriors in the prime of life, splendidly arrayed, with bonnets or headdresses of war eagle feathers and bearing lances decorated with plumes and penons of scarlet and blue cloth. They of course paid us a visit and danced in the fort, singing and firing off their fuses [fusils?] in the air. A present was given them after the dance was finished, as is the custom.[9]

THE BLOTA'UNKA

The Lakotas had other officers similar to those of the warrior societies, but who served only in war. They were known as Blota'unka. War parties went out in numbers of eight to sixty, forty being considered ideal. When the entire tribe went to war the chiefs and *akicita* societies provided all the leadership necessary. But in a smaller party, the man leading it needed assistance, so Blotaunka were appointed. These assistants were usually members of warrior societies, but also were practically a society in themselves. The Blotaunka, in turn, appointed other marshals to help carry out orders, or rather instructions, for genuine orders were almost unknown to an Indian war party. There was usually one Blotaunka to three "privates," or ordinary warriors. Blotaunka was the highest honor, next to being actual leader of the party.

The Blotaunka and akicita, when going to war, painted their faces with a black diagonal stripe from eyes to cheeks, or with a couple of black spots on the cheeks.

Before entering enemy territory the Blotaunka held a dance. A large fire was built at night, the warriors all painted for war and tied up their ponies' tails, while the two leading Blotaunka instructed eight younger men in the art of "killing" enemies, which in reality meant the counting of coups. Four of these young men formed a line on one side, four on the other, and they were presented with medicine articles' which would enable them to strike the enemy.

Then the Blotaunka brought out two crooked lances wrapped with wolf or coyote skin and decorated with crow feathers tied in four different places, along with bunches of owl feathers. Two buffalo-hide rattles and the lances were presented to warriors who had already counted coup, and a pipe was given to a fifth man. *These Blotaunka lances were more important than any of the society lances* and were made by a man who had dreamed of a wolf. The wolf knows everything, the crow can find anything, and the owl knows everything at night.

Volunteer singers sang the proper songs, and since no drum was carried on the trip the time was set with rattles. The lines of dancers sashayed through each other, feigning attack and battle actions.

The actual leader of the party carried his pipe, which had been consecrated by a holy man, sealed with tallow from a buffalo's heart and wrapped in a wolf skin, throughout the journey. The war leader was known as the one "who carried the pipe," but when he was returning home from a successful war party, before entering the village, this pipe bundle was slung on the back of one of the boys who had accompanied the party as a servant. He was followed by all those who had counted coup in the fight. Afterward the seal on the pipe was broken, and the entire party smoked it in token of victory. If there was not enough tobacco in it to go around, it was not refilled, but each one went through the motions of smoking just as if it were still lit.

The two leading Blotaunka wore black-painted buffalo robes on returning from a victorious warpath. Following the serious homecoming rituals, the Scalp or Victory Dance was given.

THE BUFFALO HEADDRESS

One Bull mentioned a society called the Buffalo Headdress for the Hunkpapa that apparently was similar to the important Chiefs' Society of the Oglalas. As its Oglala name implies, its members were the various chiefs of the tribe. They wore head-dresses consisting of buffaloskin caps with horns attached. The horns were painted red, blue, or white. When putting on their dances the members carried shields and lances. It is possible that this society had some relationship to the Bull Society of the Mandans and Village tribes.

Sometimes the members wore the headdresses into battle. Otherwise they were used only for dancing and between times were carried in rawhide cases, which with the shields and lances were hung on tripods outside of the tipis of the owners. Because they were believed to be so powerful, however, they were hung about a hundred feet away, except in case of expected attack, when they were brought up closer. Most Sioux medicines were hung on tripods behind the tipi during the day and were brought in at night, or in bad weather. The Chiefs' Society paraphernalia, however, were too potent ever to be brought inside for fear of being contaminated by the presence of women.

The members of the society included the four head chiefs, or councilors, who originally were the only ones to wear the so-called "scalp shirts." Later other members also wore them. The hair on these hair-trimmed shirts, which were made of skins of mountain sheep with the dewclaws on, was not necessarily from enemy scalps. But it was human hair, sometimes donated by one of the wearer's friends. Each lock symbolized a war honor, not necessarily a coup and not necessarily the wearer's own honors. As a chief he represented the people and his costume symbolized the combined honors of the tribe.

The dance of the Buffalo Headdress, or Chiefs', Society should not be confused with the Chiefs' Dance. When the society danced, the members did not wear the sheepskin shirts but painted their bodies white and acted the parts of buffalo bulls. Each man counted coup and then danced alone, using a scraping step, with low-bent knees and hunched-over back, snorting and pawing like an angry buffalo bull. The entire group followed him, alternating the scraping step with jumping in place, and they butted each other, as buffalo bulls do. The dance was repeated until every man had danced alone.

On the march the headdress case hung at the front of the saddle, the shield at the rear, and the lance was carried in the hand.

THE CHIEFS' DANCE

The Chiefs' Dance was given at almost any public gathering. It is still given today, but the real chiefs are gone. Not even old men, chiefs or otherwise, any longer have war stories to enact in their dancing, so the present Chiefs' Dance is merely Straight-Up Dance. But in the old days, when a chief's song was sung, all the chiefs arose to dance, those with special stories to depict doing so all at once, so that the dance was certainly varied; it might even be considered confusing by some.

One time at Standing Rock we had endured a long intermission of speeches and give-away when the singers finally started a song. Flying Cloud said to me, "Come on, One Bull, let's get in on this. We're wasting a good song." The rhythm was strong and steady, moderately fast, and we began to dance. Then one old man after another joined us until several old men were dancing and we were the only young fellows on the floor. Flying Cloud worked his way over toward me and said in a low voice, "I made a mistake that time. We'll catch it now. That's a chief's song they're singing and we'll have to give away a horse, or something." If we were going to dance with the chiefs, we were expected to act like chiefs, and that meant being very generous. Near the end of the song, Flying Cloud approached me again and whispered, "I'll fix it up all right. I'll tell them I am dancing for my grandfather, Chief Flying Cloud, and you are dancing for your father, Chief One Bull. That'll fix it up just good." That's what he did, and everyone accepted the explanation.

WAR BONNETS

The chiefs wore their full regalia—war shirt, leggings, and war bonnet—when they danced. The war bonnet, which today is popular among Indians all across the country, originated on the Plains, probably with the Sioux, although the Crows also had the same style of headdress at least as far back as Catlin's day. Nothing quite comparable to it was found elsewhere.[*] Among the Lakotas, after a man had earned three eagle feathers, his companions might have decided that he was brave enough to wear a war bonnet—just the cap with its circle of eagle feathers. It seems that originally the bonnet was made from two eagle tails, or twenty-four feathers, but later, as the bonnets became more and more elaborate, it was customary to use more feathers, sometimes as many as three tails.

The bigger the chief, the bigger the bonnet he could wear, for he represented more people. A tail, or trailer, was added to the crown to hang down behind, and feathers

---

[*]Eastern Indians had feather headdresses, often of turkey instead of eagle feathers, but the feathers were set straight up in a headband and sometimes did not even go all the way around. In another style the feathers slanted to the back, so that from the side it might remind one of the Plains bonnet, but it had no spread, or "throw," as collectors call it, and the feathers went only across the front and along the sides of the head.

No feather headdress was practical for wearing through the forests of the East. Even when wearing only one feather, the Woodland warrior usually wore it hanging down rather than straight up, making it easier to move through the trees. The warrior's cap, the *gustoweh* of the Iroquois, mentioned for the Great Feather and Eagle dances, might be termed a war bonnet, and it did have a straight-up feather. But the real war bonnet of the East was the porcupine-hair or turkey-beard roach, combined with hair from the tail of the white-tailed deer, described earlier, under "War Dance." Although evidence of its use among the Iroquoian peoples is meager or lacking, it was found all through the Woodland area and was mentioned in the earliest reports. It was already as far west as the Missouri River by the time the first white men arrived.

Even on the Plains the right to wear one or two feathers in the roach had to be earned in war. The Sioux sometimes call the roach a "Pawnee war bonnet," because they say that they first got it from the Pawnees. Or they call it a "shako," because it looks much like the crests on dress helmets of the cavalry during the period of the Indian Wars.

Chief One Bull, Laubin's Indian "father." See pages 208 and 209. Photo by Gladys Laubin.

were laced on it as they were on the crown. Before the coming of the horse, such a tail was only about waist long, but mounted warriors sometimes had tails long enough almost to touch the ground from horseback. When on foot such tails had to be carried over the arm or looped up and tied to one leg. Shortly after the development of the longer tails the higher chiefs began to wear bonnets with two tails, the most elaborate and beautiful of all. When he was raised to the chieftainship, Sitting Bull was presented with such a bonnet, containing over one hundred feathers from the tails of young golden eagles, which were white with black tips.

Every feather in the bonnet represented an honor, a coup. It was not unusual for a man to earn all the feathers in his bonnet, but he was not expected to be quite as brave as that. He was expected to earn some of them but the rest might have been donated by companions in token of *their* achievements. So the bonnet, to the man wearing it, was a challenge. Through it he represented the combined honors, strength, and valor of his people and showed that he was regarded as one of their bravest men. He was now looked upon in the light of a chief and expected to behave like one, to show the qualities of courage, fortitude, generosity, and fidelity—the four virtues so admired by the people.

As with almost every article of finery or decoration, the war bonnet involved much symbolism. The feathers, arranged in a circle, are said to be warriors sitting in council, awarding honors to the man who is wearing the bonnet, he being represented by the long plume in the center—a stripped primary wing feather, wrapped with ribbon, quillwork, or beadwork and tufted at the tip with down or fluffy feathers. This center plume also represents the Sun Dance pole, with the "eagle" or "thunderbird nest" at the top, and supposedly shows that the bonnet wearer has taken part in that great ceremony. Certainly in earlier days anyone rising high enough to wear a bonnet had taken part in the Sun Dance.

Feathers of the young golden eagle, not over two years old, were preferred for the finest bonnets, but older men often had bonnets made from feathers of the older birds, which were completely dark. Such birds were known as "old man eagles," even though the female has the longest feathers.[*]

---

[*]Golden eagles are now on the protected list of endangered wildlife along with the bald eagle, which was placed on the list many years ago. Such protection was necessary not because Indians were exterminating eagles—far from it. Indians have always venerated both eagles. Even when they were killed for their feathers, only specially trained men, with eagle power, did the killing, and the dead eagle was treated with great reverence. Flying Cloud said ceremonies were held in its honor, and the body was usually painted, decorated, and buried in a manner befitting a warrior. To this day, some of the Pueblo Indians raise their own eagles to supply the ceremonial feathers.

Eagles were threatened by white hunters. Some states offered bounties on eagles, and they were not only poisoned deliberately but also suffered, as has other wildlife, from the effects of poison sprays and poisoned rodents on which they preyed. When hunters in Alaska and some of the western states began to hunt them from airplanes, the eagles were really hard-pressed.

When it was decided that a man was entitled to wear a war bonnet, he invited war-riors of importance to a feast. Although he may have collected all the necessary feathers himself from an Eagle Seizer, he distributed them to the assemblage. Then each man handed him one or more feathers, counting a coup on each one as he did so. The feathers were then usually turned over to a man who specialized in making war bonnets, and he took the feathers to his own tipi. He sang a song as he deco-rated each feather. When the bonnet was finally completed it was presented to the candidate with another ceremony and feast.

There were occasions when a war bonnet was presented to a young man who had no real war experience but bragged of what he intended to do when he took the warpath. This was regarded in an altogether different light than telling of something already accomplished. The bonnet was given as a challenge, as much as to say, "You have been talking too much. Now prove your words."

The young man's parents usually went into deep mourning, as if he were already lost in battle. They painted their faces black, cut off their hair, and wore old, ragged clothing. For the bonnet set him apart as a chief and made him a special target for the fiercest and most experienced of the enemy warriors. Without previous battle experience, it was doubtful that he would come back alive. Such an inexperienced young fellow would hardly have belonged to any warrior society, but, if he were killed, his companions would have held a dance in his honor after a proper period of mourning. If he did return successfully he could keep the bonnet, and of course he became the envy of all his young acquaintances and received invitations to join any number of societies.

One Bull, as chief in his uncle Sitting Bull's place, had the right to wear a full double-tailed war bonnet. He was one of the last of the real chiefs, and he could do the Chiefs' Dance with realism and conviction. He was also one of the last of the old-timers to retain the custom of recounting his coups in public. We watched and heard him do this on many occasions, which were always thrilling experiences to us. He was credited with leading the charge against Major Reno in the Battle of the Little Big Horn. He told of his engagements with Crow warriors and of his part in the fight against Custer—how his horse was shot out from under him and after catching and mounting another he rescued his friend Good Bear, who had been wounded.

Following his recitation, he portrayed all these experiences as he danced. He showed his anger by growling like a grizzly bear and sometimes would strike his chest and grunt like a buffalo bull. Sometimes he danced like a buffalo bull, as mentioned for the Chiefs' Society, for the chiefs led the people, just as the bulls led the herds of buffalo upon which the people depended.

He struck with his war club, showing how he knocked three soldiers off their horses as they were running away, and he imitated the groans they made as they were struck. Even when in his late eighties and on into his nineties he could still shake his head and shoulders and snort and stamp like a buffalo bull. It was stirring to watch an old man like that, who had a story to tell and a feeling for his performance. You might think the Custer Battle took place last week!

18.   Society Dances: Dream Cults, Other Societies

Plains tribes had other societies quite different from the warrior societies and sometimes confused with them. Many of them had a purpose such as that of the Sioux Hunkayapi, which involved the adoption of a ceremonial son or daughter and was tied up directly with the ancient Calumet, or Pipe Dance. The Crows had another, the Tobacco Society, which also was built around ceremonial adoption.

Tribes all across the country also had dream cults, the members of which were rather loosely united through the sharing of dreams of particular animals or personages. Among the Sioux the most important of these cults was the Heyoka, or Thunder Dreamers.

THE HEYOKA (THUNDER DREAMERS)

The dog, horned lark, swallow, nighthawk, frog, lizard, and dragonfly were all associated with Thunder, and anyone dreaming of any of these things had to become Heyoka, that is, join the society and take part in the ceremonies. The new dreamer took part as a clown and did everything backward. He "talked backward," saying the opposite of what he really meant, and "did things backward." The Heyoka took meat from a boiling kettle with their bare hands and ate it piping hot, exclaiming how cold it was and shivering.

A bow and arrow were also associated with Thunder, the bow being the sky and the arrow the lightning. So often the clowns carried make-believe bows and arrows, the more ridiculous the better. A few years ago we saw a young man at Standing Rock do the Heyoka Dance. He had been very ill and in a coma had seen some representative of Thunder. Thunder himself is shapeless, but has huge four-jointed wings, a beak with teeth like a wolf, and a lake in the middle of his back, from which comes the rain. His voice is thunder, and rolling thunder is the beat of his wings. Lightning is the glance from his eye. So, one seldom sees Thunder himself, just one of his representatives.[*]

This young man had on a pair of shabby leggings, made of old canvas, a Levi jacket, a mask of black cloth which covered his entire head, with a long pointed nose from which projected a little pink fluffy feather. He carried a bent stick with a string across it for a bow and a couple of crooked sticks for arrows. He danced in the center of the ring while the rest of us were doing the Grass Dance. Pivoting from one

---

[*]Because of Thunder's indescribable appearance the Lakotas refer to him in the plural and speak of Thunderers, Thunder Beings, Thunder Birds—not as "the Thunderbird."

spot, he drew his bow and pointed an arrow at the sky, the ground, and the four directions, circling right to left instead of "with the sun." He did many exaggerated, angular movements with his body, arms, and legs. We thought he was a remarkable dancer (see page 213).

Most of the people present knew the identity of the dancer. It was no secret. A person who dreamed of Thunder and did not take the part of a clown would surely be struck by lightning. Later we met this young dancer and he gave us all the paraphernalia he had used. He was perfectly willing to tell us of his dream. He believed it made him well and his dance was one of thanksgiving, using the conventional form of the Heyoka. Such a dreamer was required to do the dance only once, but often such clowns appeared in repeat performances, expecially in earlier days, when the Heyoka Society was more active.

At a later Grass Dance this same dancer danced with the rest of us, in Grass Dance costume. He was really not a good dancer at all. In fact, one would never have recognized him as the same dancer. His Heyoka dream must have inspired him and fired his imagination, for his Heyoka Dance was outstanding and we shall never forget it.

The next year we saw another Heyoka dancer, whose costume was made of burlap—leggings and fringed shirt. He wore a mask similar to the first one, but had cut out ends of tin cans for ears and had no feather on the nose. He did some funny antics, but on the whole his dancing was far inferior to that of our first Heyoka dancer. He seemed more intent on his role as clown, rather than trying to portray any particular story or experience, and consequently was not as funny. But it was interesting to us that such beliefs still exist when so many of the old ways have been forgotten.

THE CONTRARIES (CRAZY DOGS WISHING TO DIE)

Among the Crows there was a certain type of behavior known as Crazy Dog Wishing to Die. It bore no relation to thunder dreams but to a man who was desperate because of failure in war or in love, loss of a friend or close relative, or some other reason announced himself as one of these Crazy Dogs. While in camp he did foolish things, talked backward, and then went to war at the earliest opportunity with the express purpose of getting himself killed. He usually got his wish. During his brief sojourn as a Crazy Dog Wishing to Die he was highly honored, not only because of his dedication but because such a man would do a great deal of harm to the enemy while courting death.

The Cheyennes called men of this sort Inverted Soldiers. Other tribes on the Plains recognized such individuals as Contraries. Whether some of them were associated with thunder beliefs we are not certain.

THE SIOUX HORSE DANCE

Among the Sioux a Horse Dance was also associated with Thunder. This was a very elaborate ritual and usually in charge of *Heyoka* members. It was described by both White Bull, of the Minikonjou, and Black Elk, of the Oglalas, who had Heyoka dreams while just youngsters. Good accounts of their visions are available in the books *War Path*, by Stanley Vestal, and *Black Elk Speaks*, by John Neihardt.[1] Wissler also reported the Horse Dance.[2]

Sixteen horses were used—four bays, four buckskins, four blue roans, and four blacks. The colors related to the four directions; although Wissler did not give this relationship, the black was probably for the West, blue for the North, bay for the East, and buckskin for the South. These colors are somewhat different from those given by White Bull and Black Elk. Both used black for West, white for North, sorrel for East, but Black Elk had buckskins for South and White Bull had light roans. Apparently, as in most Sioux ceremonies, there was some liberty in details.

The horses were painted with red zig-zag lines with forked endings down each leg, and the riders' paint matched the horses. The riders wore hood masks of cloth or buckskin, with long eagle primary feathers attached to look like horns. Wissler said there were four singers, each carrying a hand drum, each singer and his drum painted in one of the four horse colors. Wissler also said there were two virgins, but Black Elk stated four, wearing red-dyed buckskin dresses, with faces painted red. They were important characters in the dance, one representing East and carrying a pipe; one West with a hoop symbolizing the nation; one North carrying a "healing herb" and a white goose wing; and the one South carrying a wand—a "flowering stick"—symbolizing the growing things of the world. These four maidens thus held in their hands the life of the Sioux nation. Each wore a wreath of sage; from it hung a long spotted-eagle tail feather.

According to Wissler, a brush arbor was erected for the center of activity, but Black Elk used a specially painted tipi. Wissler said the leader rode a black horse and was himself painted black, with white spots representing hail. But Black Elk rode a bay horse and was painted red, with black lightning down his arms and legs. Either way, it must have been a spectacular and impressive thing to watch. The horses also had the long eagle-feather primaries inserted in their bridles in such a way that they looked like horns.

The painting of the leader, riders, and maidens was all done inside the sacred tipi. In Black Elk's ceremony there were six singers, all old men, whom he called the Grandfathers, for they represented the Four Directions, the Sky, and the Earth.

First the riders went out. When the Grandfathers began to sing about the West, the black-horse riders mounted and lined up, four abreast, on the west side of the lodge, facing West. Next they sang of the North, and the white horses and riders lined up on that side of the tipi. Then followed the sorrels, with their red riders to the East, and the buckskins, with yellow riders to the South.

The leader sang now along with the drumming and singing of the Grandfathers, while the virgins stepped outside, carrying their sacred emblems. They were followed by the leader, who mounted his horse and stood behind them, facing West. After the leader came the Grandfathers, standing abreast behind the leader on his bay horse. They sang again of each direction and of the horses representing them, and as they did each troop in turn wheeled and fell into position, four abreast—first the blacks, then the whites, sorrels, and buckskins, and all pranced in time to the song.

The procession started out, the maidens running ahead a pace, pausing, running and pausing, while the lines of horses moved into position. First the black horses circled around to take the lead and headed for the west side of the camp circle. There they wheeled, came back, and followed the buckskins, while the white horses went around the maidens to take the lead to the north side of the camp. This procedure was followed also by the sorrels leading to the eastern side and the buckskins to the southern side, when the blacks once more took the lead. Each time a troop reached its side of the village, the singers sang about that direction and its power. This parade, with its wheeling and changes of position, circled the village four times. On the second time around many of the people, mounted on their own horses, joined in the procession, bringing up the rear, so that it was a great festive occasion for everyone.

After the fourth time around, the procession stopped again on the west side, all facing back toward the sacred tipi in the center. The virgins were first again, four abreast, then the leader, followed by the six Grandfathers, also abreast, and the horsemen lined up in a company front on either side of them, the blacks and whites on their left, the sorrels and buckskins on their right. The leader raised his hand and called out four times, the fourth time being a signal for all to charge the sacred tipi. All endeavored to count coup on it, the first four expecting to receive special good luck as a result.

Wissler mentioned that just previous to this final charge, which ended the public ceremony, the painted riders dismounted, holding their horses by their halter ropes, and danced. He said also that they circled the camp twice, but, four being the sacred number, we feel that four was the customary number of times. He also said this ceremony was given in preparation for war, but Black Elk said he gave it to fulfill his vision and to bring good fortune to his people. Just before the Grandfathers left the sacred tipi, they smoothed the ground within. On returning after the ceremony they found tiny horse tracks all over the interior—the tracks of the spirit riders who had guided the ceremony.

Wissler said that during the parade a guard was posted over the ceremonial arbor, but that after the ceremony horse and moccasin tracks were found all over the ground inside. A holy man then predicted the fate of the next war party by studying these tracks.

THE SANTEE (ISAYANTI) THUNDER CEREMONY

The Eastern, or Santee (Isayanti), Sioux had an elaborate ceremony connected with Thunder, in addition to Heyoka rites. They called it Round Dance, but it bears no resemblance to the social Round Dance held in connection with the Grass Dance. A central brush arbor was built and thatched so tightly that no one could look through. An entrance was left open at each of the four directions. There was a center pole, as in other dances we have discussed. On this occasion it was painted red, and from its top hung a bark effigy of an eagle, representing Thunder. West of the pole a large pit was dug, and about twenty feet from the pit was a bark wigwam, or shelter.

At the foot of the pole stood two boys, painted red and carrying clubs, and two girls, with faces painted with blue clay. The boys represented war and the girls peace.

The leader of the ceremony was in the wigwam. His face was painted black, with white lightning streaks, and he wore a veil of black beads, a crown, or wreath, of slough grass, with two eagle primary quills to represent horns, and a robe with the hair out. He came out of the wigwam on all fours, singing, and sang four songs on his way from the wigwam to the pit. In the pit was a drum. The leader would rise up halfway out of the pit, singing and drumming.

Men dancers entered the arbor from three entrances and women from the fourth. The leader sang four more songs, while the dancers danced to the rhythm. At the end of each song all the male dancers gave a shout, and at the end of the fourth song the dancers all scurried off the dance ground while the leader jumped out of the pit and chased after them.

The first song was rather slow, but each time it was repeated it was faster than before. The performance was repeated twice. The fourth time the women did not come back, because the men brought their weapons—bows and arrows and guns— and the women might destroy their potency. This time, at the ending of the last song, the men instead of running away all fired at the bark eagle. When it fell, all ran to count coup on it.

At the foot of the pole was a bowl of water colored with blue clay, which the male dancers then drank, emptying the bowl. Ten of them then grabbed the boys and girls and threw them roughly to the ground, rolling them in the dirt, to destroy the power of Thunder. Everyone wailed and cried, as would be done in mourning a close relative. This would be the proper way to show joy and satisfaction in dealing with Thunder, where everything is done backward.

Stephen Riggs, an early missionary to the Santees, said this ceremony was given by a war leader preparing to gather a war party, which sounds as if it bore some relationship to the Horse Dance of the Oglalas described by Wissler. Dr. Charles Eastman, a Santee Sioux, told of the Bear Dance, which was conducted in much the same way, but it was a medicine ceremony for healing. The shooting at effigies, or images, on the center pole, as well as drinking from a bowl at its foot, are also parts of the Sun Dance.

The Santees had still another Thunder Dance, not Heyoka, in which the dancers flapped their arms like wings, but we know little else about it.

THE ELK DREAMERS

It is a strange thing, but Thunder is personified by many peoples around the world as a captor of women and as being very jealous of lovers. Most Indian tribes had similar beliefs. The various tribes, or bands, of Sioux all had an Elk Cult, or Elk Dreamers Society, associated with love power, or love medicine. When the Elk Dreamers had a ceremony, Heyoka dancers would gather to disturb them. They pretended to make medicine to harm them, but the elk medicine was too strong. In the Santee Elk Dance, an effigy hung on the center pole represented Thunder, but instead of shooting this effigy down, it was knocked down with saplings about twelve feet long, with tufts of leaves at their tips.

The Elk Dreamers were among the few Plains dancers to wear masks. They were triangular, made of rawhide, with branches attached to look like antlers. These were wrapped with otter fur to represent the bull elks in velvet. The dancers carried small hoops of wood, with crossed strings in the center to which were attached small mirrors. The hoop represented the rainbow, for we see half the hoop in the rainbow itself. The dancers stamped their feet and flashed the sunlight, representing their power, not only in love-making but in overcoming Thunder. With such a mirror a dancer could throw the light into a girl's eyes and win her heart. Mirrors were also set in the masks for eyes; Alice Fletcher reported one with a mirror in the center of the forehead.

As with all the dream cults, the Elk Dreamers were required to enact their visions or suffer some dire consequence. Miss Fletcher saw an Elk Dreamer put on the ceremony in 1882, which may have been one of the last times it was given.[3]

A new tipi was set up by the women members of the society on the west side of the camp, some distance from it. It was decorated with four black bands at the top and a red elk painted across the doorway, so that on entering one had to pass through the elk's body. The doorway faced east. A pole nearby held offerings of calico and little bunches of tobacco tied up in cloth.

Inside the tipi was an altar of mellowed earth, representing the unappropriated power of the earth, power which man might obtain. Ceremonies inside the tipi occupied the entire morning. Four virgins dressed in green sat near the door on the north and assisted with the singing. Two pipes were purified in incense, ceremonially smoked by the men members, then placed on either side of the altar. When these ceremonies were over, the pipes were handed to two of the young women, who stepped out of the tipi with them, followed by the other two maidens. They led the procession, followed by the Elk Dreamers, and headed north. The Elk acted like elk, cautious and wary.

In his vision each member was supposed to be given a color—a "white cloud," "red cloud," "blue cloud," or "yellow cloud." The young initiate Miss Fletcher saw was painted yellow and carried a hoop with the mirror. Other members did likewise, but one had a square within his hoop from which hung a fringe of deer hoofs. All the male dancers were nude except for clouts. One had a blue circle painted on his back, with an eagle feather fastened in the center to a splinter through his skin. This was a prayer that any wound received in battle would not be serious.

The dancers leaped, crouched, trampled the dirt hard, or trod noiselessly. They went three or four miles like this, sometimes doubling back, as wild game does. The four girls never looked back, although the men capered all the time. "The whole movement of this long dance in its queer posturings and actions was not without untrammeled grace and spirited action that produced a lasting impression," Miss Fletcher wrote.[4] As the dancers passed by, women and children from the village followed, but never closer than fifty feet. The actual distance traveled was between six and seven miles, but because of the circling and doubling back was considerably longer.

On the return to the sacred tipi a rainbow was seen in the East, which was a good omen. It showed that the young candidate had acted out his vision properly, that it was true, and that his prayers had been accepted. The virgins entered the tipi, placed the pipes back beside the altar, and the other members followed after them, taking their places within the lodge. The last to enter was the candidate. He came in, still acting like an elk retiring to a place of safety. A period of silence followed, then all unmasked and put on blankets, and shortly afterward all filed out again to take part in a feast. The tipi was taken down at sunset.

It was claimed that one who followed the trail of the Elk Dreamers found real elk tracks in the wake of the dancers.

The Assiniboins had a Female Elk Society that was a women's organization with religious significance.

When a band camped near a wooded creek, the women of this society went into the timber and changed their garments to short dresses with short sleeves. Then they would smear their exposed legs from the knees down and their arms to the elbows, with white clay. Head-dresses of leaves were placed over their hair. An older woman, who was the Medicine Woman, led the group in which young women and girls were considered as young female elk, with the older women representing older female elk.

Two men, as bull elk, with wooden horns fastened to their heads, stayed far behind the females and danced, blowing on whistles at frequent intervals. They never joined the group of women but always kept far in the rear.

As the parade passed within the camp circle it was customary for warriors to join it. They would walk on each side and shoot arrows at the "Female Elk," being careful not to hit any of them. When an arrow fell among them, the group ran and scattered just as a herd of elk would do.

After a parade completed the camp circle, they returned to the woods and changed their costumes. The Female Elk Dance was then over until the same time a year later.[5]

Among the Oglalas, in addition to Heyoka, Horse, and Elk, there were dream cults of those who had dreamed of wolves, buffalo, bears, black-tailed deer, the Double Woman, mountain sheep, rabbits, and dogs. The Double Woman was a being with one beautiful face and one horrible one. If a person saw the horrible face he might go mad. But the Double Woman could assist the womenfolk in doing embroidery in porcupine quills and beads.

The Santees had these same cults and in addition had Raw-Fish Eaters, Dog-Liver Eaters, Fire Walkers, the Round, or Thunder, Dance just described, and a Mocking Dance, which we shall take up later.

THE BERDACHES

Perhaps the strangest of all the dream cults was that of the *berdaches,* or men-women. In almost every tribe there were a few of these individuals—men who had dreamed of being women and henceforth dressed and behaved as women, usually

A *winkta* on the
Standing Rock Sioux Reservation.
Laubin Collection.

for the rest of their lives. Instead of being despised or rejected by the rest of the community, they were highly respected and often had important roles in ceremonies. Often one of these *winkta*, as the Lakotas call them, went to war and were credited, strangely enough, with being extremely brave. They brought good luck to a war party.

Occasionally one of these people is found even in this day and age. We knew one at Fort Yates. One evening, while visiting Flying Cloud, a young woman came over to talk with him about some bead work he wanted done. She was a beautiful woman, with a soft, pleasant voice. She showed us some of her beadwork and sat and talked for some little time. After she left, Flying Cloud asked, "What do you think of it?"

"Think of what?" we answered. "She seems to be a very capable and attractive young woman."

"She," he replied, "is a man, a *winkta.*" Then he told us more about "her." When about eighteen years of age, Patrick Rattling Hail had a *winkta* dream. He had been a good student and finished high school, but sometimes the old beliefs still have a strong hold. All of a sudden he began to dress like a girl; he let his hair grow and wore it like a white woman. He began to use "women's talk"—among many tribes the women use different words for some things and a different phraseology and have a different manner of speaking than men. Patrick now became Patricia. *She* became one of the best bead and craft workers on the reservation. She made such an impression upon us that to this day, we still think of him as "she." After some inquiry we learned that such persons were fairly common in earlier times and usually had the reputation of being fine craft workers.

A few years ago someone finally convinced Rattling Hail that he should discard his woman's role and be a man. He was in trouble from then on. He seemed to be genuinely confused, whereas before he had seemed entirely content. From his appearance, actions, dress, quality of voice, and manner of talking we would have defied anyone who did not know him to have suspected he was not really a woman.

But, for all his woman's role, it seemed strange that when he attended a dance he usually dressed in man's dancing costume. And yet he still acted like a woman and danced as some of the modern Indian women do when they try to imitate men's dancing.

THE BEARS

The Bears had powerful medicine for healing. Most of the people belonging to dream cults were regarded as shamans—medicine men or women—but the Bear Men were most powerful of all. Some wore the entire skin of a bear and when giving a ceremony acted fierce, growling. Sometimes they dug up prairie turnips with their bare hands and ate them raw, and they have been known to tear a dog apart and eat its liver raw. They acted in this same way in battle to frighten the enemy. Such performance would be enough to frighten anybody.

Members of the Bear Cult among some of the northern tribes made knives with iron or steel blades, obtained from the Hudson's Bay Company, and handles from one of the lower mandibles of a grizzly bear's jaws, the teeth serving as decoration. These knives were about fifteen inches long over all, with blades eight or nine inches long. The Blackfeet had such a knife in a Bear Knife Bundle. When the bundle was sold, or "passed," the new owner had to bare his chest and catch the knife in his hands when it was thrown to him.

THE WOLVES

The Wolves also had great medicine power. Sometimes Wolves and Bears danced together, each depicting the animal they represented and simulating their movements and actions in the dance.

NON-AKICITA SOCIETIES

In the discussion of warrior societies we told how new members went through the ceremony of being "captured." The non-akicita societies did notify candidates in advance, but they, too, sometimes went through the mock escape and capture as part of the general entertainment. Poor warriors or poor hunters with no reputation were seldom asked to join any society, because they were regarded as having no ambition. The societies took responsibility for the welfare of their own members and of the public as well. Care of the needy was stressed, and so they did not want members who could not, or would not, live up to that responsibility. Men who had won reputations through their own efforts were the ones most sought after.

These societies, made up of warriors as they were, nevertheless can hardly be called military societies, for their purpose was largely social and fraternal:

By conserving the food source, by preserving the unity and integrity of the tribe, and by obtaining supernatural sanction for these activities, the societies functioned to maintain tribal order. Societies in Plains Indian culture may be characterized, then, as associations of men who by protecting the material welfare, the unity and integrity, and the supernatural relations fo the tribe, maintained the tribal order.[6]

WOMEN'S SOCIETIES

The women in most tribes had societies, or clubs, just as the men did, but pertaining to "women's business." In fact, among the Sioux women belonged to most of the dream cults—all except the Bears. They said that women never dreamed of bears.

On the chart (in chapter 17) we listed women's societies only among the Oglalas and Mandans, the Mandan list coming from Maximilian. We have made no attempt to give a comprehensive report on women's societies, but a few words about some of them may be of interest. The Owns Alone, for example, was made up of women who had had only one husband and had been faithful to him.

THE WINYAN TAPIKA

The Winyan Tapika was a sacred society of young women. They met in a large tipi, the rear of which was covered with sage. In some ways this society was the nearest to being like the men's warrior societies. It owned a pipe, two drums, two rattles, and required the services of a medicine man who owned a medicine bag. The women wore buckskin dresses, with their hair loose and wreaths of sage and an eagle feather—permitted for an occasion as important and unusual as one of their meetings. Their hands, arms, and faces were painted red; on the faces were also blue lines, up and down on the forehead and chin, crosswise on the cheeks. They carried a bunch of sage and an eagle feather in each hand. (Such sage wreaths and sage in the hands were also used in the Sun Dance.) Men singers were invited to drum and sing for the dance. It was seldom, if ever, that women handled drums, even in their own societies. The women stood in a row and danced, using the customary women's steps. Following the dance they had a feast, which consisted mainly of a soup prepared in a sacred manner.

On occasion they also held a Tea Dance, when men partners were invited in. It was like the Shuffling Feet, Social, or Round Dance, the dancers moving in a circle. They served an herb tea.

THE SHIELD BEARERS

The Shield Bearers were women whose husbands and sons were great warriors with many deeds to their credit. They were special women indeed, for they carried the shields of their warriors in parades. Ordinarily women were not allowed to touch weapons, particularly shields. Their dance was held to give special honor to some hero, and in the dance they all carried bows, arrows, or other weapons and wore regalia of the men honored. This ceremony is much like the Scalp, or Victory, Dance of the Crows, Blackfeet, Shoshonis, and other tribes. The only men to take part were four singers. With the exception of the hero's regalia worn or carried, the women had no special costume, but they blackened their faces, which again sounds like Scalp Dance. They danced near the tipis of head men, forming a circle, where they stood singing, then advanced toward the center. Their dance was sometimes known as Wounded Dance and was carried down until recently, when it has occasionally been given not as a society dance but as a social activity with other dances at the time of a big "doings."

THE QUILL WORKERS

Among the Sioux, Cheyennes, and Arapahos, and earlier among the Crows and Blackfeet, there was a society of important women who did all the porcupine-quill embroidery. This society has been extinct a long time among the Crows and Blackfeet, but there are a few Lakota women who do a *very little* porcupine-quill work. At least they still know how to do it. A similar society among Sioux, Cheyennes, and Arapahos made and decorated tipis.* We understand that a few of these women are still to be found among the Southern Cheyennes and Arapahos in Oklahoma, but the society has died out in the north.

We were told that formerly, when the society was active, it held feasts and dances as the other women's societies did.

The study of societies and dream cults has given us another example of the importance of dance in Indian life. Even though, as we have seen, the dancing itself was usually quite simple and to most of us today would be considered monotonous as well, it was an integral part of these societies. With the exception of the Silent Eaters, which after all was not really a society in itself, the Indians could hardly have conceived of a society where no dancing took place. The movement of the dance was an expression of the sincerity, enthusiasm, and vitality of the members, and the rhythm united then all in a bond of comradeship and common purpose.

---

*For more information on these decorated tipis, see Reginald and Gladys Laubin, *The Indian Tipi.*

19. Bird and Animal Dances

THE PRAIRIE CHICKEN DANCE

The Indians, living close to nature and being keen students of its ways, learned much of their dancing by watching the birds and animals. Anyone acquainted with wildlife knows that many creatures actually dance. The entire universe is governed by an all-pervading rhythm, and the urge to respond is inherent in all nature. So it is little wonder that mankind has always liked to dance. Only one or two areas of the world have been reported where no dance is known.

In nature and among primitive people the dance is part of the process of court-ship. Havelock Ellis, in *The Dance of Life*, considered dancing as the first of all the arts and stated that it "is the primitive expression alike of religion and love."[1] He said also that "among some peoples, as the Omaha, the same word meant both to dance and to love."

All nature lovers have heard of the courting dances of the grouse and turkey. We look forward to watching the sage grouse dance early each spring. Once they came strutting out of the sage brush and danced right up to our very door. The cocks, so enraptured with their own appearance and importance that little else seems to interest them, allow us to move slowly right up to their strutting circle with-out taking alarm. Under a faint new moon, with the dramatic skyline of the Teton mountains as a backdrop, we quietly watch them in the twilight. These sage grouse, or chickens, are not as active and violent as the prairie chickens and sharp-tailed grouse, but what show-offs they are! At the moment only four cocks are dancing. They face into a circle about fifteen feet across. Slowly each cock turns, stopping at each quarter to swell up his white breast until it looks as if it would burst. As he puffs out his chest to display his thick, furry-looking vest, there is a faint sound as of rustling silk. He stretches his neck and bobs up and down, making a kind of gurgling noise that develops into a popping sound and ends in a deep "glug," trailing off in a barely audible whistle.

Sometimes the cocks turn to the left, sometimes to the right, then two cocks face each other and glare for minutes without moving. The white tips on the ends of their spread tail feathers shine out in the dark, reminding us of the white tips on the feathers of some of the old Indian dance bustles. It is a thrilling sight!
The prairie chickens and sharp-tailed grouse may not have as spectacular "cos-tumes" as the sage grouse, but they are much better performers. Many Indian tribes had dances to honor and to imitate them. They combine the antics of both birds in their Prairie Chicken dances.

We heard about this dance years ago, on our first visit to the Lakota country. One

Sage cock dancing

old warrior, during the Grass Dance, used a figure which was pointed out to us as the Prairie Chicken. On our early visits to the Sioux reservations a number of older men, while dancing Grass Dance, represented animals and birds and executed figures formerly belonging to other dances which had not been given in many, many years. The Prairie Chicken was one of them.

Later, Flying Cloud demonstrated the Prairie Chicken Dance for us as he had seen it when a small boy. The dance, as he portrayed it, was quite different from the Prairie Chicken Dance mentioned by Clark Wissler in his report "Dance Organizations of the Oglala Sioux." He said the dance belonged to a woman's society and that the only men to take part were the singers. The women hopped about and made noises like prairie chickens. One woman prepared a feast to follow the dance and gave presents to an old woman to call out invitations to those who were expected to attend.[2]

But according to Flying Cloud the men, as usual, were the dancers. In the animal kingdom the male is usually outstanding in appearance and must display his beauty, energy, and skill to win the approval of the female. So, as among the birds and animals, the Indian man did most of the dancing and wore the most spectacular costume.

Dancing prairie chicken cocks

Flying Cloud said a large circle was formed for the Prairie Chicken Dance, but the older women sat on the north, where the men usually sat. Since the male prairie chickens danced to "honor" the hens, the men danced to honor the women and, for this reason, changed places with them. Younger women formed an inner, complete circle, leaving an open center in which the men performed.

The leader of the men started off, dancing through the inner circle of young women toward the older women, but before breaking through the line of young women on the opposite side he began to strut and dance around the inner ring, acting like a real prairie chicken. Finally breaking through the inner circle, he made a guttural, rolling sound in his throat, "g-g-g-u-u-ih'," representing the booming sound made by the birds' inflated air sacks and the beating of their wings. As he danced, he uttered another call, "ka-tuk'-a-tuk, ka-tuk'-a-tuk," the "clucking" of the chickens. This first dancer, after showing off in the center and outside the ring in front of the old ladies, then crossed through the inner circle again and returned to the men. Thereupon he repeated the entire performance, and the other men then took their turns to strut.

Later, two men at a time entered the ring and the actions became more amusing. The movements of head and shoulders, the rapid stamp of feet in time to a tremolo on the drum, an occasional jump into the air with a turn halfway round, stopping to glare at each other, brought laughter from everyone. Sometimes the dancers quivered and shook all over.

The women bounced up and down in place, as they sat, making the same "ka-tuk'-a-tuk" sounds as the dancers. Everyone had a wonderful time. But the dance was not only a form of entertainment and relaxation. It served also the serious functions of expressing gratitude for safely surviving the winter and was a prayer for fruitfulness and abundance.

After Flying Cloud's demonstration, I began to practice the Prairie Chicken Dance myself, but I soon discovered it to be one of the most difficult dances to master. The shaking of the shoulders and quivering of every muscle is very tiring and requires much practice. Most people are amazed at the great length of time that Indians can dance without becoming exhausted, even though they may dance only a few times a year. There is a subtle relaxation in the movements that saves the dancer's strength. But the Prairie Chicken Dance is one that demands tense, strained muscles while the dancer must appear even more relaxed than in other dances, making its mastery exceptionally difficult (see page 215).

Not yet having seen the real prairie chickens dance, we were under the impression that, comical and interesting as the Indians' imitation was, they had, nevertheless, taken a great deal of liberty in their portrayal. Later, when we saw moving pictures of the courting dances of the prairie chickens and sharp-tailed grouse at the University of Wisconsin and the American Museum of Natural History in New York, we were astonished to find that the movements and even the sounds were identical to those we had learned from the Indians! The birds chose a circular, flat open space for their dance ground, much as the sage grouse do. The hens hovered about the edge of the space, and the cocks moved in to strut and dance. Several cocks danced at once, but each had his own little circle within the larger one. They stamped their feet, ruffled their feathers, inflated their throat pouches, and made the booming sound. Each one turned and glared at his neighbor. Then he would jump completely off the ground, turn halfway round in mid-air, and come down to glare at the cock now facing him from the other side.

Sometimes two cocks jumped up together in a sort of sham battle, each within his own circle. Dropping back to the ground, they glared at each other, hopped up again and came down with tails together, heads thrust out, glaring at dancers in neighboring circles. With every feather aquiver, they stamped and shook their bodies in precise and rapid rhythm.

Wissler states that the Blackfeet had a Prairie Chicken Society,[3] and Lowie says the Plains Crees had a Prairie Chicken Dance in which both men and women participated.[4]

Among the Blackfeet there were two leaders in the Prairie Chicken Society. These two leaders set up their tipis together so as to form a huge dance lodge. Two old men served as drummers. Each member of the society carried a rattle and painted his face yellow, with red between the eyes. The leaders carried staffs about four feet long, painted red and blue and decorated with feathers and white weasel skins. Four dances were given at sunrise. (The chickens dance at sunrise and at sunset.) The dancers sat on their knees in a circle. The drummers, in the center, beat the drum rapidly to imitate the prairie chickens. The two leaders did a running dance around the circle, changing places as they returned to their starting point, while the lay members thrust their heads out toward one another as they sat and occasionally changed places with each other.

The Plains Cree dance belonged to a Prairie Chicken cult and was a religious ceremony under a leader who had dreamed of prairie chickens. Both men and women belonged. The dancers strutted and hopped in ludicrous fashion, as the real chickens do. The singers used hand drums, with red suns painted on them, instead of the usual big dance drum. The ceremonies lasted all day until sunset.

According to Edward Curtis, the Crees had another Prairie Chicken Dance that was given to fulfill a vow made to combat sickness or bad luck. A special lodge was erected, with tripods at each end supporting an aspen pole of four or five inches diameter, like a ridge pole. Over it tipi covers were hung and spread out, similar to an A tent, but with an oval ground plan. There was much smoking, praying, and a feast of dog flesh was served.

To special songs the women danced, but no drum was used for them. When the men danced they imitated the movements and sounds of prairie chickens. They carried fancy beaded and feathered "stakes," or wands, about thirty inches long, which were thrust into the ground between dances and later used for lifting the dog meat from the kettles onto the plates. The drum and fancy wands were property of the society. After the ceremony, offerings were left at the place where it had been held. Later, if one came upon them, he could take them, providing he left others in their stead. To take them otherwise was a grave insult to Kitci Manitou, the Master of Life.[5]

The Sarsis had a special prairie chicken medicine tipi but sold it to the Blackfeet.

The Prairie Chicken Dance was already a thing of the past among the Oglala Sioux in Wissler's day, the early 1900's. We were fortunate that Flying Cloud, at Standing Rock, remembered it.

As recently as the 1920's some of the Canadian Indians were still doing the Prairie Chicken Dance, but apparently it had become a contest dance by that time. And well it might, for it requires much practice, skill, and imagination. We have seen an illustration from an old *Mentor Magazine*, taken about 1923, of a little Indian boy, champion Prairie Chicken Dancer at the Calgary Stampede. He is decked out with an eagle tail, eagle wings on his shoulders, and a porcupine-hair roach.

The last time we saw anything resembling a Prairie Chicken Dance among the Indians was about 1940 at the Crow Fair. The Crow Fair, held each summer at Crow Agency, Montana, for three days, is one of the finest Indian gatherings in the country. At that time over one hundred tipis in a huge circle, half a mile in diameter, made up the great camp. Old-timers were still alive, and singing, feasting, parades, and dances were the order of the day.

Two brothers did a sort of Prairie Chicken Dance all the time the other dancers were doing the so-called War Dance. These two young men, being big and heavy, did nothing very active, but they were oh so dignified and at the same time so comical! Their very obesity enhanced the illusion that they were prairie chickens. They danced toward each other, bowed, turned tails (bustles) together, and bowed outward to the audience, with little shaking movements of the arms and head. Everyone was rocking with laughter! Anyone who thinks Indians never laugh should have been there.

But the real fun came when an old Sioux woman (the Crow women would never think of such a thing) slipped up behind the two dancers, who were so interested in their own antics that they never noticed her. She mimicked everything they did to perfection, never letting them see her. The laughter she caused made the two boys think it was all for them, and they fairly outdid themselves to keep up with it.

With the passing of the old-timers, the interest in Crow Fair waned for a number of years. Some of the young people would rather have a rodeo or carnival. The few Indian celebrations to be seen today are far different from those of a few years ago, when the old "long hairs" kept traditions alive.

The Blackfeet and Crees, along with Sioux, Assiniboins, and other tribes of the Northwest, all take part in the Calgary Stampede, but to our knowledge the Prairie Chicken Dance is no longer on the program, nor is it done at any of the Indian gatherings in the United States. Prairie Chicken Dance songs are still sung in Canada, but are now part of the Grass Dance. Assiniboins, or Stonies, once had a Prairie Chicken Dance, which some say was borrowed from the Crees. A solo dancer, using two rattles and in a crouching position, imitated a prairie chicken.

From the account given here we can see that Prairie Chicken dances were common enough throughout the country where that bird is found, and except for ritualistic differences there was naturally a great deal of similarity, regardless of tribe. In the parts of the country where the prairie chicken is unknown, other birds were featured in dances. The Kiowas, in Oklahoma, still have a Humming Bird Dance, which is very fast and agitated, as would be expected in portraying that little feathered bumblebee, and takes a great deal of skill to perform.

THE QUAIL DANCE

In the East the Cherokees had a Quail Dance, which we were fortunate enough to see before it was discontinued. It was one included in the series of "stomp" dances, so used the simple shuffle-running step, counterclockwise, as is usual with Eastern dances. The accompaniment was by a singer with a water drum. At a certain place in the song, the dancers all huddled in the center, arms spread partly to the side, palms outstretched and flat. The "quail" were hiding from an eagle. On another signal all scattered wildly in all directions, after which the circle was reformed and the dance repeated as long as interest lasted.

It is probable that tribes throughout the East had dances in imitation of grouse, quail, and perhaps other birds.

COSTUME

The most popular and spectacular dance ornaments have been developed mainly from the observance of birds. The colorful porcupine hair roach, common from the Atlantic Ocean to the Rocky Mountains, is certainly an imitation of the perky crests we see on so many birds. Both the dance bustle and the familiar war bonnet are patterned after spread tail feathers of strutting birds. From the beginning, Indians, in their love of finery and decoration, decided that a fancy tail, as displayed by so many creatures in the animal world, would be a great asset to their personal adornment when dressing for special occasions. But you could not wear a tail just because you admired one. You had to earn the privilege. Just where the dance bustle originated is not definitely known. The one brought back by Lewis and Clark seems to be Yanktonai Sioux, but it is known that tribes around the Great Lakes also had them.

The center rosette is a direct copy of the spread tail of the strutting turkey gobbler or the dancing cock grouse. Turkeys and grouse are not ordinarily considered warlike, but the rosette represents a battlefield, and the bustle itself has always been associated with war. It was entirely a warrior's ornament until recently. Only the bravest warriors were permitted to wear them. Now every dancer thinks he has to have one to be properly attired.

The Grass Dance costume of hair roach, bustle, and arm wheels is ideal for the Prairie Chicken Dance, the wheels giving the impression of wings. The old warlike symbolism is lost to most present-generation Indians.

Whenever the Prairie Chicken Dance is presented on our program, it is always a favorite. Even people who know little or nothing about dance react enthusiastically to it because it is all so obvious. Dance is an international language, like music, and

Mandan *Buffalo Dance*, by Catlin, from his *North American Indians.* It is interesting to note how Catlin and Bodmer, painting in the same period, saw differences in the same dance.

there is no mistaking the movements of this one. The Prairie Chicken Dance was without a doubt one of the Indian's most colorful and picturesque dances, which few living today have been privileged to see.

THE BUFFALO DANCE

The importance of the buffalo in Plains Indian life has been mentioned a number of times. We have told about the portrayal of buffalo in the animal dances of the Sioux, Cheyennes, and Mandans, the Buffalo Dance of the chiefs, the Buffalo Societies, and the buffalo cults. The cults often included women members, and there were women's buffalo societies among many tribes.

The Plains Indian admired the qualities that the buffalo represented and he sought to develop those same qualities—great strength, courage, endurance, generosity. The buffalo gave the Indian everything he needed. Buffalo meat was the staple food of the people. From tanned hides with the hair on they made robes and blankets; with the hair removed they were used for the covers of their dwellings, clothing, and all sorts of camp and household equipment. Buffalo rawhide made shields, moccasin soles, packing cases; it served as hammer, nails, string, and glue in the manufacture of numerous articles.

Not a particle was wasted. Horns were used for decoration, spoons, and dishes. Hooves were used for dangles and rattles. Both horns and hooves were boiled to make glue. Hair was used for ropes, baskets, and woven bags and sashes. Children made sleds of buffalo ribs and used them for sliding not only on the snow in winter but down grassy hillsides in summer. When they returned home, tired and hungry, their mothers had dinner cooked for them in a buffalo paunch, which was used in place of a kettle before the traders brought iron and brass kettles; it served also as a water bag. The tail made a fly brush. Even the snort and stamp of the buffalo were used in the ceremonial dances!

When the white man began ruthlessly slaughtering millions of buffalo and leaving tons of the finest meat in the world to rot upon the prairies, the Indians began to starve. The destruction of their "commissary" forced them to surrender and come in to settle on the reservations. They were plunged, suddenly, from the midst of plenty to the depths of poverty and despair. The blow was sudden and complete. They have never recovered from it. But we have expected them to jump suddenly, from a primitive stone age, into the midst of a complicated machine age, in the matter of two or three generations, when it has taken us and our type of civilization thousands of years to arrive where it is today.

The buffalo roamed as far east as the Appalachian Mountains; even tribes on the East Coast had buffalo dances in former times. White men began the senseless slaughter of the shaggy animals upon the first contact, so that by the late 1700's they had been exterminated east of the Mississippi River.

THE PLAINS INDIANS

Within each Plains tribe there were usually several Buffalo dances. Some were almost entirely social in nature, serving largely as entertainment, while others were completely serious in purpose. One of the important Sioux Buffalo dances involved thirty separate ceremonies, one each day. In the social type, men, women, and children all took part. In all of them there were some dancers dressed as buffalo, with great headdresses—sometimes a complete mask—of buffalo hide and horns. Often these headdresses included a strip of fur that extended all the way to the tail, worn down the dancer's back. Other dancers might wear a headdress and a tail, arched by sewing it over a bent stick so that it looked like the tail of a challenging buffalo bull.

Mandan Bull Dance, by Bodmer, in Prince Maximilian's *Travels*. Other tribes, including the Sioux, used similar costumes. Both Bodmer and Catlin pictured the Bull Society Dance rather than a tribal dance for calling the buffalo. Smithsonian Institution, Bureau of American Ethnology.

Sometimes a dancer painted his body black, as mentioned in Catlin's description of the Mandan Bull Dance. Old Makes Trouble,[*] at Standing Rock, wore a suit of black-dyed underwear with a buffalo headdress containing one eagle feather hanging at the back and a tuft of pheasant feathers on the side. In earlier times sage chicken or prairie chicken feathers would have been used instead, since the pheasant is a newcomer, not native to this country. Makes Trouble's face was painted green, with white circles around his eyes—green for the earth (and grass) from which the buffalo came, and white to exaggerate his own eyes.

---

[*]Wakiyuŝicapi really means "They Make Trouble for Him!"

Gladys Laubin and Makes Trouble at a dance at Bull Head, South Dakota. Photo by Laubin.

In all Buffalo dances the dancers endeavored to simulate the activities of a herd, butting, fighting, snorting, bellowing, pawing the ground, and grunting. Even the social Buffalo dances helped to call buffalo and were pleas to the Buffalo Spirit, controller of the herds. They were prayers for fertility and of thanksgiving. The dancers not only called the buffalo but gained strength and courage from them. They thanked the Buffalo for his great generosity and sacrifice and thanked the Great Mystery for providing the buffalo. Male buffalo dancers carried weapons, for they took the parts of hunters as well as of buffaloes.

Some Buffalo dances were highly organized—we might almost say choreographed—and were presented in set patterns and formations.

The Grass Buffalo Dance is one of the social types, with little pattern. It is seldom, if ever, performed in buffalo costume; the dancers wear their usual Grass Dance costumes, but even here there is some naturalistic representation of buffalo. The drum rolls and the dancers get into a low squat, shaking their heads, arms, and shoulders and rapidly moving their heels to make an almost continuous ringing of their ankle bells. This is much the same as the beginning of a contest dance, the Stop, or Get Down, dances. On another change in the song and signal by the drum, the dancers butt against each other, striking shoulders together. The drum changes again, this time to forceful, steady beats, and the dancers spring to their feet and jump in time to it, both feet striking the ground at once. Arms are either in thrust position or hands on hips. During this jumping they also use head and shoulders to imitate buffalo. Some dancers snort and grunt to make the portrayal more naturalistic, and some make feinting movements, as if they were butting heads and shoulders again.

These movements are sometimes repeated during one dance. At other times there may be a slight intermission in between. Many times an entire evening of Grass dancing may go by without a single performance of the Grass Buffalo Dance. On other occasions, if audience or dancers demand it, it may be given several times during the evening.

THE PUEBLO INDIANS

The cultures of the Pueblo and other Southwestern Indians are still very strong, but because of efforts to prohibit their ceremonies most of these tribes are reluctant to talk about their beliefs and do not encourage visitors to attend many of their functions. In earlier days there were occasions when non-Indian friends were even invited into the kivas, but this is no longer permitted, and they are able to see only public performances.

Because Santo Domingo, in New Mexico, is one of the most conservative pueblos, we felt quite fortunate to be invited by friends from that village to attend their Buffalo, or Animal, Dance and to have a feast in their home afterward. It was a gray, raw Sunday morning in February when we drove into the little town of adobe houses. Only a few dogs roamed the dusty streets; not a soul was in sight. We happened to arrive during one of the intermissions, for the dancing took place periodically throughout the day. Later we learned that the ceremonies began at dawn, with the arrival of a group of runners who made a four-mile run before anything else got under way.

Suddenly in the distance we heard the great drums booming, the singing of the chorus, and the jingling of the dancers' bells. The Antelope dancers, in gay yellow-and white-painted costumes, each leaning on two sticks, were weaving from side to side, leading the procession. The dancers came so close we could see the sweat on the Buffalo dancers' black-painted faces and the sparkle of their eyes. Except for a few Indians from neighboring pueblos and the Santo Domingos themselves, we were the only ones watching the ceremony.

As suddenly as the dancers had appeared, they turned between two adobe houses and disappeared again. Then from another alley they returned, this time led by two Hunters, who wore beautiful quivers of mountain-lion skin over their shoulders and carried bows and arrows in their hands. Way in the rear came a crowd of singers and drummers and still farther behind were men with guns, who fired them off as the dancers entered the plaza.

Following the Hunters came the four Antelope dancers, then four Deer dancers and two Mountain Goats, with two male Buffalo dancers and one woman Buffalo between them. The woman represented Mother Earth, mother of all game animals. Even to these farming people game was important. The animal dancers lined up on each side of the three Buffalo, who always took the center.

The Pueblo songs sound extremely complicated rhythmically, but every movement of the dancers was in perfect time, following the songs exactly. Each group took various positions during the singing. The singers entered the plaza last, in such a mass that it was impossible to count them, but there must have been at least a hundred. They grouped so tightly around the drums that we could not even see them, but later we counted four of them—huge cottonwood-log drums, all sounding as one, each great boom throbbing right through us. Frances Densmore said they used as many as ten drums.[6] The chorus marched across the plaza, then stood and sang in one close body, guns going off at the beginning of some of the songs.

It was amusing to see the Antelope standing with their rears all in a row, their tiny little white tails behind them. They would turn and pivot, the leader first stamping, just as wild antelope do in giving an alarm, then all four turning at once. The dancers were boys, teen-agers, smaller than the Deer dancers. The Deer dancers had long deer antlers on their heads and tufts of white down or cotton shading their faces.

The two male Buffalo dancers, wearing huge buffalo headdresses, were stripped to the waist and painted black. The headdresses each had four eagle feathers hanging down behind, with little bunches of parrot feathers at the quill ends. Parrot feathers play an important role in many dances of the Southwest, where parrots once lived, it is said. Their feathers represent the colors of early morning light shading into the blue sky.

The male Buffalo dancers also wore armbands and leg bands of buffalo hair and on their kilts was a figure of a plumed water serpent. Each dancer carried a bow and arrows in his left hand and a rattle made of the skin of a buffalo's tail in his right. Evenly spaced along each bow were four eagle feathers.

A third man, who always stayed with them, had on a buckskin shirt. His long black hair hung below his knees as he danced; his face was also painted black.

The Buffalo Mother, or Earth Mother, also wore a buffalo headdress, but a much smaller one than those of the men, and her face was painted yellow. She was dressed in the usual Pueblo fashion, in a dark woven dress covering her left shoulder and leaving the right arm bare. Her hair was long, hanging down her back, but not as long as the man's. Dangling from her right elbow a bunch of orange feathers fluttered, making a spot of brilliant color between the large turquoise beads around her neck and the turquoise-colored sash around her waist. Her skirt, like the kilts of the men, was white with blue, black, and red woven on the borders.

Her left hand rested on her sash, and Densmore reported that in the left hand of the Buffalo Mother was concealed a little stone animal, but of course we could not see that.[7] In her right hand was a bunch of herbs and several kinds of feathers— eagle, blue jay, red bird, yellow bird, and parrot, all representing the dawn light and the coming of a new day.

The Buffalo dancers exert far more energy than any of the other animal dancers. They raise one foot in place, stamp, and repeat several times, suddenly jumping sidewise twice, sometimes running in place, in perfect time and pattern with the seemingly erratic rhythm of the music.

The Deer dancers wore the entire skin of a deer, the head with the antlers forming a cap, the rest of the skin down their backs. The Elk had caps apparently of deer-skin, with cotton on the crown between two real, but small, elk antlers. The animal dancers carried green branches which they waved at intervals to the four directions.

On leaving the plaza the Hunters went first. The Antelope and Deer made an alley for the Buffalo to pass through, then, turning, followed them off. The crowd of singers and drummers wound up the procession. Some of these latter, in appearance, were rather disappointing, for even in this most conservative of all the Pueblos they wore war bonnets, deer-tail roaches, even a few "pony" crests. One had on a Sioux scalp-lock ornament, a type not even seen among the Sioux any more, and another a black hair roach, like a Woodland Indian. Perhaps this motley array had some significance, such as peace and unity with other tribes. Most of the singers wore plain khaki trousers or Levis, shirts, and moccasins. But few of these moccasins were of Pueblo style. Some were beaded Plains moccasins, some commercial puckered-toe type, some canvas sneakers. However, all were wearing something pretty in their hair and most had eagle down sprinkled in it, symbolizing snow. Even this Animal, or Buffalo, Dance is a prayer for moisture—snow or rain—as are all ceremonies of the Southwest.

The procession and dance lasted about twenty minutes. It was repeated about twice each hour, with a fifteen- or twenty-minute rest between appearances. After the thunder of the drums, the gunfire, the powerful chants, the strenuous dancing, and the color and excitement of each performance, the complete quiet and solitude of

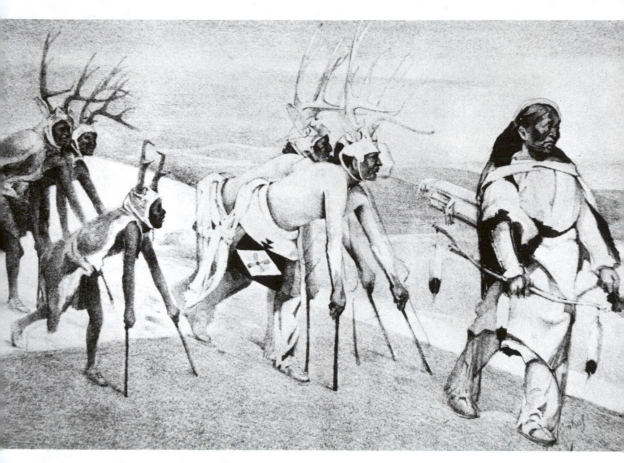

Taos Deer Dance, from a lithograph by J. A. Imhof. Deer dancers of other pueblos were similarly portrayed. (The lithograph was reversed, and so the archer appears to be left-handed.) Courtesy of A. W. Erkins.

the intermissions was an incredible contrast. It never failed to create a dramatic effect for the next entrance of the dancers.

The dance was presented twelve times during the day, once for each month. It was never changed, being repeated the same way each time, but everyone waited in anticipation for the reappearance of the dancers.

Blue mountains in the distance, groups of Indians in bright blankets clustered around the ancient adobe buildings and watching from the rooftops, provided an incomparable setting for the colorful drama. On the final dance the sun broke through the clouds once more—a brilliant spotlight on the performers, casting their long dark shadows across the plaza as they left the unforgettable scene. The pageant was over and suddenly all was as still as when we arrived.

According to Curtis, back in the days when there were still buffalo, the Keresan Pueblos, which include Santo Domingo, gave a Buffalo Dance similar to the one we saw before each buffalo hunt. Some of the Pueblos still have Buffalo dances that are highly naturalistic, the dances giving very realistic portrayals of the actions of the animals themselves. At San Juan, the Buffalo Girl dances with amazing vigor and agility, using incredibly rapid footwork.[8] In this and a number of villages the dancing is so strenuous that two alternate groups of dancers do the performing. At Taos as many as one hundred and forty dancers have been reported as taking part in one Buffalo Dance. Taos has always been much influenced by the Plains tribes, but other Animal dances of the Southwest must also have some relationship to the old Animal dances formerly so important among Plains tribes.

The Santo Domingo Buffalo Dance takes place only in winter, usually in February and, according to several reports, never before the first snow storm. Four nights of practice were held before the actual dance began, and then the dancers partially fasted for three more days and nights. The dancers all had to be Turquoise People, the Winter half of the tribe. The Pueblos are divided into Summer and Winter groups, Summer People being known as Squash People. Shortly before midnight of the fourth day the animal representatives ran "swiftly to various points as much as twenty miles distant, each party, Deer, Elk, Buffalo, Antelope, followed by a war-chief's deputy with bow and arrows."[9] Curtis reported that the Deer dancers were once mistaken for real deer in the half light of dawn and were shot at by Mexican hunters as they crossed the road.

The female Buffalo dancer, sometimes called the Buffalo Girl, was not required to make this run, but waited outside the village at a special sun shrine. When the dancers arrived at their destinations, they made prayers to the controlling spirits of the animals they represented, then returned on a run to the village.

Miss Densmore said that they went out about an hour and a half *after* midnight of the fourth day of preparation, formerly running as much as thirty or forty miles altogether. They went in different directions to make their offerings, then returned to within about a mile of the village just before dawn. About 4:00 or 4:30 the drummers and singers went "after the game," taking up a position about halfway between the council house and the known hide-out of the Animals. Four shots from the village signaled the Animals, and they made their appearance, acting wild and running about. Members of the Warrior's Society and some old men approached them, finally touching them, as the drummers and singers stood in place and sang the appropriate songs for this part of the ceremony. The Buffalo Girl stayed near them. The entire party then returned to the council house.[10] In earlier days the Animal, or Buffalo, Dance was also a prayer to call game for food and for increase in the game, for fruitfulness, as well as for snow or rain.

Miss Densmore reported the Buffalo Girl as having a headdress made from the breast feathers of a duck, from which protruded the tips of antelope horns. It had small white beads across the brow and pendants of beads hanging at each side of the face.[11]

Curtis said there was another winter Animal Dance in which only Summer, or Squash, People took part. In it there were two Deer, two Antelope, two Elk, two

Buffalo, two Mountain Sheep, and two girls associated with the Buffalo, but wearing Hopi costume and no buffalo headdresses. In the dance we saw there were four Antelope, four Deer, two Elk, two Mountain *Goats*, but no Sheep. Curtis mentioned that the Squash People asked the Turquoise People permission to give their own dance, which request was always granted. The fact that various observers have reported differences in numbers and types of performers as well as in starting time tends to show that Pueblo dances are not as rigidly "set" as some people believe, although there is no doubt that most dance movements, recitations, and songs must be exact.

The Animal Dance we saw was exciting, colorful, dramatic, and at the same time elemental and dignified. We did not try to question our friends about it. All Pueblos, and especially Santo Domingo, have bans against giving information on their religion and way of life to outsiders. Curtis cites a number of instances of not only severe punishment but execution of those who violated the bans and served as informants. He and others have reported how they had to secure information under cover. Personally we have known a few Indians from various pueblos who have given up life among their own people to live in the cities. Some of them have told us that people back home who serve as informants to outsiders usually have "accidents."

THE YAQUI DEER DANCE

A dance which has won some attention in recent years in the Southwest is the Yaqui Deer Dance; it seems to be the only really Indian dance left among these people. The Yaquis are to be found in southern Arizona and northern Mexico. They were thought at one time to be relatives of the Apaches, but they are of Uto-Aztecan stock and more closely related to the Papagos. The only relationship they bear to the Apaches is that they were also warlike and gave the Mexicans plenty of trouble until very recently.

At one time the Deer Dance had a great deal of religious significance. Among these people, as so many others, the deer was regarded as having magic power and could either cause or cure sickness. The deer was also associated with flowers, in an annual cycle, the deer pertaining to the dry season, flowers to the wet. The Deer Spirit, or controlling power of the deer, was regarded as a deity, and the dance was originally given to honor the Deer Spirit; to acquire its power; to insure good hunting, deer being an important source of food; to cure the sick; and to insure fertility of both the tribe and the animals. The dance could also bring rain and make thunder and lightning. So the over-all ceremony was concerned with growth and well-being.

The Deer Dance today is given largely as entertainment and as a test of skill on the part of the Deer dancer. Although there is little or no emphasis on the former religious aspects, the fact that the dance exists at all shows something of its former importance. According to the songs that remain, there may have been several forms of the Deer Dance at one time, but only one is left, and it no doubt is the simplest.

As given today, the Deer Dance is a solo dance and the dancer holds his audience, or receives its criticism, through his ability as a performer and the strength of his personality. He is still required to follow a certain set pattern and to perform certain conventional movements, but most of the Deer dancers today have seldom if ever seen a real deer, so a realistic portrayal is a rare occurrence. Formerly such a simulation was expected, along with other dramatic elements associated with hunting and killing the deer. The symbolical making of thunder, lightning, and rain was also included.

It has been reported that formerly the ceremony began with a number of dancers acting out the planting of their fields, when they saw deer and decided to go hunting. They tracked the deer, finally sighted it, killed it, and skinned it. Then followed moments of comedy and finally the serious aspect of making rain, so important to any desert people. It seems strange, but as the dance has lost its religious significance it has become more ritualized in form.

The peculiar drum used in this ceremony has been described in the chapter on music and instruments. In addition to the drum, the "orchestra" consists of two men with *moraches, or raspadors,* which are held against inverted half gourds as resonators. One resonator is larger than the other, producing a lower tone. The songs in existence today pertain primarily to flowers rather than to deer.

The Deer Dancer wears a small deer head, with antlers, as a headdress. The deer head is stuffed and fastened on top of a cap, which is held in place with a white kerchief. The antlers are wrapped with red cloth. The dancer wears rattles made of dried cocoons around his ankles. In each hand he carries a gourd rattle, the one in the right hand being a little larger and more oblong than the one in the left hand, which is nearly round. Both are painted red, but one has a red handle, the other blue.

This dance is another example of a dancer taking more than one part at a time. In earlier days the Deer Dancer was expected to act like a deer—to pause, look, quiver his nostrils, jerk his head, tremble all over, jump, leap, stand still, watch again. At the same time he followed the song with his rattles, which were used in a prescribed way. For that matter, they still are. The left-hand rattle is rotated in a small circle counterclockwise. The right-hand rattle beats the rhythm and is moved in a large circle or with rapid motions up and down and across the right side of the body. To be able to handle each rattle differently in this way is an accomplishment in itself.

Otherwise the dance is repetitious and monotonous. The step is a rapid toe-heel shuffle of one foot while pointing or resting the ball of the other foot on the ground. The foot action changes every four to six beats.

The Deer Dance used to be given many times a year at all sorts of fiestas, but in recent times has been limited to four times a year. There is no longer either hunting or agricultural significance to the performance. There is no longer any curative aspect, although a slight suggestion of magic persists. The dancer himself is more important as an entertainer than for any religious implication, and the entire dance reflects the change in Yaqui culture and the nearly complete loss of some of its most important aspects.[12]

THE UTE BEAR DANCE

One Indian animal dance still to be seen today is the Ute Bear Dance. The dance is usually given in late March on the Ute reservations in eastern Utah and southern Colorado. Formerly it was given earlier, in late February or early March, the time when bears were supposed to come out of hibernation. This was also the time just previous to the break-up of the winter camp, when the tribe moved out in search of game. Sometimes small villages visited larger ones for the Bear Dance instead of putting on one of their own.

Nowadays the Bear Dance seems to be mainly a social occasion, but long ago it combined religious and practical motives. The dance was considered the same as the ones the bears themselves did in the mountains, and so was expected to please them, gaining their friendship and kindliness. Later, if necessary to hunt them, it conciliated their spirits. Today it still provides an opportunity for medicine men to make prayers and doctor patients.

The dance takes place within a circle of boughs about one hundred feet across and six or seven feet high. Frances Densmore saw a circle two hundred feet across in 1914. The entrance is usually to the east, but has been reported also on the south. A new corral is built each year and the old one burned, although no ceremonial reason is attached. It is merely a way of clearing the ground of dried-up brush.

The Bear Dance is in charge of a special Bear Dance Chief, who is chosen by the men of the tribe, and he has two assistants. There is no ceremonial number of days involved now but it is usually held for seven or eight days.

The "orchestra" sits opposite the entrance to the circle of boughs. There, formerly a large shallow round basket was placed over a hole in the ground as a resonator for the *raspadors,* sometimes called *moraches,* or notched sticks which are used to accompany the Bear Dance. Each singer held one of these in his left hand, resting it against the basket, and scraped it with a round bone, or sometimes with the scapula of an antelope or mountain sheep. The resulting noise was said to sound like a bear.

But for the dance, the more noise, the better, so the next development in the orchestra was to dig a trench about five feet long, two feet wide and two feet deep and cover it with a sheet of zinc. This hole was said to represent a bear's den. Then they discovered that even more noise could be produced by digging a round hole large enough in which to set an overturned metal wash tub, on which was placed an open wooden box, with a sheet of tin on top of it.

Then came the way that is still used to this day, as far as we know. Instead of a hole in the ground, a wooden frame about a foot high, two and half feet wide and six feet long is built on the ground, on which the zinc or tin is placed and the singers sit around it on benches. They find this more efficient and more comfortable than sitting on the ground.

Up until recently, and perhaps even now, new songs were made up each year for the Bear Dance and old ones were used only if they ran out of new ones.

In the old days children did not take part in the dance, but lately the first day has been devoted to them. The singers are boys, and the dancers are boys and girls. Later the men take over the singing, but children still dance. They have several "drivers"—boys armed with switches—who go after the laggards, but there are no drivers in the adult dance.

As in most Indian gatherings, men are on the north side of the corral, women on the south. The first song is accompanied by rapid and irregular rubbing of the raspadors and then is repeated in steady 2/4 or 4/4 time as women march across the corral to choose their dancing partners by waving a hand at them. They then line up east and west, locking arms. The music pauses and begins rapidly again, and the men saunter out to form their line, clasping hands and facing their partners. The next movement consists of two long steps ahead and three short ones back, alternated on each foot. When the rhythm becomes steady again, the men go forward with this sort of rocking step as the women retreat. Then women move ahead as the men retreat.

White men are sometimes invited to dance, but they are expected to pay their partners. Indian men do not pay.

About the seventh day the real interest develops. The women wear their best clothes, and the young fellows who have been riding around get off their horses and come into the corral, hoping to be chosen to dance. The dancing starts about noon. During intermissions there are speeches and give-aways, as at almost any Indian "doings," and everyone is invited to stay for the next day, which will be the biggest of all. The children take part again, forming their own lines on the side.

The eighth day is the big day. The women wear calico dresses and brilliant shawls, beaded belts, and beaded high-top moccasins similar to those worn by Shoshonis and Crows. Some have Navajo jewelry, and others have old-time cloth dresses with elk-teeth trimming. The men wear cowboy hats, sometimes with beaded bands, bright-colored shirts, dark trousers or new Levis, beaded and fringed gauntlets. Those with long hair may wear a silk scarf around their heads, under their high "reservation" hats. The young fellows often wear a bright scarf about their necks.

The dancing is dignified at first, the women stepping lightly, the men carrying themselves proudly, prancing forward and backward. Now the lines advance toward each other, instead of one advancing and the other retreating, and occasionally they even bump each other. Sometimes couples break out of line and dance back and forth across the corral, the man on the woman's right, right arms around each other's waists. Sometimes a popular young man is chosen by two women. They dance till sunset and then all partake of a feast. In the morning the dance is resumed, lasting until about noon, when it breaks up and everyone goes home.

In earlier days it lasted all night until dawn, when two "bears" appeared upon the scene—a man and a woman, wearing bearskins, with red paint around their mouths to represent blood dripping from their jaws to suggest the ferocity of bears.

The Bear Dance is what we might call a women's dance, since they take active part and choose their partners. In keeping with the occasion, the female bear pursued the male around the corral. They acted ferocious toward anyone who laughed at them, giving as realistic a portrayal as possible. They played around for an hour or so, then went off, and the people resumed their dancing.

Formerly this last day was the only time the lines advanced toward each other and retreated, and at the end the women approached the men and tried to force them backward, each woman endeavoring to push her partner, the man opposite her. There was no couple dancing originally, this being a modern intrusion. Finally the women succeeded in pushing the men back across their side of the corral. This was the only time the men and women touched each other, and the dance ended then.

Sometimes the dance was brought to an early end by someone falling down as he danced. As with most tribes, it was believed to be bad luck to fall in a dance. Formerly the fallen dancer was treated by a medicine man, this being one occasion when he was not paid for his services. Now if anyone falls during the dance, one of the singers passes a raspador over him, beginning at his feet and continuing to his head, points it to the sky, and makes a brushing motion with it. All this is to ward off any evil effect.

An observer of the Bear Dance in 1893 declared that then the dance was sacred. The Utes believed they were descended from bears, so bear rites tinged many ceremonies. Long ago they probably would not hunt bears; in fact, many tribes had taboos against hunting them and would not eat bear meat or use bear skins. The Utes believed the mountain lion to be braver than the bear (which is unusual), but the bear was wiser and could practice magic, another belief held by many tribes.

The dance was given partly to aid the bears in coming out of hibernation and to gain power from them, as bears could cure sickness and help one send messages to friends and relatives in the Spirit World. The ground within the corral was sacred. No horses or dogs were allowed to enter. All people who came inside were invited to dance and were expected to dance if requested. The songs were believed to carry the noise of the raspadors to the bears in the mountains, where the noise changed to thunder and woke the bears up.

Even by 1893 some of the old beliefs were changing and some of the sacred character of the ceremony was already lacking. But at that time there was no gambling during the Bear Dance, whereas now hand games are going on at the same time. There was also some couple dancing, the arms around the waists being the "bear hug." Then, as now, the dance gradually worked to greater pitch and the last day was the time of most activity. But at that time it lasted four days and one night instead of the seven or eight days of more recent times. The participants danced only a short time the first day, for the bears were not supposed to be awake yet. They danced all night following the third day, fires being lit around the corral for light. They took time out only for supper. Then they danced until noon of the fourth day, and followed with a feast. By then the bears were supposed to have come out of their dens, mated, and found food.

During the first couple of days the dancers in each line joined hands, but as the dance grew in intensity they moved their arms like the forepaws of bears. If a woman stepped on a man's foot everyone laughed, for it was a sign that they would fall in love.

At intermissions, the song leader made an invocation with a corn-husk cigaret, then all the singers did the same, observing a long moment of silence after rolling their cigarets, then lighting them and blowing puffs of smoke to the sky. During this time the men stood on their side of the corral and the women sat on theirs. Some people talked with the "shades" of the dead. Anyone could do this, but only medicine men could hear the replies.

After the first day, a beaded medicine pipe was brought out two or three times a day, lit, and passed from one man to another, each one puffing a few times and passing his fingers over the stem, like playing a flute. They smoked with the spirits and believed the pipe would protect them from pneumonia and tuberculosis.[13]

Even when the Bear Dance was still considered religious, some dancers attended just for pleasure, while others hoped to obtain magic power. And even recently, simple as this dance is, people got together a week before the main Bear Dance to rehearse, which shows that the dance was important enough that a proper performance was considered desirable.

CADDO DANCES

The Caddoes, or Hasi'nai, were moved to Indian Territory from Louisiana and east Texas just before the Civil War. They still do a variety of dances that seem to be related to those of the Gulf tribes and quite different from those of other tribes of Oklahoma. At the same time they have borrowed some dances since their arrival in Oklahoma, but, although located near Plains groups—Kiowas, Cheyennes, Arapahos, and Comanches—their borrowed dances are mainly from the East—Creek, Delaware, and Shawnee.

They have an entire series of animal dances, but the Turkey Dance seems to be the most important from the standpoint of historical tradition. They also have Duck, Fish, Alligator, Bear and Coon dances, as well as others they call Bell, Corn, Quapaw, Cherokee, Swing and Ghost dances.

The Turkey Dance, although loosely grouped with these others, is considered a dance in itself, for it is always given on an afternoon, usually starting between 3:00 and 5:00 and lasting until sunset, but never after darkness. The Turkey Dance is mainly a women's dance and would seem to take the place of the Scalp and Victory dances of other tribes, although the Hasinai claim it has no relationship to these dances. But formerly there were periods in it when various women recited incidents of historical significance and past glory.

In dressing for the Turkey Dance, in addition to wearing the traditional long full skirts and pretty blouses typical of the Caddo, the women put on a sort of beaded hour-glass shaped ornament at the back of the head from which hangs a wide cloth and ribbon pendant, with mirrors down the center and little bells on the lower end.

They call this a *dus' toh*. It is similar to the ornaments worn in the Creek Ribbon Dance and the Shawnee Bread Dance, except that it is made up of several layers, the lowest layer being the widest, each successive layer being narrower and of a different color. Their dresses are more like those of Woodland tribes than those of the Plains.

Formerly several families owned dance grounds and these families offered them for the tribal dances. Someone wishing to "put on" a dance but not owning his own dance ground could get permission and usually got the cooperation of these owners, who assisted with the ceremonies and feasts.

The songs of the Turkey Dance pertain to former tribal history and periodically some woman could "stop the drum" temporarily taking over to recite a story from the past, but this was last done about 1930. The woman who led the Turkey Dance used to carry a long, carved cane but this is not often used nowadays.

The Turkey Dance might be divided into five parts. It used to begin with an old man going through the camp, calling the dancers together. The women were already in their dance dresses, but might be engaged in various camp activities, such as making bread, but they immediately put on their *dus' toh,* which is regarded as a special headdress used only in the Turkey Dance. No one seems to know why. They started for the dance ground, dancing as they went, even though their hands might still be covered with flour. They formed a single line as they arrived. (Nowadays they do not begin dancing until they arrive on the dance ground.)

With the long dresses it is difficult to observe the foot work, but they first move ahead with a subtle little slide step, circling to the left or clockwise. For the second part of the dance the song changes and they move into a side step, which seems to be a double beat with each foot, but sliding along the ground, barely lifting the feet. They turn a little, with some hesitation, from one side to the other, as the drum changes to an accented 2/4 beat. The drum is similar to that once used by other tribes, a large, flat, double headed drum hung from four tall stakes.

On the third change of song, the dancers lift their arms, bent at the elbows and shoulder high, to represent wings, and move around without any particular order, occasionally bumping one another, as if the turkeys were jostling each other. Both feet come down together, the weight is shifted to one foot, both feet come down again, and the weight is shifted to the other foot.

The fourth part of the dance is accelerated and gives the impression of a forward limp step, with the left foot forward, but it is really more of a little kick than a limp. They are now formed in a large circle and move towards the center with this kick step. On a signal from the drum, which then goes into a steady beat, they retreat to the edge of the circle with a sort of flat-footed single step to each foot. This forward and backward motion is continued during this entire song, when there is a break in the dance and the women go after partners.

Up to now the Turkey Dance has been very serious, but there is some relaxation during this "man hunt." If the man chosen does not wish to dance, the woman takes his hat and wears it for the final section of the dance. Sometimes the men will run and try to hide behind trees, but the women go right after them. At the close of the dance the man has to buy his hat back.

Once in the dance again, all is serious once more. Each woman faces her partner, and on a change in the song the man turns to face the opposite way. The men are the only ones to turn this way until the last three songs, when both men and women turn around. When this last part of the Turkey Dance is finished, just before sundown, all return to the camp for an evening meal.

In the evening, following a Drum Dance, which is always the first to be given, some of the old animal dances may still be seen. A Bear Dance is done in couples, starting off with the man on the right, the woman on the left, facing forward, the man moving with right foot ahead, the woman with left ahead. When the song changes, they dance obliquely and on the next change dance forward again. They change to single file, the men dancing backward now, then forward again, and so on until the drummers bring it to an end. As with many other tribes, the main difference in some of the dances is to be found in the songs. A similar dance might be given to a different song, but if it is not a bear song, it is not a Bear Dance.

The Duck Dance is another done by groups of couples, two couples to each group, the women going backward, facing their partners. The step is rather flat-footed, and the men sometimes quack like ducks as they dance. They dance in a circle, counterclockwise for a time. Then the men split, dancing around the women, matching up with the next pair of women, much as in a square dance. On another signal the women move forward in a clockwise circle, and the men open ranks to let them through. All continue around until meeting again, when the entire routine is repeated.

They have similar dances called Coon, Fish, and Alligator dances. Another dance that might be considered with the animal dances is the Stirrup Dance, which portrays riding a horse. It is another couple dance, and at certain signals in the song they cross hands, the woman puts her inner foot on the man's inner foot, and they hop around on their outside feet. There are two songs for this dance, both fast. It is a fast and strenuous dance with little rest, but when the song changes, each partner goes back on two feet in a sort of trot step for a brief interval. The next time they do the "stirrup" part of the dance they change sides, so that the opposite feet do the hopping.

During the winter season the Caddoes have hand games almost every weekend, men playing against the women. Since they prefer to dance outdoors, the hand games, requiring no costume and yet giving an opportunity for much singing around the drum and accompanied by feasts and raffles, serve in the same recreational capacity that the dances do in summer. It is rather remarkable that they still have a knowledge of so many old dances and still enjoy doing them.

Animal, bird, and even fish dances have been listed for the Yuchis, Creeks, Seminoles, and Shawnees. The Cherokees also had similar dances, which in recent times were given during the winter when the Booger Dance was featured. In the same category with the stomp dances were a Lizard Dance and an Ant Dance.

The Ant Dance was especially amusing, the dancers using the first two fingers of their right hands, near their foreheads, moving them to represent the feelers of the ants, turning now this way, now that way, sometimes facing each other and approaching each other with their "feelers" as they shuffled about.

THE LAKE INDIANS' SWAN DANCE

The Winnebagos and other Lake Indians have a Swan Dance in which only women and girls take part. They begin by forming a V, like a flock of flying geese, and dance with a slight limp step in 3/4 time, as in most women's dances, moving sometimes directly forward, sometimes in a circle to the right. It is a very simple dance, but, when all wear old-style buckskin dresses with the wide, fringed sleeves or capes, it presents a very charming and beautiful appearance.

THE NOOTKA WOODPECKER DANCE

Animal and bird representations played a large part in the dances of the Northwest Coast. When gathering for one of the winter performances, the Nootkas formed in groups according to the kind of dance in which they would participate. One from each group then arose and announced which dance it would give the following day.

Men performed such dances as Deer, Killerwhale, Hair-Seal, Kingfisher, and Crane. But birds were usually represented by women, and their repertoire included Snipe, Woodpecker, Butterball Duck, Sawbill Duck, and Mallard.

After the announcements a tattoo was beaten on the sounding boards, and the groups paraded around the dance hall, pantomiming motions suggestive of their particular dances, thus giving a preview of the following day's performance.

In the Woodpecker Dance the women wore only bark aprons. Their breasts and underarms were painted red, backs and outer arms were painted black, and under their arms they also fastened pieces of matting, painted red underneath and black on top, to simulate wings. On their heads they wore masks to further give the impression of the birds they portrayed. They danced first at the home of the chief and then performed all through the village. The various dance groups appeared one after the other all night long, and if visitors came before they were finished they had to repeat them again.[14]

PART IV.   **Dances of Other Areas**

20. Dances of the Pacific Coast

THE NORTHWEST COAST

Many tribes, stretching a thousand miles along the Pacific Coast from northern California to the Aleutian Islands, developed similar cultures, based largely on fishing or whaling, or both. In many ways these Indians of the Northwest Coast were entirely different from Indians of other parts of the country, and even within this area there are many differences in languages and customs. We think of the Haida, Tlingit, Kwakiutl, Nootka, and Chinook, as typical tribes of the Northwest, but actually there were about fifty tribes associated with this culture, and they represented at least seven linguistic families.

The dense timber to the east of them prevented much contact with inland tribes, and the heavy rainfall and lush abundance of many kinds of edible plants and berries made agriculture unnecessary or even impracticable. In three months' time, through the bounties of nature, they could lay up enough supplies for the rest of the year, so they were left with extra time for artistic development, for ceremonies, and for warfare, which was also largely ceremonial.

They did not follow the democratic ideas found among most North American Indians, but instead put much emphasis upon wealth and family connections. They were perhaps the most aristocratic of all, with a class system of free men, which included chiefs, nobles, and common people, and of slaves, who were really not a class at all, for they had no rights or privileges. Slaves were captured in war, bartered in trade, or sometimes brought into servitude by debt. The difference between those we might call nobles and commoners was largely one of wealth, which meant possessions, and these were largely acquired through personal industry and ingenuity. The wealth possessed by a leader consisted of the holdings of his entire family group. Even in this aristocratic society a chief did not have the autocratic power associated with European royalty.

These Indians of the Northwest Coast developed wood carving to a high art and created the famous totem poles and the remarkable and spectacular masks used in their elaborate potlatches and winter ceremonies. They also produced great, beautifully built war canoes and large houses of split cedar slabs.

Generally it can be said for the entire area that obtaining *spirit power* was a primary drive among these people; it was sought by both boys and girls at puberty. Boys often wandered alone for days through the deep forests, hoping for contact with some spirit, preferably one which was not already represented in his family. If he was unsuccessful, however, the power or powers already in the family might be handed down to him. In some groups the family power was handed down to the youngest son. Eventually the acquisition of power was acknowledged in a public performance, but sometimes a person waited a number of years before making such an announcement, because it was very expensive.

There were many recognized powers, but even so most of them had already been acquired by a number of people, so a person newly receiving one of these was expected to join a cult, or secret society, of those having the same power. To make a public announcement of spirit power meant that one had to stand the expense of paying tutors, already well acquainted with this certain power, for a long period of training; of providing a feast for the entire village; and of buying ceremonial paraphernalia; as well as make many sacrifices of property and go through harrowing tests of courage.

Originally men hoped for special power largely for success in war, but in more recent times it was desired for success in any field of endeavor—fishing, hunting, whaling, carving, craftsmanship, or being a shaman—but mainly it was sought for prestige, which was most important of all. Prestige here was more important even than on the Plains, but was acquired in an entirely different way. Women desired power for success in basket making, weaving, and other skills necessary to their mode of life.

The final announcement of having acquired a power meant having a spirit song, supposedly given in the vision, and giving a dance performance portraying what one had learned from the spirit visitor. The novice taught the song to tribal singers, who sang it for him as he danced.

The greatest power one could receive was said to be Eagle, recognized here as elsewhere as greatest of all the dwellers in the heavens, most powerful in the spirit realm. The Grizzly Bear was also great power, but usually not desired because it was too warlike and made its possessor short-tempered and disagreeable, hard to live with. Strangely enough, Duck was also a war power and one of the greatest, requiring a period of forty nights' preparation. Wasp, Loon, Black Bear, Cougar, and Wolf were all important powers. So were Deer, Killer Whale, Hair Seal, Kingfisher, Crane, Otter, Raven, and a Winged Human. All these were largely men's powers, although sometimes women received them. Women usually got their power from various birds—Snipe, Woodpecker, and several kinds of ducks.

Often before deciding to give the public dance, the novice became sick, because of his belief that the spirit had come to pay him a visit and the only way he could recover his health was to give the dance. Apparently most of the spirits were supposed to appear in about the same fashion, for spirit dancers were supposed to dress as the spirit had appeared to them and all dressed much alike. Most had some sort of shredded cedar-bark crown, with long streamers, often decorated with dentalium shells. But some wore hemlock fronds around head, neck, waist, arms, and legs. They wore a blanket belted around the waist, went barefooted, and painted their faces and often their entire bodies with red or black or both colors, sometimes adding mica dust for a glittering effect. Sometimes a cape with long human hair or goat hair hanging down over the shoulders was worn. Recently costumes of black cloth have been used instead of the dancers painting their bodies.

Although the candidate, or novice, was not supposed to tell what his power was for fear of losing it, he could give hints so that a medicine man, or shaman, could recognize it and obtain the proper assistants to help him with his ordeal. When they came to dress him he usually acted crazy, out of his head. He ran away from them, or tried to, but they tied a long rope to him. He might dash about blindly, run into trees, hurl himself into the sea. He tore around like this until exhausted, and it might take several days to calm him down enough that he could sing his song and teach it to the chorus. They must sing it exactly right, or he would become sick.

SPIRIT DANCES

The Spirit dances were held in the winter, which in that region is a time of rain, fog, and dampness. There was something going on almost every night from November until March. The dances were held in a large community building, with several fires burning on the earthen floor for light and heat. At one end of the building a space was partitioned off with curtains to serve as "backstage" quarters for the performers.

Formerly the representation of a spirit power in a dance was not realistic, for if it were it would be recognized and someone could destroy it, especially a jealous shaman, for a shaman had the greatest power of all. His power could travel to the country of ghosts and bring back lost souls and could even retrieve powers which had been lost, or captured. With such power the shaman could also cause or cure sickness.

The dance itself was a frenzied demonstration of whirling, hysterical movement, full of contortion, with rapid breathing, muscles tense, eyes sometimes closed— every gesture violent and erratic. The dancer sometimes moved in a counterclock- wise circle. If he stumbled or fell, it was not only regarded as a bad omen but made him feel ridiculous, and he must give away presents in order to feel reinstated in the good graces of the village. He believed such a misfortune was caused by a malignant shaman. If he lost any article of apparel, he was also expected to give away. To lose his headdress was the worst possible calamity, for it meant certain death would follow.

Isolated as these people were, they nevertheless had a number of customs similar to those of the Plains Indians, such as this give-away for a lost or dropped article. Also, the number four was important, and in ceremonies there were three feints before the actual movement was made. And, as on the Plains, a stick was often used to symbolize the present made at the give-away.

Certain people of wealth and power symbolized their station at a public gathering such as the Spirit Dance with a pole ten to twelve feet long, which had an ornament of shredded cedar bark and mountain-goat hair adorning its center. This particular pole had magic power to lead its handlers around the hall, into the fire, through the crowd—any place. Sometimes it would dance up and down.

The dancing usually began about 8:00 in the evening and lasted until around 6:30 in the morning. As many as forty-five Spirit dances might be given over this period in one night.

The singers for some dances beat upon boards with sticks, or batons, and for others used a wooden box drum, about five feet square and two feet deep, which was sometimes hung from the ceiling. Split-stick clappers and fancy carved wooden rattles were also used.

There were occasionally some daytime performances, associated with the initiation of candidates into secret societies. Several might be going through the initiation at once. These novices made their preparation behind the screen in the community house, then came bursting out, swinging their arms wildly, sometimes getting down on all fours and sniffing the ground, then rising up again, striking out at everything and everybody within reach. Each had a rope around his waist or chest that extended eight feet or so behind and was held by an assistant, so that he could not run away. The novices made their way outside, sometimes running down to the beach, sometimes into the wood, eventually being half dragged, half carried, back to the building. This was all accompanied by men shaking rattles, beating drums and singing.

Sometimes there was a dance outside around a pole. One circle was formed around it, about twelve feet in diameter, everybody holding hands. Another circle was formed outside of the first one, going the opposite way around, and a third outside of this one, going the same way as the inside circle, everyone keeping time with the singing and drumming. Then they formed two lines and endeavored to push each other from their positions. All seemed to enjoy this sport to the utmost, and it ended in a hearty laugh.

During intermission in the Spirit dancing the novices were held down on the ground by their assistants, who kept them from rising while other dances took place. A man who had demonstrated his spirit power on some other occasion arose from the spectators and marched clockwise around the room four times, singing and shaking a hollow wooden rattle. When he pointed it toward someone, that person jumped up, ran around, throwing his arms wildly about, bending almost to the ground, going through all sorts of antics. Eventually ten or fifteen men would be on the floor at once, all performing in similar fashion. Sometimes two or three would take hold of each other and all jump up and down together. Or a couple would seize the man with the rattle and try to take it from him, feigning great exertion and violence. When this performance was over, all took their seats and another man picked up the rattle and started a similar performance. Then a couple of the novices would struggle to their feet, followed by their attendants at the ends of the ropes, and dance the length of the house and back again.

Sometimes the novices were painted with red water color on the legs, which was occasionally moistened to look like blood. Some of them actually did make blood run over their chests and arms from little cuts made on their chins and under their tongues.

When the Spirit dancing was over, there was usually another give-away. Then fifteen or twenty young men came dancing into the house. They stood in a row, dancing for a time in place, then danced forward and backward the length of the house, then in place at one end again. A solo dancer now came forward, dancing in front of the rest, shaking a rattle, jumping up and down and around, sometimes squatting deeply, then jumping up again.[1]

It happened sometimes that a person was suspected of having special power that he never publicly demonstrated. He might then be "captured" by members of a secret society possessing the same power and forced to join them. This also reminds us somewhat of the Plains and the "capture" to make one join a warrior society or for making a chief. Such a "capture" was sometimes made with the use of eagle down, which was very potent. The captor approached his intended captive and threw eagle down at him four times, whereupon the captive either went into convulsions or went completely unconscious and was carried away.

The Cannibal Spirit, considered one of the most powerful of all by some of the Northwest Coast people, could not be obtained through a spirit-seeking vigil or a vision, but had to come from the society itself. To join, one had to pay high dues to the society and give a big feast, so only the sons of rich men were able to join, but the members had great prestige, and it was said that they could stand any kind of pain without feeling it. The Cannibal Spirit was also known as the Black Tamanous, or Spirit. It was wild and terrible, but members of the society were highly respected—and feared.

The Kwakiutls in particular considered the Cannibal Ceremony of great importance, but so did other tribes. After a father had made the necessary payments to insure a visit from the Black Spirit, his son gave a dance to announce his desire to belong to the Cannibal Society. Whistles were heard all around the village, supposedly made by the Cannibal Spirit, and members of the society then came to sing for the boy. While dancing, a whistle was heard again, and other members of the society appeared in their huge, grotesquely carved and painted masks, surrounded the boy, and carried him off behind the curtain, whence he supposedly disappeared, taken by the Cannibal Monster. The dances and rituals of the Northwest Coast were full of magic trickery, and he was probably taken through a secret door or may have been secluded in his own house.

According to one story, he was supposed to travel completely around the world in the next four days. Another says he was devoured alive by the Monster. When the Spirit Monster threw him up again he was filled with supernatural power.

A family rich enough to afford membership in the Cannibal Society had a house large enough that the final ceremonies were held within it. While the boy was hidden from the villagers, he was actually visited by a member of the society, who gave him instructions and told him how to behave.

Four days after his disappearance the whistles were heard again, signaling the novice's return. He appeared on the beach across from the village and two dancers were sent to discover who this demented being was, for that is the way he acted— wild, uncontrolled, and crazy, obsessed by the spirit which had carried him away.

When the dancers returned with news of the boy's identity, other men were sent to capture him and bring him in. When they finally caught him, he went unconscious and "died" again. They sang over him and raised him up four times, and he came to, looking wild and crazy again, once more trying to elude them. He ran around biting people, for, being possessed of the Cannibal Spirit, he now had a taste for human flesh. When finally captured again, he was carried unconscious into the house and placed behind the curtain.

The other society members, wearing great masks and cedar-bark costumes, danced through the village. These masks represented beings which lived with the Cannibal Monster. One was a huge bird, with a great beak for crushing men's skulls. He was portrayed by a dancer wearing a tremendous mask with a beak about six feet long. The masked dancers used their arms and torsos, but usually did little footwork. The masks were bulky and heavy, so doing vivacious, active dancing with them would have been quite a feat.

That night a great dance was held in the house of the boy's family in an effort to bring him back to normal behavior. He was dressed much as other Spirit dancers described before, naked, with blackened face, cape with long cedar-bark fringe, and bark fringe on his knees and ankles. When he appeared before the gathering he again tore around, biting at people, staring wildly about, not recognizing anyone, avoiding anyone who tried to touch him. He danced in a low squat, one foot in advance of the other, arms extended, fists clenched and thumbs sticking up. Then he moved forward with long leaps, both feet together, throwing his arms to the side, hands and fingers trembling.

A woman dancer appeared, bearing in her arms what looked like a mummy, or corpse, which she held out to the crazed Cannibal Dancer. He was immediately attracted by her offering of the food he craved and followed her as she danced backward around the fire four times. Then he disappeared, going again behind the curtain.

Gradually the Cannibal came back to his senses. When he appeared next he was wearing a blanket. He danced not quite as wildly, and little by little drew himself more erect, but again followed the woman with the corpse. The step he now used was one of drawing one knee almost up to his chest while slightly lowering the other. After circling the fire four times, he again "disappeared."

Twice more he came back, each time dancing erect and with more subdued action. On the last time around, the woman made motions of placing the "corpse" on an overturned drum. When the Cannibal Dancer disappeared this time, other members of the society took over the dancing.

The entire performance was repeated four nights, and on the last night the novice, the Cannibal Dancer, was supposed to have regained his entire human aspect and become like other people. Throughout the entire drama singers and audience participated, the latter at least to the extent of encouraging the dancers, clapping their hands in time with the songs, pounding on benches, tables, and drums. Some of them became so excited they nearly rivaled the dancers, whose frenzy became more intense with this sympathetic response. The beating of the singers' batons on the boards, with periodical changes in tempo, volume, and musical pitch, resulted in an ecstasy in which everyone took part. At some moments of climax the din was enough

"Medicine Mask Dance of the Clal-lum Indians of the Northwest Coast at Esquimalt," by Paul Kane. Royal Ontario Museum.

to nearly drown out the voices of the singers. At such performances, some members of the society showed their power over pain by exhibiting various fresh cuts on arms, chests, or legs; by having bone skewers thrust through noses, lips, or ears; or sometimes by having arrows, spears, or harpoon points piercing arms, legs, sides, or backs.

Following the performance on the fourth night, gifts were made to the society and the singers, and a feast was prepared for the entire village.

Other societies—Grizzly Bear, Wolf, Crazy Man, Warrior—all held similar performances to that of the Cannibal Society, but none of these others seem to have rated as highly. The Wolf was highly esteemed, for its members had healing power. So the entire society was sometimes called upon to cure a sick person, but it was very expensive. When they were invited to perform for a patient, whistles were heard in the woods. Each society had its own peculiar whistles, which were recognizable to all who were acquainted with them.

The Wolves came bounding out of the woods, dressed in wolfskins, wearing wooden wolf masks or blackened faces. They paraded and danced through the village, dancing for the patient four, sometimes five, nights. They were feasted during the day. On the fifth night they cut and pierced themselves in the same way the Cannibals did, and finally a medicine man appeared, with a whalebone knife in each hand, and pretended to kill the Wolves. When the Wolves disappeared, another group of men wearing all sorts of monstrous bird and animal masks representing spirits with healing power, came on the scene and danced around the patient, who handed out gifts to them. This personal contact with such miraculous beings could make him well or enable a medicine man to find his lost spirit and return it to him.

The paramount theme in all these societies seemed to be one in which the novice died and was brought back from the spirit world to live again in this life. All sorts of trickery was used to demonstrate this underlying idea and make the claims seem real to the uninitiated. Sometimes the novice was placed in a box and apparently burned alive and his blackened bones were shown. Then later, when the fire burned out, he came up out of the ashes. This was all done with underground tunnels, substitutions, and boxes with false bottoms. There were fake drownings and all sorts of calamities, but the novice, through the power he acquired from the spirits, was able to overcome all hazards and return to the people.

Members of the Warrior Society had power from the War Spirit of the North which made them invulnerable and enabled them to throw disease at an enemy, or to catch his spirit. Because physical prowess was so important in war, dancing was particularly important to one demonstrating warrior power. The dancer made a display of technical virtuosity in portraying his skill as a warrior and the vitality he could command in battle. Again the dancer usually wore black face paint and sometimes had his body heavily coated with grease, with duck down sprinkled over it.

A report from the Puget Sound area from about 1878 tells of Klallam Indians doing a War Dance they had borrowed from the Makahs. By this time Indians had already given up native dress for ordinary wear:

There were nearly twenty-five dancers, mostly men, who were dressed in American style, except that they had no shoes and wore parti-colored shawls and blankets thrown around them. One man carried an open umbrella. Their heads were bound with head-bands of cedar bark or kerchiefs, in which were long white or gray feathers generally tipped with red. Much feathery down was sprinkled over them. They had hollow wooden rattles and tails and wings of hawks or eagles in their hands. Their faces were blacked in various ways. With the music of the drum and singing they jumped around in a space twenty feet in diameter, throwing their arms wildly about, now up, now nearly to the ground, with movements quick as those of a cat in the midst of hot fire.[2]

A report as recently as 1939 for the Swinomish of the same area, the only ones apparently keeping alive the Spirit dancing, sounds as if it had become more conventionalized in the meantime and not quite as wild. Some of the animal impersonations were much more naturalistic, such as demonstrating eagle power by portraying an eagle in flight. So many things were involved in the presentation of a dance—formal patterns, music, conventionalized movements, audience participation, and the like—that this writer did not consider the performance dance drama, but it sounds as if it were very much so.

In the case of the War Dance, it was depicted as solo. Swinomish dancers carried nothing in their hands, wore headdresses with three feathers so attached that they moved with the dancer's movements. Costumes were black velveteen or flannel shirts and short trousers, trimmed with little carved wooden paddles or war clubs, with fluttering feathers sewed on to represent the down formerly stuck to the grease on their bodies. They also wore capes much like the old-time ones, made of buckskin or cedar bark, and long hair that cascaded over the shoulders. Sometimes feathers also hung from the sides of the capes.

The dancer began by standing, trunk slightly forward and knees bent, shifting weight back and forth from one foot to the other to a rapid beating of the drum. He advanced slowly, turning his body in different directions but progressing in a counterclockwise circle. Often he used peculiar "warrior gestures," one arm straight out from the shoulder, straight ahead or at an angle to the floor, the other arm bent at the elbow with its palm facing the shoulder, then reversing positions as he moved ahead. This is an abstract movement representing an attack with weapons of some kind. He jerked his head, a movement of defiance, signifying his willingness to fight and making the feathers in his headdress move. This first section of the dance was sometimes finished with a rapid twirl and jump.

In the second part of the dance he sometimes threw his arms to the side, hands open, to represent the swoop of an eagle. Then he might cross them in front of his body in a gesture that meant he was on the lookout. On a change of drum rhythm to an accent on every third beat and rest on the fourth beat, he faced the center and jumped on both feet to the right on each count, holding his position on the rest. This figure he repeated to the left in the same way. In moving right he might cross his left arm over his body, and vice versa in moving left.

There were other movements to represent birds. A fish hawk was represented with positions the opposite of the above. In moving right he extended his left arm to the left, with right arm bent at shoulder level and hand close to his head, with his head bent slightly forward, gazing down. He reversed these positions in moving to the left.

To represent a white owl he held his arms bent with his elbows to the side and forearms extended waist high. When he jumped right he faced right, when he jumped left he faced left. When the beat was accented he extended his arms nearly straight, opening his fists to look like claws. On the pause he went back to the original position, but swinging his body in a right angle to the left, then repeated swinging right. His jumps to the right were longer than those to the left, so that the dance continued in a counterclockwise circle.

The dancer then sang the next verse of his song, still holding his tense body position, and when the drummers took up the song he moved his arms and body in rhythm. Then the whole performance was repeated, but slower and with a change of rhythm to single accented beats.

A person's spirit power was supposed to increase with use, so most of those having acquired power performed at each winter festival.

Clowns played important parts in the ceremonies of the Northwest Coast, as they did in most regions. Here, as also in the Southwest, they pretended to abhor cleanliness and rationality and to hold contempt for custom. But in the Northwest they did little that would appeal to our sense of humor. They carried swords and lances as emblems of office and, to our notion, acted more frightening and terrible than funny. They scattered food about; called people by wrong names; acted irresponsible in general; showed contempt for rank, dignity, and property; and went around breaking furniture and terrorizing people. In the northern villages they wore peculiar wooden masks with a queer-shaped nose, for their power was supposed to rest in the nose.

ENTERTAINMENT DANCES

Throughout the long, rainy winter many dances were given just for pleasure and to entertain spectators. There were many demonstrations of supposedly magic power—wooden images worked by strings, like puppets, the performers aided by assistants up on the roof, in tunnels, or scattered through the audience; sleight-of-hand tricks; supernatural visitations; scenes of horror and violence. Some of these performers must have been able to rival anything our magicians do in the theater today. Victims apparently suffered anything from disembowelment to decapitation, but were made whole again and brought back to life.

The Nootkas even had an Echo "Dance." It was used to greet visitors from another village and at the same time confuse and drive away any evil spirits accompanying them. When their canoe approached it was met by two men who waded up to their armpits to prevent its landing. Land-otter impersonators cavorted and tumbled about like otters on a slide, then rushed toward the canoe, splashing it full of water until it was swamped, and the visitors had to swin to shore. They were brought to the house of the chief who was giving the dance and were presented with gifts—sea-otter skins, dentalium shells, even slaves.

The following morning as many as forty or fifty young men went out into the woods, shouting here and there to represent echoes, or spirits which cause people to lose their way. They wore cedar-bark blankets, doubled and belted at their waists, and masks with long cylindrical mouths. A group of them forced their way into the chief's house, each pair grasping a visitor by the wrists. The visitors were led into the forest, round and round, and other "spirits" called back and forth, doing everything possible to confuse the visitors. Finally they were released, the captors running swiftly away from them in all directions, but continuing the deceptive calls. Sometimes the visitors became truly lost and wandered about the rest of the day and even through the night. Next morning they were "rescued" by friendly village fishermen.

The visitors were then entertained with other performances, some of them real dances. A great whale was impersonated by two men carrying a huge whale mask. They went through the movements and gyrations of a whale rising, spouting, and diving, and then being attacked by other performers representing killer whales.

At such an entertainment women dances, such as the Woodpecker Dance described under Bird and Animal Dances, were also performed.

This was the country of the potlatch, the greatest give-away of all. But here the give-away was an establishment in itself, rather than a supplement to other ceremonies. In an effort to establish or retain prestige, wealthy people tried to outdo each other in making presents and in destroying their own property. It was an elaborate and complicated system. At some of these potlatches not only the local village was involved but visitors might come from villages far and near. It must have been a breathtaking sight to see the great carved and painted canoes arrive, paddled by naked slaves. Sometimes they came in one at a time, sometimes in flotillas, their occupants ceremonially dressed in beautiful Chilkat blankets, furs, and ornaments, clan emblems displayed, and wearing elaborate masks and headdresses.

Here we have an audience as spectacular in appearance as the players on the stage. Among the Nootkas, for instance, some in the audience wore deer horns on their heads and black stripes across their eyes. Warriors appeared with wolf skins or bearskins over their shoulders and some wore horns of burning cedar bark projecting from their heads.

Chiefs often owned dances. Some of these were inherited, passed down from one generation to another, but such inheritance has not been respected in recent years. Other dances were purchased. When it came a chief's turn to put on a demonstration, he presented an entire drama by selected young people whom he paid to enact their parts, and he furnished all the costumes and properties. Nowhere in America could be found more dramatic elements than those of the Northwest Coast, but by 1900 it was all but gone. With the passing of the old culture went the weaving and carving, the work in abalone shell and mountain-sheep horn. The old whaling and war canoes disappeared, often being used as coffins for their former owners, and in their places are now to be seen modern boats with outboard motors.

But there are reports of some Spirit dances being given even nowadays during the winter months, and as we have found in other areas, women are now playing an important part, often being possessed with a war spirit and dancing with every bit as much frenzy and excitement as the men.

Recently several dedicated groups have been attempting to revive some of the costumes and dances of the Northwest Coast. There are a few old people who remember details enough to make creditable performances possible. Perhaps other areas will do the same thing.

THE ESKIMOS

Although Eskimos are not, strictly speaking, Indians, they are native Americans, and so we should say a word about their dancing. Bancroft wrote in the 1880's that

dancing, accompanied by singing and violent gesticulation, is their chief amusement. In all the nations of the north, every well-regulated village aspiring to any degree of respectability has its public or town house. . . . It consists of one large subterranean room, better built than the common dwellings, and occupying a central position, where the people congregate on feast days. . . . A large portion of the winter is devoted to dancing. Feasting and visiting commence in November. . . . The dancers, who are usually young men, strip themselves to the waist, or even appear in *puris naturalibus,* and go through numberless burlesque imitations of birds and beasts, their gestures being accompanied by tambourines and songs. Sometimes they are fantastically arrayed in seal or deerskin pantaloons, decked with dog or wolf tails behind, and wear feathers or a colored handkerchief on the head. The ancients, seated upon benches which encircle the room, smoke, and smile approbation. The women attend with fish and berries in large wooden bowls, and upon the opening of the performance, they are at once relieved of their contribution by the actors, who elevate the provisions successively to the four cardinal points, and once to the skies above, when all partake of the feast. Then comes another dance. A monotonous refrain, accompanied by the beating of an instrument made of seal intestine stretched over a circular frame, brings upon the ground one boy after another, until about twenty form a circle. A series of pantomimes then commences, portraying love, jealousy, hatred, and friendship. During intervals in the expression, presents are distributed to strangers. In their national dance, one girl after another comes in turn to the center, while the others join hands and dance and sing, not unmusically, about her. The most extravagant motions win the greatest applause.[3]

He also added a footnote from the explorer Otto Kotzebue, which said, "They make the most comical motions with the whole body, without stirring from their place."

The above sounds a good deal like an Indian gathering, even to the give-away. One thing is different, however, and that is the drum. The Eskimo tambourine drum which Bancroft described is struck on the side and not on the head.

Friends who have lived with the Eskimos tell us they are the happiest and most carefree people in the whole world. It has been reported that Eskimo dances have no religious significance, but they do portray ancient myths and legends, even though they are apparently given only for recreation. They are dramatic storytelling dances and as such have also served to preserve and perpetuate the history of the people. Eskimos sometimes use extremely grotesque and fantastic masks, representing mythical or imaginary beings, but apparently these are only to enhance the storytelling of the dances. However, the masks at one time must have had some power, for often they were destroyed at the end of the performance.

Peter Freuchen wrote that for small informal gatherings in an igloo (which is not necessarily of snow blocks, being merely the Eskimo word for "house") two men would entertain. One used the tambourine, the other sang and danced to it. It was struck in 4/4 time, three beats in succession, and a pause. There was not much room for dancing with the feet, so the movement was with the body, swaying from side to side with gyrating hips and emphasizing the rhythm with head and even face. Sometimes the audience, seated on the bunks around the wall, joined in with a kind of refrain after each verse of the song. The singer-dancer might even go into a sort of trance, the rhythm becoming wilder and wilder and the song rising in pitch until the drummer brandished the beater in front of his face, bringing him back to some semblance of normality. Then they traded places, the drummer becoming the singer-dancer. Freuchen also said that among the Hudson Bay Eskimos women took part in these song fests. Some Eskimos did not think that women should take part, except to sing the refrain, but the rule was not enforced.

The Eskimos had many poets whom they admired, and their poems were often put to music. Some of these songs were of a sacred nature and sung in honor of the

Eskimo drummers. University of Alaska Archives, Charles Bunnell Collection, Fairbanks.

great game animals upon which the Eskimos depended. There was dancing also, at some of these recitations, but it was rather an accompaniment to the song than the other way round. Completely new songs were demanded for each new ceremony.[4]

Freuchen wrote mainly about the Polar and Hudson Bay Eskimos, but Captain MacMillan told us years ago that the Eskimos are really all one people and the only differences in either language or custom is due to contact with white people. In Alaska this contact was with Russians and later Americans. The other Eskimos were exposed mainly to English influence.

Although Eskimo celebrations seem in many ways to be like Indian celebrations, some of the Alaska Indians were considerably influenced by the Eskimos. This is especially true of the Tinehs,* an Athabaskan tribe distantly related to the Navajos

---

*More recent spellings have been Tinne, Tinneh, and Déné, which is similar to the Navajo Diné—"People."

Eskimo Big Dance. University of Alaska Archives, Charles Bunnell Collection.

and Apaches. They had dances in which the feet were not moved, but they turned their heads from side to side while swinging and swaying their bodies.

But the Eskimos were also affected by the cannibal myths of the coastal Indians. One of the favorite dances represented two cousins, one of whom lived on the top of the mountain, the other at the base. They were supposed to entertain passers-by with their dances, then catch them and eat them.

They had a Ruffed Grouse Dance in which the principal performer wore a mask to represent one of these birds. He danced on his knees and imitated a grouse drumming. Two women and a clown wearing a grotesque mask crept up behind him and imitated his actions.[5] We remember that the Blackfeet had a Prairie Chicken Dance in which the men went through chicken movements while on their knees. The Blackfeet once ranged far north into Canada. We wonder whether they ever contacted the Tinehs and, if so, who learned the dance from whom.

CALIFORNIA

Linguistically, the Indians of California were perhaps more diversified than any other peoples in the world, some twenty-one distinct linguistic families being represented. Culturally they ranged from very primitive desert dwellers in the south to aristocratic hunters and fishermen in the north, who showed considerable ties with the Northwest Coast tribes. The people in the central part of the region were among the most peaceable ever encountered. They supposedly had a low culture, depending upon acorn meal and other plant foods as staples. They were despised by the Spaniards, who hunted them down with dogs from horseback, making great sport of lancing them when they were overtaken. American gold seekers were even worse, surrounding entire villages and wiping them out in one great orgy of slaughter.

The California Indians were certainly among the best basket makers in the world, and they did beautiful work with feathers and in obsidian chipping. Dancing was very important to them, but they did mainly dances to help fulfill hopes for peace, prosperity, and abundance, prosperity meaning acquisition of such simple things as quantities of obsidian, woodpecker scalps, flicker feathers, and skins of albino deer, all used ceremonially for costumes and decoration. In some localities dancers wore beautiful headbands of hummingbird feathers.

Dances also placated evil spirits who brought devastating storms or sickness, and supplicated the spirits controlling fish and game. Following a successful hunt, there were also dances to appease the spirit of the slain animal so that it would not take offense and make hunting difficult in the future. Some dances lasted five, ten, or even more days, but most had died out by 1900, so it is difficult to learn much about them.

THE NORTHERN TRIBES

The most important dance of the Hupas was the Dance of Peace, but for the area of northern California generally the Salmon Dance, Jumping Dance, and White Deerskin Dance were considered most important, or at least they were best known to outsiders. And yet, while most of the dances celebrated peaceful pursuits, the most important dance of the Yukis seems to have been the Scalp Dance, in which the entire scalp of an enemy, from eyes to ears, was carried on a stick.

The Yukis also had an Acorn Dance and a Feather Dance, the latter displaying showy feather capes, bands of flicker feathers, and feathered wands. Another minor dance of northern California was the Brush Dance, held to cure an ailing child. The dancers wore no ornaments, but danced holding boughs of foliage from dark until dawn.

The Hupas had a Friendship Dance, as well as a Dance of Peace, but the latter was more important. The Friendship Dance served to welcome visitors, but the Dance of Peace symbolized the tribe's friendly relationship with neighboring tribes.

Bancroft said that for the Karoks and Shastas an annual feast of thanksgiving was important. In the dancing, each individual displayed his personal wealth in the decoration of his costume. The participants slowly circled the fire. At the conclusion of the dance an old man arose and made a thanksgiving oration, enumerating the blessings of the past year and exhorting his listeners to be worthy of even greater benefits by proper living and moral behavior.

In central and northern California the dancers were usually naked, or nearly so, with face and body painting being important parts of costume. Bancroft wrote:

They use broad stripes drawn up and down, across, or spirally round the body, for the favorite device; sometimes one half of the body is colored red and the other blue, or the whole person is painted jet black and serves as a ground for the representation of a skeleton, done in white, which gives the wearer a most ghastly appearance. The dancing is accompanied by chanting, clapping of hands, blowing on pipes of two or three reeds and played with the nose or mouth, beating of skin drums, and rattling of tortoise shells filled with small pebbles. This horrible discord is, however, more for the purpose of marking time than for pleasing the ear. The women are seldom allowed to join in the dance with the men, and when they are so honored, take a very unimportant part in the proceedings, merely swaying their bodies to and fro in silence.[6]

Bancroft compiled his material largely from reports of actual observers. Just where the skeleton painting fitted in is not certain, for he does not name the dance and it certainly would not belong in anything of a festive or playful character.

We have already seen that Indian music generally was unappreciated. Bancroft also mentioned skin drums, but California is otherwise reported as a drumless area, except for the foot drums discussed in the chapter on music and instruments.

Some of the northern California tribes did only the Jumping Dance as their "great dance," but others did both White Deerskin Dance and Jumping Dance, the White Deerskin Dance being performed first, followed by the Jumping Dance. In these dances they displayed their richest costumes, as well as wealth in the form of great blades of obsidian, seashells, and albino deerskins.

These northern California tribes were somewhat affected by the ideas of wealth held by the people farther up the coast. Position in life depended upon the possession of material things, but the prized possessions were quite different from those desired by Northwest Coast Indians and were really visible manifestations of spiritual blessings. The regalia worn by the dancers were standardized by custom; if any symbolism had been attached to it, it had long ago been forgotten.

The White Deerskin Dance

The White Deerskin Dance, although given in the fall, might be considered a new year's dance, for it had to do with the renewal of life and the traditions of the beginning of the world. The dance showed that everyone was happy, that no one held any ill feelings, and that consequently they should not expect storms, earthquakes, or other calamities to befall them.

The dancers in the White Deerskin Dance were all men. They wore white tanned deerskins as kilts, or sometimes draped over the left shoulder, and necklaces of dentalium shell, abalone, and elk teeth. Some blew upon bone whistles. Otherwise the dance was accompanied by singing only. Some of the dancers wore headdresses which had the appearance of fur hats, being made of large bands of wolf fur held in place with smaller bands of embroidery. On some of these, great long feathers of the condor stood erect at the back. Four special dancers had head-dresses made of a dozen or more sea-lion tusks turned upward and attached to a headband.

The barefoot dancers lined up abreast, facing the audience of men, women, and children. At the time of a White Deerskin Dance, neighboring villages gathered to watch and take part. Rich men handed their treasures over to the dancers to display, and the dance became a sort of contest as to which village had the richest men.

The dance was conducted so as to produce a climactic effect. It varied in length with the tribe. The Klamaths held it for twelve days, the Hupas for six, some tribes for ten. It gradually built up in intensity, splendor, and duration of performance. The treasures actually began to appear only toward the end, and the finest were saved for the very last performance.

In the center of the line of dancers was the chief singer, with an assistant on each side. The remainder of the line formed a sort of chorus, not singing, but grunting and shouting as sort of accompaniment.

All but the four men wearing the tusk headdresses carried long poles on each of which was mounted the skin of an albino deer. The entire skin was saved except for the antlers, and the head and neck were stuffed. A long strip of leather was sewed to the mouth to represent the tongue, and it, as well as eyes and ears, were decorated with woodpecker scalps.

As the dance progressed, some dancers carried other decorated skins, and some carried raccoon skins mounted and decorated just as were the deerskins. The objects they carried were swayed and swung in time to the music. The dance movements varied from swaying in place, with a short stamp on one foot, to slow walks and long leaping steps.

The most spectacular part of the dance came at night, the firelight reflecting from the glittering obsidian blades and the brilliant translucent abalone shell of necklaces and headpieces. In front of the men carrying the deerskins danced the four with the tusk headdresses, carrying the great obsidian blades, some over a foot long, and blowing their bone whistles. They paired off and danced toward each other, in front of the long line of dancers, clicking their blades as they met, striking sparks and making glasslike tinkling sounds which could hardly be heard above the din of the whistles, the singing, and shouting. They sashayed past each other, a pair going to each end of the line and returning. Sometimes they displayed the beautiful short, wide, sinew-backed and painted bows of the region, brandishing them and the obsidian blades in a threatening manner.

At times the dance became quite wild, the dancers going into weird contortions and using vehement gestures, the song rising to a shrieking pitch as the excitement mounted and the emotion became more intense. It ended in a wild orgy of physical abandon.

Hupa Indians of Pekwan, Lamath River, California, performing the Jumping Dance. The dancers are wearing flicker-feather headdresses. From a photo by A. W. Ericson, about 1890–1900. Smithsonian Institution, Bureau of American Ethnology.

The Jumping Dance

The dancers in the Jumping Dance wore beautiful headdresses of wide bands of flicker feathers. They also wore shell necklaces and deerskin kilts and carried in one hand a beautifully woven basketry tube. Just what they carried in these tubes was not learned, but they were an important part of the regalia. The dance was given to ward off sickness and evil. According to Dr. Kroeber, it varied between two steps, each used with a different song.

In the first the hand holding a dancing basket is raised, then swung down and the knees bent until the fingers touch the ground, whereupon the dancer hops about half a foot into the air. In the second form of dance one foot is stamped violently as the basket descends. The drop or stamp coincides with the beat of the music, the leap itself is therefore begun at the end of a bar of song.[7]

414

THE CENTRAL TRIBES

A century or more ago, a secret society known as the *Kuksu*, or Big Heads, was prominent among the tribes of central California. They danced from October to May and believed that if the dances ceased the world would disintegrate, and certainly theirs did. Some of their dances were held in a great round meeting house, at the back of which was placed a hollow-log drum, which was held to be very sacred, and they danced on it with their bare feet. Some of their dancers wore tremendous head-dresses, reminding one of a huge pincushion, made of long rods beautifully decorated with down and brilliant feathers. They also wore fiber or grass kilts with belts woven of tiny feathers. Some carried bows and quivers made of deerskins with heads attached; others had bone whistles, gourd rattles, and magic staves.

THE SOUTHERN TRIBES

On the south, mainly in Arizona but partly in California, were the Mohaves, a desert people, without many dances, but showing some interesting features in the few they had. Particularly interesting was their drum. A shallow trench about four feet long and a few inches wide was scooped out of the sand. Its walls were sprinkled with water to make them compact. At one end of this trench a tray-shaped basket was overturned. At the other end a large pot or jar was laid to serve as a resonance chamber. The basket was struck with a palm beater and the jar gave out a deep boom.

Their favorite dance seems to have been one to do with the water birds, cranes and herons, which would have had a great appeal for desert dwellers. They also had a dance for the Pleiades, but it was a fun dance held in the daytime. Desert people see wonderful star-filled skies at night, and they must have felt an urge to honor some of the constellations, but why they did it in the daytime, when it is hot, is somewhat perplexing.

In the Bird Dance, the singer knelt at his drum, and in a line facing east, abreast of him, knelt several elderly men. Behind him were two women, selected for their strong voices, their bodies painted red and their hair, white. In front of him, facing the sun, sat three rows of young men, forty or fifty of them, wearing tufts of white heron or crane feathers on their heads and strings of them down their backs. A path was left open through the three rows.

An old man, with one arm raised behind him and the other pointing forward and down, ran down this path, shouting, as the drummer banged on his basket and all others clapped their hands. This running through the seated young men was repeated, then the singer raised his hand and the row of elderly men stood up. Each had a staff his own height and merely nodded his head in time with the music. When the singer signaled again, all the young men went into a kneeling position. Next the first row arose to its feet and joined in the singing, and when the leader of that row raised his arms the second row stood up and joined in the song. Then the leader of the second row called the third to its feet, so all were singing, and finally the two women began to sing, their shrill voices rising above the whole chorus.

The young men danced first by merely flexing their knees, arms hanging slack at their sides. But when the leader of each row raised his hand, the knees were dropped lower and lower, until they were dipping and rising twelve inches or more at a time, and they kept this up until everyone was so tired they all had to quit. Using only two songs, feet never leaving the ground, they all thought it was lots of fun and someimes kept it up for hours.[8]

In southern California the missions ruined Indian culture long ago. For a time the Indians were allowed to do some of their dances as innocent amusement, but the dances gradually disappeared as the culture disintegrated. As late as 1906 there was one old man among the Diegueño, near the Mexican border, who still remembered the songs and ritual for a dance for the dead. This in itself is remarkable, for such a dance was surely bound up in religion, and all forms of their religion had been suppressed for a hundred and fifty years by the Spanish padres. And at this late date there were still a few who remembered a Red Feathered Bird Dance of social nature. It should have been done by a double line of men and women, but three men joined the leader and another sang the woman's part in a high falsetto voice. These were old people, but they danced all night. They stamped their feet in place, according to the varied rhythm of the song. They would bend and sway their bodies, then straighten up with a grunt or a groan, because of their age, and pause between songs.

There are some reports that would indicate that formerly there were some very active and interesting dances. One from Mesa Grande began with the dancers entering the circle and the leader starting a song in a soft voice. The others followed, and then the women chimed in. The music grew louder and louder, becoming energetic and even frenzied, with body movements corresponding.

At first the dancers moved in an irregular circle, stamping feet and occasionally emitting expressive grunting sounds to emphasize the song. Then arms were extended, flexed, and relaxed. As the music grew in intensity the stamping became more violent, the grunting louder, and muscles more tense. The women sang louder and louder and the dancers raised bent arms above their heads. Now and then one dancer would break away from the others and circle like a dervish, clapping his hands and uttering a wild "ha-ha" as he whirled, then return to his place. The song ended with a shuddering expiration of breath on a downward cadence, and the dance suddenly stopped. After a brief intermission it was given all over again.[9]

The Mission Indians had animal dances in which dancers entered on hands and knees, with wild cries, depicting the animals they represented. The chief stood in the center and touched each one with a feathered staff as if to exorcise some evil power.

Speaking of the Yumas, another desert tribe, Bancroft wrote:

Dancing and masquerading is the most favorite pastime. They have feasts with dances to celebrate victories, feasts given at marriage, and when girls attain the age of puberty; a ceremony is observed at the burial of noted warriors, and on other various occasions of private family life, in which both men and women take part. The dance is performed by a single actor or by a number of persons of both sexes to the accompaniment of instruments or their

416

own voices. All festivities are incomplete without impromptu songs, the music being anything but agreeable, and the accompanying corn-stalk or cane flutes, wooden drums, or calabashes filled with stones and shaken to a constantly varying time.[10]

So we find that even desert people, living rather drab, uninteresting lives, with most of their time devoted to searching for food, had dances to relieve the monotony, and some of these were interesting and colorful. Disintegration of dance and culture went hand in hand, and the people themselves came finally to the verge of oblivion.

21. Dances of the Southwest

THE HOPI SNAKE DANCE

Perhaps the most popular ceremony for the tourist in the Southwest is the Hopi Snake Dance, which apparently has a fascination because of its (to whites) weird, spectacular, and somewhat horrible aspects. Every Pueblo tribe has elaborate ceremonies, and dances for bringing rain and the Snake Dance of the Hopis is one of the most important. Each Hopi village gives the Snake Dance every other year, alternating with the Flute Ceremony, also given to bring rain, in the in-between years. So we can find the Snake Dance being given every year, but in different villages. According to Hopi legend, the Flute Chief was younger brother of the Snake Youth, who brought the ceremony to the people.

The beginnings of the Snake Dance doubtless trace back to the snake cults of Mexico and Central America. It is certain that many other Pueblo tribes had similar dances at one time. There may be thriving snake cults among them even today, although the Hopis are the only ones still performing an actual dance with snakes. Formerly some of the villages kept large snakes in special pits and ceremonially fed them. The prolific nature of the snakes was supposed to induce like fruitfulness among the people, promoting the numbers and welfare of the tribe.

The spectacular dance of which everyone hears is actually only a small part—the windup—of ceremonies that extend over a period of sixteen days, with preliminary preparations even before that.

The Spaniards apparently never saw the Snake Dance, or they surely would have reported it. But rumors about it began to be heard in the middle 1800's, usually to be classed as tall tales of the early visitors to the Hopi country.

The Hopis, as well as some other Pueblo tribes, believed that they originated in an underworld; consequently their deities and the spirits of their ancestors all dwell down there. They call the snakes their "brothers" and believe they carry their prayers to the Rainmakers beneath the earth. Their own name for the ceremony means "rattlesnakes," and these do predominate in the ritual, although they use any kind of snake they can catch.

Over the years there has always been argument whether or not the snakes have had their fangs or poison sacks removed. Snakes just released after the ceremony have been sent to the Smithsonian Institution and found to have poison sacks and fangs intact. But herpetologists claim that a rattlesnake will regrow fangs in a very few days, and it would take several days to ship the snakes to Washington.

Edward Curtis claimed to have documented reports from former Snake Priests asserting that the snakes were defanged, with a full account of how it was done.

418

The Zuñi Rain Dance, photographed by A. C. Vroman in 1900. The ultimate purpose of most Pueblo Indian dances is to bring rain. Smithsonian Institution, Bureau of American Ethnology.

He even took moving pictures of the Snake Dance back in 1906. Not long after that the Hopis, like most of the other Pueblos, refused to permit pictures to be taken.

The average member of the Snake Fraternity knew nothing of the defanging of the snakes and handled them as if they were completely deadly. They were skillfully handled by all who came in contact with them—gatherers; "whippers," sometimes called "huggers," because they place their left arms over the shoulders of the dancers and apparently control the snakes with their feather "whips," or wands; and dancers, who carry them in the hands and in their mouths. A dancer carrying a snake in his

419

mouth is imparting to it the prayer which is to be delivered to relatives in the underworld.

The Snake ceremonies are conducted jointly by the Snake and Antelope fraternities. They are held during the month of August or in early September, depending upon the moon. It is claimed that rain has always followed. The Antelope Chief must be a member of the Snake Clan. Lay members of either fraternity can apparently belong to any clan. Although the Snake Priests are the ones who handle the snakes, they are really servants of the Antelope Chief, and the Antelopes are in charge of the ceremonials connected with the Snake Dance. Preparations begin in the winter, when the two fraternities prepare offerings which are placed to the four directions.

Boys join one of the fraternities early in life, and it would seem that the more timid ones become Antelopes, although later they may change over to membership in the Snakes. For, as well as being a prayer for rain, the Snake Dance is also an exhibition of manliness and fearlessness. A certain "man medicine" is even contributed by the Warrior Fraternity. The Antelopes sip some of this medicine, as do the women members of the Snake Fraternity. What is left over is used for mixing the paint which the Snake Priests wear for their public appearance in the Snake Dance. So it is possible that the Snake Dance originally had significance in acquiring power in war.

The members of the Snake Fraternity also serve as doctors, and sometimes a person joins in order to be healed of some illness.

Six days before the public dance, the Snake Priests go out after the snakes, spending most of four days at this task. The first day they go north of the village, the second day west, the third day south, and the fourth day east. Bodies painted red, they travel in loincloth only, their nakedness being an additional prayer that rain may cool their sunburned bodies. On the fifth day they make the "man medicine," and on the morning of the sixth, which is really the fifteenth day of ceremonies, an Antelope race is held. Actually, anyone can participate. The race is started by a special officer, who himself sometimes runs as much as three miles to a certain spring, where he fills a gourd with water and ooze from its bank. This he smears on the left foot of each runner, then he smashes the gourd, which is the signal for the race to start. The racers represent the rain gods bringing water directly to the village.

In the afternoon, the Antelopes gather green boughs and construct a *kisi*, a sort of circular shade or booth, and in front of it they dig a shallow pit and cover it with a cottonwood board. It represents the entrance to the underworld. At sunset the Antelope Dancers come out of their kiva and march four times around the plaza. Each time they pass the board they sprinkle corn meal on it and stamp on it with the right foot, the sound representing thunder; the rattles they shake, made of antelope skin, are the sound of rain. The sound of their stamping on the cottonwood board also lets the dwellers in the underworld know that the ceremonies are being properly performed.

The Snake Priests appear and repeat the same performance. The two fraternities then line up, facing each other and singing, first softly, but gradually louder, shaking their rattles harder, simulating an approaching storm.

An Antelope Priest of the Corn Clan and a Snake Priest of the Cloud Clan go into the *kisi,* returning with green stalks and vines with which the Antelope Priest dances around the plaza, just as the Snake Priests will dance with the live snakes on the following evening. He drapes the greens around his neck and carries them in his mouth, while the Snake Priest dances behind him with his arm around his neck in positions similar to those of the coming snake ritual, except that the role of the Snake Priest will be reversed. After four times around, the Antelope Priest gathers up a second bunch of greens from the *kisi* and dances around four times more, after which the fraternities return to their respective kivas and the Antelopes are served food by the women. The Snake Priests also eat, but it is their last meal until the ceremonies are ended. After the meal the Assistant to the Antelope Chief gathers up the greens from the *kisi* and carries them out to the corn fields in supplication for mature crops.

On the morning of the sixteenth, or last, day, another race is run, similar to the Antelope race of yesterday, but this time to honor the snakes. A preliminary race seems to be an important part of many of the dances of the Southwest. Also that morning in the Snake kiva the Snake Chief makes a medicine of certain roots, including soapweed, or yucca, for washing the snakes. The actual washing, done early in the afternoon, is conducted by a man of the Cloud Clan. Curtis said the reasons for washing the snakes were threefold:

. . . because the snakes are our children; because we think that by washing the snakes, who are very powerful, we may be repaid by them in the form of rains, which they will send to wash us in return; because we wish the bodies of the snakes to be clean when we put them in our mouths.[1]

Following the washing of the snakes, the Snake Priests paint for the ceremonial dance, mixing the paints with the "man medicine" made two days before. Pink clay is smeared on moccasins, forearms, calves, and the upper right side of the head. The chin is painted white and the rest of the face, black.

The snakes are carried in two bags, one for rattlers and one for other kinds, taken to the plaza, and deposited in the *kisi.* The Antelopes come out of their kiva, dance four times around, each time stamping on the board, as they did the day before, and scattering meal upon it. The Snake Priests, each wearing a turtle-shell rattle below his right knee, follow in like manner, and both fraternities line up facing each other for a period of singing. Then the Snake Priests, each accompanied by a whipper and a catcher, or gatherer, dance over to the *kisi,* where each Snake Priest is presented with a snake, which he first carries in his hands, then places about his neck and in his mouth, holding it with his teeth, imparting to it his prayer. The whipper dances behind him, with left arm around the dancer's neck, calming the snake with movements of his feathered wand, as if stroking it, and preventing it from coiling. Each snake is danced four times around the plaza, then tossed aside, and the catcher picks it up. These catchers thus hold all the snakes that have been discarded until all have been danced with, when an Antelope Priest draws a circle of meal on the ground and casts meal to the six directions (four world quarters, up and down). The catchers then throw the snakes inside the circle, and the Snake Priests scramble wildly to grab handfuls of them, then run swiftly over various trails out of the village to turn the snakes loose to carry their messages to the dwellers of the underworld. It was decided the night before which trail each Snake Priest would take and at what place he would deposit his snakes.

While the Snake Priests are engaged in freeing the snakes, all men and boys of the village who have not taken active part in the ceremonies march around the plaza four times, followed by the Antelope Priests, who do likewise. The Snake Priests then bathe in a special medicine which has been brewing all day and drink some of it too. It is an emetic and purgative, used to purify themselves and overcome any evil influence of the snakes. So the Snake Dance ends; it will not be given again for two years in this village. The rain is sure to follow, bringing grass for the game and livestock, maturing the corn, ripening the orchards, revitalizing the people both materially and spiritually.

Strange as the Snake Dance is in comparison to Indian rituals elsewhere, there are yet some interesting comparisons. The number four is sacred here, as everywhere, among Indians. We have also seen the Priest make offerings to the six directions. At many intervals during the Snake Dance and its time of preparation such offerings are made, using the fluffy "breath feathers" of the golden eagle. Many tribes have similar terms for these and put them to similar ceremonial use. They represent the breath of life, life itself. The idea of dancing for power, to signify unity of purpose, to establish harmony with all creation, is not strange to Indians all over the country.

The snake, to many peoples around the earth, is an ancient symbol of wisdom, and also of sexual power, which must be used with wisdom. The snake also symbolizes lightning. Indians everywhere represent lightning as a zigzag line, but southwestern Indians often add a head and rattle tail to the zigzag line as the lightning symbol.

The dualities, the opposites of nature, are also represented in the Snake Dance, as in many Indian ceremonies elsewhere—male and female, night and day, heat and cold, peace and war, matter and spirit, and so on. The antelope is a contrast to the rattlesnake, representing the gentler aspect of nature, the feminine, the timid, the elusive, the subtle life in the present world rather than in the underworld. Indians generally associate horned animals with divine power, and deer and antelope play important roles in ceremonies of healing and magic.

So, while the antelope may represent feminine power on earth, the Antelope Chief represents masculine power among the divine, and he leads the ceremony. All the way through, the Antelopes take precedence over the Snakes. Antelope also represents fruitfulness. But the snake also has a dual representation. It is the symbol of Mother Earth. Union of Antelope and Snake represents creation. The

Snake Dance has many elements of beauty, with great depth of meaning and significance, if we have some understanding of its underlying reasons and motives.

NAVAJO DANCES

Almost everyone who has heard of the Navajos* associates them with Night Chant, Fire Dance, and Squaw Dance, but few realize that at one time they had many dances, few of which are performed any longer.

THE SQUAW DANCE, AND ENEMY WAY

"Squaw Dance" is a white man's term. Originally it was part of a war ceremony, the Enemy Way, which lasted three days and nights. As has happened so often, now that the Indian Wars are at an end, the ceremonies are put to other uses, often to healing. The Squaw Dance now is part of a healing rite, disease being the enemy to be defeated. The actual dance is merely the public part of the ritual and is done for fun. The women are in charge, the ones taking part being unmarried. They select their own partners, who must pay them after each dance if they want their freedom. Each one leads her partner in the dance, and holds on to him until he pays.

The Enemy Way involves a number of myths pertaining to the earth and sky and the relationship of natural forces—mountains and clouds, men and animals—and the Squaw Dance comes from a related legend in which two captive girls were set free and danced around the two warrior heroes.

On the second morning of the ceremony, the hogan where the patient is being treated undergoes a mock attack and sham battle. The attackers camp north or west of the hogan and so attack toward east or south. They carry staffs made from fresh-cut juniper and charge in a great rush, amidst much confusion. They are blackened with mud which, being a mixture of earth and water, symbolizes these natural forces and also the Hard Flint Boys, who in the sky are the Pleiades and on earth are the whirlwinds and waterfalls.

Since this was formerly a war ceremony, an old scalp is still used in the ritual and the patient himself is blackened with a special charcoal, which has much the same meaning to the Navajos that we have discussed for other tribes. In the old days, a warrior who had killed an enemy blackened himself all over so that the spirit of the slain one could not recognize him. At the same time black was the color for mourning and expressed a lament for the loss of a brave soul. If the warrior was not overcome by the enemy's spirit, he then acquired his power for himself.

During the three-day ceremony the patient and the performers are not allowed to eat meat, salt, or anything sweet or hot.

Navajo is a Tewa word for a cultivated area. The people we know today as Navajo (or Navaho) were called Apaches del Navajo by the Spaniards, Apache being a Zuñi word for "enemy." The tribes known now as Apaches and Navajos were already raiding the Pueblo villages when the Spaniards arrived.

The war ceremonial drove away all enemy ghosts, which were also identified with the ghosts of monsters slain by ancient legendary heroes. Today, in driving away these ghosts, sickness is driven from the patient and he regains his health through the magic of the sacred sand paintings, songs, rituals, and dances. The drum used in the Enemy Way is a water drum made from a pot. It in itself represents a ghost. It is tapped with a cherry or cedar-wood beater bent to form a hoop on one end, and the ghost is beaten into the ground.

Each evening the so-called Squaw Dance takes place, but we should remember that it is only an interlude and a very small part of a long and complicated ceremony.[2]

THE MOUNTAIN CHANT

When the thunder sleeps is the time for the Mountain Chant, or Mountaintop Way. Many tribes had taboos against telling myths and legends during the summer, but in the winter nature is asleep and so the spirits will not be offended by hearing something said of them they might not like. The Navajos believed that if they held the Mountain Chant during seasons when thunder was active they would be struck by lightning or bit by a rattlesnake, symbolical of lightning.

The ceremony lasts nine days. The Navajos speak of their ceremonies as "sings," and a sing is a great social occasion as well as a time of ceremony and healing. It is like a fair, where the people go to be entertained, to exchange gossip, and to renew tribal solidarity, for there is no real tribal center and a sing is the only opportunity of getting together.

The ceremonies are held in a sacred hogan, which faces east. A new sand painting is made each day, the paintings as well as the songs dramatizing the legend of a mythical hero. Sometimes as many as twelve medicine men work at one time on a sand painting. At times different medicine men compete with each other, displaying their magic.

Formerly, on the ninth night, eleven or twelve different dances were held. They were given outside in a big corral, or arbor, made of cedar and pine branches, opening to the east. Families sat around the inner edge of this, each one having its own little fire. The entire nine-day ceremony is mainly one of healing, and on this occasion the patients are brought inside the big circle.

In an early account, the very first dance of the series was a Fire Dance, although at that time, instead of dancing with burning cedar brands, each dancer carried a magic wand, with eagle down attached to its tip. The fire in the center was built up so high that flames sometimes soared a hundred feet in the air, but the dancers had to approach close enough to light the down on their wands. At the end of this dance they deftly flipped a ring of fresh down, hidden in their palms, up over the burned tip, and all looked fresh and new again.

The last dance was the now famous Fire Dance with which many people are familiar, as it is given every year at the Gallup Ceremonials. It is hardly a dance, the performers, painted all over with white clay, brandishing burning cedar brands, switching themselves and each other with them, running and jumping around the fire.

The First Dance

A 1934 report gave the first dance as one by a pair of performers, each wearing a conical cap with imitation buffalo horns and hanging feathers attached. They had strips of bright cloth hanging at elbows and knees, wore red moccasins, and each carried a long, heavy arrow, with long feathering and stone head. They danced to the left around the central fire, circling six times. Then patients were brought out and placed on blankets to the southwest of the central fire, and the dancers danced between them and the fire, first facing each other, then turning east and west, north and south, finally east and west again.

They made noises like a hawk, spat on their arrows, rubbed them between their lips, then threw back their heads and proceeded to swallow them. It looked as if they were swallowed for about eight inches, but in reality these were "trick" arrows, the feathered end being hollow and the forward part of the shaft telescoping into it. There was much acting and pantomime with this, with weird cries and noises, when finally the arrows were "withdrawn" and applied to the patients. They were placed on the feet, pointing first one way, then the other, then on the knees, abdomen, chest, shoulders, and head in the same fashion.

The dancers then picked up their arrows, pranced backward a few steps, waved them skyward and to the four directions, and swallowed them again. Once more they placed them over the patients as before, then danced backward and forward, facing each other, waved the arrows at the fire, and made their exits, going north of the fire.

The Second Dance

When they returned, they were accompanied by a file of fifty or more people, in everyday clothes, who sang as they danced around the fire. At every sixth step they waved bunches of twigs held in their hands. They circled twelve times, then sat in a row east and west, southwest of the fire, while the two arrow dancers performed as before.

The Third Dance

The next set was introduced by singing, whistling, and strange noises from outside the arbor. A file of fifty-five men entered, circling around the fire, "chanting, gesticulating, prancing, turning this way and that." Some shook gourd rattles, others a peculiar sort of woven rattle, held within a bunch of twigs.

The Fourth Dance

They were followed by another pair of dancers, barefoot this time, otherwise dressed like the first two, but carrying in each hand peculiar triangular ornaments with eagle feathers dangling from them. They waved them in the same manner as the arrows,

Wand Dancer
(Fourth Dance)

Setting Sun Dancer
(Eighth Dance)

Cactus Dancer
(Eighth Dance)

Lightning Dancer
(Ninth Dance)

Navajo Mountain Chant dancers, redrawn from native drawings.

circling the fire six times while the seated group of men sang for them. The pair danced six steps forward with a light, gliding, pacing step, then retreated with seven steps. Again they advanced and retreated, first to the east, then south, north, south, and east again. Moving toward the fire, they waved the ornaments toward it and departed north of the fire.

The Fifth Dance

Again came the Arrow Dance, but this time with eight performers, in two groups of fours, facing each other. Wheeling, they danced to the four world quarters, then placed their arrows on the afflicted parts of the patients and swallowed them as before. When they left, all the performers who had been "on stage" so far followed them off.

The Sixth Dance

Another procession entered, led by a masked dancer accompanied by the two triangle bearers. The dance was similar to their former performance, but more vigorous now, and the masked dancer took an emphatic part. Lining up abreast, they faced east, south, west, north, and east again, making a complete circle almost in place, then pranced off.

The Seventh Dance

Next, two dancers entered, wearing large shieldlike feathered ornaments in front of their chests and carrying triangles similar to those used before. They were the Rising Sun and Moon. They alternated with two masked performers, then were replaced by masked performers carrying the same sort of triangles. The masks were similar to those worn by Pueblo Indians, but were somewhat simpler. The triangle bearers danced with a "hopping, tripping, graceful step."

The Eighth Dance

After the Rising Sun and Moon came the Cactus dancers, at first a pair, then two sets of four each, carrying in each hand "finger" cactus tied to sticks. Following them was a pair representing the Setting Sun and Moon, each wearing a feather disk bustle. So the sun and moon rose on the front of the dancers and set on their rears!

The Ninth Dance

The Lightning Dance was performed by a number of dancers, each one wearing a horned cap with four eagle feathers standing erect from its crown and carrying in each hand the "lightning," made of eight light strips of wood pinned at four crossing points, like "lazy tongs," which when collapsed were only a few inches wide but could be pressed in such a way that they would shoot out eight or ten feet. These "lightnings" were each tipped with three eagle feathers, and the dancers wore armbands from which long dangles with more eagle feathers nearly dragged the ground. They posed, postured, and strutted as they manipulated their lightning.

The Tenth Dance

In between performances of the Lightning Dancers came four with bull-roarers on poles, called by the Navajos "groaning sticks," which obviously represented thunder and wind.

The Eleventh Dance

Just before dawn the patients were brought forward again. Four dancers carrying little trees entered, circling the fire and performing over the patients much as the Arrow dancers did. A whole group of them came next, dancing vigorously around the fire twelve times, gesticulating and waving twigs of cedar and piñon toward the fire, the earth, and the heavens. They filed to the southwestern side of the corral, where the patients were lying, and formed a screen around them, chanting and waving the twigs. Then all sat in a big angle, open to the fire, and two medicine men made a feather dance in a dish in front of the patients. As they waved their hands in time to the song, the feather raised up and danced.

The Twelfth Dance

The final dance was the Fire Dance, on which we have already commented. It took place as the first early light appeared in the east. As in the other dances of this series, they circled to the left, or clockwise.[3]

In the Mountain Chant, as with other ceremonies in other tribes, the dances may not be given exactly the same every year, for the earlier account mentions the fourth dance in the series as one with "piñon wands." There were three principal dancers, wearing masks representing characters also portrayed in the *Yeibichai* Ceremony. They were accompanied by two other performers, one with a bull-roarer, or "groaning stick," and the other shaking a rattle. The three "danced a lively and graceful jig, in perfect time to the music, with many bows, waving of wands, simultaneous evolutions and other pretty motions which might have graced the spectacular drama of a metropolitan theater."[4]

Although the number and types of dances may differ, it is nevertheless important that every phase of the nine-day ceremony be carried out properly. Otherwise it would fail, its purpose of healing and of bringing prosperity to the people would not be fulfilled, and it would all have to be started over again. The Navajos truly follow the Trail of Beauty, and beauty is the underlying power in all rituals to transform a sick person into a healthy one. One of the songs translates:

> *In the house of long life, there I wander.*
> *In the house of happiness, there I wander.*
> *Beauty before me, with it I wander.*
> *Beauty behind me, with it I wander.*
> *Beauty below me, with it I wander.*
> *Beauty above me, with it I wander.*

Beauty all around me, with it I wander.
In old age traveling, with it I wander.
On the beautiful trail I am, with it I wander.

THE YEIBICHAI, OR NIGHT CHANT

This ceremony was given in November and also lasted nine days. The Yei are gods, and Yeibichai is "Grandfather of the Gods." He and his mate were both portrayed by men; in many Indian tribes men often took female parts in important rituals. Both of these dancers were masked. The Yeibichai mask, of white buckskin, had red and yellow hair and a fan of eagle feathers across its top from ear to ear.

In the Night Chant little boys were initiated with sacred meal and ceremonially whipped with yucca whips by the Yei. Girls were blessed with meal but not whipped. Afterward the "gods" removed their masks and allowed the children to put them on, so that they too would feel like gods. In order to qualify for performance as a god in the Night Chant, a person had to take part in the ceremony at least four times; sometimes he participated a number of years before he felt eligible.

East of the sacred hogan was an arbor of brush, which served as headquarters for the dancers, and between this arbor and the hogan was left a path or lane, with a large fire halfway between the two. On the ninth evening the medicine man, or "singer," in charge of the ceremony, usually an elderly man, came out of the hogan and sat on the ground near the door. The patient was brought out and seated upon a buffalo robe. This was the time when, years ago, four masked figures representing gods of war appeared on the scene, brandishing bows and arrows and knives to scare evil spirits away from the patient. He, if able, rose from his robe and sprinkled meal upon them as they chanted, danced, and cavorted around him.

Then the medicine man arose and sprinkled the path to the arbor with sacred corn meal. A little jingle of bells was heard and from the arbor came the Yeibichai, wearing his mask and a buckskin robe, a wreath of spruce over his shoulders, and carrying a magic basket. The buckskin for this ceremony was prepared from the skin of a deer from which no blood was shed. The deer was trapped and smothered with corn meal. The Yeibichai was followed by a file of four more dancers, draped in blankets and wearing white kilts and deerskin hoods, blue for the sky, with a yellow band across the bottom for the evening glow and black perpendicular stripes for falling rain. They also had red and yellow hair, with two feathers coming out of a bunch of owl fluffs over the right ear. The owl feathers helped to distinguish them as gods, for the Navajos, as well as many other tribes, fear the owl, and the average person will have nothing to do with it.

The Yeibichai's mate does not come out at night, which is a time when evil spirits are about, and although he has the power to overcome them, apparently she does not.

The rhythm for the dancing was furnished by a drummer beating on a ceremonial basket. The four dancers carried sprigs of evergreen in their left hands, rattles in their right, and spruce twigs were held with black hands below their knees. They stopped in front of the medicine man and his patient, who sprinkled them with meal, and they all turned to face the east. The medicine man chanted a long invocation, the patient repeating it after him, line for line. Then a loud whoop was heard and the Yeibichai dashed away down the lane to the arbor, twirling his basket as he ran. The line of dancers pivoted to face West again, and then the Yeibichai came bounding back, followed by a whooping clown who suddenly came bursting out of the arbor. He too was masked, but wore poor clothes, with a fox skin down his back. He was the Water Sprinkler, God of Rain and Snow, and why wear good clothes if going out in the rain? He caused much mirth and laughter, for the rain brings joy and happiness. He went through all sorts of antics, kicked his bare legs, yelled, shrieked, and flirted his tail at the fire. He brought a breath of relief to the people after the long seriousness of the invocation. Later on, although he might not be taking as active part in the festivities, his whippoorwill call was still heard.

The dancers had been standing quietly, but now lifted their hands in unison waist high and slowly began to shake their rattles, lifting and stamping first their right feet, then their left, hesitatingly at first, but suddenly swinging into full rhythm, the Yeibichai chant breaking from their lips, the eerie song rising higher and higher, each phrase ending with the "hu hu hu HU!" of the Yei, who never speak to men with human words. The rattles now swung emphatically and the dancers, as well as listeners, became enthralled with the powerful, piercing chant.

Another character now put in an appearance, the Humpback. He too, was masked, and on his back he wore a hump made of a sheepskin over a hoop, painted with white spots and decorated with feathers. Inside were supposed to be black clouds and all kinds of seeds.

Once again we find the sacred number four. The Yeibichai chant was repeated four times; then another group of singers and dancers appeared. This time there were six, wearing similar masks, but white, and they represented male gods. Although it may have been cold and snowing, they were nearly nude, the upper halves of their bodies smeared with gray paint, wearing beautiful hand-woven kilts and streamers of colored cloth down their backs.

The story is that these gods also have mates, and at one time they were also portrayed by male dancers, but in later years it seems that they were no longer to be seen. There were times during the night when women danced, but in their usual dresses of heavy flounced skirts, velveteen blouses, and heavy silver jewelry. They danced in a long line, then in two lines, with movements something like the Virginia reel. Edna Ferguson reports that, when they danced with the "gods," each god "swoops up his goddess with an angular gesture, prances with her to the end of the line, drops her and moves back into his own line."[5]

When the six dancers retired, a team of eight came on. Following them, the first four reappeared. Each time a new team arrived, the medicine man and his patient arose to greet them. And so it went, all night long, hour after hour, until dawn. The last of the dancers had left the ground and for a brief interval all was quiet as the faint light in the east grew stronger. The medicine man dropped his blanket and rose to face the early glow, the patient also rising to stand beside and slightly behind him. Suddenly the dancers' bells were heard again and a new team, made up of exceptionally big fellows, stripped and freshly painted, came trotting in. They stamped with power and vigor and sang in clear, loud voices the last song, the song to the dawn, "In beauty it is finished." The new day, new life and light, brings its promise of health and joy. Patient, participants, and audience were all reborn, and, although life would go on as before, it would be accompanied with new strength, new beauty, and deeper appreciation.

At one time the Navajos had more "sings" than were ever counted. How many are still being performed may not be fully known. They run from one to three, five, or nine nights. All are different, and yet each incorporates certain elements of the others. Each one is under one "singer," who took an apprenticeship as a boy and spends his life at this vocation. Songs and ceremonies are property, just as much as are more tangible things, and the apprentice pays his teacher over the years for the privilege of learning the mysteries from him. The teacher holds one song and one sand painting for his own as long as he lives, so that only on his passing does the apprentice come into full possession of the entire ceremony. So a man may spend as many as twenty years before he is a full-fledged "singer."

The fact that the Navajos speak of the ceremonies as "sings" instead of dances would indicate that to them the singing is more important than the dancing. But recent translators claim that "way" would be a more accurate interpretation than "sing," so speak of the Mountaintop Way, the Night Way, and the like. Regardless of what they are called, we wish to point out that the Navajos had many dances, and some of them were extremely interesting, even from the standpoint of pure dance.

PART V. Indian Dances Today

22. The Grass, or Omaha, Dance

One of the last surviving dances of early days among Plains and Northern Woodland tribes is the popular Grass Dance, usually called "War Dance" by white people, because most of them think it is the *only* Indian dance. Even some of the Pueblo Indians in the Southwest have dances which incorporate movements and costumes of the Grass Dance.

The Grass Dance is known by many different names among the various tribes and has an interesting history. Today it is merely a "good time dance," but at one time it involved a great deal of ritual and symbolism. Certain phases of it definitely trace back to the war dances we have already talked about, but it also has elements of victory celebration and of old animal and bird dances. Although we cannot strictly call the Grass Dance a war dance, it was a warriors' dance, for originally only experienced warriors could belong to the Grass Dance Society.

ROACHES AND BUSTLES

Among the Omaha, Osage, Iowa, Pawnee, and other Missouri River tribes certain military ranks were designated by crest headdresses, or roaches, of deer and porcupine hair and by feather belts, or bustles, known sometimes as crow belts. The bustle was always associated with great bravery, and its wearers often served as camp policemen. In its earliest form the bustle was merely a stuffed crow or raven skin fastened to the rear of the belt so that it stood out horizontally from the back of the wearer. One of these belts from the Winnebagos—a very old one—is to be seen at the Chicago Museum of Natural History. The raven skin is attached to a very elaborately quilled belt. A Winnebago who wore a bustle showed that he had killed an entire enemy family in its own lodge.

In 1664 La Potherie reported a party of twenty young men from the Great Lakes region, faces and bodies painted black and "wearing girdles of otter skin to which were attached the skins of crows, with their plumage." The ceremony was in preparation for a long journey to Montreal and involved a great feast with ten kettles. Each man danced in turn, singing his own song. When he ended his song the others yelled, their voices gradually dying away.

Some took firebrands, which they tossed about everywhere; others filled their dishes with hot coals, which they threw at each other. . . . I was present at a like entertainment among the Iroquois at the Sault of Montreal, and it seemed as if I were in the midst of hell.[1]

Another early mention of the bustle was by Antoine Denis Raudot in 1709, when writing about the Discovery Dance of the same region.[2]

A specimen of the crow belt was brought back by Lewis and Clark and may be seen at the Peabody Museum of Harvard. It is made of four raven skins which pro-

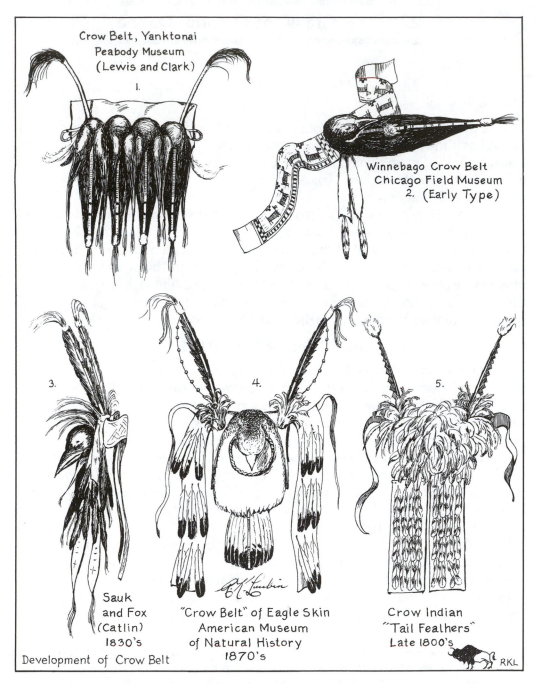

Crow Belt, Yanktonai
Peabody Museum
(Lewis and Clark)

1.

Winnebago Crow Belt
Chicago Field Museum
2. (Early Type)

3.

4.

5.

Sauk
and Fox
(Catlin)
1830's

"Crow Belt" of Eagle Skin
American Museum
of Natural History
1870's

Crow Indian
"Tail Feathers"
Late 1800's

Development of Crow Belt

RKL

The development of the crow belt, or bustle. 1. A Dakota crow belt, brought back by Lewis and Clark, in the Peabody Museum, Harvard University, drawn as it would look if the "horns" were properly erected. 2. A Winnebago crow belt, another early design, in the Field Museum. The belt is decorated with porcupine quills. 3. A crow belt such as Catlin portrayed for Sauks and Foxes in the 1830's. 4. A Gros Ventre bustle, worn by the Spoon Bearer in the Grass Dance, in the American Museum of Natural History, New York City. Although an eagle was substituted for a raven, it was still called a "crow belt." 5. A bustle of the type used by various tribes in the late 1800's and still worn by Crow Indians.

trude horizontally, side by side, from the back of the girdle. However, an observer unfamiliar with such an ornament would hardly realize how it is supposed to look from the way it is displayed in the case with the horns hanging down. The black raven skins are beautifully decorated with porcupine quills which are still nicely colored after all these years. The wearers of these belts which Lewis and Clark saw also had a stuffed raven attached to each elbow and wore another on the head, with the beak over the forehead, and their entire bodies were painted black, as La Potherie had reported a hundred and forty years before.

These men were assigned by the Sioux chief to guard the explorers' boat and not let it move without his permission. The adventurers learned that the reason they were being held was that they had given the Indians no tobacco, so were not considered friendly, or at least had offered no proof of their friendship. Once they understood that such a little ransom was all that was necessary to bring about their release and at the same time establish their friendship, they made the requested donation of tobacco, the bustle wearers let go the cables, and the expedition was on its way again.

The wearing of raven skins is even reported for the Cherokees, whose scouts displayed them.[3] Catlin has a number of paintings showing Sauks and Foxes wearing ornaments of stuffed raven skins with two erect, decorated sticks, spikes, or "horns" projecting from the pad to which the raven was fastened. Tixier mentioned a *corbeau* for the Osages and Long, for the Otos, each describing it in similar fashion.

THE OMAHA HETHUSHKA CEREMONY

Although the crow belt, or bustle, is quite old, it has undergone much change and development. The Omaha, a tribe living on the Missouri River in earth lodges, had a warrior society known as Hethu'shka, whose objective was "to stimulate an heroic spirit among the people and keep alive the memory of historic and valorous acts."[4] By the time of the Omaha Hethushka, the bustle was usually the entire skin of an eagle, stuffed, with the two "horns" and the further addition of two trailers, or panels, from which small, fluttering feathers dangled. (There used to be one on display in the American Museum of Natural History in New York.)

Only the leader of the Hethushka wore a crow belt. The other members wore bunches of grass in their belts, to symbolize scalps or honors taken in battle. The ceremony was held in a large earth lodge. The leader sat opposite the door, the traditional place of honor among all tribes, so far as we know, and other members were graded in rank on either side of him, the lowest rank nearest the door. The meetings were held about once a month, a feast giver being selected as host for each meeting. The host sat in a lowly spot to the right of the door, with two appointed or volunteer servants to assist him. The servants were famous warriors, so even among Indians there was a ceremonial humility on certain occasions. But at the same time a place near the door, in a military society, symbolized a place of danger—the guard post of a fortification.

437

The drum was on the leader's left, in the position of greatest honor, and two to four men singers sat around it, sometimes assisted by a few chosen women singers. The first song was about black paint and clouds filling the sky overhead.

Before me stands, awaiting my touch, coal-black paint. Heavy black clouds are filling all the sky over our heads. Upon our faces now we put the black, coal-black cloud. Honoring war, wearying for the fight, warrior's fight. Waiting to go where the Thunder leads warriors on.[5]

In many tribes war was regarded as a great fire, so the colors red and black were both symbolic of war, red for the flames, black for the charcoal and ashes remaining after the fire was extinguished. Hence black was the color of victory.*

The leader dipped the fingers of his right hand into a dish of charcoal paint, touched his forehead, cheeks, chin, and both sides of his chest. A servant then passed the dish to the others, the song being repeated each time the paint was applied.

Prayer songs were sung and ceremonial pipes smoked around the circle. One pipe started at the door, circling left to the rear. The other pipe started in the rear and traveled left to the door on the other side. Dancing then preceded the feast, the dancers enacting personal war experiences, and dancing followed the feast.

Several fire tricks were known to the shamans, or medicine men, of many tribes. These consisted of handling hot coals, hot rocks, and flames and often of dipping the bare hands into boiling water.

Thunder was associated with fire and with war and also with black paint. Thunder, to Omahas, was God of War, and Thunder was honored in the Hethushka ceremonies.

THE SIOUX BUY THE OMAHA DANCE

Dances and songs were regarded as property, either tribal or personal, and so were bought and sold through an exchange of presents. The Yanktons bought the Hethushka ceremony from the Omahas about the time of the Civil War. De Smet wrote about it in 1867 as he found it among them, and they seem to have already passed it on to their western relatives, the Lakotas, by that time. The Lakotas call it Oma'ha Kai'yotag, Oma'ha Wacipi, or Peji Mignaka Wacipi—Omaha Society, Omaha Dance, or Grass Bustle Dance. Because they did not understand the symbolism of the grass they spoke of it as Omaha Dance, in honor of its former owners, or merely as Grass Dance. (The Sioux accent the second syllable, Oma'ha, to designate the tribe. O'maha, in Lakota, means "something that sticks.") They im-

---

*These colors also had other meanings. Red is the color of the sun and consequently symbolized life, as well as blood and fire. Black is the color of the earth and also represents ignorance. It was used in mourning. Painting the face black, whether for mourning or for victory, served as a disguise so that vengeful spirits would not recognize the wearer.

Laubin portraying an initiate in the Grass Dance Society. Laubin Collection.

mediately began to make changes. Being great singers, they created new songs, and being great dancers, they stressed the dancing.

They knew that the Omahas had associated the ceremony with Thunder. To them Thunder implied the boiling water trick, so they incorporated it into the ritual. No doubt they were familiar with the hair roach, and now they accepted it as the standard headdress of the Omaha Society, and even shaved the heads of initiates, imitating neighboring tribes to the east, who wore the roach with shaven heads. According to Lewis and Clark, the Sioux also shaved their heads, but apparently they later gave up the practice, except for incorporating it into the Grass Dance and continuing it with initiates into their Fox Society.

439

Lakota Grass dancers about 1900. Left to right: Little Horse, Lone Elk, Left Hand Bear, Bone Necklace, and Eagle Shirt. Smithsonian Institution, Bureau of American Ethnology.

Hunkpapa and Yanktonai Sioux informants say there were two bustles, but Wissler, in one account, says there were four for the Oglalas. Another time he mentions but two, so apparently his informants were not quite sure. The Sioux added rosettes of feathers to the centers of the bustles, but held to the Omaha tradition of using only feathers from birds of prey, particularly the crow, buzzard, magpie, and eagle. The crow has the keenest scent, so was first to arrive on a battlefield, and the bustle was named after him. The eagle could afford to be last, for he was big enough to chase the others away.

The entire bustle represented a battlefield. The two horns were warriors—the one on the left, nearest the heart, a friend, the one on the right, an enemy. Horsehair tassels on their tips were the scalp locks of the two warriors. The rosette represented arrows sticking in the fallen warriors, the fluttering feathers on the panels symbolized feathers fluttering to earth from the birds flying above the battlefield.

The deer hair on old roaches was always dyed red. The Sioux, to this day, call all roaches *wapeṡa*, meaning a red-hair headdress, regardless of color, even though they have been made in many colors for a long time. The Pawnees said that the red-dyed deer hair represented a fire. One or two eagle feathers were worn in the roach, depending upon the standing of the wearer. They were attached in bone sockets, so that they twirled as the dancer performed. The feathers represented medicine men dancing in the fire, and the bone sockets were the medicine that protected them from being burned.

The roach soon became the standard headdress for all members of the Grass Dance Society although one story said that originally the Sioux had only seven. For some reason now unknown, the number seven was connected with Thunder.

Eventually the bustle also became standard costume for any Grass dancer, and from about 1900 on everyone has been permitted to wear one.

In recent years the Grass Dance has become tribal property and anyone is free to dance, but originally the Omaha, or Grass, Dance Society was made up only of brave warriors with battle experience. It was not a true warrior society, however, for its members were not called upon for special police duties, either in camp or while at war. But it had officers, nevertheless. In addition to the Bustle Wearers there were two Whistle Men; two Spoon Carriers; one Whipper, or Driver; one Drum Keeper; and usually a Master of Ceremonies. Except for wearers of bustles and roaches, no clothing was worn but breechclouts and moccasins.

Dog meat was a requirement for the feast of the Grass Dance among the Lakotas, the dog also being associated with Thunder. In the early days of the Lakota Grass Dance, the meat was taken from the kettle with bare hands, as in the Heyoka ceremony. In later years, however, this was dispensed with, and the meat was handled only with a forked spit (representing lightning), the fork elaborately decorated with bead wrappings and feathers, and a spoon of buffalo horn.

One story goes that when the original Lakota leader of the Grass Dance died, he told his followers that anyone who dreamed of making changes in the ritual could do so. A new leader claimed such a dream and made some innovations, but lightning struck and killed several dancers following the ceremony. So they left out the innovations. But lightning struck again. This time tobacco was placed in the hills for Thunder, and there was no more trouble from lightning.[6]

SPREAD OF THE GRASS DANCE

After the Lakota developed the dance and ritual it passed from tribe to tribe, eventually coming back to the Omahas themselves. The Assiniboins and Blackfeet also called it Grass Dance. The Crows and the Hidatsas, from whom the former learned the dance, called it Hot Dance,[*] perhaps because they also knew the boiling water trick. Apparently the dance as taught to the Hidatsas included it, but it was not retained by them. The Indians around the Great Lakes called it Dream Dance; the Arapahos, Wolf Dance; the Utes, Turkey Dance; the Kiowas, O'homo Dance. Although each tribe has added or taken away from the original version of the ceremony, the dance itself, the songs, and costumes are similar all over Indian country. All the tribes credit the Sioux with the spread of the ceremony, and all have incorporated many Sioux songs into it.

There is good reason to believe that it all started with the Pawnees, who taught the Omahas what the latter called *Hethushka*.

As we have noted, Omahas, Iowas, Osages, and Otos contributed to the spectacular costume. The Omahas passed these and the fundamental ritual to the Lakotas, who added other features before passing it on until it came back to the Omahas and Pawnees, who could hardly have recognized their old acquaintance. When the Crows originally learned the dance from the Hidatsas, it called for four sacred bustles, which they increased to eight. The Assiniboins had seven. The Kiowas had only one, which they say they got from the Sioux, but they still have it and care for it in the sacred manner prescribed to them. It is doubtful if any of the other tribes still possess sacred bustles.

These sacred bustles originally were cared for just like other sacred or medicine bundles. Certain it is that the bustle no longer has any special significance. The Kiowas and other Oklahoma Indians have made bustles recently which are simply immense and have been copied by many other tribes.

THE SIOUX GRASS, OR OMAHA, DANCE

Since the Sioux developed the Grass Dance and caused its spread throughout the country, perhaps we should take up their dance in more detail as being more or less typical of the dance everywhere.

The Lakotas even built a dance lodge similar to the earth lodge of the Pawnees and Omahas for the Grass Dance. It eventually was changed to a large log building, circular or octagonal in shape, with a dirt floor, which became the favorite place for any Indian "doings" until just the last few years, when more modern structures have been taking over. The Crows, and later the Indians near the Great Lakes, also used these large log or wooden buildings for their dances. The doors invariably faced east, just as the tipi and most ceremonial lodges did.

---

[*]This was not the same Hot Dance listed by Maximilian for the Arikaras.

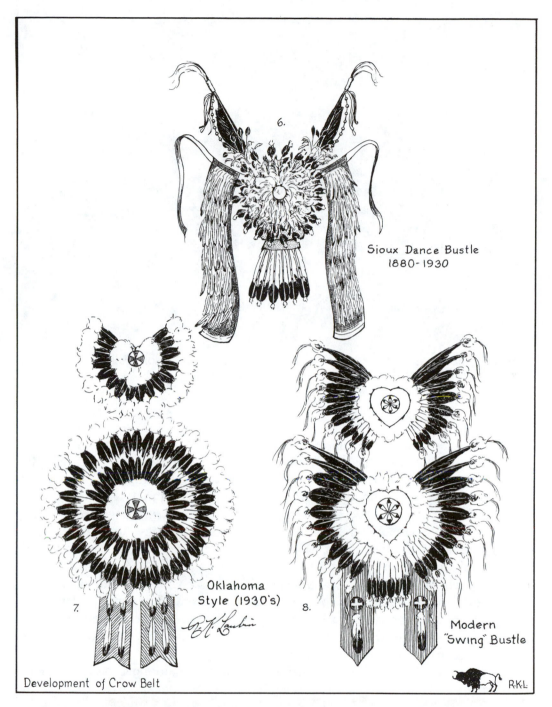

6.

Sioux Dance Bustle
1880-1930

Oklahoma
Style (1930's)

7.

Development of Crow Belt

8.

Modern
"Swing" Bustle

R·K·L

The further development of the crow belt, or bustle. 6. A Sioux Grass Dance bustle, in the style of the late 1800's and early 1900's, showing the addition of a small rosette, but still made from feathers of birds of prey. 7. The exaggerated rosette and addition of a neck "bustle" that appeared in the 1930's and is still worn. 8. The swing bustle and neckpiece are currently popular. The Aztecs had similar ornaments at the time of the Spanish conquest.

A Sioux dance house, photographed about 1890. John A. Anderson Collection, Nebraska State Historical Society, Lincoln.

Opposite the door sat six officers, or head men. To the north of them hung the two (or four) sacred bustles on a rack of poles. Still farther to the left hung the big dance drum, on four decorated stakes, around which the singers sat, the women assistants sitting or standing behind them. Two of the head men were to wear the bustles. One of them had a decorated buffalo-horn spoon, and one carried a whip with a saw-toothed wooden handle and two long leather lashes. Another head man carried the decorated forked spit. The man who served as Dance Leader carried a long *heḣaka śi' yotanka,* or elk whistle.

Such a whistle does sound like a bull elk bugling. *Śi' yotanka* really means a big prairie chicken, a designation the Sioux use for several different whistles. Why? No one knows for certain, any more than we say an elk "bugles," when he sounds much more like a flute. But his call is a series of harmonics, such as a bugle makes, and the prairie chicken does make a kind of whistling sound.

We have seen these long wooden whistles in recent use among Crows in Montana and Indians of Oklahoma, but it is a long time since we have seen one among the Sioux.*

---

*We have one of these elk whistles, made of box elder, with an eagle feather hanging to it on a long thong, just as Maximilian described it a hundred and thirty or more years

After four sacred bustles were adopted, the opinion seems to be that the Elk Whistle Man and the Spit Keeper were the other two to wear them.

North of the door sat another Whistle Man, wearing an eagle-bone whistle on a cord around his neck, and another man with a plain buffalo-horn spoon. On the south sat the lay members.

De Smet, writing in 1867, seems to have actually seen the Grass Dance among the Yankton Sioux. He mentioned some of the important concepts associated with the ceremony and not understood by the average observer. The Grass Dance Society had already become the principal association among the Yanktons.

All the braves, or men of heart, as the Indians express it, belong to this fraternity. All the members enter into a solemn engagement: first, to avoid quarrels among themselves, and to submit any differences which may arise to the arbitration of two or three wise men. This is their supreme court, improvised for the occasion, and there is no appeal from its decision; the result is generally happy and they live in good understanding and great harmony: second, the society undertakes to give aid and assistance to the weak, to protect the widow and the orphan and to succor the sick and the stranger in need.

At the ceremonial dances each member carries a long bunch of grass, which is among them emblem of abundance and charity. It is the grass that nourishes their horses and domestic animals, and fattens the buffalo, the deer, the elk, the bighorn and the antelope of the plains and mountains. . . .

It is especially in the spring, when the grass is tender and sweet, that their ceremonial dances take place. The badge or distinctive mark of the society is the bunch of grass braided and attached to the waist of each member in the form and appearance of a long tail.[7]

By this comment is it easily seen that the Sioux did not learn that the braided tails represented scalps, for De Smet would have seized upon that symbolism, being prone to write detrimentally of any "pagan practices."

The Winnebagos also say that the dance was done in the spring, when the grass was short and green, but the Lakotas gave the ceremony, as had the Omahas, about once a month.

The Sioux developed an old man's and a young man's Grass Dance, which they now speak of respectively as Slow and Fast Grass Dance and which other tribes now call Slow and Fast War Dance.

---

ago. We got it from a trader on the Crow reservation. Carrying it in my hand while walking down the road we met an old friend, White Arm.

Pointing to the newly acquired whistle, he asked, "Where you get 'im?"

I replied, "From that trader back there."

"Me make 'im. No good," White Arm said.

We knew the whistle would not "work" when we bought it, but such whistles are now so rare that we thought we should get it anyway. I tinkered around with the bird quill which controls the sound hole and finally got it to play. So old White Arm knew the principle of making the whistle but just had not taken the time to adjust it properly.

When the singers started a dance song, the Driver with the whip was first to rise. If other dancers did not respond immediately, it was his duty to see that they did. Usually he merely threatened with his whip, largely to amuse the spectators, ranged around the walls behind the seated dancers. Occasionally he lashed a particularly slow or stubborn dancer on the legs, but if he drew blood, he was expected to make a present to some old person.

The Song Leader decided on the songs to be used — slow, fast, in honor of some individual, and so on. Individuals enacted war experiences as they danced, and between dances distinguished warriors were given an opportunity to recount their coups. In those days only men who had struck the enemy were allowed to "sit at the drum," and when a man wished to tell a war experience he went to the drum and struck it with his hand, a stick, or his war club, showing that he had struck the enemy. Striking the drum no doubt took the place of the earlier custom of striking the post.

After a man had finished "counting his coups," the singers thumped a number of times on the drum in approval and the onlookers applauded with exclamations of "Hau! hau!" His women relatives gave a high-pitched trill, made by vibrating the tongue rapidly against the roof of the mouth. It sounds something like tapping the mouth with the hand, but the hand is not used. The men tapped the mouth only in a charge against the enemy, or as a victory call used in a few warrior society dances.

De Smet had an interesting comment on the dancing of the Yanktons.

At the first signal given by the master of ceremonies all the brethren are on foot carefully painted and in their finest costumes. They form a large circle, brandish their weapons, whether guns, lances, war-clubs, bows and arrows or any other arms which have been the instrument of some heroic act either in war or in the chase. All their movements are in strict time to the sound of the drum, tambourine, flute and gourd filled with pebbles. While they leap and dance with fantastic gestures and capers, each brother in turn sings his *dowanpi,* or song, recounting his lofty deeds of valor or his heroic charities. The choruses in which all join are full of sarcasm of cowardice and avarice. *Each dancer seems to have a pirouette and to take a position all his own.* [Italics ours.] They jump up and down and the ground seems to tremble beneath the beating of their feet. They wind in and out and turn in every direction, right and left, in an admirable confusion, keeping time with the deafening sound of the wild music.[8]

The above remarks could apply to any of the Sioux divisions, or for that matter to any Indians doing Grass Dance, even in its present form, except for leaping and the use of the "tambourine, flute and gourd filled with pebbles," which certainly have not been used in any Grass Dance in recent years. De Smet's mention of their use here may be his effort to describe the effect of Indian music. It is possible that by "flute" he means the *ši'yotanka,* or eagle-bone whistle.

The Indians told General Howard that the Omaha dance was a dance of peace. What they probably meant was that they did it during times of peace, trying to correct the white man's impression that everything was a war dance. Howard wrote:

Most of the Indians who took part were naked, except for the breech-cloth, and various ornaments, made of feathers, wings of birds, or evergreen branches, worn upon their heads or hanging around their necks. The dancers were fantastically painted from head to foot.

We could not trace anything very distinctive in the dance, nor very well interpret what it meant. They used the same odd steps characteristic of nearly all Indian dances. The men, when together, retained sufficient space for individual movement. A man would take two steps first with one foot and then with the other, then putting his hands together he would bend down and look on the ground as if searching for something, all the time keeping step with the beat of the tom-toms. The antics of one Indian were not always like those of another. One would indicate the chase and represent a deer, antelope, or buffalo, and others would represent wild geese, turkeys, or ducks.

After most of the dancers had ceased their performances, one—sometimes two or three— would jump up and dance for a long time, going through with all kinds of movements and gyrations, and looking down and up, and off.* Mingled with the sound of the tom-tom was the incessant chanting of the lookers-on, who sat with their heads thrown back. The chant was participated in to some extent by the dancers, but they confined themselves mostly to punctuating it with whoops and yells, which made the dance, though intended to symbolize peace, almost as startling as that which portends war.[9]

It is difficult to understand the evergreen branches, unless on this occasion the Indians were trying to emphasize, for an army officer, that they were at peace. We have never heard of evergreens being used in the Omaha Dance. But certainly the general would not confuse grass with evergreen branches, unless he was observing the dance from a long way off.

De Smet and Howard both imply that various dancers were doing various things. It is always puzzling to strangers to watch a group of Indian dancers all doing something different. They think the dance unorganized and the dancers untrained. This is far from true, but the Plains Indians were, and still are, individualists and they show it in their dancing. To them it is bad taste for one dancer to imitate the style of another. To the trained observer, this variety of figures and patterns is exciting and interesting. It is enchanting to watch the performances of individual dancers as each works his way around the dance ground and comes into view again. A dancer may look over one shoulder and then follow it around in a turn, or he may bend low and "look for something that isn't there." He "dances to his fingers" or "to his toes," and uses his feet almost as if they were hands.

Whatever the song, one characteristic of the Grass Dance is that the dancers must end exactly on the last beat of the drum. The singers give the cue so they know when the end is coming. Formerly, if the Dance Leader wanted the dance to be longer he gave a signal with his whistle and the song was repeated again. This is the only time we know of when a dancer could tell the singers what to do. Otherwise, the Song Leader, or Drum Chief, decides what songs to use and how long they should be sung.

---

*This is the first mention of "dancing the tail," to be taken up later.

Each dancer usually tries to get in a special flourish all his own for the ending. A good dancer has a sort of "dance signature" which no one else would think of copying. This flourish at the end of the dance is still carried out by good dancers. With the old meaning of the Grass Dance nearly forgotten and contest dancing almost taking over, a proper ending is more important than ever. No matter how many steps you know or how fancy you dance, if you miss the last beat of the drum and make another step, everybody laughs at you. It is not always easy to end properly. With many dancers and many bells ringing, it is hard enough even to hear the song, let alone anticipate its ending. But a good dancer always gets it right, and this is one of the main reasons he is considered good.

Occasionally some of the modern flourishes are very amusing, being copied from an "aesthetic" or "interpretive" dance routine seen on trips away from the reservation. Once we saw a champion Sioux dancer perform before a gathering of Crows and end his dance with a leap, landing on one knee with his arms outstretched. The Crows were convulsed with laughter.

The dances are usually short, but so usually are the rests in between until they take a real break for a give-away, a Woman's Dance, or some other diversion that we will bring up later. Occasionally the singers fool everyone by singing an extremely long time, trying to tire the dancers out.

One thing that the Lakotas almost always do, which many tribes nowadays do not do, is "dance the tail." What is the tail of a dance? The end, of course. The dance apparently comes to an end. Each dancer brings his dancing to a sudden stop with his favorite flourish as the song ends, and all start to walk to their seats. Then the singers begin to drum again and the dancers quickly reassemble, to dance as the song is sung once more. Again they make their fancy endings and the dance is really finished.

In the old days, only certain brave warriors were selected by the *Ikoncan,* Master of Ceremonies, to dance the tail. They were ones who had been left behind as rear guard on an expedition or had rescued comrades under fire. The tail dancers usually dramatized their experiences with a great deal of realism and gusto, adding to the general entertainment. Sometimes, instead of dancing to a song by the singers, the dancer sang his own song as he danced, the singers merely keeping time on the drum. It takes a good pair of lungs to be able to dance and sing at the same time.

As the old warrior days receded further and further into the past and fewer men remained who were entitled to dance the tail, the custom, like so many others, gave way, and for many years now anyone has been permitted to dance it, so all the dancers usually take part in it now. But the tail is seldom danced among the Crows, and "Sioux" dancers, like ourselves, miss it. It is seldom seen in Oklahoma, either, except among the Osages, who still designate a few dancers to dance the tail in the old way. A Comanche dancer told us that his people, as well as the Poncas and Pawnees, dance the tail only twice a year, but on these occasions all the dancers are permitted to take part.

Another custom was that if a dancer lost some article of costume, the other dancers approached it, danced around it, and several struck it, as if counting coup on an enemy. The "coup strikers" were then each required to make a gift, such as a horse, a pipe, or other valuable present, to someone, usually to an old and distinguished person, and the dancer who lost the article, if he wanted it back, also had to "give away."

Generosity was regarded in the same category with bravery as one of the supreme virtues. No one was considered really brave unless he was generous at the same time, so in this Give-away the dancers expressed their courage. If a song were sung in honor of an individual, that person was expected to get up and dance when he heard his name in the song, and to respond at the end of his dance by giving away to someone.

A dancer who had been wounded in battle wore a brass trade bell to call attention to it, a red tip on the end of one of his roach feathers, and sometimes a red feather in his bustle, if a bustle man. The bells sounded so nice that all the other dancers wanted them. There would be many dancers with many wounds if all the bells worn today still had the same symbolism. The brass sleigh bells have become a standard part of every dancer's costume, and although once more difficult to obtain are still available if one knows the right channels. Some dancers not only wear straps of them around their ankles, but around their knees, down each leg from waist to ankle, and sometimes even around the waist.

THE ORIGINAL RITUAL

Once a person had entered the dance hall he was not supposed to leave until the ceremonies were completed, and they lasted several hours. If one did have to leave he had to pay a forfeit in the form of a gift to an old man. Then he could dance his way out of the lodge, which obviously called attention to his leaving, but he was not supposed to go out otherwise.

During all these preliminary dances the feast of dog meat was being prepared by the womenfolk of the member who had been selected to provide it. A man was not asked to provide a feast more than once. Since the entire Grass Dance has become more or less tribal property and everyone is welcome to attend, the feast is furnished nowadays by a number of volunteers, and dog is reserved for very special occasions. It is always a mark of distinction to be served dog. We have told how the Iroquois and other Eastern tribes used dog flesh or dogs' heads to represent the enemy. But dog meat had also another symbolism. Before the Indians had horses, the dog was their best animal friend. So if a man sacrificed his favorite dog for his visitors he was really demonstrating in what high esteem he held them.

When the meat was ready, the brass kettle containing it was removed from the fire by the Whistle Man near the door, who smoked it over a sweet-grass smudge, swung it around four times, and set it down in the center of the dance ring. Nearly everything was done in a series of four, four being the sacred number to most tribes. There are four directions, four winds, four seasons—one could go on and on with the number four as found in nature.

449

The singers then began the series of songs for taking down the sacred bustles. The two Whistle Men took the bustles from their rack, purified them in the sweet-grass smoke, and laid them on the ground, behind the altar of incense, facing the door and not far from the kettle. On the next song, the two Bustle Men came forward, took places kneeling behind the bustles, and swayed their bodies in time to the music. When the bustles were mentioned in the song they rose on their knees and outstretched their arms toward them.

After extending their arms, hands open, the fourth time, a different song was sung. This time they arose, each approaching his bustle in a low crouching position, right hand extended toward the bustle, left arm outstretched in back. They advanced almost to touching the bustles, then retreated with relaxed arms to their initial position. This advance and retreat was repeated three times. The fourth time they grabbed the bustles, held them aloft, then offered them to the four winds and resumed the dance, tying the bustles on as they danced, circling counterclockwise now, looping around the kettles. They came back the other way around, going clockwise, and continued circling. On the fourth time around they were joined by the two Whistle Men, who followed them. As the two leaders passed the kettle this last time they extended their right hands over it. The first Whistle Man pretended to reach into the kettle and the second Whistle Man picked it up, dancing with it to complete the circle, then continued alone until he had set it down again in its original place.

The next song called the Spit Keeper to dance. He held the decorated forked spit in his right hand, point forward, and at first danced slowly, almost in place. As the song became faster he began circling to the left. He completed half the circle on the third "verse" and finished the circle on the fourth. The second song was faster yet. He began to dance back and forth on the path to the kettle. The second half of this song was extremely rapid and he danced to the kettle, almost touching it with the point of the spit, then returned to his starting point. This action was repeated three times. The fourth time he actually tried to spear the dog's head in the kettle, leaving the spit in it, and circled the kettle to the end of the song.

Next, the Whistle Men, who always acted as servants, came to the kettle, the first one taking the dog's head with the decorated spit and placing it in a dish made of turtle shell near the head men in the rear of the lodge. The second Whistle Man had a less fancy, smaller forked spit, with which he also served meat. The heart, liver, and breast were also placed in the special dish, and meat was served first to the leaders in the rear—the Bustle Men, Drum Keeper, and Singers.

During the next song the Spoon Carriers brought soup to these same men and offered it to their lips. If their conduct had been beyond reproach, they accepted the soup. If not, they turned their heads away, refusing it. To accept when unworthy might bring later misfortune.

A prayer of thanksgiving for the food was next offered by one of the head men. Four men with coups to their credit were selected to eat the choice parts which had been placed in the turtle dish. Everyone else brought his own dish and spoon, a custom still observed at Indian feasts. In the case of a large meeting, more food was brought in and distributed. The bones of the dog were saved, gathered up by the Whistle Men, and placed in another dish.

The head Whistle Man took the dog skull, held it over sweet grass incense, then set it facing the door. The other Whistle Man placed the bones in a pile to one side. The first one of the brave men, who had eaten the meat from the head, then danced, portraying the exploit which had won him his coup. On his fourth time around he struck the skull, which now represented an enemy, held it up, and narrated the exploit, then gave away a horse. The other three brave men went through the same routine, but were not expected to give away as much value as a horse. Next, all four danced together, circling the pile of bones with right hands extended over it, as in a blessing.

Following this ceremonial feast, the Driver called another general dance, which lasted as long as the assembly was interested. The singers were the ones who usually decided when the session would end. They sang the closing song, the officer in charge of this closing part of the ceremony danced alone and gave away, then all the dancers joined in this last dance, dancing around four times before rushing for the door as if attacking an enemy.

Members of the Omaha Society gave the ceremony before going to war. In the dances they pantomimed battle actions—fighting, scalping, scouting, spearing, shooting, and the like. This is the nearest thing the Sioux had to a war dance. Other tribes that took up the Grass Dance did not do this, so far as we know.

The above account and much of what follows is largely from our own research, gathered over the years as we interviewed old-timers and tried to put the various elements, still occasionally seen, together. The reports of ethnologists have been sketchy and incomplete. Even Wissler may never have seen the entire ceremony, for his best days among the Oglalas were in the early 1900's when the government suppression was at its height. Actually dancing with the Indians gives one an opportunity to learn details that may not be given in an interview.

Nowadays it is customary to use a bass drum, and the drum is seldom "hung," that is, supported from the four decorated stakes. When the dancing is outdoors, the drum is often placed on one side of the dance arena, under the arbor, for it is much more important that the singers be comfortable than the dancers. When they are dancing at night, however, the drum is usually placed near the center pole, under the gasoline lamp or electric lights hanging from it. Indoors the drum is usually placed at one side of the room to give the dancers more space.

Although it is no longer required that a singer be a coup striker, or even have war experience, he is still an honored person. Today the singers usually wear ordinary, or "white man's," clothes and large cowboy hats. When we first went to the reservation years ago, the tall "reservation" hats were popular, but one seldom sees them anymore. They still wear cowboy sombreros, and the singers wear them indoors as well as outdoors.

WOMEN'S ROLE

After the Omaha Dance had been established for a number of years, the women were invited to participate. Since that time there have always been intermissions in the routine when the women's dances were performed. Among all the tribes we have visited except the Crows the same drum is used for the women's dances, but the singers stand up when singing for them. They are seated for all the men's dances.

The women "have the floor" in their dances, and the old custom, still occasionally carried out, was for the women to invite partners to dance with them. Usually when a Round, or Circle, Dance was called, the women first danced alone. They formed a segment of a circle, depending upon the number in attendance, shoulder to shoulder, and moved to the left, lifting the left foot slightly higher than the right, dragging the right to come up to the leading left foot. Sometimes they moved in half time for a while and then increased to a step on every beat.

The rhythm for the women's dances is always, anywhere, in 3/4 time, with a heavily accented first beat and the third beat soft—no second beat at all. The men's dancing is to a slightly accented or steady 2/4 rhythm.

There is a slight flexing of the knees in the Round Dance which gives a fascinating and graceful movement when it is done properly. Sometimes an inner circle is formed, the dancers facing those in the outer circle, which makes one circle go opposite to the other, for they are both moving to the left. Very rarely a circle will be led to the right.

The women's dance is also known as the Dragging Feet Dance. Sometimes for a bit of variation the left foot is moved forward slightly while stepping to the left, the right "dragging" to catch up with it, and on the next step the left foot is moved backward, the right foot always being dragged or shuffled to catch up. This gives an interesting back-and-forth as well as sidewise movement to the dance.

After dancing to the first song, some of the women choose men to dance in the circle with them. Formerly a woman made this choice by going to the man and tapping his foot with her toe. Occasionally some men, uninvited, would break into the dance, forcing their way into the circle. The men placed their arms over the shoulders of the women on either side of them, and the women put their arms around the men's waists. This was the nearest thing to couple dancing in the early days. In recent years the Rabbit Dance, the Indian Two Step, and other modern dances have been included in the Grass Dance gatherings. These are decidedly takeoffs on white-style dancing in couples.

Since the women have been admitted to the Grass Dance meetings, they usually sit on the south side of the lodge. The head men are still on the west, the other men on the north side. During the typical men's dancing in the Grass Dance, the women dance in place or move slightly to the left and back to the right, but always on their side of the lodge. They rise slightly on their toes, with knee action, or merely "bounce" in place, and sometimes use a twisting step of shifting the weight alternately from toes to heels, their moccasins making figure eights in the soft earth.

There is a fascination in watching the women dance, for good dancers among

Gladys Laubin dancing with Sioux and Crow Indians during a Hot Dance at a Crow fair. She is wearing a buckskin dress made for her by Chief One Bull's daughters Regina and Margaret. Laubin Collection.

them exhibit as much of a sense of rhythm as do the men. They have simple steps, gliding forward or backward or sideways, sometimes alternating left and right feet, sometimes dancing with both feet together, twisting from toes to heels. As they bounce, the long dresses and fringes sway rhythmically. And they have standards for good dancing, holding contests for best dancers, just as the men do. But we have never seen women of any other tribe dance as vigorously as the Sioux women, especially the older women.*

In Oklahoma the women sometimes dance as a group, circling around the hall with a forward shuffling step, outside the compact circle of men dancing in the

---

*Indians and we personally object to the word "squaw." It is the Narraganset word for "woman" and came into use through Roger Williams and the English settlers, but it has been used in such a derogatory manner that it offends Indians today. After all, each tribe had its own word for "woman," so why use a Narraganset word to designate them?

center. This style has now worked its way north, and Sioux women are also doing it. The men sometimes circle to the right instead of dancing melee fashion (when they move every which way, with no attempt at formation). Moving to the right is contrary to the old Plains custom in which many dances "followed the sun," but the direction in which the dancers move seems to be set by the Dance Leader. Sometimes the women follow the men around in a mass, a column of fours, or a column of sixes. At other times the women work to the left, circling outside the men. Sometimes they move diagonally across the floor, the men giving way to them as they pass.

THE SONGS

So far we have not been able to find any one who claims to know all the songs of the Grass Dance ritual. It is doubtful that any such singer survives. Although singing is perhaps as popular with Indians today as it ever was, the style of singing is gradually changing and the number of types of songs decreasing. The new songs are generally social in nature and, to non-Indian ears, more melodious, but they lack the charm and character of the older songs. Many of these newer songs have been and are being recorded, but so far as we know no one ever recorded or transcribed the seven important ceremonial songs used in the Lakota Grass Dance ritual.

Frances Densmore, who did such a remarkable job of collecting Indian music all over the country, had the opportunity to collect all the old Grass Dance songs, but at the time did not understand enough of the significance of the Grass Dance to do so. She was first at Standing Rock in 1911 while there were plenty of "real Indians" alive. But at that time Indians were seldom permitted to dance, and Miss Densmore told us that she would not ask the agent to grant them permission. She had some idea of the importance of dancing, for the Indians did not want to sing any songs without the proper accompanying dances and rituals but she convinced them that the old days were gone forever and that through her efforts they could at least keep a memory of their music. However, she did not collect these particular Grass Dance ritual songs, and they have probably been lost forever.

ANIMAL DANCES

General Howard mentioned the various animal and bird dancers he saw at the Omaha Dance. Animal Dances were still being performed by some tribes at least as recently as the time of the Civil War. Henry Boller, who was in the West between 1858 and 1866, told of one he saw among the Hidatsas.

On the afternoon of the third day the most thrilling part of the ceremonies occurred. The rattles sounded, the drums beat, and the bulls executed their stamping, jarring dance with unwonted energy. . . . All eyes were turned towards the Medicine Lodge, whence came pouring forth, and dispersing in all directions, a band of antelopes, fifty or sixty in number. They were men and boys of all sizes, entirely naked and painted all over with white clay. Willow twigs were bound on their heads in the shape of and to represent horns. There were also frogs and several nondescript animals.[10]

The Sioux once had an animal dance similar to that of the Mandans, Hidatsas, and other Western tribes. The last time that it was given was in Chicago for Buffalo Bill's Wild West Show at the Columbian Exposition in 1893! Ralph Hubbard saw it with his father, the writer Elbert Hubbard. He was only eight years old then, but he never forgot the spectacle. The dance was given on a special request, and since the show was located in Chicago for an extended stay there was time enough to prepare for it. The Cheyennes in the show also took part. The Indians sent home to the reservations for the necessary animal headdresses and other paraphernalia.

The dance was given, as far as the Indians were concerned, not for the show at all. They took advantage of an opportunity, otherwise denied them, to put on this dance which they hoped would bring back the game. Buffalo, deer, antelope, even coyotes were all represented. The dance took up the entire show time, lasting all afternoon, and was repeated again that night. Few in the audience realized they were seeing the temporary revival, the last presentation, of a ceremony now lost, even in memory, to most Indians.

Even in Howard's time, the Grass Dance was beginning to take over many older ceremonies. During the time that the dances were suppressed and Indians were given only rare permission to dance at all, the Grass Dance was the one always given. White men, on these occasions, wanted to see *the* War Dance, of which they had formerly been so afraid. The brilliant costumes, painted bodies, wild music, and whirling dancers satisfied them in this respect, and the Indians used the opportunity to keep alive all the types of dancing they knew.

With the passing of the last survivors of the buffalo days, one seldom sees features reminiscent of those times. We were fortunate in being on the reservations a number of years ago, while those old people were still alive. Both at Standing Rock and at Pine Ridge we saw snatches of various animal dances. A few old men had buffalo headdresses and imitated buffalo while the younger fellows were merely doing fancy Grass Dance steps. One old man danced like a wolf, another like a bear. Once in a while we saw one do prairie chicken movements. Even some of the younger dancers imitated birds, shaking heads and shoulders, quivering all over, moving their arm wheels like wing feathers.

The present-day Grass Dance also incorporates a Buffalo Dance, which the Sioux call the Grass Buffalo Dance. Many people, even Indians, mistake this for the old buffalo dances, of which there were often several, even in one tribe. The Grass Buffalo is quite different, but is another example of the way the animal dance motifs have been included in the Grass Dance.

COSTUME CHANGES

Although the original Grass Dance costume was only breechclout and moccasins, plus roaches, grass tails, and bustles (for those having the right to wear them), other ornaments gradually crept in. The addition of arm wheels, sometimes incorrectly referred to as "arm bustles," was made in the late 1800's, but they did not become really popular until between 1920 and 1950. (A bustle is something worn on the

Laubin wearing old-style "cactus-blossom" arm wheels, a porcupine-hair roach, and a traditional bustle, opening the Charging-the-Kettle Dance. Photo by Ned Hockman.

rear; how can it be a *bustle* on the arm?) They are rosettes made much like the center rosettes added to the bustles about 1875 or 1880. The Lakotas call them *un' kcila,* or cactus blossoms, and they do look something like the blossoms on the prickly pear.

An otter skin cape or collar became popular. This was sometimes worn like a necklace, hanging in front instead of resting on the shoulders. Matching armbands and garters of porcupine-quilled work were added, then a full breastplate of quill-work instead of the otter skin. And about the same time beaded armbands and cuffs began to appear. Bone "hair pipes" became available and breastplates of them were worn. Women also began wearing them, but the men's breastplates are always strung with the hair pipes crosswise, the women's perpendicular, and the women's breastplates or necklaces were made very wide and long.

Anklets of white angora-goat hair also became popular and have been accepted as standard in Indian dancing costumes ever since. The idea of anklets was not new; some type had been used for generations. Those made of the long white hair of the Rocky Mountain goat were particularly prized, for that animal is surefooted, fleet, agile, and extremely difficult to hunt. So he symbolized qualities admired and coveted by every warrior. The hair of the domestic Angora goat is used as a substitute; much of it at one time came up from the Navajos, who raise them (see page 216).

CHANGES IN CEREMONY

For many years it has been customary to build a brush arbor for summer dances. It is constructed exactly like the Sioux Sun Dance lodge, except that the center pole is undecorated, and usually from its top flies Old Glory. The only other difference is that the Grass Dance arbor is usually smaller, although we have seen a particularly large one at Fort Yates, which was about sixty-five or seventy feet in diameter.

We doubt that there has been a full Grass Dance since 1900. Occasionally snatches of the old ritual have been given, sometimes for the Indians' own entertainment, occasionally to entertain tourists. In 1936 we attended a Fourth of July celebration at Bull Head, South Dakota, and were invited to a dog feast. It followed a long afternoon of dancing. There was no ceremony connected with it, but several old people made prayers, and following the feast there was a give-away. We learned that actually we were in on the leftovers. The real dog feast had been held the day before, in honor of the old men, but there was no ceremony then either.

We have seen two varieties of the Feast, or Charge the Kettle, Dance. The first time we saw it, there were four dancers instead of a solo dancer, as described by the old men. The first two each carried three feathered wands about three feet long. On the opening song the four danced slowly and with some hesitation, taking their places side by side in a line. A new song with a quick beat followed. The dancers approached the kettle, a big iron one, still in "company front" formation, hands extended as described earlier. The song got still faster as they neared the kettle and then stopped, the dancers holding their positions with hands outstretched. When the song started again, the dancers retreated to their original position. This advance and retreat was made three times. On the fourth time they turned to the left as they neared the kettle and danced around it single file, the two in advance thrusting their wands into it as they passed. The dance ended as they circled the kettle.

There was no explanation why the two dancers each carried three wands, but it can be seen that the dance was similar to the dance with the forked spit. These young dancers did not seem to be sure of themselves, but the mere fact that they knew something of it showed that all is not yet lost.

The next time we saw the Kettle Dance, I was chosen to dance with the group, making the fourth dancer. White Buffalo had the forked spit, and I danced on his right, the other two dancers following me. It was much like the first time, except that as we passed the kettle White Buffalo pretended to spear the dog, leaving the spit in the kettle, and the last man picked up the kettle and carried it off as we left the dance ground.

Chiefs and dignitaries entitled to wear eagle-feather war bonnets used the occasion of a Grass Dance to display them, and the chiefs also wore their full beaded buckskin costumes of leggings and war shirts. This was probably the origin of the "straight up" and "fancy" dances, or Slow and Fast Grass Dance, for it has never been considered proper to "dance fancy" in a chief's regalia. Some of these dignitaries carried feathered staffs. Both crooked and straight lances were also seen, which properly belonged not to the Grass Dance but to the older, true warrior societies.

At the Grass dances we attended in the 1930's and early 1940's we saw old men like One Bull, White Bull, Makes Trouble, and Young Eagle, all veterans of the Custer Battle and of the Indian Wars, actually recite their war deeds, or count coup. With their passing the custom went out of existence. Iron Bull had a Strong Heart bonnet of split buffalo horns and the ring rattle of that society. And so we had an opportunity to see particles of old dances which were no longer being given in their entirety and since have ceased almost completely.

The Driver was still an important officer when we first went to Standing Rock; Charging Eagle then held the office. We have not seen one since. Rosebud was a Whistler and carried an elk whistle. Occasionally an older dancer wore an eagle-bone whistle around his neck, which was permissible in the old days of the Grass Dance. These whistles are similar to those used in the Sun Dance, but are not decorated in the same way. They were used in battle and represented the scream of an eagle, or even of a Thunderbird.

CONTEST DANCES

A number of contest dances are usually included in today's Grass Dance gatherings. One is called the Braided Tail, and traces back to the days when the braided grass tails were worn on the belts. Other contest dances are known as Stop, Drum, and Get-Down dances. The main difference among them is the songs to which they are danced. These songs stop periodically, and when they do the dancer must stop, holding whatever position he is caught in, until the music begins again. Other times the song stops, but the drum keeps going. Each one of these dances establishes a different mood, but all are usually very fast and the songs, stops, and changes of drumming and rhythm are entirely up to the whims of the singers.

Another contest dance that was once popular in Oklahoma is the Feather Dance, known also as Cheyenne Feather Dance. Today the Grass Dance, or "War Dance," itself is called "Feather Dance" because of the big feather bustles and neck pieces worn by the dancers. The old Feather Dance has been briefly mentioned in connection with the Iroquois Eagle Dance. Small fluffy feathers are struck into the ground, and the dancers must pull them up with their lips without touching any part of the body to the ground, except their feet, of course. They can get the feather in either of two ways: They bend one knee as low as possible, extending the other leg almost straight out, and lean far over to the side until they can get the feather. This way is like the Iroquois Eagle Dance. The other way is to jump straddle-legged, legs as far apart as possible, then lean forward to grab the feather with their lips or teeth. Either way takes not only great agility but timing and judgment, for the dancer must be exactly the right distance from the feather in order to get it and it must be done in time with the music, with leg bells ringing. It also takes sure balance, or he goes over on his face.

One Assiniboin dancer was so good that he could pick up the feather balancing on only one foot, the other extended, shaking its bells but not touching the ground!

This may be a Cheyenne dance, but the first time I saw it was as a boy, when it was done by a Pequot Indian from Rhode Island, only he picked up a handkerchief from the floor instead of a feather. This dance is seldom seen nowadays, but we may have been responsible for reviving it among the Northern Arapahos, for recently, after seeing one of our performances, some of them have been doing it for tourists.

When I first became interested in the Feather Dance, I asked Acee Blue Eagle if he would teach it to me. He said, "Oh! You can't do Feather Dance. Only the very young ones do Feather Dance." But I learned it nevertheless and have been doing it ever since.

One contest dance brought to our attention years ago by the Crows is one they call Ruffle Dance. It is now becoming popular at Indian gatherings all over the country. Nowadays some of the "Fancy War Dance" contest winners are from tribes that formerly never heard of this type of dancing—Zuñis, Navajos, and Hopis.

For the Ruffle Dance the drum throbs rapidly to start and the dancers "ruffle their feathers," shaking shoulders and bodies to make the feathers in their modern "swing bustles" vibrate. Then the singers take up a fast 2/4 time, getting faster and faster, and suddenly stop, which requires great control on the part of the dancers who have been moving so rapidly. This sequence may be repeated several times before the contest is brought to a close.

In addition to these special contest dances, Fast and Slow War dancing as well as Straight-up dancing are judged for best performers. In fact, at some contests for deciding best dancers in these classes, the contest dances play a minor role and may not be given at all.

Indians judge the contests today much as they always have. The most important consideration is keeping the rhythm—following the song. Carriage of the body is important. The steps must be in time with the drum. The dancer must end exactly on the last beat, and if he has a fancy flourish it adds to his credit. Judges in Santa Fe, South Dakota, and Montana have told us that a variety of steps does not get too much consideration and neither does a too-gaudy costume. When judging "traditional" contests, no fancy steps or "getting down low" are permitted. Losing a beat, dropping an article or part of a costume, missing the ending—any one or all of these points disqualify a contestant.

One present-day judge we know was formerly a fancy-dance champion himself, and he told us that most of the judges have been champion dancers. In the fancy-dance finals, each judge watches one particular dancer. He holds in his hand a bunch of little willow sticks, or even matches, and lays one stick aside for each point he awards his dancer. Does he keep strict rhythm with the drum? If so, he gets a stick. Does he move his shoulders like a bird? A stick for each shoulder. How about shaking his head? Does he make his feathers and entire body quiver like the leaves in the wind? Can ge get down low or do some other fancy movement without loss of rhythm? At the end of the dance the judges count their sticks and the dancer who was given the most wins.

For Straight-up Dance,[*] points are given for traditional costume, designs, braided hair, hair wraps of otter skin, and facial designs. Sometimes a Straight-up dancer is awarded the prize not for any particular dancing ability at all but just because he looks "most old time." One time such a dancer won first place just because he had his own long braided hair.

At the present moment the contests seem to be holding the principal interest in Indian dancing. Formerly, on the reservations contests played a very small part at Indian gatherings, although both of us have won contests among the Sioux and Crows. It seems today more as if the highlight of the gathering is the final contest and choice of the winner, who then follows the "powwow circuit" in the hope of becoming national champion. But some attend in much the same way that non-Indians go to the gym for a workout. Boys come, each bringing his costume and participating as long as he feels like it. When he is tired, he changes back into his street clothes and either goes home or he sits around and waits for the feast which follows in the long intermission between the afternoon and evening dancing. But a present-day "War Dance" or "PowWow" is still an opportunity of being with friends and relatives and the most certain way of bringing Indians together.

---

[*]In Oklahoma it is referred to as Straight Dancing.

MODERN TRENDS

In recent years the Grass Dance has become merely a good-time dance. Since the warriors of old have gone, there are no war experiences to enact, and each dancer uses his favorite steps, and everyone dances for his own enjoyment.

Indians like style changes and "being modern," like anyone else, but some of the modern trend in costuming is a far cry from the beauty and dignity of the earlier articles. The old symbolism is gone, and feathers of all types are used in the bustles. The construction has changed. Larger and larger bustles have been made, and more and more colors used; they are becoming "louder" all the time. Roaches of deer and porcupine hair came to be dyed in many colors and then gave way almost entirely to great crests of artificially lengthened stripped feathers, with perhaps purple, green, or magenta fluffies at their tips.

This was the Oklahoma, or southern, style. It gradually crept north and became popular among the Arapahos of Wyoming. A useless type of beaded suspenders, tracing back originally, no doubt, to the beautifully quilled or beaded strips formerly sewed over the shoulders of a war shirt, is still worn.

When we first went to visit the Sioux at Standing Rock, they were in the depth of depression and drought. The bans on dancing had just been removed. The few costumes that remained were usually made of dyed long underwear with buttons down the front—red, blue, black, yellow, green—all colors. To this was added breechclouts with no flap on the back, which gave the appearance of a ribbon-decorated diaper. The reason for no flap, they told us, was that it was only in the way and did not show when the dancer was wearing the bustle. But almost none of them owned a bustle.

About 1936 the underwear began to give way to suits made of pajamas or sweat shirts or sweaters and trousers, decorated with white chainette or upholstery fringe, sequins, beadwork trimming with hearts, spades, clubs, and diamonds as motifs, but the diaper-shaped breechclout was retained. This style, they said, was introduced by Indians still farther north, from Fort Berthold and Fort Totten. These costumes usually included a shoulder yoke, or cape, of satin (sateen) or velveteen, also decorated with the fringe, sequins, and playing-card designs.

The capes trace back to the beautiful ones formerly made of the skins of foxes, coyotes, and otters. Even the chainette fringe is a substitute for earlier buckskin fringe. Bustles are seldom used with this costume, but at least the dancers retain the hair roach, and some owners are proud of exceptionally nice ones. No longer having the right to wear eagle feathers (war honors), many dancers now use fluffy plumes attached to thin coiled springs from automobile chokes and wrapped with ribbon or beadwork. These are really quite pretty, as they bounce and wave with the movements of the dancer.

The Sioux never did go in for the super-elegant feather crests, and now the dancers in Oklahoma are tired of them. They say that they look like "Zulu hats" and make the dancers look like circus horses. Some of their roaches are made of

Laubin (center) with Magpie Eagle (left) and Flying Cloud (right) wearing the Northern Plains type of costume, at a Grass Dance at Fort Yates, North Dakota. Photo by Gladys Laubin.

sisal fiber—rather removed from porcupine hair but better than the "Zulu hats." Porcupine hair is difficult to obtain, and good roach makers are harder to find, but it is good to know that there is a revival of interest in this old-style headdress.

Until the last four or five years the Oglalas of Pine Ridge retained the dyed underwear and bustles of the turn of the century. But changes are now creeping in. Northern dancers are going bare-legged or are wearing "breed leggings," a short knee-length legging used in early days by trappers and mountain men to protect the lower part of their trousers and take the place of riding boots. Another popular trend all over the Indian country is a set of leggings of Angora goat hair. Today's dancers are also wearing silk shirts, over which we see the beaded suspenders, and

Modern Oglala Sioux dancers, wearing "breed leggings," such as were worn long ago by trappers and mountain men. Photo by Gladys Laubin.

Oklahoma-style "swing bustles," often made of eagle wings, or even a more recent style of huge tail and neck ornaments—great circles of highly decorated feathers of all colors of the rainbow, with a triangular segment missing at the top of the one that fits around the neck.

About the turn of the century, with war no longer the Plains way of life, the symbolism of the bustle began to change. Bustles of that period often had jack-rabbit ears attached to the tips of the long horns, or spikes—an ear to each horn—and the rosettes were made of grouse, sage chicken, and wild-turkey feathers, representing the tails of these birds as spread in their courting dances. The panels were now made of a myriad of small feathers of such birds and were said to represent the low-spread wings of the birds dancing.

The Crows added to the center, in place of a rosette, a sort of disheveled-looking cluster of split and drooping feathers, representing sage or prairie chickens hiding in the brush. The rabbit ears also suggested rabbits hiding, only the tips of their ears showing. Such was the change-over from a purely military significance to one entirely peaceful. The Crows still use this kind of "tail feathers," as they call the bustle.

Even in the old days, the movements of the dancers were said to represent those of graceful birds. White Buffalo Man always began to dance with a movement of his head and shoulders to represent a bird. He wore a new swing-style bustle, just up from Oklahoma, which opened and shut as he danced, like a butterfly's wings. Other good dancers also use much head and shoulder movement.

If one watched twenty different dancers, he would probably see twenty different figures being executed. Flying Cloud, although wearing the Northern-style fancy dance costume which permitted him to dance any way he pleased, always danced "straight up," like a chief, because his grandfather after whom he was named was a chief. Occasionally, just to show that he was having a good time, he made a fancy spin.

On our first trip to Standing Rock, some of the younger fellows who had never had a chance to dance were anxious to try it. Big Horn did one simple step almost all night long that he must have seen some old-timer do years before. It was much like the old Bear Dance step.

Antelope, son of the famous Sioux chief Running Antelope, always carried a fancy mirror. Such mirrors were an early introduction into the Grass Dance. Originally a mirror was used for flashing signals while on a war party—the original heliograph—later adopted by the army. But a mirror was also used in the Elk Dance, which was a dance for making love medicine. The dancer flashed the mirror into the eyes of the young woman he was interested in. The light rays were supposed to blind her to any aversion she might have and open her heart. In Antelope's time the mirror was evidently connected with the old Elk Society idea, for it was said that the one who carried it was a "lady killer." As he danced, Antelope would look into the mirror, adjust his headdress, and otherwise put it to use, to the amusement of the spectators. Every once in a while he would call out, "Maki′li!" ("I'm a cracker-jack!").

464

The Assiniboins say that the one who carries the mirror is so shy that he looks in it, seeing only himself, so he is not embarrassed or made bashful by the eyes of the audience.

Nowadays a few dancers among the Crows and also in Oklahoma still have fancy mirrors—a sort of hand bag, fully beaded, with a mirror in the center—but they carry them by the handle, hanging down, and never look into them. They are merely ornaments.

Young Eagle, really a very old man, had been a scout at the time of the Custer Battle and had been wounded in the leg. He was also known as Callous Leg because of his old wound. He never missed a dance and danced for hours at every gathering. He was one of the first to begin and last to quit, although nearly ninety years old. He always danced acting the part of a scout, watching, looking, following the trail, always ready for action. We never saw him put his hand to his forehead to shade his eyes—the usual conception of a scout. He sometimes danced in place, hardly moving at all, or merely lifting one foot a bit, stretching his neck way out, sometimes shaking his head, but his actions always fit the character of the song. It was a pleasure to watch him.

At Pine Ridge, Robert Horse was one of the best dancers. He ended every dance with a spin, then moved his right leg back and forth, his final movement being to hit his right heel on the ground and lift his foot high, always exactly on the last beat of the drum. He never missed!

Running Eagle had a fancy bustle. The rosette was spread, not with a mirror, which you may think modern enough, but with a 1934 Ford V-8 hub cap! On the horns, instead of the customary dyed horsehair, he had tiny American flags flying! And so the old days passed.

THE CROW HOT DANCE

Robert Lowie gives a good account of the Crow Hot Dance.[11] He says they had two Whippers, eight crow belts (although formerly there were only four), and also two buffalo-horned headdresses, topped with eagle feathers and decorated with white weasel skins.

The first song was for taking down the bustles, the second in honor of the chiefs, the third for the Crier, or Announcer, the fourth for the Drum Keeper, and the fifth for the Drumstick Owner. Each of these groups, or individuals, got up and danced during their songs, and then "gave away."

Among the Crows we have never seen a Whipper, or the horned bonnets, although when we first went among them they had the most beautiful war bonnets that we had ever seen, and more of them. We were told that at one time a woman was given the office of Whipper. When we wanted to give a concert version of the Hot Dance in our program overseas, we had a hard time getting any of our Crow dancers to take the part of Whipper realistically. They said they never had such an officer and that it was contrary to their customs to strike anyone with a whip. But when one of their own women reminded them of the old woman who used to be Whipper at some of the dances held during their youth, they recanted, and we had no more difficulty in getting a convincing performance.

For some very special occasions the Crows still put on both the Kettle Dance and the dance for taking down the bustles. We have also seen them do the solo Dance of the Forked Spit, but have only heard about it among the Sioux. It is an extremely fast dance, with much fancy footwork, and requires a dancer with good wind and much agility. Generally the Crows dance much slower than the Sioux, but not in the Forked Spit Dance.

The Crows in their dance regalia are much more conservative than many other tribes. They wear tight-fitting dyed underwear and capes, and these have been used so long now that they are traditional. Other ornaments and their style of dancing are unchanged.

Although the Crows have always spoken of Hot Dance rather than Grass Dance, we saw some evidence of grass being associated with the dance. On one occasion one of the older men, whom they called John Adams, appeared with a great long tuft of slough grass fastened to the rear of his belt. It was not braided, as formerly worn by Omahas and Sioux, but hung loose behind, almost touching the ground. John was making a special effort to look "old time," was not wearing dyed under-wear, as the others were, but was painted from head to foot with red ochre, wore a porcupine roach, and had long straps of bells from his waist to his ankles. He and I were the only ones stripped to clouts and moccasins. Then he topped it all off by wearing sunglasses!

During Crow Fair they had a horseback parade all around the camp, and peri-odically the dancers dismounted and danced in front of their horses. During a pause in the dance, John's horse reached over and grabbed the grass in his teeth, raising old John completely off the ground and shaking him as a dog would a rabbit. And he was a big man! Everyone howled with laughter. Poor John struggled in the air for several moments before the horse bit through the grass and dropped him to the ground again. The Indians made jokes about this all the rest of the fair (see page 217).

On our very first visit to the Crows we were aware that something was different in Crow "war dancing." Dancing with them, carefully watching, we realized that they accent the *off* beat—they put the heel down on the accented beat instead of the toe. Their Owl Dance, which is nearly the same as the Round Dance of other tribes, is done the same way. The foot is raised on the accent instead of lowered. Sioux sometimes called their Round Dance a Crow Dance, but never dance it the way the Crows do. For the Owl Dance the singers leave the big drum and go to the center of the circle, each using a single-headed hand drum. They choose drums which "sing well together."

On our first visit to the Crows, they recognized right away that we danced "Sioux style." They sang a Sioux contest song for me, then gave me a silver dollar as a prize. Every once in a while they would ask me to "do Sioux dance" for them.

There was some suggestion that the Crow Hot Dance included snatches of older

Left to right: Laubin (wearing an old-time costume), Henry Old Coyote, Gladys Laubin, Paul Nomi, Hugh Little Owl, and Simon Old Crow, at a Crow fair. Note how the Crows flatten their porcupine-hair roaches. Laubin Collection.

bird and animal dances. We saw a pair of "prairie chicken" performers, and the first few years we were with them there were still four men, belonging to a kind of fraternity, who always wore eagle wings at any of the celebrations. A golden eagle wing hung over each shoulder. No such fraternity is mentioned by Lowie, and our Crow friends told us merely that they "were like brothers."

The Crow dancers wear golden-eagle feathers in their roaches. The only Sioux to do this had to have earned the right to wear them. Later, descendants of coup strikers were permitted to wear eagle feathers, thus passing along the family glory, but other dancers have to be content with the stripped feathers or springs and fluffies previously mentioned.

The Crows not only wear golden-eagle feathers—they demand the two center tail feathers of the year-old bird, white with black tip, and even before the ban on killing eagles went into effect paid as much as five dollars apiece for them.

THE GIVE-AWAY

The give-away is an important part of any present-day Indian dance. The gifts are

467

The Crow Owl Dance, the Crows' version of the Round Dance, at the Crow Indian Agency, Montana. Joseph Medicine Crow (left) and Donald Deernose (center) are prominent Crow leaders. Office of Indian Affairs, Washington, D.C.

Laubin (seated, second from left) and Crow Indian dancers during an intermission. Photo by Gladys Laubin.

usually made not only to someone but in honor of someone, which is sometimes difficult for an outsider to understand.

For instance, during World War II we attended a dance at Standing Rock in honor of the boys in the service. The dances were constantly interrupted by give-aways, and some of the dancers were wishing that they had more opportunity to dance instead of sitting out these long intermissions. But, since giving seemed to be the order of the occasion, I made a donation to the singers—who are just about the most important people at a dance—in honor of the parents of the Indians overseas. I tied up the dance for half an hour. There were only half a dozen singers. First, they sang a song in my honor, using my Indian name, Tatanka Wanjila, and I was required to dance to it alone. Then all the parents of servicemen, both men and women, lined up and solemnly filed past me to shake my hand. Since almost every adult at this gathering was a soldier's parent, it took a long time.

To the white man's way of thinking, the singers, having been the ones to receive the gift, should have shaken my hand, and it would all have been over with very quickly. But no, the gift was *in honor* of the parents, so *they* shook my hand. Had I made the gift in honor of the soldiers themselves, it would have been the same, for they, not being present, would have been represented by their parents and relatives.

The Indians were always giving moccasins to Gladys—but they fit *me.* In this way they supposed they were making us both happy, and she had double pleasure—receiving the moccasins and then giving them to me.

OTHER TRIBES

The most nearly complete account of any Grass Dance we have seen is to be found in *Land of Nakoda,* the story of the Assiniboin Indians, by James L. Long, himself a member of that tribe.[12] Although the account is very similar to what we have learned from the Sioux, and the Assiniboins claim to have received the dance directly from the Sioux, their relatives, there are a few things that are very different. In the first place, they used seven bustles and apparently have no tradition of their real meaning. They believe that the dance was "dreamed" by a Sioux, who received it from a great rooster he saw in the dream. The bustles represent roosters' tails. The origin of such a story can hardly be very old, for there were no domestic chickens before the white man came, and no native bird that could possibly be mistaken for a rooster. It is almost certain, however, that the center rosettes were copied from the spread tails of turkeys and grouse.

The Assiniboins also claim two Whippers, or Drivers, but we have seen and heard of only one for the Sioux.

The Kiowas still have their one sacred bustle and a Keeper for it. We were fortunate in having him tell us about it. The Keeper does not wear the bustle himself but merely takes care of it. That is a job in itself, for there are rituals and taboos connected with it. It is kept in a buckskin bag, with a drawstring to close it. It is the old-style bustle, with no rosette, and the Kiowas claim to have received it from the Sioux long ago. The last time the full ritual was given was in 1922. The bustle was used once following World War II, but it was used without permission and without the proper ceremonies, and the incident has been embarrassing ever since.

With the Kiowas the Bustle Keeper is also the Whistle Man, but he does not have an elk whistle. His is like the war whistle previously described.

When it was decided to hold an O'homo Dance, four days were set aside for it. The bustle was removed from its case in a ceremonial manner and handed to two virgins, who put it together, smoothed its feathers, and handed it back to the Keeper. He then purified it over cedar smoke and offered it to the four directions—east, west, north, south. Offering in this manner is unusual; ordinarily it is done in a circle. Sioux usually offer west first, but other tribes offer first to the east.

Prayers were then made for the people, prayer songs sung, and the bustle placed on the ground. Two dancers approached it and retreated, as we have recounted for other tribes, four times. The whistle was blown during these approaches and during certain songs afterward. The dancers sat "like eagles" between approaches, which raises the possibility that phases of the Grass Dance may even trace back to the old Calumet Dance.

The Wearer, a very brave man, then came forward and the Keeper tied the bustle on him. He danced outside the circle, everyone giving him plenty of berth, for the bustle was too sacred for anyone else to touch. After the bustle was tied on him, other dancers could wear ordinary bustles, and the Kiowas developed some dandies! There were two groups of Grass dancers, whom our friend the Keeper called "clans"—Ravens and Eagles. The Ravens wore bustles of raven feathers, the Eagles of eagle feathers.

The Doorkeeper had a special "ax." If he laid it on the floor across the doorway, everyone had to stay inside. He could keep them there the entire four days if he wished to. The dancers generally danced in a circle to the left. If they were led to the right, they had to "unwind" before stopping.

After the four days' ceremonies were over, the bustle was put back in its case with ritualistic movements and proper songs, and members of the O'homo Society were reminded to live right even in everyday life out of respect for the bustle.

When we produced our pageant, *Arrows to Atoms,* in Oklahoma City, representatives of fifteen different tribes took part. One of the dances we presented was the Grass Dance. In talking with several old men—Kiowa, Comanche, Kiowa-Apache, Pawnee, and Oto—it was decided that the best way to get the "sacred" bustles into position was to have them placed by young women. It was also decided to use four bustles, hence four virgins.

Our friend the Bustle and Whistle Keeper of the Kiowas refused to take an active part, but had no objection to others doing so and no aversion to the dance, since we were not using real sacred bustles, but only "making believe." Afterward he was much pleased with the presentation and, in fact, that is when he volunteered the information we have been giving you. He said we made it seem "real."

Although the Oklahoma Indians do have very fast dances, they, like the Crows, generally set a pace much slower than do the Sioux, Northern Arapahos and some of the other Northern Indians. One no longer makes a serious attempt to separate Oklahoma dancing into tribal styles. Cheyennes, Southern Arapahos, Kiowas, Comanches, Otos, Poncas, Caddoes, Wichitas, Pawnees, Delawares, Sauks and Foxes— all dance together. The Osages hold pretty much to themselves, but even an Osage is occasionally seen at the big gatherings. Generally all the tribes in the western half of the state mix at the dances. The eastern half—people who were once from the Eastern Woodlands, with the exception of the Delawares and Sauks and Foxes— do not attend as frequently. Since all the above-mentioned tribal groups have different languages, the songs are sung to vocables only. Even the singers are of mixed tribes. Some recent songs, like "Forty-Niners," are sung in English. English is taking the place of the old sign language of the Plains, which was the intertribal medium of communication before school days.

"POWWOWS"

Indian gatherings around the country, and especially in Oklahoma, are usually spoken of as "powwows." Older Indians designate them, in English, as "doings." "Powwow" is an example of how an Indian word has been taken into English and then back by the Indians as an *English* word. Many Indians use the words *"papoose,"* "squaw," and "powwow" believing them to be English, for these words came from tribes far to the east, with languages as different from some of the western tribes as Chinese is from English.

According to Roger Williams, "powwow," in Narraganset, means a shaman, priest, or medicine man. When the medicine man gave a demonstration of his power he attracted a large crowd. While gathering, the Englishmen heard the word "powwow" used so frequently that they misinterpreted it to mean the occasion rather than the medicine man, the cause of the occasion. The word has been misused ever since.[13]

Regardless of what name the Indians call their present-day dancing, to us, because of our early association with the Sioux and the old-timers' stories of the origin of the dance, it is Omaha, or Grass, Dance. And, because it traces so far back into history, we feel that it is an important dance, no matter how diluted and changed from its original sources it may be. Actually it was once more like a series of dances, most of which are no longer performed. Some of the old-timers who are left are resigned to the loss of the old ways and would rather have them gone forever than carried on haphazardly or without meaning or understanding. One can hardly blame them, but it seems a pity, nevertheless.

The Grass Dance is an interesting example of the way a ritual developed into a dance; in the way it was formerly given it contained elements of true choreography. The version of the Hot Dance, or Grass Dance, that we presented with our Crow troupe in Europe was one of our most popular presentations, enjoyed not only by the audience but by the dancers themselves.

Ritual was also responsible for costume development, but the over-all result in the early costumes was beauty. Art and beauty were seldom the *aims* of any Indian dance but were often the result. For this reason most Indian dances contain artistic elements that can be highly satisfying to any audience, even when the underlying symbolism and meaning may not be understood.

Although most of the accompanying dances and ceremonies are no longer to be seen, the Grass Dance is still an extremely interesting dance not only to students but also to most observers because of its action, footwork, and striking costumes.

It appears that the Grass Dance is one Indian dance that will survive, regardless of changes and of what may happen to all other Indian dances.

23. Other Dances Today

THE RABBIT DANCE

When we first went to Pine Ridge Reservation, the Rabbit Dance had just about taken over everything else. One reason for this may have been that there had been no opposition to it during the days of the ban on dancing, because it was considered a white dance. Another reason was that few men on the reservation still had dance costumes and Rabbit Dance was danced in "white man's clothes."

It is certain that the dance came from the whites, for in the old days men and women did not dance together, arm in arm, as they do in the Rabbit Dance. It looks to us as if they copied the fox trot or the waltz or combined the two.

We first heard about this dance from a Winnebago boy, White Wing. His demonstration of it, with Wíyaka Waštewin as partner, was somewhat different than we later saw among the Sioux. But wherever we have seen it, the partners face each other, the man holding the woman's right hand in his left, other arms around each other's waists, in the position of the fox trot. Most of the dancers even executed the old "pump-handle" movement with the two clasped hands.

White Wing moved his left foot twice ahead and then once to the rear and taught Gladys to move the opposite way, right foot ahead twice and then back once. The inner feet, man's right and woman's left, drag much as in typical Round, or Woman's, Dance. He said that the pattern the feet made on the ground looked like the tracks of a rabbit, hence the name of the dance.

But among the Lakotas, both man and woman advance their left feet twice and step back once. No one we knew had any idea why it was called Rabbit Dance. Sometimes, in talking English, they called it Bunny Dance. They said it was a "new" dance they had learned only twenty-five or thirty years before. The songs are always humorous, and in talking of the Rabbit Dance people always laugh, but in the actual dancing they look as serious as if they were doing the most important of dances.

The 3/4 rhythm is the same as for other "women's dances," including the even more recent Forty-niner, and many of the songs are sung in English. Sometimes they are first sung in Lakota, then in English. They used to sing, "You get the Model-T license and we'll go to a Bunny Dance." Others were, "I'll take you to a Rabbit Dance in my one-eyed Ford"; "Dearie, when we go to Bunny Dance, don't you tell anybody"; and "Dearie, don't you worry, when we go to Bunny dances you know I love you."

The dance moves in a circle to the left, clockwise, for as long as the singers feel necessary. Usually, during the singing of each repetition of the song, there is one place where they drum three steady beats in contrast to the usual accented first beat, silent second, and unaccented third beat, and every couple immediately turns completely around. The only way to know when this is to take place is to know the song, for some songs place it differently than others, and the turn, when done properly, is on the three steady beats, so there is no time to listen for them and then turn.

The Rabbit Dance never became popular among the Standing Rock Sioux and the few times we have taken part in it there it lacked the enthusiasm with which it was given at Pine Ridge. They did not even do the back step, and they seldom did the turns. At Standing Rock they rather favored the older Kahomni Dance, which looked much the same as the way they do the Rabbit—no back step—and they turned around when the leader called, "Kahomni!"

When the singers for the Rabbit Dance finally decide to end the dancing to the left, they bring the song to a close. The couples drop hands and walk around the circle together, side by side, while the drum sounds softly. They may walk around like this for several circles. Then the singers begin once more. The couples join hands and this time face the opposite direction, moving to the right, usually once around, when the dance ends.

Many tribes in the Northwest took up the Rabbit Dance, but we never saw it among the Crows. There, what they call a Two-Step takes its place. It is much like the old-fashioned two-step of the whites and certainly must have come from that source. It is also popular in Oklahoma, and that is probably where they learned it, for the Crows visit in Oklahoma frequently. Some couples wear matched costumes. The boy may wear a blue silk shirt, for example, with a blue scarf tied around his hat, and the girl a blue silk dress. Some insert little variations in the dancing to make it interesting.

In the Rabbit, as in other women's dances, it used to be that a man seldom asked a woman to dance. It was not considered quite proper. A woman selected her partner, usually by advancing toward him and touching his foot with the toe of her moccasin. When the dance ended, the man was expected to make a little present to the woman who had asked him to dance. His wife was not supposed to be jealous over this, for the invitation was really a compliment to her too, showing that she had picked a good man.

But in Oklahoma we were told the Rabbit Dance was no longer popular because it broke up so many families. Some couples used it as an excuse for some real philandering. The dance even spread as far as the Senecas in New York State, where the same thing happened. Although the Sioux had the Rabbit Dance in the early 1900's, the Senecas did not get it until about 1952, and it was abandoned in 1958. Too many wives were lost in the meantime. It was done to Sioux songs sung in Iroquois style and using a little water drum and horn rattles.

Finally we learned that all indications point to the Crees as the originators of the Rabbit Dance. They are known as the Rabbit Skin Wearers because some of their winter clothing was made of rabbit skins. So the dance was originally the Rabbit Skin Wearers' Dance, but was shortened to Rabbit Dance, and Bunny Dance (after the bunny hug?) and most tribes forgot, or never knew from where it had come.

THE FORTY-NINER

The Forty-Niner is one of the most recent dances and is often done during intermissions of the "War Dance" in some parts of the country. The songs are of much the same character as those for the Rabbit Dance and in the same rhythm, although somewhat faster. The step is the usual limp step of women's dances, with the left foot raised higher than the right, but the dancers move forward instead of sidewise. A line is formed, alternating partners, a man followed by a woman, couples lined up in this fashion. They dance in a circle to the left, left hands on left shoulders all along the line. At least this is the way they used to do it, but even this new dance has changed recently. Couples now line up as for a Round Dance, linking arms, and about the only difference is that it is faster and they often form several concentric circles, all as close and tight together as they can get.

This dance shows its modern aspects in several ways. The songs, so far as we know, are always sung in English. The dance is for fun, and the dancers show their enjoyment by laughing, giggling, and whooping as they go around—something entirely different from any other Indian dance we have ever heard of. In fact, the Arapahos have a fun dance called the Slug Dance, similar to Rabbit or Two-Step, and the songs are silly, but if anyone laughs or giggles during the dance, he or she is pummeled, in fun, afterward. Hence its name, in English, Slug Dance.

One favorite Forty-Niner song, known up and down the country, says, "I love you honey. I don't care if you been married sixteen times, I'm goin' to get you yet!" Another is, "I want to see you tonight in the moonlight. You know the place where we meet every night." It is hard to keep a straight face during such songs when sung for Rabbit Dance, and in Forty-Niner no effort is made to do so.

When we danced Forty-Niner with a group of young people representing several tribes at Sheridan All American Indian Days, they even "wound up" like a Snake Dance or Shawnee Stomp Dance, although they did not "crack the whip" at the end.

This dance has been reported sometimes as a true couple dance and, like the Rabbit, is reputed to have broken up marriages, but we have never seen it performed so. It is hard to believe that the dance, as described above, could break up families.

There are several stories about the origin of the dance and of its name. It is certain that is has nothing to do with the gold rush of 1849. Mason said that it originated in Wisconsin among the Chippewas, who claimed that fifty young men went to World War I and forty-nine came back. So they made up this dance in their honor.[1]

We believe that the dance originated in Oklahoma and have heard a similar story down there. The Northern Cheyennes say that they learned it from their southern relatives, and the Lakotas say that they learned it from their friends and allies the Northern Cheyennes. Furthermore, with so many tribes represented in Oklahoma and now using English as a universal language, the fact that the songs are composed in English helps to bear this out. Acee Blue Eagle told us that the dance was made up by the girls back home to honor boys of the Forty-ninth Division in World War I. So this must be the period of its origin.

There are still other stories of the Forty-Niner. The Southern Cheyennes formerly regarded it as a sort of victory dance and say that placing the hands on the shoulders represents a united people working together for a common cause.

THE HOOP DANCE

One of the most popular of present-day Indian dances is the Hoop Dance. Good dancers of many tribes now perform it, but it is certainly a recent innovation. Because our own interpretation of it has been considered one of the highlights of our presentations, we have often been asked about its origin.

Its present popularity began among Indians at Taos a number of years ago. One authority on the Indians of that region believes that it started at the Century of Progress Exposition in Chicago in 1933, with a troupe of Chinese jugglers who did some fancy manipulations with rings, or hoops. A big Indian village was a feature of the exposition, and many tribes were represented. But Taos already had a Hoop Dance before that time, for we had already seen Taos performers, a father and son, each with two hoops, do it several years before the exposition, and it was also at that time that Thunder Cloud, an Ottawa Indian from Michigan, a descendant of the great Pontiac, taught his version of it to us. Now it may be possible that Taos, or other southwestern Indians, saw a performance of Chinese jugglers at the World's Columbian Exposition in Chicago in 1893, but they certainly knew of the Hoop Dance before the exposition of 1933.

We believe that the Hoop Dance originated among the Indians around the Great Lakes. We first heard about a dance with two hoops from friends who had lived with the Bad River and Nett Lake Chippewas before the dance became internationally popular. Our first contact with this two-hoop dance was, as we mentioned, from the Ottawas, another Greak Lakes tribe.

Densmore reported a one-hoop dance for the Menominis.[2] It was an acrobatic dance, but much simpler than some of the present-day versions. It was associated with the story of the origin of tobacco. The Creator gave tobacco to one man, who passed it out to other Indians. They wanted more, so he made them dance to get it. The dance they did had to be acrobatic, but a hoop was not always used. Some dancers danced on their hands, with feet in the air; some danced "lying down." It seems to have been a sort of "trained-animal" dance, all sorts of stunts being used to beg for tobacco. Finally the culture hero Manabush, himself, wanted the tobacco, and he is the one who invented the Hoop Dance and passed it on.

Dancers also imitated rabbits, partridges, fish, frogs, crawfish, and owls in this tobacco ceremony, and Miss Densmore thought the whole thing a sort of "degenerate form of the Calumet." For that matter, these comic dances may have been performed as the "light motif" to break the monotony and bring relief to the seriousness of the full Calumet ritual, just as the clowns perform in other serious rituals.

476

We have been unable to find references to hoop dancing in the very early reports from any part of the country, but that does not prove that it did not exist. Few of the writers were present at intimate tribal gatherings. They may have missed seeing it performed or may merely have neglected to report it, as they did so many other things. We know a ring, or hoop, was important in the symbolism of tribes all across the country.

Among the Sioux a hoop was featured in many ceremonies. A hoop about two feet in diameter, with two strings crossing its center, was important in the Bear Dance of the Santees. Members of the Oglala Sacred Bow Society wore small hoops, three inches in diameter, with crossed strings of rawhide dyed blue, slung over their left shoulders by thongs. The man who envisioned the society was a noted shaman named Black Road, and he used a hoop when doctoring.[3]

The Elk Society, as we have already seen, also made use of hoops with crossed strings. The Santees had another dance known as the Mocking Dance, in which followers of a man named Bukuna imitated his dancing, all wearing similar costumes of varied colors. Bukuna painted his face "whitish," wore a large-sleeved jacket of reddish-colored muslin, and had a cap of mallard skin. All others wore caps of otter, mink, or other fur, peaked in front. Each dancer carried a hoop about a foot across, with two crossed strings, a bunch of eagle feathers hanging from the center, and colored down around the circumference. When the song began, all raised their hoops high. The leader, who had a hoop about five feet across, walked along the diameter of the dance circle blowing a whistle about six feet long, and the dancers circled about the circumference. The leader held his big hoop in one hand and jumped through it.[4]

Various games employed hoops, one in particular being used as part of the ritual to call buffalo, and this hoop game was also an important symbol in the Ghost Dance.

When we first went to Standing Rock years ago there was usually at least one dancer in the Grass Dance who carried a hoop. It was large, three or even four feet across, and occasionally during the dancing he would step into it, or pass it over his body, or do a few simple tricks with it. It was large enough that he could pass it over his tail feathers, roach and all. On one occasion James Magpie Eagle came out carrying a very small hoop, not over a foot in diameter, wrapped in fur. He danced around, holding it in his hand, and all of a sudden it was at least three feet across! It was made from the bead of a truck tire, wrapped in fur, then coiled up into a small hoop. The fur disguised it so that it looked like one little hoop. Magpie Eagle would dance in and out of it for a while, then coil it again and once more have a little fur hoop.

But none of these Lakotas did what we would call a Hoop Dance today. Nevertheless, the fact that they did execute occasional fancy figures with the hoop shows that a fully developed hoop dance might have existed there in the past.

Just how the Hoop Dance got to the Southwest is hard to say, but Indians everywhere have always been great travelers and visitors, so, if they did not learn it from the Chinese jugglers, they no doubt picked it up on a visit to some northern tribe. Taos people, in particular, have long had contact with Plains Indians and do many dances in Plains costume and Plains style. There is no doubt but that Indians of the pueblos are the ones who made the Hoop Dance popular. Tourists have been visiting the pueblos for many years and have given the Hoop Dance, as well as many other dances of that area, publicity that the Indians themselves would never have dreamed of.

The Southwestern version of the dance is usually very fast, and since the Indians learned of its appeal to non-Indian visitors they have worked to make it more and more spectacular. At first they used two hoops, which was the supreme achievement of only a few dancers around the Lakes. The Lake Indians, however, were not allowed to touch the hoops with their hands, and they used *very small hoops*. This is the version Thunder Cloud taught us, and he said a dancer's hoops should come only from the ground to his knee, just below the kneecap. Naturally, the smaller the hoops, the more difficult it is for the dancer.

Although the southwestern style is fast and spectacular, Indians there do not use small hoops. In fact, most of their dancers are small people, but they use very large hoops that come way above the knee, some even reaching the thigh.

Before long, Southwestern dancers were using four hoops, which nevertheless were still within the old symbolism, the number four being sacred to all tribes. Even six is a sacred number to many tribes, and to some seven also is a ceremonial number. But nowadays dancers use ten, twelve, or even fifteen hoops, so the dance has become merely a stunt, and the symbolism as well as the style and beauty of movement has all but disappeared. We just heard of a hoop dancer who is using twenty-four hoops!

When the dance first started in the Southwest, with two hoops and later even with four, there were certain rules, although the dancers were allowed to touch the hoops with the hands. Still, they could hold only one hoop in a hand at a time and the hoops had to be picked up from the ground with the feet alone. Later, as more hoops were added, it was permissible to hold two hoops in one hand, but they had to be separated, grasped in such a way that one hoop turned one way and one the opposite way. They could not be together. But now, using the great number of hoops, all rules except picking them up with the feet seem to have been abandoned, and the dancer ends up with hoops hanging all over him.

The Southwestern style of Hoop Dance has spread all across the country. Even so, no two hoop dancers dance exactly alike. It still is an individual affair, and each dancer incorporates whatever tricks he likes best and in whatever order he desires, so we cannot speak of *the* Hoop Dance as if it exists in only one form or pattern. It is now an intertribal dance, as most Indian dances have become, and belongs to no one tribe or district but to Indians all over the United States.

Even the Hoop Dance songs now have a similarity, whether sung by Yakimas in Washington or Navajos in Arizona. The song we use is Yakima, but we learned it from a Crow friend. It was a rainy day, so we all had to stay in the house. He got out his drum, lay on his back on the couch, and sang the song over and over, almost all day long so that we could learn it. We would have liked to learn it a phrase at a time, but Indians do not break their music down that way. When we asked him to repeat a phrase he repeated the whole song. So, although we did learn it a phrase at a time, we had to go through the entire song each time in order to do so. But it is a good song!

In the Northwest some dancers started using three hoops interlinked like a chain. To an uninformed observer these look difficult to maneuver, but actually are simpler to handle than if all are separate, for it is impossible to lose one.

To the Sioux, and to many other tribes as well, the hoop symbolizes the world and even the universe. It represents a united nation. All power is in a circle. Time and the seasons move in a circle. Most Indian homes were round. The Indian says that when he moved out of his round house into a square house he lost all his power.

So, even today, although the Hoop Dance seems just a contest dance for fun and for a good time, to the dancers who really know, this old symbolism of the hoop is still connected with it. Furthermore, the gyrations and figures the dancer executes in manipulating the hoops over and about his body symbolize the difficulties that must be overcome in life, and the competent dancer overcomes them successfully.

THE NEW YEAR DANCE

The New Year Dance, in which we have taken part with the Crows, is an interesting example of how Indians have changed and adapted dances to conditions. They have a big get-together usually every night between Christmas and New Year's Day, all of these being an Indian way of celebrating the white man's holidays. Before the activities begin, old men sit around and smoke what they call "Nez Purse" (Nez Percé) tobacco, which is a root they obtain from that tribe. It has a fragrance like celery leaves, and it is shaved and scraped and placed in the pipe bowl. One elderly man takes the long-stemmed pipe, lights it with a match, holds it aloft toward the ceiling, and then passes it to the left to the other men, each of whom smokes it in turn.

There are the usual "War dances" and give-aways, but a different dance, one they call Buckskin Dance, plays an important part in the evening's festivities. All the participants, both men and women, wear beautiful white buckskin costumes. Crow women's dresses are more or less conventional in pattern, although now they are usually beaded in floral designs. Men usually wear a buckskin "suit"—trousers instead of leggings and a sort of coat or jacket instead of the old-time war shirt, and floral-beaded. Two or three wear war bonnets, but most wear long hair, some with a beaded headband and a rooster feather. No roaches or bustles are worn in the Buckskin Dance, but all carry feathers in their right hands.

When we first went to live with the Crows, most of the men, even young ones, had long hair. Then for a number of years we seldom saw long hair, but Crow dancers usually wore braids attached to a headband so that they looked more like old-time Indians than do most of the modern Indian dancers. In the last few years, however, many young Indians of various tribes are wearing long hair again.

The Christmas–New Year dances are held in a big community hall. At Lodge Grass, where we were the only non-Indians present, there was a pot-bellied stove in each corner. It was cold every night—once it was twenty-four degrees below zero outside. Inside it was chilly, although all four stoves were kept almost red-hot. Dancing was the only way to keep warm.

The singers sat around the big bass drum in the center of the dance floor. There are a number of things peculiar to these yuletide dances. One is that the rhythm for the Buckskin Dance is in 3/4 time, which is usual for women's dances, but it was the first time we ever heard the Crows use this rhythm on the big drum. Another peculiarity is that the men start the dance on the beat; as we have mentioned before, the main thing that impressed us about Crow dancing is that they normally dance *off* the beat.

The men dance around to the left. Women who want to take part form a line. As the men dance past them, they seize their hands and pull them into the line, in which they are interspersed in no particular order. This is not a partner dance. Sometimes there are two or three men followed by several women, sometimes a man and a woman.

Just before midnight on New Year's Eve the elderly man with the long-stemmed pipe lights it again, holds it up to the ceiling, and passes it around as was done earlier in the evening.

The singers stand this time, with hand drums, and begin a lively song in steady rhythm. The dance leader comes from the back room, dressed in black underwear with roach and tail feathers and swinging an old-fashioned brass school bell, to the handle of which is tied an otter skin. He uses a sort of running step. Men and women dance up to each other and shake hands. As they approach, each waves the feather he or she carries and holds it up as if giving a toast. While men circle to the left, the women form another line circling to the right, inside the men's circle, and as they pass each other, all shake hands again. After everyone has shaken every-one else's hand, the women swing around, and their line joins the tail end of the men's line and the entire extended line keeps on dancing clockwise. By now every-one in the audience is on the dance floor, and the dancers wind in and out among them, shaking hands all around and calling out, in English, "Happy New Year!" Audience as well as regular dancers are now supposed to dance, and sometimes they make quite a big circle.

This dance is called the Long House, or Long Tipi, Dance, and it, too, is stepped on the beat. There is a lot of knee action, and everyone swings the feathers in his right hand in time with the music.

We learned that this dance was obtained from the Nez Percés, hence the use of the Nez Percé tobacco. The Nez Percés do the dance for funerals. The Crows dance it only at New Year, although they say there is no restriction against doing it at some other time. The Nez Percés used to make a long house similar to that of the Iroquois in the East, which apparently accounts for the name of this dance. Following the Long House Dance there are usually Owl and Push dances and then a second phase of the Long House, which is a couple dance, this time led by the man with the bell. The couples lead left or right, depending upon the bell leader, who moves ahead, turns around, leads back and forth, as he feels.

The Owl Dance is the Crow version of the Round Dance, the dancer lifting the left foot on the beat instead of putting it down, as among most tribes. The Push Dance is Crow Two-Step; the men "push" the women, who dance backward all the time. The songs are similar to Sioux Rabbit songs. One translates, "I used to behave myself, but not now, since I met you." All with a straight face. The women choose their partners in these dances.

At the end of the dancing, which may last till nearly dawn, there is a big feast. On this New Year morning it consists mainly of Indian foods—pemmican, buffalo stew, bitterroot pudding, "fry" bread, and of course the now Indian stand-by, coffee. No one worries about the food being cold. It was brought in hot, many hours earlier.

On New Year night, the festivities may open with a Crow "War Dance," with variations of a fast beat, one like a very fast women's dance. Sometimes the dancers start slowly, getting faster and faster. Sometimes the singers just trail off at the end; sometimes they keep singing, but stop the drum until the last five or seven beats. One time they stopped, then throbbed rapidly on the drum while the dancers crouched, then as they raised up and stretched forward to move ahead, the drum came into action again.

Owl Dance and Push Dance are again favorites, and of course the give-aways. As in other tribes, the custom is for the one who receives the present to shake hands with the giver. The Crows, as well as other Indians, have always been extremely generous with us and with other visitors. We have received silk scarfs, quilts, blankets, beaded armbands, furs, and silver dollars.

The Crows have an Honor Dance like that of the Lakotas. They sing a song, using a person's name, who then gives away and dances alone for a time, when the same song is repeated much faster and everyone joins in the dance. For a special honor the drum throbs at the end of the song, while the dancers remain still, then it starts all over again.

On New Year's night the Long House Dance is given again, in both its line-up and couple versions, but this time the couples dance in a circle, usually to the right, but sometimes to the left, following the leader with the bell. Some move the left foot alternately ahead and back, others ahead only. The circle becomes tightly packed, moving in one direction, then all turn around, going the opposite way until, on a signal from the leader, the direction is reversed again—but this time everyone dances backward.

The New Year programs are among the few occasions when one can see the Bustle Dance and Feast Dance that were formerly part of the old Hot Dance ceremonies.

Just before the final feast I was invited to take part in the Get Down Dance, which is like the Sioux Stop Dance. The dancers squat as low as possible, dancing in time to the drum, which stops occasionally, and they must hold whatever position they are caught in, regardless of how difficult or ridiculous it is.

Following the dancing comes the feast, this time mainly white man's foods— potato salad, boiled meat, store bread, mixed canned fruits, oranges, sweet rolls— but you may be lucky enough to have some buffalo-berry jelly and more fry bread.

In recent years there have been two dancing societies among the Crows that bear some resemblance to the old warrior societies. One is known as the Rees, sometimes called Big Holes-in-the-Ears. The other society is called Night Warriors. They try to outdo each other in everything, but especially in giving away and in dancing. When someone is invited to join one of these clubs he is usually given presents, but later he pays dues.

At Christmastime one year each Ree gave away two pounds of butter, while each Night Warrior gave away a pound of coffee and five pounds of sugar. The members of one society invite the wives of the men of the other society to dance, then give them these presents. One time the Rees had all sorts of gifts tied to strings which crisscrossed all over the hall. Visitors and Night Warriors were each given a string to follow, and you should have seen the resulting confusion and entanglement!

With dancing societies like these still active, the Crows still have many good dancers. Such societies can do much to encourage an interest in the lore of the past and to keep alive some of the old ways.

Often during the Christmas holidays we have visited other tribes, but the Crows were the only ones with the special dances just described. The others celebrate the "White Man's Give-Away" (Christmas) too. Usually they have a Christmas tree and sometimes even a Santa Claus, but the dances are the usual Fast and Slow War Dance and social dances, with nothing especially ascribed to the Christmas or New Year season.

PART VI. **In Retrospect**

Laubin portraying a vision from the Ghost Dance.

24. Concert Dancing

Indian dancing has been labeled "monotonous" by people who witness only the fast and slow "War Dances" of today's "powwows." Such people might go to a modern dance and think nothing of the monotony there, because they go not to be entertained but to take part in the festivities. The same might be said for the Indians. They go to a dance not to entertain or to be entertained but to take part in a social occasion. Furthermore, those who are acquainted with Indian dance, even the modern version, find far more monotony in current television dance programs and even in concerts of ballet and modern dance.

In ballet the principal dancer may pick up the ballerina, swing her around, and hold her for fancy poses. No doubt this is a great exhibition of skill, strength, and grace, but it is offensive to Indians. To their minds it is an affront to human dignity. When we were in Europe with our Crow dancers, we attended a number of ballets. The Indians fell asleep during some of the performances or commented as above on what they saw. They were more interested in those with the most pantomimic display. These fitted in with their own ability as pantomimists and sign talkers.

Over two hundred years ago, when Timberlake took members of the Cherokee tribe to England, he found that their favorite diversion was to go to a performance of the Sadler's Wells Ballet, "the activity of the performers and the machinery of the pantomime, agreeing best with their notions of diversion."[1]

In short, Indians and non-Indians like what they are familiar with and tend to find the unaccustomed boring or monotonous. But even balletomanes may enjoy Indian dancing. A gentleman from Chicago, who had sponsored classical ballet for many years, told us, after seeing a concert we gave in Thorne Hall at Northwestern University, that "it was like a breath of fresh air after the ballet."

In reading the comments of early writers on Indian dancing, we have seen that the descriptions run from "crude and uncouth" to "agile and graceful." It is apparent that such comments are based entirely on the observer's understanding, likes, and dislikes. Those repelled by Indian dancing found it so different from what they understood as dancing that they were at a loss to appreciate it or describe it.

There is good reason to believe that the actual execution of Indian dancing changed little over the years, until prohibition of the dances by the government and the attendance of Indian children at schools where they learned something of "white man's dances." Even the most modern and deteriorated Indian dancing retains an Indian flavor quite different from the dancing "on the outside" that has influenced it.

The Laubins following a performance at Jackson Lake Lodge, in Grand Teton National Park, where they have appeared each summer since the dedication of the lodge. Laubin Collection.

RECORDING INDIAN DANCES

Several authors have tried to "teach" Indian dancing through writing on the subject. In recent years a system of notation has been developed for ballet and modern dance, and an adaptation of this system has been used in an attempt to transcribe Indian dances. No doubt such transcriptions can be made with a good deal of accuracy insofar as patterns, formations, and footwork are concerned. Ballet and modern dance have set figures and patterns that can be used in almost every dance, in varying proportions and placement, which have made them comparatively simple to transcribe. But Indian dancing, even in one area or within one tribe, has no such exactness, except perhaps in the case of some of the strictly ceremonial dances of the Southwest.

As we have pointed out, footwork, although important, is not really the essence of Indian dance. There are other factors—attitudes, spirit, underlying meanings, personal mannerisms—that are impossible to communicate in either writing or notation.

Furthermore, even if it were possible to record Indian dances accurately, the system of notation itself is so complicated that only a true student would ever bother to learn it, and he would have to spend much time becoming proficient in its use. One proficient in the use of the notation might be able to make valuable notes on the dances of the Southwest, but most of the southwestern dances are of such a sacred nature that the Indians do not even allow photographs to be taken. There the Indians so far are preserving them. We hope that they continue to do so.

If one finds a dance worthy of recording, the best possible way to do so is with motion pictures. So far almost nothing has been done along this line. But the real repertoire of dances that we have been writing about—Greeting dances; Harvest dances; Warrior Society dances; Scalp, Hunting, Pipe, and Buffalo dances—have already passed away and are not even memories in the minds of most of the oldest living individuals. The important time for a good system of notation, or motion-picture equipment, ended more than fifty years ago.

We believe that, regardless of the benefits of pure entertainment, most people would rather see the dances presented honestly. They would rather see *real* things than imagined things having no basis in fact. Certainly, in our experience, the genuine, considering anything Indian, is far more interesting and exciting than trumped-up versions have ever been or ever could be.

A dancing teacher came to us and wanted to know if we would teach her some Indian dances so that she, in turn, could teach some of the fundamentals of Indian dancing. We offered to try. We started out with a few basic steps. After some practicing she said, "I think I can do some of these steps after a while. But how do you get the rest of it?"

"What do you mean by that?" we asked.

"Well, the entire use of the body is different from what we are accustomed to. The attitudes are different. The underlying reasons for dancing are different. The very spirit is different. How do you learn these things?" she replied.

487

Laubin in the Brave Heart Dance—a dance of greeting—from information received from White Eyes, an aged Cheyenne Indian. Photo by Gene Petersen.

"Now that is something we are afraid we cannot teach you," we said. "These things have to come to a person through study, association and understanding. Indian dance, like any other true dance, is not merely a matter of motion or exercise, of moving feet and body, but must be accompanied by thought and emotion. It expresses emotional and spiritual needs even more than physical. We don't think that these things can be taught. They must be felt and experienced."

We believed that living and associating with old-timers, who were saturated with the lore of the past, was the best way to learn and to understand the real spirit, character, and style of true Indian dancing. We felt that to portray Indian dances with conviction we would have to be able to think and act like Indians. We could acquire these qualities only through long association with the people themselves.

As far as we know, we were the first to present authentic Indian dances on the concert stage. "Authentic" is a word very much misused, so much so that we hesitate to use it. But by it we mean that our dances are based on thorough study of only genuine Indian material. We deliberately stayed away from a study of any other form of dance in an effort to keep the purity of the Indian material. We developed our dances from actual firsthand information received from the old Indians, supplemented with that gathered from historical accounts of earlier observers. We have merely condensed and edited original material.

Our work carries conviction because we have actually "lived it," associating with Indians over a period of many years. Speck called us "assimilated Indians." He said that for years it was expected that Indians would become assimilated into our culture. If Indians could become "white men," there was no reason why white men could not become Indians if they cared to. In fact, it has happened many times throughout history.

"Culture is not a matter of blood," he stated, "but a matter of association and training."

In our efforts to gather material, we were often given helpful advice and information by museum directors and ethnologists, but never any encouragement except from Speck. The others felt that what we wanted to do was impossible. All we could do was learn a superficial technique of Indian dancing, which would be meaningless. Much Indian dancing was ritualistic, lasting for hours, or even days, so how could one put it on the stage?

Speck said that we could do it but that it would not be easy. It would require much study, effort, understanding, and close association with Indian people. Years later, after seeing one of our recitals, he made the remark about us as "assimilated Indians" and said, "You are no longer white, Redge and Gladys. You *are* Indians."

John Martin, former dance editor of the *New York Times,* said that we had upset all his theories. He had supposed that to do ethnic dances one must be of the race or nationality he portrayed. But he told us that he was completely under the impression that he was watching "real Indians" at our performances.

Our effort, from the start, has been not so much to reproduce an Indian dance step by step and movement by movement as to portray the underlying spirit and feeling of it, the essence of it, and consequently the very character of the people. We have been using the medium of Indian dance to bring about a better understanding of the Indians, and many Indians have been warm in praise of our work.

Once we gave a program for the old-timers at Little Eagle, South Dakota, to show them what we were doing with the material they had been helping us with over the years. Anthropologists told us that it would be impossible, for example, to give a stage presentation of the Sun Dance, which in actuality lasted several days. But One Bull and Kills Pretty Enemy, who had taken part in the real Sun Dance many years before, and were leaders in its recent revival, told us that they liked our Sun Dance best of all. They caught the spirit of what we were trying to do right away. And recently anthropologists have been influential in bringing us to their campuses for concerts and seminars.

Although we have been doing Indian dancing professionally for years, we do not feel that it is a career to be recommended to non-Indians. In the future, if Indian dancing is to be preserved, the Indians must be encouraged to do it themselves. One of our purposes has been to call the attention of the public to the beauty and worth of the dancing and to try to stimulate interest in its survival as an art form.

We feel that our efforts have met with some success, for we were presented the Capezio Dance Award in New York—the highest national dance recognition—for having

learned, loved, preserved and presented to vast audiences the ancient dance art of the first Americans, the Indians. In our theatres, lecture halls and classrooms, it is the individual who serves as ambassador of a dance culture. The oldest and most universal expression in the world [is] ethnic dance. . . .

But this was the first time the award was given to ethnic dancers.

The Capezio Dance Award is a memorial to Salvatore Capezio, the dancer's cobbler whose shop, opened in 1887 near the old Metropolitan Opera House in New York, became the meeting place for famous artists of the dance and theater. It is given for long-range accomplishment in the field of dance, not for an isolated event or "best" performance of any specific year.

As a project Indian lore has its values, even when it is not carried on to its highest or fullest development. It is a fascinating hobby, to say the least, and can be put to constructive use. It cultivates an interest in the Indians, and such an interest is necessary if any real Indian lore is to be preserved.

But some of these groups who claim to be preserving Indian dances have often done more to hold back a true understanding and appreciation of them and have actually prevented their acceptance as fine art. This may be through no lack of sincerity on their part but because of ignorance on the part of the public. People see an amateur performance of Indian dances, whether by a non-Indian or an Indian group, and their interest wanes. They cannot visualize it as a truly fine art, comparable to other forms of the dance, because they cannot seem to realize that they are seeing merely demonstrations by students or amateurs.

Gladys Laubin in the Sun Dance. Some tribes chose a Holy Woman as Leader of the Sun Dance. Laubin Collection.

In many societies men had the monopoly on dancing, but in the United States the usual opinion of a male dancer has been that he is a "sissy." Ted Shawn did much to reinstate dancing as a man's art when he toured with his troupe of all-male dancers some years ago. More superb physical specimens would be hard to find. A dancer's body must be elastic and supple, not muscle-bound. Until recently much physical training tended to develop large, bulging muscles, but not agility and suppleness. Because of his pioneer work in physical training Shawn was once engaged by a well-known college of physical education to put the football squad through a period of training. The boys had the usual idea that a dancer must be a sissy, but within half an hour Shawn had them begging for mercy. He was twice as old as any of them, but their hard, tense muscles tired quickly.

Indian life in the past developed sound, beautiful bodies. Amost every explorer who came in contact with Indians was generous in his praise of their physique and endurance, even when he could see little else to admire. Captain John Smith wrote of one "Savage eight score [160] years olde [who] was as lustie and went as fast as any of us; which was strange to behold."[2]

GENERAL CHARACTERISTICS

Although there is no such thing as a typical Indian, there were certain customs and characteristics common to most of the Indians of North America. Many tribes had similar religious beliefs and played similar games. The use of the pipe and tobacco was regarded as sacred, as was the number four. Grace was offered before meals. A ceremonial post, or pole, was important in many rituals. The steam bath and the give-away were almost universal. So it is no great wonder that dancing was often much the same from tribe to tribe.

Consequently there are certain phases of Indian dancing that we can describe in general terms. From our observations among Indians of Woodlands and Plains tribes, as well as some in the Southwest, we would say that all have a similar way of handling their bodies and feet. In other words, all have a similar manner of execution. The characteristic position is with knees slightly bent and backs straight. There is a great freedom of movement, almost a loose-jointedness, and except in a few dances or for accent the dancer always seems to be relaxed.

We find that some of the best dancers among Indians today are overweight, even obese.* Our old friend Acee Blue Eagle, the famous Oklahoma artist, was a fine dancer. He was one of the biggest men we ever knew but as light as a feather as

---

*Indians today often admire obesity. Many Indian women take pride in being fat. It is a sign of prosperity. But Pretty Shield said that when she was a girl there was only one fat woman in the entire Crow tribe, and the people made fun of her.

Formerly in many tribes the chiefs and elders were known as "Big Bellies." Their fighting and hunting days over, they sat around in council most of the time and became paunchy.

Laubin (center) dancing with Sioux and Crow Indians at a Crow fair in Montana. Photo by Gladys Laubin.

he danced. Some of these heavy men dance only a few times a year, and yet they stay with it for hours. They can dance long and well because they are relaxed and enjoy dancing. There are few moments of extreme tension. Even in the most strenuous dances the good dancer gives the impression of never quite extending himself. This is something very difficult for a white person to learn. It is part of the charm and fascination of Indian dancing.

In most dances the arms are used little or not at all. In earlier days in many dances the hands were placed on the hips, fingers extended, making a straight line from fingertips to elbows—not palms on the hips and wrists bent, as we sometimes see today. Or one might hold a fan or other article in one hand and place the other hand on the hip. Today hands often hang at the sides or are held with bent elbows. But they never appear to be dangling or "flopping" and are never thrown wildly about, as in American black and African dancing.

In fact, even the most active dancing is generally dignified and controlled. There may have been exceptions to this, as among tribes of the Northwest Coast and some of the medicine men's performances. But by and large the above statements hold. This may sound as if the dancing is stilted, and we know that many of the early observers felt it to be, but actually a good Indian dancer uses every muscle of his body. When imitating birds and animals, he shakes his head and shoulders, moves his back muscles, and sometimes brings his arms, hands, and fingers into play.

The Indian has a duplicate or a substitute for almost every known dance step. The very simplicity with which some of these steps seem to be executed is a compliment to the grace and skill of the performers.

There is a subtlety of motion that is usually completely lost to the casual observer but is one of the most interesting aspects of Indian dancing. Even when it is noted, it is difficult to acquire. But it makes the difference between a genuine and a false interpretation.

Sudden but subtle shifts in weight add to the difficulties of trying to imitate Indian dancing. For these reasons so many observers, especially show producers, have tended to discount authentic Indian dance as show material. They want exaggerated movement, spectacular leaps and jumps, great masses of performers, uniformity, and girls with little on but their figures. Indian dancing is generally the opposite of these demands.

Many people think of Indian dancers as being always in a crouched position. The only continuous "crouch," if it can be called that, would be the slightly bent knees. On occasion the dancers get down into such a squat as to be nearly resting on their heels, but this cannot be considered a typical position. It is used nowadays mainly in contests, to test endurance and agility. In the old days the squat position was also used in part of the Scalp, or Victory, Dance and in the Eagle Dance. Even in such a position, the back is straight and the head up. The back is seldom hunched, unless in imitation of buffalo or in order to tell a story. One of the most discouraging things to see is some of the young Indians who do let their shoulders sag and their heads hang as they dance. This is not an old-time Indian dance attitude.

The well-known anthropologist Clark Wissler spent much time with Indians in the early 1900's. He remarked that he used to enjoy watching the important old men walk, for it would put the slouching gait of the white man to shame. But even then the young people were taking on the awkwardness of the whites.[3]

The beautiful posture of the old Indians made a great impression upon us. It was

Laubin in the Brave Heart Dance. Laubin Collection.

thrilling to watch each one, standing erect, or walking as if his moccasins barely touched the earth, or dancing with his head up and back straight.

Indians all across North America had dances connected with the various animals and birds with which they were familiar. Several of these animal and bird dances have been taken up in detail. Curt Sachs, in his *World History of the Dance*, says that "the people influenced by the animal dance have a variety of movements and dance with enthusiasm; those who do not know the animal dance have few movements and show little zest for dance."[4]

495

The Buffalo Dance as presented by the Laubins and their Crow Indian dance troupe on their tour of eleven countries in Europe and North Africa, and in Israel. Left to right: Susie Yellowtail (Bear), Laubin, Thomas Yellowtail, Henry Old Coyote, and Joseph Medicine Crow. Laubin Collection.

Indian dancing has sometimes been criticized because it lacks great jumps and leaps, but, as we have seen from early writings, leaping and jumping have been prominent in several accounts. Several California tribes had dances in which they leaped into the air from a squat position. One of the typical dances of that area is the Jumping Dance described earlier. It is doubtful, however, that any Indians ever developed finished leaps such as we see in ballet or in modern dance. Today one no longer sees leaping in Indian dancing, but we know that it existed, and we personally saw examples of it years ago.

We once saw a Cheyenne Indian do a series of leaps. In the firelight he looked lithe as a boy. He was naked except for a long, narrow breechclout that nearly dragged the ground, moccasins, bells, and a red roach headdress. The other dancers were in the usual dyed underwear. He whirled and leaped around the fire so rapidly and had such perfect control of his agile body that it seemed that his constant spinning and turning were timed to the leaping flames. He kept up the wild, vigorous dancing far into the night, after many other dancers had quit. When we went to talk with this marvelous dancer afterward, we were overwhelmed to discover that he was an old, old man. His face was lined and wrinkled. But he had the figure, the carriage, the suppleness of a boy. He knew not a word of English, but you should have seen his face light up when a young Cheyenne translated our compliments to him. He said that his name was Lone Wolf. He certainly had the grace and endurance of a wolf.

We have always noticed, from our very first trip to the reservation, that the best dancers among Indians often are the very old people and the young children. White Bull and One Bull, when in their nineties, would dance all evening. When One Bull danced the Chief's Dance, he sometimes acted like a buffalo bull, snorting, bellowing, and pawing the ground. When Makes Trouble was in his eighties, he did the best Buffalo Dance we have ever seen. Another old Sioux—and, strange to say, his name was Long Wolf—did a marvelous Buffalo Dance, even though he had a wooden leg.

Some years ago we saw two "companies" of Apaches give the Crown Dance. The first presentation was by the "professional" group—the older men—the acknowledged portrayers of the Mountain Spirits. Some were big and heavy, but how they could dance! They performed with a precision and perfection almost unbelievable. Shortly afterward, the younger, "amateur" group performed. They were being trained by the "professionals" and were really very good. If one had not seen the others first, he would have been quite satisfied with their efforts, but having seen both troupes, there was not the slightest doubt that the older men were far superior. They danced with more power, finesse, grace, and conviction.

In the modern Grass Dance one sometimes sees a sinuous, crouching movement that he would have seen in some warrior dances of long ago. But the chiefs and dignitaries almost always dance *straight up* and insist that this was the old-time position for most dances. The chiefs do not do the exaggerated "fancy dancing" that some of the younger dancers indulge in.

In warrior and solo dances the individual was allowed a great deal of liberty in his movements, even to inventing his own. A good dancer developed his own style, and no one else would think of copying him. This is carried out to some extent even today but it is not as noticeable as it used to be.

Religious dances, of course, were ritualistic and sometimes had their own peculiar steps, used for no other dance. Often there is little that non-Indians would call dancing in these rituals. There is movement, to be sure, but sometimes only a swaying of the body, or slight flexing of the knees, or raising of the heels. But the mere fact that they spoke of these rituals as dances shows the important position given to dancing.

To Indians the song and costume often determined the dance, rather than any great change in step or pattern. Every dance, whether religious, social, or ceremonial, had its own special songs associated with it. In many dances bells were worn by the dancers about the knees and ankles to add to the rhythmic effect. From about the time of the Civil War sleigh bells have been the most popular bells, but when it has been difficult to obtain them other kinds have been used. Sheep bells are worn by many dancers nowadays. They are shaped like cowbells but are much smaller and so can be worn, several around each ankle, in comfort. The Sioux word for bell, *ma'zahlahla*, means "iron rattle."

Many dances, especially those for war and hunting, were punctuated by yells and shouts of great variety, which astonished and even frightened non-Indian observers. Exuberance in social dances also led to occasional sharp yelps and cries, but even in his yelling the Indian is dignified. The yells and calls have meanings and symbolism and are not used promiscuously. When used as the Indian uses them, they add zest and interest to the dance. Dances of other peoples are also occasionally accented with yells of various kinds, but none of them seem to have the force and effect of those of the Indians.

Even social dances were involved with the religious beliefs of the tribe; at one time probably all dances had religious significance. Dancing by men, here on earth below, portrayed the actions of spirits in the afterworld. When the spirits were happy, the people danced happy dances. When the spirits were unhappy, angry, or alarmed, men's dancing corresponded. When the spirits were unconcerned for man's welfare, the Indians danced to revive their interest in them and their affairs.

Possible exceptions as far as having spiritual interpretations for their dances were tribes of the extreme Northeast—Naskapis, Montagnais, Penobscots—whom Speck said showed no evidence of having dances with religious aspects at the time he visited them in the early 1900's. But even in this area he thought that before contact with Christians dance and song were important in the religious beliefs. He wrote that the missionaries did not seem to understand

how essential such emotional outlets are to the natives' mental balance, or how much better adapted to native mentality these are than the but half-comprehended Mass.
Aside from the social benefits, which they fully appreciate, the Indians recognize certain physical stimulus in the dance which they interpret as an awakening of the soul-spirit and a development of strength. Sweating is one of the objects of dance exertion. It tends to cultivate strength and bring good luck, for "dancing is a remedy, it lies in the sweating."[5]

Wissler said that nothing could be more erroneous than the idea most people have that there is no order or design to Indian dancing. "Their dances were rigidly fixed in pattern," he wrote, "and call for the precision and art that come with long training." He also stated that some of the ritualistic dances required skill in acting and that some parts were as vividly portrayed as if upon a "civilized" stage. He even went so far as to claim that, since all dances and rituals were performed to appropriate music, had the Indian the proper stage settings for them, they could be classed as opera. One of our operas might mean little to an Indian, seeing it without knowing

Laubin in the Brave Heart Dance. Laubin Collection.

its background, but at the same time he might appreciate it better than some white people "because he sensed the spirit of it."[6]

The sad part has been that as Indian children became older, most of them became ashamed of their heritage. Then, with old age approaching, they looked back and realized that they had lost something important, and so they tried to recapture it. Many of today's old people, who are apparently the most conservative Indians, are Carlisle graduates, or victims of other old-style Indian schools, who have come to appreciate what they were forced to give up in earlier years and so have leaned over backward to make up for the loss. Twenty or more years ago the old people were the real old-timers, who had never lost anything but the outward aspects of their culture. They were the best dancers in those days because they truly understood what they were doing.

One time while I was dancing with the Crows, an old man named Bird Horse surprised me by taking me by the hand and leading me all around the circle. He called out loudly in Crow, "Look at this young man here! He is nothing but a white man but he looks more real, more Indian, than some of you young Crows do. What's the matter with you? You dress like cowboys. Are you ashamed of being Indians? I appreciate this young man and his woman and welcome them to our celebration."

Now many of the younger people are regaining an interest in their own lore and heritage. Some are extremely good dancers. The pity is that there are so few left to help them.

REGIONAL CHARACTERISTICS

Indian dances ran the gamut of emotional experience and covered practically every phase of life: birth dances, children's dances, puberty dances, dances to celebrate weddings, medicine dances of magic and of healing, dances for games and for pleasure, humorous dances, religious dances. There were dances to welcome strangers, to cement alliances, to honor the dead.

Dances were given to assure good hunting and to celebrate the resultant success. There were dances of planting and of harvesting; of preparation for war and of victory and peace. When a chief was "raised," there were dances to honor him. There were dances of sacrifice, of appeal for future blessings, of thanksgiving. Many dances had their origins in dreams and portrayed the dream experiences. There were also times when dancing was mainly social.

Each area of the country had dances typical of the culture and activities of the region. In the East there were special strawberry festivals when the wild strawberries were ripe. In the North, Snowshoe dances celebrated the arrival of winter and its enveloping blanket of white. On the Plains there were many Buffalo dances. In the thick, dark forests of the Northwest, where a gloomy religion full of powerful, often dread, spirits, developed, there was even an Echo Dance, intended to confuse malevolent spirits and keep them away from the villages. In the arid Southwest almost every dance had the bringing of rain as its primary purpose.

Bird Horse leading Laubin around the dance circle, calling out: "Look at this young man! He is nothing but a white man, but he looks more Indian than some of you young Crows do!" Photo by Gladys Laubin.

The Indian, wherever he was found, was a product of his environment and his culture was built around it. Indians of all the heavily wooded regions had religions with gloomy concepts. The people of the open plains and prairies seem to have been happier. Perhaps happiest of all, with the least reason to be so, were the Eskimos. But, regardless of tribe or cultural development, all seemed to be content with their lot. Each tribe believed itself to be "the People," and the only personal desire was to be worthy and recognized among one's own. (Enemy tribes were usually designated as "Snakes" or "Adders.")

The Indian culture of the Southwest remains strong but that of the Plains, the Woodlands, California, and the Northwest Coast is nearly gone. The culture of the Woodlands was built upon war, farming, and hunting; that of the Plains, on war, the horse, and the buffalo. With the extermination of the buffalo and the cessation of the wars, the incentive for most of the dances was lost. This, coupled with the general discouragement of the people, plus the actual prohibition of the dances, has left little but memory of the old days, and that memory is fast fading with the younger generations.

The dances of hunters and warriors naturally differ in spirit and character from those of farmers or people with a different way of life. The Village Tribes of Plains Indians were still farmers and retained planting and harvest dances similar to those of the Woodlands. Thus in both areas we find dances common to hunters and farmers. From what we have been able to learn, the Plains and Woodlands can be roughly grouped together for dance styles. We find quite different patterns and formations, and even some difference in execution, in the Southwest, California, the Northwest Coast, and Alaska.

The Plains and Woodland peoples were individualists in name and in deed, and their dancing shows it. Dancing in the Plains area was probably the most active and spectacular of all, both in content and in costume, with much Siouan influence in evidence.

The Southwestern Pueblo Indians live a communal existence, which is evident in their dancing. It is characterized by few solos, by well-organized group dances and processionals. Their dancing might best be compared to the chorus line and the ballet.

On the Plains certain distinguished women—those who had gone to war and counted war honors like men—were allowed to participate in men's dances. There were few of these, of course, but we knew Mary Crawler, Tašina Maniwin, who fought in the Battle of the Little Big Horn. She was then only a teen-age girl, but she "counted coup" on the soldiers, just as the warriors did, and so she danced with the men.

Generally speaking, it seems that most of the Plains dances moved in a circle to the left, or clockwise, "following the sun," for the sun was the highest manifestation of the Great Mystery. On the other hand, the Woodland people, both north and south, usually moved to the right, "with their hearts toward the fire," for to them fire was the all-important gift to man and symbolized light and life, truth, renewed strength and vigor, purification, and power. Fire had much the same meaning to the Prairie tribes, but the sun, to which they were exposed continually, took the most important part in their symbolism. Both areas featured many solo dances, but footwork seems to have been more elaborate on the Plains.

It may be interesting to note that most of the Pueblo dances also move to the right, or counterclockwise. Does the fact that they are also farming people have anything to do with it? But Navajos also farm, and among them we find dances moving in clockwise circles again, with some dances in opposing lines. To add to the confusion, we now occasionally find Plains Indians dancing to the right, as mentioned in the account of the Grass Dance.

On the Northwest Coast and among the Eskimos, the dances are largely solo, but with much audience participation. There is almost a cult of frenzy, with much exaggerated movement, not too much footwork, but swinging of arms, jerking of head, spasmodic moving of muscles, and a preoccupation with the fantastic and horrible.

In California we find dancing in lines again, with beautiful and detailed accouterments, some jumping and leaping, but not the virtuosic footwork we find on the Plains.

It seems that everywhere we find some circle dancing, for in the final analysis it is the most logical formation for group dancing. With the exception of something like the Sioux Elk Mystery, which progressed literally for miles, dancing is generally limited to a small space, either surrounded by an audience or with an audience on one to three sides. A dancer is almost forced to dance in place, move in a circle left or right, or dance forward and backward. The same applies to a group, with the additional feature of forming lines that move forward and backward, face each other, or sashay through each other. Or a group can also move in a spiral, which we find in the Stomp dances.

Indian men and women did not dance arm in arm, as white people do, until learning it from them. In the social dances men and women did dance side by side, or in the same circle together, but generally men and women had separate dances, with the men having by far the greater number and variety of steps and movements.

While dancing served as spectator entertainment, it was not done for that purpose. Largely it was the participation that was important. Even solo dances were given either as contests or as parts of ceremonies and rituals.

COSTUME

Originally Indian men, and, in many areas, women, wore little clothing. The Indian's body was his dancing instrument, as it should be in any dance, and he did not hide it or restrict its movements with unnecessary clothing. His body was toughened to withstand exposure in all kinds of weather, and he danced with no more clothing in winter than in summer. Indians who met the first white men were puzzled about why they wore so much clothing. They thought, "These white men must be very weak people, or else they have such ugly bodies they have to hide them like that!"

The Laubins in an old social dance. Laubin Collection.

Once an old Sioux Indian was standing outside a government building at Fort Robinson, Nebraska, in subzero weather, with only a buffalo robe wrapped around his waist, completely bare from there up. An officer's wife hurrying from one house to another, stopped to stare at him.

"My goodness! Aren't you cold?" she asked.

The Indian looked at her and asked, "You face cold?"

"Why, no, but my face is always exposed, and is used to the cold," the lady answered.

"Me face all over," replied the Indian.

But in recent years the Indians have accepted the white man's standards in nearly everything, including false modesty. The white man said, in effect, "It isn't proper to paint your body and dance in your bare skin like that." So the Indian did the next-best thing. He danced in dyed underwear. Years ago I was lectured to by several Indians because I insisted on dancing the old-time way, clothed mainly in breechclout and moccasins. They told me that it was immoral. Certainly that is what they have been taught by missionaries and government employees. The nudity of the Indian dancers upheld the contention of prudish Victorian observers that the dancing was immoral and gave another excuse for prohibiting it. With as little mingling of the sexes as we find in Indian dancing, it can hardly be considered immoral from that standpoint. The Indian dancer did not need a partner in his arms to attain the satisfaction dancing could bring to him.

To our way of thinking, one of the greatest losses in the cultural transition the Indian has been undergoing is the loss of the feeling for beauty. In the old days he was surrounded by beauty and constantly created things of beauty. The loss of the sense of true beauty is evidenced in some of the present-day costumes. The change began with the first contact with Europeans. From the very beginning Indians admired the goods the strangers brought to trade. To be able to possess them set a man above his fellows, for he had to be an exceptionally good hunter and warrior to obtain the necessary trade articles. Since personal prestige was the goal of every man in an individualistic society, such as that of most of the tribes of the Woodlands and Plains, obtaining the new goods was often considered important.

Cloth was early substituted for buckskin, commercial dyes for native colors, beads for porcupine quills, brass kettles for clay pots, iron arrowheads for stone, steel knives for flint. Even bows and arrows gave way to inferior guns, almost entirely as a matter of prestige. (The bow was a superior weapon for hunting or Indian-type warfare until the latter part of the nineteenth century, when the breech-loading repeating rifle was developed.)

Ribbons and mirrors, ostrich and peacock feathers were added to personal adornment. Lewis and Clark gave out army officers' coats, complete with epaulets and braid, to the men they "made" chiefs. Included also were swords and cocked hats. Catlin made a remarkable portrait of one chief, who came back from Washington decked out in beaver hat and plume, an officer's coat, and an umbrella. Imagine what a figure he cut in the Chief's Dance!

Of course these extremes were not common. The over-all change was gradual and of the Indian's own choosing. Consequently Indian costume was often enhanced rather than spoiled by the addition and substitution of new things. On the whole, the development was in good taste and the results charming and dignified.

We wish that we could say the same thing for some of the present-day costumes. The emphasis now seems to be mostly on ornate display. Color combinations, materials, and patterns are often disturbing. Such changes have sometimes been encouraged by spectators, who seem to think that anything made with beads or feathers is "beautiful." Many have never seen the real beauty of the traditional things. As long as it is garish, gaudy, spectacular, or just "different" they seem to be satisfied.

Apropos to this trend of thought, Kroeber wrote in his *Handbook of the Indians of California:*

Since most people have not the interest to familiarize themselves with the art of their own civilization they are wholly incapable of knowing what a remote foreign one is about. Hence they prefer Indian baskets with bastard European patterns, and though they may find something vaguely pleasing in many primitive works of decoration—if seen sufficiently rarely—the quality which appeals is that of strangeness and the grotesque.[7]

Even in movement, particularly in the "War Dance," the desire is often for fancy, meaningless flourishes and eccentric steps. The beauty and dignity of the old-style dancing are hard to find. Some girls have been dancing the old Round, or Woman's Dance, in modern shoes, without leggings, unheard of in former times. This may be partly for economic reasons, for beaded moccasins and leggings are very expensive. But Indians still love to dance, and something outstanding may still develop. There is no reason why Indians cannot become interested in reviving and sustaining good taste. In fact, some of them are doing just that, and the recent trend is to encourage the use of traditional things once more. Women are beginning to wear leggings and moccasins again and to dress their hair in old-time ways. We do not see so many of them wearing fancy headbands and eagle feathers, as they have been doing for a number of years. There is still more dignity at an Indian dance than at most non-Indian dances.

THE IMPORTANCE OF DANCING

Something of the importance ascribed to dancing by Indians, even in these times, may be understood when we realize that a dance is the one sure way of getting Indians together. Some of the old intertribal jealousies and animosities persist, but Indians from diverse tribes will show up for a dance, and in the Indian centers of our big cities the dances are now tending to ameliorate the old feelings and bring about understanding among the Indians. They are beginning to recognize themselves as an entity, rather than as small reservation or tribal groups. On the reservations, however, just the opposite often takes place. There the dancing is instrumental in retaining both tribal identity and isolation and is the heart of cultural preservation.

The Sun Dance as presented by the Laubins and their Crow Indian dance troupe. Left to right: Gladys Laubin, Thomas Yellowtail, Joseph Medicine Crow, Henry Old Coyote, and Laubin. Laubin Collection.

Many writers have stated how fond Indians were of dancing, feasting, and gambling. The three usually went together. Sometimes games were played in such a ritualistic manner that they might almost be considered dances. The Indians themselves seemed to regard the two in the same light, and it is certain that they enjoyed taking part in ritualistic and religious dances, these too, serving function as diversion and entertainment.

The Indians usually took part in religious ceremonies for personal reasons rather than because of any sense of being required to participate. In what we might call secular dances (although, as already mentioned, many of these had religious significance), participation was largely one of self-satisfaction, of dancing for the sheer joy to be found in rhythmic movement.

Lewis Morgan, writing in 1851, said that with the Iroquois,

as with the red race at large, dancing was not only regarded as a thanksgiving ceremonial, in itself acceptable to the Great Spirit, but they were taught to consider it a divine art, designed by *Hä-wen-ne'yu* for their pleasure as well as for worship. It was cherished as one of the most suitable modes of social intercourse between the sexes, but more especially as the great instrumentality for arousing patriotic excitement, and for keeping alive the spirit of the nation. The popular enthusiasm broke forth in this form and was nourished and stimulated by this powerful agency. These dances sprang, as it were, a living reflection from the Indian's mind. With their wild music of songs and rattles, their diversity of step and attitude, their grace of motion, and their spirit-stirring association, they contain within themselves both a picture and a realization of Indian life. The first stir of feeling of which the Indian youth was conscious was enkindled by the dance; the first impulse of patriotism, and the earliest dreams of ambition were awakened by their inspiring influences. In their patriotic, religious and social dances, into which classes they are properly divisible, resided the soul of Indian life. It was more in the nature of a spell upon the people than of a rational guiding spirit. It bound them down to trivial things, but it bound them together; it stimulated them to deeds of frenzy, but it fed the flame of patriotism.

The Iroquois had thirty-two distinct dances. . . . Their overpowering influence in arousing the Indian spirit, and in excluding all thoughts of a different life, and their resulting effects upon the formation of Indian character, cannot be too highly estimated.

The tenacity with which the Iroquois have always adhered to these dances furnishes the highest evidence of their hold upon the affections of the people. . . . The body of the Senecas, Onondagas and Cayugas, upon their several reservations, still cling to their ancient customs, and glory in the dance as ardently as did their forefathers. *When it loses its attractions, they will cease to be Indians* [italics added].[8]

The Iroquois in New York State and Canada retain much of their traditional culture and as late as 1974 were still performing many of their ancient dances.

HOLDING A DANCE

All across the country there seems to have been a more or less universal pattern for the presentation of a dance, regardless of the kind of dance it was. Usually a feast was involved, as well as speeches, harangues, and a give-away. The harangues usually took the pattern of the recounting of personal exploits, or "counting coups," but might also be grouped under four other categories: stories for amusement, speeches in honor of individuals, speeches of a political nature, and long prayers for the welfare of the people. The give-away might be anything from a simple exchange of presents to the elaborate potlatches of the Northwest Coast.

The present-day pattern of holding a dance still has many elements of the earlier form. First the spectators gather, the men sitting on one side of the room, usually at the right of the door, the women on the other side. They may just sit quietly for a time before anything happens, enjoying the peaceful tranquillity that seems to permeate them all. Sometimes the children run around and play, but they are seldom boisterous, and, if they are, a word from some older person is enough to send them shyly off the scene.

When one attends an Indian dance today, he expects to find "War Dance" as the principal item on the agenda, with fast and slow variations, and occasionally a championship contest for best "fancy" dancer. Interspersed will be "women's

Oklahoma "Fancy Dancers." Left to right: Dixon Palmer, Little Horse Waller, and George Palmer. Photo by A. C. Hector.

dances"—Round, Two-step, or Rabbit Dance, sometimes a Forty-Niner. Round Dance is called Owl Dance by the Crows and sometimes Shuffling Feet, Crow Dance, or Circle Dance by the Sioux. Densmore also referred to it as Cheyenne Dance. The fact is that all Plains and some Woodland tribes do a dance so similar that it would be difficult to say where it originated. The Sioux must have had it for a long, long time, and yet do not claim it as their own.

And there may be what is still called Chiefs' Dance, although the real chiefs are gone, and sometimes an Honor Dance. Always there are give-aways, sometimes raffles, and usually a feast.

But no longer do women just sit on the sidelines or dance in place while the men are cavorting out in the center in the "War Dance." Nowadays we often find some girls or young women right out on the floor, attired as men and doing full-fledged men's dancing. This was unheard of in early days. In the old days the Sioux believed that a woman dancing like a man would bring bad luck (unless she was a warrior woman).

We saw the first suggestion of this sort of thing years ago at Standing Rock. The young women formed a sort of society, and all made dark cloth dresses very much alike, heavily decorated with tin-cone fringes. The skirts were much shorter than those of typical Indian dresses, and they wore no leggings. They developed a very fancy and vigorous step, similar to one used by the best men dancers, and all danced the same step at the same time, very fast, tin cones jingling. It was fascinating for a while, but soon became monotonous. It seemed strange to see them with bobbed hair, bare legs, and short skirts. It turned out to be a mere passing fad and did not last long. And at least they never dreamed of wearing eagle feathers!

Even the Indians joke about their dances being on "Indian time." A dance may be announced for 2:00 in the afternoon, and no dancers show up until 9:00 in the evening. We heard there was to be a dance at No Heart's one afternoon. We arrived about 3:00, thinking that it would be well underway, but not a soul was to be seen. We wandered in the woods along the Missouri River, enjoying the songbirds and the fragrance of the wild roses that saturated the air. Finally we heard a wagon approaching. It was No Heart and his wife with a big load of groceries. We went over to greet them.

"Big dance tonight," No Heart said. "First we have feast at 5:00. You come."

It was after 5:00 o'clock then, but we said nothing, just thanking him for the invitation. The feast actually came off about 8:00, the dancers began to arrive about 9:00 and by 11:00 a good dance was in progress, which lasted until the wee small hours.

Once we were with the Crows when a dance was announced for 5:00 p.m. At 5:00 the dancers came to a big tipi next to ours and began to get ready. Some of them came over to our tipi to borrow a mirror and paint. They spent all the time between then and 8:00 dressing and painting their faces. As far as dressing goes, all they had to put on were their dyed underwear, capes, clouts, moccasins, bells, and a few little ornaments. Most of the time was given to telling jokes and singing new songs a couple of them had just learned in Oklahoma. These social preparations were part of the dance as far as they were concerned and almost as important. About 8:00 they went to their own tipis for supper, and it was 9:00 or after before they gathered again for the actual dance.

While the audience and dancers are gathering, the singers sometimes rehearse songs as they sit around the drum—a large bass drum—which is often placed directly on the ground, not hung from four tall stakes, as were the old drums.

510

Sometimes the feast is held before the dance, but more often it serves as an intermission. While waiting for the dancers to appear, we sometimes hear speeches, often political in nature, but usually having something to do with tribal welfare. We have been to many a dance at which the preliminary invocation was a long prayer given by one of the leaders.

When a few of the bolder dancers arrive on the scene, the singers drum for them, and they usually dance for several songs. Their dancing tends to draw other dancers, who wait to see how things are going before they put in an appearance.

After a half-hour or more of dancing, there is usually an intermission, during which time honor songs are sung for certain individuals, who respond by "giving away." Money, handmade quilts, flour, canned fruit, sugar, and coffee often take the place of the horses, war bonnets, moccasins, and blankets that were given away in earlier times and are sometimes given away even today.

This intermission may be followed by a set of women's dances. The afternoon is spent in men's and women's dances, give-aways, and speeches, with a longer intermission for the feast. Then the entire procedure will be repeated in the evening, as long as the dancers and the audience—or rather the singers—are interested. Usually there are dancers who will perform as long as the singers will sing.

The singers are often older men who in their younger days had been fine dancers. Certainly they understand the dance for which they are singing, and they also understand human physical makeup, attitudes, and emotions. They really make the dance, for upon them depends the performance of the dancers and the enjoyment of the spectators. In present-day Grass dances the dancing usually starts out rather slowly but seems to gather momentum as both singers and dancers become more interested. The pulse of the drum seems almost to follow the pulse of the dancers, so that as the evening moves on the dances become faster and more furious.

For a much needed rest and change of pace, a Round Dance or Rabbit Dance is interposed, after which the men are given the floor again. No matter how fast the pace becomes, it is usual to introduce each new song with a slower tempo, and then the rapid rhythm is again brought into play. So it goes throughout the night, and, just before the dance is to break up, the singers make a final effort to tire the dancers out. And with most dancers they are successful. The furious pace, lack of rest, and strenuous exertion force one dancer after another to withdraw. Eventually only a few are left, the singers sing the final song, and the dancers and audience disperse. After the roar of the drum, the high-pitched voices of the singers, the clanging of myriad sleigh bells, the stamping of many feet, it is suddenly so quiet! In the distance a dog barks or an owl hoots, and the tinkling of the bells trails off to a whisper as the dancers wend their way to their tipis under a starlit sky. In contrast to the noise and action we have just been a part of, the silence is now so deep we can almost hear *it.*

A similar program routine is, and has been from time immemorial, followed by both Plains and Woodland tribes and, we believe, was also followed to some extent in other parts of the country.

According to the early accounts many of the dances of the Plains and Woodlands were solo. From such reports and our own observations it seems that, except for the social Round dances, there was little in the way of "chorus" dancing in these areas. Even when the people danced en masse, it was still individualistic. This has always been confusing to the average white observer, accustomed to watching group dancers doing the same thing at the same time. Among the Indians one sees a great variety of steps all at once.

THE GRAND FINALE: CONCERT DANCING

If Indian dancing is to be "staged," or concertized, it should be done on a rather intimate basis, because of the personalized quality. Another reason is that the really fine costumes have so much detail that much of their beauty is lost if they are seen from too far away or if too many dancers are seen at once. We feel that the dancing is at its best when done solo or in small groups. A huge company may be spectacular, but it is not nearly as beautiful, as artistic, or as satisfying.

There are those who argue that Indian dance should always be seen outdoors in its natural setting, but we do not feel so. It can no longer be seen in its natural setting. There are no longer the great camps to provide the setting. Indian fairs and rodeos are now cluttered with automobiles, wall tents, present-day clothing, and all sorts of other intrusions to destroy the atmosphere that prevailed when the Indians were living their own kind of life.

Most Indian shows today are presented at a fairground on the race track, which can hardly be considered a natural setting. Even in the early days, thrilling as it must have been to see the dances in their native surroundings, they would nevertheless be classed as folk art and we are trying to show that they are good concert material, to be presented in theaters and fine concert halls. If they are, then they do not need much setting to make them interesting. The costumes and movements are beautiful enough in themselves, and good lighting helps create the atmosphere that otherwise has been lacking for a hundred years and more.

The idea of a recital of Indian dances is a new one to Indians, and most of them still have no understanding of a real concert presentation. Their dances were always given for special occasions. Preparations for *one* dance might take days or weeks, and each dancer might spend hours getting ready for his part. Years ago a group of dancers from San Ildefonso Pueblo were presented in New York at an exhibition of Indian art and painting. The newspapers listed the program of dances for each performance. There were Braiding-of-the-Belt, Butterfly, Buffalo, Comanche, Eagle — six to eight different dances to be given each time.

We wondered. It did not sound right to us, and we doubted that any such performance would be given. We got there early on the opening day and bought the very first tickets sold. We waited almost two hours after show time for the performances to start. The lady presenting the Indians was very apologetic and tried to explain the seriousness of the dances, how much they meant to the Indians, and

The Boastful Warrior Dance—Laubin in the costume of the Lakota Strong Heart Society. Photo by Ned Hockman.

the great length of preparation involved—but she should have known that in the first place, for she came from the Indian country.

Finally the Indians were ready, and the lady came forth to make another apology. Only one dance would be presented today, the Braiding-of-the-Belt, because the entire cast had to prepare for it. It was presented periodically all afternoon. On succeeding days the company was divided in half, and each half did one dance, making two dances possible each day. Our tickets served as "season tickets" and entitled us to admission on each of the following days. In other words, it took an entire week to present the "recital" that had been scheduled for each day.

So, although this was in our early experience with Indians, we could not believe that they were ready to give a "dance recital." The Indians were so intent on doing things right that the Navajos in the group insisted on having a carload of sand sent from the reservation for their sand paintings. But at least, these Indians were presented in New York as artists—a new experience for them and for the audience.

In training our troupe to go overseas, we impressed upon them the necessity of doing many dances in one performance, which meant changes of costume for each. They were simply wonderful. We never have seen any artists who could get ready for the next dance as quickly. But it was all a new experience to them. Hitherto they had danced only for their own "doings," or for local rodeos, where they did only two or three dances a day, all in the same costume.

Indian dancing is more alive today than it has been in many years. It is being done much as it always has been in the Southwest, where it is still strong and active. But in other parts of the country the dancing has suffered, not only through discouragement, but because the entire change of culture has made it meaningless and unnecessary. In these areas the dancing that is left is almost entirely social. The dancers usually know little or nothing about the rituals and traditions formerly associated with the dances they are doing. Such dances are only shells of what they formerly were.

Many Indians are still proud of being Indians. Many of them, however, are trying to prove that they can be successful in the white man's world without losing their Indian identity. They are not quite willing to give up all their "Indianism," but at the same time they are doing little, if anything, to preserve it.

The problem of preserving Indian dance has two sides. It is necessary to interest the Indian himself in the artistic value of his dances, and it is necessary to educate the public to appreciate them if they are to take their places as a recognized art within a great American heritage. Until recently the average American has not been much interested in dance as art. He knew little and consequently cared little about Indian dancing.

Dancing served the Indians as drama and theater in the early days, but could hardly have been considered as drama as whites understand the term. Each individual Indian dramatized his personal experiences but, with few exceptions, seldom portrayed roles other than his own.

Non-Indian observers have always looked for something that was not there. They have tried to cast the Indian in their own molds. They have made little effort to understand what the Indians were doing and could not see the charm and beauty that was there, whether or not they understood the deeper significance.

Even Lewis and Clark, who were much more tolerant and understanding than most of the explorers, mentioned several occasions when dances were going on but apparently were not interested enough to see them. In one instance the *Journals* report that "this being the day of adoption and exchange of property between them all, it is accompanied by a dance, which prevents our seeing more than two Indians today."[9] We think that they missed a great Calumet Dance and Give-away that present-day students of Indian lore would give almost anything to see.

Many people go to watch Indians dance just to be entertained. They seem to have no idea that the Indians are not trying to entertain them—that they are merely amusing themselves. They seem unable to understand that even now, with the dances as diluted and deteriorated as they are, there is nevertheless material there of potential concert caliber, with great artistic possibilities.

And yet, all of the finest classical and concert dancing we see today originated in the same sort of material. La Argentina and other Spanish dancers following her took the dances of the cabarets, towns, and villages of Spain and adapted them to the concert stage. Shan Khar did the same for India. We have been trying to do something similar for American Indian dance, for, after seeing some of the finest dancers from around the world, we were convinced that the dances of our own native Indians before the advance of the conquering white man, had been the equals of any for color and action and beauty.

The possibilities of preserving Indian dance as art often seem discouraging, but the mere fact that Indians still have the desire to dance, or that they are dancing at all after all the years of persecution, is encouraging in itself. Much of the dancing presented for white people at fairs, rodeos, and other tourist attractions is poor. But a little interest and understanding on the part of the public could help bring good dancing back—not only bring it back but give it importance, perhaps not of the religious and ceremonial nature it formerly possessed, but in aesthetic value, which would mean even more in these times.

Fifty years ago, during the period when government opposition was at its height, Marsden Hartley, an observer writing primarily in regard to the Southwest, said: "In the life of the American Indian all expression symbolized itself in the form of the dance. It is the solemn high mass of the Indian soul, to which he brings his highest gifts for adoration."[10]

His words apply just as well to all Indians. They show that there have always been a few people with perception enough to recognize beauty and value, even though they were opposed by the popular trend of the time.

In closing, a comment by Walter Terry, now dance editor of *Saturday Review*, written when he was with the *New York Herald-Tribune*, may be appropriate:

In these dances . . . we see suggested in steps and body movements the activities of free and independent men, men of dignity; we see feet caress the earth or pound power from it;

Laubin performing a Hoop Dance, using very small traditional hoops, not the large hoops used today. Photo by Ned Hockman.

we see arms and head raised to face a horizon, a frontier; we feel man's closeness to nature in the imitation of birds and animals, in the stance which is as firm as the deeply rooted oak; we see capers as well as processional, humor as well as profound dedication and above all we see in the body of Indian dance a love of beauty and simplicity. At least the Laubins, dedicated to the task of creating greater unity between the first and the later Americans, make us feel, through their dances, that this is so. . . .

The technical, the choreographic, and thematic areas of Indian dance appear to be endless, and these aspects of the dance are to be respected, but more important is the richness of spirit which underlies these dances and which leaves the modern theater-goer refreshed, stimulated and, if I may speak for myself, cleansed in heart and in spirit. Surely this dance of the American Indian is worthy of cherishing by all Americans, for it is obviously not a neolithic hangover, but a great dance of contemporary force and significance, as Reginald and Gladys Laubin are reminding us.

Wana le yuśtan!   Hecetu yelo!

Notes

Preface

1. See the pamphlet by Felix Cohen, *Americanizing the White Man* (Washington, U.S. Office of Indian Affairs).

2. Samuel Champlain, *Voyages of Champlain, 1604–15* (Boston, Publications of the Prince Society, 1880), II, 124. Hereafter cited as Champlain, *Champlain Voyages.*

3. John Long, *Journal, 1768–1782* (Vol. II of Thwaites, *Early Western Travels,* 32 vols., Cleveland, Arthur H. Clark, 1904–1907), 65.

4. Louis Hennepin, *A New Discovery of a Vast Country in America* (2d London issue, 1698; reprint, ed. by R. G. Thwaites, Chicago, A. C. McClurg & Co., 1903), I, 468.

5. Quoted from Paul A. W. Wallace, *The White Roots of Peace* (Philadelphia, University of Pennsylvania Press, 1946), 3.

6. Quoted from *American Heritage* flyer announcement of *The Book of Indians* (New York, 1961).

Chapter 1. The First Explorers

1. Henry S. Burrage (ed.), *Early English and French Voyages* (New York, Charles Scribner's Sons, 1906), 19–21.

2. Edward Gaylord Bourne (ed.), *Narratives of the Career of Hernando de Soto* (New York, Barnes, 1904), I, 106, 153.

3. Edward Gaylord Bourne (ed.), *The Voyages of Columbus and of John Cabot* (New York, Charles Scribner's Sons, 1906), 181.

4. *Ibid.,* 201–202.

5. *Ibid.,* 335.

6. *Old South Leaflets,* Vol. II, No. 37, and Vol. V, No. 115 (Boston, Old South Association.

7. Charles C. Willoughby, *Antiquities of the New England Indians* (Cambridge, Peabody Museum, Harvard University, 1935), 269.

8. Henry R. Schoolcraft, *The American Indians* (Philadelphia, 1851), 332, 335.

9. Burrage, *Early English and French Voyages,* 19–20.

10. *Ibid.,* 23.

11. *Ibid.,* 47.

12. *Ibid.,* 49, 51.

13. *Ibid.,* 57.

14. Champlain, *Champlain Voyages,* I, 51.

15. *Ibid.,* 241, 247.

16. *Ibid.,* II, 46.

17. Samuel Champlain, *Champlain's Expedition of 1615,* translated from French text of 1619 (Magazine of American History, 1885), 563.

18. Champlain, *Expedition,* 81.

19. Morris Bishop, *The Odyssey of Cabeza de Vaca* (New York & London, The Century Company, 1933), 67.

20. *Ibid.,* 68.

21. *Ibid.,* 80.

22. *Ibid.*, 83, 95, 96.

23. *Ibid.*, 107, 118.

24. George Parker Winship, "Narratives of Casteñada and Francisco Vásquez" (1540–42), Bureau of American Ethnology, *Fourteenth Annual Report*, 1892–93)

25. Bourne, *Narratives of . . . De Soto*, II, 18.

26. *Ibid., passim.*

27. *Ibid.*, II, 97.

28. *Ibid.*, 121.

29. *Ibid.*, 123.

30. Robert F. Heizer, *Francis Drake and the California Indians, 1579*, University of California Publications in American Archaeology and Ethnology, Vol. XLII, No. 3 (Berkeley, University of California Press, 1947).

31. James Cook, *Capt. James Cook, Voyages to the Pacific Ocean, 1776, 1777, 1778, 1779* (London, 1785), II, 266, 283, 305.

Chapter 2. The Colonial Period

1. John Smith, *The Generall Historie of Virginia, 1584–1626* (London, 1627), 3.

2. *Ibid.*, 30.

3. Edward Arber (ed.), *Travels and Works of Captain John Smith*, I, lxix.

4. *Ibid.*, lxiv.

5. *Ibid.*, lxxi.

6. *Ibid.*, cxiv.

7. *Ibid.*, 21.

8. *Ibid.*, 76.

9. *Ibid.*, 123.

10. Champlain, *Voyages*, I, 241.

11. Roger Williams, *A Key to the Language of America* (London, 1643), 112.

12. William Wood, *New England's Prospect* (1629–34; introd. by Eben Moody Boynton, West Newbury, Massachusetts, 1898).

13. John Josselyn, *New England Rarities Discovered* (London, 1672).

14. Daniel Gookin, *Historical Collections of the Indians in New England, 1674* (Boston, 1792).

15. Lt. Henry Timberlake, *Memoirs, 1756–1765* (London, 1765; reprint, Johnson City, Tennessee, Watauga Press, 1927), 102.

16. James Adair, *The History of the American Indians* (London, 1775; reprint, Johnson City, Tennessee, Watauga Press, 1930), 102, 116.

17. William Bartram, *Bartram's Travels* (Philadelphia, 1791; reprint, New York, Macy-Masius, 1928), 298–300.

18. *Ibid.*, 395–96.

19. Edna Kenton (ed.), *The Indians of North America*, from *The Jesuit Relations and Allied Documents, 1610–1791* (New York, Harcourt, Brace & Co., 1927), I, 24.

20. *Ibid.*, 37.

21. *Ibid.*, 128, 129.

22. E. H. Blair, *Indian Tribes of the Upper Mississippi Valley and Region of the Great Lakes* (Cleveland, A. H. Clark, 1911), I, 84, 134, 135.

23. *Ibid.*, 337–38.

24. Hennepin, *A New Discovery*, I, 239.

25. *Ibid.*, 462–63.

26. *Ibid.*, 233.

27. *Ibid.*, 236.

28. *Ibid.*, 222–38.

29. *Ibid.,* 195.

30. *Ibid.,* 168.

31. W. Vernon Kinietz (ed.), *The Indians of the Western Great Lakes, 1615–1760* (Ann Arbor, University of Michigan Press, 1940), Letters 26 and 27, "Memoir Concerning the Different Indian Nations of North America," by Antoine Denis Raudot.

32. Antoine Simon Le Page du Pratz, *The History of Louisiana* (English translation, London, 1774).

33. *Ibid.,* 327.

34. *Journals of La Vérendrye* (Toronto, Publications of the Champlain Society, 1927).

Chapter 3. The Late 1700's and Early 1800's

1. Jonathan Carver, *Travels Through the Interior Parts of North America, 1766, 1767, 1768* (London, 1778; reprint Minneapolis, Ross & Haines, Inc., 1956), 266–83.

2. *Ibid.,* 279.

3. Kinietz, *The Indians of the Western Great Lakes, 1615–1760.*

4. Blair, *Indian Tribes of the Upper Mississippi Valley,* I, 344–45.

5. *Ibid.,* II, 230.

6. Count Francesco Arese, *A Trip to the Prairies, 1837–38* (trans. by Andrew Evans; New York, The Harbor Press, 1934), 88–89.

7. Long, *Journal, 1768–1782,* 70–71.

8. *Ibid.,* 72.

9. Edwin James, *A Narrative of the Captivity and Adventures of John Tanner, during Thirty Years Residence among the Indians* (1830; reprint, Minneapolis, Ross & Haines, 1956), 9.

10. Alexander Mackenzie, *Mackenzie's Voyages, 1789–1793* (Toronto, Radisson Society, 1927), 101, 109, 127, 130.

11. *Ibid.,* 180, 210.

12. Meriwether Lewis, *History of the Expedition of Captains Lewis and Clark, 1804–5–6* (ed. by Nicholas Biddle, Philadelphia, 1814; reprint, Chicago, A. C. McClurg & Co., 1902–1903), I, 160–61; Pierre-Antoine Tabeau, *Tabeau's Narrative of Loisel's Expedition to the Upper Missouri* (ed. by Annie Heloise Abel, trans. by Rose Abel Wright; Norman, University of Oklahoma Press, 1939), 196.

13. Tabeau, *op. cit.,* 191.

14. *Ibid.,* 215.

15. Lewis, *Expedition of Lewis and Clark,* I, 41, 109.

16. *Ibid.,* 62.

17. *Ibid.,* 162.

18. *Ibid.,* 159.

19. *Ibid.,* 392.

20. *Ibid.,* 353.

21. *Ibid.,* 407, 408.

22. *Ibid.,* II, 11.

23. *Ibid.,* 266, 271.

24. *Ibid.,* 409.

25. John Bradbury, *Travels in the Interior of America, 1809–11* (Vol. V of Thwaites's *Early Western Travels*), 159.

26. Alexander Ross, *Adventures of the First Settlers on the Oregon or Columbia River* (Vol. VII of Thwaites's *Early Western Travels*), 128, 136–38, 143, 148.

27. Philip Ashton Rollins (ed.), *The Discovery of the Oregon Trail, Robert Stuart's Narratives, 1811–12* (New York, Charles Scribner's Sons, 1935), 13.

28. Tilly Buttrick, *Voyages, 1812–19* (Vol. VIII of Thwaites's *Early Western Travels*), 149, 151, 152.

29. William Faux, *Memorable Days in America* (in Vol. XII of Thwaites's *Early Western Travels*), 51.

30. Edwin James, *Accounts of S. H. Long's Expedition from Pittsburgh to the Rocky Mountains, 1819–20* (Vols. XIV–XVII of Thwaites's *Early Western Travels*), XIV, 209.

31. *Ibid.*, XV, 114.

32. *Ibid.*, 114, 123, 127, 129.

33. *Ibid.*, XVII, 170.

Chapter 4. The Best Observers

1. Maximilian, Prince of Wied, *Travels in the Interior of North America, 1832–34* (Vols. XXII–XXIV of Thwaites's *Early Western Travels*), XXIV, 27–31.

2. *Ibid.*, 33.

3. George Catlin, *North American Indians* (1841; reprint, Edinburgh, 1926), I, 98.

4. *Ibid.*, 142.

5. *Ibid.*, 274–77.

6. Wisconsin Historical Society Collections, cited in Hodge *Handbook of the Indians North of Mexico*, Bureau of American Ethnology *Bulletin 30* (Washington D.C., Government Printing Office, 1910).

7. Catlin, *North American Indians*, II, 155, 156, 159.

8. *Ibid.*, 241–44.

9. Henry R. Schoolcraft, *The Indian in His Wigwam* (Philadelphia, 1848), 195.

10. *Ibid.*, 221.

11. Francis Parkman, *The Oregon Trail* (1849; reprint, New York, New American Library, 1950), 97.

12. *Ibid.*, 222.

13. Hiram Martin Chittenden and Alfred Talbot Richardson (eds.), *Life, Letters and Travels of Father Pierre-Jean De Smet, S.J., 1801–73* (New York, Harper, 1904), I, 165.

14. *Ibid.*, 168.

15. *Ibid.*, III, 914, 917.

16. *Ibid.*, I, 680.

17. *Ibid.*, III, 1061.

18. Josiah Gregg, *Commerce of the Prairies, 1831–39* (Vols. XIX–XX of Thwaites's *Early Western Travels*), Part II, XX, 325, 345.

19. Edwin Thompson Denig, "Indian Tribes of the Upper Missouri, 1854," Smithsonian Institution, Bureau of American Ethnology, *Forty-sixth Annual Report*, 1928–29, 556.

20. Rudolph Friederich Kurz, "Journal . . .: An Account of his Experiences Among Fur Traders and American Indians on the Mississippi and the Upper Missouri Rivers During the Years 1846 to 1852" (ed. by J. N. B. Hewitt), Bureau of American Ethnology, *Bulletin 115* (1937), 41, 42.

21. Maj. Gen. O. O. Howard, *My Life and Experiences Among Our Hostile Indians* (Hartford, 1907), 305.

22. *Ibid.*, 369, 460, 539.

Chapter 5. The Ghost Dance

1. James Mooney, "The Ghost Dance Religion," Smithsonian Institution, Bureau of American Ethnology, *Fourteenth Annual Report*, 1892–93.

2. *Ibid.*, 829.

3. *Ibid.*, 777.

4. *Ibid.*, 789.

5. *Ibid.*, 917.

6. *Ibid.*, 920. See also David H. Miller, *Ghost Dance* (New York, Duell, Sloan and Pearce, 1959).

Chapter 6. Concepts of Indian Dancing

1. Timberlake, *Memoirs*, 137–42.

2. George Catlin, *Eight Years Travel and Residence in Europe* (London, 1848), I, 113.

3. Julia Frather, "Fourth of July at Klamath Reservation," *Overland Monthly*, Vol. XLII, No. 2 (August, 1903).

4. Caleb Atwater, *The Indians of the Northwest* (Columbus, 1850), 129–32.

Chapter 7. Music and Instruments

1. Frank G. Speck, *The Iroquois*, Cranbrook Inst. of Science Bulletin No. 23 (Oct. 1945), 79.

2. *Ibid.*, 79.

3. Wood, *New England's Prospect*, 102.

4. Adair, *The History of the American Indian*, 437.

5. Carver, *Travels Through the Interior Parts of North America*, 152.

6. Atwater, *The Indians of the Northwest*, 112.

7. *Ibid.*, 131.

8. Arese, *A Trip to the Prairies, 1837–38*, 91–92.

9. Frances Densmore, "Musical Instruments of the Maidu Indians," *American Anthropologist*, n.s., Vol. XLI (1939), 113–18.

10. *Ibid.*

11. Smith, *The Generall Historie of Virginia*, 73.

12. Frances Densmore, "Music of Acoma, Isleta, Cochiti and Zuñi Pueblos," Smithsonian Institution, Bureau of American Ethnology, *Bulletin 165* (1957).

13. Densmore, "Music of Santo Domingo Pueblo," 41–43.

14. Speck, *The Iroquois*, 77–78.

15. Hodge, *Handbook of North American Indians*, 170, 171.

Chapter 8. Masks and Paint

1. J. G. Swan, quoted by Clark Wissler in *Masks*, American Museum of Natural History Guide Leaflet Series, No. 96 (1938), 3.

2. See also Frank G. Speck, *A Study of the Delaware Indian Big House Ceremony* (Harrisburg, Pennsylvania Historical Commission, 1931), II.

3. Curtis, *The North American Indian*, XII, 29–31.

4. Wood, *New England's Prospect*, 69.

5. Thomas Auburey, *Travels through the Interior parts of America* (London, 1777), I, 292–94.

6. James Buchanan, *Sketches of the History, Manners and Customs of the North American Indians*, (London, 1821), 94–95.

7. Arese, *A Trip to the Prairies*, 91, 97.

8. Adair, *The History of the American Indians*, 19.

9. Philip Stedman Parkman, *The Culture of the Luiseño Indians*, University of California Publications in American Archaeology and Ethnology, Vol. VIII, No. 4 (Berkeley, University of California Press, 1908), 224, 226.

10. William Simons (ed.), Third Book, *The Proceedings and Accidents of The English Colony in Virginia* (1608; reprint, Edinburgh, 1910), 400, 405.

11. Gookin, *Historical Collections of the Indians in New England*, 153.

Chapter 9. Dances of the Life Cycle

1. M. R. Harrington, *Religion and Ceremonies of the Lenape, Indian Notes and Monographs* (New York, Heye Foundation, 1921).

2. Capt. John G. Bourke, "The Medicine-Men of the Apache," Smithsonian Institution, Bureau of American Ethnology, *Ninth Annual Report*, 1887–88, 584.

3. Morris Edward Opler, *An Apache Life Way* (University of Chicago Press, 1941).

4. John Collier and Ira Moskowitz, *Patterns and Ceremonials of the Indians of the Southwest* (New York, E. P. Dutton & Co., 1949), 81.

5. Harrington, *Religion and Ceremonies of the Lenape*, 92–97. See also Frank G. Speck, *Delaware Indian Big House Ceremony* (Harrisburg, Pennsylvania, Pennsylvania Historical Commission, 1931).

6. John J. Matthews, *Wah'kon-tah* (Norman, University of Oklahoma Press, 1932), 288–300.

7. Frank G. Speck and Leonard Broom, *Cherokee Dance and Drama* (Berkeley, University of California Press, 1951), 12.

8. Lewis H. Morgan, *League of the Iroquois* (Rochester, New York, 1851; reprint, New Haven, Human Relations Area Files, 1954), I, 276.

Chapter 10. The War Dance

1. Thomas L. McKenney and James Hall, *History of the Indian Tribes of North America* (Philadelphia, E. C. Biddle, 1837–44), *Atlas* volume, 3, 4.

2. Le Page du Pratz, *The History of Louisiana*, 353–55.

3. Timberlake, *Memoirs*, 102.

4. *Ibid.*, 92.

5. Morgan, *League of the Iroquois,* I, 258–68.

6. William N. Fenton and Gertrude Prokosch Kurath, "The Iroquois Eagle Dance," Smithsonian Institution, Bureau of American Ethnology *Bulletin 156* (1953), 103–105.

7. *Ibid.*, 105–106.

8. Frank G. Speck, *Ethnology of the Yuchi Indians* (Philadelphia, University of Pennsylvania Press, 1909).

9. Victor Tixier, *Travels on the Osage Prairies, 1839–40* (ed. by John Francis McDermott, trans. by Albert J. Salvan; Norman, University of Oklahoma Press, 1940), 210–15.

10. *Ibid.*, 210n.

11. Speck and Broom, *Cherokee Dance and Drama*, 62–63.

12. Rollins, *Overland Monthly*, 1903.

13. Robert H. Lowie, *The Crow Indians* (New York, Farrar, 1935), 215–36.

14. John G. Bourke, *An Apache Campaign* (New York, Charles Scribner's Sons, 1958), 33, 34, 114.

15. Catlin, *North American Indians*, I, 143, 144.

Chapter 11. Victory and Scalp Dances

1. Frank G. Speck, *Penobscot Man* (Philadelphia, University of Pennsylvania, 1940).

2. Lewis, *Lewis and Clark Expedition*, I, 91–92.

3. Lowie, *The Crow Indians*, 225–27.

4. Maximilian, *Travels in the Interior of North America*, XXIII, 388.

5. James, *S. H. Long's Expedition*, XV, 123–26.

6. William N. Fenton, "The Iroquois Eagle Dance an Offshoot of the Calumet Dance," Smithsonian Institution, Bureau of American Ethnology, *Bulletin 156* (1953), 191.

7. De Smet, *Life, Letters and Travels*, II, 580.

8. Bradbury, *Travels in the Interior of America*, 66, 159.

9. Tabeau, *Narrative of Loisel's Expedition*, 204–207.

10. Maximilian, *Travels in the Interior of North America*, XXIII, 352.

11. Denig, "Indian Tribes of the Upper Missouri, 1854," *loc. cit.*, 557–58.

12. Schoolcraft, *Personal Memoirs, 1812–42* (Philadelphia, 1851), 386.

13. Judge Ricker Papers, at the Nebraska Historical Society, Lincoln, Nebraska.

14. *Voyages of Champlain*, I, 237–38.

15. Speck, *Ethnology of the Yuchi Indians.*

16. Speck and Broom, *Cherokee Dance and Drama*, 64.

17. Hubert Howe Bancroft, *The Native Races* (San Francisco, 1886), 281.

18. George Catlin, *American Indian Collection* (London, 1848), II, 22.

Chapter 12. The Green Corn Dance

1. Bartram, *Travels*, 399.

2. Hodge, *Handbook of American Indians*, 176–77.

3. Speck, *Ethnology of the Yuchi Indians.*

4. William A. Galloway, *Old Chillicothe* (Xenia, Ohio, The Buckeye Press, 1934).

5. *Ibid.*, 192.

6. Timberlake, *Memoirs*, 88.

7. Morgan, *League of the Iroquois*, I, 269.

8. Tabeau, *Narrative of Loisel's Expedition*, 216.

9. Alice Fletcher, "The Omaha Tribe," Smithsonian Institution, Bureau of American Ethnology, *Twenty-seventh Annual Report*, 1905–06.

10. John L. Cowan, "Indian Ceremonial Dances," *Overland Monthly*, Vol. LIX, 2nd series (January–June, 1912).

11. Erna Ferguson, *Dancing Gods* (New York, Alfred A. Knopf, 1931), 49.

Chapter 13. Calumet and Eagle Dances: In the East

1. Blair, *Indian Tribes of the Upper Mississippi Valley*, 182, 186.

2. *Ibid.*, 325–30.

3. Fenton, "The Iroquois Eagle Dance . . . ," Smithsonian Institution, Bureau of American Ethnology, *Bulletin 156* (1953), 185–96.

4. *Ibid.*, 209.

5. James, *S. H. Long's Expedition*, XV, 126.

6. Kinietz, *The Indians of the Western Great Lakes*, Letter 27.

7. Catlin, *North American Indians*, II, 243.

8. R. G. Thwaites (ed.), *Jesuit Relations* (Cleveland, Burrows Bros. Co., 1896–1901), "Relation of 1666–67," LI, 47.

9. Kinietz, *The Indians of the Western Great Lakes*, 192.

10. *Ibid.*, Letter 26.

11. Fenton, *The Iroquois Eagle Dance*, 163.

12. Jacques Le Sueur, S. J., *History of the Calumet and of the Dance* (1734–64). *Contributions from the Museum of the American Indian* (New York, Heye Foundation, 1952), Vol. XII, No. 5, 9–11.

13. Hennepin, *A New Discovery of a Vast Country in America*, I, 236; II, 653–56.

14. Timberlake, *Memoirs*, 63–65.

15. Adair, *The History of the American Indians*, 63, 176–77.

16. Timberlake, *Memoirs*, 103, 107.
17. Speck and Broom, *Cherokee Dance and Drama*, 33.
18. *Ibid.*, 28.
19. John Lawson, *History of Carolina* (London, 1714; reprint, Raleigh, 1860), 68.
20. Catlin, *North American Indians*, II, 126–27.
21. Fenton, *The Iroquois Eagle Dance*, 163.

Chapter 14. Calumet and Eagle Dances: In the West

1. Tabeau, *Narrative of Loisel's Expedition*, 215.
2. Sidney J. Thomas, "A Sioux Medicine Bundle," *American Anthropologist*, Vol. XLIII (1941), 605–09.
3. American Museum of Natural History *Papers*, I, Part 2.
4. *Ibid.*
5. Paul Kane, *Wanderings of an Artist* (reprint, Toronto, 1925), 278–83, 300.
6. James, *S. H. Long's Expedition*, XV, 123–26.
7. John Comfort Filmore, "Wawan Ceremony of the Omaha," *Land of Sunshine*, Vol. X (December, 1898–May, 1899), 332–33.
8. Robert H. Lowie, *The Crow Indians* (New York, Farrar and Rinehard, 1935), 269–73.
9. Hennepin, *A New Discovery of a Vast Country in America*, 237.
10. Frances Densmore, "Teton Sioux Music," Smithsonian Institution, Bureau of American Ethnology, *Bulletin 61*, 68–77; also AMNH papers, op. cit., Melvin R. Gilmore, *Prairie Smoke* (New York, Columbia University Press, 1929).
11. AMNH, ibid.
12. Hodge, *Handbook of American Indians*, 381.
13. Catlin, *North American Indians*, 62–63.
14. *Ibid.*, II, 154–56.
15. Ferguson, *Dancing Gods*, 48, 49.

Chapter 15. The Sun Dance: Teton Sioux

1. Densmore, "Teton Sioux Music," *loc. cit.*, 86.
2. J. R. Walker, "The Sun Dance of the Oglala Division of the Teton Dakota, *Papers of the American Museum of Natural History*, Vol. XVI, Part II (1917), 51–221. See also in the same volume Pliny Earle Goddard, "Notes on the Sun Dance of the Sassi," Part IV (1919), 273–82; W. D. Wallis, "The Sun Dance of the Canadian Dakota," Part IV, 323–80.
3. Walker, "The Sun Dance of the Oglala," *loc. cit.*, 97.
4. J. Owen Dorsey, "A Study of Siouan Cults," Smithsonian Institution, Bureau of American Ethnology, *Eleventh Annual Report*, 1889–90, 361–544.
5. Joseph Epps Brown, *The Sacred Pipe* (Norman, University of Oklahoma Press, 1953), 92–93.
6. Densmore, "Teton Sioux Music," *loc. cit.*, 126.
7. Brown, *The Sacred Pipe*, 86, 95.
8. Frithjof Schuon, *A Message on Indian Religion*.
9. Stanley Vestal, *New Sources of Indian History* (Norman, University of Oklahoma Press, 1934), 146–47.

Chapter 16. The Sun Dance: Other Tribes

1. Catlin, *North American Indians*, I, 175–208.
2. Hjalmar R. Holand, *Westward from Vinland* (New York, Dover, 1940).
3. Maximilian, *Travels in the Interior of North America*, XXIII, 326–33.

4. Told to Ralph Hubbard many years ago by a Ute friend.

5. George Bird Grinnell, *The Cheyenne Indians* (New Haven, Yale University Press, 1923), II, 212–13.

6. Edward S. Curtis, *The North American Indian* (Norwood, Massachusetts, Plimpton Press, 1930), XIX, 121.

7. Grinnell, *The Cheyenne Indians*, 285–336.

8. Curtis, *The North American Indian*, 128–31.

9. Leslie Spear, "The Sun Dance of the Plains Indians," *Anthropological Papers of the American Museum of Natural History*, Vol. XVI, Part VII (1920).

10. Marvin K. Opler, "The Integration of the Sun Dance in Ute Religion," *American Anthropologist*, Vol. XLIII (1941), 550–72.

11. Lowie, *The Crow Indians*, 297–326.

Chapter 17. Society Dances: The Warrior Societies

1. Lowie, *The Crow Indians*, 173.

2. *Ibid.*, 174–75.

3. Maximilian, *Travels in the Interior of North America*, XXIII, 115.

4. Denig, "Indian Tribes of the Upper Missouri," *loc. cit.*, 558–61.

5. Karl N. Llewellyn and E. A. Hoebel, *The Cheyenne Way* (Norman, University of Oklahoma Press, 1941), 99–100.

6. Clark Wissler, "Some Protective Designs of the Dakota," *Papers of the American Museum of Natural History*, Vol. I, Part II, 50–52; Helen H. Blish, "The Ceremony of the Sacred Bow of the Oglala Dakota," *American Anthropologist*, Vol. XXXVI (1934), 180–87.

7. Densmore, "Teton Sioux Muxic," *loc. cit.*, 320.

8. Maximilian, *Travels in the Interior of North America*, XXIII, 291.

9. Henry A. Boler, *Among the Indians, 1858–66* (Chicago, Lakeside Press, 1959), 287.

Chapter 18. Society Dances: Dream Cults, Other Societies

1. Stanley Vestal, *War Path* (New York, Houghton, Mifflin Co., 1934); John Neihardt, *Black Elk Speaks* (New York, William Morrow, 1932).

2. Clark Wissler, "Societies and Ceremonial Associations in the Oglala Division of the Teton Dakota," *Anthropological Papers of the American Museum of Natural History*, Vol. XI, Part I (1912), 95–98.

3. Alice Fletcher, "The Elk Mystery of the Oglala," *Peabody Museum Papers*, Sixteenth and Seventeenth Annual Reports, Vol. III, Parts II, IV, Cambridge, 1884.

4. *Ibid.*, 286.

5. James L. Long, *Land of Nakoda* (Helena, Montana, State Publishing Company, 1942), 190; illustration, 186.

6. Norman D. Humphrey, "Characterization of Plains Associations," *American Anthropologist*, Vol. III (1941), 436.

Chapter 19. Bird and Animal Dances

1. Havelock Ellis, *The Dance of Life* (New York: Modern Library, 1929), 34, 35, 44.

2. Wissler, "Societies and Ceremonial Associations in the Oglala Division," *loc. cit.*, 1–99.

3. *Ibid.* "Societies and Dance Associations of the Blackfoot Indians, *Anthropological Papers of the American Museum of Natural History*, Vol. XI, Part IV, 359–460.

4. Robert H. Lowie, *Anthropological Papers of the American Museum of Natural History*, Vol. XI.

5. Curtis, *The North American Indian*, XVIII, 85–87.

6. Frances Densmore, "Music of Santo Domingo Pueblo," *S.W. Museum Papers*, #12–15, 1938, 145.

7. *Ibid.*, 147.

8. Curtis, *The North American Indian*, XVI.

9. *Ibid.*, 137.

10. Densmore, "Music of Santo Domingo Pueblo," *loc. cit.*, 148–49.

11. *Ibid.*, 147.

12. For further information, see Carleton Stafford Wilder, "Yaqui Deer Dance," unpublished M.A. thesis, University of Arizona, 1940; Samuel Marti, *Instrumentos Musicales Precortesianos* (Mexico City, Instituto Nacional de Antropologia, 1955).

13. Verner Z. Reed, *The Ute Bear Dance, American Anthropologist*, Vol. IX (1896). See also Albert B. Reagan, "The Bear Dance of the Ouray Utes," *Wisconsin Archives*, Vol. IX (1930), 148–50; Julian H. Steward, "A Uintah Ute Bear Dance," *American Anthropologist*, Vol. XXXIV (1932), 263–73; Frances Densmore, "Northern Ute Music," Smithsonian Institution, Bureau of American Ethnology, *Bulletin 75* (1922); Robert Lowie, "Dances and Societies of the Plains Shoshone," *Anthropological Papers of the American Museum of Natural History*, Vol. XI (1915), 823–31.

14. Curtis, *The North American Indian*, XI.

Chapter 20. Dances of the Pacific Coast

1. Myron Eells, "The Twana Chemakum, and Klellam Indians of Washington Territory," Smithsonian Institution, *Annual Report*, 1887, Part I, 614–68.

2. *Ibid.*, 665. See also Joyce Annabel Wike, "Modern Spirit Dancing of Northern Puget Sound," unpublished M.A. thesis, University of Washington, 1941; Ruth Underhill, *Indians of the Pacific Northwest* (Washington, Bureau of Indian Affairs, 1944); Ralph W. Andrews, *Indian Primitive* (Seattle, Superior Publishing Co., 1960); Curtis, *The American Indian*, X, 11.

3. Bancroft, *The Native Races*, I, 66–67.

4. Peter Freuchen, *Book of the Eskimos* (New York, Bramhall House, 1961).

5. McIlwraith, *Bella Coola Indians*, II, 7–38.

6. Hubert Howe Bancroft, *The Native Races* (San Francisco, 1886), I, 352, 392.

7. A. L. Kroeber, "Handbook of the Indians of California," Smithsonian Institution, Bureau of American Ethnology, *Bulletin 78* (1925), 56.

8. *Ibid.*, 764–65.

9. T. F. McIlwraith, *Bella Coola Indians* (Toronto, University of Toronto Press, 1948), II, 135–37.

10. Bancroft, *The Native Races*, 515.

Chapter 21. Dances of the Southwest

1. Curtis, *The North American Indian*, XII, 152. See also Ferguson, *Dancing Gods*; Frank Waters, *Masked Gods* (Albuquerque, University of New Mexico Press, 1950) and *Book of the Hopi* (New York, Viking Press, 1963); Earle R. Forrest, *Snake Dance of the Hopi Indians* (Los Angeles, Western Lore Press, 1961); John G. Bourke, *The Snake Dance of the Moquis of Arizona* (New York, Scribner's, 1884); Jesse W. Fewkes, "Snake Ceremonials at Walpi," *Journal of American Ethnology and Archaeology*, Vol. IV; Dr. Frederick W. Hodge, "Pueblo Snake Ceremonials," *American Anthropologist*, Vol. IX (April, 1896).

2. Gladys Reichard, "War Dance," *Colorado University Contributions to Anthropology*, No. VII (1928). See Frank Waters, *Masked Gods*.

3. Albert B. Reagan, "A Navaho Fire Dance," *American Anthropologist*, Vol. XXXVI (1934), 434–37.

4. Washington Matthews, Smithsonian Institution, Bureau of American Ethnology, *Fifth Annual Report*, 1883–84, 436.

5. Ferguson, *Dancing Gods*, 206.

Chapter 22. The Grass, or Omaha, Dance

1. Blair, *Indian Tribes of the Upper Mississippi Valley*, 337–38.

2. Kinietz, *The Indians of the Western Great Lakes*, Letter 27.

3. Fenton and Kurath, "The Iroquois Eagle Dance, *loc. cit.*, 198.

4. Fletcher, "The Omaha Tribe," *loc. cit.*

5. *Ibid.*

6. Wissler, "Dance Organizations of the Oglala Sioux," *loc. cit.*, 13–99.

7. De Smet, *Life, Letters and Travels*, III, 1058–61.

8. *Ibid.*

9. Howard, *My Life and Experiences Among Our Hostile Indians*, 460–63.

10. Henry A. Boller, *Among the Indians, 1858–66*, Lakeside Classics (Chicago, Lakeside Press, 1959), 107.

11. Robert Lowie, "Societies of the Crow, Hidatsa and Mandan Indians," *Anthropological Papers of the American Museum of Natural History*, Vol. XI, Part III (1913), 200–206.

12. Long, *Land of Nakoda*.

13. Williams, *A Key to the Language of America*.

Chapter 23. Other Dances Today

1. Bernard Mason, *Dances and Stories of the American Indian* (New York, A. S. Barnes & Co., 1944), 141.

2. Frances Densmore, "Menominee Music," Smithsonian Institution, Bureau of American Ethnology, *Bulletin 102* (1932).

3. Blish, "The Ceremony of the Sacred Bow of the Oglala Dakota," *American Anthropologist*, Vol. XXXVI (1934), 180–87.

4. Lowie, "Dance Associations of the Eastern Dakota," *Anthropological Papers of the American Museum of Natural History*, Vol. XI (1913).

In Retrospect

1. Timberlake, *Memoirs*, 136.

2. Smith, *The Generall Historie of Virginia*, I, lxviii.

3. Wissler, *Indians of the United States*, 273.

4. Curt Sachs, *World History of the Dance* (New York, W. W. Norton & Co., 1937), 17.

5. Frank G. Speck, *The Naskapi* (Norman, University of Oklahoma Press, 1935), 179.

6. Clark Wissler, *Indians of the United States*, American Museum of Natural History Science Series (New York, 1940), 270.

7. A. L. Kroeber, "Handbook of the Indians of California," *loc. cit.*, 95.

8. Morgan, *League of the Iroquois*, 249–51.

9. Lewis, *Lewis and Clark Expedition*, I, 135, 160, 161.

10. Marsden Hartley, "Tribal Esthetics Dance Drama," *El Palacio*, November 16, 1918, *Journal of the Museum of New Mexico*, Vol. VI, No. 4 (February 8, 1919), 53.

Index

531